RESEARCH HANDBOOK ON ENTREPRENEURSHIP AS PRACTICE

HANDBOOKS OF BUSINESS AND MANAGEMENT RESEARCH AS PRACTICE

The Elgar Handbooks of Business and Management Research as Practice series aims to take steps to bridge the gap between theoretical research on a given subject and its relevance to practitioners and corporate trainers. They will be rigorous and research-led but will be accessible to and informed by practice. These *Handbooks* are both stimulating to researchers and pertinent to practice-based teachers and higher level students.

Titles in the series include:

Handbook on Intuition Research as Practice
Edited by Marta Sinclair

Research Handbook on Entrepreneurship as Practice
Edited by Neil Aaron Thompson, Orla Byrne, Anna Jenkins and Bruce T. Teague

Research Handbook on Entrepreneurship as Practice

Edited by

Neil Aaron Thompson

Associate Professor, Department of Management and Organization, Vrije Universiteit Amsterdam, the Netherlands

Orla Byrne

Assistant Professor of Entrepreneurship, UCD College of Business, University College Dublin, Ireland

Anna Jenkins

Senior Lecturer in Entrepreneurship and Innovation, Department of Strategy and Entrepreneurship, The University of Queensland, Australia

Bruce T. Teague

Associate Professor of Entrepreneurship, Florida Gulf Coast University, USA

HANDBOOKS OF BUSINESS AND MANAGEMENT RESEARCH AS PRACTICE

 Edward Elgar
PUBLISHING

Cheltenham, UK • Northampton, MA, USA

Published by
Edward Elgar Publishing Limited
The Lypiatts
15 Lansdown Road
Cheltenham
Glos GL50 2JA
UK

Edward Elgar Publishing, Inc.
William Pratt House
9 Dewey Court
Northampton
Massachusetts 01060
USA

Paperback edition 2023

A catalogue record for this book
is available from the British Library

Library of Congress Control Number: 2022932130

This book is available electronically in the **Elgar**online
Business subject collection
http://dx.doi.org/10.4337/9781788976831

ISBN 978 1 78897 682 4 (Hardback)
ISBN 978 1 78897 683 1 (eBook)
ISBN 978 1 03532 205 3 (Paperback)

Printed and bound by CPI Group (UK) Ltd, Croydon, CR0 4YY

Contents

Contributors

Tor Helge Aas	NORCE and University of Agder, Norway
Camilla Eline Andersen	Stockholm University, Sweden
Henrik Berglund	Chalmers University of Technology, Sweden
Karl Joachim Breunig	Oslo Business School, OsloMet, Norway
Orla Byrne	UCD College of Business, University College Dublin, Ireland
Betsy Campbell	Pennsylvania State University, USA
Suwen Chen	University of Edinburgh Business School, UK
Boukje Cnossen	Leuphana University of Lüneburg, Germany
Thomas Cyron	Jönköping University, Sweden
Thomas Davis	University of Liverpool Management School, UK
Dimo Dimov	University of Bath, UK and Reykjavik University, Iceland
Tamim Elbasha	Audencia Business School, France
Steffen Farny	Leuphana University of Lüneburg, Germany
Miriam Feuls	Copenhagen Business School, Denmark
William B. Gartner	Babson College, USA
Silvia Gherardi	University of Trento, Italy
Vern L. Glaser	University of Alberta, Canada
Nicole Gross	National College of Ireland, Ireland
Lars Hamacher	Maastricht University, the Netherlands
Richard T. Harrison	University of Edinburgh Business School, UK
Magnus Hellström	University of Agder, Norway and Åbo Akademi University, Finland
Inge Hill	Royal Agricultural University, UK
Katja Maria Hydle	NORCE and University of Oslo, Norway
Deniz Iren	Open University of the Netherlands, the Netherlands
Anna Jenkins	The University of Queensland, Australia
Bengt Johannisson	Linnaeus University, Sweden
Ewald Kibler	Aalto University, Finland
Irina Liubertė	ISM University of Management and Economics, Lithuania
Dominik Mösching	University of St. Gallen, Switzerland
Jarrod Ormiston	University of New South Wales, Australia
Theodore R. Schatzki	University of Kentucky, USA and Lancaster University, UK

Hallur Thor Sigurdarson   Reykjavik University, Iceland

Chris Steyaert   University of St. Gallen, Switzerland

Bruce T. Teague   Florida Gulf Coast University, USA

Lisa Thomas   Audencia Business School, France

Neil Aaron Thompson   Vrije Universiteit Amsterdam, the Netherlands

Karen Verduijn   Vrije Universiteit Amsterdam, the Netherlands

Julian Dominik Winter   Leuphana University of Lüneburg, Germany

Foreword
William B. Gartner

I believe this book marks a "turning point," actually, the metaphor might be more aptly stated as, a "fulcrum" that leverages the entrepreneurship field towards a theoretical and methodological focus on the processes of entrepreneurial becoming, rather than that of entrepreneurship being. As the editors of this book state, so clearly, an "entrepreneurship as practice" perspective is grounded in the world of verbs. It appears to be an inherent problem in the study of human endeavors to focus on nouns: the entrepreneur (Gartner, 1988), the organization (Weick, 1979) or the environment (Hannan & Freeman, 1977) rather than on the verbs that actually animate these phenomena. The processes of becoming that are inherent in "entrepreneuring" (Steyaert, 2007), have, indeed, always been an intrinsic aspect of the study of humanity (Nayak & Chia, 2011), yet, the transitory nature of process is much more difficult to cling to (Campbell, 1974). It is odd, really, that in every moment, we are in the present only as we step out of the past and into the future. Yet, our notions of "now" tend to remain fixed – we "be" rather than "become." We tend to minimize the fluidity of the present – both in recognizing the value of the past (Wadhwani, Kirsch, Welter, Gartner & Jones, 2020; Wadhwani & Lubinski, 2017) and the future (Dey & Steyaert, 2015; Gartner, 2007; Thompson, 2018) in the processes of the present. This book provides a roadmap for staying in the processes of entrepreneurship.

More to the point, one of the challenges of current scholarship in entrepreneurship is in finding where to focus one's attention when exploring the various facets of the entrepreneurial phenomenon (Dimov, Schaefer & Pistrui, 2021; Shepherd, Wiklund & Dimov, 2021). As such, I believe that our attention must be on practices when studying the phenomenon of entrepreneurship if we want to stay within a process perspective (Helin, Hernes, Hjorth & Holt, 2014; Hjorth, Holt & Steyaert, 2015). I hope that one might see the connection between a focus on "entrepreneurship as practice" and "entrepreneurial behavior" (Gartner, 1988). The focus on practices is not to ignore the practitioner of those practices, just as the focus on entrepreneurial behavior is not to ignore the entrepreneur (Gartner, 1985), but, rather to focus on practices (or behaviors) is to appreciate the value of starting with the "doings and sayings" (Schatzki, 2016) of what is occurring – that is the verbs of the phenomenon of entrepreneurship. If, for a moment, we are to take on the role of entrepreneurship educators, it would seem apparent, to me at least, that as educators, our primary interest is in training individuals to engage in entrepreneurial practices. Our courses are about the verbs of entrepreneurship rather than about the noun of entrepreneurial being. Our educational processes are based on Aristotle's aphorism "We are what we repeatedly do." So, we begin with practices, not a focus on the practitioner. And, the focus on practices is not to ignore the context (Welter, 2011; Welter & Gartner, 2016) in which practices occur. Rather, again, the emphasis, the focus, begins with practices, rather than with the practitioner or context.

When we are willing to look at the many different practices that occur in entrepreneuring, and when we recognize the many different contexts in which entrepreneurial practices occur, it is critical to emphasize the necessity of celebrating the value of variation in these entrepreneurial practices. As such, the entrepreneurship as practice field, is, from my perspective, both theoretically and methodologically capable of a more systematic ability to recognize and document variation in entrepreneurship. I have attempted to champion a more systematic approach (McKelvey, 1982) to recognizing variation in the entrepreneurial phenomenon which I have labeled the "critical mess" (Gartner, 2004; Gartner & Birley, 2002) that asks for more documentation of the phenomena of entrepreneurship and less concern for developing a theory of the phenomena of entrepreneurship. From a "critical mess" perspective, the goal is to simply study the phenomenon and describe it in ways that others can gain an understanding and insights from. I would suggest that an entrepreneurship as practice perspective is similar in its intentions. The goal, at this point, is to understand the various practices that exist in entrepreneuring across the many different contexts and practitioners that engage in these practices. Inherent in an entrepreneurship as practice perspective, then, is that there is no "one best way" in which entrepreneurial practices are practiced. Therefore, scholars must study and document this variation. Variation matters, particularly in entrepreneurship, where the creation of differences, both in the practices and outcomes of practices, appear to be critical to whether these practices and their outcomes are sustainable over time.

Be that as it may, this book is an important milestone in the development of entrepreneurship as practice as a central aspect of entrepreneurship scholarship. I hope that this book finds its place on the shelf of every entrepreneurship scholar's library.

REFERENCES

Campbell, D. T. (1974). Evolutionary epistemology. In D. T. Campbell (Ed.), *Language, Development and Culture* (pp. 413–463). New York: John Wiley & Sons.

Dey, P., & Steyaert, C. (2015). Tracing and theorizing ethics in entrepreneurship: Toward a critical hermeneutics of imagination. In A. Pullen & C. Rhodes (Eds.), *The Routledge Companion to Ethics, Politics and Organizations* (pp. 231–248). Abingdon: Routledge.

Dimov, D., Schaefer, R., & Pistrui, J. (2021). Look who is talking … and who is listening: Finding an integrative "we" voice in entrepreneurial scholarship. *Entrepreneurship Theory and Practice, 45*(5), 1176–1196.

Gartner, W. B. (1985). A framework for describing and classifying the phenomenon of new venture creation. *Academy of Management Review, 10*(4), 696–706.

Gartner, W. B. (1988). Who is an entrepreneur? Is the wrong question. *American Journal of Small Business, 12*(4), 11–32.

Gartner, W. B. (2004). Achieving "critical mess" in entrepreneurship scholarship. In J. A. Katz & D. Shepherd (Eds.), *Advances in Entrepreneurship, Firm Emergence, and Growth*, vol. 7 (pp. 199–216). Greenwich, CT: JAI Press.

Gartner, W. B. (2007). Entrepreneurial narrative and a science of the imagination. *Journal of Business Venturing, 22*(5), 613–627.

Gartner, W. B., & Birley, S. (2002). Introduction to the special issue on qualitative methods in entrepreneurship research. *Journal of Business Venturing, 17*(5), 387–395.

Hannan, M. T., & Freeman, J. (1977). The population ecology of organizations. *American Journal of Sociology, 82*(5), 929–964.

Helin, J., Hernes, T., Hjorth, D., & Holt, R. (2014). Process is how process does. In J. Helin, T. Hernes, D. Hjorth, & R. Holt (Eds.), *The Oxford Handbook of Process Philosophy and Organization Studies* (pp. 1–16). Oxford: Oxford University Press.

Hjorth, D., Holt, R., & Steyaert, C. (2015). Entrepreneurship and process studies. *International Small Business Journal, 33*, 599–611.

McKelvey, B. (1982). *Organizational Systematics: Taxonomy, Evolution, Classification*. Berkeley, CA: University of California Press.

Nayak, A., & Chia, R. (2011). Thinking becoming and emergence: Process philosophy and organization studies. In Haridimos Tsoukas & Robert Chia (Eds.), *Philosophy and Organization Theory* (pp. 281–309). Research in the Sociology of Organizations vol. 32. Bingley: Emerald Publishing.

Schatzki, T. (2016). Sayings, texts and discursive formations. In A. Hui, T. Schatzki, & E. Shove (Eds.), *The Nexus of Practices: Connections, Constellations, Practitioners* (pp. 126–140). Abingdon: Routledge.

Shepherd, D. A., Wiklund, J., & Dimov, D. (2021). Envisioning entrepreneurship's future: Introducing me-search and research agendas. *Entrepreneurship Theory and Practice*, *45*(5), 955–966.

Steyaert, C. (2007). "Entrepreneuring" as a conceptual attractor? A review of process theories in 20 years of entrepreneurship studies. *Entrepreneurship & Regional Development*, *19*(6), 453–477.

Thompson, N. A. (2018). Imagination and creativity in organizations. *Organization Studies*, *39*(2–3), 229–250.

Wadhwani, R. D., Kirsch, D., Welter, F., Gartner, W. B., & Jones, G. G. (2020). Context, time, and change: Historical approaches to entrepreneurship research. *Strategic Entrepreneurship Journal*, *14*(1), 3–19.

Wadhwani, R. D., & Lubinski, C. (2017). Reinventing entrepreneurial history. *Business History Review*, *91*(4), 767–799.

Weick, Karl E. (1979). *The Social Psychology of Organizing* (2nd edition). Reading, MA: Addison-Wesley.

Welter, F. (2011). Contextualizing entrepreneurship: Conceptual challenges and ways forward. *Entrepreneurship Theory and Practice*, *35*(1), 165–184.

Welter, F., & Gartner, W. B. (Eds.) (2016). *A Research Agenda for Entrepreneurship and Context*. Cheltenham, UK and Northampton, MA, USA: Edward Elgar Publishing.

Introduction to the *Research Handbook on Entrepreneurship as Practice*

Neil Aaron Thompson, Orla Byrne, Anna Jenkins and Bruce T. Teague

INTRODUCTION

Over the past decade, Entrepreneurship as Practice (EaP) has steadily gained momentum as a scholarly community (Champenois et al., 2020; Teague et al., 2021; Thompson et al., 2020). Beginning with Steyaert's (2007, p. 456) declaration that practice theories "hold the greatest potential for those who conceive of entrepreneuring within a creative process view", scholars from around the world have begun a new movement to explore how theories of practice can enable a different mode of engagement with and understanding of entrepreneurial phenomena (for full reading list see https://www.entrepreneurshipaspractice.com). This Handbook is a product of this ongoing momentum and collective movement.

EaP travels the pathway laid down by previous scholars who take seriously the notion that creative and collaborative organizing activities are the root of entrepreneurial phenomena (hence the verb entrepreneuring) (Hjorth et al., 2015; Johannisson, 2011; Verduyn, 2015). This stands in contrast to contemporary research that continues to denote and reduce entrepreneurship studies to the quality of a person (Gartner, 1988; Ramoglou et al., 2020), or to contextual features of environments, over process. Thinking of entrepreneuring as ongoing creative organizing means, broadly speaking, that scholars prioritize the arrays and varieties of collective activities in their research (Fletcher, 2006; Gartner, 2016; Hjorth, 2012). Entrepreneuring thus unites scholars in their rejection of the idea of entrepreneuring as anything but genuinely social, relational and collective, whether in market or in other settings. What is more, entrepreneuring denotes a unique social phenomenon as it takes place "in-between or along the edge of established human practice" (Farias et al., 2019, p. 555). Entrepreneuring exists in a liminal time and space between "what is" and "what could become" (Garcia-Lorenzo et al., 2018). Consequently, entrepreneuring brings into focus the importance of organization creation (intensity, potentiality, and movement) that stands in contrast to organization (hierarchy, functionalism, monologue) (Hjorth, 2003, p. 5).

However, while walking along this pathway, EaP also offers a distinctive theoretical framework based on its adoption of contemporary theories of practice (see Thompson & Byrne, 2020 for more background). In the first part of this introduction, we begin with a review of the core features that make entrepreneurship as practice a distinct domain to understanding entrepreneuring. In particular, we outline the fundamental ontological and epistemological features of the framework from a Schatzkian perspective (Schatzki, 2012), and discuss how it compares and contrasts to existing onto-epistemological frameworks in entrepreneurship studies. EaP scholars advocate for, draw on and contribute to the broader 'practice turn' ongoing in contemporary social theory (Schatzki et al., 2001). In short, theories of practice are a category of philosophical arguments and social theories that have emerged in the past few decades, and have become influential across the social sciences. Theories of practice offer new ways of understanding and explaining social phenomena (Nicolini, 2012) by providing a robust conceptual means of exploring and explaining how and why people go about their daily work (Reckwitz, 2002; Rouse, 2006). In doing so, they provide the theoretical means for scholarship to go beyond problematic dualisms (action/structure, human/non-human, mind/body, subjective/objective) that persist in much of current entrepreneurship scholarship (Gherardi, 2012, 2017).

While this review lays out a basic groundwork for defining what makes EaP a distinctive approach to entrepreneurship research, in the second part of this introduction, we introduce four chapters in which leading scholars propose novel ways to understand and conceptualize a domain-specific practice theory of entrepreneuring. In the third part, we introduce five chapters that provide more evidence that EaP is an active, exciting and distinct domain. The contributing authors in this section all push the boundaries of how to conceptualize EaP in new and fruitful theoretical directions. In the fourth part of this introduction, we introduce six chapters that propose novel and insightful methodologies and methods for studying entrepreneuring practices. The fifth part of this introduction introduces four chapters that adopt theories of practice as a lens to empirically research an aspect of entrepreneuring, which demonstrates another way to develop innovative and novel insights. We conclude with final thoughts about the future of entrepreneurship as practice research.

THE DISTINCTIVE DOMAIN OF ENTREPRENEURSHIP AS PRACTICE

To those scholars unfamiliar with the rich intellectual history of theories of practice, the combination of 'practice' and 'theory' sounds impossible. As Johannisson (2011) notes, 'practice' is often used as a commonsense term in scholarship to denote the local, situated, specific, concrete and detailed, while 'theory', on the other hand, is a form of propositional knowledge that is ideally supposed to be universal, abstract and generic. However, as we will discuss next, theories of practice carve out new ontological and epistemological arguments about the nature of social life, doing away with the dualism between theory and practice in the process, which has a great many fruitful implications for the study of entrepreneuring.

Ontological Considerations

Ontology is a particular theory about the nature of social phenomena. EaP presents a novel ontological perspective of entrepreneuring by positing that entrepreneuring occurs in and through social practices (Thompson et al., 2020). Put another way, EaP views social practices as the ontological basis of all entrepreneuring phenomena and processes. Any entrepreneuring phenomena, such as new venture ideation, investment pitches, family business succession, internationalization strategy, etc., is fundamentally grounded in real-time, contextually situated social practices conducted by entrepreneuring practitioners. Consequently, because all practices are social by definition, it is common to drop the 'social' adjective.

Since practice is at the core of EaP, it is helpful to review what scholars mean by the concept because the term has a specific theoretical meaning in practice theories. In the Schatzkian (2001, 2006) view, a practice is "an organized, open-ended spatial-temporal manifold of actions". On the one hand, practices are constituted by 'manifold of actions', which are multiple and sequential actions carried out by practitioners for practical purposes and concerns in certain spatial and temporal locations. They are 'open-ended' in that they are continuously evolving so they may develop in different and indeterminable ways. In carrying these actions out, practitioners not only try to achieve their practical ends, but also compose instances of the practice – albeit in new and discontinuous conditions. Thus, it is helpful to think of a practice as composed "each time for the first time," so to speak (Garfinkel & Sacks, 1970).

To illuminate this point, take the following thought example of an instance of a 'pitch practice'. We can imagine the practice is carried out through multiple and sequential actions carried out by practitioners for practical purposes and concerns. For example, a potential investor invites an entrepreneur to an office location to learn about their venture over email software, having heard about her from a colleague. The entrepreneur replies to the email and takes further steps to organize the logistical details with the investor for the presentation. On the day of the presentation, the investor and colleagues welcome the entrepreneur to the office, the entrepreneur introduces herself and then uses a prepared slide deck to cover the attractive investment details of the venture. This is followed up with a question–answer series of interactions and ends by a conclusion to the pitch meeting ('thank you for your time', 'we'll stay in touch', or 'we'd like to know more, please send us the details we requested'). Here we can glean the manifold and sequential actions (invitation, meeting and conclusion) taken by practitioners for practical purposes (possible investment relationship). Importantly, in carrying out these actions, the practitioners also compose another instance of 'pitch practice' – the entrepreneuring practitioners mutually extend the practice's existence in time and space.

Additionally, practice theorists also argue that to carry out the actions that constitute a practice, practitioners simultaneously draw upon and are guided by pre-existing organizing dimensions of the practice, namely practical understandings, explicit rules, and teleo-affective structures. Practical understandings (aka habitus (Bourdieu, 1990), practical knowledge (Strati, 2007) or practical consciousness (Goldenstein & Walgenbach, 2021)) are tacit ways of knowing how to participate in a practice – an embodied understanding of what to do learned by engaging in the practice. It is knowing how to do something and having the skill or capacity to do what is understood by the practice. Through engaging in a practice, practical "understandings are established, acquired, sustained, and transformed through the actions that compose these practices" (Schatzki, 2002, p. 135). Rules are codifications of action taking the form of explicit formulations that prescribe, require, or instruct that such and such be done, said, or is the case. They are conceived to regulate existing activities or introduce new activities. Teleo-affective structures are an array of ends, projects, uses (of things), and even emotions that are acceptable or prescribed for participants in the practice. A teleo-affective structure provides a configuration and way of organizing across multiple practices. Taking these three dimensions together, practices present what Taylor (1985) calls 'semantic spaces', aka clearing (Heidegger, 1978) or sites (Schatzki, 2005), in which entrepreneuring practitioners interact and coexist intelligibly. This means that any entrepreneurial action, mental state, and use of language that has previously been performed to compose a given practice, also may articulate and hand down a semantic repertoire to subsequent practitioners. This repertoire establishes and structures the meaningfulness of interactions, but does not determine whatever transpires in a subsequent instance of a practice.

To illustrate this, we return to our previous 'pitch practice' thought example. Any individual action, such as the entrepreneur's responses to investor questions, is only intelligible for the practitioners present (and any observers as well), when practitioners share practical understandings, rules and teleo-affective structures. For instance, how to appropriately request and respond to a meeting request; engage in greetings; prepare and use a slide deck and presentation. The 'pitch practice' may also be structured by formal instructions, requirements and guidelines about the pitch. These can include legal regulations that govern non-disclosure, the timing and detail presented in the presentation, or other explicitly stated expectations about sales figures, projected numbers and legal agreements. Finally, a teleo-affective structure coordinates the purposes and ends and emotions of engaging in a practice, such as gaining investment, investing on behalf of investors for returns, receiving good feedback from investors about the pitch, and enjoying a successful career; and includes acceptable uses of such equipment as PowerPoint, computers, telephones, printers, scanners, etc.

As we can see in this simple thought example, the ontological status of any one 'entrepreneurial action' is contextually dependent on, but not determined by, a semantic space (i.e., practical understandings, explicit rules and teleo-affective structures). To say that entrepreneurial actions (actions taken by the entrepreneur and stakeholders) are organized by these matters is to say that their actions express a shared understanding, broadly observe the same rules, and pursue ends and projects included in the shared structure of acceptable teleologies. Any significant deviation from these shared tacit understandings and acceptable teleologies will produce unease, confusion, miscommunication and even social sanctions by other practitioners – and, in this case, the entrepreneur or investors are more likely to fail to come to an agreement. In sum, the duality between agency (collective performance of a practice) and structure (dimensions that shape collective performance) is endogenous to the situated, turn-by-turn, moment-by-moment interaction of entrepreneuring practitioners.

While this explanation defines the concept of a single practice, it is important to note that EaP scholars view entrepreneuring as inherently transpiring as part of and within nexuses of many practices. These nexuses, or intersections and overlaps, between practices, articulate and hand down a multiplicity of 'semantic spaces', which, in turn, are reproduced and renewed through their collective performances. Entrepreneuring thus ontologically exists through the joint performance of an interwoven texture of practices, drawing upon material objects, which link and overlap with each other across temporalities and spatial locations. In turn, we can view a venture as a larger net of practice-arrangement bundles that is tied relationally to the similar nets that are other ventures (competition or cooperation), as well as to those that compose local and state governments, foundations, incumbent firms and the broader ecosystem.

The ontological perspective that EaP brings to the table is a distinctive approach which has a few key differences with existing ontologies in entrepreneurship studies. On the one hand, EaP differs from the ontology of individualism that underpins much of contemporary entrepreneurship research. First, individualism is an ontological view that argues entrepreneurship is a function of individuals and their relationships. Entrepreneurial phenomena, such as new venture ideation, networking, resourcing, opportunity evaluation, etc., are either instituted in or composed of entrepreneurs' actions and mental states situated in context (social, geographical, political, cultural), in which context is other individuals' actions, mental states, and relations. However, unlike EaP, individualists do not believe that the identity of entrepreneurial actions, mental states, and relations is intrinsically wedded to an interpersonal context. This is to say that an entrepreneur's action and mental states might be contingently and causally connected to others in contexts, but not inherently defined by them. What mostly shapes entrepreneurial action and mental states are not 'semantic sites', as in EaP, in other words, but the entrepreneurs' own independent intentions, purposes, perceptions, and other actions. Hence, individualists do not recognize that entrepreneurial action and mental states are dependent upon practices that commune 'semantic spaces', instead they rather hold that social contexts are ontologically independent from entrepreneurial action and mental states.

On the other hand, entrepreneurship scholars also have drawn upon societist ontologies that recognize contexts as determining entrepreneurial action, which differ from EaP in significant ways. Entrepreneurship scholars, for instance, commonly argue that entrepreneurial activities are embedded within, and are determined by, market, political and cultural structures. These structures are encompassing phenomena that help determine what occurs within it by subjecting entrepreneurs to certain conditions and outfitting them with particular interests and motivations. This differs from an EaP perspective, however, by assuming that the societal phenomena are fundamentally different in kind from the activities, mental states and relations of entrepreneurs. Entrepreneurs' actions, mental states, and relations might be determined by, and even inseparable from, societal structures, but entrepreneurial action, mental states and relations are not seen as playing a part in composing these phenomena. An EaP perspective similarly positions entrepreneuring in a wider, distinctly social setting in the absence of which entrepreneuring would not exist. However, the properties of entrepreneurial action, mental states and relations are ontologically *continuous* with the distinct social contexts in which they exist (Schatzki, 2005). In short, EaP provides a middle road in which an entrepreneur's actions, mental states and relations are shaped by social practices (through 'semantic spaces' constituted by practical understandings, rules and teleo-affectivity), while entrepreneuring practitioners are simultaneously involved in their reproduction and renewal.

Epistemological Considerations

EaP also draws on theories of practice to recast theories of knowledge and its role in entrepreneuring process, which carries with it significant implications for the scholarly field of entrepreneurship research. Epistemology concerns a theory of the nature of knowledge. As already stated in the previous section, the manifold of actions that compose a practice anew also, in part, draws upon, is shaped by and reproduces or renews practical understandings. Hence, it is more precise to say the practice theories are onto-epistemological frameworks since the distinction between ontology and epistemology is blurred, given that epistemological practices shape the object we are studying (Gherardi, 2000; Nicolini et al., 2003).

Practical understandings are a form of knowledge that is concerned with practical 'knowing how' or knowing-in-situation (Hindmarsh & Pilnick, 2007; Nicolini et al., 2003), which differs in kind from propositional knowledge based on facts. Entrepreneurship scholars typically strive for propositional knowledge in which entrepreneurial phenomena are theoretically explained based on arguments and facts, which can be arrived at through a rigorous empirical research process. Practical understandings, in contrast, are a form of tacit knowing-how to engage with others, which is held collectively (dispersed among people) and rooted directly into the human body (Thompson & Illes, 2020). For example, when an expert entrepreneur performs a pitch, she does so not by explicitly referencing propositional knowledge about pitches in the moment, but by using practical understandings that are shared with audiences. Audiences in their part need not know any propositional knowledge about pitches or persuasion explicitly to understand and resonate with the entrepreneur's meaning in the moment. While propositional knowledge can be used as a reference point in preparation of practice (which is itself a practice), the performance itself is conducted according to shared and tacit practical understandings. Unlike propositional knowledge, practical understandings do not reside in the mind, and can be difficult or impossible for practitioners to fully describe and codify. The good news is that because practical understandings are shared publicly through their use in and through practices, scholars do have ways to observe practical understandings in the moment. In this sense, practical understandings pervade entrepreneurial action, mental states and relationships, yet are not 'things' these people own. Rather, practical understandings are a collective phenomenon that are only observable, significant and meaningful when practitioners undertake mutual action for practical purposes and concerns.

By introducing and positioning practical understandings as central to entrepreneuring literature, EaP augments and contrasts significantly with existing research in a number of ways. First, EaP is similar to studies that emphasize experiential knowledge when theorizing entrepreneurial learning (Pittaway & Cope, 2007; Politis, 2005). These studies posit that entrepreneurial learning is not so much a function of learning 'theory' (propositional knowledge) about the entrepreneurship process (such as, men are more likely than women to start new companies in most parts of the world; or it's better to have many weak ties than strong ties for new ideas). Rather entrepreneurial learning occurs when individuals act as entrepreneurs by engaging in 'real' or simulated tasks and projects (creating a business model, generating prototypes, testing markets, etc.). Individuals gain experiential knowledge by experiencing first-hand 'what it is like' to act entrepreneurially and reflecting upon these events. EaP augments this view by redefining experiential knowledge as practical understandings, which are transmitted among practitioners tacitly via their participation in specific practices. As such, individual minds are not the location of entrepreneuring knowledge, developed through individual reflection, but rather this knowledge is shared, tacit and embodied and revealed only through engagement in practice. Individuals come to 'know-how' to perform entrepreneuring by their continued participation with others in carrying out entrepreneuring practices, while, at the same time, their participation in carrying out entrepreneuring practices is shaped, but not determined, by the particularities of certain practical understandings. Accordingly, which practices practitioners are (not) co-composing with others matters a great deal to the forms of practical understandings being observed and enacted. This nuance clarifies the academic conversation on experiential knowledge by illuminating which form of knowledge is being experienced in the moment (practical) and how it is intrinsically related to particular practices.

Second, EaP is similar to, but adds more nuance to, studies that posit prior knowledge is a predictor of entrepreneurial motivation, intention and action (Ardichvili et al., 2003; Arentz et al., 2013; Shane, 2000). In these studies, prior knowledge is said to be formed from previous education, business and entrepreneurial experiences, which individuals can consciously access, evaluate and act upon to engage in entrepreneurial activity. Hence, prior knowledge is commonly seen as a key predictor of an individual's engagement in entrepreneurial activity. EaP similarly views prior knowledge as endowed by prior experiences but differs in that prior knowledge is split into either propositional knowledge or practical understandings. In its practical form, knowledge is not consciously accessed and utilized by individuals in mental decision-making processes. Rather, EaP argues that this practical form of prior knowledge cannot be reduced to the cognitive process of individuals as this knowledge exists as a distributed and tacit phenomenon written into human bodies. Prior knowledge, in this sense, is equivalent to an individual's practical ability to participate with others to carry out certain practices. Hence, practical understandings are a form of prior knowledge that is meaningful and significant when enacted in the presence of others.

Finally, and perhaps most significantly, EaP's epistemological arguments have implications for entrepreneurship scholarship itself. As previously mentioned, most entrepreneurship scholarship aims at developing propositional knowledge about entrepreneurial phenomena using rigorous reasoning and empirical methods. And yet, EaP leads to critical questions about whether practical understandings can be neatly transformed into propositional knowledge without losing significance and meaning. By definition, practical understandings are tacit and embodied, and fundamentally linked to specific practices, thus not easily codified and reified into words communicated in academic articles. Any explanatory theory of an entrepreneuring phenomena which recognizes practices, however, will be able to observe the performances of practices that evidence practical understandings and, with patience, it is possible to show how practical understandings have consequences for entrepreneuring in specific settings. It remains challenging or impossible, however, to transform these situated and complex insights into reified propositional knowledge (general theory) without stripping practical understandings of their content and meaning. In this vein, it is important to note that the research process itself depends on the utilization of practical understandings that are intrinsic to research practices. This suggests that certain research practices carry with them certain practical understandings on the unstated ways of gathering data, making judgements about quality of data, how to perform a certain analytical technique, write up findings in an attractive way, and the like. Alternative research practices thus continue different and varied modes of practical understandings of the research process and outcomes. This calls into question whether it is possible that the field will or could arrive at consensus not only about methodological procedures, but also general theory, given that the ways in which research is conducted shape the way scholars think and act.

Based on these challenges, EaP follows practice theorists who advocate for a performative view of social science (Latour & Woolgar, 1979; Pickering, 1992; Rorty, 1979) in which the academic endeavor does not seek to provide propositional knowledge. Rather this way of doing research takes the contextualization of knowledge seriously and uses research practices to uncover different forms of tacit and shared practical understandings as they relate to various nexuses of practices, and how this helps explain various entrepreneuring phenomena in certain circumstances. Theoretical contributions, hence, are recast as uncovering previously unknown forms of tacit and shared practical understandings as they relate to various nexuses of practices, how practices circulate and shift across contexts, how practice relationships are formed to maintain a venture (or not) and/or how new nexuses of practice may have positive or negative consequences for other nexuses (Nicolini, 2017).

NEW FOUNDATIONS

While the previous section lays out a basic groundwork for defining what makes EaP a distinctive approach to entrepreneurship research, as noted by Gherardi (Chapter 1, this volume), there are a great many opportunities for EaP to develop foundations in new and fascinating directions. In fact, existing EaP research has predominantly applied practice theories, such as Bourdieu, Giddens and Schatzki, that have been well established in the social practice theory literature. While recognizing the value in these contributions, to date, there remains an opportunity to use foundations as a point of departure to ask what would happen if we approached things from the reverse direction. Gherardi (Chapter 1, this volume) argues that it is time to think more about how entrepreneurship scholars can contribute to practice theory by calling for a domain-specific theory of practice. In her chapter, she distinguishes realist ontologies that ask what an opportunity *is* from relational ontologies that ask what opportunity *does*. Reframing 'opportunity' in terms of a *statu nascenti* – the moment in-between when all potentialities and energies and affective forces are present and not-yet fully realized – suggests that entrepreneuring is a collective and knowledgeable resourcing activity taking place within a domain of situated practices. In particular, she introduces the concepts of *agencement*, formativeness, and everyday creativity. *Agencement* considers agency that occurs as part of the connections between humans, non-humans, materialities, discourses and knowledges, that happen within the practice itself. The concept of *formativeness* is a way of knowing/doing that, in doing, invents the way of doing. It is the process in which an object – material or immaterial – takes form and its forming is a process of invention. The third concept, *everyday creativity*, points to the dynamics of a practice in which stability and change is always in an unstable equilibrium and practical creativity is deployed within everyday activities. In developing these concepts, Gherardi argues that EaP has potential to contribute to theories of practice by adding insight into how a (new) practice comes into being, how it gets resourced (with financial, economic, social capital and legitimacy) and how it achieves a more or less stable existence or change over time, given that the empirical research on how practice becomes 'a' practice is still in its infancy.

Alternatively, Schatzki (Chapter 2, this volume) devotes attention towards positioning entrepreneuring within a broader practice theory of social change. In his chapter, he identifies two ontological phenomena responsible for all changes in social affairs – activity chains and material events and processes. First, he argues that social change is caused by activity chains – sequences of actions – that include participation of multiple people. Social changes that appear in a particular bundle of practices and material arrangements arise from the interrelated chains of activity that pass through the bundle. As a result, explaining these changes centers around mapping the nature of these activity chains responsible. Second, Schatzki attributes social changes also to material events and processes, which recognizes the important material dimension of bundles of practices. Social change is thus a function of particular activity chains and particular events and processes of material arrangements. Similar to Mösching and Steyaert (Chapter 19, this volume), Schatzki posits that any analyses of entrepreneurship (and of the efforts of particular entrepreneurs) must attend to the practice-material arrangement bundles, within or in the context of which people bring about ('create') new products, new organizations, new techniques of production, new forms of organization, new funding, new items of social value etc. Accordingly, analyses of entrepreneurs should not examine persons as such (i.e., individual traits, mental states or other individualized properties), but instead people's lives, as it is here that the activities that are of interest can be seen. However, he cautions that focusing solely on individual lives leads to erroneous views that individuals bear sole responsibility for social change. For while particular lives can be credited with instituting new headings in chains of action, whether these chains continue on and yield social changes depends on the (re)actions of others. This realization directs researchers' attention towards the contexts in which individuals act, thus to such matters as activity chains, practices, materiality, normativity, collective actions, and connections among bundles, in explanations of entrepreneuring and relations to social change.

Johannisson (Chapter 3, this volume) develops entrepreneurship-specific practice theories by focusing on the integration of both process and practice perspectives. Entrepreneuring provides the umbrella under which this conceptual unification occurs. While creating this theoretical integration, Johannisson deftly avoids becoming trapped in an individualist-centric explanation of social change by highlighting the organizing context which shapes the practices and processes of entrepreneuring. The author goes on to contemplate how researchers might effectively access the phenomena of interest. He does this by elaborating on his prior work (Johannisson, 2011) in which he proposed enactive research as a means through which to access the experience of the entrepreneur directly. His enactive research method allows researchers to benefit from the strengths of both direct observation and autoethnography. He then offers two examples of enactive research as a means of understanding the practices and processes associated with entrepreneuring.

Finally Sigurdarson and Dimov (Chapter 4, this volume) call upon researchers to fully recognize entrepreneurial diversity and explore the meaning of this diversity for researchers who study entrepreneuring practices. They begin by exploring the emergent patterns of research found in the disciplinary histories of biology and culture studies. In both cases, they demonstrate the critical role of thick description studies in the development of each field. They then make a compelling argument that entrepreneurial diversity must compel entrepreneurial researchers to build a 'thick' understanding of different types of entrepreneuring practices. In essence, they call for a body of research upon which the field could produce a parallel to a cladistic classification system. Subsequently, the authors take a step further by exploring and unpacking that which makes entrepreneuring practice unique from other practices. They highlight contextual sensing, problematizing, and envisioning better solutions to the problems identified within particular contexts. They leverage these conclusions to suggest that the field of entrepreneurship cannot be fully understood by relying upon individual-centric approaches – contextual responsiveness is too important. Additionally, they demonstrate how the field would benefit from studies in which emphasis is placed on understanding how entrepreneurs sense problems, envision solutions and learn as they engage with others in practice.

NEW THEORETICAL ADVANCES

Providing more evidence that entrepreneurship as practice is an active, exciting and distinct domain comes from the next five chapters of this Handbook, in which contributing authors push the boundaries of how to conceptualize EaP in new and fruitful directions. As Verduijn and Andersen (Chapter 5, this volume) caution, similar to Schatzki (Chapter 2, this volume), there is always the looming danger that EaP scholars will slip back into individualism by prioritizing the presence, roles and intentions of entrepreneurs for explanations of practices observed. This creates a risk of generating overly simplistic explanations of the entrepreneuring that does not consider other practitioner agency, how practices form, connect and produce particular outcomes. As a way of pre-empting this danger, Verduijn and Andersen encourage EaP scholars to fully embrace practice theories to understand the heterogeneous, relational forces that together 'produce' entrepreneuring processes, and initiatives, not as some final outcome, but as prone to further materializing, as an in-between, or yet-to-become. To embrace their approach, they encourage EaP scholars to take a more critical stance by anchoring their work in a critical posthuman framework (Braidotti, 2015, 2019a, 2019b; Gherardi, 2009; Manning, 2016). Such a view of EaP enables scholars to tackle difficult questions such as who/what gets to produce knowledge, and what practices to perhaps resist, or alter, in producing a more just world.

Similar to Verduijn and Andersen, Elbasha and Thomas (Chapter 6, this volume) provide a clear argument for EaP scholars to avoid slipping back into individualism by adopting and furthering a Strong Structuration Theory (SST). SST retains the interrelated duality of structure and agency of Giddens's Structuration Theory, while bringing a stronger focus to the activities and processes that take place in situ, making it ideal for the study of entrepreneurship as practice. Drawing on SST, Elbasha and Thomas outline a framework for studying how actions and activities are shaped by the context in which the entrepreneur operates and how entrepreneurs, in turn through their actions and activities, shape this context. Using the example of a small independent French winery, the authors illustrate the range of research questions that can be asked when taking an SST approach at different levels of analysis, shifting from the macro institutional environment including the social and technological environment through to the micro internal structures of the firm including the entrepreneur's knowledge and values. These research questions have a process element to them enabling the duality of structure and agency to be explored over time.

In their chapter, Harrison and Chen (Chapter 8, this volume) explore another alternative way to conceptualize EaP research by drawing upon a framework of improvisation and routine. Harrison and Chen draw on an extensive body of literature from social practice theory, strategy-as-practice, routine theory and improvisation. Taking inspiration from how jazz musicians improvise in performances, they develop a framework for understanding entrepreneurship as practice centered on how different forms of improvisation influence the routines in situ and how routines respond to the need to improvise through flexing (the adaptation of existing familiar actions), stretching (the application of actions that not all participants are familiar with), and inventing (the creation of new activities and emerging patterns). This furthers literature by viewing entrepreneuring as a transpositioning, zigzagging improvisational practice, that is always a work in process. Similar to Schatzki (Chapter 2, this volume), EaP should thus put aside the word 'entrepreneurship' and look and see which practices produce enduring or recurring events that eventually turn into 'things' or 'events' that are later deemed as 'entrepreneurship'.

In entrepreneurship studies that adopt individualism, it is common to explain observations of entrepreneurial entry and activity by reference to an entrepreneur's intentions. As stated by Verduijn and Andersen (Chapter 5, this volume), entrepreneurship scholars can easily slip into a mode of attributing entrepreneuring practices to individual mental states, including intentions of entrepreneurs. Farny and Kibler's chapter (Chapter 7, this volume) specifically takes aim at this issue by reconceptualizing intentionality from an individualist towards a collective phenomenon. Drawing on Tuomela's 'we-perspective' of intentionality, the authors conceptualize different forms of joint intentionality in collaborative forms of business venturing, such as ecosystem development, social enterprises and community-based enterprising. They build on the premise that EaP is based on entrepreneurs' engaging in collaborative practices and activities shifting focus from the entrepreneur as an individual agent, to the entrepreneur being part of a functional group of agents that act collectively to achieve desired outcomes.

In particular, this distinguishes between shared intentions where the entrepreneur is driven to act based on private motives which happen to be shared by others; joint intentions where entrepreneurs are collectively and mutually committed to acting jointly; and we-intentions involving a strong sense that they are working together as a group. Drawing on insights from their fieldwork across a number of research projects, Farny and Kibler offer a lens through which new theoretical understanding of collective action in EaP research can be studied.

Finally, Berglund and Glaser (Chapter 9, this volume) advance EaP theory in a novel way by bringing to the fore the central role of artifacts in entrepreneuring practices that have been surprisingly overlooked, with the exception of the pitch, in existing research. Although the use of artifacts has become mainstream in entrepreneurial education around the world (such as the Business Model Canvas), there has been limited study of them in EaP research specifically and the academic domain more broadly. To address this shortcoming, the authors develop a typology of artifacts and provide suggestions for how these different types of artifacts can be studied in future EaP research. In particular, they classify artifacts into three board categories: (i) Abstract – conceptual devices that help entrepreneurs develop and communicate theories of their ventures, examples include the business model and entrepreneurial identity; (ii) Material – tangible devices which are central to the emerging venture, examples include physical and digital prototypes; and (iii) Narrative – sensemaking devices that enable the relation of individuals, objects, and events in meaningful accounts, examples include the pitch and the rhetorical devices used in them and business plans. Their chapter suggests artifacts as an alternative unit of analysis for studying new venture development to the opportunity construct which has become conceptually and pragmatically problematic. Artifacts and the practices that are intertwined with them provide an approach to studying how an emerging venture interacts and connects with their surrounding context (customers, users, partners, regulators, institutions, technologies). Drawing on principles of design, Berglund and Glaser suggest that practices of experimentation and transformation are particularly suitable for coupling with the study of artifacts and entrepreneuring practices.

NEW METHODOLOGICAL ADVANCES

The Handbook also makes a significant contribution to the methodological decisions researchers must make, as they undergo empirical EaP studies. Hill (Chapter 15, this volume) positions ethnographic studies as being best placed to capture the multimodality of entrepreneurial practices. Hill draws on her experience of conducting ethnographic studies, and Bourdieu's practice theory, to present guidelines in conducting ethnographic studies. The chapter outlines how a researcher can gather insights into the complex multiplicity of processes and social relations, by combining observations, interviews, with action research and online secondary research. Hill continues by outlining several methods for capturing entrepreneurial practices, the choices that researchers have, and discusses the advantages and limitations of different research strategies. She also explains the different levels of intervention of the researcher, from observation to documentary data collection, when investigating business processes. Hill's chapter also outlines how to work with material artifacts and social relations that matter for entrepreneurial practices, in particular, how a researcher can identify what is important for enacting the particular entrepreneurial practice under investigation. The chapter also delves into the complexities of presenting ethnographic research findings and addresses the challenges researchers face in doing this, when trying to publish their work. This can be particularly challenging when capturing socio-materiality, when document coding must include how material artifacts and social relations are integrated into entrepreneurial activities to become relevant for entrepreneurial practices. Drawing from her own learning journey in conducting these studies, as well as her analysis of the literature, Hill concludes by outlining fundamental questions any researcher should ask before considering ethnographic methods.

Continuing the discussion of socio-materiality in ethnographic studies, Gross (Chapter 12, this volume) takes an alternative perspective. Again, drawing on her own experience of conducting an ethnographic study, Gross discusses the theoretical and empirical role of silence in socio-material assemblages. Silence is a key feature, not only in our conversations but also in our everyday life. It is a prominent feature of an ever-increasing range of work activities in open as well as collective spaces. However, the behavioral cues provided by silence are often highly ambiguous and researchers are prone to misattributing the motives that lie behind silence. This raises very real practical challenges for the researcher, such as what happens if practices are hidden in and through silence? How does silence play out in the field? And how can researchers study 'things' and their use, if individual entrepreneurs or entrepreneurial teams sit fixed in position and quietly for hours on end? Through the use of vignettes based on her own fieldwork, we see that studying what people do, and trying to uncover the technological and non-technological objects and artifacts embedded within practices, is difficult when their work is done in complete silence. Gross puts forward methodological insights and means through which unsilencing can be achieved. She encourages researchers to acknowledge the presence of silence and to observe it, reflect on its meaning as well as impact on the research, and to discover the materials, objects and practices which are hidden in and through the silence. Deriving a model of unsilencing silence in socio-material assemblages, she recommends that future research should consider acknowledging, understanding and contextualizing the silence before attempting to challenge it.

In addition to socio-materiality, researchers can also focus on conversation as part of their ethnographic study. Campbell (Chapter 10, this volume) argues that conversation is not merely a way to transfer information; but a fundamental means of accomplishing shared goals and engendering social life. Adopting an ethnomethodological tradition of conversation analysis (EM/CA) highlights the importance of language to social practices and everyday working life. It probes the complex and repeated patterns of saying and doing that occur in routine conversations between team members in private. CA has evolved since the 1960s, and has been used in other disciplines to understand how professional accomplishments are conversationally produced and understood by members in action. Identifying a gap in our understanding of the role of conversation in entrepreneurial practice, Campbell explains how CA can add new details to existing constructs and entirely new ways of understanding entrepreneurship. These insights can reveal the dynamic, complex and idiosyncratic aspects of ordinary entrepreneurial work in action, and the practical means by which founders build new ventures. Campbell also outlines guidelines of how to conduct a study using CA. As CA is concerned with the structure of interaction rather than the content, it does not guess about the thoughts, feelings or motivations of research subjects. Instead, it looks for evidence in the observable data that is available to members. Campbell talks us through how to analyze CA data using Jeffersonian Notation to capture audible details of interactions. Once transcribed, the researcher searches for how turns are constructed, sequences ordered, or identities categorized in other similar instances, before connecting the interactional data with wider social theory.

Despite the popularity of ethnographies for researching practices, Liubertė and Feuls (Chapter 14, this volume) argue that the value of any methodology for learning about practices lies not in the specific methods used but in how researchers engage with these methods. With that, they propose that interview*ing* can be adapted in line with the onto-epistemological assumptions of practice theory. However, to do this, EaP researchers must move beyond the interview-as-an-instrument approach and adapt interviewing practices to their onto-epistemological assumptions. This requires delving into the social and collaborative nature of interviewing, using 'interviewing' as opposed to 'interview' to highlight the active and interactive nature of the practice. Drawing on Davidson's account of first-, second-, and third-person knowledge, they position interviewing as a social practice. In this way, interviewing can be seen as an interactive, purposeful and affective engagement that allows for the co-creation of knowledge by researchers and research participants. This means recognizing the interactive elements of interviewing and scrutinizing the performance or 'hows' of interviewing. Liubertė and Feuls explain further by determining six essential principles of interviewing as social practice. These principles offer methodological reflections and guidance on how researchers can encourage participants to reveal the more tacit elements of their practices during the interview encounter, and analyze the interview material afterwards. The method demands embeddedness and a reflective process of creating research materials for interpretation. By doing this, the authors suggest we gain access to the layers of practices that are not directly observable, affording us a more complete insight into these practices from the people who enact them. Therefore, Liubertė and Feuls argue that by using the methodological principles of interviewing as social practice, a deeper theoretical understanding of entrepreneurial practices can be achieved.

As we see a significant rise in remote working, and greater activity on digital spaces, entrepreneurial practices are becoming increasingly digital. There are more entanglements of physical and digital entrepreneurial practices across digital and physical sites. Consequently, there is a growing need to better understand digital methods of data collection and analysis. Cyron (Chapter 11, this volume) encourages and guides researchers in how to grapple with the digitization of entrepreneurial practices lying at the heart of how people create, develop, organize and implement new ventures. Cyron outlines how digital data sources include everything from semi-public profiles and blogs on social networking sites, to back channels including private conversations on social networking sites, productivity software, data storage files and digital tools and devices such as emails, messaging services, and video communication applications. Cyron outlines best practices in collecting these sources of data. He addresses the opportunities these digital methods hold such as being able to zoom out from digital sites and their entanglements with physical sites to view the physical and embodied enactment and entanglement of practices across larger nets of practices. He also addresses the challenges involved in collecting information from each of the digital data sources, especially the risk of becoming overwhelmed by the volume of data and the decision as to which data sources to use, how and why. Cyron also cautions researchers to be reticent and adhere to best practices in negotiating access, ethics, trust, and data security including GDPR (General Data Protection Regulation) requirements.

Moving away from specific methods used to carry out empirical studies of entrepreneurial practice, Davis (Chapter 13, this volume) outlines a methodological agenda for studying entrepreneurship through spatial inquiry. Discussing the importance of time and space for practice research, Davis identifies a gap in our understanding of the role of space in entrepreneurship as practice research. These questions include what is the relationship between space and entrepreneurial practicing? How can we explore the influence of a space in relation to its current entrepreneurial activity? How might we understand the different aspects of space – this confluence between structural (space as objectively existing) and experiential (space as felt and understood) aspects? And methodologically, how can we begin to synthesize these different spatial aspects in a dynamic and unfolding entrepreneurial process? Addressing these concerns, Davis uses Henri Lefebvre's 'spatial triad', a conceptual and analytical frame for studying spatial phenomena over time that incorporates three interrelated 'spaces' in society: perceived space ('real' physical properties of space), conceived space ('imagined' mental representations of space) and lived space (the 'lived' experience of space in-between the real and imagined). Davis uses his own research exploring the relationship between space and entrepreneurship at Cains Brewery in Liverpool, UK, to outline four guiding principles for operationalizing Lefebvre's triad. These principles emphasize researcher immersion and historicized methods, as well as the importance of attending to wider geographical forces and the political implications of human action. As he discusses this process, Davis mobilizes the three interrelated aspects of the triad, unfolding the continuous interplay between the conceived, perceived, and lived. In doing this, Davis's primary contribution is to show how EaP scholars might utilize spatial inquiry to continue to unsettle structure–agent dichotomies, where space is treated as a dynamic and unfolding phenomenon actively shaping and in turn shaped by entrepreneurial practices and activities over time.

NEW EMPIRICAL ADVANCES

As the previous section demonstrates, EaP remains a lively, unique and growing perspective to understanding entrepreneuring in terms of a coherent 'package' of philosophical foundations, theory and methodology. In the final section of this Handbook, we have included four chapters that adopt a practice theory lens to examine empirical research as an aspect of entrepreneuring, which demonstrates another way to develop innovative and novel insights.

Hamacher and colleagues (Chapter 16, this volume) note that prior entrepreneurship research on entrepreneurial pitching has tended to explain pitching outcomes based on judges' perceptions of both entrepreneurial impression management, rhetoric or non-verbal communication and/or the coherence and plausibility of their business plans. However, this narrow focus fails to appreciate the complex practices that play out between judges as they attempt to reach a consensus in their decisions. Drawing on audio recordings of judging discussions at a three-day hackathon event involving 250 contestants across 30 entrepreneurial teams, the authors examine the relational and temporal conversational practices that play out in judging discussions to understand how judges move from individual perceptions of pitches towards consensus decisions. Their findings show the importance of examining the role of non-entrepreneur actors, such as judges, in determining entrepreneurial outcomes. This advances work begun by Teague et al. (2020) by highlighting how it is not only interactions between entrepreneurs and the judges that shape pitching outcomes, but also interactions between the judges themselves, providing motivation for future scholarship to examine practices that involve others in entrepreneurship pitching including teammates, other teams, mentors, coaches, sponsors, organizers and audiences.

Similarly, Hydle and colleagues (Chapter 17, this volume) adopt practice theory to challenge the existing assumption of individualism in corporate entrepreneurship (CE) literature. Rather than CE be conceptualized as an aggregate of individuals' actions, the authors study CE practices in the context of servitization – when manufacturers move from products to services. Drawing on data from five manufacturing firms in Norway within an industrial cluster of suppliers to the energy and maritime sectors, they identify and examine four interrelated entrepreneuring practices (bundles): prospecting the ecosystem; developing the new service-oriented business venture; transforming the organization; and establishing the new service-oriented business venture. This contributes to CE theory by exposing four important CE practices in the context of servitization, as well as highlighting the mutual participation of senior engineers, development engineers, middle managers and service employees in the practices-arrangement bundles. The authors conclude that practice theory is a useful tool for CE research as it enables researchers to further grasp and uncover entrepreneuring activities within corporations.

Another example of innovative insights being developed through using practice theories as a theoretical lens comes from Cnossen and Winter (Chapter 18, this volume). In this chapter, the authors investigate the practices that maintain and develop a coworking space, specifically investigating the practices enacted by a mother and daughter partnership. The authors note that while family and enterprise are typically understood as separate entities or domains, each with their own aims and rules, these boundaries are not so clear in cases of early-stage family enterprises, where family members put unpaid labor into the business, or in enterprises where the service or product sold is offered in a home-like place with a familial atmosphere. Using ethnographic fieldwork in a newly founded coworking space in Hamburg, the authors examine not only the management practices involved in reproducing a coworking space but demonstrate their entanglement with the realm of family through care-taking practices. In particular, the authors render visible how the everyday care-taking practice of installing a cupboard, breakfast events, and curing a cold intersect with management practices of financial decision-making, recruiting clients, and facilitating networking. The authors conclude that practice theories offer a new way to conceptualize and investigate how practices can contribute to both the doing of family and the doing of entrepreneurship, which weaves together the realms of business and family.

This section of the Handbook concludes with a contribution by Mösching and Steyaert (Chapter 19, this volume). In their chapter, the authors seek to understand how, and under which conditions, entrepreneurship can constitute a 'disruptive' force that brings about transformative change, given pressing needs to respond to rising inequality and ecological degradation. Applying practice theory, they note that entrepreneurial 'world making' often needs to overcome existing and often dominant organizational practices. However, whether or not this depends on introducing new practices or altering existing relations among practice is little understood. They conduct a multi-sited ethnography that focuses on an entrepreneurial project aiming to change the dominant form of coffee production, distribution and consumption by turning to alternative, more sustainable and socially equal forms of organizing. By tracing and comparing the connections among dominant and marginal practices in the industry, they demonstrate that 'world making' plays out in the different ways that practices (and their components) are associated across time and space, whereby new (modes of) associations enable different worlds to become. Overall, their analysis suggests that novel agential potentials in world making can develop even when singular practices themselves are not changing.

CONCLUSION: LOOKING TO THE FUTURE

Following in the footsteps of scholars who have developed 'entrepreneuring' as an alternative model to individualism, entrepreneurship as practice, as can be seen in this Handbook, is a new and exciting domain of entrepreneurship research. Continuing the tradition laid down by Fletcher, Gartner, Hjorth, Steyaert, Anderson, and Johannisson among many others, this research community takes seriously practitioners' practices when building theory of entrepreneuring processes, whilst boldly acknowledging the great diversity that this entails. EaP continues to chip away at the individualism assumption that supports much of contemporary entrepreneurship research. It does so by stressing the importance of contextualizing not only entrepreneuring, but also knowledge itself. Hence, EaP, perhaps humbly, does not offer a 'grand' theory of entrepreneuring, but rather a well-articulated conceptual means through which scholars and practitioners can understand important challenges (such as forming new practices, accomplishing collective intentionality, disrupting and altering practice-bundle relationships, and transformation of practical knowledge). Accordingly, EaP contributes by offering a convincing framework for developing detailed insights into complex processes and relations that resonate with practitioner experience, rather than being removed from them.

Despite these gains, in many ways EaP is still in its infancy and there are many opportunities to contribute further. We see the future of EaP developing simultaneously in three ways. First, EaP still holds a relatively marginal voice in the entrepreneurship research community. The danger is that scholars will abandon (or never apply) theories of practice on the grounds that the peer review system rejects the framework and insights developed through it. After all, EaP scholars' practices also exist relationally to other dominant practices in the field. To prevent this, we see the future of EaP as the continued expansion of collective participation through which a broad community of scholars interact to write, review and publish practice theory-led research. While EaP will remain a core contributor, it is important that entrepreneurship scholars acknowledge and work with other practice theory-led communities within the academy (such as organization, strategy, leadership innovation and information scholars). These communities all share a common epistemological and ontological foundation, and thus have an ability to come together to support practice theory scholarship more broadly. This will occur as this community overall continues to deepen its commitment to the ontological and epistemological arguments of practice theories, and use the framework to develop rich and convincing accounts of entrepreneuring that are not possible through any other means. As the relations among writers, readers, reviewers and editors expand, EaP will play a role in carving out a sustainable trajectory for future scholars to advance practice theory research as a distinct domain.

Second, we echo Gherardi (Chapter 1, this volume) that EaP scholarship also poses a unique opportunity to contribute to theories of practice in ways that other domains do not. While applying practice theories in new ways in new contexts will continue and should be encouraged, scholars can also think deeply about how EaP can contribute to under-developed aspects of practice theories, in particular, how new practical knowledge – the formation and assembly of actions, mind/bodies, materials, meaning, normativity and identity – is possible from performances of pre-existing practical knowledge. Very few studies investigate the formation of new practices from a practice theory standpoint, and it remains little understood how new practices may emerge given that practitioners use pre-existing practical knowledge, rules and teleo-affective structures to do so.

Finally, EaP research has the potential to close the gap between practitioners and scholars by recognizing, elevating and understanding the nuances of performing practical knowledge in various situations and circumstances. However, most research has continued to focus on applying theories of practice to develop insights for a scholarly audience, and has limited the involvement of practitioners in the process. This does not need to be the case, as practitioners can take a role in research practices to make visible the tacit understandings being used to coordinate interactions, and collectively help unpack their origins and complexities. The results of this process make practical knowledge available for discussion and transformation by collectives of practitioners, which can reflexively help to bring about positive social change in the process. We see future EaP research developing this potential by engaging more seriously with practitioners to produce mutually beneficial insights and explanations. In summary, the near future holds many potential opportunities for EaP to contribute not only to the entrepreneurship research domain but also to scholarship on organizations, strategy, leadership and innovation among others, for those scholars willing to pursue them.

REFERENCES

Ardichvili, A., Cardozo, R., & Ray, S. (2003). A theory of entrepreneurial opportunity identification and development. *Journal of Business Venturing*, *18*(1), 105–123.

Arentz, J., Sautet, F., & Storr, V. (2013). Prior-knowledge and opportunity identification. *Small Business Economics*, *41*(2), 461–478.

Bourdieu, P. (1990). *The Logic of Practice*. Cambridge: Polity Press.

Braidotti, R. (2015). Posthuman affirmative politics. In S. E. Wilmer & Audronė Žukauskaitė (Eds.), *Resisting Biopolitics: Philosophical, Political, and Performative Strategies* (pp. 30–56). New York: Routledge.

Braidotti, R. (2019a). *Posthuman Knowledge*. Cambridge: Polity Press.

Braidotti, R. (2019b). A theoretical framework for the critical posthumanities. *Theory, Culture & Society*, *36*(6), 31–61.

Champenois, C., Lefebvre, V., & Ronteau, S. (2020). Entrepreneurship as practice: Systematic literature review of a nascent field. *Entrepreneurship & Regional Development*, *32*(3–4), 1–32.

Farias, C., Fernandez, P., Hjorth, D., & Holt, R. (2019). Organizational entrepreneurship, politics and the political. *Entrepreneurship & Regional Development*, *31*(7–8), 555–566.

Fletcher, D. E. (2006). Entrepreneurial processes and the social construction of opportunity. *Entrepreneurship & Regional Development*, *18*(5), 421–440.

Garcia-Lorenzo, L., Donnelly, P., Sell-Trujillo, L., & Imas, J. M. (2018). Liminal entrepreneuring: The creative practices of nascent necessity entrepreneurs. *Organization Studies*, *39*(2–3), 373–395.

Garfinkel, H., & Sacks, H. (1970). On formal structures of practical actions. In J. C. McKinney & E. A. Tiryakian (Eds.), *Theoretical Sociology* (pp. 337–366). New York: Appleton-Century-Crofts.

Gartner, W. B. (1988). Who is an entrepreneur? Is the wrong question. *American Journal of Small Business*, *12*(4), 11–32.

Gartner, W. B. (2016). *Entrepreneurship as Organizing: Selected Papers of William B. Gartner*. Cheltenham, UK and Northampton, MA, USA: Edward Elgar Publishing.

Gherardi, S. (2000). Practice-based theorizing on learning and knowing in organizations. *Organization*, *7*(2), 211–223.

Gherardi, S. (2009). Introduction: The critical power of the practice lens. *Management Learning*, *40*(2), 115–128.

Gherardi, S. (2012). *How to Conduct a Practice-Based Study: Problems and Methods*. Cheltenham, UK and Northampton, MA, USA: Edward Elgar Publishing.

Gherardi, S. (2017). Sociomateriality in posthuman practice theory. In S. Hui, E. Shove, & T. R. Schatzki (Eds.), *The Nexus of Practices: Connections, Constellations, Practitioners* (pp. 38–51). London: Routledge.

Goldenstein, J., & Walgenbach, P. (2021). "How on earth did this happen?" The relationship of practical consciousness and institutional evolution. *Organization Theory*, *2*(3), https://doi.org/10.1177/26317877211020324.

Heidegger, M. (1978). *Being and Time*. Oxford: Blackwell.

Hindmarsh, J., & Pilnick, A. (2007). Knowing bodies at work: Embodiment and ephemeral teamwork in anaesthesia. *Organization Studies*, *28*(9), 1395–1416.

Hjorth, D. (2003). *Rewriting Entrepreneurship: For a New Perspective on Organisational Creativity*. Copenhagen: Liber.

Hjorth, D. (Ed.) (2012). *Handbook on Organisational Entrepreneurship*. Cheltenham, UK and Northampton, MA, USA: Edward Elgar Publishing.

Hjorth, D., Holt, R., & Steyaert, C. (2015). Entrepreneurship and process studies. *International Small Business Journal*, *33*(6), 599–611.

Johannisson, B. (2011). Towards a practice theory of entrepreneuring. *Small Business Economics*, *36*(2), 135–150.

Latour, B., & Woolgar, S. (1979). *Laboratory Life: The Construction of Scientific Facts*. Princeton, NJ: Princeton University Press.

Manning, E. (2016). *The Minor Gesture*. Durham, NC: Duke University Press.

Nicolini, D. (2012). *Practice Theory, Work, & Organization: An Introduction*. Oxford: Oxford University Press.

Nicolini, D. (2017). Practice theory as a package of theory, method and vocabulary: Affordances and limitations. In M. Jonas, B. Littig, & A. Wroblewski (Eds.), *Methodological Reflections on Practice Oriented Theories* (pp. 19–34). Cham: Springer International Publishing.

Nicolini, D., Gherardi, S., & Yanow, D. (Eds.). (2003). *Knowing in Organizations: A Practice-Based Approach*. Armonk, NY: M. E. Sharpe.

Pickering, A. (1992). *Science as Practice and Culture*. Chicago: University of Chicago Press.

Pittaway, L., & Cope, J. (2007). Simulating entrepreneurial learning: Integrating experiential and collaborative approaches to learning. *Management Learning*, *38*(2), 211–233.

Politis, D. (2005). The process of entrepreneurial learning: A conceptual framework. *Entrepreneurship Theory and Practice*, *29*(4), 399–424.

Ramoglou, S., Gartner, W. B., & Tsang, E. W. K. (2020). "Who is an entrepreneur?" is (still) the wrong question. *Journal of Business Venturing Insights*, *13*(1), e00168.

Reckwitz, A. (2002). Toward a theory of social practices: A development in culturalist theorizing. *European Journal of Social Theory*, *5*(2), 243–263.

Rorty, R. (1979). *Philosophy and the Mirror of Nature*. Princeton, NJ: Princeton University Press.

Rouse, J. (2006). Practice theory. In D. M. Gabbay, P. Thagard, & J. Woods (Eds.), *Handbook of the Philosophy of Science* (Vol. 15, pp. 500–540). Amsterdam: Elsevier.

Schatzki, T. R. (2001). Practice theory: An introduction. In T. R. Schatzki, K. K. Cetina, & E. von Savigny (Eds.), *The Practice Turn in Contemporary Theory* (pp. 1–14). London: Routledge.

Schatzki, T. R. (2002). *The Site of the Social: A Philosophical Account of the Constitution of Social Life and Change*. University Park: Pennsylvania State University Press.

Schatzki, T. R. (2005). Peripheral vision: The sites of organizations. *Organization Studies*, *26*(3), 465–484.

Schatzki, T. R. (2006). On organizations as they happen. *Organization Studies*, *27*(12), 1863–1873.

Schatzki, T. R. (2012). A primer on practices. In J. Higgs, R. Barnett, M. Hutchings, & F. Trede (Eds.), *Practice-Based Education: Perspectives and Strategies* (pp. 13–26). Rotterdam: Sense Publishers.

Schatzki, T. R., Knorr Cetina, K., & Savigny, E. von (Eds.) (2001). *The Practice Turn in Contemporary Theory*. London: Routledge.

Shane, S. (2000). Prior knowledge and the discovery of entrepreneurial opportunities. *Organization Science*, *11*(4), 448–469.

Steyaert, C. (2007). "Entrepreneuring" as a conceptual attractor? A review of process theories in 20 years of entrepreneurship studies. *Entrepreneurship & Regional Development*, *19*(6), 453–477.

Strati, A. (2007). Sensible knowledge and practice-based learning. *Management Learning*, *38*(1), 61–77.

Taylor, C. (1985). Interpretation and the sciences of man. In *Philosophy and the Human Sciences: Philosophical Papers* (pp. 15–58). Cambridge: Cambridge University Press.

Teague, B. T., Gorton, M. D., & Liu, Y. (2020). Different pitches for different stages of entrepreneurial development: The practice of pitching to business angels. *Entrepreneurship & Regional Development*, *32*(3–4), 334–352.

Teague, B. T., Tunstall, R., Champenois, C., & Gartner, W. B. (2021). Editorial: An introduction to entrepreneurship as practice. *International Journal of Entrepreneurial Behavior & Research*, *27*(3), 569–578.

Thompson, N. A., & Byrne, O. (2020). Advancing entrepreneurship as practice: Previous developments and future possibilities. In W. B. Gartner & B. T. Teague (Eds.), *Research Handbook on Entrepreneurial Behavior, Practice and Process* (pp. 30–55). Cheltenham, UK and Northampton, MA, USA: Edward Elgar Publishing.

Thompson, N. A., & Illes, E. (2020). Entrepreneurial learning as practice: A video-ethnographic analysis. *International Journal of Entrepreneurial Behavior & Research*, *27*(3), 579–599.

Thompson, N. A., Verduijn, K., & Gartner, W. B. (2020). Entrepreneurship-as-practice: Grounding contemporary theories of practice into entrepreneurship studies. *Entrepreneurship & Regional Development*, *32*(3–4), 247–256.

Verduyn, K. (2015). Entrepreneuring and process: A Lefebvrian perspective. *International Small Business Journal: Researching Entrepreneurship*, *33*(6), 638–648.

PART I

NEW FOUNDATIONS

1. Under what conditions is a domain-specific practice theory of entrepreneurship possible?

Silvia Gherardi

INTRODUCTION

The rediscovery of practice theories, since the 2000s, has also affected entrepreneurship studies and has become an emerging social phenomenon visible under the label 'entrepreneurship as practice' (Thompson & Byrne, 2020). The rediscovery of practice theories in social sciences in general is due to several factors, mainly to go beyond problematic dualisms (action/structure, human/non-human, mind/body), to displace mind as the central phenomenon in human life, to see reason not as an innate mental faculty but as a practice phenomenon, and to question individual actions and their status as building blocks of the social (Schatzki, 2001, p. 11).

In a systematic literature review of the articles published between 2002 and 2018 and identified as belonging to the field of entrepreneurship as practice (Champenois, Lefebvre, & Ronteau, 2020), we find a definition of the knowledge interests of the field, formulated as follows: 'The Entrepreneurship as Practice perspective entails investigating entrepreneurship as emerging/creative organizing that consists of a bundle of practices (structural and processual), performed (enacted, and embodied) by a constellation of entrepreneurial practitioners who are intertwined and embedded.' Consequently, the main focus of the field is defined in terms of practices, practitioners, and processes, where practitioners – according to this definition – constitute the central focus from which intentional action springs.

In my opinion, at the beginning of an emerging stream of research in any field, it is crucial to bring legitimacy by emphasizing a supposed homogeneity and create a bandwagon effect, but once the newness of the stream is acknowledged, difference and differentiation should be recognized (Corradi, Gherardi, & Verzelloni, 2010). In my reading of the literature on entrepreneurship which has a sensibility towards practice theories and the contemporary debate surrounding practice-based studies, it is important to value what I consider the antecedents of Entrepreneurship as Practice, i.e. those studies that made possible the rediscovery of practice theories and that ground the specificity of the scientific debate on entrepreneurship.

Many studies in Entrepreneurship as Practice follow the mainstream influences of a specific practice theory in an attempt to *apply* it in the context of an entrepreneurial practice. We can easily trace the application of activity theory (Jones & Holt, 2008), pragmatism (Watson, 2013), structuration theory (Chiasson & Saunders, 2005; Fletcher, 2006; Jack & Anderson, 2002; Mole & Mole, 2010), Bourdieu praxeology (Anderson, Dodd, & Jack, 2010; De Clercq & Voronov, 2009; Dodd, Pret, & Shaw, 2016; Foley & O'Connor, 2013; Hill, 2018; Karataş-Özkan, 2011; Spigel, 2017; Tatli et al., 2014; Vincent, 2016), ethnomethodology (Chalmers & Shaw, 2017), a Foucauldian practice perspective (Dey & Steyaert, 2016), a Schatzkian approach (Keating, Geiger, & McLoughlin, 2014), an Orlikoswkian approach (Rittenhofer, 2015), an actor-network sensibility (Barinaga, 2017; Gherardi & Nicolini, 2005; Korsgaard, 2011; Murdock & Varnes, 2018) and a critical practice theoretical perspective

(Houtbaeker, 2016; Parkkari, 2019). Moreover, we can trace a conjunction of Giddens and critical realism (Sarason, Dillard, & Dean, 2010) and of Bourdieu and critical realism (Vincent & Pagan, 2019).

We have evidence of attention towards what theories of practice may offer to entrepreneurship studies, and in this panorama of variegated theoretical grounding and methodological takes there is also a voice that calls for developing a consequential methodology for practice-based studies, starting from three commonalities that together constitute practice theory as an ontological approach: '(a) practices are organized, materially mediated and collaborative activities; (b) practices are fundamental to all social phenomena; and (c) performances of practices draw on embodied and practical knowledge' (Thompson & Byrne, 2020, p. 31). Which image of what constitutes a practice is implicit in such a framing? We can notice how the term practice does not simply refer to what entrepreneurs do and say, rather it refers to multiple activities – performed not only by entrepreneurs – that are socially recognizable in particular social and material contexts. Moreover, all practices are social practices in the sense that they are meaning-making, identity-forming, and order-producing activities (Nicolini, Gherardi, & Yanow, 2003), and finally that practical knowledge is kept and transmitted within practices.

A theoretical framework based on those three commonalities has the great advantage of formulating a simple and clear picture of how to define a practice ontology and it should be noted that such ontology may be either a realist, a social constructionist, or a critical realist one, and sometimes it is very difficult to understand which one sustains the author's theoretical frame. However, my intention in briefly sketching the state of the art of Entrepreneurship as Practice literature is not to articulate further what has already been elaborated, but rather to propose a different (and somewhat parallel) line of argumentation. It states that entrepreneurship as practice does not need to apply practice theories elaborated by the 'big fathers' (as Verduyn & Tillmar, 2019 call them), rather it may explore and develop an autonomous practice theorizing of entrepreneurship (a domain-specific practice theory) that may contribute to practice theories. My aim is therefore to turn the issue upside down on the assumption that the task of applying practice theories has been done, whilst I wish to encourage other scholars to experiment with the task of theorizing on the grounded knowledge of the entrepreneurship field.

The chapter is organized as follow: first a definition of domain-specific theory of practice is introduced, then I propose to conceive entrepreneurship as a collective knowledgeable doing and entrepreneuring as a situated activity. I proceed to formulate a proposal for theorizing entrepreneuring as a *statu nascenti* in which resourcing takes place and I conclude by focusing on three concepts that may become the building blocks for a domain-specific practice theory of entrepreneuring: *agencement*, formativeness and everyday creativity.

COMMONSENSICAL UNDERSTANDING OF PRACTICE, GENERAL THEORIES OF PRACTICE, AND DOMAIN-SPECIFIC THEORIES OF PRACTICE

As Alvesson and Sandberg (2011) noted, understanding the philosophical assumptions underlying a theory is crucial for being able to further develop it. This development may take place within the same framework or may disrupt it by problematizing taken for granted assumptions. The authors argue that what makes a theory interesting and influential is often that it challenges our assumptions in some significant way. Nevertheless to receive attention a theory must be significantly different from, and at the time be significantly connected to, established literature in order to be seen as meaningful. While a 'gap-spotting' attitude (finding a gap, filling the gap), is rather diffuse and under-problematizes existing literature – thus reinforcing rather than challenging already influential theories – the authors suggest 'problematization' as a methodology for generating new research questions. They indicate how certain theoretical orientations, such as some version of social constructionism, postmodernism, feminism, critical theory (and I shall add more recent debate on posthumanism and new materialism), are oriented to disrupt rather than build on existing literature, thus running the opposite risk of over-problematizing it. This dynamic between 'gap-filling' and problematization can also be traced within practice-based studies.

Considering the literature on practice theories in organization studies, Sandberg and Tsoukas (2015) distinguish three approaches: commonsensical theories of practice, general theories of practice and domain-specific theories of practice. A commonsensical approach to practice that regards 'practice' simply as 'what people do' is largely diffuse and it is basically a-theoretical. It perpetuates the useless distinction between abstract theory as juxtaposed to concrete practice, rendering practice derivative of theory. Commonsensical theories of practice are not even promising within entrepreneurship as a practice field, as Sandberg and Tsoukas argue for organization studies. Nevertheless, since the dichotomy theory/practice is so widespread, it is worth spending a few words on the theories of knowledge behind a certain understanding of theory based on scientific rationality and a certain understanding of practice based on the logic of practice.

The ongoing discussions about a supposed theory/practice gap and a claim that practice should mirror theory is based on the implicit assumption that theory is the product of scientific rationality. Positivism is the theory of knowledge that, in assuming the separation of subject/object sustains scientific rationality as opposed to the logic of practical rationality. Nevertheless, the upsurge of practice theories is related to the discrediting of positivism in the 1960s and the loss of credibility of its main assumptions: scientism (scientific method as the only valuable source of knowledge); naturalism (the unity of method across the social and the natural sciences); regularity as the notion of causality (the regular association of x and y is both necessary and sufficient to talk about causality); an assumption that explanation entails prediction (and vice versa); a rejection of explanations in terms of mental or subjective states (like intentions or motives); a predilection for quantification and sophisticated statistical analysis; and finally a sharp distinction between facts and values (Baert, 2005). A renewed interest in meaning, language and critique arose in the late twentieth-century social sciences (Baert and Domínguez Rubio, 2009) when naturalist philosophy of social science was challenged by three intellectual strands: hermeneutics, Wittgensteinian philosophy, and critical theory. The liberation of meaning from logic brought into focus the relations between meaning, practices and language (Gherardi, 2018). Moreover, the interest in meaning-making led to the rediscovery of the phenomenological tradition – Heidegger and Merleau-Ponty in philosophy – and in particular of Alfred Schutz's work (1962, 1964) in sociology, which focused on the everyday 'common-sense world'. Different from scientific rationality, the practice rationality (Bourdieu, 1990) operates within a taken-for-granted world where people suspend disbelief. Schutz's phenomenological sociology, Bourdieu's, and Berger and Luckmann's (1966) constructionist research institutionalized the assumption that the categories, through which people interpret social reality, help as well to create the world. Social constructionism has contributed to the empirical investigations of what counts as genuine knowledge and why. Therefore, knowledge becomes an observable and researchable phenomenon rather than a merely imagined normative ideal, and within practice as a theory of knowledge, in the 1970s several general theories of practice were elaborated and today are considered classic or first wave theories.

In Sandberg and Tsoukas's understanding, the most extensive general theories of practice are those developed by Bourdieu, Giddens and, more lately, Schatzki and they have in common a reference to Heidegger's existential ontology. What characterizes general theories of practice is that they provide a systematic and comprehensive conceptualization of what defines practice and how it may be explained, thus providing a more accurate account of the logic of practice, in contrast to both individualism and structuralism.

Nevertheless, the more recent debate, especially within organization studies (OS), moves further to consider practice within domain-specific theories of practice and Sandberg and Tsoukas (2015, p. 193) give the following examples:

> Several domain-specific theories of practice can be found in OS. These, inter alia, include a performative approach to routines (Feldman and Pentland, 2003), understanding strategy as practice (Whittington and Vaara, 2012; Golsorkhi *et al.*, 2010), a stucturationist approach to technology (Orlikowski, 2000), and a practice-based view on organizational knowledge and learning (Gherardi, 2006; Nicolini *et al.*, 2003; Sandberg and Pinnington, 2009; Tsoukas, 1996, 2009, 2011).

My interest here is not to propose a classification of practice theories; several authors have proposed interesting and useful criteria for distinguishing for example an empirical, a theoretical, and a philosophical approach (Feldman & Orlikoswski, 2011), a weak and a strong approach (Nicolini, 2012), or three waves of practice research (Rinkinen, 2015). Rather, I wish to propose a compelling understanding of the category 'domain-specific theories of practice', in which it is not so much the topic that organizes a cluster of studies, rather it is the process of theorizing, grounded in a corpus of practice-based studies about a topic, that becomes a specific practice theory of a phenomenon. I am proposing to elaborate 'entrepreneurship as practice' not as the application of practice theories to entrepreneurship, but as a practice theory of entrepreneuring and I wish to explore under which assumptions such a theory may be developed.

ENTREPRENEURSHIP AS A COLLECTIVE KNOWLEDGEABLE DOING AND ENTREPRENEURING AS A SITUATED ACTIVITY

A common point of departure in all practice theories is the assumption that practices have to do with activities, and many practice scholars are concerned with what people *do* (Shove, Pantzar, & Wilson, 2012). Nevertheless, I argue that *doing* is not enough for defining a practice and that the concept of practice is more useful both for empirical research and for theorizing when it is conceived of as a *knowledgeable doing*.

The rationale for looking at a practice as a collective and knowledgeable doing is dual. In the first place it brings a renewed conception of knowledge as an activity, rather than as an object (as the information and understanding about a subject which a person has) and, in the second place, it connects with the corpus of knowledge (entrepreneurship in our case) that has been socially and historically elaborated and will be further elaborated while being practised.

As Kenneth Gergen (1985, p. 270) reminds us, 'knowledge is not something that people possess in their heads, but rather, something that people do together'. In this simple and straightforward definition of knowledge we can see the epistemological move from knowledge as a noun to knowing as a verb and the displacement of knowledge from the cognitive domain to the domain of the performative. Moreover, the collective activity of knowing takes place in situated practices and in practising it performs the social and historical knowledgeability of a domain of practice. In our case, entrepreneurship is conceptualized as a collective and knowledgeable activity taking place within a domain of situated practices that are socially recognized as pertaining to entrepreneurship, and that perform a body of social and historical knowledge that has been elaborated and institutionalized under the label entrepreneurship and that in being used responds to a transformative logic of practice. Knowledge in its being used, transforms itself, thus knowing can be conceived of as always performative of its conditions of production and reproduction. In other words, entrepreneurship as a corpus of knowledge changes not only under the pressure of external events, but also as a consequence of the standards of excellence created by the practitioners through their knowing in practice.

To illustrate more effectively what it means to study entrepreneurship as a collective and knowledgeable doing I would like to propose an analogy with so-called laboratory studies. In the 1970s, 'science', i.e. the social construction of scientific facts and scientific knowledge, became studied as a field of social practices like any other. Ethnographic methodologies were used in laboratory studies (Callon, 1986; Clarke & Fujimura, 1992; Knorr Cetina, 1981; Latour & Woolgar, 1986) resulting in rich descriptions of the mundane practices related to science, scientists, technologies and innovations. Knowledge practices were looked at, paying attention to the unique relations between things that are brought together in laboratories' activities: scientists, technologies, artefacts, discourses, live and non-live materials, expert and non-expert knowledges, everything that, in becoming connected, gives shape to a practice. Entrepreneurship may be studied according to the same methodological principle as situated practices and as a body of knowledge that follows a transformational logic.

Laboratories studies and science and technology studies made visible how the concept of practice connects 'knowing' with 'doing'. Not only does knowing move knowledge away from the cognitive, but also the boundaries between knowing and learning are blurred once a situated social learning theory (Lave & Wenger, 1991) proposes a concept of learning as competent participation in a situated practice within a community of practitioners. Similarly, laboratories studies and science and technology studies refer to the Latin verb *facere*, to stress the social and technological manufacturing of knowing: Knorr Cetina (1981) uses the term 'facticity' and Bruno Latour (1987) the 'fabrication' of scientific facts and technical artefacts. Knowledge consequently is fabricated by situated practices of knowledge production and reproduction, using the technologies of representation and mobilization employed by practitioners. The term 'knowing-in-practice' (Gherardi, 2001; Orlikowski, 2002) has sanctioned the passage from the noun to the verb, suggesting how knowing is an enactment and an accomplishment, rather than a thing or a static property. What is known constitutes itself in knowledgeable doing, in purposeful activities, and it is 'situated in practice' (Suchman, 2007). Knowing-in-practice only becomes meaningful in relation to a distinct social practice. Due to its embeddedness in social practice, knowing is necessarily in permanent flux, and it entails a procedural understanding of the ability to act of all the practice elements once connected and reconnected. In other words, knowledge emerges from the context of its production and is anchored by (and in) material supports in that context.

The epistemic change that the passage from nouns to verbs entails is also linked to the processual understanding implicit in the idea of knowing as an activity and as an ongoing process of achievement. The epistemology of 'becoming' is widely used within process studies for stressing the temporality of practising and its situatedness; nevertheless this change is particularly evident in the passage from 'entrepreneurship' to 'entrepreneuring', in which we can individuate the same sensibility towards an epistemological switch even before the vocabulary of practice made its appearance in Entrepreneurship as Practice literature. Appreciating entrepreneurial phenomena processually opens up the field to an understanding of entrepreneurship as organizational creation, meaning 'not simply the creation of new organizations but also experiments in new organizational forms' (Hjorth, Holt, & Steyaert, 2015, p. 599).

There is a pioneer body of knowledge about entrepreneurship and small business research that has been developed by Bengt Johannisson since the late 1970s and 1980s that may be clearly defined as the antecedents of the 'entrepreneurship as practice approach' since in his work the idea of entrepreneurship as a 'contextualized practice' is illustrated by the connection between networking and local development, and by his methodological choices while conducting contextual, interpretive and action-research approaches (Steyaert & Landström, 2011). In contrast with a dominant voluntarist understanding of entrepreneurship as the effect of individual actors and against the rhetoric of the entrepreneur as the lonely (and male) hero, Johannisson's work uses the network metaphor for suggesting a more subjectivist approach in which 'venturing means organizing through personal networking' (1995, p. 215). His work is representative of the epistemological tensions between objectivism and subjectivism, realism and social constructionism, that appeared in entrepreneurship studies as well as in organization studies after the linguistic turn, when a sensibility towards interpretive, anthropological research became widespread. In methodological terms, Johannisson (2011) proposed a new genre – 'enactive research' – based on the aim at being present when a new enterprise is conceived of (or imagined), so that he suggests that the best way to study entrepreneurship is to try it out. We can value Johannisson's contribution as pioneering the logic of practice for the effort he devoted to de-centre the (individual) entrepreneur as the central focus and agent of entrepreneurship and in doing this to implicitly move from the individual to the activity. Moreover, we can prize his continued efforts considering how even within the Entrepreneurship as Practice literature, practices are considered as stemming from the entrepreneur, in a conception and methodology for empirical research where the focus and the beginning of the research is on the entrepreneur – the image I call 'the entrepreneur and his (sometimes her) practices' – as if the entrepreneur were outside the practices of entrepreneuring. The heritage of methodological individualism imported from economics and psychology is hard to get rid of. To this is added the persistent genderism that pervades the birth of the discipline and that has been the subject of careful and continuous criticism (Ahl & Marlow, 2012). Gender as a social practice and entrepreneuring may be conceived of and empirically investigated as two intertwined practices (Bruni, Gherardi, & Poggio, 2005).

To better understand the differences that Entrepreneurship as Practice literature may operate within we have to remember that the turn to practice, after the 2000s, has been done mainly for de-centring the human subject as the main source of action and moving from a formulation of practice theory as 'humans and their practices' to a vision of practice as the entanglement of humans, materialities, discourses, knowledges and any other relevant element in situated activities. Even when Johannisson writes about a practice theory of entrepreneuring – as in the title of his 2011 article – his pioneering work targets practice in contrast to the image of entrepreneurship as an intentionally planned and dramatically staged activity that characterizes rationalistic approaches to entrepreneurship. In his work practice is rather conceived of as an organizing context, a container of improvisational and personal networking activities, guided by phronesis, the relevant guiding intellectual virtue in the knowledge-creating process.

The concept of entrepreneuring slowly moved in further translations 'from slow motion to a conceptual attractor?' in the words of Steyaert (2007) who used a question mark in sceptically reflecting on the term after twenty years of being in use. In my opinion, years later we can leave the question mark out since the process approach has been widely accepted and what is more important is that the concept as a conceptual attractor has pointed entrepreneurship studies towards a social ontology of relatedness, and towards a social ontology of becoming. This move has been done appropriating the term 'only for those process theories formulated within the so-called creative process view (Sarasvathy et al. 2003), leaving out the discovery perspective (Shane and Venkataraman 2000) and the evolutionary perspective (Aldrich 1999) which both speak of processes in an entitative and equilibrium-based way' (Steyaert, 2007, p. 454). Thus, the term entrepreneuring, as a travelling concept, has paved the way for how entrepreneurship scholars can embrace different ontologies, epistemologies, and practices of researching and knowing. It has been the attractor also for practice theories and the emergence of the Entrepreneurship as Practice movement.

It is within the above state of the art and the cultural climate around entrepreneuring and the creative process view thus introduced that I propose to develop a domain-specific practice theory of entrepreneurship grounding it in the most central and traditional concept: that of opportunity.

THE *STATU NASCENTI* OF ENTREPRENEURING

I propose to explore the concept of opportunity as the leading way into the formulation of a domain-specific practice theory of entrepreneurship. My choice of this concept is in relation to the long and articulated elaboration in literature where entrepreneurship is often defined in terms of the identification and pursuit of opportunities. I feel therefore authorized to consider it as foundational of the discipline and as a travelling concept that may change its meaning in its being used and moved into other terrains. Moreover, from the point of view of practice theories, I wish to stress how a concept of opportunity is almost absent and with it the issue of how new practices enter into use and how the process of resourcing of the nascent practice initiates its trajectory, is not fully developed. An exception is the work in energy and consumer culture where new practices (showering instead of bathing, or Nordic walking diffusion) have received attention (Shove & Pantzar, 2005).

In choosing the concept of opportunity I wish also to reverse the direction of theorizing and open a reflection on what entrepreneurship studies may offer to practice theory.

The idea that entrepreneurs exploit opportunities to create economic wealth is well grounded in literature and with the growing interest in social entrepreneurship, the economic definition of opportunity has been enlarged to consider its social value and the opportunities for social change as well. In the contemporary context of social, environmental and economic transformation (in the geological epoch of the Anthropocene) fundamental changes in human/anthropocentric modes of being in the world are sorely needed (Calás, Ergene, & Smircich, 2018) and therefore the concept of opportunity may acquire a different space of signification.

A rich research tradition has evolved that examines both how entrepreneurs – acting alone or in groups – exploit these opportunities and the implications of these actions for a wide variety of sustainable social and economic practices. Within this tradition the concept of 'opportunity' may be enlarged to cover also the idea of 'necessity'. Nascent necessity entrepreneurs are defined as those people whose motivation for initiating the business start-up has emerged out of contextual necessity, such as lack of other sources of income or employment. Beyond economic concerns, for many of the unemployed, 'liminal entrepreneuring' is also the means for regaining recognition and social acceptance for individuals living in precarious conditions (Garcia Lorenzo et al., 2018).

In the literature, two perspectives on the processes by which opportunities are formed have been dominant: either opportunities are formed by exogenous shocks to pre-existing markets or industries that entrepreneurs then discover (Shane, 2003), or they are formed endogenously by the entrepreneurs who created them (Alvarez & Barney, 2007). Sustaining these two formulations of opportunities there are distinct epistemological assumptions: critical realism in the discovery process and evolutionary realism in the creation process (Alvarez, Barney, & Anderson, 2013). In both cases opportunities are objectified and understood within a realist ontology. Moreover, since the phenomenon of entrepreneurship necessarily involves the dynamic interplay of opportunities and resources, it is assumed that it cannot be understood without due attention to resource mobilization, and, also in this case, financial, human, and social capital are resources objectified and commodified (Keating et al., 2014).

We can notice the relationship of interdependence between two separate processes: discovering or creating opportunities and resourcing them and how this interdependence is foundational of entrepreneuring. Nevertheless, within the relational epistemology that Steyaert (2007) has outlined for a creative process of entrepreneuring, the entitative view of opportunities and resources may be abandoned in favour of a relational view that focuses on how entrepreneurs, opportunities and resources establish links that bring forward the process of relating. An epistemology of practice will go a step further by proposing not to look at interactions and interdependencies, rather to reformulate their relations with the concept of intra-action. I shall come back to this epistemological change shortly, once I have introduced a change in the concept of opportunity following a certain style of theorizing about practice.

Instead of putting the question 'what an opportunity is', I prefer to ask 'what an opportunity does', since theorizing practice moves from questions of ontology to questions of epistemology and to be more precise I should say to questions of onto-epistemology since the distinction between ontology and epistemology is blurred once we accept not only the linguistic turn, but also the practice turn in which our epistemological practices shape the object we are studying (Gherardi, 2019; Gherardi & Strati, 2012).

My answer to the question is that an opportunity takes shape and performs a *statu nascenti* (a nascent state). The concept of *statu nascenti* has been proposed by the Italian sociologist Francesco Alberoni who carried out numerous studies on social movements (their start, development and end) and on individuals (on the nature of love and relationships among individuals and groups). The principles of his thought are to be found in *Movement and Institution* (1984), where he developed the concept of *statu nascenti*, to indicate the moment in which leadership, ideas, and communication come together and fuel the birth of movements. Similarly, falling in love is seen as a collective movement made up exclusively of two people and falling in love is in essence 'the ignition state of a collective movement' (Alberoni, 1983, p. 3).

The basic assumption of the nascent state is that individuals who go through the same experience or have participated in the same *statu nascenti* share an understanding that makes them profoundly similar. This experience is created by the sensation of sharing objectives and ideals such as in the case of organizations that are aiming to introduce change. A *statu nascenti* entails the restructuring of the fields of experiences to new ends so that participants share an affinity that also marks their distinction. A nascent state may be also linked to the concepts of creative networks and cultural improvisation, in which energy is spread out and fuelled into a new project, concept or experience. It is the state of the movement that precedes the institution and it is the moment in which the associations and the affects take form. In the *statu nascenti* of the process of entrepreneuring, we can trace how the knowledgeable process of resourcing, in its socio-material becoming, links the ideational, affective and socio-material forces within situated activities.

When we take 'opportunity' to denote the *statu nascenti* of a knowledgeable way of associating socio-material relations, we can look at the creativity of everyday life in situated practices of resourcing for an entrepreneurial project.

AGENCEMENT, FORMATIVENESS, AND EVERYDAY CREATIVITY

In developing the idea that opportunity is at the core of a domain-specific theory of practice in entrepreneuring, I am implicitly relying on a conceptualization of practice as an *agencement* of heterogeneous elements (humans, materialities, knowledges, affects) that, in their being connected achieve agency. Humans are not external to the practices in which they participate, nor are material arrangements external to the practices that humans carry out, nor is the researcher's subjectivity external to the practices s/he studies. Taking seriously the principle of considering practice as the unit of analysis implicitly denies the prioritization of individual or materials, or discourses or knowledges, in favour of an idea of entanglement (Orlikowski, 2007, 2009) or intra-action (Barad, 2003) or socio-materiality (Mol, 2002), or *agencement* (Gherardi, 2016). This means a different conceptualization of agency, not as a privilege of humans and their cognitive and reflective capacity, nor as the extension of agency to non-humans, rather as an ongoing process of connecting and disconnecting through which agency emerges as *agencement*, as a process of associations.

In a previous work in which I delineate the contribution of a practice-based theory of organizing inspired by an actor-network sensibility (Gherardi, 2016), I propose two concepts – *agencement* and formativeness – that address two 'blind spots' in the conversation on the turn to practice. The first blind spot concerns how we can talk of practices as having agency; the second concerns how we can articulate knowing in practice as a 'doing while inventing the way of doing', i.e. the creative entanglement of knowing and doing.

Agencement is a word currently used in French as a synonym for 'arrangement', 'fitting' or 'fixing', and it has been used as a philosophical term by Deleuze and Guattari (1987) with the sense of 'in connection with'. For Deleuze and Guattari, a philosophical concept never operates in isolation but comes to its sense through the connection with other senses. This meaning of 'being in connection with' gives a first good approximation of the term. The problem, however, is that its translation into English as 'assemblage' has changed the original meaning suggesting a final state, rather than a process of assembling. In Deleuze and Guattari's vocabulary, *agencement* re-codes emergence and becoming (Venn, 2006, p. 107) 'namely, (de/re)-territorialization (in relation to topology), the machinic (in relation to autopoiesis), multiplicity, "agencement machinique" (in relation to differentiation, compossibility). [...] It focuses on process and on the dynamic character of the inter-relationships between the heterogeneous elements of the phenomenon. It recognizes both structurizing and indeterminate effects.' Therefore, the term *agencement* can recast the structure/agency division pointing to the process of linking heterogeneous elements in an open-ended process, and it connects also with Foucauldian influences in practice theories in which the de-centring of agency is related to more positive and emancipatory discourses that redefine the relationship between agency and change, power and resistance, intentional agency and embodied agency (Caldwell, 2007).

In the context of focusing on the *statu nascenti* of the practice of entrepreneuring and its resourcing through the mobilization of material resources and immaterial forces, the concept of *agencement* enables us to notice how agency is situated and distributed within a practice and how the association of heterogeneous elements gives birth to a practice and a certain way of practising entrepreneurship. The concept of *agencement* can prove useful for a practice-based study of the *statu nascenti* of an entrepreneurial project, since in studying the becoming of a way of practising, the researcher may empirically follow and describe the process whereby humans, artefacts, rules, technologies, sensible knowledge, legitimacy and any other practice resource, become connected thanks to a collective knowledgeable doing (Gherardi, 2019). At the same time, any single and situated practice is connected to other practices, and it is the process itself of *agencement* that makes practices agential. When studying the practices of organizing and resourcing, both materiality and the process of construction matter, since multiple realities may be enacted through different spacings, timings, and actings. We need to produce narratives of *agencements* that capture the materiality, the passions and beliefs, the practices of attraction and engagement within these complex assemblages which underlie such nests of associations.

Moreover, since I introduced a distinctive relation between knowing and doing as foundational of a certain practice theory, I have to account for knowing in relation to ordering 'things' and the open-ended process of becoming. This is where the concept of formativeness makes its appearance.

In studying the biographies of learning and knowing of women entrepreneurs and thus focusing on their engagement in practical creativity, the concept of formativeness was introduced to illustrate how in forming the object of practice, the way of doing is invented (Gherardi & Perrotta, 2014).

In order to see how socio-materiality is embedded in an ongoing entrepreneurial project and to investigate the process whereby doing and knowing unite into a form, it is useful to turn for inspiration to organizational aesthetics (Strati, 1999, 2019; Gherardi & Strati, 2017a) and particularly to the Italian philosopher Pareyson. The aesthetic theory formulated by Pareyson is an aesthetics of production – as opposed to an aesthetics of contemplation – and it concerns the becoming of the form, i.e. the outcome of a formation process. Pareyson is fascinated by the idea of human life as the invention of forms which acquire lives of their own: they detach themselves from their creators and become models, engendering styles. There is hence a formative character in the whole of human industriousness, and art is a specific domain of this formativeness: it is more a 'doing' than an expressing or a contemplating. Formativeness is defined as 'a doing' such that while it does, it invents the 'way of doing' (Pareyson, 1954, p. v). Both in art and industriousness there is the tentative feature of intrinsic tension and union between production and invention. Simultaneously invented in doing is the 'way of doing': realization is only achieved through proceeding by trial and error to the result, thus producing works that are 'forms' (Pareyson, 1954, p. vi). Forming also requires a relationship with materiality, because forming means forming a material, and the work is nothing other than formed material. In the process of the formation of matter, the work also acts as a formant even before it exists as formed.

In the *statu nascenti* in which opportunity and resourcing became an *agencement* of heterogeneous elements that achieve agency in their being in connection, there is formativeness since an entrepreneurial project becomes a situated practice whose form is shaped by a knowing that invents its way of doing while connecting to the institutionalized body of knowledge and institutional practices that we name 'entrepreneurship'.

A domain-specific practice theory of entrepreneurship grounded in the concepts of practice as *agencement* and knowing in practice as formativeness, enable us to make a link with the body of knowledge that in the study of entrepreneuring (meaning here how organizations achieve being entrepreneurial) has focused on everyday creativity and play (Hjorth et al., 2018).

A socio-material conception of creativity in everyday life focuses more on describing improvisation's generative character and less on creativity's newness value and it is based on three principles: 'that creativity is an everyday phenomenon; that there is a close relationship between human beings and material tools in the creativity process; and that there is a close relationship between continuity and renewal' (Tanggaard, 2013, p. 29). To think in terms of creative practices enables us to think in terms of how knowledge is *invented* while knowing (formativeness). There is no prepared script for creativity and cultural improvisation, for social and cultural life – Hallam and Ingold (2007) state, rather, that people work it out as they go along. The metaphor of wayfarer (Ingold, 2000, p. 229) – a way of knowing is itself a path of movement through the world – has inspired several thinkers (Cunliffe, 2018) in relation to our own research practices and as 'wayfinding' in relation to a practice-based conception of organizational learning (Chia, 2017).

The attention to everydayness has consequences not only for the conception of mundane practical creativity practices but also for the consideration of the temporality and rhythms of everyday entrepreneuring. Also, as Verduyn (2015, p. 646) argues, an attention to 'how disruptions of existing rhythms lead to smaller or larger changes to reality, but also how such changes are not neutral'. The micro-politics of power is more easily noticed in the small details of the everyday (Weiskopf & Steyaert, 2009).

While the theme of practical creativity, creative practices and formativeness has made its way in entrepreneuring literature, the concept of play – which gave rise to a call for papers on organizational creativity, play and entrepreneurship (Hjorth et al., 2018) and subsequently to two volumes in the journal *Organization Studies* – has been explored only recently. In their introduction Hjorth et al. (2018) identify play as an affirmation of chance, a speculative movement towards the future, and a pragmatic action-event (play lives in playing, like lightning lives in the flash) that embraces becoming (Manning & Massumi, 2014) and affect. Play is also producing and a product of openness and affect and invites one to engage in a multiple language experience that provides knowledge that is rich and not just representational (Beyes & Steyaert, 2012; Gherardi & Strati, 2017b; Linstead, 2018; Thrift, 2007). For thought to move in new ways, new relationships with concepts or the formation of new relationships to new concepts need to happen (Massumi, 2002) and imagination (Thompson, 2018), heterogeneity and openness help, as we can see in the relationship between aesthetics, art and entrepreneurship (Beyes, 2009; Pallesen, 2018), or work and play (Sørensen, 2008), or performative art (Scalfi Eghenter, 2018). The issue of arts-based research methods in entrepreneurial studies proposes a new challenge that highlights the relevance of the creation of texts in doing research, and focuses on the topics of the playful, of the artistic and of the performative in order to stimulate 'critically affective performative texts' that are inspired and formed by play and mystery (Linstead, 2018).

In engaging with the concept of practical creativity we can learn interesting and exciting lessons not only about our object of knowledge – Entrepreneurship as Practice – but even more insightful discoveries about our own epistemic practices in conducting research and forming the known object.

AS A WAY OF CONCLUDING

In this chapter, acknowledging that much research has been done on the contribution that several practice theories may offer to the entrepreneurship literature, I ask myself if and what entrepreneurship studies contribute to practice theories. This question came to my mind in considering how Entrepreneurship as Practice literature has been dominated by an applicative style of reasoning in which some fully fledged thought, either following the classic philosophical stream like phenomenology or pragmatism, or some of the big fathers of practice theories, were applied to the empirical study of a practice or to the construction of a theoretical framework. My questioning was supported by the way in which Sandberg and Tsoukas (2015) categorize practice theories in organization studies, distinguishing between a commonsensical understanding of practice – mainly a-theoretical – a general theory of practice (Bourdieu, Giddens and Schatzki), and domain-specific theories of practice that I understand as ways of theorizing about a knowledge object informed by a practice sensibility.

Is it possible to develop a domain-specific theory of practice and the necessary conditions for building a coherent theorizing of Entrepreneurship as Practice? I contextualized such a space for theory building, beginning from the assumption that it is not enough to look at practice for what people simply do and say, rather it is more promising to consider a practice as a collective knowledgeable doing and focus on how knowing and doing are inextricable. Therefore, a practice is always a situated practising, always socially sustained, and practice theorizing is developed within a processual understanding, the same expressed in the passage from nouns to verbs: from knowledge to knowing, from practice to practising. Such an epistemic move has been present in entrepreneurship literature much earlier than the label 'entrepreneurship as practice' was coined. In my opinion, it is important to position new developments of a field of study in continuity with the social and historical elaboration of the past. For this reason, I like to acknowledge how important it was to theorize entrepreneurship within the process approach that has developed over the last twenty years of practice theorizing, after the general theories of practice. This move is part of a wider change in the epistemology of social sciences that took place after the discrediting of positivism and the language turn that blurred the separation between ontology and epistemology. This is now expressed in different ways, as onto-epistemology (or ethic-onto-epistemology), following Barad, as relational epistemology (Fox & Alldred, 2016), or simply as becoming. It became difficult to see a phenomenon – organization or enterprise – as static and defined by a fixed number of characteristics, rather a relational and processual epistemology has been the road for constructing entrepreneurship as a knowledge object that unfolds in researching epistemic practices.

In proposing to develop a domain-specific practice theory I relied again on the history of the discipline and the concept that in literature gathers the greatest consensus on the definition of entrepreneurship: the discovery or creation of opportunities and their resourcing processes. Opportunity may be read in several different ways and a practice theorizing prefers to replace questions of ontology – what an opportunity *is* – with questions of epistemology: what an opportunity *does*. My proposal is therefore to frame 'opportunity' in terms of a *statu nascenti*, as the moment in-between when all potentialities and energies and affective forces are present and not-yet fully realized. It is the dynamic moment in between movement and institution, in between falling in love and loving. In the *statu nascenti* of the process of entrepreneuring, we can trace how the knowledgeable process of resourcing, in its socio-material becoming, links the ideational, emotional and material forces within situated activities.

A domain-specific practice theorizing of entrepreneuring can be grounded in the resourcing practices called into question by a *statu nascenti*. Entrepreneuring as practice literature may contribute to practice theories having something to say about how a (new) practice comes into being, how it gets resourced (with financial, economic, social capital and legitimacy) and how it achieves a more or less stable existence or change over time. This is an important contribution for theorizing practice focusing on its nascent state and for developing a methodology for the empirical study of emergent practices, since the empirical research on how practice becomes 'a' practice is still in its infancy (Bjorkeng, Clegg, & Pitsis, 2009; Lindberg, Walter, & Raviola, 2017).

However, there are necessary conditions to be met for elaborating a theoretical framework grounded both on previous knowledge on entrepreneurship and on practice concepts. I advance three concepts that may sustain a practice theorizing on entrepreneurship and its onto-epistemological positioning. These concepts are: *agencement*, formativeness and everyday creativity.

What are the consequences of conceptualizing entrepreneurial practices as *agencement*? To say that a practice is an *agencement*, implies considering practices (and not humans) as the unit of analysis and that the connections between humans, non-humans or more-than-humans, materialities, discourses and knowledges, happen within the practice itself. Practitioners (entrepreneurs and non-entrepreneurs), material and non-material resources, emotional energies, knowledges and discourses are not separate/separable (they are entangled) within a practice. Moreover, the concept of *agencement* illustrates not only the connections within a practice, but also the connections among practices that are interwoven to form a texture of practices (Gherardi, 2006). Agency is attributed to the practice and not only or exclusively to humans or non-humans.

The concept of formativeness is proposed in relation to the definition of practice as a collective knowledgeable doing that establishes connection(s) and is emergent from ways of being connected and adds to it a further dimension. Formativeness is a way of knowing/doing that, in doing, invents the way of doing. It is the process in which an object – material or immaterial – takes form and its forming is a process of invention. Entrepreneurial knowing is more similar to an artistic process than to a scientific one.

The third concept, everyday creativity, points to the dynamics of a practice in which stability and change are always in an unstable equilibrium and practical creativity is deployed within everyday activities. Connections are done and undone in a contingent way, in the everyday-ness of a practice; stability is the problem and not the solution.

From the Entrepreneurship as Practice literature we may expect, in the future, empirical studies more process-oriented, socio-material, and with a more fine-grained vocabulary for describing the rhythms and the intra-actions of the elements that compose a practice and a texture of practices. Practice may prove itself as a powerful concept.

As a final consideration I like to stress that the engaged character of all practices, including those of academic theorizing, and theorizing as an engaged and critical practice (Zundel & Kokkalis, 2010) opens a new space for reflecting on methodological choices when empirical entrepreneurial practices are the object of research and researchers are internal to the practices they study and the partial and situated knowledge (Haraway, 1988) they produce, instead of reproducing 'the God trick' and portraying an abstract knowledge from nowhere.

REFERENCES

Ahl, H., & Marlow, S. (2012). Exploring the dynamics of gender, feminism and entrepreneurship: Advancing debate to escape a dead end? *Organization, 19*(5), 543–562.

Alberoni, F. (1983). *Falling in Love*. New York: Random House.

Alberoni, F. (1984). *Movement and Institution*. New York: Columbia University Press.

Aldrich, H. (1999). *Organizations Evolving*. Newbury Park, CA: Sage.

Alvarez, S. A., & Barney, J. B. (2007). Discovery and creation: Alternative theories of entrepreneurial action. *Strategic Entrepreneurship Journal, 1*(1–2), 11–26.

Alvarez, S. A., Barney, J. B., & Anderson, P. (2013). Forming and exploiting opportunities: The implications of discovery and creation processes for entrepreneurial and organizational research. *Organization Science, 24*(1), 301–317.

Alvesson, M., & Sandberg, J. (2011). Generating research questions through problematization. *Academy of Management Review, 36*(2), 247–271.

Anderson, A. R., Dodd, S. D., & Jack, S. (2010). Network practices and entrepreneurial growth. *Scandinavian Journal of Management, 26*(2), 121–133.

Baert, P. (2005). *Philosophy of the Social Sciences: Towards Pragmatism*. Cambridge: Polity Press.

Baert, P., & Domínguez Rubio, F. (2009). Philosophy of the social sciences. In B. Turner (Ed.), *The New Blackwell Companion to Social Theory* (pp. 60–80). Oxford: Blackwell Publishing.

Barad, K. (2003). Posthumanist performativity: Toward an understanding of how matter comes to matter. *Signs, 28*(3), 801–831.

Barinaga, E. (2017). Tinkering with space: The organizational practices of a nascent social venture. *Organization Studies, 38*(7), 937–958.

Berger, P., & Luckmann, T. (1966). *The Social Construction of Reality*. Garden City, NY: Doubleday.

Beyes, T. (2009). Spaces of intensity: Urban entrepreneurship as redistribution of the sensible. In D. Hjorth & C. Steyaert (Eds.), *The Politics and Aesthetics of Entrepreneurship: A Fourth New Movements in Entrepreneurship Book* (pp. 92–112). Cheltenham, UK and Northampton, MA, USA: Edward Elgar Publishing.

Beyes, T., & Steyaert, C. (2012). Spacing organization: Non-representational theorizing and the spatial turn in organizational research. *Organization, 19*(1), 45–61.

Bjorkeng, K., Clegg, S., & Pitsis, T. (2009). Becoming (a) practice. *Management Learning, 40*(2), 145–160.

Bourdieu, P. (1990). *The Logic of Practice* (trans. R. Nice). Stanford, CA: Stanford University Press.

Bruni, A., Gherardi, S., & Poggio, B. (2005). *Gender and Entrepreneurship: An Ethnographical Approach*. London: Routledge.

Calás, M. B., Ergene, S., & Smircich, L. (2018). Becoming possible in the Anthropocene? Becomingsocialentrepreneurship as more-than-capitalist practice. In P. Dey & C. Steyaert (Eds.),

Social Entrepreneurship: An Affirmative Critique (pp. 267–281). Cheltenham, UK and Northampton, MA, USA: Edward Elgar Publishing.

Caldwell, R. (2007). Agency and change: Re-evaluating Foucault's legacy. *Organization, 14*(6), 769–791.

Callon, M. (1986). The sociology of an actor-network: The case of the electric vehicle. In M. Callon, J. Law, & A. Rip (Eds.), *Mapping the Dynamics of Science and Technology: Sociology of Science in the Real World* (pp. 19–34). Basingstoke: Macmillan.

Chalmers, D. M., & Shaw, E. (2017). The endogenous construction of entrepreneurial contexts: A practice-based perspective. *International Small Business Journal, 35*(1), 19–39.

Champenois, C., Lefebvre, V., & Ronteau, S. (2020). Entrepreneurship as practice: Systematic literature review of a nascent field. *Entrepreneurship & Regional Development, 32*(3–4), 281–312.

Chia, R. (2017). A process-philosophical understanding of organizational learning as 'wayfinding': Process, practices and sensitivity to environmental affordances. *The Learning Organization, 24*(2), 107–118.

Chiasson, M., & Saunders, C. (2005). Reconciling diverse approaches to opportunity research using the structuration theory. *Journal of Business Venturing, 20*(6), 747–767.

Clarke, A., & Fujimura, J. (Eds.) (1992). *The Right Tools for the Job: At Work in Twentieth-Century Life Sciences*. Princeton, NJ: Princeton University Press.

Corradi, G., Gherardi, S., & Verzelloni, L. (2010). Through the practice lens: Where is the bandwagon of practice-based studies heading? *Management Learning, 41*(3), 265–283.

Cunliffe, A. L. (2018). Wayfaring: A scholarship of possibilities or let's not get drunk on abstraction. *M@n@gement, 21*(4), 1429–1439.

De Clercq, D., & Voronov, M. (2009). The role of cultural and symbolic capital in entrepreneurs' ability to meet expectations about conformity and innovation. *Journal of Small Business Management, 47*(3), 398–420.

Deleuze, G., & Guattari, F. (1987). *A Thousand Plateaus: Capitalism and Schizophrenia*. Minneapolis: University of Minnesota Press.

Dey, P., & Steyaert, C. (2016). Rethinking the space of ethics in social entrepreneurship: Power, subjectivity, and practices of freedom. *Journal of Business Ethics, 133*(4), 627–641.

Dodd, S. D., Pret, T., & Shaw, E. (2016). Advancing understanding of entrepreneurial embeddedness: Forms of capital, social contexts and time. In F. Welter & W. B. Gartner (Eds.), *A Research Agenda for Entrepreneurship and Context* (pp. 120–133). Cheltenham, UK and Northampton, MA, USA: Edward Elgar Publishing.

Feldman, M., & Orlikowski, W. (2011). Theorizing practice and practicing theory. *Organization Science, 22*(5), 1240–1253.

Feldman, M., & Pentland, B. (2003). Reconceptualizing organizational routines as a source of flexibility and change. *Administrative Science Quarterly, 48*(1), 94–118.

Fletcher, D. E. (2006). Entrepreneurial processes and the social construction of opportunity. *Entrepreneurship & Regional Development, 18*(5), 421–440.

Foley, D., & O'Connor, A. J. (2013). Social capital and the networking practices of indigenous entrepreneurs. *Journal of Small Business Management, 51*(2), 276–296.

Fox, N., & Alldred, P. (2016). *Sociology and the New Materialism: Theory, Research, Action*. London: Sage.

Garcia-Lorenzo, L., Donnelly, P., Sell-Trujillo, L., & Imas, J. M. (2018). Liminal entrepreneuring: The creative practices of nascent necessity entrepreneurs. *Organization Studies, 39*(2–3), 373–395.

Gergen, K. (1985). The social constructionist movement in modern psychology. *American Psychologist*, March, 266–275.

Gherardi, S. (2001). From organizational learning to practice-based knowing. *Human Relations, 54*(1), 131–139.

Gherardi, S. (2006). *Organizational Knowledge: The Texture of Workplace Learning*. Oxford: Blackwell.

Gherardi, S. (2016). To start practice-theorizing anew: The contribution of the concepts of *agencement* and formativeness. *Organization, 23*(5), 680–698.

Gherardi, S. (2018). Practices and knowledges. *Teoria e Prática em Administração, 8*(2) (special issue), 33–59.

Gherardi, S. (2019). *How to Conduct a Practice-Based Study: Problems and Methods* (2nd edition). Cheltenham, UK and Northampton, MA, USA: Edward Elgar Publishing.

Gherardi, S., & Nicolini, D. (2005). Actor-networks: Ecology and entrepreneur. In B. Czarniawska & T. Hernes (Eds.), *Actor-Network Theory and Organising* (pp. 285–306). Copenhagen: Liber.

Gherardi, S., & Perrotta, M. (2014). Between the hand and the head: How things get done, and how in doing the ways of doing are discovered. *Qualitative Research in Organization and Management, 9*(2), 134–150.

Gherardi, S., & Strati, A. (2012). *Learning and Knowing in Practice-Based Studies.* Cheltenham, UK and Northampton, MA, USA: Edward Elgar Publishing.

Gherardi, S., & Strati, A. (2017a). Pareyson's *estetica: Teoria della formatività* and its implication for organization studies. *Academy of Management Review, 42*(4), 745–755.

Gherardi, S., & Strati, A. (2017b). Talking about competence: That 'something' which exceeds the speaking subject. In J. Sandberg, L. Rouleau, A. Langley, & H. Tsoukas (Eds.), *Skillful Performance: Enacting Capabilities, Knowledge, Competence, and Expertise in Organizations* (pp. 103–124). New York: Oxford University Press.

Golsorkhi, D., Rouleau, L., Seidl, D., & Vaara, E. (Eds.) (2010). *Strategy as Practice.* Cambridge: Cambridge University Press.

Hallam, E., & Ingold, T. (2007). *Creativity and Cultural Improvisation.* Oxford: Berg Publishers.

Haraway, D. (1988). Situated knowledges: The science question in feminism and the privilege of partial perspective. *Feminist Studies, 14*(3), 575–599.

Hill, I. (2018). How did you get up and running? Taking a Bourdieuan perspective towards a framework for negotiating strategic fit. *Entrepreneurship & Regional Development, 30*(5–6), 662–696.

Hjorth, D., Holt, R., & Steyaert, C. (2015). Entrepreneurship and process studies. *International Small Business Journal, 33*(6), 599–611.

Hjorth, D., Strati, A., Drakopoulou Dodd, S., & Weik, E. (2018). Organizational creativity, play and entrepreneurship: Introduction and framing. *Organization Studies, 39*(2–3), 155–168.

Houtbaeker, E. (2016). *Mundane Social Entrepreneurship: A Practice Perspective on the Work of Microentrepreneurs.* Helsinki: Aalto University.

Ingold, T. (2000). *The Perception of the Environment: Essays on Livelihood, Dwelling and Skill.* London: Routledge.

Jack, S. L., & Anderson, A. R. (2002). The effects of embeddedness on the entrepreneurial process. *Journal of Business Venturing, 17*(5), 467–487.

Johannisson, B. (1995). Paradigms and entrepreneurial networks: Some methodological challenges. *Entrepreneurship & Regional Development, 7*(3), 215–232.

Johannisson, B. (2011). Towards a practice theory of entrepreneuring. *Small Business Economics, 36*(2), 135–150.

Jones, O., & Holt, R. (2008). The creation and evolution of new business ventures: An activity theory perspective. *Journal of Small Business and Enterprise Development, 15*(1), 51–73.

Karataş-Özkan, M. (2011). Understanding relational qualities of entrepreneurial learning: Towards a multi-layered approach. *Entrepreneurship & Regional Development, 23*(9–10), 877–906.

Keating, A., Geiger, S., & McLoughlin, D. (2014). Riding the practice waves: Social resourcing practices during new venture development. *Entrepreneurship Theory and Practice, 38*(5), 1207–1235.

Knorr Cetina, K. (1981). *The Manufacture of Knowledge: An Essay on the Constructivist and Contextual Nature of Science.* Oxford: Pergamon Press.

Korsgaard, S. (2011). Entrepreneurship as translation: Understanding entrepreneurial opportunities through actor-network theory. *Entrepreneurship & Regional Development, 23*(7–8), 661–680.

Latour, B. (1987). *Science in Action: How to Follow Scientists and Engineers Through Society.* Cambridge, MA: Harvard University Press.

Latour, B., & Woolgar, S. (1986). *Laboratory Life: The Construction of Scientific Facts.* Princeton, NJ: Princeton University Press.

Lave, J., & Wenger, E. (1991). *Situated Learning: Legitimate Peripheral Participation.* Cambridge: Cambridge University Press.

Lindberg, K., Walter, L., & Raviola, E. (2017). Performing boundary work: The emergence of a new practice in a hybrid operating room. *Social Science & Medicine, 182*, 81–88.

Linstead, S. A. (2018). Feeling the reel of the real: Framing the play of critically affective organizational research between art and the everyday. *Organization Studies, 39*(2–3), 319–344.

Manning, E., & Massumi, B. (2014). *Thought in the Act*. Minneapolis: University of Minnesota Press.

Massumi, B. (2002). *Parables for the Virtual: Movement, Affect, Sensation*. Durham, NC: Duke University Press.

Mol, A. (2002). *The Body Multiple: Ontology in Medical Practice*. Durham, NC and London: Duke University Press.

Mole, K. F., & Mole, M. (2010). Entrepreneurship as the structuration of individual and opportunity: A response using a critical realist perspective. *Journal of Business Venturing, 25*(2), 230–237.

Murdock, K. A., & Varnes, C. J. (2018). Beyond effectuation: Analysing the transformation of business ideas into ventures using actor-network theory. *International Journal of Entrepreneurial Behavior & Research, 24*(1), 256–272.

Nicolini, D. (2012). *Practice Theory, Work, and Organization: An Introduction*. Oxford: Oxford University Press.

Nicolini, D., Gherardi, S., & Yanow, D. (2003). Introduction: Towards a practice-based view of knowing and learning in organizations. In S. Nicolini, S. Gherardi, & D. Yanow (Eds.), *Knowing in Organizations: A Practice-Based Approach* (pp. 1–31). Armonk, NY: M. E. Sharpe.

Orlikowski, W. J. (2000). Using technology and constituting structures: A practice lens for studying technology in organizations. *Organization Science, 11*(4), 404–428.

Orlikowski, W. J. (2002). Knowing in practice: Enacting a collective capability in distributed organizing. *Organization Science, 13*, 249–273.

Orlikowski, W. J. (2007). Sociomaterial practices: Exploring technology at work. *Organization Studies, 28*(9), 1435–1448.

Orlikowski, W. J. (2009). The sociomateriality of organizational life: Considering technology in management research. *Cambridge Journal of Economics, 34*(1), 125–141.

Pallesen, E. (2018). Creativity play and listening: An auditory re-conceptualization of entrepreneurial creation in the context of new public management. *Organization Studies, 39*(2–3), 191–207.

Pareyson, L. (1954). *Estetica: Teoria della formatività*. Turin: Edizioni di Filosofia. [Partial English trans.: *Existence, Interpretation, Freedom: Selected Writings*, ed. P. D. Bubbio. Aurora: The Davies Group, 2009.]

Parkkari, P. (2019). *Doing Entrepreneurship Promotion: A Critical, Practice Theoretical Study of Entrepreneurship*. Helsinki: Aalto University Press.

Rinkinen, J. (2015). *Demanding Energy in Everyday Life: Insights from Wood Heating into Theories of Social Practice*. Helsinki: Aalto University Press.

Rittenhofer, I. (2015). The reflexive case study method: A practice approach to SME globalization. *International Journal of Entrepreneurial Behavior & Research, 21*(3), 410–428.

Sandberg, J., & Pinnington, A. H. (2009). Professional competence as ways of being: An existential ontological perspective. *Journal of Management Studies, 46*(7), 1138–1170.

Sandberg, J., & Tsoukas, H. (2015). Practice theory: What it is, its philosophical base, and what it offers organization studies. In R. Mir, H. Willmott, & M. Greenwood (Eds.), *The Routledge Companion to Philosophy in Organization Studies* (pp. 184–198). London: Routledge.

Sarason, Y., Dillard, J. F., & Dean, T. (2010). How can we know the dancer from the dance? *Journal of Business Venturing, 25*(2), 238–243.

Sarasvathy, S. D., Dew, N., Velamuri, S. R., & Venkataraman, S. (2003). Three views of entrepreneurial opportunity. In Z. J. Acs & D. B. Audretsch (Eds.), *Handbook of Entrepreneurship Research* (pp. 141–160). New York: Springer Science.

Scalfi Eghenter, A. (2018). Organizational creativity, play and entrepreneurship. *Organization Studies, 39*(2–3), 169–190.

Schatzki, T. R. (2001). Introduction: Practice theory. In T. R. Schatzki, K. Knorr Cetina, & E. von Savigny (Eds.), *The Practice Turn in Contemporary Theory* (pp. 1–14). London and New York: Routledge.

Schutz, A. (1962). *Collected Papers I: The Problem of Social Reality*. Dordrecht: Springer.

Schutz, A. (1964). *Collected Papers II: Studies in Social Theory*. The Hague: Martinus Nijhoff.

Shane, S. A. (2003). *A General Theory of Entrepreneurship: The Individual–Opportunity Nexus*. Cheltenham, UK and Northampton, MA, USA: Edward Elgar Publishing.

Shane, S. A., & Venkataraman, S. (2000). The promise of entrepreneurship as a field of research. *Academy of Management Review*, *25*, 217–226.

Shove, E., & Pantzar, M. (2005). Consumers, producers and practices: Understanding the invention and reinvention of Nordic walking. *Journal of Consumer Culture*, *5*(1), 43–64.

Shove, E., Pantzar, M., & Wilson, M. (2012). *The Dynamics of Social Practice: Everyday Life and How It Changes*. London: Sage.

Sørensen, B. M. (2008). 'Behold, I am making all things new': The entrepreneur as savior in the age of creativity. *Scandinavian Journal of Management*, *24*(2), 85–93.

Spigel, B. (2017). Bourdieu, culture, and the economic geography of practice: Entrepreneurial mentorship in Ottawa and Waterloo, Canada. *Journal of Economic Geography*, *17*(2), 287–310.

Steyaert, C. (2007). 'Entrepreneuring' as a conceptual attractor? A review of process theories in 20 years of entrepreneurship studies. *Entrepreneurship & Regional Development*, *19*(6), 453–477.

Steyaert, C., & Landström, H. (2011). Enacting entrepreneurship research in a pioneering, provocative and participative way: On the work of Bengt Johannisson. *Small Business Economics*, *36*(2), 123–134.

Strati, A. (1999). *Organization and Aesthetics*. London: Sage.

Strati, A. (2019). *Organizational Theory and Aesthetics Philosophies*. London: Routledge.

Suchman, L. (2007), *Human–Machine Reconfigurations: Plans and Situated Actions* (2nd edition). Cambridge: Cambridge University Press.

Tanggaard, L. (2013). The sociomateriality of creativity in everyday life. *Culture & Psychology*, *19*(1), 20–32.

Tatli, A., Vassilopoulou, J., Özbilgin, M., Forson, C., & Slutskaya, N. (2014). A Bourdieuan relational perspective for entrepreneurship research. *Journal of Small Business Management*, *52*(4), 615–632.

Thompson, N. (2018). Imagination and creativity in organizations. *Organization Studies*, *39*(2–3), 229–250.

Thompson, N., & Byrne, O. (2020). Advancing entrepreneurship as practice: Previous developments and future possibilities. In W. B. Gartner & B. T. Teague (Eds.), *Research Handbook on Entrepreneurial Behavior, Practice and Process* (pp. 30–55). Cheltenham, UK and Northampton, MA, USA: Edward Elgar Publishing.

Thrift, N. (2007). *Non-Representational Theory: Space, Politics, Affect*. London: Routledge.

Tsoukas, H. (1996). The firm as a distributed knowledge system: A constructionistic approach. *Strategic Management Journal*, *17*, 11–25.

Tsoukas, H. (2009). A dialogical approach to the creation of new knowledge in organizations. *Organization Science*, *20*(6), 941–957.

Tsoukas, H. (2011). How should we understand tacit knowledge? A phenomenological view. In M. Easterby-Smith & M. A. Lyles (Eds.), *Handbook of Organizational Learning and Knowledge Management* (2nd edition) (pp. 453–476). Oxford: Blackwell.

Venn, C. (2006). A note on assemblage. *Theory, Culture & Society*, *23*(2–3), 107–108.

Verduyn, K. (2015). Entrepreneuring and process: A Lefebvrian perspective. *International Small Business Journal*, *33*(6), 638–648.

Verduyn, K., & Tillmar, M. (2019). Enacting resistance: Introduction to 'founding mothers of practice theories'. 4th Entrepreneurship-as-Practice Conference, 3–5 April, Nantes, France.

Vincent, S. (2016). Bourdieu and the gendered social structure of working time: A study of self-employed human resources professionals. *Human Relations*, *69*(5), 1163–1184.

Vincent, S., & Pagan, V. (2019). Entrepreneurial agency and field relations: A realist Bourdieusian analysis. *Human Relations*, *72*(2), 188–216.

Watson, T. J. (2013). Entrepreneurship in action: Bringing together the individual, organizational and institutional dimensions of entrepreneurial action. *Entrepreneurship & Regional Development*, *25*(5–6), 404–422.

Weiskopf, R., & Steyaert, C. (2009). Metamorphoses in entrepreneurship studies: Towards an affirmative politics of entrepreneuring. In D. Hjorth & C. Steyaert (Eds.), *The Politics and Aesthetics of Entrepreneurship: A Fourth New Movements in Entrepreneurship Book* (pp. 183–201). Cheltenham, UK and Northampton, MA, USA: Edward Elgar Publishing.

Whittington, R., & Vaara, E. (2012). Strategy-as-practice: Taking social practices seriously. *The Academy of Management Annals*, *6*, 285–336.

Zundel, M., & Kokkalis, P. (2010). Theorizing as engaged practice. *Organization Studies*, *31*(1), 1209–1227.

2. The determinants of social change, including entrepreneurs

Theodore R. Schatzki

This chapter is not, in the first place, about entrepreneurs or entrepreneurship. It is, instead, about the determinants of change in social life, or stated in less conventional terms, about what drives social change along, that is, keeps it going. However, the main topic has significant implications for how one thinks about entrepreneurs. For entrepreneurs have often been accorded responsibility for certain social changes. Joseph Schumpeter's (2002, 2003; see Swedberg, 2006) contention that entrepreneurs are responsible for economic development – defined as economic changes that arise within the economy "by its own initiative" and not from or in response to external phenomena – is a paradigm of such attribution. Schumpeter, moreover, generalizes his contention: in *any* sector of social life (e.g., economy, politics, art, science) a select group of individuals is responsible for the development of that sector. As a result, an analysis of the determinants of social change such as the one presented in the current chapter is bound to shed light on entrepreneurship.

As indicated, the chapter primarily examines what keeps change going. In line with the Handbook's theme of entrepreneurship as a practice, I focus on different ways that theories of practices can and do approach this topic. Only after mapping these ways and how my own account approaches the matter will I turn, at the end, to the implications of my account for theorizing entrepreneurs and entrepreneurship.

One might wonder whether anything drives change or keeps it going. Many theorists think that (social) change is nearly an omnipresent feature of the world. It takes many forms and occurs or unfolds at many different speeds, tempos, and rhythms. It is nigh high inevitable. Why, then, think that anything keeps it going? Maybe nothing is required. Or maybe the number of things that keep it going is vast.

My view is that it is possible to identify a small number of types of things that are responsible for social change. My conviction on this point is informed by my philosophical background, which inclines me to look for common denominators and to compile short lists of fundamental factors or components. Many social theorists seeking to identify the causes or origins of change have likewise produced short lists of factors, including technological development, conflict, social movements, culture (ideas), and demographic changes. My list will look more ontological than these: my aim is to identify the *ultimate* phenomena responsible for changes in social affairs, making these ultimate phenomena as comprehensive as possible. Indeed, my list will contain just two items. The relation of these two items to the list of causes that social theorists compile is that these two items, in the myriad forms and combinations they assume, fill out what is going on when the phenomena social theorists pick out determine change. Indeed, terms such as "technological development" and "conflict" are in effect names for general types of complicated combinations of these two items. Just one of these two items, moreover, principally clarifies the significance of entrepreneurship for change.

Ultimateness does not always connote usefulness. A longer list of more specific factors might be more useful than a short list of ultimate factors to social researchers. As indicated, however, the shorter list reveals what is going on when instances of phenomena on the longer lists contribute to changes in social affairs. Discussing the shorter list thereby deepens researchers' comprehension of how the world works. Most important, it undergirds greater appreciation of the implications of how the world works for social research and the explanation of social change.

THE NATURE OF SOCIAL CHANGE

Before getting to the main topics, I need to discharge two preliminaries. The first is to sketch my view on the relationship among change, difference, and persistence. The second is to specify what social changes amount to in the world. Both these matters inform the remainder of the discussion.

Change, metaphysically speaking, arises from events and processes. For present purposes, I construe events as things happening and treat processes either as integrated whole nexuses of continuous events (see Rescher, 2000) or as unfolding advances (see Bergson, 1911 [1907]). Examples of the two sorts of process are, respectively, taking a test and sharpening a pencil with a pencil sharpener. To say that changes arise from events and processes is to imply that a world composed solely of substances, relations, or structures could, in principle, be changeless, that is, static. Whatever substances, relations, and structures exist could simply go on existing – in principle, forever. Events and processes introduce dynamism into the world: things happening or unfolding. A world that boasts events and processes cannot be static.

To be more precise about the matter: events and processes automatically introduce differences into the world. When I revise a paragraph of my essay, the actions I perform introduce differences into the world: not only is the paragraph different after each act of revision (as are my fingers, the keys, the monitor, etc.), but the acts themselves, by adding to the stock of events in the world, automatically instate differences from the state of the world prior to their occurrence. Processes typically introduce even more differences, due to their temporally extended and unfolding nature. Some theorists say that difference *is* change. If this were true, the continuous production and prodigious volume of differences would problematize the existence of persistence: as Heraclitus saw, it would not be possible to step into a river once, let alone the same river more than once. I think, however, that it is intuitively better, first, to distinguish between difference and change and, second, to affirm the existence of persistence. One way of doing this is to place conditions on which differences amount to changes. My suggestion in this regard is that significant differences alone amount to changes. As I work on it, for instance, the paragraph continually becomes different. But it is only when it has become significantly different that it has changed. I should add that the significance of difference depends not just on the magnitude of difference but also on judgment and what difference is juxtaposed with.

Difference underlies change. But difference underlies persistence, too. I define persistence as the continued existence of something over time. My paragraph, for instance, persisted while I worked on it (and afterwards). It persisted even though it continually became different and eventually changed. Indeed, persistence requires difference: for the continuing existence of something over time is its continuing existence at *different* times. Change and persistence, consequently, are compatible: the paragraph that exists at the beginning of the revision process exists at the conclusion, even though it has changed "in the process." Of course, revisions can be so great that the paragraph ceases to persist: the paragraph that exists at the start of the process no long exists at its conclusion. In this case, change dissolves persistence.

The main topic of this chapter is what keeps social change going. I have now explained that change arises from events and processes. The topic, therefore, can be reformulated as, What events and processes keep social change going? Before tackling this issue, however, we must consider which changes are social changes, that is, what qualifies a change as a social one.

Elsewhere (e.g., 2002) I have argued that social phenomena consist in slices or aspects of interwoven practices and material arrangements. An organization, for instance, consists in certain related practices that are connected to particular linked arrangements. Racial discrimination, moreover, consists in a slew of components of practices and arrangements – actions, thoughts, rules, general understandings, signs, locations, etc. – that over time hang together with one another in different combinations. Social changes, meanwhile, are by definition changes in social phenomena. It follows that social changes are changes in slices and aspects of linked practices and arrangements. This proposition, in turn, implies that social changes embrace changes, or just differences, indeed often myriads of, even labyrinthine, changes, or just differences, in linked practices and arrangements. This is as true of a change in a particular interpersonal relation as a change in an economic system, as true of changes to groups or organizations as of those in fads or exchange rates. In each case, what there is in the world to a given social change is a collection of changes to (differences in) practice-arrangement bundles.

In sum, the principal issue for this chapter is what sorts of events and processes produce changes (significant differences) in social phenomena, that is, changes in bundles of practices and arrangements, where these changes themselves embrace collections of differences in the linked practices and arrangements involved.

MEET THE CANDIDATES

In line with the basic division in social ontology between individualism and everything else, the basic option in analyzing what keeps social change going is individualism or nonindividualism. Individualism attributes social changes to the activities of collections of individuals (such as Schumpeter's entrepreneurs), whereas nonindividualism acknowledges that individuals contribute something to change but attributes considerable responsibility for this to social phenomena or to some nonindividualist component of social life such as systems, structures, institutions, or orders. I should explain that by "individuals" I mean persons or people. I do not build into the notion such ideas as that individuals are bearers of rights or executors of economic calculations, though there might be contexts in which these things are true. In any event, individualism concentrates on actions as well as the mental apparatus that determines actions (preference schedules, utility calculations, reasons, motivations and ends, habits, etc.). It is typically unspecific about how individuals' actions compound and are responsible for large or sustained social changes. In addition, this approach often homogenizes people's mental apparatuses, thereby facilitating model building and computability. Most accounts that highlight the contribution entrepreneurs make to social change are individualist in nature.

It is hard to generalize about nonindividualism on these scores since the category includes quite disparate positions on the significance of individuals' actions for change and on what phenomena beyond individuals determine change. But social theory has regularly distinguished two camps. The first camp encompasses positions that highlight so-called "meso-level" phenomena such as interactions, local situations, values, and routines. The second camp embraces positions that emphasize "macro-level" phenomena such as systems, orders, or societies. The dividing line between the two "levels" is imprecise since matters such as complexity and size form continuums. What unites approaches of both rough sorts is the idea that social changes depend on processes, principles, relations, or mechanisms that befall or concern nonindividualist entities. Parsons's (1951) systems theory provides a clairvoyant example: although a system, according to this theory, is composed of actions, its functioning and evolution are determined by "pattern variables." More contemporary examples are Deleuze and Guattari's notion of abstract machines, the use of attractors in dynamic systems theory and assemblage theory, the institutional substances of the institutional logics approach, and even the idea of the exigencies of situations.

I do not believe (see Schatzki, 2016) that it is sensible to distinguish among micro, meso, and macro levels. Social phenomena share the same basic composition and, as stated, form continuums on the registers of spatial size and number of components (complexity). Still, given the pervasiveness and familiarity of the three level scheme, I want now – drawing on my own practice ontology – to distinguish three analogous options for a practice theoretical account of what drives social change. The three options highlight, respectively, lives, practices (bundles), and constellations as the locus where social change is kept going.

The first option parallels the idea that the actions and compounded actions of individuals determine change. It highlights, however, individual lives instead of individuals. The term "life" emphasizes the continuity and temporal extendedness of existence in a way that "individual" does not. It also suggests accomplishment, as in the idea of conducting or leading a life (cf. Dreier, 2007). Lives, moreover, bear a close relationship to persons or subjects. And the word, as an erstwhile biological concept, points toward the many corporeal processes that underlie and contribute to human existence. All this and more makes the term eminently fungible for social thought (see also, e.g., Dilthey, 2002 [1910]; Ingold, 2015). Content-fully, furthermore, a life, as I use the term, is an ongoing series of occurring, perduring, and persisting activities and "mental" (*seelische-geistige*) ways of being, which are performed, expressed, and signified through the performance of bodily actions and the occurrence of other bodily goings-on (e.g., gestures, expressions, physiological reactions) and whose existence constitutionally depends on how things are in the world. An example of the existence of an activity constitutionally depending on the state of the world is a wave of a hand constituting a greeting on the occasion of seeing a friend across the street. Note that a life is always the life of an individual, that is, a particular person.

The second option treats practices as the locus where social change is kept going. Treating practices thus usually involves envisioning what might be called a "practice dynamics." A practice dynamics is set of processes, relations, principles, or mechanisms that apply to practices as such, through whose occurrence or operation practices and, thereby, social phenomena change. An example of such a dynamic is Stanley Blue's (2019) Lefebvrian idea that practices repeat and, in repeating, change (see Lefebvre, 2004 [1992]). Blue envisions social life as composed of a multitude of practices that, by virtue of interconnectedly repeating, constantly change. This dynamic is located in the practices themselves. For Blue, even though practices are performed by people, people are, so to speak, carried along by practices, not the other way around as on the first option. A parallel picture is found in Shove, Pantzar, and Watson (2012). The authors distinguish several forms of change: recombinations of elements, switches in who carries out which practices, and alterations in how practices are related (e.g., coexist, compete, and are dependent or codependent). Changes of these sorts are interrelated. Although, moreover, the elements that compose practices are joined in the activities of individuals, individuals are not responsible for – e.g., intentionally pursue – these changes in practices but instead simply carry them out.

Some theorists of practices, for example, Reckwitz (2002) and Shove et al. (2012) treat materials as components of practices. Others such as Bourdieu, Kemmis, Giddens, and myself distinguish practices and materiality and highlight the intimate relation between them (various conceptions of sociomateriality in cultural and organizational theory advance parallel ideas). This division among practice theorists cleaves understandings of what keeps social change going. When materials are included in practices, practice dynamics concern ontologically hybrid entities. Materiality is thereby subsumed into and subject to these dynamics. When, by contrast, practices are distinguished from but yoked to materiality, bundles are open to dynamics that pertain to activity, materiality, or both. Not only does the existence of plural categories of dynamics open the door to greater complexity. It is possible that these dynamics can work against one another or come into conflict, a situation well known to engineers, generals, sports trainers, and developers of technology.

The third and final option espies processes, relations, and mechanisms that work at a larger scale. As noted, on my view practices and arrangements link as bundles. Teaching practices, for example, join with material arrangements at schools or universities such as classrooms, offices, and labs to form bundles. Bundles, too, connect and form constellations. In the US, teaching bundles connect to administrative bundles, residential bundles, food provision bundles, transportation bundles, and sports bundles (etc.) to form the constellations that constitute universities. Such constellations are larger than bundles in the dual senses of containing more components – more practices, arrangements, and relations (compare Latour, 1993; DeLanda, 2006) – and forming more spatially far-flung entities.

As noted, a prominent form of social theory posits processes, principles, relations, or mechanisms that happen to or concern "macro" or large social phenomena and that determine, or help determine, how these and other phenomena change over time. Neoclassical accounts of markets provide a fine example (even though many markets, especially in previous centuries, have been meso rather than macro in scale). Other examples are systems theoretical processes that govern the boundaries, organization, and development of systems, and the attractors and processes of territorialization, deterritorialization, coding, and decoding that DeLanda (e.g., 2006) holds responsible for changes in assemblages.

To date, few theories of practices have identified processes, mechanisms, or principles that pertain to large phenomena (constellations) and are responsible for their functioning or evolution. Practice theoretical accounts of the functioning, emergence, or evolution of constellations have tended to envision these phenomena as put together from, and dependent on linkages among, smaller phenomena: individuals (or lives), practices, and bundles. They thereby prioritize processes and mechanisms that pertain to these smaller phenomena, especially individuals and practices together, conceptualizing larger entities as effects of these (e.g., Giddens, 1979; Shove et al., 2012). This is, in my opinion a sensible way of theorizing. Examples of empirical work informed by this perspective include Bueger and Gadinger (2014), Jarzabkowski et al.

(2015), and Kemmis et al. (2014). Much practice theoretical work on entrepreneurs and entrepreneurship also adopts this procedure, though some follow Bourdieu.

Bourdieu connected the first and third options, ignoring the second. A kind of large social entity that Bourdieu often examined is fields (more generally, spaces), for example, educational fields, art or literary fields, economic fields, and religious fields. Bourdieu (e.g., 2005 [2000]) analyzed fields as composed of distributions of capital, the positions thereby constituted, the strategies adopted by those who occupy these positions, the stakes they pursue, the struggles that ensue, and the action-generating habituses and material layouts that reflect, reinforce, and reproduce these fields, distributions, and positions. All these matters bear on social change. As a result, Bourdieu's recognition that conflicts transpire in fields accords individuals and groups a role in keeping change going.

Bourdieu also held that fields are not self-propagating wholes that precisely sculpt action. People with habituses shaped in certain fields can enter others. External events can bear on fields. And habituses honed within a given field are always spontaneous, meaning that they do not simply slavishly regenerate what people in the past have done in that field but instead produce activities appropriate to present circumstances that – apart from unusual situations such as people suddenly finding themselves in radically different circumstances – are broadly consistent with past activities. The result is that practices continually drift and evolve. For Bourdieu, consequently, change results as much from individual lives as from processes and mechanisms that concern fields as such. Lives prosecute conflict and are a prominent source of internal deviation and change

Still, practice theories are ambivalent about processes and principles that apply to large phenomena. Recognition of such processes and principles clashes with the inclination of theories of practices to stay close to activity and to acknowledge its causal and constitutional centrality. At the same time, such theories broadly decenter the individual as the unit composing social phenomena and as the motor of social change.

WHAT KEEPS SOCIAL CHANGE GOING

This section outlines the account of social change that I have developed elsewhere (Schatzki, 2019). This account does not exemplify any of the three options just outlined. It might seem to combine elements of options one and two. In reality, however, it rejects all three.

My basic thesis is that social changes result from nexuses of activity chains and material events and processes. At first blush, according activity chains this responsibility seems to instantiate the first option discussed in the previous section: for action chains resemble lives and their trajectories. This impression, however, is false (see below). At the same time, the claim that material events and processes keep change going does reflect the ontological centrality of bundles in social life; it thus recalls the second option discussed in the previous section. As we will see, however, recognizing the responsibility of material events and processes for changes differs greatly from attributing processes, relations, and mechanisms to bundles or practices as such.

Let me first dispel the suspicion that my thesis about chains of activity instantiates the first option. The difference between chains of activity, on the one hand, and lives and life trajectories on the other comes out in their different relationships to bundles and, thus, to changes in bundles, i.e., social changes. Whereas both lives and activity chains bear constitutional relations to bundles, only activity chains have a causal relation.

To begin with, note that lives and bundles, in particular, lives and practices, are constituted by the same phenomena. Bundles are interwoven practices and arrangements. Practices, meanwhile, are open, organized arrays of doings and sayings. And doings and sayings are activities: they are performances of actions. Consequently, doings and sayings are at once components of practices and moments of lives: practices and lives are centrally composed of the same basic phenomena.

This coincidence does not distinguish lives or life trajectories from activity chains. For activity chains, too, are composed of activities. But there is a big difference: activity chains contain the activities of *multiple* people, whereas lives contain the actions of *particular* persons. This difference is crucial to the different relationships that lives and chains respectively bear to social changes, that is, to changes in bundles, in particular, changes in activity.

To see this, consider that lives pass through different bundles. This phenomenon assumes multiple forms. First, lives can move among practices. Second, a life trajectory passes amid mutable material arrangements, tracing a spatial path through the objective spaces they define. And third, lives proceed amid arrays of places and paths that are anchored at these material arrangements. To proceed amid such arrays is to act sensitive to them, X-ing at or in relation to material entities at which places to X are anchored (for example, sleeping in beds or on a couch that is cleared off for this purpose).

Individual lives pass through multiple, in fact, through potentially myriad bundles. As lives pass through bundles, they help compose the bundles. Similarly, the totality of life trajectories laid down during a given period of time in a given geographical expanse coincides with the totality of practices (bundles) enacted in that chunk of space–time: there is no component of an enacted practice in this chunk that is not a moment of someone's life trajectory, and at least almost all of the actions that help compose any of these trajectories are components of practices. As a result, any social change that encompasses changes in the activities that compose these practices – as opposed to changes in what organizes these activities – involves components of the lives involved. But the trajectories of these lives do not *determine* these changes in activities. These trajectories simply *contain* the changed activities. As a result, the trajectories are not responsible for changes in social life, that is, in bundles (and constellations). Instead, what is responsible for social changes is whatever *is* responsible for the changed actions. All this, note, follows from the coincidence of trajectories and practices.

What I just said about constitution – a life contains one person's actions, life trajectories coincide with practices/bundles – lacks the element of causality. Activity chains, by contrast, encompass causality. I realize that the concept of causality has fallen into disrepute in certain circles and that some thinkers believe that the social, and also the natural, sciences can do without it. I work, however, with an expansive notion of causality derived from Aristotle as interpreted by Heidegger (1977; see also Woodward, 2003) and think of the causes of something as what is responsible for it. The cause of a forest fire is whatever is responsible for the fire, the cause of a spike in the inflation rate is whatever is responsible for the spike, and the cause of an action is whatever is responsible for its performance. This is a very noncommittal conception of causality that corresponds to the fact that entities depend on other entities in the cascades of events and processes that happen in the world.

Consider lives and practices. Where is causality located in them? Lives contain activities, which are also components of practices. Many activities are interventions in the world that leave an altered world behind. This intervening in the world and altering it is one form of causality – one general way in which something, in this case, activity is responsible for something else, in this case, changes in the world. In acting, moreover, people react to things or act in their light. When people react to something that something induces activity. This inducing is another form of causality – another general way entities, in this case, events and states of affairs, are responsible for other entities, namely, people performing actions. A third form of causality is teleology, people acting for the sake of something. This is a form of causality because a state of affairs or way of being for the sake of which a person acts bears responsibility for what she does on that occasion.

The first two of these forms of causality underlie the phenomenon of activity chains. Chains of activity are series of activities, each component of which reacts to the previous component or to a change in the world brought about by that previous component. Such chains are causal threads: prior activities and states of the world inducing activities, and activities bringing about changes in the world. These chains, more specifically, the nexuses they form, are also one of the two phenomena responsible for social changes, that is, for sets of changes in practice-arrangement bundles: changes in bundles are causal effects or nominal results of activity chains. This is as true of the founding of a start-up by a couple of friends as of a revision in government regulations, as true of a sudden reversal of a firm's market fortunes as of a spike in the inflation rate or the collapse of a given country's currency (to stick to economic examples). The major differences in the present context among these cases are the extensiveness and complexity of the nexuses of activity chains that lead to or result in change.

Another way of putting this idea is that chains of action lead to and leave behind changed bundles. The steady or punctuated advance of myriad linked, metamorphosing, cascading, resonating, reinforcing, or colliding action chains deposits endless differences and changes in bundles and, hence, social phenomena. It follows that all social changes are historical: the progression of events and processes over time leaves social changes in its wake.

Chains of action pass through lives, just as they pass through, while also circulating within, bundles, constellations, and hence social phenomena. Chains, consequently, can escape both the intentionality and awareness or knowledge of individuals and collections thereof. Chains of activity can, of course, be regimented by organizations and institutions, and individuals, for example, those in positions of authority, can individually or collectively initiate them intentionally. This is an important fact about how many social phenomena begin or persist. At the same time, social reality is plied by numerous chains that are haphazard in the sense of being contingent and only partially or scarcely known to, overseen by, or intended by participants. People are typically aware of the events and states of affairs to which they react on particular occasions but often unaware of the events and states of affairs that had given rise to these. People possess knowledge of only a part, or sliver, of the complex activity nexuses that their own activities are part of.

In short, although lives and activity chains alike help compose bundles of practices and arrangements, activity chains also contain the causality responsible for changes in bundles. A specific set of (moments of) life trajectories coincides with any specific bundle during a particular time period. But the changes that appear in this bundle during this period arise from the interrelated chains of activity that pass through both the bundle and the lives involved. As a result, explaining these changes centers around mapping the chains responsible. It also follows that to attribute social changes to nexuses of activity chains is not to propound a practice theoretical version of the micro approach to social determination and explanation outlined in the previous section. Indeed, chains of action jump in space and time and can move throughout the practice plenum. They are not micro phenomena.

The phenomenon of activity chains decenters the subject. It also avoids treating actors as mere executors of practices that are greater than and arrayed "above" them. Rather, as just explained, subjects are caught up in the proliferating nexuses of activity chains that result in social changes. At the same time, particular individuals can be responsible for changes in bundles, although some people never contribute anything. Individuals bear responsibility for changes when (1) they perform actions that set new headings for the chains that these performances are part of and (2) significant differences in social phenomena arise from these new headings (see Schatzki, 2019, pp. 86–87). Actions that fulfill these two conditions are "originary." A curious feature of originary activities is that status as originary depends on the reactions of others – for it is others' reactions to an action, together with subsequent reactions to their reactions, that give rise to the changes in social life that retrospectively qualify an action as originary. Activity chains thus qualify activities as originary after the fact.

Chains of action, however, are not the only phenomenon keeping social change going. Chains of action that pass through particular bundles help compose the practices that are part of those bundles. For example, chains of action that floriate from a CEO's decision to develop a new ad campaign help compose practices (calling, planning, contracting, advertising, sketching, brainstorming, etc.) that are part of the bundles of the corporation or its ad agency. This fact about the composition of bundles concerns their practice dimension. But bundles, and thereby social phenomena, also possess a material dimension. The second overall factor responsible for social changes is material events and processes that happen to the material arrangements with which practices are interwoven.

This category covers a wide variety of phenomena. Earthquakes, for instance, destroy lives and built environments. Bacteria contaminate food supplies and devastate indigenous populations. The creation of new electromagnetic processes enables people to see and talk to one another over great distances and the development of new types of human association (e.g., players of Pokémon Go). And innovation in processes of alcohol extraction, condensation, and aging yields new liquors that shift alcohol dependency and the numerous practices and bundles attendant to this. Meanwhile, the development of new materials leads to new types of settings and bundles (such as those in airplane compartments or cryotherapy clinics). And on and on. The world we live in is full of material events and processes, including ones that happen to the bundles of practices and arrangements through, as part of, dependent upon, and on the background of which people live their lives and coexist with others. Responsibility for the differences and changes in bundles and constellations that make up social changes falls not just to chains of activity but also to material events and processes that occur to the material arrangements with which practices are interwoven.

This phenomenon is so pervasive, and so much the focus of science, engineering, and design, that it is easy for social theorists not to attend to it. I am not claiming, however, that all social changes arise from material events and processes, too. I am simply pointing out that a surprising range of social changes depends on such occurrences and that certain changes largely result from them. I am also maintaining that theoretical formulations must acknowledge and accommodate these facts. By a "material entity," incidentally, I mean anything with a physical-chemical composition. Events and processes are material if they arise solely from the physical-chemical composition of the entities to which they occur. The material world, accordingly, can be defined as the sum of material entities, events, and processes.

When material events and processes all by themselves are responsible for social changes, the changes typically concern material arrangements: earthquakes leveling buildings and killing inhabitants is a dramatic example. Most social changes, however, result from action chains and material occurrences in combination. For instance, the changes that result from earthquake rescue and reconstruction efforts arise from both; in addition to numerous action chains, these efforts might embrace the functioning of motors, the use of sonar technology, gravity-caused settling of collapsed buildings, physical exhaustion, and the physiology of smell. Note that the social effects of many material events and processes are mediated by practices. The differences, for example, that effects of alcohol on the human body make to social affairs depend on practices and how people react to these effects. Even the effects themselves can depend on bundles. Similarly, the difference that new materials make to social life depends on contemporaneous bundles and what is done with the materials in them.

Material events and processes also contribute to social change by mediating activity chains. This fact is built into the definition of a chain as a series of activities, each of which reacts to the prior activity or to a change – possibly a material change – in the world brought about by that prior activity. Another way materiality mediates chains is by providing avenues through which people learn of actions, events, and states of affairs to which they react. Examples of such avenues are satellite transmissions, written texts, and air serving as a medium for the transmission of sound. Reactions to prior activities can also be essentially tied to material entities, events, and processes, as when a broker reacts to other brokers' purchases by hitting the purchase button on his keyboard and initiating the purchase of stock.

Attributing social changes – changes in bundles of practices and arrangements – to material events and processes recognizes the important material dimension of bundles, in particular, that they are composed of material arrangements and thus subject to events and processes that befall such arrangements. But attributing social change to material occurrences is not an instance of the second option discussed earlier in the chapter, meso explanations: invoking processes, mechanisms, or principles that apply to bundles as such. For what is responsible for changes is always particular sets of components of arrangements and particular sets of events and processes that happen to them. So recognizing the causal role of such events and processes does not amount to erecting a practice theoretical meso explanation.

One implication of the claim that social changes result from nexuses of activity chains and material occurrences is that what is actually going on when *other* alleged determinants of change operate is that numerous nexuses of this sort are progressing, proliferating, and metamorphosing. Prominent examples of alleged determinants of change include dependence, codependence, coevolution, power, mechanisms, conflict, collective action, social movements, technological innovation, contagion, feedback, governance, and cascades of activity. Extensive discussion of this point is found in Schatzki (2019).

WHAT ABOUT LARGER CHANGES?

The claim that social changes result from nexuses of activity chains and material occurrences applies to social changes generally regardless of their character or scale. Small and large changes, as well as simple and complex ones, economic and political changes, and ancient and modern ones, too, are determined thus. Of course, the larger or more complex the change the larger or more complex the responsible nexus is likely to be. This fact freights explanations of large or complex changes. It also implies that the art of explaining large or complex changes is the art of fashioning overviews (*Übersichten*; see Wittgenstein, 1958) of the large and complex nexuses that lead to them (see Schatzki, 2019).

What I want to do in this section is to consolidate my picture of what keeps social change going by very briefly explaining why it is implausible to think that the motor of larger or more complex changes is processes, mechanisms, or principles that apply to bundles as such (meso explanations). There is no space to provide parallel thoughts about macro explanations. I do not think that one can *prove* that practice theoretical meso explanations should be abandoned. Ultimately, the goodness of ontological ideas lies in the quality of the empirical research they inform. The goodness of my claims about the determination of change are ultimately certified by the insight and illumination afforded by research they inform. Theories, however, also have to pass the test of intellectual plausibility and cogency (see Schatzki, 2019). Consequently, identifying conceptual issues with a theory decreases its presumptive goodness.

I do not reject tout court the idea that so-called meso phenomena can be the locus of social change. Interactions, for example, are a promising candidate. Good examples of processes that occur to interactions and determine social changes are the emotional contagion and exchange that Randall Collins (2004) ascribes to interactions under the name "interaction ritual chains." These processes especially determine changes that connect to group membership, for example, changes in sex, smoking, and social stratification. Note that Collins's account of interactions is not a rival to my accounts of practices and change. On the contrary: his theory can form an alliance with mine to yield a more complete account of social life (see Schatzki, 2021 for the idea of a theoretical alliance). Collins's account analyzes aspects of interactions – and the contributions these aspects make to social life – that a theory of practices is not going to detail. At the same time, his account is compatible with the thesis that activity chains are responsible for social changes. For interactions are a general kind of activity chain; what Collins has done is provide an account of this kind. So his account is not at odds with my own view but instead at once illustrates and goes beyond it. Similarly, Collins's attention to dimensions of the material world that support (e.g., the body) or mediate (e.g., symbols) emotional contagion and exchange illustrates the idea that material events and processes are part of the nexuses that are responsible for social change.

Unlike interactions, however, bundles are not something to which processes, mechanisms, or principles apply as such. Or, more carefully stated, processes or principles that pertain to bundles as such are inert – they do not determine social changes but are themselves products of what determines change. As indicated, bundles are hybrid entities, composed of practices and material arrangements. Examples of processes that happen to bundles as such are expansion, bifurcation, coalescence, and connecting to other bundles. These processes are nothing beyond sets of changes in bundles: terms such as "expansion" or "bifurcation" simply characterize the overall form, character, or import of a set of changes taken as a set. Now, these sets as sets (i.e., as such) do not determine anything; the only exception is when activities react to them as unities. Nor are these sets of changes qua sets determined by anything. Each set is simply a nominal unity that results from all the nexuses of activity chains and material occurrences that are responsible for the changes that compose it. In short, the real action lies in activity chains and material occurrences: everything else is ultimately a matter of nexuses of chains and occurrences, the differences these nexuses leave behind in the world, and the changes in social phenomena these differences constitute.

Repetition, as mentioned, is another process possibly connected to change that has been ascribed to bundles, or rather, practices. Blue (2019), as noted, writes that practices change as they repeat – for each repetition is at least a little different from prior ones. Since, furthermore, practices hang together, and relations among them affect how they repeat and, thus, how they are different with each repetition, the social field embraces a labyrinth of interconnectedly repeating and continually changing practices. As I conceive of them, however, practices and bundles do not repeat. The occasions on which, according to Blue, practices repeat are, according to me, occasions when (1) a bundle's practices are extended in the sense that additional constituent activities occur and (2) its material arrangements possibly evolve. The practice and bundles thereby become different, but difference does not amount to repetition. Extension and evolution, furthermore, bear no inherent connection to change. Extension and evolution are simply the persistence through time of a bundle through occurrences of additional or altered components. Whether change results is a further, contextual matter.

Changes in social phenomena arise from the intertwining of two phenomena: series of reactions to prior reactions and to events in and states of the world, and material events and processes. Processes and mechanisms that pertain to practices as such either are inert or simply denote combinations of these two phenomena. My account might seem so much to ontologically reduce what keeps social change going as to render the account useless to social researchers. But this analysis, among other things, keeps researchers alive to the possibility of chains and occurrences moving social life in new directions; teaches them to look for originary actions, haphazard determining chains, and the roles played by material occurrences; reinforces the conviction that empirical work is irreplaceable; and helps researchers understand that the task of explanation in social science is to give overviews of complex nexuses of chains and occurrences.

ENTREPRENEURS AS VECTORS OF CHANGE

This concluding section redeems the contention stated at the start that an account of social change has implications for conceptualizing entrepreneurs and entrepreneurship. This contention, I wrote, arises from the close association, dating to the early work of Schumpeter, of entrepreneurs with change.

I am not going to dwell on the issue of how to define entrepreneurs and entrepreneurship. Informed by Gartner (1988) and Shane and Venkataraman (2000), I will simply define entrepreneurs as enterprising individuals who seize opportunities to bring about new phenomena in organizational, including economic, situations; entrepreneurship, then, is this phenomenon occurring. Nor will I explore what determines opportunities to bring about novelty. Anyone reading this chapter will appreciate that, on my view, analyses of entrepreneurship and of the efforts of particular entrepreneurs must attend to the practice-arrangement bundles, within or in the face or context of which people bring about ("create") new products, new organizations, new techniques of production, new forms of organization, new funding, new items of social value, etc. Analyses of entrepreneurs and entrepreneurship cannot focus on heroic individuals alone but must also consider the contexts in which individuals act, thus such matters as practices, materiality, normativity, collective actions, and connections among bundles. Otherwise such analyses are incomplete. The present chapter has also suggested that analyses of entrepreneurs and entrepreneurship should not examine persons as such but instead these people's lives. For the activities that are of interest in such analyses are components of their lives. This overall position qualifies as a version of what Hardy and Maguire (2008) call a "process-centric narrative" of entrepreneurship.

The inception of new products, organizations, techniques, funding, or values often qualifies as social change. As discussed, social changes arise from nexuses of activity chains and material occurrences. It follows that nexuses of chains and occurrences are what lie behind the inceptions of new phenomena that prominent theories hold entrepreneurs responsible for. The mere fact that the activity chains involved always pass through the lives of particular persons, in particular, the lives of those called "entrepreneurs," does not, as explained, qualify those lives – as opposed to the activity-occurrence nexuses – as the source of these changes. Generally speaking, of course, the lives of particular people *can* be responsible for changes, for instance, the appearance of new phenomena: individual people bear responsibility for social changes when these changes arise from chains, new headings for which were set by these people's activities. What's more, the set of people who are widely credited with bringing about new phenomena and situations in organizational, including economic, situations (i.e., entrepreneurs) probably more or less coincides with – or is a very large subset of – the set of people in those situations whose actions establish new headings for action chains that in turn lead to (possibly proliferating) collections of changes in bundles. So Schumpeter is right to hold entrepreneurs responsible for certain social changes, namely, for many changes that consist of inceptions of new phenomena. At the same time, I doubt that such individuals are responsible for all such changes; drift, for example, can also be responsible. What's more, this thesis, as Schumpeter argues, holds of social life more generally: anywhere in social life individuals bear responsibility for many of the new phenomena that appear there.

At the same time, individuals do not bear *sole* responsibility even for those social changes, those inceptions of new phenomena, for which they bear responsibility. For while particular lives can be credited with instituting new headings in chains of action, whether these chains continue on and yield social changes depends on the (re)actions of others. Even to the extent that entrepreneurs are rightly characterized as instigating change, they do not attain this status on their own, by virtue of their own actions alone. The cooperation, so to speak, of others is required. This realization once again directs investigators toward the bundles and constellations of bundles within which people act. For the formation of chains of action, and thus of chains of action leading to social change, depends on these, too.

REFERENCES

Bergson, H. (1911 [1907]). *Creative Evolution*. Trans. A. Mitchell. New York: Henry Holt and Company.
Blue, S. (2019). Institutional rhythms: Combining practice theory and rhythmanalysis to conceptualise processes of institutionalization. *Time & Society*, *28*(3), 922–950.
Bourdieu, P. (2005 [2000]). Principles of an economic anthropology. In N. J. Smelser & R. Swedberg (Eds.), *Handbook of Economic Sociology* (2nd edition, pp. 75–89). Princeton, NJ: Princeton University Press.
Bueger, C., & Gadinger, F. (2014). *International Practice Theory: New Perspectives*. London: Palgrave Macmillan.
Collins, R. (2004). *Interaction Ritual Chains*. Princeton, NJ: Princeton University Press.
DeLanda, M. (2006). *A New Philosophy of Society: Assemblage Theory and Social Complexity*. New York: Continuum.

Dilthey, W. (2002 [1910]). *The Formation of the Historical World in the Human Sciences*. Trans. R. A. Makkreel & F. Rodi. Princeton, NJ: Princeton University Press.

Dreier, O. (2007). *Psychotherapy in Everyday Life*. Cambridge: Cambridge University Press.

Gartner, W. B. (1988). Who is an entrepreneur? Is the wrong question. *American Journal of Small Business*, *12*(4), 11–32.

Giddens, A. (1979). *Central Problems of Social Theory*. Berkeley, CA: University of California Press.

Hardy, C., & Maguire, S. (2008). Institutional entrepreneurship. In R. Greenwood, C. Oliver, K. Sahlin, & R. Suddaby (Eds.), *The Sage Handbook of Organizational Institutionalism* (pp. 198–217). London: Sage.

Heidegger, M. (1977). The question concerning technology. In *The Question Concerning Technology and Other Essays* (pp. 3–35). Trans. W. Lovitt. New York: Harper.

Ingold, T. (2015). *The Life of Lines*. Abingdon: Routledge.

Jarzabkowski, P., Bednarek, R., & Spee, P. (2015). *Making a Market for Acts of God: The Practice of Risk-Trading in the Global Reinsurance Industry*. Oxford: Oxford University Press.

Kemmis, S., Wilkinson, J., Edwards-Groves, C., Hardy, I., Grootenboer, P., & Bristol, L. (2014). *Changing Practices, Changing Education*. Singapore: Springer.

Latour, B. (1993). *We Have Never Been Modern*. Trans. C. Porter. Cambridge, MA: Harvard University Press.

Lefebvre, H. (2004 [1992]). *Rhythmanalysis: Space, Time and Everyday Life*. Trans. S. Elden and G. Moore. London: Athlone.

Parsons, T. (1951). *The Social System*. New York: Free Press.

Reckwitz, A. (2002). Toward a theory of social practices: A development in culturalist theorizing. *European Journal of Social Theory*, *5*(2), 243–263.

Rescher, N. (2000). *Process Philosophy: A Survey of Basic Issues*. Pittsburgh: University of Pittsburgh Press.

Schatzki, T. (2002). *The Site of the Social: A Philosophical Account of the Constitution of Social Life and Change*. University Park: Pennsylvania State University Press.

Schatzki, T. (2016). Practice theory as flat ontology. In G. Spaargaren, D. Weenink, & M. Lamers (Eds.), *Practice Theory and Research: Exploring the Dynamics of Social Life* (pp. 28–42). Abingdon: Routledge.

Schatzki, T. (2019). *Social Change in a Material World*. Abingdon: Routledge.

Schatzki, T. (2021). Forming alliances. In M. Lounsbury, D. Anderson, & P. Spee (Eds.), *On Practice and Institution: Theorizing the Interface* (pp. 119–138). Bingley: Emerald Publishing.

Schumpeter, J. (2002). New translations: *Theorie der wirtschaftlichen Entwicklung*. Trans. M. C. Becker & T. Knudsen. *American Journal of Economics and Sociology*, *64*(2), 405–437.

Schumpeter, J. (2003). The theory of economic development. Trans. U. Backhaus. In *Joseph Alois Schumpeter*, ed. J. Backhaus (pp. 61–116). Boston: Kluwer.

Shane, S., & Venkataraman, S. (2000). The promise of entrepreneurship as a field of research. *Academy of Management Review*, *25*(1), 217–226.

Shove, E., Pantzar, M., & Wilson, M. (2012). *The Dynamics of Social Practice: Everyday Life and How It Changes*. London: Sage.

Swedberg, R. (2006). Social entrepreneurship: The view of the young Schumpeter. In C. Steyaert & D. Hjorth (Eds.), *Entrepreneurship as Social Change: A Third Movements in Entrepreneurship Book* (pp. 21–35). Cheltenham, UK and Northampton, MA, USA: Edward Elgar Publishing.

Wittgenstein, L. (1958). *Philosophical Investigations* (2nd edition). Trans. G. E. M. Anscombe. Oxford: Blackwell.

Woodward, J. (2003). *Making Things Happen: A Theory of Causal Explanation*. Oxford: Oxford University Press.

3. Paradigmatic foundations of the enactive approach to entrepreneuring as practice

Bengt Johannisson

INTRODUCTION

All scholars dream of creating a model of the phenomenon they study that is generic as well as distinct. Entrepreneurship researchers are no exception and this is highlighted in the poem by Karin Boye 'On the Move' where she talks about roads to goal achievement being the most worthwhile part. The generic approach implies that the model covers all appearances of entrepreneurship, from everyday smartness to path-breaking achievements such as the introduction of a radical innovation that changes everyday life for many people. A model is distinct if it makes entrepreneurship stand out as unique when compared with other social phenomena. However, in their ambitious review of extant process models of entrepreneurship, Moroz and Hindle (2012) could not find any framework that qualified as both generic and distinct. An inventory made in July 2018 of studies that had so far referred to Moroz and Hindle's article showed that no researcher had made a serious attempt to take up the gauntlet.

In present digital times, both everyday life and organizational and societal practices change incessantly. A way forward in the quest for the ideal model of entrepreneurship may be to amalgamate a process perspective with a practice view on entrepreneurship. Burgelman et al. (2018), for example, demonstrate that strategy-process research becomes vitalized if combined with a practice approach. Compare also Chia and MacKay (2007). While processes organize activities in time, practices structure spatial, social and mental activities (Hernes, 2003). Considering contemporary advances in each field, such a hybrid approach to entrepreneurship is timely. The philosophical foundations of a process view on organization have recently been systematically scrutinized by Helin et al. (2014) and Hernes (2014) and the philosopher Theodore Schatzki (2001, 2002, 2005) has contributed to a thorough conceptualization of organization as practice.

Here I[1] take the process/change and practice/doing perspectives on entrepreneurship to heart. Considering its generic dynamic features, I will henceforward, with reference to Steyaert (2007) and Hjorth et al. (2015), refer to the 'entrepreneuring' denomination. This implies that practicing entrepreneurship means considering ongoing change to be a natural state in line with what the poem in the vignette implies. Compare also Langley et al. (2013). A further proposition claims that not only is the overall emergence of the entrepreneurial process and its outcome unique. The separate practices in terms of organized activities that constitute the process and produce this outcome are equally unmatched, since the concrete situations they deal with have to be locally treated. This makes entrepreneuring materialize as a stream of situated practices that enact ventures and careers as well as the environment in parallel. The boundary between these venturing activities and the environment is permeable and constantly negotiated. Drawing upon the notion of improvisation, Orlikowski (1996) has suggested a 'situated' approach to organizational change. However, situated practices as improvisations are in her approach rather considered as easy options for making organizations chained by routines more able to deal with change. In contrast, such practices are here considered as the basic elements in the conceptualizing of entrepreneuring. The challenge taken on is thus to find out *how* situated practices are enacted across boundaries in time and space, given that entrepreneuring is defined as *creative organizing of material and human resources for new economic, social, cultural and/or ecological value creation.*

Studying the very becoming of entrepreneuring calls for a close-up approach. A number of issues have to be dealt with in order to qualify for the proposed '*enactive*' approach: (1) identifying the ontological pillars of the model's main elements – process and practice – as the basis for an integrated framework; (2) stating the epistemological foundations for associated empirical research; (3) presenting an appropriate methodology for leading an empirical inquiry that validates the proposed conceptual framework; and (4) providing an axiological, i.e. evaluative, audit of the overall approach.

The chapter is organized as follows. To begin with, the features of entrepreneuring as creative organizing are positioned against dominant views concerning organization process and practice (*the ontological challenge*). This section concludes with a conceptual model that highlights the proposed distinct and generic features of entrepreneuring. The following section reviews the conditions for gaining insight into the processes and practices that enact entrepreneurial phenomena (*the epistemological challenge*). After this, the enactive methodology is presented, which implies that the researcher also takes on the identity of an entrepreneur becoming, in other words, an '*entresearcher*' by launching a venture and reflecting on the experiences being made (*the methodological challenge*). This section also summarizes the field research that generates the induced formative dispositions of entrepreneurs which transform the modeling into the proposed generic and distinct theory of entrepreneuring. Then, an axiological review of the enactive approach in terms of what value the research process itself and the enacted ventures have created for its stakeholders and society at large is presented (*the ethical challenge*). The chapter concludes with ontological and methodological reflections on the differences between the practices of entrepreneuring and those of management, according to Mintzberg's (1980 [1973]) seminal study of managers at work.

CONCEPTUALIZING ENTREPRENEURING AS PRACTICE

Ontological Foundations

The view that the environment is enacted rather than objective or subjective (Weick, 1979; Smircich & Stubbart, 1985) originates in the image of reality as socially constructed (Berger & Luckmann, 1966; Gergen, 1999). This ontological position has, for example, been adopted by Starr and MacMillan (1990) and Gartner et al. (1992) when inquiring into entrepreneurship. Entrepreneurs enact their environment by convincing themselves as well as others that their image of the world is true by acting accordingly. Enactment frameworks vary, though, with respect to what human capabilities – cognitive, affective and conative (Hilgard, 1980) – are activated in the world-making. Weick's (1979) and Hernes' (2014) frameworks are cognitively biased, while Smircich and Stubbart (1985) as well as Gartner et al. (1992) also recognize the role of emotions in the enactment process. See also Baron (2008). The conative faculty was brought up as early as 1912 (published in English in 1934) by Schumpeter, who stated that the entrepreneur's will is crucial and others have underlined the role of passion as a motivating force (Cardon et al., 2009). Being also existentially driven, the entrepreneur oscillates between desire for freedom and the pain of anxiety over a life-long career (Olson, 1962). Anchoring an inquiry into existential philosophy also means reflecting "not with the reason only, but with the will, with the feelings, with the flesh and with the bones, with the whole soul and with the whole body. It is the man that philosophizes" (Macquarrie, 1973, p. 15).

Process frameworks that draw upon the image of the world as socially constructed are founded on an ontology of becoming (Chia, 2002; Nayak & Chia, 2011; Langley et al., 2013). Helin et al. (2014) in their survey of process philosophers who have inspired organization studies, argue that entrepreneurial phenomena are especially well suited for process research. Moroz and Hindle's (2012) review, however, shows that existing frameworks modeling entrepreneurship as process mainly consider entrepreneurs as change-makers. In a world that itself constantly is on the move, as originally stated by Heraclitus, the challenge for entrepreneurs is, though, not to instigate change. It is rather about temporarily holding the world long enough to deal with upcoming situations and to be able to create new value through venturing. The dynamics of entrepreneuring is reflected in the very movement from coping with one situation to the next and in the mobilization of additional resources beyond everyday coping that is needed when enacting a new venture. Entrepreneuring then appears as a constant flow of local dealings with upcoming situations and this is intensified due to new projecting. Empirical research also confirms that successful venturing calls for a high level of activity (Carter et al., 1996). Over time, instrumental and situated practices and ventures accumulate into an entrepreneurial career as an existential endeavor.

Studying entrepreneuring through a practice lens as the organizing of concrete activities is well founded. Joseph Schumpeter (1987 [1943]) stated that entrepreneurship is about "getting things done" and Peter Drucker (1985) declared that "entrepreneurship *is* practice". Although practices thus include not only doings but also sayings that may be performative (Latour, 1986) and thus appear as deeds (Gartner, 1993), concrete action is what counts. Smircich and Stubbart (1985, p. 726), accordingly, point out that "[e]nactment implies a combination of *attention and action* on the part of the organization members" (italics in original). Schatzki (2002, p. 71) states that "a practice is a 'bundle' of activities, that is to say, an organized nexus of actions". This suggests that a social-constructionist world-view becomes more productive as a paradigmatic platform for entrepreneuring if combined with a practice framework.

Hernes (2014) and Schatzki (2002) thus both provide philosophically well founded and complementary contributions to theorizing entrepreneuring as a processual practice. Where Hernes focuses on different modes of articulating meaning structures, Schatzki sees articulation of intelligibility as only one mode of agency that generally concerns doings which "are incidents of accomplishment or carrying out" (2002, p. 191). Even if Schatzki more explicitly than Hernes recognizes the importance of affection in addition to cognitive capabilities, his conceptualization of practice and human agency still does not call attention to the role of conation, implying will and desire. While Hernes illustrates his framework with stray examples from his own previous research, Schatzki combines his modeling with systematic reflections on two rule-driven, institutionalized settings, one of which is a historical community and the other one a contemporary market structure.

Although Schatzki's conceptualization of practice is both analytically convincing and empirically validated, it reveals little about how practices, including ventures and organizations, let alone entrepreneurial careers, come into being. Practices are by Schatzki also mainly

Table 3.1   Positioning entrepreneuring as creative organizing

Feature	The Process View (Hernes, 2014)	The Practice View (Schatzki, 2002)	Entrepreneuring as Creative Organizing
Ontological standpoint	Meaning structures being the world	Human coexistence as a nexus of arranged entities and organized activities	The world as ambiguous inviting the creation of enacted structures through dialogue
Temporal order	Becoming as an overarching principle	Causal and teleological – making things happen	Kairotic – alert timing, drawing upon the past, enacting the future
Agency	The present as enacting the past and the future	That which gets something done, human or nonhuman	The entrepreneur as an orchestrator, embedded in an organizing context
Organization/order	Temporary pattern of event formations	Hierarchically ordered tasks, projects, ends	Situations and ventures as enveloped in a career
Recognized human faculties	Cognitive (affective)	Cognitive and affective	Cognitive, affective and conative
Rationale(s)	Instrumental	Instrumental	Instrumental and existential

associated with regularities, even if he also opens up for a broader interpretation: "A practice's actions, above all its tasks and projects, do invariably exhibit regularities. A practice, however, also embraces irregular, unique, and constantly changing doings/sayings, tasks and projects" (Schatzki, 2002, p. 74). Even practice theory as applied in organization research mainly concerns institutionalized routines involving recurrent practices (with)in existing formal organizations (Feldman, 2000; Orlikowski & Yates, 2002; Nicolini, 2012). This view makes practices appear as standardizing and disciplining, representing a centripetal force that by reducing variety runs the risk of prolonging temporary stability into inertia. In contrast, a practice framework feasible for inquiring into entrepreneuring as a processual phenomenon has to consider situated practices as the rule and routines as exceptions.

Table 3.1 summarizes key aspects of Hernes' and Schatzki's conceptualizations of process and practice as well as corresponding features of the proposed modeling of entrepreneuring. The latter stands out in three respects: by considering the world as enactable; viewing human agency as enforced by desire and willpower; and presenting entrepreneuring not only as an instrumental endeavor but also as an existential commitment. Schumpeter (1934, p. 93) succinctly states the ongoing balancing of instrumental and existential forces when summarizing the entrepreneur's prime movers: "First of all, there is the dream and the will to found a private kingdom, usually, though not necessarily, also a dynasty. ... Then there is the will to conquer: the impulse to fight, to prove oneself superior to others, to succeed for the sake, not of the fruits of success, but of success itself. ... Finally, there is the joy of creating, of getting things done, or simply of exercising one's energy and ingenuity."

Hernes' understanding of "the agency of the present" (2014, p. 4) signals a chronological image of time, but in the context of entrepreneuring the expression rather associates with entrepreneurs' spontaneous and resolute response to occurrences in their context. Dealing with an ambiguous complex and becoming world, entrepreneurs are rather guided by an event-based kairos logic (Rämö, 1999; Orlikowski & Yates, 2002) that triggers dialogue and action. Time-consuming articulation in terms of documentation and planning is accordingly rationed by entrepreneurs (Johannisson, 2008). Written words pave the road for standardization and routinization, in turn eroding attention to details and preserving the illusion that it is possible to hold a world on the move.

On the face of it, the enactment of situated practices and improvisation as "occurring when the design and execution of novel action converge" (Baker et al., 2003, p. 255) are identical phenomena. After all, they both instigate "*creactivity*" by combining creation and action on the spot. Both 'situated practice' and 'imitation' thus seem to be productive when inquiring into entrepreneurship/ing. However, Baker et al. (2003) (implicitly) adopt an ontology of being and, accordingly, position the proposed conceptualization of improvisation against a model that assumes that design precedes action and that imitations as 'local' tactics over time sediment into strategies. An ontology of becoming states, in contrast, that (situated) practices can neither be considered as improvisations that make up for the rigidity of routines, nor be predestined to become part of planning for the future. Still, these practices often appear as creative imitations of previous practices and may in the future themselves be creatively imitated when upcoming situations call for them.

Modeling the Entrepreneuring as a Weaving Process

Being in constant motion and busy with concrete issues is the life-blood of entrepreneurs – whether dealing with specific situations, launching ventures or practicing entrepreneuring as a way of life. When drawing upon practice theory it is logical, however, to start this conceptualization of entrepreneuring from below, at the level of the individual activity, and then map how activities combine into situated practices, each one being "an organized nexus of actions" (Schatzki, 2002, p. 71). These intermittently combine into new ventures, which in turn furnish the life-long career of the entrepreneur. The pragmatic, instrumental view – 'what works is true' – that guides hands-on dealing with situations as well as the launching of new ventures, is subordinate to entrepreneurs' existential drive. Although it sometimes makes businesspersons reorient their interest and organizing capabilities towards the production of cultural, social or ecological values, the way these are accomplished remains the same.

A social-constructionist perspective does not mean that entrepreneurs are in total control of their own development conditions or able to enact any environment. Powerful institutions reduce their freedom of action. In a world of becoming, environmental disturbances also impose themselves on the entrepreneur, thereby becoming "constitutive of action" (Joas, 1996, p. 160). Operating in an enacted world is therefore a mighty task for entrepreneurs, since it implies continuous sense-making of environmental change, heedful attention to upcoming situations and energetically taking necessary action. Still, the entrepreneur is not totally dependent on his own attention, competences and resources when it comes to enacting a feasible environment. Support is provided by the entrepreneur's personal network of trusted others, which spans the boundary between the entrepreneur(ial organization) and the enacted environment. Elsewhere, we address this network as an "*organizing context*" (Johannisson, 2000; Johannisson et al., 2002). Mutuality builds strong ties that make the network members provide the entrepreneur with solicited as well as unsolicited information, resources and legitimacy (Aldrich, 1999). The organizing context thus is self-organizing and its ontological status is that of a 'site' (Schatzki, 2005). This implies that the units, here the entrepreneurs and their organizations, simultaneously constitute the context and are themselves produced by it. The organizing context stands out in perspective of other images of context as far as its members intermingle with each other's 'internal affairs'. In her thorough review of the context concept Friederike Welter (2011, 2019) structures contexts into 'where' contexts – business, social, spatial and institutional – and 'when' contexts – temporal and historical. Gaddefors and

Anderson (2017) take a more radical standpoint by ascribing entrepreneurial agency to the (local) context itself.

Research on 'industrial districts' provides well-documented cases of contexts where the social and cultural embedding fosters individual and collective entrepreneurship. Physical, social and mental proximity trigger intense social exchange between the small traditional firms that inhabit such settings. This favors the owner-managers' ambitions as businesspersons while simultaneously institutionalizing a way of life that corresponds to their existential urge. See for example Becattini et al. (2009). Usually, a minority of the firms in the industrial districts are entrepreneurial enough to take advantage of local colleagues to extend their own growth ambition. Their personal networks often go beyond the spatially demarcated industrial district. Challenged by an emergency, network mates who are able to help out with their experience from similar situations are selectively addressed. Access to the experience of trusted members of the organizing context thus enlarges the action repertoire of the entrepreneur.

The proposed framework for conceptualizing entrepreneuring as practice thus suggests a tripartite agency: the entrepreneur, the members of the organizing context and an environment that calls for attention. Compare Bouchicki (1993). This multiple agency orchestrates both the instrumental dealing with upcoming concrete situations and the effectuation of the entrepreneur's existential drive. Metaphorically, this process appears as the weaving of a rag-rug whose warp is constituted by the entrepreneur's personal network and the weft of situated practices and their socio-material outcome.

In Figure 3.1, those personal relations in the organizing context that are activated appear as horizontal lines that make the warp of the rag-rug. Some of these relations carry the entrepreneur throughout the career, while others are established and/or terminated as the entrepreneurial career evolves. The weft primarily consists of measures for dealing with

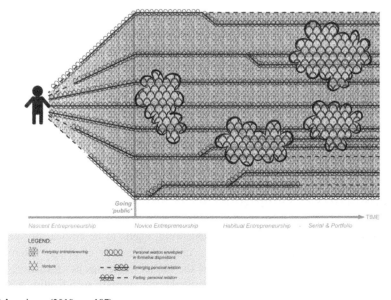

Source: Johannisson (2018a, p. 187).

Figure 3.1   *The entrepreneurial career as a weaving practice*

everyday situations and corresponds to the traditional rag-rug where previous, yet modified, inlays combine with new material (practices). When, however, the entrepreneurial process is intensified because a new venture is being launched, the otherwise rough, yet plain, surface of the rag-rug is elevated because of the piling up of activities (in weaving vocabulary addressed as 'tabby with tufted inlay'). Once this new venture has become 'everyday business' its resources and practices are absorbed by the emerging weft. When the venture is closed down, its resources are recycled to feed new situated practices, and sometimes also new ventures. These over time enact habitual, sequential/serial as well as parallel/portfolio, entrepreneurship (Westhead & Wright, 1998; Rosa & Scott, 1999).

This modeling of entrepreneuring as a socio-material weaving process, which is also energized by desire and will as well as serendipity, implies that it lies beyond rational, intended action. Instead, the evolving entrepreneurial career is orchestrated by the entrepreneur's '*formative dispositions*' as representing an existential drive. These appear as a set of general attitudes to the practice of entrepreneuring. In Figure 3.1, these dispositions envelope the strong relations between the entrepreneur and the members of the personal network. Identifying these dispositions calls for empirical research, whose methodology will be presented below.

Comparing this image of entrepreneuring as practice with the (four) models that Moroz and Hindle (2012) review in detail brings Sarasvathy's (2001, 2008) causation model of the entrepreneurial process to mind. Sarasvathy's conceptualization and the one proposed here certainly have similarities, the major one being the rejection of the entrepreneurial process as the product of explicit planning. There are, however, also a number of differences between the two approaches. To begin with, they are ontologically each other's opposites. Besides, where Sarasvathy argues that available resources frame the direction and scope of further venturing, the focus here is on how experience from previous coping with situations is used when dealing with new ones. While Sarasvathy models how successful/expert entrepreneurs organize individual ventures, the present concern is the making of entrepreneurial careers which encompass everyday entrepreneuring (Steyaert, 2004) as much as dramatic venturing. The latter difference is distinctly exposed in the contrasting use of metaphors for modeling the phenomenon. Both of them originate in textile handicraft when Sarasvathy uses the quilting image to illustrate the emergent (expert) entrepreneurial process as an assemblage of contributions by stakeholders which, like patches of a quilt, connect loosely to each other. The rag-rug metaphor, in contrast, presents the entrepreneurial process as a life-long commitment whose continuity is guaranteed by the warp, in other words, the social embedding of the entrepreneur in the organizing context.

EPISTEMOLOGICAL CHALLENGES IN THE QUEST FOR ENTREPRENEURING AS PRACTICE

Any modeling of a phenomenon, here entrepreneuring, needs to be empirically verified in order to qualify as a theoretical contribution to its field. Here the challenge taken on is to empirically state what the conceptualization of the model addresses as 'formative dispositions'. They are a product of the individual's ascribed traits, primary socialization and experiences that accumulate over time in his private and public life. Formative dispositions replace explicit goal-setting (compare Chia & MacKay, 2007) and, mobilizing cognitive, emotive as well as conative capabilities, they direct *how* entrepreneurs practice their trade. Although

Bourdieu (1977, p. 214) associates dispositions with re-active behavior and habits, disposi-tions that are able to produce effective situated action, the core of entrepreneuring, should be "indefinitely heterogeneous" (Ryle, 1949, p. 44). As Figure 3.1 indicates, they also regulate the entrepreneur's exchange with members of the organizing context and, consequently, the way the entrepreneur uses it to deal with the enacted environment.

The ontological positioning of entrepreneuring as a flow of situated practices defines the range of potential epistemologies that concern how to feature the insight that both brings out the uniqueness of every situation and advises how to deal with it. As indicated the everyday doings of entrepreneuring are as important to pay attention to as dramatic events such as the birth of a new venture. "[W]hen we take a *practical* attitude to the world we seek to go out-wards a concrete situation in all its richness and particularities. What is required here is not analysis but appreciation – to … explore it from within" (Shotter & Tsoukas, 2014, p. 387) (italics in original). Early on, systems theory taught us that even minor accidental events may cause radical change by way of self-enforcement (Maryama, 1963). Such insight has become especially important currently, when New Public Management (NPM) with its message that only what can be measured and thus categorized matters has invaded all sectors of society (Rose, 1999).

Flyvbjerg (2001) has taken on the challenge to vitalize and implant courage in the social sciences to make them adopt feasible epistemologies. He points out that Aristotle's intellectual capabilities 'episteme' and 'techne' with their belief in knowledge that is accumulative and possible to generalize are not feasible in social research. Flyvbjerg instead calls attention to another capability that Aristotle brings up, namely 'phronesis', that is, to use experience to heedfully consider concrete situations. What resolutely gets 'things done', even in opposition to established norms, as is the case in entrepreneuring, is however 'metis' (cf. Johannisson, 2011). Metis originates in Greek mythology and connotes shrewdness or "cunning intelli-gence" (Letiche & Statler, 2005). Metis is closely tied to action. "When a person is described by one or other of the intelligence epithets such as 'shrewd' or 'silly', 'prudent' or 'impru-dent', the description imputes to him not the knowledge, or ignorance, of this or that truth, but the ability, or inability, to do certain sorts of things" (Ryle, 1949, p. 27). This makes phronesis and metis into key entrepreneurial capabilities, since they, in contrast to formal knowledge, inform about *how* to act in specific situations. Ryle (1949, p. 44) illustrates this argument by stating that being informed about the rules of chess is only the beginning of the beginning of becoming a clever chess-player.

Sustainable entrepreneuring thus calls for an ability to balance phronesis and metis across situations and ventures into an entrepreneurial career. In a world on the move there is no time for preceding reflection about what to do – immediacy is called for. "It is now or never" Elvis Presley once sang. Quoting Goethe's *Faust*, Flyvbjerg (2001, p. 134) argues that "Am Anfang war die Tat" (In the beginning was the deed), stating that action precedes thinking. Since each upcoming situation must be individually dealt with, a series of situated practices does not accumulate into general knowledge. When challenged by a new situation, the entrepreneur instead ransacks his available repertoire of previous concrete dealings with similar incidents in the past. By creative imitation, or analogical reasoning (Nilsson, 1998), the entrepreneur creatively modifies such local experience to enable it to deal with the new situation.

Entrepreneurial learning is thus experiential, in that it draws upon previous experiences, as well as experimental by being tried out in the making of new realities (Politis, 2005). Hence, in entrepreneurial settings, the bricolage metaphor is as applicable to 'actionable knowledge'

(Jarzabkowski & Wilson, 2006) as to the recycling of material resources (Baker & Nelson, 2005). This makes failures that are lived through into an asset, since a situated practice that failed in the past may, modified or not, be able to deal with future situations. The entrepreneur's action repertoire is further enlarged, as the strong trust relationships to members of the organizing context make their experience of situated coping accessible to the entrepreneur as well. The members of the personal network may even on their own initiative act on behalf of the entrepreneur which makes entrepreneuring genuinely collective that aligns with the social-constructionist image of knowing and learning (Nonaka & Takeuchi, 1995).

The fact that knowing and doing are tightly intertwined in an enactment framework (Cook & Brown, 1999; Alvarez & Barney, 2007) has decisive implications for how to inquire empirically into entrepreneuring as practice. In order to be able to feature the creation of the situated practices that constitute entrepreneuring, as well as tracking the constitutive formative dispositions, the scholar has to be not only mentally but also physically involved in the very becoming of the practices. Only then is it possible for the researcher to grasp *how* situations are dealt with hands-on. It is thus not enough to metaphorically 'get under the skin' of entrepreneurs by engaging in 'thinking-from-within' (Shotter, 2006; Shotter & Tsoukas, 2014) – the researcher's own skin is at stake.

Referring to Heidegger, Chia and MacKay (2007) propose "indwelling" as a mode of getting the necessary insight, not the least into practices (Chia & Rasche, 2010; Nayak & Chia, 2011). Drawing upon pragmatist philosophy, Cook and Brown (1999) differentiate between 'knowledge' that can be possessed, whether explicit or tacit, and 'knowing', which is integrated with the action itself. Compare also Gherardi and Perrotta (2014). Cook and Brown invite us to a 'dance' between knowledge and knowing since it would be 'generative', as a "source of *new* knowledge and knowing lies in the use of knowledge as a tool of knowing within situated interaction with the social and physical world" (Cook & Brown, 1999, p. 383, italics in original). To my mind, Cook and Brown's metaphor recommends us as scholars to arrange an encounter between the formal knowledge possessed by the academic world and the embodied knowing that is integrated with the practices themselves.

There are two well-established ways of inquiring into the inner life of organizations: direct observation and auto-ethnography. While the former adopts an outside-in perspective where scholars invite themselves to the subjects' world, the auto-ethnographic approach scrutinizes this world from the inside. Barbara Czarniawska (2007, p. 17) uses the umbrella concept "shadowing" for different ways of "following selected people in their everyday occupations for a time" in order to reveal their doings and sayings. In a classic study in a field close to that of entrepreneurship, Mintzberg (1980 [1973]) recorded managers' work, a study that I will come back to in the concluding section. However, for a number of reasons, shadowing is not appropriate for tracking the doings of entrepreneurs. First, their creative organizing implies that the situation at hand directs what the entrepreneur does and how he does it. Still, this insight is usually out of reach even if the researcher performs as an assiduous follower and a brilliant interpreter. Second, the entrepreneur is not just intellectually involved when taking action but affectively and conatively as well. These human qualities are often hidden even from the entrepreneurs themselves, let alone from the shadowing researcher. Third, as also existentially motivated, entrepreneurs take action not only in order to instrumentally deal with the situation at hand but also with the long-term commitment to an entrepreneurial career in mind.

Auto-ethnography as a mode of self-reflection is well established as a methodology in social research; see for example Hayano (1979), Young (1991), Patton (2002), Alvesson (2003) and van Maanen (2011). These studies, however, focus more on the authors' intellectual and/or emotional experiences than on their concrete doings, or embodied practices. Nevertheless, some ethnographic studies report how researchers invite themselves as observing participants to existing organizations, e.g. Orr (1996). However, in order to catch entrepreneurs' incessant dealings with detailed and concrete situations they have to be lived through, cf. Berglund (2007).

Establishing a symbiotic relationship between practitioners and researchers may be another possible way forward to inquire into practices. Over the last 50 years, there have been a number of attempts in organization research to bridge between epistemic, or scientific, formal knowledge, and practical, embodied knowing. See Johannisson (2018a, Table 3.1, p. 67) for an overview of approaches. Such joint knowledge-creation, however, easily becomes dominated by academic norms. What therefore remains for the researcher studying situated entrepreneurial practices is to become involved, personally and hands-on, in entrepreneuring. Immediately flags of warning are hoisted. The first protest concerns the risk of 'going native' and thereby losing the ability to reflect on experiences gained. Cf. Czarniawska (2007). However, that risk is considerably reduced in studies of contemporary phenomena in modern societies, since the researcher remains embedded (also) in his original social context. A second obstacle is the desperate, yet hopeless, pursuit of the neutral scholar who engages in social research without any prejudice and personal interests. Traditional interpretive research methodology, nevertheless, takes sides with this defensive approach and accordingly suggests detailed 'cleaning' procedures for avoiding potential biases. Alvesson and Sköldberg (2009) are, under the label of 'reflexivity', especially assiduous and systematic in this respect. The purification process that they present tries to neutralize all subjectivities that can be associated with the researcher's personal impact on the findings. Yet, in qualitative research only inter-subjectivity can be accomplished.

There is yet another way of dealing with the fact that scholars are human beings, not robots. Rather than being looked upon as a liability, the personal involvement of the researcher can be considered an asset for increasing our understanding of the world. Törnebohm (1979) thus argues that personal interests and associated competences should be included in a researcher's paradigm in addition to ontological and epistemological ones, when designing an appropriate methodology for social research. Certain personal capabilities and experiences may condition gaining access to useful accounts and certainly have ethical/axiological implications. It would be against common sense to reject social-research findings because the scholar has been knowledgeable and clever enough to become able to establish a dialogue with the subjects concerned.

If the need for special personal qualities and experiences is not recognized in the social sciences, inquiry into human affairs had better be carried out incognito by other investigators than researchers. The German journalist Günter Wallraff managed to get himself employed in different disguises, for example as a miner, which enabled him to reveal a number of inferior working conditions. An experiment closer to enactive research was staged by the Swedish artist Anna Odell in the early 2000s. Still a student, she posed as mentally disordered and acted as if she was going to commit suicide by jumping from a bridge in Stockholm. This 'installation' made it possible for her to reveal practices among the institutions involved that no 'straight' social research would have accomplished. It seems to be about time that also social researchers, and especially scholars in the field of entrepreneurship, take courage and break new ground for gaining an insight into the world.

THE ENACTIVE METHODOLOGY: TRACKING THE ENTREPRENEUR'S FORMATIVE DISPOSITIONS

Building embodied knowing, critical of entrepreneuring as practice, calls for personal involvement in the processes concerned. This goes for practitioners who want to improve their competences as well as for external investigators, including researchers who want to inquire into situated practices. The argument is thus that learning *how* such practices materialize requires that the researcher integrates his professional identity with that of an entrepreneur and lives through the becoming of situated practices and their structuring into ventures. This means that the scholar has to engage as an *"entresearcher"* (*entre*-preneur *and* re-*searcher*) by enacting a venturing process. Only by adopting such a hybrid identity can the scholar become a successful explorer of the dialogue between knowing and acting. By making the scholar into an (inter-)active *and* reflective contributor to the world a bridge is built between the ontological and epistemological foundations of inquiry into entrepreneuring as practice, on one hand, and encounters in the field, on the other.

In the proposed 'enactive' approach, the scholar's idiosyncrasies, his personal experience, capabilities, interests and values are recognized, organized and, if needed, completed. The capable entresearcher has to be (1) acquainted with the empirical field concerned; (2) socially competent enough to create a dialogue with the subjects concerned; (3) able to turn the commitment of the subjects who are involved into action; (4) sufficiently resolute to enact events that generate value for those involved as well as for society at large; and (5) reflective and imaginative enough to use field accounts to induce the formative dispositions that craft situated practices.

The enactive researcher is expected to mobilize all his capabilities, cognitive, affective as well as conative, professional as well as personal. Practicing as an entresearcher is thus about becoming increasingly authentic (Eriksen, 2012), a 'complete human being', in other words, without disconnecting from his professional academic identity. Having experienced creative organizing in terms of his own venturing, even if 'only' in his own academic context, adds to the credibility of the entresearcher. Such academic initiatives preferably cover all the tripartite missions of a public university in Sweden: research, education and outreach activities.

My practical experience as an entrepreneur or creative organizer is also concentrated on the academic setting. As researcher, I have initiated and led research programs (within my own universities and beyond), established a research institute (with a colleague), organized (inter)national conferences, and edited an international journal in the field. As educator, I have launched a unique entrepreneurship program including internship in small (entrepreneurial) firms, initiated and organized nationwide post-graduate courses and co-directed an international doctoral program. My involvement in outreach activities includes engaging as an activist in community and social entrepreneurship, initiating and organizing a series of national conferences on local development, and publishing frequently in daily newspapers.

Table 3.2 provides the agenda for the enactive approach to entrepreneuring as practice. The empirical research covers two enacted projects, and the design of their reporting draws upon van Maanen's (2011) triads of tales – realist, impressionist and confessional. Overarching

Table 3.2   *Identities/roles and practices over the phases of enactive research*

Research phase	Entresearcher role	Research practices
Familiarization	Explorer/learner	Hanging around
		Building legitimacy
		Getting involved as an activist
Initiation	Visionary/entrepreneur	Imagining
		Reviewing the personal network
		Launching
Actualization	Manager/executor	Organizing – committing people
		Doing – arranging activities
		Closing the venture(s)/project
Separation	Communicator/observing participant	Hanging around
		Providing advice
Reflection	Scholar/moralist	Condensing (confessional tale embedding realist and impressionistic tales)
		Ethical concerns

Source: Johannisson (2018a, p. 87).

reflections on the enactive approach constitute a confessional tale which embeds realist tales presenting in chronological order 'facts' about the two cases as well as impressionist tales which describe how 'situations' as critical incidents in the enactment processes are dealt with. Reflection on the latter has produced the proposed formative dispositions of the entrepreneur that generate situated practices. See Johannisson (2018a, Chapter 4) for details.

The two venturing projects were both enacted in a regional setting but were different with respect to created value, structure and 'enactability'. The original Anamorphosis project[2] concerned a holistic and organically structured venture that was launched in an ambiguous and therefore permissive setting where creative ideas about what to do and how were almost unlimited. Embracing three ventures, the second SORIS[3] project was, in contrast, hierarchically structured and launched in a more or less institutionalized context with the university and further external parties as influential stakeholders. While I could as entresearcher in the Anamorphosis project give free rein to my spontaneity and imagination, in the SORIS project I had to restrain myself and also to mobilize my capabilities as a negotiator in order to make the venturing process enactable. In order to indicate the academic affiliation of the ventures and also draw upon the university's concrete and symbolic resources, the Anamorphosis project was accommodated in the vicinity of the university campus, while the majority of the SORIS activities were enacted on the campus itself.

The task environment of the two projects, both lasting for about a year, was deliberately chosen to provide a complementary insight into entrepreneurial practices beyond market entrepreneurship. The aim of the Anamorphosis project was to inquire into an encounter between culture and science and its potential contribution to regional development. Considering its ambition to produce cultural value, this project took place in 1999 in a spectacular old building that also housed a community of artists. The project was realized as an art exhibition of anamorphosis and a series of public dialogue seminars led by volunteering experts. Its enactment was triggered by my disillusionment when the university withdrew from another proposed venture (aimed at celebrating the new millennium). SORIS materialized in 2014 and was designed to make social entrepreneurship into an integral part of the public regional innovation and development policy. While the Anamorphosis project, besides its emotional arousal, originated in my genuine curiosity, SORIS was inspired by my action research into soci(et)al entrepreneurship. See for example Berglund et al. (2012). It was also designed to acquaint a cohort of freshmen on a business program with social entrepreneurship.

The resourcing of the enacted projects focused on human and social capital (which even market-oriented entrepreneurs consider more important than financial capital, cf. Johannisson, 2008). Compare also Davidsson and Honig (2003). Consequently, drawing on my personal network, I mobilized in both projects a team staffed with knowledgeable and committed practitioners. In the Anamorphosis project, the team operated as a 'task force', and its members thus volunteered hands-on and whole-heartedly with their versatile professional competences. In addition, the few (three) students involved as apprentices carried out complementary activities. In the SORIS project, the members of the 'steering committee' were also enthusiastic volunteers who mainly contributed with professional advice. Here our meetings were documented by a salaried secretary, who also assisted the leaders of the three ventures embraced by the project. One venture, led by a consultant, organized a network between regional work-integrating social enterprises, while another venture, initiated by two unemployed persons, was concerned with launching a social enterprise in the tourism industry. The third venture, coordinated by a volunteer associated with a local social enterprise, aimed at arranging a job-creation event for and by unemployed young people. Altogether, about 40 students were involved in the SORIS venturing activities.

The two projects were institutionalized to a different degree. The Anamorphosis project had no example to follow and was only loosely connected to the university. Experimenting was the dominant modus operandi, but the inevitable mistakes that occurred were easily overcome. Seminar themes were spontaneously and gradually generated. The freedom of action that the project team allowed itself was even large enough for the original objective of the project to be retrospectively changed to justifying the activities that had de facto been carried out. In contrast, the SORIS project's scope for enactment was relatively restricted. First, the objective of the project had to be negotiated with regional and state authorities. Second, because of the extensive involvement of students, formal rules regarding organizing, lecturing and examination had to be attended to. Third, since the SORIS project took place on the premises of the university, its rules concerning practical arrangements had to be followed. Fourth, the project pushed itself further into formal structuring because of the complexity of its three parallel ventures. Fifth, my own role accordingly involved paving the road for ventures, by providing a supportive context for them rather than contributing to their hands-on enactment. These caring activities included warding off threats, amplifying opportunities and offering the venture leaders a sounding board.

In addition to providing an insight into entrepreneuring as practice and educating students, the projects also had the ambition to establish a dialogue with extramural interest groups. In the Anamorphosis project, information about the art exhibition and the seminars was widely circulated in Växjö, where the university is located, using posters as well as advertising and further promotion in the regional newspaper. The message of the SORIS project was communicated to the regional community at seminars and conferences which were broadcasted by a local television company, which was also run as a social enterprise.

As the proposed framework suggests, any venturing initiative includes situations of a different origin and magnitude with respect to their contribution to the evolving entrepreneurial process. Even minor incidents are important to consider, since they may grow into more severe disturbances. Time, however, puts restrictions on the number of incidents that can be attended to by the entresearcher. Since the entresearcher spends considerable time on embodied action, there remains less time for reflecting while the entrepreneurial process is still evolving. However, the limited scope of the Anamorphosis project gave me, in spite of my deep involvement in its materialization, time to produce ethnographic accounts. I even gave way to the temptation to interview my team mates about their experiences of the project. Their typical comment was: 'Why do you ask? You staged everything yourself and should already know!' Since I could not be personally involved in hands-on venturing activities in the SORIS project, the interpretation and reflection accounts were, in addition to formal and informal encounters with mainly students, supplied by proceedings from staged meetings and mailed conversations.

Three kinds of dramatic situations that triggered emotional tensions and caused anxiety but also resolute action were identified in the field research and thus reported as impressionistic tales: 'circumstances', 'predicaments' and 'experiments'. *'Circumstances'* concerned environmental disturbances that had to be dealt with urgently before growing into disasters. *'Predicaments'* were about coincidences that are encapsulated in the enacted venture but which might have made the enactment move in an unfavorable direction if not actively dealt with. If properly managed, these deviations could instead be redirected to subsequently make significant contributions to the overall eventing. The third kind of impressionistic tales that were registered reported *'experiments'*. These interventions were deliberately staged by me, the entresearcher, in order to mobilize the energy needed to forestall threats to the enactment of the project.

Reflecting back on the Anamorphosis and SORIS projects, six *formative dispositions*, i.e. generic attitudes associated with entrepreneuring as practice, were induced from the qualitative accounts. Jointly with my capabilities – cognitive, affective as well as conative – these dispositions provided the embodied insight, direction and energy needed to enact the projects. These formative dispositions are: (1) considering change and experimenting a natural state; (2) experiencing the personal network as a bodily extension; (3) recognizing venturing as a collaborative undertaking; (4) rationalizing and imputing agency to one's own actions over random events; (5) safeguarding room for maneuvering; and (6) regarding institutions as competitors, indifference as an enemy and resistance as an energizer. In Johannisson (2018a, pp. 164–174), these dispositions are reflected on in detail.

AN AXIOLOGICAL AUDIT OF THE ENACTIVE APPROACH

Axiological issues, i.e. value-related reflections on empirical inquiry, are as important as ontology, epistemology and methodology to attend to in social research. From an axiological point of view, the key question is: In what respect does the research contribute to the making of a better world in terms of individual freedom, equality, and solidarity. According to Hill (1984, p. 67), projects with the highest axiological principles/ambitions are those that attend to "human rights and dignity", basic democratic values, in other words. Not only economic value but also social, cultural and ecological values have then to be attended to. Rescher (1969) on his part, states that a hard-core axiological approach which only relates to one intrinsic, or ultimate, value is not productive. Referring to Perry (1926), he argues that anything that is an object of somebody's interest has a value (Rescher, 1969, p. 50). Enactive research into entrepreneuring involves many stakeholders, all with their own idiosyncratic interest in the enactment concerned: members of the entrepreneur's personal network, students, external stakeholders including the financiers, the university to which the entresearcher is affiliated and, of course, the entresearcher himself.

What makes enactive research stand out among other social-constructionist approaches is that the entresearcher does not content himself with being an observer and interpreter of the world who communicates his findings verbally. For three reasons, the enactive researcher also engages concretely in world-making. First, only such engagement can generate the genuine, embodied knowing about the world that makes enactment possible. Second, the enactments concerned may well be designed to produce value that contributes to the making of a better, more human, world. This ambition, ultimately a responsibility that all scholars have, is here represented by the launching of the cultural Anamorphosis and the social SORIS projects. Third, Michael Polanyi (1974 [1962]) promotes a view on the researcher's responsibilities that is even more far-reaching. Not only should the competent scholar mobilize his personal skills as Törnebohm (1979) suggests. According to Polanyi the scholar must in addition demonstrate a genuine *commitment* that generates the 'personal knowledge' needed to direct both the research process and the validation of its findings. This view provides a bridge between epistemology and axiology when inquiring into entrepreneuring. On one hand Polanyi's framework justifies the deep personal involvement of the scholar in the research process that the enactive approach suggests. On the other it supports the conceptualization of entrepreneuring as instrumentally and existentially driven enactment in terms of creative organizing for the production of new value, social, cultural and environmental as well as economic.

Axiological issues, however, occur rarely in extant entrepreneurship research, whether as a perspective on *what* is being studied or on *how* that research is carried out (Kyrö, 2015). There are three main reasons for this deficiency. First, entrepreneurship is a young research field, institutionalized through conferences and journals only in the 1980s. Second, the field is still dominated by positivist research where the researcher's ambition is to mirror an objective reality as accurately as possible. Third, when values are taken into consideration in qualitative social research, they are usually assigned to the researchers' ideology (Alvesson & Sköldberg, 2009; Lindgren & Packendorff, 2011) and considered as a bias to control for. Just as entrepreneurial activity is charged with contributing to economic wealth mainly in the interests of the entrepreneur himself, entrepreneurship researchers are accused of lacking reflexivity and of playing the capitalists' game. Critical inquiries into entrepreneurship, e.g. Ogbor (2000), remain, however, discursive and detached exercises concerning the destruction of contemporary conceptual images of entrepreneurship. Enactive research instead provides a 'constructive' contribution to an emerging field of research by inviting the researcher to the practitioner's game.

An axiological review of enactive research must include an appreciation of the entresearcher's involvement both as scholar and practitioner. Considering that the entresearcher is expected to also mobilize idiosyncratic insights and capabilities such as familiarity with the field of study, general sociability and empathy and endurance, even intersubjectivity is in practice inaccessible in enactive research. What remains for the entresearcher is, first, to communicate trustworthiness, both as a practitioner and as a scholar, and, second, to praise those involved in the hands-on enacted venture for their contributions to the enactment as an academic knowledge-creating exercise. Here I will comment on two complementary ways of inspiring confidence in general, and with contributing practitioners and students in particular: carefully considering what value to create through the enacted activities and embedding the project concerned in preparatory and following-up activities. For a number of reasons, profit-oriented ventures were not launched (compare above). First, associating entrepreneurship/ing with economic value creation alone would undermine the ambition to induce a generic model of entrepreneuring. Second, as also stated above, a focus on economic value creation is for ideological reasons a legitimate target for criticism. Third, had I enacted profit-oriented projects rather than cultural and social ones, the suspicion would have arisen that my objective was to line my pocket at the students', the volunteers' and the public's expense. Entrepreneuring as economic value creation is, however, indirectly taken into consideration by anchoring its conceptualizing in extant entrepreneurship research, which is definitely dominated by inquiry into economic activity.

The entresearcher can also build confidence by embedding the enacted activities in a more general concern for the subjects and their communities before and/or after the enacted project. After all, the researcher is accountable for both the intervention per se and for the interpretation of its materialization and outcome. This responsibility is both personal and associated with the researcher's role as a member of the academic community. When I launched the Anamorphosis project, some of the trusted people whom I enrolled in my task force formed my only association with the artists' cooperative residing in the premises, the 'Italian Palace', where the event took place. The majority of the artists were even skeptical of the project, an attitude that only slowly changed as the venturing activities assumed a more definite form. However, at the closure of the Anamorphosis project, I was invited to become a member of the board. For a decade I engaged in different public activities together with the artists, and for some years I also had an office in the Italian Palace. As regards my early contacts with people involved in the SORIS project, I had met with several of them in my research into work-integrating social enterprises. At the time the SORIS project was launched I even chaired a voluntary association that supported a social enterprise. This association also became the formal owner of SORIS. When that project ended I stayed involved in the social enterprise (and later in its supportive organization as the enterprise went bankrupt in 2020). Researchers cannot build confidence if they rush in and out of hands-on involvement in social change processes.

A further ethical issue is how to balance the pretentious and bold imposition as an (ent) researcher of a (socially constructed) reality on further project members, on one hand, with strong personal commitment and self-assumed responsibility for the initiation, organizing and completion of enacted ventures, on the other. An adequate point of departure for such an audit is formed by the responsibilities of a university's academic staff: contribute to the research field, educate students, and engage in outreach activities. However, the interfaces between these three obligations are seldom considered, let alone regulated in detail – leaving out of account that academic education in Sweden is expected to be generally supported by research. This means that launching a project with a focus on research, education or reaching out to society does not automatically pay attention to the other two responsibilities.

The enactive approach invites a unique integrative approach to the three missions of universities. Representatives of the three targeted missions were invited to a joint learning exercise where explicit and tacit, formal and informal knowledge met in ongoing dialogues. I and the students jointly represented the university and its concern for research and education, while 'society' as the target of outreach activities was primarily represented by the practitioners on the projects' expert boards but also by the projects' external financiers. In the Anamorphosis project, the seminars provided concrete arenas where further researchers, students and the general public could meet. In the SORIS project, leaders and involved students jointly reported the enactment of each venture at a concluding seminar. A panel of experts representing different communities then cross-examined the presenters in front of an audience that included further students and university staff. Since this event was locally broadcasted it also reached the general public.

The practitioners who staffed the task force in the Anamorphosis project and the steering committee in the SORIS project all volunteered. As members of my personal network they all immediately and enthusiastically contributed to the enactment of the events. I can see a number of reasons for their spontaneous and deep engagement. First, they were intrigued by the possibility to enact a venture that with respect to its objective adjoined those of their own organization but, with respect to mode of organizing, contrasted their professional work. In the Anamorphosis project, the artists on the task force thus appreciated the spontaneous, yet tight, organizing that contrasted their own anarchic work environment. In contrast, the members who represented established organizations, often public institutions, enjoyed the experimental and playful mode of organizing. In the SORIS project, the meetings of the steering committee were esteemed because its members shared the same strong commitment to social entrepreneurship. Second, many of the volunteers were in a transitional phase of their professional career and therefore considered participation in the projects an opportunity to reflect upon their work situation. Third, at the time of the Anamorphosis project in 1999, the university was upgraded to become a full university. Only a few years before the SORIS project was launched, the university had grown radically by merging with another university. Consequently, the regional practitioners could share the attention that the university received on these occasions.

The entresearcher's responsibility for participating students goes beyond that of a traditional educator as it also includes the roles of a coach and a guardian. Both projects were integrated parts of an undergraduate course in entrepreneurship, and for each project the students' involvement lasted for its first four formative months. The few (three) students in the Anamorphosis project worked very closely and informally with me and the other members of the task force as 'legitimate peripheral participants' (Wenger, 1998). Therefore, for good or for bad, they could experience the 'heat of entrepreneuring' (compare Stewart, 1989), in other words, the immediacy of the situated practices that enact venturing. On one hand, this meant close and rewarding collaboration with the task force members on practical matters and, on the other, that they had to personally experience the reluctance of established institutions to new ideas. This aversion included the skepticism of the university administration vis-à-vis the Anamorphosis project as an event that was not formally sanctioned. A controversy occurred, for example, when the students proposed that a link between the project's and the university's homepage should be established in order to promote the event. The harsh treatment that the students experienced at the computer office forced me to intervene and defend the students' initiative.

The students who enrolled in the SORIS project could choose to participate in any of the three ventures. Once having made their choice, they were formally organized by the venture leaders. The students were enrolled in the SORIS project for two reasons: to experience the practice of collectively launching a venture and the need for experiencing 'conscientization' (Freire, 2001), in other words, making the students aware of entrepreneuring as a road to other than economic values and the need for practicing solidarity and empathy. However, both objectives turned out to be difficult to reach. The students participated in a Bachelor program in Enterprising and Business Development, and those who considered an entrepreneurial career had starting their own business in mind. My constructive-critical approach created a number of controversies between the students, on one hand, and me and the venture leaders, on the other. However, a qualitative course evaluation revealed that, when reflecting back on the experiences gained during the enactment process, the majority of the students had reconsidered the role of entrepreneuring in a societal context and the benefits of experiential learning. See also Achtenhagen and Johannisson (2018).

Hill's (1984) foundations of an axiological audit of social research are, first, that the ontological and epistemological assumptions and proposed methodology, i.e. the knowledge-creating system, must correspond with the issue being addressed. Second, that an emancipatory position is adopted implying that "[s]ocial projects which oppress, disenfranchise, or denigrate fellows humans" (Hill, 1984, p. 68) are turned down. These two requirements are, I argue, met in the two enacted projects as products of enactive research that make both the researcher and the students into potent but also responsible contributors to social change. A complementary axiological principle adopted here is that the enactive approach redirects the dominating view on entrepreneurship from being considered as a kind of management for increasing economic value to a mode of enhancing human value, cultural as well as social. Also, by actively involving the subjects concerned in the venturing process, its outcome appears as a joint product of dialogues between members of the research, education and societal communities.

CONCLUSION: THE NATURE OF ENTREPRENEURIAL WORK

Summarizing their search for a distinct and generic model of entrepreneurship as process, here entrepreneuring, Moroz and Hindle (2012, p. 811) are worried about the lack of empirical studies and absence of "practical implications that address the 'how' of entrepreneurship". The enactive approach deals with both these shortcomings by, first, amalgamating process and practice frameworks in a social-constructionist ontological setting and, second, proposing an epistemology and associated methodology that make the researcher live through, or practice, the very becoming of entrepreneuring. The six 'formative dispositions' of the entrepreneur that were induced from the empirical inquiry (see above) condense into the duality *conscientiousness* and *grit* (Johannisson, 2018a, p. 190). See also Duckworth et al. (2007). It maintains the entrepreneur's ability to combine concern for details through situated coping with endurance that lasts beyond individual ventures and builds an entrepreneurial career. This provides a model of entrepreneuring that, I argue, is distinct as well as generic, as it equips the phenomenon with a specific and universal style (Spinosa et al., 1997, p. 20).

The argument that the model is generic is of course closely associated with how entrepreneuring as a social phenomenon is defined, here as creative organizing across borders in order to create new value. Here, I want to provide further support for the argument that the model is also distinguished by being positioned against management. This elucidatory discourse has been saved for these concluding remarks since, from a different perspective, it brings to attention the compatibility of the elements that constitute the adopted enactive approach. Entrepreneuring and management are often presented as closely related phenomena, making the former into just a special kind of management. Elsewhere I argue, however, that entrepreneuring and management rather represent contrasting ideologies (Johannisson, 2002, 2018b). A relevant question here then is: What implications do proposed ideological differences have on how managers and entrepreneurs practice their trade?

I define ideology as "*a consistent and permanent way of perceiving and appreciating the world that, charged by emotional commitment, generates a specific mode of conduct*" (Johannisson, 2002, p. 48, italics in original). The management ideology states that managers are expected to behave rationally, adopt chronological time as a temporal order and, guided by quantitative goals and plans, draw upon routines that translate plans into action. The discourse here has clarified that the entrepreneurial ideology, in contrast, states that entrepreneurs acknowledge the role of emotions and will and associated 'irrational' behavior, practice a kairos temporal order, are (also) existentially driven and, drawing upon previous concrete experiences, deal with concrete challenges by situated practices. While managers 'make' decisions that others are expected to translate into action, entrepreneurs 'take' action that directly addresses the situation at hand. Managers and entrepreneurs thus relate differently to the world, and adopt contrasting basic attitudes. Henry Mintzberg (1980 [1973]), in his iconic study *The Nature of Managerial Work*, originally submitted as a PhD thesis in 1968, stated that managers have to submit to an internal and external (objective) environment (Mintzberg, 1980 [1973], p. 55). I here argue that entrepreneurs co-produce a supportive organizing context and enact the environment.

It should thus come as no surprise that such ontological differences make management and entrepreneuring appear as contrasting practices. Mintzberg (1980 [1973], pp. 28–53) identified six characteristics of chief executives' everyday doings – "much work at unrelenting pace"; "activity characterized by brevity, variety and fragmentation"; "preference for live action"; "attraction to the verbal media"; "between his organization and a network of contacts"; and "blend of rights and duties". Surprisingly enough, these practices jointly echo what is here generally associated with the practice of entrepreneuring: constantly being on the move, and being involved in pro- and inter-active dealing with upcoming concrete situations. Mintzberg, however, sees acting as an entrepreneur as only one out of ten managerial roles, a role that he associates with acting "as initiator and as designer of important controlled change in his organization. This change takes place in the form of improvement projects, many of which are supervised directly by the manager and all of which come under his control in one way or another" (Mintzberg, 1980 [1973], p. 81). This image of *what* managers do when performing as entrepreneurs obviously contrasts against Mintzberg's own image of *how* managers generally work.

An obvious key question is: How come that managers and entrepreneurs, in spite of contrasting ideologies, do what they do in similar ways? I argue that this paradox is a product of the different ontologies that managers and entrepreneurs cultivate. Sune Carlsson (1951), Mintzberg's major source and inspiration, argued that managers typically re-act, that is consider themselves as externally controlled by an objectified environment. Entrepreneurs, in contrast, see the environment as enactable, as socially constructed, and therefore are pro-active as well as inter-active. Managers use their energy and ability to move as reflected in their practices to tread water in order to survive, while entrepreneurs use similar practices to explore new waters. Mintzberg (1980 [1973], pp. 50–51), however, touches upon an attempt to break out of this dejection by arguing that it is 'only' a matter of attitude whether the work situation is considered to be out of control or not. In his opinion, the manager can take control over his life by being 'smart', which in the vocabulary used here means becoming entrepreneurial. However, since Mintzberg as a researcher is tied to an objectivist approach, he could not elaborate upon this hunch; his paradigm simply produced managers as slaves to the circumstances.

The field reports on the Anamorphosis and SORIS projects reveal that, while entrepreneurs' feeling for the situatedness of action remains strong and general, the enactability of their environment varies with its institutionalization. An inquiry into entrepreneurs' use of time also informs us about how they adapt to different environmental conditions. In the 1970s, the years when Mintzberg published his findings, I conducted the first of a series of field studies of how successful entrepreneurs allocate their time. This investigation was repeated on different samples over three decades the last of which (2004) covered Swedish Gazelles. See Johannisson (2008). While the entrepreneurs in the 1970s invested a dominant share of their available time in either hands-on action or envisioning their future, in the turbulent 2000s time was reallocated in favor of concrete action. This suggests that entrepreneurs realize that envisioning the future is futile in a liquid world. Over the three-decade period, the time spent on planning activities by the entrepreneurs remained low. The work and practices by chief executives, as reported by Mintzberg, focused instead on planning and hands-on doings. Presumably, the latter activities were triggered by attempts to make up for the inability of routines to deal with upcoming unexpected situations. Without referring to Mintzberg (1980 [1973]), let alone to entrepreneurship research, organization scientists such as Feldman (2000) persist in performing the Houdini trick of breaking out of bonding routines, even making them into a source of change.

Whether managers view themselves as defensive trouble-shooters who are slaves to the circumstances or as germinating entrepreneurs waiting for their deliberation will certainly remain a cherished subject in organization research. Optimists from Pinchot III (1985) to Hjorth (2012), focus on the potentials of organizational entrepreneurship. Pessimists like Alvesson and Spicer (2016), in contrast, consider contemporary organizations as hit by "functional stupidity", which makes them unable to be alert and reflective. Once this stupidity is overcome, it still remains for managers as would-be entrepreneurs to consider their use of time. Such attentiveness should result in more heedful coping also with minor incidents, not just because they are potential sources of structural change, but also since such alertness is accompanied by an increased awareness of the need to constantly be on the move in a liquid world.

NOTES

1. Throughout this chapter 'I' and masculine pronouns are used. This may be provocative in contemporary 'metoo' times but is a consequence of the adopted methodology.
2. Anamorphosis is an art form where an original three-dimensional object is distorted into a two-dimensional image that is, however, restored by properly locating a cylindrical, pyramidal or conic mirror in the painting.
3. **SO**cial **R**egional **I**nnovation **S**ystem (SORIS).

REFERENCES

Achtenhagen, L., & Johannisson, B. (2018). The reflexivity grid: Exploring conscientization in entrepreneurship education. In K. Berglund & Karen Verduyn (Eds.), *Revitalizing Entrepreneurship Education: Adopting a Critical Approach in the Classroom* (pp. 62–81). Cheltenham, UK and Northampton, MA, USA: Edward Elgar Publishing.
Aldrich, H. (1999). *Organizations Evolving*. London: Sage Publications.

Alvarez, S., & Barney, J. (2007). Discovery and creation: Alternative theories of entrepreneurial action. *Strategic Entrepreneurship Journal*, *1*, 11–26.

Alvesson, M. (2003). Methodology for close-up studies: Struggling with closeness and closure. *Higher Education*, *46*, 167–193.

Alvesson, M., & Sköldberg, K. (2009). *Reflexive Methodology: New Vistas for Qualitative Research* (2nd edition). London: Sage Publications.

Alvesson, M., & Spicer, A. (2016). *The Stupidity Paradox: The Powers and Pitfalls of Functional Stupidity at Work*. London: Profile Books.

Baker, T., Miner, S., & Eesley, D. (2003). Improvising firms: Bricolage, account giving and improvisational competencies in the founding process. *Research Policy*, *32*, 255–276.

Baker, T., & Nelson, R. (2005). Creating something from nothing: Resource construction through entrepreneurial bricolage. *Administrative Science Quarterly*, *50*(3), 329–366.

Baron, R. (2008). The role of affect in the entrepreneurial process. *Academy of Management Review*, *33*(2), 328–340.

Becattini, G., Bellandi, M., & De Propris, L. (Eds.) (2009). *Handbook of Industrial Districts*. Cheltenham, UK and Northampton, MA, USA: Edward Elgar Publishing.

Berger, P., & Luckmann, T. (1966). *The Social Construction of Reality: A Treatise in the Sociology of Knowledge*. New York: Doubleday.

Berglund, H. (2007). Researching entrepreneurship as lived experience. In H. Nergaard & J. P. Ulhöi (Eds.), *Handbook of Qualitative Research Methods in Entrepreneurship* (pp. 75–93). Cheltenham, UK and Northampton, MA, USA: Edward Elgar Publishing.

Berglund, K., Johannisson, B., & Schwartz, B. (Eds.) (2012). *Societal Entrepreneurship: Positioning, Penetrating, Promoting*. Cheltenham, UK and Northampton, MA, USA: Edward Elgar Publishing.

Bouchicki, H. (1993). A constructivist framework for understanding entrepreneurship performance. *Organization Studies*, *14*(4), 549–570.

Bourdieu, P. (1977). *Outline of a Theory of Practice*. Cambridge: Cambridge University Press.

Burgelman, R., Floyd, S., Laamanen, T., Mantere, I., Vaara, E., & Whittington, R. (2018). Strategy process and practices: Dialogues and intersections. *Strategic Management Journal*, *39*, 531–558.

Cardon, M., Wincent, J., Singh, J., & Drnovsek, M. (2009). The nature and experience of entrepreneurial passion. *Academy of Management Review*, *34*(3), 511–532.

Carlsson, S. (1951). *Executive Behaviour: A Study of the Work Loads and the Working Methods of Managing Directors*. Stockholm: Strömbergs.

Carter, N., Gartner, W., & Reynolds, P. (1996). Exploring start-up event sequences. *Journal of Business Venturing*, *11*, 151–166.

Chia, R. (2002). Essai: Time, duration and simultaneity: Rethinking process and change in organizational analysis. *Organization Studies*, *23*(6), 863–868.

Chia, R., & MacKay, B. (2007). Post-processual challenges for the emerging strategy-as-practice perspective: Discovering strategy in the logic of practice. *Human Relations*, *60*(1), 217–242.

Chia, R., & Rasche, A. (2010). Epistemological alternatives for researching strategy as practice: Building and dwelling worldviews. In D. Golsorkhi, L. Rouleau, D. Seidl, & E Vaara (Eds.), *Cambridge Handbook of Strategy as Practice* (pp. 34–46). Cambridge: Cambridge University Press.

Cook, S., & Brown, J. (1999). Bridging epistemologies: The generative dance between organizational knowledge and organizational knowing. *Organization Science*, *10*(4), 381–400.

Czarniawska, B. (2007). *Shadowing and Other Techniques for Doing Fieldwork in Modern Societies*. Malmö: Liber.

Davidsson, P., & Honig, B. (2003). The role of social and human capital among nascent entrepreneurs. *Journal of Business Venturing*, *18*, 301–331.

Drucker, P. (1985). *Innovation and Entrepreneurship*. New York: Harper & Row.

Duckworth, A., Peterson, C., Matthews, M., & Kelly, D. (2007). Grit: Perseverance and passion for long-term goals. *Journal of Personality and Social Psychology*, *92*(6), 1087–1010.

Eriksen, M. (2012). Facilitating authentic becoming. *Journal of Management Education*, *36*(5), 698–736.

Feldman, M. (2000). Organizational routines as a source of continuous change. *Organization Science*, *11*(6), 611–629.

Flyvbjerg, B. (2001). *Making Social Science Matter: Why Social Inquiry Fails and How It Can Succeed Again*. Cambridge: Cambridge University Press.

Freire, P. (2001). *Pedagogy of Freedom: Ethics, Democracy, and Civic Courage*. Lanham, MD: Rowman & Littlefield.

Gaddefors, J., & Anderson, A. (2017). Entrepreneurship and context: When entrepreneurship is greater than entrepreneurs. *International Journal of Entrepreneurial Behavior and Research, 23*(2), 267–278.

Gartner, W. (1993). Words lead to deeds: Towards an organizational emergence vocabulary. *Journal of Business Venturing, 8*, 231–239.

Gartner, W., Bird, B., & Starr, J. (1992). Acting as if: Differentiating entrepreneurial from organizational behavior. *Entrepreneurship Theory and Practice, 16*(3) 13–32.

Gergen, K. (1999). *An Invitation to Social Construction*. Thousand Oaks, CA: Sage Publications.

Gherardi, S., & Perrotta, M. (2014). Between the hand and the head. *Qualitative Research in Organizations and Management: An International Journal, 9*(2), 134–150.

Hayano, D. M. (1979). Auto-ethnography: Paradigms, problems and prospects. *Human Society: Journal of the Society for Applied Anthropology, 38*(1), 99–104.

Helin, J., Hernes, T., Hjorth, D., & Holt, R. (2014). Process is how process does. In J. Helin, T. Hernes, D. Hjorth, & R. Holt (Eds.), *The Oxford Handbook of Process Philosophy & Organization Studies* (pp. 1–16). Oxford: Oxford University Press.

Hernes, T. (2003). Organization as evolution of space. In B. Czarniawska & G. Sevon (Eds.), *Northern Lights: Organization Theory in Scandinavia* (pp. 267–290). Copenhagen: Liber.

Hernes, T. (2014). *A Process Theory of Organization*. Oxford: Oxford University Press.

Hilgard, E. R. (1980). The trilogy of mind: Cognition, affection and conation. *History of the Behavioral Sciences, 16*, 107–117.

Hill, M. R. (1984). Epistemology, axiology, and ideology in sociology. *Mid-American Review of Sociology, 9*(2), 59–77.

Hjorth, D. (Ed.) (2012). *Handbook on Organisational Entrepreneurship*. Cheltenham, UK and Northampton, MA, USA: Edward Elgar Publishing.

Hjorth, D., Holt, R., & Steyaert, C. (2015). Entrepreneurship and process studies. *International Small Business Journal, 33*(6), 599–611.

Jarzabkowski, P., & Wilson, D. (2006). Actionable strategy knowledge: A practice perspective. *European Management Journal, 24*(5), 348–367.

Joas, H. (1996). *The Creativity of Action*. Cambridge: Polity Press.

Johannisson, B. (2000). Networking and entrepreneurial growth. In D. Sexton & H. Landström (Eds.), *The Blackwell Handbook of Entrepreneurship* (pp. 368–386). Hoboken, NJ: Wiley-Blackwell.

Johannisson, B. (2002). Energising entrepreneurship: Ideological tensions in the medium-sized family business. In D. Fletcher (Ed.), *Understanding the Small Family Business* (pp. 46–57). London: Routledge.

Johannisson, B. (2008). The social construction of the disabled and unfashionable family business. In N. Gupta, N. Levenburg, L. Moore, J. Motwani, & T. Schwarz (Eds.), *Culturally-Sensitive Models of Family Business in Nordic Europe: A Compendium Using the Globe Paradigm* (pp. 125–144). Hyderabad: ICFAI University.

Johannisson, B. (2011). Towards a practice theory of entrepreneuring. *Small Business Economics, 36*(2), 135–150.

Johannisson, B. (2018a). *Disclosing Entrepreneurship as Practice: The Enactive Approach*. Cheltenham, UK and Northampton, MA, USA: Edward Elgar Publishing.

Johannisson, B. (2018b). Making entrepreneurship research matter: The challenging journey to an academic identity. In R. Blackburn, D. De Clercq, & J. Heinonen (Eds.), *The SAGE Handbook of Small Business and Entrepreneurship* (pp. 578–593). Thousand Oaks, CA: Sage Publications.

Johannisson, B., Ramirez-Pasillas, M., & Karlsson, G. (2002). Institutional embeddedness of inter-firm networks: A leverage for business creation. *Entrepreneurship & Regional Development, 14*(4), 297–315.

Kyrö, P. (2015). The conceptual contribution of education to research on entrepreneurship education. *Entrepreneurship & Regional Development, 27*(9–10), 599–618.

Langley, A., Smallman, C., Tsoukas, H., & Van de Ven, A. (2013). Process studies of change in organization and management: Unveiling temporality, activity and flow. *Academy of Management Journal, 56*(1), 1–13.

Latour, B. (1986). The powers of association. In J. Law (Ed.), *Power, Action and Belief: A New Sociology of Knowledge* (pp. 264–280). London: Routledge & Kegan Paul.

Letiche, H., & Statler, M. (2005). Evoking metis: Questioning the logics of change, responsiveness, meaning and action in organizations. *Culture and Organization*, *11*(1), 1–16.

Lindgren, M., & Packendorff, J. (2011). On the temporary organizing of entrepreneurial processes: Applying a project metaphor to the study of entrepreneurship. *Revue de L'Entrepreneuriat*, *10*(2), 45–67.

Macquarrie, J. (1973). *Existentialism*. Harmondsworth: Penguin Books.

Maryama, M. (1963). The second cybernetics: Deviation-amplifying mutual causal processes. *American Science*, *51*, 164–179.

Mintzberg, H. (1980 [1973]). *The Nature of Managerial Work*. Englewood Cliffs, NJ: Prentice Hall.

Moroz, P., & Hindle, K. (2012). Entrepreneurship as a process: Toward harmonizing multiple perspectives. *Entrepreneurship Theory & Practice*, *36*(4), 781–818.

Nayak, A., & Chia, R. (2011). Thinking becoming and emergence: Process philosophy and organization studies. In H. Tsoukas & R. Chia (Eds.), *Philosophy and Organization Theory* (pp. 281–309). Bingley: Emerald Group Publishing.

Nicolini, D. (2012). *Practice Theory, Work, and Organization: An Introduction*. Oxford: Oxford University Press.

Nilsson, A. (1998). *The Analogy as a Management Tool*. Luleå, Sweden: Luleå University of Technology.

Nonaka, I., & Takeuchi, H. (1995). *The Knowledge-Creating Company*. New York: Oxford University Press.

Ogbor, J. (2000). Mythicizing and reification in entrepreneurial discourse: Ideology-critique of entrepreneurial studies. *Journal of Management Studies*, *37*(5), 605–635.

Olson, R. (1962). *An Introduction to Existentialism*. New York: Dover Publications.

Orlikowski, W. J. (1996). Improvising organizational transformation over time: A situated change perspective. *Information Systems Research*, *7*(1), 63–92.

Orlikowski, W., & Yates, J. (2002). It's about time: Temporal structuring in organizations. *Organization Science*, *13*(6), 684–700.

Orr, J. (1996). *Talking about Machines: An Ethnography of a Modern Job*. Ithaca, NY: Cornell University Press.

Patton, M. (2002). *Qualitative Research & Evaluation Methods*. Thousand Oaks, CA: Sage Publications.

Perry, R. (1926). *Realms of Value: A Critique of Human Civilization*. Cambridge, MA: Harvard University Press.

Pinchot III, G. (1985). *Intrapreneuring*. New York: Harper & Row.

Polanyi, M. (1974 [1962]). *Personal Knowledge: Towards a Post-Critical Philosophy*. Chicago: University of Chicago Press.

Politis, D. (2005). The process of entrepreneurial learning: A conceptual framework. *Entrepreneurship Theory and Practice*, *29*(4), 399–424.

Rämö, H. (1999). An Aristotelian human time–space manifold: From Chronochora to Kariotopos. *Time & Society*, *8*(2), 309–328.

Rescher, N. (1969). *Introduction to Value Theory*. Englewood Cliffs, NJ: Prentice Hall.

Rosa, P., & Scott, M. (1999). The prevalence of multiple owners and directors in the SME sector: Implications for our understanding of start-up and growth. *Entrepreneurship & Regional Development*, *11*(1), 21–37.

Rose, N. (1999). *Powers of Freedom: Reframing Political Thought*. Cambridge: Cambridge University Press.

Ryle, G. (1949). *The Concept of Mind*. London: Hutchinson.

Sarasvathy, S. D. (2001). Causation and effectuation: Toward a theoretical shift from economic inevitability to entrepreneurial contingency. *Academy of Management Review*, *26*(2), 243–263.

Sarasvathy, S. D. (2008). *Effectuation: Elements of Entrepreneurial Expertise*. Cheltenham, UK and Northampton, MA, USA: Edward Elgar Publishing.

Schatzki, T. (2001). Introduction: Practice theory. In T. Schatzki, K. Knorr Cetina, & E. von Savigny (Eds.), *The Practice Turn in Contemporary Theory* (pp. 1–14). London: Routledge.

Schatzki, T. (2002). *The Site of the Social: A Philosophical Account of the Constitution of Social Life and Change*. University Park, PA: Pennsylvania State University Press.

Schatzki, T. (2005). The sites of organizations. *Organization Studies, 26*(3), 465–484.

Schumpeter, J. (1934). *The Theory of Economic Development*. Oxford: Oxford University Press.

Schumpeter, J. (1987 [1943]). *Capitalism, Socialism and Democracy* (6th edition). London: Allen & Unwin.

Shotter, J. (2006). Understanding process from within: An argument for 'withness'-thinking. *Organization Studies, 27*(4), 585–604.

Shotter, J., & Tsoukas, H. (2014). Performing phronesis: On the way to engaged judgement. *Management Learning, 45*(4), 377–396.

Smircich, L., & Stubbart, C. (1985). Strategic management in the enacted world. *Academy of Management Review, 10*(4), 724–736.

Spinosa, C., Flores, F., & Dreyfus, H. (1997). *Disclosing New Worlds: Entrepreneurship, Democratic Action and the Cultivation of Solidarity*. Cambridge, MA: MIT Press.

Starr, J., & MacMillan, I. (1990). Resource cooptation via social contracting: Resource acquisition strategies for new ventures. *Strategic Management Journal, 11* (special issue), 79–92.

Stewart, A. (1989). *Team Entrepreneurship*. Thousand Oaks, CA: Sage Publications.

Steyaert, C. (2004). The prosaics of entrepreneurship. In D. Hjorth & C. Steyaert (Eds.), *Narrative and Discursive Approaches in Entrepreneurship* (pp. 8–21). Cheltenham, UK and Northampton, MA, USA: Edward Elgar Publishing.

Steyaert, C. (2007). Entrepreneuring as a conceptual attractor? A review of process theories in 20 years of entrepreneurship studies. *Entrepreneurship & Regional Development, 19*(6), 453–477.

Törnebohm, H. (1979). *Queries about Inquiries*. Gothenburg: Department of Philosophy of Science, University of Gothenburg.

van Maanen, J. (2011). *Tales of the Field: On Writing Ethnography* (2nd edition). Chicago: University of Chicago Press.

Weick, K. (1979). *The Social Psychology of Organizing* (2nd edition). Reading, MA: Addison-Wesley.

Welter, F. (2011). Contextualizing entrepreneurship: Conceptual challenges and ways forward. *Entrepreneurship Theory and Practice, 35*(1), 165–184.

Welter, F. (2019). *Entrepreneurship and Context*. Cheltenham, UK and Northampton, MA, USA: Edward Elgar Publishing.

Wenger, E. (1998). *Communities of Practice: Learning, Meaning and Identity*. Cambridge: Cambridge University Press.

Westhead, P., & Wright, M. (1998). Novice, portfolio, and serial founders: Are they different? *Journal of Business Venturing, 13*(4), 173–204.

Young, M. (1991). *An Inside Job*. Oxford: Oxford University Press.

4.   Entrepreneurship as practice and problem

Hallur Thor Sigurdarson and Dimo Dimov

INTRODUCTION: DIVERSITY AND DIFFERENCE IN ENTREPRENEURSHIP

We widely acknowledge that entrepreneurship is a diverse activity, a 'critical mess' (Gartner, 2004). The hundreds of millions of nascent entrepreneurs and new business owners that the Global Entrepreneurship Monitor study identifies every year (e.g. Bosma et al., 2020) do not do the same thing or speak with a single voice. Whether it is the particular practices associated with making a particular product or service (from bread to accountancy and satellite-launching rockets), the business practices associated with an industry or culture, or the social practices that underpin market needs or economic value, entrepreneurs around the world blend in with the community in which they operate yet stand apart to be identified as entrepreneurs. However, our scientific knowledge of entrepreneurship does not do service to the diversity of this activity.

Diversity challenges scientists to develop coherent frameworks for understanding the world that gives rise to it. In biology as well as culture – two domains of awe-inspiring diversity – this scientific endeavour has proceeded broadly in two steps. The first step involves detailed observation or 'thick description' (Geertz, 1973) of particular animals or human cultures. The second step aims to place these observations into an intelligible frame or theoretical framework.

In biology, the detailed and systematic observation of life forms has led to a rigorous classification into taxonomic ranks. Thus, a lion (*Panthera Leo*) is a *species* within the *genus Panthera*, which in turns belongs to the *family Felidae*, to the *order Carnivora*, to the *class Mammalia*, to the *phylum Chordata*, to the *kingdom Animalia*, to the *domain Eukaria*, and ultimately to *Life*. A species is a unit of biodiversity and signifies the largest group of organisms in which two mating individuals can produce fertile offspring. The taxonomy of organisms is based on the articulation of patterns from the thick observation of morphology, genetics, and behaviours. The decomposability of the classification systems implies that within adjacent hierarchical relationships, the behaviour of the component subsystems is independent of other components (Simon, 1962). On the basis of such classification as systematic diversity, the theory of evolution helps explain speciation – the evolution of new species – through the interplay of a population of organism and their environments.

Human cultures introduce an additional, semiotic level of complexity. As Clifford Geertz states, 'Believing with Max Weber that man is an animal suspended in webs of significance he himself has spun, I take culture to be those webs and the analysis of it to be therefore not an experimental science in search of law but an interpretive one in search of meaning' (1973, p. 5). In this sense, the aim is to gain access to the conceptual world in which our subjects live so that we could converse with them. 'Theoretical formulations hover so low over the interpretations they govern that they don't make much sense or hold much interest apart from them' (Geertz, 1973, p. 25). For Geertz, the essential task of theory building is not to codify abstract regularities but to make thick description possible, not to generalize across cases but to generalize within them, i.e. achieve clinical inference. 'Rather than beginning with a set of observations and attempting to subsume them under a governing law, such inference begins with a set of (presumptive) signifiers and attempts to place them within an intelligible frame' (Geertz, 1973, p. 26).

This brief foray into biology and anthropology inspires to see the diversity of entrepreneurship as a looming frontier in our understanding of it. As a human activity, entrepreneurship is contiguous with human culture and thus bound with the diversity of human practices. In this sense, we can speak of how entrepreneurship manifests itself within a particular culture. At the same time, entrepreneurship can be seen as *type* of human activity, whereby its different manifestations across human cultures can be deemed to have something in common and to differ from activity that we can deem 'non-entrepreneurial'. This invokes the metaphor of a matrix organizational structure, in which one belongs to a particular business unit (with its distinct scope or purpose) while also engaged in a particular functional role (marketing, operations, finance). In this structure, one is accountable to both a business unit head and a functional head. By the same token, entrepreneurship is accountable to both the context of its manifestation and its functional or conceptual stance towards that context.

In what follows, we seek to unpack this metaphor as a way of making the diversity of entrepreneurship intelligible. Entrepreneurship varies in the sense that launching a coffee shop is different from launching a software business or a logistics service. It also varies in the sense that starting a business in China is different from starting one in Uganda, Iceland or Mexico. At the same time, entrepreneurship represents variation from non-entrepreneurial business-related activities such as administration. In the former sense, entrepreneurship is a practice, implicated in our understanding of different social practices. In the latter sense, entrepreneurship is a problem, a type of inquiry within a given practice that creates space for new value.

Our arguments will start from the latter sense, seeking to establish entrepreneurship as a distinct type of activity. We prepare the ground by discussing classificatory structures and distinguishing formal and substantive conceptions of entrepreneurship. We then proceed to articulate a formal conception of the entrepreneur as a conceptual architect, i.e. someone who problematizes current activity and thus articulates new space for meaning and value. The sections that follow unpack the notion of problematizing and connect it with envisioning. Finally, we articulate the substantive conception of entrepreneurship as practice enmeshed with other social, business and management practices.

PREPARING THE GROUND

Classification categories form a branching-out structure that can be understood in two directions. An outward direction is about drawing finer distinctions among objects or organisms that share a set of key properties. Thus, within the order *Carnivora* we can distinguish different families, and so on. An inward direction is about finding commonalities amongst a diverse set of objects or organisms, finding the lowest common denominator of properties that can define a category to subsume all these organisms. We can see the former direction as contextualization or fragmentation, i.e. multiplication of categories; and the latter as decontextualization or unification, i.e. merging of categories. In this sense, each position or viewpoint renders a particular category salient as the lowest common denominator of the group of organisms it subsumes – a point of distinction from other organisms within the broader category to which it belongs. This salient category plays a dual role: from without, it is unifying; from within, it is a launchpad for further distinction.

Such a dual role is implicit in the distinction between formal and substantive conceptions, as outlined by Polanyi (2001 [1957]) for the term 'economic'. In a formal sense, the term offers a framework for understanding economic decisions as means–ends choices. In a substantive sense, it is rooted in the empirical reality of how people earn their livelihood, an 'instituted process of interaction between [people and their] environment, which results in a continuous supply of want satisfying material means' (Polanyi, 2001 [1957], p. 34). In other words, there are so many different ways in which people conduct economic activity. A substantive conception prompts us – upon hearing the term 'economic' – to ask for the specific details and descriptions. In contrast, a formalist is happy to subsume all this diversity under a generic concept.

In a sense, the formalist stance is equivalent to the functional pillar in the matrix structure. It seeks to unite particular activities performed in different units or contexts as being of the same functional type. The substantivist stance recognizes that these activities are performed in different contexts and thus their specifics can vary. This distinction reflects the broader Wittgensteinian idea that the use of words is embedded in a 'game' – a language-game – which encompasses the whole of language and the way of life with which it is entwined. Meaning is thus holistic and contextual, suggesting that otherwise uniform words can take on different meanings depending on where and how they are used. Consider the simple example of handles, where each meaning of handle is associated with particular activities and embedded in different technical systems:

> It is like looking into the cabin of a locomotive. We see handles all looking more or less alike. (Naturally, since they are all supposed to be handled.) But one is the handle of a crank which can be moved continuously (it regulates the opening of a valve); another is the handle of a switch, which has only two effective positions, it is either off or on; a third is the handle of a brake-lever, the harder one pulls on it, the harder it brakes; a fourth, the handle of a pump: it has an effect only so long as it is moved to and fro. (Wittgenstein, 1958: §12)

We can similarly think about the term 'captain' – whether of a ship, sports team, or school debating team – whereby the practice of 'captaining' (if there is one), just like the practice of handling or economic practice takes on different forms. We could thus say that the words 'economic', 'handle', and 'captain' are formal descriptions while their substantive meaning is derived from the context in which they are used or operate. One may be prone to suggest that a society is full of economic activity, the cabin of the locomotive is full of handles and all organized groups have captains. These become ways of focusing attention, of implying that a society has other activity, that the cabin of the locomotive has other gadgets and that organized groups have other members, which are not the subject of our interest. Equally, these terms then become launchpads for further distinctions, based on specific context and practices.

By the same token, we can distinguish formal and substantive conceptions of 'entrepreneurship'. In the former sense, we can think of the world as full of entrepreneurial activity, as a way of indicating our interest and diverting attention from other, non-entrepreneurial activity. In the latter sense, we recognize that it is difficult to describe what this involves without recognizing the empirical diversity that exists amongst entrepreneurial activities and thus engaging with the specific context in which entrepreneurship is manifested.

IN SEARCH OF FORM

We can deem entrepreneurship as belonging to a broader class of economic activity, which in turn belongs to a broader class of social activity. In this sense, we need to identify the point within the broader classes of social and economic activities at which the category 'entrepreneur' branches out. When we view entrepreneurship as the generation or creation of new economic activity (Davidsson, 2003), we use dispositional words such as generate or create to describe what entrepreneurs do. There are two important clarifications necessary in this regard.

First, some dispositional words are generic or determinable (as opposed to specific or determinate), i.e. they signify the doing not of things of one particular kind but of things of lots of different kinds (Ryle, 2009 [1949]). In this sense, there are different ways to create – scientists, engineers, artists, and designers all are involved in creating things and they do so in many different ways, engaging in different activities. Similarly, the profession of lawyer does not imply that there is a single activity called 'lawyering'. Indeed, lawyers do many different things: drafting wills or contracts, witnessing signatures, defending clients, etc. In the same manner, entrepreneurs make products, sell to customers, negotiate contracts, hire employees, analyse financial statements, and make investment decisions. Many (or even most) of these activities could also be done by non-entrepreneurs.

Therefore, faced with someone whom we see as engaged in entrepreneurship, there are many things that they are actually doing and perhaps not everything they do is an exclusive or unique marker of entrepreneurship. In order to get a sense of the formal marker of entrepreneurship, it is helpful to start with a practising entrepreneur and begin to 'peel away' activities or practices that s/he performs that are not (exclusively) entrepreneurial in the sense that they can be seen as broader economic or social practices.

As someone engaged in business, an entrepreneur performs a number of core business practices – accounting and bookkeeping, financial management, marketing, production, customer service, brand building, operations management, service delivery, human resource management, selling, negotiation, etc. We can lay these aside given that they are performed by any person engaged in business. In this sense, every entrepreneur is a business person, but not every business person may be an entrepreneur.

As someone managing an organization, an entrepreneur performs a number of core management practices – planning, staffing, communication, control, development. We can lay these aside given that they are performed by any person engaged in managing others. In this sense, every entrepreneur is a manager, but not every manager may be an entrepreneur.

Finally, as someone embedded in particular society and culture, the entrepreneur also performs a number of social/cultural practices associated with being with and dealing with others. These include building relationships, observing rituals, celebrating achievements, etc. We can lay these aside given that they are performed by all members of that culture. In this sense, every entrepreneur is a member of a culture, but not every member of that culture may be an entrepreneur.

What are we left with? While we can peel away constituent activities as belonging to individual business/management/cultural practices, what remains is the sense of meaning that these practices have when bundled together by the entrepreneur – the irreducible first-person ontology of the entrepreneur's intentionality (Dimov et al., 2021). The meaning of the activity that would lead us to describe someone as 'entrepreneur' arises from the 'imaginary' situation in which the person operates, acting under the guidance of real but intangible markers such as beliefs, aspirations, and desired future that collectively provide a sense of opportunity that the person articulates (Dimov, 2020). In this sense, entrepreneurship entails an intentional stance towards the world. States of consciousness and intentionality are emergent or epiphenomenal in nature: although they would not exist but for certain neurophysiological processes, they are ontologically irreducible to such processes (Searle, 1994). In other words, they have a distinct first-person ontology. An entrepreneurial stance is always someone's stance.

With this in mind, we come to the second clarification. To the extent that entrepreneurs bring things and processes (production and exchange relationships) into being, we can deploy the Aristotelian idea of four causes of why things come into being (Aristotle, 1981). A *final* cause represents a desired outcome, for the sake of which the thing is. An *efficient* cause represents the agency that initiates the change. A *formal* cause pertains to the mechanism that operates as a shaping force. A *material* cause represents the context providing the immanent elements. Aristotle offers the example of the making (or coming into being) of a chair. The final cause reflects the purpose for which the chair is made. The efficient cause pertains to the agency of the carpenter. The formal cause represents the shape and style of the chair. Finally, the material cause pertains to the materials of which the chair is made.

It is the setting of the final and formal causes that channel the entrepreneur's intentional stance towards the world. In theory, if one possessed unlimited financial resources, having set the final and formal causes, one could source all the necessary materials and completely outsource the execution to others. In this sense, we can see entrepreneurship as the setting of problems to be solved as well as the blueprint for their solution. This entails problematization and framing.

As an activity that involves creativity and an expansion of what can be done and perceived, the capacity of entrepreneurship cannot be limited to the current order of things. In other words, a theory and an approach to entrepreneurship as practice has to become a 'field of practice' involving the capacity to move beyond the already ordered, its maintenance and rationality. This, on the surface, simple insight draws attention to the content of entrepreneurial practice – how it can be perceived and studied – but also its limitations as a catalyser of entrepreneurial action. The setting of final and formal causes involves the construction of meaning and vision as useful indicators for an understanding of new differences and their incipiency in an entrepreneurial field of practice.

In this sense, the entrepreneur acts as a conceptual architect – relating and organizing things in imaginary ways to produce new meaning that can be instituted to become a new actuality (e.g. the product is produced, the customer is engaged, the money is obtained). This reflects Vygotsky's (1978) idea that the development of abstract thought leads to meaning dominating action. Action becomes a pivot through which a person moves in a field of meaning. It is in this sense that the meaning of an entrepreneur's action arises from the imaginary situation (field of meaning) in which the person operates. Such imaginary situation is well captured by the notion of 'opportunity' as the entrepreneur's articulation of what he or she is trying to do. A person becomes an entrepreneur by virtue of envisioning such an imaginary situation and acting under its guidance. The person can meaningfully refer to 'opportunity' in this sense. The label 'imaginary', thus, implies that the earliest articulation of what an entrepreneur is trying to do is nothing but a linguistic act (Dimov, 2020).

The attraction of the conceptual architecture presented as a vision can be very powerful, as when Elizabeth Holmes' vision for Theranos ('one tiny drop changes everything') attracts over $1bn of funding and a stellar board of directors. Even when the implementation efforts are exposed as a fraud, the vision remains attractive (Liuberté and Dimov, 2021). Also, consider the anecdotal interaction attributed to President Kennedy when seeing a janitor sweeping the floor. Asked what he was doing, the janitor replied, 'Well, Mr. President, I'm helping put a man on the moon.' Actions have different descriptions (e.g. sweeping the floor, maintaining the building, helping put a man on the moon). Only under the aspects of the individual's purpose or vision of what they are doing, can such actions be described as intentional in the sense that the individual can provide reasons for what they do (Anscombe, 2000 [1957]). Until articulated, these visions are invisible to others, to those not privy to the first-person ontology of the person in question. The practice of entrepreneurship becomes a practice of envisioning, involving the creation of new concepts, articulating new meaning and connections – disclosing new worlds (Spinosa et al., 1997). Notably, envisioning involves something different and not-yet-actual. It is entwined with a notion of difference and distinctions as something that emerges and the 'problematization' this involves.

PROBLEMATIZING

As we argue for problematizing as a distinguishable activity in entrepreneurial practice, involving both final and formal causes, we do so with a reference to Gilles Deleuze's conceptualization of problems. With Deleuze comes a radically processual ontology, where difference and diversity are immanent (e.g. Colebrook, 2002; Kristensen et al., 2014; Steyaert, 2007). Hence, being can only be comprehended as a process and emergence, i.e. as a becoming. The perception of a being or thingness is considered only as a momentary stability in a continuous flux – a movement of perceived sameness (May, 2005). Subsequently, any moment or event has a transformative capacity and the capacity to become something different and unanticipated. In an ontology of becoming and process, attention shifts from being and stability to movements, ruptures, relations and novelty, to how something emerges and its ability to transform (Helin et al., 2014). This radically processual ontology makes Deleuze's thought particularly relevant for studying entrepreneurship, but also organizational practices (e.g. Hjorth, 2015; Hjorth et al., 2015; Linstead and Thanem, 2007; Scott, 2010; Sigurdarson, 2021; Steyaert, 2007).

Deleuze found creativity to be intertwined with sensing and working at problems (Jeanes, 2006). He and Guattari, Deleuze's collaborator, understood philosophy to be a creative practice and an 'art of forming, inventing and fabricating concepts' (Deleuze and Guattari, 2009, p. 2). In turn, concepts have the dual capacity, on the one hand, to maintain current order, and on the other, to change the ways in which we experience and act in the world (Porter, 2010; Sigurdarson, 2021).

Problems are the catalysers of new concepts and shape the space in which new ideas, connections, visions and meaning get developed (Deleuze and Guattari, 2009). Deleuze draws on an evolutionary parallel of living beings emerging in processes of responding to problems. The flower's photosynthesis and the human eye are both responses to and enactments of the shared problem of light, and so even is the artist's capture of light in colours on a canvas. In addition to conveying the vitality of problems, these examples indicate a close connection between problems and opportunities, i.e. how the awareness or sensing of a problem becomes an opportunity to make something new – new connections and distinctions.

Thus, the sensing and attending to problems connects with ways of living, as a potentiality to introduce new differences. Deleuze (1983, 2013) draws on Nietzsche and Spinoza to show how sensing and working at a problem connects to a will or desire. It is a desire, not defined or limited to a lack of something, but a productive and affirming force that has the capacity to *add* to the world. It is a longing for more than what is already here, it is affectual. It is a desire that finds 'joy' in heterogenic and unexpected encounters, as they are events that can increase desire's ability to act in new ways. It is this desire that drives working at problems in ways that introduces new differences and distinctions, and new concepts.

Jeanes (2006) indicates a key notion of the vitality of problems and desire for entrepreneurial creativity, by linking it to personal crisis and intensity, and knowing that one has not succeeded, yet. The problem has not been solved and a novel difference (e.g. a new product, service or organization) has not been actualized to the entrepreneur's satisfaction. In this respect, a familiar metaphor would be the entrepreneur as the one still striving towards a moving target. Which is qualitatively different from the administrator's maintenance of order, balance, and predictability in outcomes. The perceived intensity and the experienced crisis of the entrepreneur expresses a desire to work at a problem, and while Deleuze describes a joyous encounter, it is easy to see how this work can be perceived, for instance, as an exhilaration, devastation or bewilderment.

Lastly, a Deleuzian understanding of problematizing, involving sensing and working at problems, resonates with the famous Schumpeterian notion of a *creative destruction*, indicating an entrepreneurial practice that disrupts and destroys market stability, when introducing radically new products, services or processes. Sensing problems others may have failed to notice, considered out of reach or unimportant, and working at them with desire towards an envisioned future is a nascent expression of a creative destruction, oriented towards practice.

PROBLEMATIZING AND ENVISIONING

Now, we connect back to visions and envisioning, but this time it becomes intertwined in a process of problematizing – of sensing and working at problems. An entrepreneurial vision is clearly not a solution to a problem, but rather a conceptualization, responding to a problem and connecting with an imagined potential future. In this the force and context of the entrepreneurial activity corresponds to the intensity and reciprocity between problems and concepts. For instance, Elizabeth Holmes' entrepreneurial vision was expressed in the slogan 'one tiny drop changes everything'. The vision responds to a problem, or a set of problems, including the problem of living a long and healthy life and the discomfort or fear of needles used to draw blood. The vision responds to the problems it intensifies as a concept, drawing attention to them and presenting a desired outcome (final cause). Which is at the same time, a framing for entrepreneurial activity and engagement (formal cause). Thus, a framing that makes a substantive concatenation of various activities meaningful for a desire to work at the problems – to add to the world by preparing it for the incipient solution. One could then argue that Holmes' envisioning was so strong and compelling that the entrepreneur(s) was unable to let go of it, even in the face of technological infeasibility. Even deception and fraud became meaningful activities, as ways of keeping the vision alive.

The entrepreneurial activities involved in working at problems, framed by conceptualizing a meaningful vision, furthermore direct desire and action towards milieus where new problems can be sensed, and new futures envisioned. Thus, problematizing is an osculating process, bringing entrepreneurial practice into contact with various activities, not characterized by the same or the expected (e.g. habits and routines), but forming a meaningful concatenation of activities. Correspondingly, in entrepreneurship, we sometimes talk about pivoting, with respect to shifts in the visions involved in the entrepreneurial process. Henceforth, as the entrepreneurial process acquires a different substantive meaning, not only content but activities and how they get organized, also change.

For Vygotsky, the development of abstract thought in children enables them to create and play in imaginary situations and thereby escape situational constraints. By the same token, through envisioning entrepreneurs evade the situational constraints of the actual states of affairs. Entrepreneurial action becomes meaningful when it responds to a problem and an envisioned future, but it is not reducible to an actual state of affairs (e.g. available resources, current skills, habits and markets).

TAKING STOCK, IN SEARCH OF SUBSTANCE

Entrepreneurs sense new problems and envision different futures. We cannot speak of 'new' and 'different' in a meaningful way without a reference point. New and different acquire their meaning only in relation to something existing, a current way of life. In this sense, to understand entrepreneurship, a researcher is prompted to ask what there is. Entrepreneurship is part of social reality as 'that part of the world to which experience gives us access that constitutes the realm of human coexistence' (Schatzki, 1988, p. 243). To say that entrepreneurship is social is to acknowledge that an entrepreneur's actions intersect the lives of other people and that their success is interdependent with the actions of other people.

We might say that people around the world live in different worlds. In one (physical) sense, the world is the all-encompassing totality of the cosmos, of which all of us are part. In another (social) sense, a world is 'an organized body of objects, purposes, skills, and practices on the basis of which human activities have meaning or make sense' (Dreyfus, 2014, p. 222). The social world constitutes a backbone of intelligibility and thus represents a background against which we can state what there is. To erect a worldview, we need a foundation of what we take as true or given. This suggests that different foundations would lead to different worldviews.

Goodman (1978) refers to this as 'worldmaking', i.e. the idea that descriptions of our world are entwined with frames of reference and that different descriptions constitute world versions: 'We are confined to ways of describing whatever is described' (Goodman, 1978, p. 3). In this sense, to make a new description is to re-make worlds already on hand: recompose, reweigh, reorder, delete, supplement or deform various aspects of descriptions we already have at hand. This is not unlike editing a photo to turn it into something else.

We could therefore say that entrepreneurs offer different descriptions of the world in which they live. But are they realistic? Could one dismiss entrepreneurs as wide-eyed mavericks who are not in touch with reality? It helps to distinguish here different senses of realism, namely habituation and revelation (Goodman, 1978). In one sense, realism is associated with familiarity. Something is realistic when it arises from habituation, from what we are accustomed to. In another sense, however, realism is associated with revelation, that is, the disclosure of new or unseen aspects of the world. These are revealed under a new system of categorization or representation. Goodman (1983, p. 271) goes even further in a third, metaphorical sense of realism: 'Taken literally, Don Quixote describes no one – there never was or will be the Man of La Mancha – but taken metaphorically, Don Quixote describes many of us who battle windmills (or windbags)'. Therefore, the descriptions that entrepreneurs offer can be seen as revealing or metaphorical, putting the familiar and habitual at a new angle or in a new light (or making new connections, as Deleuze would have it).

Let's turn our attention to the familiar and habitual as the starting point for the operation of entrepreneurship. Within a range of practice perspectives (e.g. Bourdieu, 1990; Giddens, 1984) and an even broader array of cultural theories (Reckwitz, 2002), we focus on the perspective, articulated by Schatzki (1996, 2002), of the site of human coexistence as a variegated and constantly evolving mesh of orders and practices. Orders refer to the configuration of things, while practices refer to organized human activities, 'temporally unfolding and spatially dispersed nexus of doings and sayings' (Schatzki, 1996, p. 89). Thus, orders exist and evolve in a context of practices, and practices exist and evolve in a context of orders. The connections between practices and orders represent the 'sinews' that hold the mesh together.

Social life is marked by social orders. For Schatzki, an order is an arrangement of things – people, artefacts, organisms, and things – that determines relative positions in terms of space (where something is), meaning (what something is) and identity (who somebody is). An arrangement is 'a hanging together of entities in which they relate, occupy positions, and enjoy meaning (and/or identity)' (Schatzki, 2002, p. 20). This conception of order goes beyond more restrictive conceptions such as regularity, stability, and interdependence in the sense that an order can be regular or irregular, stable or unstable, and encompass one- or two-way dependency. To the extent that an entrepreneur engages with things, these things can be seen as part of existing social order(s).

Social life transpires through practices. What holds together the doings and sayings that comprise a given practice are four mechanisms: (1) practical understandings of what to say and what to do (intelligibility); (2) explicit rules, principles, precepts, and instructions; (3) 'teleoaffective' structures such as ends, projects, beliefs, emotions, etc.; and (4) general understanding of how the world makes sense (Schatzki, 1996, 2002). We can therefore see much of what entrepreneurs do and say as the performance of a practice, a way for those doings and sayings to have certain meanings.

This perspective enables us to see entrepreneurs (and their visions) as arising from and entangled in a web (mesh) of orders and practices. The invisible threads of the web enable us to 'see' how the life of the entrepreneur hangs together or interrelates with other human lives. One form of such interrelation relates to how mentality and practical intelligibility are organized across people. Schatzki (2002) outlines two modalities in this regard, namely commonality and orchestration. Commonality reveals itself when the same understanding, rules or teleoaffective structures are expressed in the actions of different people. For example, entrepreneurs in San Francisco, London, Sofia, Lagos or Bangalore can talk about pre-money valuation, minimum viable product (MVP), or raising Series A funding. Orchestration reveals itself when the understanding, rules and teleoaffective structures that guide the actions of different people are non-independent. In this sense, entrepreneurs prepare funding pitches on the understanding that such pitches are part of the investment selection practices of business angels or venture capitalists.

A second form of interrelation relates to when the actions or situation of one person are objects of another person's actions. In this sense, what entrepreneurs do is directed at or is about other people. Entrepreneurs see other people as 'customers', 'suppliers' or 'employees' when those other people become the objects of the intentional stance of selling, buying or hiring. When an entrepreneur solicits feedback from a potential customer it is with the intention of ultimately creating something that the customer would want to buy.

A third form of interrelation arises through the settings in which lives hang together. Different people can find themselves in the same setting. At certain networking events, entrepreneurs find themselves face to face with corporate executives, other entrepreneurs, students or industry experts. Conversations are shaped by the interactions that ensue and, in this way, initial entrepreneurial efforts that are nebulous, open-ended, and accidental can eventually become scalable, focused, and deliberate (Nair et al., 2020). Similarly, the particular arrangement or physical set-up of a given setting, such as an open office space in a venture incubator or accelerator, can facilitate conversations or interactions. Setting also matters in the sense that actions performed in the same setting over time can be non-independent. For example, a client file updated with the overnight work of one person, can inform and structure the work of another person starting work in the morning. Equally, work done in different settings at the same time can also be non-independent. Product development activities can take place in the same office across time or at different locations at the same time. Many start-ups outsource software development work to teams based in other countries and different teams can work simultaneously on different aspects of the software code.

Finally, lives hang together through chains of actions, whereby each action is performed in response to previous actions. Although entrepreneurs set out on their venturing journey with a specific purpose and blueprint in mind, their subsequent actions evolve in response to feedback and reactions by potential customers, suppliers, employees and investors.

Revisiting Aristotle's four causes as discussed earlier, sensitivity to and understanding social life enables us to appreciate the *efficient* and *material* causes of the outcomes of entrepreneurship. Entrepreneurs do and say things that are congruent with the lives of other people. They also work with things from existing orders. But, by virtue of being entrepreneurs, they also do and say new things as well as shape new orders.

LOOKING AHEAD

The views we have expounded in this chapter suggest that entrepreneurship scholars should exhibit dual sensitivity in their engagement with the world of entrepreneurship, tantamount to enacting a matrix type of accountability. On the one hand, they need to illuminate the threads of orders and practices that make entrepreneurs part of a particular community. In this sense, the answer to the question of what entrepreneurs do acquires specific meaning only in the specific practice context in which entrepreneurs operate. Such a meaningful answer requires identification and deeper understanding of specific practices. On the other hand, scholars need to appreciate that entrepreneurs as such make new worlds within their communities – they sense new problems and imagine different futures. Problematizing addresses the dynamic nature of entrepreneurial practices and informs of their distinctiveness. We identify the entrepreneurial in the reciprocal process of problematizing and providing a meaningful framing for a dynamic and substantive entrepreneurial activity.

In Aristotelian terms, entrepreneurship is made possible through its *efficient* and *material* causes that ground it in a particular social life (present and history) as well as through its *final* and *formal* causes that commit it to a different future. Entrepreneurs define and create new value, but such value rests on something given. In time, the value entrepreneurs create becomes given, taken for granted, dissolved in an evolved social life. This happens in the same way that metaphors become stale over time, incorporated in the ever-evolving mainstream language. While social life transpires in a milieu, its horizon is ever evolving (Schatzki, 2002). Entrepreneurship is the dynamic force that keeps eyes on the horizon and feet on the ground. There are important implications here for theorizing and studying entrepreneurship.

First, an understanding of entrepreneurship as practice involving problematizing and conceptualizing suggests a genealogy of problems. It involves the ability to sense problems, to intensify them in a conceptualization of an imaginary desired future, and to work at them without respecting the boundaries of a normative (actualized) practice (e.g. routines and habits) and the order of things, but still emanating from these. Problematizing demystifies entrepreneurship and its relationship to creativity as being something transcendental and mysterious. Instead, creativity in entrepreneurship as practice involves a process of sensing, conceptualizing and working at problems.

From the researcher's point of view a substantive genealogy of entrepreneurial problems indicates a non-individualistic approach to doing research, attentive to how entrepreneurial practice is an expression of different sensed problems. This involves the researcher asking questions resembling the following: 'What are the problems the entrepreneur is attempting to solve and how?' 'How do the problems become conceptualized and meaningful?' or 'How does working at a problem introduce new problems?' These questions are processual involving attentiveness to variability and change; intensity and desire; and indicate how a concatenation of activities emerges and becomes meaningful. Correspondingly, attentiveness to such questions accounts for the criticality of new meanings, differences or distinctions, and relationality in entrepreneurship as practice, while allowing for the contextual variability in the 'fields of practices' in which entrepreneurship takes place (Schatzki, 2003).

Attention to problems and their genealogy in entrepreneurship complements a so-called 'second-person perspective' (Dimov et al., 2021, p. 1177) to doing entrepreneurship research. In other words, it involves drawing the researcher's attention to problematizing as a purposeful space for engagement and a potential 'mediated accountability' between researcher and entrepreneur. It is purposeful because of its importance – guiding and connecting activities – for entrepreneurship as practice. Thus, the plea here to the researcher is to enter and engage with the entrepreneurial process of problematizing and meaning-making.

A second implication connects to the epistemology of doing entrepreneurship. It directs theorization and inquiry into how entrepreneurs learn and gain insights into what it is they desire and do. It is an epistemology that emerges from the prolific reciprocity of problems and concepts giving meaning to action. Here, Deleuze's understanding of problems as a 'mode of being of difference' becomes relevant (Wasser, 2017, p. 50). It emphasizes the mentioned transformative potentiality of problems, making them a point of departure when attempting to carve out a space or a field, which is still not bound by the current order of the world or a market. To an extent, this resonates with Knorr Cetina's (2001) *epistemic objects* which she coins in the context of scientific discoveries and which are characterized by a lack of completeness. The concept of epistemic objects conveys dynamic, interactive, constructive and creative practices, and provides useful insights to entrepreneurship. However, epistemic objects, as portrayed, lack in attention to problems and problematizing as an oscillating process moving towards a desired, imaginary and dynamic future. These provide a frame and meaning to a (rhizomatic) selection of entrepreneurial activities.

What do entrepreneurs do? Again, they sense problems and develop new concepts (e.g. ideas, slogans and narratives) as they envision new and desirable worlds, which frame activities in meaningful ways within the communities in which they operate. Arguably, there is something poetic to entrepreneurial practice – the sensing and disclosing of something novel, not entirely actual but still communicable and desirable. Still, inventing, adjusting and reorganizing concepts and creating visions is not enough in entrepreneurship; a corresponding approach to activities needs to be made available.[1]

NOTE

1. In Icelandic the word 'athafnaskáld' means entrepreneur, but the literal meaning is 'action-poet'.

REFERENCES

Anscombe, G. E. M. (2000 [1957]). *Intention* (2nd edition). Cambridge, MA: Harvard University Press.
Aristotle (1981). *Aristotle's Metaphysics*. Trans. and ed. W. D. Ross. Oxford: Clarendon Press.
Bosma, N., Hill, S., Ionescu-Somers, A., Kelley, D., Levie, J., & Tarnawa, A. (2020). *Global Entrepreneurship Monitor: 2019/2020 Global Report*. London: Global Entrepreneurship Research Association.
Bourdieu, P. (1990). *The Logic of Practice*. Cambridge: Polity Press.
Colebrook, C. (2002). *Gilles Deleuze*. London: Routledge.
Davidsson, P. (2003). The domain of entrepreneurship research: Some suggestions. In J. A. Katz & D. A. Shepherd (Eds.), *Advances in Entrepreneurship, Firm Emergence and Growth*, Vol. 6 (pp. 315–372). Oxford: Elsevier.
Deleuze, G. (1983). *Nietzsche and Philosophy*. London: Athlone Press.
Deleuze, G. (2013). *Expressionism in Philosophy: Spinoza*. New York: Zone Books.
Deleuze, G., & Guattari, F. (2009). *What Is Philosophy?* London: Verso.
Dimov, D. (2020). Opportunities, language, and time. *Academy of Management Perspectives, 34*(3), 333–351.
Dimov, D., Schaefer, R., & Pistrui, J. (2021). Look who is talking … and who is listening: Finding an integrative 'we' voice in entrepreneurial scholarship. *Entrepreneurship Theory and Practice, 45*(5), 1176–1196.
Dreyfus, H. L. (2014). *Skillful Coping: Essays on the Phenomenology of Everyday Perception and Action*. Oxford: Oxford University Press.
Gartner, W. B. (2004). Achieving 'critical mess' in entrepreneurship scholarship. In J. A. Katz & D. Shepherd (Eds.), *Advances in Entrepreneurship, Firm Emergence, and Growth* (pp. 199–216). Greenwich, CT: JAI Press.
Geertz, C. (1973). *Interpretation of Cultures*. New York: Basic Books.
Giddens, A. (1984). *The Constitution of Society*. Cambridge: Polity Press.
Goodman, N. (1978). *Ways of Worldmaking*. Indianapolis: Hackett Publishing Company.
Goodman, N. (1983). Realism, relativism, and reality. *New Literary History, 14*(2), 269–272.
Helin, J., Hernes, T., Hjorth, D., & Holt, R. (2014). Process is how process does. In J. Helin, T. Hernes, D. Hjorth, & R. Holt (Eds.), *The Oxford Handbook of Process Philosophy & Organization Studies* (pp. 1–16). Oxford: Oxford University Press.

Hjorth, D. (2015). Sketching a philosophy of entrepreneurship. In T. Baker & F. Welter (Eds.), *The Routledge Companion to Entrepreneurship* (pp. 41–58). New York: Routledge .

Hjorth, D., Holt, R., & Steyaert, C. (2015). Entrepreneurship and process studies. *International Small Business Journal*, *33*(6), 599–611.

Jeanes, E. L. (2006). Resisting creativity, creating the new: A Deleuzian perspective on creativity. *Creativity and Innovation Management*, *15*(2), 127–134.

Knorr Cetina, K. (2001). Objectual practice. In T. R. Schatzki, K. Knorr Cetina, & E. von Savigny (Eds.), *The Practice Turn in Contemporary Theory* (pp. 184–197). London: Routledge.

Kristensen, A. R., Sørensen, B. M., & Lopdrup-Hjorth, T. (2014). Gilles Deleuze (1925–1995). In J. Helin, T. Hernes, D. Hjorth, & R. Holt (Eds.), *The Oxford Handbook of Process Philosophy & Organization Studies* (pp. 499–512). Oxford: Oxford University Press.

Linstead, S., & Thanem, T. (2007). Multiplicity, virtuality and organization: The contribution of Gilles Deleuze. *Organization Studies*, *28*, 1483–1501.

Liuberté, I., & Dimov, D. (2021). 'One tiny drop changes everything': Constructing opportunity with words. *Journal of Business Venturing Insights*, *15*, e00242.

May, T. (2005). *Gilles Deleuze: An Introduction*. Cambridge: Cambridge University Press.

Nair, S., Gaim, M., & Dimov, D. (2020). Toward the emergence of entrepreneurial opportunities: Organizing early-phase new-venture creation support systems. *The Academy of Management Review*. In press.

Polanyi, K. (2001 [1957]). The economy as instituted process. In M. S. Granovetter & R. Swedberg (Eds.), *The Sociology of Economic Life* (pp. 31–50). Boulder, CO: Westview Press.

Porter, R. (2010). From clichés to slogans: Towards a Deleuze–Guattarian critique of ideology. *Social Semiotics*, *20*, 233–245.

Reckwitz, A. (2002). Toward a theory of social practices: A development in culturalist theorizing. *European Journal of Social Theory*, *5*, 243–263.

Ryle, G. (2009 [1949]). *The Concept of Mind: 60th Anniversary Edition*. Abingdon: Routledge.

Schatzki, T. R. (1988). The nature of social reality. *Philosophy and Phenomenological Research*, *49*, 239–260.

Schatzki, T. R. (1996). *Social Practices: A Wittgensteinian Approach to Human Activity and the Social*. Cambridge: Cambridge University Press.

Schatzki, T. R. (2002). *The Site of the Social: A Philosophical Account of the Constitution of Social Life and Change*. University Park, PA: Pennsylvania State University Press.

Schatzki, T. R. (2003). A new societist social ontology. *Philosophy of the Social Sciences*, *33*(2), 174–202.

Scott, T. (2010). *Organization Philosophy: Gehlen, Foucault, Deleuze*. New York: Palgrave Macmillan.

Searle, J. (1994). *The Rediscovery of the Mind*. Cambridge, MA: MIT Press.

Sigurdarson, H. T. (2021). Reboot and repeat: Political entrepreneurship and the Icelandic Pirate Party. *Ephemera: Theory and Politics in Organization*. Forthcoming.

Simon, H. A. (1962). The architecture of complexity. *Proceedings of the American Philosophical Society*, *106*(6), 467–482.

Spinosa, C., Flores, F., & Dreyfus, H. (1997). *Disclosing New Worlds: Entrepreneurship, Democratic Action and the Cultivation of Solidarity*. Cambridge, MA: MIT Press.

Steyaert, C. (2007). Entrepreneuring as a conceptual attractor? A review of process theories in 20 years of entrepreneurship studies. *Entrepreneurship & Regional Development*, *19*(6), 453–477.

Vygotsky, L. S. (1978). *Mind in Society*. Cambridge, MA: Harvard University Press.

Wasser, A. (2017). How do we recognise problems? *Deleuze Studies*, *11*(1), 48–67.

Wittgenstein, L. (1958). *Philosophical Investigations* (2nd edition). Trans. G. E. M. Anscombe. Oxford: Blackwell.

PART II

NEW THEORETICAL ADVANCES

5. Cautiously creating a future-oriented manifesto for thinking entrepreneurship as practice

Karen Verduijn and Camilla Eline Andersen

INTRODUCTION

As the title of this chapter hints at, our concern is to create a manifesto for how to process towards the future of entrepreneurship as practice (EAP) thinking. While manifestos have appeared in diverse forms and for various purposes through history, they often materialized as written public reactions to a past that had created a somewhat blameworthy present state of something. In these written statements or declarations, a person or group would typically describe principles, policies, motives, intentions, views and/or rules concerning changes that the author(s) believed should be made[1] for further cause of action towards progress (Latour, 2010). Some may be acquainted with the avant garde-like filmmaking movement established by the Danish directors von Trier and Vinterberg in 1995 and their radical 'Dogme 95 Manifesto'. Like many other manifestos created within the aesthetic realm, 'Dogme 95 Manifesto' was a response to dominant cultural values at the time of its creation. This particular manifesto was a publicly stated reaction against what they saw as absurd plotlines and over-elaborate visuals of mainstream cinema, formulated as rules that could aid themselves and other directors to work artistically from more traditional values such as story, acting, and theme, and further help them avoid getting lost in special effects and technology. One of the ten rules making up the 'Dogme 95 Manifesto' reads: 'Shooting must be done on location. Props and sets must not be brought in (if a particular prop is necessary for the story, a location must be chosen where this prop is to be found)'.[2] Although the practice of creating manifestos in very recent history may be associated with aesthetic groups or artists, and therefore may cause some doubt regarding the timeliness of such a practice in scholarly work, it can be interesting to know that *manifesto*[3] etymologically refers to a public declaration that explains reasons for actions done or planned, and that to *manifest* refers to making something comprehensible and visible to a public,[4] something we set out to do further albeit in a more stuttering manner than in the 'Dogme 95 Manifesto'.

If turning our gaze some hundred years back, manifestos were a common practice in war-related, religious and/or political matters. A very famous example of the latter is Marx and Engels' Communist Manifesto published in 1848. Furthermore, at least over the last forty years, scholars in different fields have taken up this practice to voice their ideas (e.g. Haraway, 1985; Latour, 2010; Willis & Trondman, 2000), also in the field of entrepreneurship (e.g. Gartner, 2016; Essers et al., 2017). Gartner's (2016) 'Entrefesto' for entrepreneurship scholars is a great example. Echoing the manifesto tradition Gartner's (2016, p. 340) entrefesto consists of several principles (or provocations?) for researchers within the field of entrepreneurship, displayed in both small and capitalized letters in different sizes composed together on one page as in a typical manifesto poster style. Here entrepreneurship researchers are urged to: 'BEGIN ANYWHERE', 'Come on! Play! Invent the world!', 'ACT "as if" and it will become', 'Learn to fail or you will fail to learn' (p. 340), and more, in an alluring manner. The entrefesto also comes with a three pages long poem-like 'concatenation' where Gartner gives some explanations, nineteen footnotes and a reference list. With this entrefesto, Gartner, in our reading of it, is responding to dominant ways of thinking in the field of entrepreneurship in an affirmative and innovative manner. To elaborate, when approaching the mentioned elements in the entrefesto as a whole, we read between the lines that this is created as an attempt to articulate complex thinking on entrepreneurial scholarship in a different manner than how it is commonly done. And further that Gartner with this elaborates on why and how scholars can go beyond traditional ways of both thinking and doing entrepreneurship research that so easily becomes the norm. Moreover, we understand Gartner's entrefesto as articulating a different starting point for research practices, suggesting that entrepreneurial research following the many solicitations in the entrefesto might offer openings to alternative ways of doing scholarship that further will create more variation in what we can know about the entrepreneurship phenomenon.

EAP is a rather new strand within entrepreneurship research that draws from practice theory in how entrepreneurship is understood. Despite that researchers within this vein seek inspiration in social practice theory to further discussions in the field and desire to go beyond a human-centred perspective in future knowledge producing processes, we are sensing that EAP as a research community seems to continue to go in similar directions as what some sought to avoid, towards the future. Said differently, the EAP community seems to remain human-centred in its endeavour to think and know entrepreneurship differently. Also, and this is the main point in this chapter, EAP researchers are rather sparingly engaging with the practice lens's *critical powers* (Gherardi, 2009). These two troubling currents, together with documented embedded and embodied 'stuck happenings' (Andersen, 2017) that the first author experienced at EAP conferences, have encouraged us to cautiously create what we think of as a future-oriented manifesto as a way to resist a potential closing-off in further expansion of EAP thinking. In doing this, we think of Gartner's (2016) entrefesto as a springboard. Despite that we have found inspiration within a different philosophical and theoretical landscape than Gartner, we are working from a similar spirit. We are not interested in finding the 'right answers', but rather to learn from the questions we can ask from exploring the entrepreneurship landscape with 'new eyes'. Hence, in this chapter, by working from posthuman affirmative modes of thinking (e.g. Braidotti, 2015, 2019a, 2019b; Manning, 2016), we critically and creatively respond to the above troublings by going beyond a problematizing of the possible (negative) consequences of EAP theorizing remaining human-centred and becoming uncritical. We are curious of the generative powers of asking: *what if* we were to be thinking EAP research inspired by critical posthuman practice theory?

A precarious practice of creation seldom takes the form of a neat and structured process. Neither does our stuttering process of articulating a future-oriented manifesto for EAP scholarship. Despite this we have here arranged the chapter in parts that when read transversally might function as a 'call to attention' (Latour, 2010, p. 473) for EAP researchers, a community the first author is an active member of. The first part concerns how we frame the practice of creating a manifesto in the present time. The next part sketches the advancing of the EAP 'movement', and elaborates on what we have termed the troubling currents. Then we introduce and elaborate our particular practice theory thinking inspired by critical posthuman theory, followed by a storying of 'stuck happenings' (Andersen, 2017) registered at EAP conferences.

We then pick up again on the idea of the manifesto, and offer some preliminary thoughts on possible future prospects for EAP thinking.

MANIFESTO AS A CALL TO ATTENTION

As mentioned in the introduction, some may question the relevance and timeliness of writing manifestos. Latour (2010, p. 472) actually suggests that 'the time of manifestos has long passed' if we think of them as declarations of how to progress in a fast-forward manner. However, he continues, if we rather think that it is *the time of time* that has passed, that 'the idea of a flow of time moving inevitably and irreversibly forward that can be predicted by clear-sighted thinkers' has vanished, a manifesto could still be of use (Latour, 2010, p. 473). Picking up on this pragmatic potentiality that Latour sees in creating manifestos we are in this chapter cautiously crafting a manifesto as a practice of caring for the future prospects of EAP. For readers this entails that instead of clear rules similar to the ones in the 'Dogme 95 Manifesto', they will encounter our stuttering attempt to act on a present that worries us as embedded and embodied scholars. A stuttering that, without predicting a certain outcome, still might be creative of transformation for EAP research. Hence, we do not intend to manifest a certain way to progress forward to avoid the currents we find troubling in the expanding entrepreneurship as practice landscape, but rather aim to explore a different way of thinking of how to '*process* forward and meet new prospects' (Latour, 2010, p. 473, italics in original) within this vein of scholarship.

Although this perhaps is a queering of the traditional idea of manifestos, Latour (2010, p. 473) suggests that a manifesto does not have to function as a statement of how to progress from what was but rather can operate as 'a warning' or 'a call to attention to *stop* going further *in the same way* as before toward the future'. With this he articulates a shift from the idea of progress to one of '*tentative and precautionary progression*' (2010, p. 473, italics in original). The latter idea still concerns movement and something is still going forward, Latour explains. However, rather than focusing on fleeing from our past as a way of moving towards a different future, he outlines a commitment to innovating with precaution 'what lies ahead, the fate of things to come' (Latour, 2010, p. 486). Hence, inspired by Latour's reframing of manifestos and what he writes of as a turn to the prospect of shaping things to come (2010, p. 486), and affirmative modes of thinking as articulated in the work of particularly Rosi Braidotti (2013, 2015, 2019a) and Erin Manning (2016), we think of our stuttering manifesto as a call to attention with respect to the above mentioned currents, and as a commitment to the practice of precarious innovation. The following section will elaborate on EAP, and what we see as the troubling currents.

SKETCHING THE ADVANCING OF THE EAP 'MOVEMENT' AND POTENTIAL CLOSING OFF-IN EAP RESEARCH

The EAP movement commenced, literally, when a few scholars sat together, had lunch, and agreed that adopting social practice theory could form a way forward to deal with some of the issues that we and others had found problematic in current entrepreneurship research (in particular, individualism, universalism, essentialism, and representationalism – see e.g.

Weiskopf & Steyaert, 2009). This was the onset for the first EAP conference, held at Vrije Universiteit Amsterdam in 2016. The first EAP conference was followed by the 2nd (Dublin, February 2017), the 3rd (Vaxjö, April 2018), the 4th (Nantes, April 2019) and the 5th (back in Amsterdam). The number of attendees grew rapidly: from approximately 30 in 2016 to approximately 60–70 during the later EAP conferences. Keynote speakers at the first conference were Davide Nicolini and Susi Geiger. Dublin welcomed Theodore Schatzki, Vaxjö Chris Steyaert, and Daniel Hjorth, and Nantes Silvia Gherardi and Richard Whittington.

Of course, when initiating all this, EAP research was already happening, already going on. Obviously, there were yet several contributions 'out there' (e.g. Anderson, Dodd, & Jack, 2010; Dodd, Pret, & Shaw, 2016; Keating, Geiger, & McLoughlin, 2014; Pret, Shaw, & Dodd, 2016; McKeever, Anderson, & Jack, 2014; Sarason, Dean, & Dillard, 2006; Tatli et al., 2014; Terjesen & Elam, 2009), but these works were not 'labelled' EAP, till we set out to do so. And the annual conferences got connected to dedicated special issues, and edited volumes, such as a special issue in *Entrepreneurship & Regional Development* (see Thompson, Verduijn, & Gartner, 2020), a special issue in the *International Journal of Entrepreneurial Behavior & Research* (see Teague et al., 2021), and this *Research Handbook on Entrepreneurship as Practice*. So, jointly we set out to create more of those EAP contributions; basically one could say that we had started to enact an entire EAP conversation, connected to an actual EAP research community. The mission of this community being, broadly, to 'contribute to the Entrepreneurship Academy by explaining existing topics of interest in new ways as well as bringing forth new topics and explanations by using a practice theory lens to study the constitution and consequences of practices' (http://www.entrepreneurshipaspractice.com, retrieved 23/1/20).

As stated previously, one of the reasons the practice theory lens is being adopted is to address entrepreneurship research's persistent individualist outlook. Entrepreneurship research traditionally makes the (individual) entrepreneur overly important in the understanding of organization-creation, as well as ascribing them special, hero-like attributes. This tradition has been interrogated. Ranging from problematizing the 'strong figure of the entrepreneur' (Weiskopf & Steyaert, 2009), 'unmasking' the entrepreneur (Jones & Spicer, 2009), and questioning the entrepreneur as a 'heroic figurehead' (Anderson & Warren, 2011; Williams & Nadin, 2013; Johnsen & Sørensen, 2017), contributions have paved the way for a less individualistic approach. EAP research aims to pick up from this by centring relational processes (Fletcher, 2006) that co-construct particular initiatives. The emerging and growing EAP research body seeks to put practices at the centre of their empirical and theoretical knowledge when creating approaches to entrepreneurial phenomena.

At the same time, and contradictorily, many of these contributions do seem to keep circling back to human-centred analysis of entrepreneurial activities, by voicing their attempts as directed towards an understanding of the *practices of entrepreneurs*, i.e. to 'what entrepreneurs actually *do*' (Sklaveniti & Steyaert, 2020). In a relational thinking, however, foregrounding practices, the interest obviously is in how such practices form, connect, and *produce* particular outcomes. Overreliance on understanding the presence, role, intentions, etc. of (some) actors involved produces simplified explanations (Weiskopf & Steyaert, 2009), that cannot account for the full complexities of what is actually actualizing. We suggest that interpreting what entrepreneurs do to understand what this might represent is not what should mainly drive EAP research.

The second troubling current, and the one that perhaps is closest to our hearts in our response to the ongoing present in the EAP landscape, is that EAP research contributions so far do not actually engage with the 'critical power' of the practice lens (Gherardi, 2009). Hence, even though practice-based theorizing more widely does come with a critical *commitment* (Sklaveniti & Steyaert, 2020), and, as such, may enable possibilities for social change, and empowerment (Sklaveniti & Steyaert, 2020, p. 330), this (important) endeavour has not really been taken up in EAP. This chapter does pay explicit attention to practice theorizing's poten- tial critical commitment. Engaging with critical thinking and thinkers is relevant not in the last place because of the pervasive and tenacious optimism being attached to entrepreneurship as a beneficial economic activity (Calás, Smircich, & Bourne, 2009), wiping off the table all else that entrepreneurship does, or can be, such as a connecting force (Gaddefors & Anderson, 2017), or an act of provocation (Hjorth & Holt, 2016).

A critical commitment in entrepreneurship research actually witnesses a consistently growing stream of contributions emerging over the last twenty years (approximately), com- monly known as the 'field' of critical entrepreneurship studies (the term being coined by Calás et al., 2009). Diverging from 'mainstream', functionalist entrepreneurship research, such contributions offer novel, radical, complexified and nuanced ways of understanding and researching entrepreneurship phenomena. They question the taken-for-granted norms and assumptions of mainstream entrepreneurship research. Critical entrepreneurship studies argue that generally the study of entrepreneurship promotes entrepreneurship as something positive and desirable in economies and societies (Rehn & Taalas, 2004; Calás et al., 2009; Jones & Murtola, 2012; Rehn et al., 2013), and problematize and *resist* this 'evangelical' (global) discourse offering a utopian view of *entrepreneurialism.* They challenge the prevail- ing (neo-liberal) way of conceiving, perceiving, 'knowing' and theorizing entrepreneurship (Grant & Perren, 2002), and they encourage a re-examination of the very nature of enterprise discourse (du Gay, 1991, 2004; Fournier, 1998; Armstrong, 2001; Jones & Spicer, 2005) so as to 'reveal' the dysfunctional and ideology-controlling effects of entrepreneurialism. In doing so, they, e.g., seek to expose the darker sides of entrepreneurial practices that are usually hidden from view (Rehn & Taalas, 2004; Wright & Zahra, 2011) and unveil relations of power and asymmetry related to gender or ethnicity (Ahl, 2004; Essers & Benschop, 2007, 2009; Banerjee & Tedmanson, 2010; Essers, Benschop, & Doorewaard, 2010).

These contributions, as Weiskopf and Steyaert (2009, p. 188) so eloquently suggest, by revealing negative consequences, and ideological or hegemonic workings, add further force to 'the cool if not cold wind of critique'. According to Braidotti (2019a, p. 167), a critique mainly stemming from negation and negative passion, 'diminishes our relational competence and denies our vital interdependence on others'. A 'negative' critique can then be said to be a critique that *maintains* negation and opposition (Bunz, Kaiser, & Thiele, 2017, p. 7). Also, such a critique risks producing other absolute truths than the ones under critique and further 'leave[s] little space for new ideas, alternative conceptions or inventions of the possible' (Weiskopf & Steyaert, 2009, p. 189). We read this thinking as in proximity to one of Latour's (2010) arguments that we pointed to earlier in this chapter, that is if we believe that the time of time has passed (or: the linearity of time), to flee from the past as a way to create movement towards a better future that we think we already know, might not be so productive. Rather, when aiming at transformation Latour suggests to commit to a more precarious innovation of things to come. This is a shift *from* the idea of creating movement to progress away from the past and in the direction of something known, *towards* the idea of creating movement from the present by innovating 'the fate of things to come' (Latour, 2010, p. 486). This practice of innovating concerns according to Latour (2010, p. 487) 'to compose – in all its meanings of the word. Including to compose with, that is to compromise, to care, to move slowly, with caution and precaution'. Hence, in our effort to cautiously create a manifesto for EAP research as an experimentation with what EAP research might look like and do if it resists the potential of becoming human-centred and uncritical, we are curious of the potential of a critique that is creative and inventive.

Critical entrepreneurship studies have also picked up on this 'other' way of formulating and enacting critique. Next to the 'negative' (sceptical) vein of critical entrepreneurship research, we witness a second one, one practising an affirmative form of critique. This latter vein of critical entrepreneurship research, seeking alternative ways of approaching what is found problematic, considers entrepreneurship as a critical force of societal production (e.g. Calás, Ergene, & Smircich, 2009; Rindova, Barry, & Ketchen, 2009; Calás et al., 2018). Contributions in this vein turn the attention to entrepreneurship's emancipatory potential (Rindova et al., 2009), as a phenomenon that not only brings about new firms, products and services, but also 'new openings for more liberating forms of individual and collective existence' (Verduijn et al., 2014, p. 98), rephrasing '"*entrepreneuring*" as part of society, and fundamentally a process of social change' (Calás et al., 2009, p. 553, italics added), (re)aligning entrepreneurship (more) with the 'common good'. The affirmative kind of critique seeks to critique to *create* (Braidotti, 2013), to intervene in the world in a more positive logic. This approach does not leave the critiquing at piercingly asking what it is that we have become, but rather continues in a more speculative manner by asking 'What if' ('what if we became this, what if we became that?'). Despite its positive 'approach', affirmative critique does not paint the kind of rose-tinted, optimistic interpretation of entrepreneurship as produced in, e.g. the media, or in mainstream entrepreneurship research. Instead, affirmation acknowledges that knowing entrepreneurship requires, as with 'negative' criticality, a critical interrogation of its premises and guiding assumptions. An example of an affirmatively critical entrepreneurship study can be found in Dashtipour and Rumens (2018), who have elaborated on the setting up of a Swedish anti-racist commercial magazine (*Gringo*) to elucidate how 'entrepreneurship introduces incongruence and newness and thus ruptures established norms, familiarity, and coherence' (Dashtipour & Rumens, 2018, p. 224). They illustrate how an initiative such as *Gringo*, by creating 'heterotopia' points at the more significant social change potential of entrepreneurship that goes beyond 'the economy', the individual venture, or the individual entrepreneur.

The affirmatively critical 'tradition' is the one we seek to connect EAP with. We further elaborate in the next section.

PRACTICE THEORIZING WITH POSTHUMAN CRITICAL THEORY AND AFFIRMATIVE CRITIQUE

In our haltering bringing into being of a future-oriented manifesto for EAP thinking we are curious of a practice theory that works from the understanding that practice is more-than-social and that is placing criticality at the core of its task. This is why we in this section lay a ground for the EAP community to engage in practice theorizing inspired by critical posthuman perspectives that seek to go beyond Western humanism and that are oriented towards justice. Contending that there is no one, unified practice approach, Schatzki (2001) indeed sketches various strands of practice theorizing, with the majority conceiving of practices as 'embodied, materially mediated arrays of *human* activity' (Schatzki, 2001, p. 2, italics added). However, he also mentions a 'significant "posthuman" minority' (Schatzki, 2001, p. 2), which posits that the activities practices are composed of 'also include those of nonhumans such as machines' (Schatzki, 2001, p. 2). Schatzki further explains how this posthuman minority is subdivided in approaches that assert that nonhuman entities mediate practices, such that 'understanding specific practices always involves apprehending material configurations' (Schatzki, 2001, p. 3) on the one hand, and on the other hand, that there are posthumanist practice theorists claiming 'that nonhumans do not just mediate, but themselves propagate practices: practices, in their eyes, comprise human and nonhuman activities' (Schatzki, 2001, p. 3). Gherardi (2016, p. 38), asserting that 'a unified theory of practice does not exist', also points at differences in approaches to practice-based understandings. In doing so she argues how *all* practice approaches incorporate 'materials' in their understandings, but that there is a difference in *how* they see them having a role in the production of practices: 'the issue is not whether or not materiality matters within practice theory; rather it is whether materiality merely mediates human activities – as in human-centred theories – or is constitutive of practice, as in posthuman practice theories' (Gherardi, 2016, pp. 38–39).

In our articulation of a manifesto as a call to attention towards a potential closing-off of possible future engagements with the criticality of/in entrepreneurship, we are drawing on the work of philosopher Rosi Braidotti and her articulation of a posthuman critical theory and affirmative critique (2013, 2015, 2019a, 2019b) and also the philosopher and artist Erin Manning's (2016) work on a 'minor gesture'. In their thinking we find both a framework for a practice theorizing that includes the more-than-human, allowing us to understand materiality as being constitutive of practice, and one that also is critical of unjust power relations and how this materializes (see e.g. Dashtipour & Rumens, 2018, as elaborated above). Further, rather than responding and critiquing in a reactive manner to what is found problematic in the world, their thinking offers an affirmative alternative. This alternative is grounded in a process ontology where what is, is always in the process of becoming something else. We will say more about affirmation later in this section, after a short presentation of a few central features in Braidotti's critical posthuman theory. However, it is important to understand that criticality from a process ontology works from another logic than the 'anti'. At the same time critical posthumanism takes negative elements in the world very seriously (Braidotti, 2019a). However, instead of working towards justice by focusing on stopping what is unjust, this philosophical vein has 'virtual potentials as its core' (Braidotti, 2019a, p. 155). Before turning to Braidotti and Manning for their thinking on affirmation, we want to stress that they are not the only ones to have thought about affirmation. Affirmative critique has multiple influxes.

For the purpose of creating a manifesto for EAP as a call to attention to address the troubles we have briefly unfolded in the previous part, we find great inspiration in Braidotti's posthuman critical theory (2013, 2019a, 2019b). In her thinking, the posthuman is both a 'historical marker of our condition' and a theoretical figuration (2019a, p. 1). She defines the posthuman condition as 'the convergence of posthumanism on the one hand, that focuses on the critique of the Humanist ideal of "Man", and post-anthropocentrism on the other, which criticizes species hierarchy and anthropocentric exceptionalism' (2019a, p. 2). In her book *Posthuman Knowledge* (2019a) she develops a 'framework for posthuman knowledge by creating a balancing act between posthumanism and post-anthropocentrism' (2019a, p. 11). As a theoretical figuration, she writes of the posthuman as a navigational tool that enables us to survey the material and discursive manifestations of the mutations that are engendered by advanced technological developments, climate change and capitalism (2019a, p. 2). The post-human figuration is, with Braidotti, 'a work in progress', 'a working hypothesis of who we are becoming' (Braidotti, 2019a, p. 2) that highlights the positive potential of the above mentioned posthuman convergence, and its project is affirmation.

For the purpose of trying to put a couple of threads from Braidotti's thinking to practice later in the chapter, we will try to outline just a few ideas from her articulation of a critical posthuman theory before we go on unfolding affirmation as a mode for critique dependent on these threads. Due to the lack of space this will be done in a non-exhaustive manner. Two threads that in our reading are running through Braidotti's posthuman thinking are an interest in 'an enlarged, distributed and transversal concept of what a subject is and how it deploys its relational capacities' (2019a, p. 40), and the possibility of knowing differently. First, Braidotti (2019a, p. 41) suggests that we need 'a subject position worthy of our times', that is 're-positioned as a dynamic convergence phenomenon across the contradictions of posthumanism and post-anthropocentrism' and that can support us in developing a 'suitable ethical framework to do justice to its multi-layered complexity'. She proposes that the key term to thinking about a posthuman subject is *relationality* (2019a, p. 45). This is 'multi-scalar relationality': we are 'variations on a common matter' as much as we are embodied and embedded beings steeped in the material world, connected but also differing from each other, yet 'structurally related to one another, to the human and nonhuman world we live in' (2019a, pp. 44–45). We suggest this connects well with Gherardi's (2016) aforementioned articulation of how materiality is constitutive of practice in her writing on posthuman practice theories.

Importantly, this relational subject challenges our common understanding of the creation of knowledge. The knowing subject, as Braidotti explains, or the entrepreneur or the entrepreneurial researcher, is not 'Man, or Anthropos alone, but a more complex assemblage' (2019a, p. 45). The capacity to produce knowledge is not a privilege that solely belongs to humans, but a capacity that is 'distributed across all living matter' and throughout self-organizing networks (Braidotti, 2019a, p. 51). This, in our argument, connects to entrepreneurship as practice theorizing's concerns to understanding thinking as a relational activity. Posthuman knowing and posthuman knowledge are about our capacity to relate and to 'produce adequate understandings of the interconnection with all matter' (Braidotti, 2019a, p. 132). Which makes us wonder: what if we are to consider EAP not as a 'fixed signifier', but rather think in terms of a becoming-EAP? Might that spark an imagination for the '"we" (we might) become' (Calás et al., 2018, p. 267)? And could liaising with critical posthuman theory spark EAP-becoming?

We have previously mentioned that the ongoing figuration of the posthuman has affirmation as its project, and further that we are curious of what an affirmative critique can be creative of in particular in relation to some present troublings in EAP. As stated before, affirmative critical research aims to explicitly go beyond opposition (Deleuze, 1962). The guiding idea of critique as affirmation is that critique should transform the object of critique: a critiquing to create (Braidotti, 2011, 2013; MacLure, 2015; Raffnsøe, 2016; Andersen, 2017). What is proposed here is a mode of critique that seeks to affirm rather than negate by wondering how we can 'work towards socially sustainable horizons of hope, through creative resistance' (Braidotti, 2019a, p. 19), and produce 'adequate knowledge in and for the world' (Braidotti, 2019a, p. 50). How can EAP research be transformed through engagement with the principle of affirmative critique and what other knowledge might be produced? There are no straightforward answers to the above questions. For more inspiration and boldness, we have turned to

Manning (2016). She writes that what negative critique does is to 'actively trace what the event cannot do' and this for-against gesture is an acting that remains in the it is, hence negative critique is reactive (Manning, 2016, p. 203). Connecting this back to what we wrote earlier, negative critique is steeped in the anti, which again is a strategy based in another ontology than a processual one. Manning (2016, p. 203) elaborates this further by writing that negation is not affirmation's 'other' because it operates in a very different logic. Manning's alternative to negations is 'the minor gesture', that is 'an operative cut that opens experience to its potential' (2016, p. 201). This operation, she suggests, 'is affirmative to its core' (2016, p. 201). What it does is to 'catalyse a reordering' without an aim, as 'affirmation does not yet know what a field can do' (2016, p. 201). 'Affirmation does not position', she continues, 'it experiments' (2016, p. 201). What is possible to think, what we can imagine, depends on how reality is assembling.

Moreover, affirmation is not about interpreting, or judging, as this is to ask 'what if' from the stance of the 'IT IS'. Rather, based in a process ontology, its 'movement towards the world is one of mutual inclusion' (Manning, 2016, p. 202) that asks 'what if' at the heart of the what else? Hence, 'affirmation is the yes of the child's "again"!' (Manning, 2016, p. 209), a pragmatic stance of experimentation that promises nothing else. From this yes! many no's will follow, as affirmation does not mean that anything goes. As Manning writes, 'the affirmative path is rocky and unsteady. No well-trodden ruts here' (2016, p. 205). Hence, one of the uncomforting modes of affirmation is that it 'promises nothing' (2016, p. 205). Hence, so far we can already suggest that EAP research might become different and create alternative knowledge through experimentation. Our driving question in the following sections is: how can we, inspired by critical posthuman theory, alter habitual thinking and doing within the EAP community? To discover something as Gartner (2016) proposes, or in our words to learn something new that can create movement towards a just future, is not about finding a new landscape, but in having 'new eyes' (Gartner, 2016, p. 340). And critical posthuman theory is our proposed new eyes.

STUCK HAPPENINGS AS POTENTIAL KNOTS FOR KEEPING EAP RESEARCH MOVING

What follows is an attempt at bringing our reader to experience EAP materializing. We offer a glimpse of certain events at EAP3, EAP4, and around (preparing) EAP5. We see, and introduce, them as Deleuzian events in that they 'carry no determinate outcome, but only new possibilities, representing a moment at which new forces might be brought to bear' (Stagoll, 2005, p. 91), and thus not as representations of a reality of any kind. We acknowledge that they cannot serve to denote 'what really happened' in some way. We understand these vignettes as accounts of presents, and as such a working against data and theory as stable (Jackson & Mazzei, 2012), and against data and theory as 'facts'. They are 'mere' accounts of experienced affects, expressing a desire for potential action. They denote a certain experienced 'stuckness' (Andersen, 2017), vis-à-vis what we have earlier voiced as hesitations with the EAP research conversation, and with Latour (2010) we think of them as something to compose *with*, a fate to come. The stuckness described below is based on the experiences of the first author, but may easily be recognized by others in the community.

So, there was this instance at EAP3 (in Vaxjö) where we had a keynote, and a panel discussion, with someone in the audience pointing at the fact that we – once again – had 'three white (older) men' sitting in front of the room. And how/why this had come about, where were the women/coloured people etc. And, people in the audience agreed, and started to wonder (we're an as-practice community after all) if and how we could change this. The very person raising the point had a solution: he ran down the steps of the theatre, and joined the (other) three men in front of the room. We were left with the – acknowledged – feeling and observation that we could not in fact change what was happening.

There was another instance at EAP3, during the introduction day of the doctoral part. This was held at Linnaeus University's 'Teleborg castle'. A lovely, elegant setting, in the midst of lakes and woods. At some point during the introduction day, some of us started to explain what was actually 'in', or rather 'out' of the EAP domain, in an attempt at demarcating the boundaries of the conversation. Something which did not feel right. After the session, I took the break to go outside, for a walk, and found it actually hard to go back in. The castle had turned into a 'gloomy' one [see Figure 5.1], the steep stairs had somehow become hard to climb … This had actually registered in my body as a form of entrapment, and I sensed that I did not want to fit some mould.

Then there was EAP4, where we [i.e. the (female) lead organizer of EAP3, and first author] tried to address the issue with some of the particular stuckness experienced at EAP3. We prepared an experimental workshop, where we set out to try and make people reflect, and sense what bodily immersion may do to change things. We drew upon Andersen (2017), Barad (2007), and Harding, Ford, and Lee (2017) to explore and practise the altering of what we phrased as '(unintentional) stuck and troublesome happenings'. We experimented with activating attendees' bodily experiences by asking them to walk around, and pass on certain items.

In wrapping up the workshop we proposed to practise four shifts with, and within, our community: (1) From critiquing (each other) to caring, and kindness; (2) From the well-known, well-practised tendency of academia to 'act superior' towards a more humble position; (3) From hierarchy ('the experts') to dialogue (which we viewed as more 'doable' from the proposed caring, humble positioning); and (4) From formulating, and offering, 'standards' (and 'fundamentals') towards embracing fluidity in our engaging with social practice theorizing.

Afterwards, we jointly agreed that we didn't manage to do more than just 'stir the soup' a bit. We could not actually register any signs of change during the discussions, and although we were confused about the lack of movement when elaborating together with open minded and engaged colleagues, we were not giving up. EAP5 could prove to provide yet other opportunity for experimenting with altering practices.

Organizing an academic event perhaps always proves to be more work than anticipated and my co-organizer and I found ourselves frantically arranging all sorts of last-minute practicalities in the beginning of March 2020, with the fifth Entrepreneurship as Practice Conference and Doctoral Symposium planned to take place, in Amsterdam, from March 30 up until April 3. Of course we were aware of COVID-19, and of there being 'break-outs' in Northern Italy, and then also in the south of the Netherlands. But mostly, at the time, people would be pretty relaxed about it all, and joke a bit about if and how this would affect our lives. But then, slowly, we received some cancellations in relation to the virus, and some initial measures being announced: some people were no longer allowed to travel, including one of the keynote speakers. We, on a daily basis, assessed the situation, and for some time continued to feel that things could still go ahead. But then it kind of collapsed – too many people cancelling, and we had to decide to postpone the conference. Followed by a partial lockdown in our country, rigorously affecting public life, and even closing schools and universities, also our own. When we decided to postpone, we would still have been 'allowed' (officially) to continue. But within the scope of just a day or two, the whole situation changed. Now we're not even sure IF postponing is at all possible.

As we have asserted above, relaying of these events should not be seen as factual, as representing something, nor as *judgement* of any kind. These are experienced affects, as sensed by the chapter's first author, who has been part of initiating this conversation, and community. It is in a way a storying of the community's experiments of altering our own practices, as an ongoing endeavour, as an attempt at an act of affirmative critique. Not per se as a result of

Figure 5.1   Teleborg Castle

human-driven intentionality though (e.g. the intervention at EAP3, the workshop at EAP4), as the first stirrings of change actually seem to come from 'outside' (the virus).

In what follows, we describe a re-turn to EAP research, the idea of creating a manifesto in relation to our current attempt at opening/altering EAP research's practices, as a desire to expand or become-other through what is more than oneself.

A STUTTERING FUTURE-ORIENTED MANIFESTO FOR EAP RESEARCH

So far, we have tried to fold out some varieties in our stuttering process of trying to articulate future prospects for EAP scholarship. In the introduction we used an example from the field of arts to exemplify the use of manifestos, and we presented Gartner's (2016) *entrefesto* as a springboard for what we have set out to do in this chapter. A variety of manifestos has been created within the area of science, and several of these have engaged with how to create knowledge (e.g. Haraway, 1985; Willis & Trondman, 2000). As with our manifesto, these seem to be less about strict rules and regulations for the creation of knowledge and more about responding (sometimes radically) to difficult questions circulating in a particular time and space. Difficult questions that we suggest are circulating in the landscape of EAP thinking have to do with EAP not engaging with practice theorizing's critical outlook, thus missing out on addressing such questions as who/what gets to produce knowledge, and what practices can serve to perhaps resist, or alter, in producing a more just world.

Gartner (2016) suggests that by opening up to a variety of methods, data sources and perspectives we are more likely to 'find' variation in the entrepreneurship phenomenon. His entrefesto thus points at variation: 'always so as to increase the number of choices' (Gartner, 2016, p. 340). It also points at 'fresh' approaches ('having new eyes'; 'traditions are solutions to yesterday's problems'), affect ('ENCHANTMENT'), and at adopting a process ontology ('it will become'). The entrefesto is thoroughly affirmative in how it does not claim that variation is to be *found*, but rather it is to be created, and worked with ('Come on!', 'ACT', 'BEGIN'). We agree with Gartner's suggestion to open up for variation in how to approach entrepreneurship, and in seeing how EAP can be(come) a driver of variation. Not by seeking to 'find' it, though, but rather by intervening in differentiation processes, by rearranging the assemblages, such that 'what lives is set free' (Deleuze, 1983).

Gartner's hope is that the entrepreneurship field continues to be open to (more) *radical* methods and outlets and our concern is to creatively, in a cautious manner, engage in future affirmative critical prospects for EAP thinking. As proposed, a practice theory anchored in posthuman thinking is currently what we find most promising for EAP to be engaging with, that is creating movement for processing forward and meeting new prospects for EAP theorizing. In particular, we are interested in what inventive lines of thoughts are possible to think for the future of EAP if we engage with a *critical* posthuman framework, and (thus) with affirmative critique. And that brings us back to suggesting an orientation towards justice to give direction to the variation Gartner proposes. Not as a 'what is supposed to be', but, rather as a differential process, in the way Braidotti (2019a, p. 9) explains: justice as 'social, trans-species and transnational', based on a relational ethics ('we are all in this together', 2019a, p. 9). Indeed, a becoming-EAP-together (Calás et al., 2018). This takes us to EAP5. Postponement indeed did not prove to be feasible. Rather, we had a series of digital seminars in September 2020. COVID-19, the more-than-human pandemic, became active in the reordering (Manning, 2016) of the event, and the possibilities of technology paved the way. Another 'mere' account of experienced affect:

> With the EAP5 digital 'Zoom' seminar series, I experienced that the emphasis came to lie on the relational. With it came a sense of happiness, it was actually so nice to meet and chat. The atmosphere was open and constructive. I have experienced that 'we' 'are' a 'people, a community, and an assemblage'. (Braidotti, 2019a, p. 18)

'"We" [...] cannot [...] act alone' (Braidotti, 2019a, p. 18). Where the little intervention at EAP4 did not manage to – in our experiences – alter 'stuck happenings' (Andersen, 2017), COVID-19 did. If, and how, this will endure, obviously remains to be seen. Alas, as per Manning, any road ahead does not come with 'guarantees'.

In our reflections, and stuttering articulations, what we envisage as way(s) forward is about a becoming-together, and a continued experimentation – tracking and analysing 'shifting grounds' (Braidotti, 2019a, p. 11). Not the 'negative' critique but a more precarious innovation to come (Latour, 2010), so as to enable possibilities for social change and empowerment. To make it that the 'gloomy castle' actually becomes a sign of an affirmative, justice-minded community!

In short: so, yes, we (EAP community) embrace social practice theories (plural!), to emphasize the heterogeneous, relational forces that together 'produce' entrepreneurial processes, and initiatives, not as some final outcome, but as prone to further materializing, as an in-between, or yet-to-become. And indeed, we as a community are also a (temporary) 'production' of heterogeneous, relational forces. Evidenced, not in the last place, and as we have previously pointed at, by the fact that the work was already going on when the incipient EAP community emerged. So, we 'have' that on board, and each of our own backgrounds, and (academic) habits, as becoming-subjects. We have the various different meeting surroundings, and their effects, and affects. And, we are yet-to-*further*-become. We concur with Calás et al. (2018) where they write: 'we believe there is merit in re-imagining what we collectively *already know*, opening possibilities for re-assembling what we collectively *already do* as practice/practicing and theory/theorizing in our field' (2018, p. 267, italics in original). This chapter, our manifesto, is at the very least meant to suggest a pause, to interrupt 'automatic stimulus-response reactions' (Weiskopf & Steyaert, 2009, p. 200). It is an invitation to stay curious, to avoid closing-off, avoid entrapment, and to avoid becoming *dogmatic* (MacLure, 2018).

So, owing once again to Gartner (2016), let's PLAY, EAP community (Figure 5.2).

EXPERIMENT. CONTINUE THE

CREATIVE RESISTANCE.

RESIST THE DOMINANT PRACTICES. TRACK THE

SHIFTING GROUNDS.

MAKE THEM PRODUCTIVE.

AND: WE'RE ALL (BECOMING) IN THIS

TOGETHER.

Figure 5.2   *A future-oriented manifesto for thinking entrepreneurship as practice*

NOTES

1. See https://en.wikipedia.org/wiki/Manifesto#Scientific_and_educational.
2. See https://en.wikipedia.org/wiki/Dogme_95.
3. See https://www.etymonline.com/word/manifesto.
4. See https://www.merriam-webster.com/dictionary/manifest.

REFERENCES

Ahl, H. (2004). *The Scientific Reproduction of Gender Inequality: A Discourse Analysis of Research Texts on Women's Entrepreneurship*. Stockholm: Liber.

Andersen, C. E. (2017). Affirmative critique as minor qualitative critical inquiry: A storying of a becoming critical engagement with what happens. *International Review of Qualitative Research, 10*(4), 430–449.

Anderson, A. R., Dodd, S. D., & Jack, S. (2010). Network practices and entrepreneurial growth. *Scandinavian Journal of Management, 26*, 121–133.

Anderson, A. R., & Warren, L. (2011). The entrepreneur as hero and jester: Enacting the entrepreneurial discourse. *International Small Business Journal, 29*, 589–609.

Armstrong, P. (2001). Science, enterprise and profit: Ideology in the knowledge-driven economy. *Economy and Society, 30*(4), 524–552.

Banerjee, S., & Tedmanson, D. J. (2010). Grass burning under our feet: Indigenous enterprise development in a political economy of whiteness. *Management Learning, 41*, 147–165.

Barad, K. (2007). *Meeting the Universe Halfway: Quantum Physics and the Entanglement of Matter and Meaning*. Durham, NC: Duke University Press.

Braidotti, R. (2011). *Nomadic Theory: The Portable Rosi Braidotti*. New York: Columbia University Press.

Braidotti, R. (2013). *The Posthuman*. Cambridge: Polity Press.

Braidotti, R. (2015). Posthuman affirmative politics. In S. E. Wilmer & Audronė Žukauskaitė (Eds.), *Resisting Biopolitics: Philosophical, Political, and Performative Strategies* (pp. 30–56). New York: Routledge.

Braidotti, R. (2019a). *Posthuman Knowledge*. Cambridge: Polity Press.

Braidotti, R. (2019b). A theoretical framework for the critical posthumanities. *Theory, Culture & Society, 36*(6), 31–61.

Bunz, M., Kaiser, B. M., & Thiele, K. (2017). Introduction: Symptoms of the planetary condition. In M. Bunz, B. M. Kaiser, & K. Thiele (Eds.), *Symptoms of the Planetary Condition: A Critical Vocabulary* (pp. 7–17). Lüneburg: Meson Press.

Calás, M. B., Ergene, S., & Smircich, L. (2018). Becoming possible in the Anthropocene? Becomingsocialentrepreneurship as more-than-capitalist practice. In P. Dey & C. Steyaert (Eds.), *Social Entrepreneurship: An Affirmative Critique* (pp. 267–281). Cheltenham, UK and Northampton, MA, USA: Edward Elgar Publishing.

Calás, M. B., Smircich, L., & Bourne, K. A. (2009). Extending the boundaries: Reframing 'entrepreneurship as social change' through feminist perspectives. *Academy of Management Review, 34*(3), 552–569.

Dashtipour, P., & Rumens, N. (2018). Entrepreneurship, incongruence and affect: Drawing insights from a Swedish anti-racist organisation. *Organization, 25*(2), 223–241.

Deleuze, G. (1962). *Nietzsche et la philosophie*. Paris: PUF.

Deleuze, G. (1983). *Nietzsche and Philosophy*. New York: Columbia University Press.

Dodd, S. D., Pret, T., & Shaw, E. (2016). Advancing understanding of entrepreneurial embeddedness: Forms of capital, social contexts and time. In F. Welter & W. B. Gartner (Eds.), *A Research Agenda for Entrepreneurship and Context* (pp. 120–133). Cheltenham, UK and Northampton, MA, USA: Edward Elgar Publishing.

du Gay, P. (1991). Enterprise culture and the ideology of excellence. *New Formations, 13*, 45–61.

du Gay, P. (2004). Against 'enterprise' (but not against 'enterprise', for that would make no sense). *Organization, 11*(1), 37–57.

Essers, C., & Benschop, Y. (2007). Enterprising identities: Female entrepreneurs of Moroccan and Turkish origin in the Netherlands. *Organization Studies, 28*, 49–69.

Essers, C., & Benschop, Y. (2009). Muslim businesswomen doing boundary work: The negotiation of Islam, gender and ethnicity within entrepreneurial contexts. *Human Relations, 62*, 403–423.

Essers, C., Benschop, Y., & Doorewaard, H. (2010). Female ethnicity: Understanding Muslim migrant businesswomen in the Netherlands. *Gender, Work and Organization, 17*, 320–340.

Essers, C., Dey, P., Tedmanson, D., & Verduyn, K. (2017). Critical entrepreneurship studies: A manifesto. In C. Essers, P. Dey, D. Tedmanson, & K. Verduyn (Eds.), *Critical Perspectives on Entrepreneurship* (pp. 1–14). Abingdon: Routledge.

Fletcher, D. (2006). Entrepreneurial processes and the social construction of opportunity. *Entrepreneurship & Regional Development, 18*, 421–440.

Fournier, V. (1998). Stories of development and exploitation: Militant voices in enterprise culture. *Organization, 5*(1), 55–80.

Gaddefors, J., & Anderson, A. (2017). Entrepreneursheep and context: When entrepreneurship is greater than entrepreneurs. *International Journal of Entrepreneurial Behavior & Research, 23*(2), 267–278.

Gartner, W. B. (2016). *Entrepreneurship as Organizing: Selected Papers of William B. Gartner.* Cheltenham, UK and Northampton, MA, USA: Edward Elgar Publishing.

Gherardi, S. (2009). Introduction: The critical power of the practice lens. *Management Learning, 40*(2), 115–128.

Gherardi, S. (2016). Sociomateriality in posthuman practice theory. In A. Hui, T. Schatzki, & E. Shove (Eds.), *The Nexus of Practices: Connections, Constellations, Practitioners* (pp. 38–51). Abingdon: Routledge.

Grant, P., & Perren, L. J. (2002). Small business and entrepreneurial research: Meta-theories, paradigms and prejudices. *International Small Business Journal, 20*, 185–209.

Haraway, D. (1985). A manifesto for cyborgs: Science, technology, and socialist feminism in the 1980s. *Socialist Review, 15*(2), 65–107.

Harding, N. H., Ford, J., & Lee, H. (2017). Towards a performative theory of resistance: Senior managers and revolting subjectivities. *Organization Studies, 38*, 1209–1232.

Hjorth, D., & Holt, R. (2016). It's entrepreneurship, not enterprise: Ai Weiwei as entrepreneur. *Journal of Business Venturing Insights, 5*, 50–54.

Jackson, A. Y., & Mazzei, L. A. (2012). *Thinking with Theory in Qualitative Research: Viewing Data Across Multiple Perspectives.* London: Routledge.

Johnsen, C. G., & Sørensen, B. M. (2017). Traversing the fantasy of the heroic entrepreneur. *International Journal of Entrepreneurial Behaviour & Research, 23*, 228–244.

Jones, C., & Murtola, A. M. (2012). Entrepreneurship and expropriation. *Organization, 19*, 635–655.

Jones, C., & Spicer, A. (2005). The sublime object of entrepreneurship. *Organization, 12*(2), 223–246.

Jones, C., & Spicer, A. (2009). *Unmasking the Entrepreneur.* Cheltenham, UK and Northampton, MA, USA: Edward Elgar Publishing.

Keating, A., Geiger, S., & McLoughlin, D. (2014). Riding the practice waves: Social resourcing practices during new venture development. *Entrepreneurship Theory and Practice, 38*, 1–29.

Latour, B. (2010). An attempt at a 'compositionist manifesto'. *New Literary History, 41*(3), 471–490.

MacLure, M. (2015). The 'new materialisms': A thorn in the flesh of critical qualitative inquiry? In G. Cannella, M. S. Perez, & P. Pasque (Eds.), *Critical Qualitative Inquiry: Foundations and Futures* (pp. 93–112). Walnut Creek, CA: Left Coast Press.

MacLure, M. (2018). Encounters and materiality in intimate scholarship: A conversation with Maggie MacLure. In K. Strom, T. Mills, & A. Ovens (Eds.), *Decentering the Researcher in Intimate Scholarship* (pp. 197–204). Bingley: Emerald Publishing.

Manning, E. (2016). *The Minor Gesture.* Durham, NC: Duke University Press.

McKeever, E., Anderson, A., & Jack, S. (2014). Entrepreneurship and mutuality: Social capital in processes and practices. *Entrepreneurship & Regional Development, 26*, 453–477.

Pret, T., Shaw, E., & Dodd, S. D. (2016). Painting the full picture: The conversion of economic, cultural, social and symbolic capital. *International Small Business Journal, 34*, 1004–1027.

Raffnsøe, S. (2016). *Philosophy of the Anthropocene: The Human Turn.* Basingstoke: Palgrave Macmillan.

Rehn, A., Brännback, M., Carsrud, A., & Lindahl, M. (2013). Challenging myths of entrepreneurship? *Entrepreneurship & Regional Development, 25*, 543–551.

Rehn, A., & Taalas, S. (2004). 'Znakomstva I Svyazi' acquaintances and connections: Blat, the Soviet Union, and mundane entrepreneurship. *Entrepreneurship & Regional Development, 16*, 235–250.

Rindova, V., Barry, D., & Ketchen, D. J. (2009). Entrepreneuring as emancipation. *Academy of Management Review, 34*(3), 477–491.

Sarason, Y., Dean, T., & Dillard, J. F. (2006). Entrepreneurship as the nexus of individual and opportunity: A structuration view. *Journal of Business Venturing, 21*, 286–305.

Schatzki, T. (2001). Introduction: Practice theory. In T. Schatzki, K. Knorr Cetina, & E. von Savigny (Eds.), *The Practice Turn in Contemporary Theory* (pp. 1–14). London: Routledge.

Sklaveniti, C., & Steyaert, C. (2020). Reflecting with Pierre Bourdieu: Towards a reflexive outlook for practice-based studies of entrepreneurship. *Entrepreneurship & Regional Development, 32*(3–4), 313–333.

Stagoll, C. (2005). Event. In A. Parr (Ed.), *The Deleuze Dictionary* (pp. 89–91). Edinburgh: Edinburgh University Press.

Tatli, A., Vassilopoulou, J., Özbilgin, M., Forson, C., & Slutskaya, N. (2014). A Bourdieuan relational perspective for entrepreneurship research. *Journal of Small Business Management, 52*, 615–632.

Teague, B., Tunstall, R., Champenois, C., & Gartner, W. B. (2021). An introduction to entrepreneurship as practice (EAP). *International Journal of Entrepreneurial Behavior & Research, 27*(3), 569–578.

Terjesen, S., & Elam, A. (2009). Transnational entrepreneurs' venture internationalization strategies: A practice theory approach. *Entrepreneurship Theory and Practice, 33*, 1093–1120.

Thompson, N., Verduijn, K., & Gartner, W. B. (2020). Entrepreneurship as practice: Grounding contemporary theories of practice into entrepreneurship studies. *Entrepreneurship & Regional Development, 32*(3–4), 247–256.

Verduijn, K., Dey, P., Tedmanson, D., & Essers, C. (2014). Emancipation and/or oppression? Conceptualizing dimensions of criticality in entrepreneurship studies. *International Journal of Entrepreneurial Behavior & Research, 20*, 98–107.

Weiskopf, R., & Steyaert, C. (2009). Metamorphoses in entrepreneurship studies: Towards an affirmative politics of entrepreneuring. In D. Hjorth & C. Steyaert (Eds.), *The Politics and Aesthetics of Entrepreneurship: A Fourth Movements in Entrepreneurship Book* (pp. 183–201). Cheltenham, UK and Northampton, MA, USA: Edward Elgar Publishing.

Williams, C. C., & Nadin, S. J. (2013). Beyond the entrepreneur as a heroic figurehead of capitalism: Representing the lived practices of entrepreneurs. *Entrepreneurship & Regional Development, 25*, 552–568.

Willis, P., & Trondman, M. (2000). Manifesto for ethnography. *Ethnography, 1*(1), 5–16.

Wright, M., & Zahra, S. (2011). The other side of paradise: Examining the dark side of entrepreneurship. *Entrepreneurship Research Journal, 1*, 1–7.

6. Strong Structuration Theory: an introduction and potentials

Tamim Elbasha and Lisa Thomas

This chapter serves to introduce Strong Structuration Theory (SST) as a theoretical and methodological guide for Entrepreneurship-as-Practice research (EaP). It is an approach which uses a practice theory lens to study the constitution and consequences of practices and represents a means for observing EaP. The chapter responds to calls for greater connection between micro-level process and practices with macro-level outcomes, an area which is gaining momentum for both process and practice scholars, in the pursuit of more managerially relevant research (Kouamé & Langley, 2018). Employing SST also addresses calls for greater methodological diversity within entrepreneurship research (Karataş-Özkan et al., 2014; Shepherd, 2015). SST represents a fruitful avenue for advancing entrepreneurship research with the potential to encourage the exploration of existing topics of interest to entrepreneurship researchers in new ways as well as encouraging new topics and explanations. Practice theories allow for moving away from a theoretical focus on the individual entrepreneur towards the importance of joint activity, performativity and entrepreneuring work. They advance the quest for stronger insight into how individual-level processes and practices connect to broader organizational- and institutional-level systems and processes. In so doing, this helps capture both structure (opportunities and constraints) and agency (the doing and the choice to do otherwise) in order to enhance an understanding of the mechanisms of an entrepreneurial system which is real, complex and dynamic (Jack et al., 2008).

SST equips EaP researchers with the tools to study entrepreneuring as a relational, in-context and open-ended process. The chapter illustrates the decoding of entrepreneurship through a social practice lens (Johannisson, 2011; Watson, 2013) to explore the dynamic links between agents (or the entrepreneurial actor-in-focus – those actors who and whose practices are the focus of the EaP study) and their wider contextual environment (structure/opportunity). It elaborates the value of Stones' SST (Stones, 2005) as a particularly beneficial theory *and* methodology for exploring recursive relations across different levels of analysis over time.

The field of entrepreneurship is ripe for exploring the unfolding links between individuals, their practices, and their rich context (Anderson & Starnawska, 2008; Suddaby et al., 2017). This context is composed of different layers that connect the micro and the macro (Gartner, 1988). Entrepreneurial agents' actions are shaped, but not determined, by social structures yet in turn they shape and modify that structure since entrepreneurship is not purely an economic, individualized act, but one that is embedded in, and draws from society and its immediate context (Dodd & Anderson, 2007). Entrepreneuring can be appreciated as a process (Gartner, 1988) which cuts across multiple levels of analysis. It is embedded and connected within a complex system of individual agents who act in often creative ways, where their action changes the context for other agents (Anderson et al., 2012a). This provides a clearer understanding of how entrepreneurial agents and structures mutually enact social systems, and social systems in turn become part of that duality.

To understand this dynamic we need to appreciate the underlying connections of the entrepreneurial system since to focus on entrepreneurial components in isolation may lead to losing sight of the 'magnificent wholeness of entrepreneurship' (Anderson et al., 2012a, p. 963). Strong structuration theory (Stones, 2005, 2012) can help shape and guide practice research in entrepreneurship through:

1. Emphasizing the different components of entrepreneurs' context.
2. Advancing a structuration cycle model that makes explicit the processual unfolding of structuration over time.
3. Proposing a methodological guidance to conduct empirical research.

The chapter unfolds as follows. It begins with an overview of SST, illustrating how it builds on Giddens' (1979, 1984) work in structuration theory. The chapter then highlights the entrepreneurial context as the background for applying SST within research. This is followed with a more detailed account of what SST entails and introduces the quadripartite framework of structuration (Stones, 2005). This framework represents the structuration process as a series of recursive cycles. The chapter then provides an illustration of the application of the framework within an entrepreneurial context. The chapter sets out a proposed methodology for SST and outlines steps in the application of the methodology in research in entrepreneurship and entrepreneuring.

STRONG STRUCTURATION THEORY

Theory of structuration (Giddens, 1979, 1984) is one of the most influential theories in the social sciences (Chatterjee et al., 2019). It explicates, at an abstract level, how structure and agency are interrelated, being a duality in which neither can exist without the other. The duality of structure stresses the interdependency between structure and agency; 'the structural properties of social systems are both a medium and outcome of the practices they recursively organize' (Giddens, 1984, p. 25). Agents draw upon structures in their conduct, and this 'drawing upon' involves reflexivity and knowledgeability of the structural context which they engage with (Giddens, 1989). Giddens (1979) claims that reflexivity enables agents to tacitly assess the relationship between the action, its reasons and its consequences. Agency refers to interventions or actions taken by agents in the ongoing process of being in the world, and thus in producing intended and unintended actions (Giddens, 1984).

Giddens debates a difference between structure, structures and social systems. Structure has a virtual existence in social practice and is 'recursively implicated in the reproduction of social systems' (Giddens, 1984, p. 377). Structures, on the other hand, are 'recursively institutionalized rule-resource sets' (Giddens, 1984, p. 25). They are structuring properties that allow time–space to be bound in social systems (Giddens, 1984, p. 17). Social systems 'comprise the situated activities of human agents, reproduced across time and space' (Giddens, 1984, p. 25). These relationships establish organized and localized social practices, and they describe different aspects and levels of the same concern (Nicolini, 2012).

Giddens' structuration theory has received considerable criticism concerning how structure(s) is/are conceptualized (e.g. Archer, 1995; Cohen, 1989; Mouzelis, 1991; Parker, 2000; Stones, 2005; Thrift, 1985). Critics also point out the difficulties in mobilizing Giddens' structuration theory in empirical research mainly due to the high level of abstraction. For instance, not everyone in a given organization shares the same interpretation of their context (Harris et al., 2016). Indeed, existing research demonstrates a 'pick and choose' (cf. den Hond et al., 2012) tendency among researchers of Giddens' theory of structuration concepts. Additionally, other scholars pointed out the lack of empirical guidance offered by Giddens to researchers (Harris et al., 2016; den Hond et al., 2012; Sminia, 2009; Archer, 1995).

Despite its critics, structuration theory's central premise (the duality of structure and giving social structure and agency equal footing) remains appealing, especially for entrepreneurship scholars (e.g. Chiasson & Saunders, 2005). The theory of structuration has been evolving ever since it was introduced by Giddens. The sociologist Rob Stones developed Strong Structuration as an elaboration in a way that retains duality of structure but has a greater sense of ontology-in-situ: a concern with social processes and events at particular times and places, and at the ontic, concrete level (Jack, 2017; Stones et al., 2019). Since the publication of Stones' work in 2005, SST has since been taken up widely in management research (Price et al., 2019; Kholeif & Jack, 2019; Cowton & Dopson, 2002; Joseph, 2006; Manders et al., 2020) and other disciplines, for example, accounting (Adhikari & Jayasinghe, 2017; Jack, 2017) and healthcare management (Greenhalgh & Stones, 2010).

Stones sees three levels of ontology that are relevant to empirical analysis (2005, p. 77). The highest level of abstraction provides broad guidance to the research, whilst the lowest ontic level is filled with substantive details informed by entities at a time and place. Stones argues for a third meso level, connecting the other two. This meso level of ontology is of interest to empirical research as it accommodates variations and relative degrees of generalized (abstract) knowledge. Methodologically, to study the interplay between structure and agency across the different levels, Stones suggests that the best place is the 'intermediate temporality' (Parker, 2000, p. 107) where structuration cycles unfold in an intermediate zone of reality. This intermediate zone is where wider external historical and societal environmental systems (context) and individual actions (content) meet, forming a bridge between ontic and abstract level analyses (Elbasha & Wright, 2017). This is of value in EaP research given entrepreneurial agents draw on their knowledge of internal and external structures when making decisions, communicating with others, transforming their organizations or resisting change (Coad et al., 2016).

THE ENTREPRENEURIAL AGENTS' CONTEXT

The structuration cycle(s) unfolds in an 'intermediate temporality' (Parker, 2000, p. 107) where wider historical systems and institutional forces manifest in forms of position-practices (Bhaskar, 1979). The social position of an entrepreneurial agent is linked to a set of expectations and roles placed upon that social position. The notion of position-practices 'can serve as a more robust link between structure and institutionalised modes of conduct' (Cohen, 1989, p. 209). For example, being the owner/manager in a small family firm imposes certain expectations of commitment and loyalty or 'familyness' born of the close connection between family members. This comes about through involvement over generations in serving to promote a long run family 'survival' orientation. As well as being useful for stability and consistency of performance, the expectations to act in such a way may both constrain and guide entrepreneuring activities (Nordqvist & Melin, 2010; Tran & Santarelli, 2014).

Entrepreneuring is an evolutionary process that takes account of, challenges and modifies changes in the shifting environment. Consequently, choice, chance and environmental circumstances may all influence situations (Anderson et al., 2012b; MacKay & Chia, 2013). The past is drawn upon and made relevant to the present which depends importantly on the social practices developed from the web of relations among historical and institutional forces within which agents are embedded (Feldman & Orlikowski, 2011; Jack et al., 2008). Change enables entrepreneuring as well as providing the milieu and outcomes from entrepreneuring (Jack et al., 2008). Consequently, structure and agency are not static or separate but are dependent upon each other and recursively related (Giddens, 1984).

From a social practice perspective, EaP focuses on entrepreneurial actions and interactions, their source, pattern making and outcomes for 'getting things done' within small firms (Johannisson, 2016, p. 406). In getting things done, actions are enabled and constrained by the external structures at the institutional level; the social and economic circumstances of the firm's context, and by the internal structure at the individual level; and the entrepreneur's worldview and experiences. Getting things done is also situated within the historical forces and the expectations of the other agents in the immediate and distant context. From an SST perspective, this translates respectively to the position-practices of the entrepreneur and the network of position-practices that entrepreneurs are situated within. This context defines the dynamic, unfolding everyday practices that guide and enable human activity across time and space (Anderson et al., 2012a; Gedajlovic et al., 2013; Whittington, 1996, 2006; Feldman & Worline, 2016).

Analytically, SST invites researchers to 'slide' on a scale from the macro institutional and societal level to the micro individual level, and vice versa. In our experience, the meso level in between the micro and the macro is composed of different meso 'layers' such as organization, departments, geographical clusters, sub-industries and sub-markets and so on. Each of these layers contains actors linked in a web of relations, where each is also bounded by position-practices (e.g. Elbasha & Avetisyan, 2018). For example, just like being an owner/manager in a small family firm entails certain obligations and expectations, being a national SME association entails certain obligations and expectations from the context – the other agents in the web of position-practices relations.

Within entrepreneurship, context is recognized as a critical factor in explaining the situatedness of entrepreneurial actions and processes where agents are embedded (McKeever et al., 2015; Anderson et al., 2012a; Gedajlovic et al., 2013). It is not constant but is itself continually reconstituted within and by processes of interaction over time (MacKay & Chia, 2013). For example, if the entrepreneurial agent decides to introduce new planning practices, this may well impact their 'professional identity' vis-à-vis other actors within their network (banks, employees, business partners, other entrepreneurs and so on), with the potential of them altering their actions and pattern of interactions in subsequent planning episodes, or alternatively, repeated enactment of the same practice will likely mean more effective performance of the same practice in subsequent episodes (Jarzabkowski et al., 2016). Structural properties emerge and change in a structuration process which may be active and historical (Champenois et al., 2020). To explore and comprehend this adaptive entrepreneurial system calls for a research approach which illuminates the nature of social practices, how they are drawn upon and constituted. Abstracting from the practices of individual entrepreneurs allows the researcher to capture both agency and structure to understand the underlying mechanisms of the complex and dynamic entrepreneurial system (Jack & Anderson, 2008). Table 6.1 presents some important external and internal contextual elements and layers within EaP research using SST.

Table 6.1   Important contextual elements and layers inspired by SST

Element	Examples
Historical institutional forces	Previous entrepreneuring stories at societal level
	Icons of entrepreneurship and their impact on society
	Risk-tolerance or avoidance built into national culture
	Government support for entrepreneurship
Institutional elements, represented in position-practices	A constructed and shared image of entrepreneurs: hard working, making sacrifices, being active, offering innovations, taking risks, presenting ideas, networking activity
	What is expected from a social entrepreneur?
	From a family entrepreneur?
	From a woman entrepreneur?
Evolving relations with other agents-in-context	Obtaining seed money would change the relation between the entrepreneur and the financial institutions
	Growing bigger will alter the relations with other founders/family
	Collaborating with other organizations/institutions to leverage resources changes an entrepreneurial agent's social capital
	Increased responsibilities borne of partnering with other organizations/institutions present new experiences
	Learning from business start-up incubators
Institutional forces, represented in general dispositions (structures internal to the agent)	What does it take to make a successful person?
	How does one categorize failure?
	What does work–life balance mean?
	How does race/colour/gender influence work?
Personal experience, represented in general dispositions (structures internal to the agent)	How did I deal with this issue in the past and to what end?
	What are my 'stocks of experience' (competencies – technical and other embodied skills)?
	What are my personal value commitments and orientations?

As will be presented later in this chapter, an SST approach incentivizes EaP researchers to incorporate these elements in their data collection and analysis.

THE PROCESS OF STRUCTURATION

SST presents structuration process as a series of recursive cycles. Stones (2005) represents this process in his quadripartite structuration framework. Each of these cycles involves four inter-twining elements: external structures, internal structure, active agency and outcomes. Figure 6.1 presents the quadripartite structuration framework.

- External structures are those macro-level 'pressing conditions that limit the agents to do otherwise' (Stones, 2005, p. 111). They represent the agent's conditions of action and establish the wider historical and field-level context which influence agents-in-focus, i.e. those closest to the practices observed and studied (Stones, 2005, pp. 93–94).
- Internal structures are social structures that exist in the agent's mind. They reflect (1) the generalized worldviews, typifications and cultural schema (habitus) that influence agents 'naturally' and unconsciously (Stones, 2005, p. 88); and (2) the agent's perception of the rules and expectations embedded in her/his position. Stones labels the first general dispositions and the second conjuncturally specific (Stones, 2005).

- The third element is the agent's agency, their creative, motivated, pervasive, intended and/or unintended actions. Agency reflects the ability of agents to choose to act and the acting itself (Stones, 2005), thus it is important to examine prioritization of concerns and the consequence of persuasive actions. Agency is enabled and/or constrained by a combination of the external and internal structures presented above and is affected by the conscious or unconscious motivations that impact the interpretations and the drawing upon structures.
- The final element is the outcomes, or the effects the structuration cycle(s) has on structures. A structuration cycle may reproduce and maintain, or challenge and change existing structural conditions, external and/or internal. The effects may be intended or unintended.

Analytically, and perhaps more importantly for EaP, we are concerned with entrepreneurial actions and interactions, what Steyaert (2007) refers to as 'entrepreneuring' – the making of adventurous, creative or innovative exchanges with other parties with whom the entrepreneurial agent engages. The entrepreneurial agent is the 'artful interpreter of practices' amending and reproducing the repertoire of practices from which they draw within their social context (Whittington, 2006, p. 615). The 'micro' level of practice includes individual or collective processes and activities taking place at a lower level than organizational level (Kouamé and Langley, 2018, p. 561). Examples include conversations, negotiations, know-how, managerial cognition, emotion, and motivational knowledge. The application of an SST theoretical lens brings to the fore the importance of agents' knowledgeability of the contexts in which they and their organizations operate (Harris et al., 2016). The activities are fundamentally relational, and it is through interactions that practices emerge (Champenois et al., 2020). As such, entrepreneuring is composed of events and experiences where each event arises out of and is constituted through its relations to other events (Thompson et al., 2016; Langley et al.,

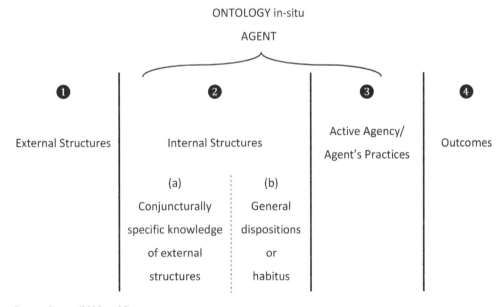

Source: Stones (2005, p. 85).

Figure 6.1   The quadripartite of structuration

2013). The agent actively and reflectively draws upon the internal structures to produce action. Entrepreneuring is thus an ongoing process of structuration over time through the assessment of the interplay between micro and macro societal levels of analysis (Elbasha & Wright, 2017). The micro activities of individual entrepreneurial agents form a 'bundle' of ways of 'getting things done' for example, product development, branding, networking and selling, which combine and coordinate change (Thompson et al., 2016). Consequently, practices are linked to the presence or absence of other practices entangled within the structural context (Jarzabkowski et al., 2016). This structural context represents an intertwining of external structures and internal structures (elements 1 and 2 of the quadripartite schema). They encompass actions which accumulate as practices throughout a firm's lifecycle (Watson, 2013) reflecting the ability of entrepreneurial agents to choose to act as well as the acting itself (Stones, 2005). It is their interdependence which shapes the outcomes, whether intended or unintended. Without close attention to the situated enactment of practices, observers are liable to overvalue formal practices, while undervaluing practice adaptations in context (Jarzabkowski et al., 2016).

The continual production, re-production and ways of 'getting things done' become an important focus within EaP research, as the use of practices involved is shaped by practical adaptations associated with specific contexts or actors' needs (Jarzabkowski et al., 2016). So, while the outcomes of practices allow us to consider their impact on firm performance, we can also consider the impacts on the practices themselves. Thus, practices are shaped at different ontological levels from the interplay of different structuration processes over time and space (Coad et al., 2016).

To further explicate these four elements in an EaP setting, and based on Greenhalgh and Stones (2010), Table 6.2 provides an example of the questions that could be asked both at the micro–meso level and the meso–macro level. The latter will likely incorporate a longer timescale and more numerous and complex relationships in exploring the interdependent relationships between structures, agency and the outcomes.

In sum, whilst the entrepreneurial agent brings into play their dispositions, knowledge and capabilities for a given situation, their action is equally shaped by numerous influences which depend on their horizon of action, and particular external contextual structures confined by time and space (Greenhalgh & Stones, 2010). SST provides a framework within which it is possible to identify and analyse structures by breaking them down into analytically separate components (external, conjuncturally specific and general dispositions). Whilst the duality of structure is integral to Stones' framework, this duality is best understood through analysis of a quadripartite framework of these interrelated components, agency and outcomes (Stones, 2005). This structuration cycle allows researchers to conceptualize entrepreneuring as a process, and combinations of processes, where the practices of entrepreneurial agents are taking place. SST is thus able to elaborate answers to what social structure is, the extent to which it exists independently of human agency and the extent to which it enables and constrains human action. SST helps inform how individuals think, work and fulfil their role allowing the researcher an alternative means to make sense of social actions within organizations (Franco et al., 2017). These questions cannot entirely be resolved at the level of abstract theorizing (Greenhalgh & Stones, 2010). Consequently, the quadripartite study of structuration involves seeking empirical evidence with which to explore and test key concepts and the relationships between them.

Table 6.2   *Applying the quadripartite framework: study exploring the interdependence of elements for a small French independent winery*

1. EXTERNAL STRUCTURES: Conditions of action – the external structural context which shapes action	
FRENCH WINE INDUSTRY	*What is the prevailing political, economic, technological and institutional context?*
Macro-level questions: The broad strategic terrain within which the macro actors apply their knowledge and act in the French wine Industry	**Technological/Environmental:** – Biodynamic farming, micro-oxygenation – Packaging innovation, compressed air – Use of drones in irrigation management – Climate change & higher alcohol levels in grapes – End of stripping process (to keep vines on leaves for shade) – Move to earlier harvests, increasing frequency of hailstones – New grapes for certain categories of Bordeaux wines **Economic & Political:** Plan National contre le Dépérissement du Vignoble 2019 (Vineyard Decline plan) Drink driving laws New World competition **Social:** 'Boire moins mais mieux': Decline in general consumption of French wine. Increase in consumption of better-quality wine.

The network of this study – which agents are represented, what are their position-practices? *What are the key relationships in the network (local agent–global agent, regional agent–local agent, local agent–local agent etc.)?* *Are these relationships changing over time?*	**Institutional Actors:** **Wine professional bodies** **Globally:** International Organization of Wine and Vine (OIV); Wine and Spirits Trade Association (WSTA); Cooperatives; IWSR-Vinexpo. **Nationally:** GROUPE ICV; Vignerons Coopérateurs de France; Institut national de l'origine et de la qualité (INAO); L'Office National Interprofessionnel des Vins (ONIVINS); French Confederacy of Wine Cooperatives (CCVF). **Regionally/Locally:** Le Comité National des Interprofessions des Vins à Appellation d'Origine et à Indication Géographique (Cniv); Vigneron Indépendante. *Local Domains* **Other macro-level actors:** **Economic:** Global competitors, World Wine Trade Group (WWTG) – promoting free and responsible international trade in wine. Global groups; National actors, National groups – e.g. Castel Frères, Pernod Ricard, Vinadeis. Global customers, Export Agents, Media. **Political:** Ministère de l'Agriculture, France AgriMer.
Questions focused on specific situation(s): Mapping the relevant part of the network-in-focus *Who are the key agents involved?*	Focus firm: 'Domaine des Deux Frères, Bordeaux' – Owner-manager – Family members – Local (neighbouring) domains/owners – Customers – Oenologists – Suppliers – Local community – Local cooperatives – Resellers, Export agents
What are the resources / infrastructure necessary to support the situation?	– Technology – Viticulture know-how – Vineyard hectarage – Soil quality – 'Terroir' – Local network relationships – National network relationships – Marketing

2. ENTREPRENEURIAL AGENTS INTERNAL STRUCTURES – relevant to the situation	
What are the agents' general dispositions (cognitive capacity, skills, 'stocks of experience', socio-cultural schemas, values)?	Owner-manager experience of working within other industries outside of the wine industry, their embodied skills, learning ability and reflexivity, sense of place and history, socio-cultural schemas
What is the agent's situation specific knowledge of relevant external structure (the strategic terrain)? How does the agent believe how other agents see this industry relevant for the immediate situation? How do they assume they are expected to act within this terrain?	Owner-manager situation specific knowledge – i.e. knowledge of wine industry, the processes, technology, traditions, the history, knowledge of the specific situation and context at hand: – Knowledge of industry 'rules' – Technical know-how of viticulture – Macro-level changes – Innovation within wine industry, by competitors – Export trends – Social trends How owner-managers are expected to position-practice relations – expectations and roles placed upon owner-managers' social position: – Main breadwinner – Analyst and advisor at local/national wine industry level – Partner/collaborator – Strategic leader/key decision-maker – Innovation catalyst – Local community referent – Debtor
3. ACTIVE AGENCY – actions and interactions	
What does the entrepreneurial agent (actor-in-focus) do?	How does the owner-manager draw on, reflexively relate to general dispositions, situation specific knowledge in an unfolding sequence of action?	– Which traditional wine-making tools and practices are employed (artefacts)? – How are the traditional tools/practices of wine-making implemented? – What is changed in how tools are used? – What new tools are tested? Which traditions are discarded? – How are resources leveraged for sustaining production, innovation, maintaining product quality? – What new innovations are introduced and implemented? – How and why are relationships developed and maintained within the local field, macro-level field for new knowledge? – What is the relationship between practices and the external structure (the strategic terrain)?

How do the social structures (rights, rewards/ sanctions, norms, duties, physical and cognitive demand) enable, influence or constrain owner-manager active agency and their strategic orientations?	**Enablers:** – Local community embeddedness – Collaboration as a source of social capital (knowledge source, helps in resource acquisition i.e. grapes, efficiency of production) – Environmental levers stimulating innovation (bio viticulture, reduction in use of machinery in viticulture) – Government's 'Vineyard Decline' plan – Soil 'terroir' quality – linked to geography **Constrainers:** – AOC rules for grape varieties – Soil 'terroir' quality – linked to geography – Decline in consumption of wine in France

4. OUTCOMES – results of the cycles

What are the immediate consequences of specific actions (intended/unintended)?	– How is the local context changed based on changes in practices, or through no modification in practices, e.g. in terms of competition, innovation, wine quality, increased sales? – Which opportunities are seized and how (linking enablers)? – How are the constraints surmounted (circumventing constrainers)? – Does collaboration alter processes of local actors, wider network actors?
How do these consequences feedback on the position-practices and other significant influences (negative and positive) in the network and wider external structures? What is the significance of the consequences for others in the network – power, legitimacy etc.?	– Does implementing innovation or collaborating with other wineries modify the legitimacy of the owner-manager vis-à-vis these local actors, other network actors? – What are the effects for competitors, cooperatives? – What are the effects on the local environmental ecosystem?

A PROPOSED SST METHODOLOGY

Giddens saw the empirical value of Structuration Theory as a sensitizing device (Giddens, 1984); a generic and unspecific way to influence research (Stones, 2005; Makrygiannakis & Jack, 2018). SST provides important methodological detail envisioning research as an investigation and a drilling down process (Stones, 2005). In this process, scholars approach their questions knowing that 'problem, theory, and data influence each other throughout the research process' (Ahrens & Chapman, 2007, p. 313). As such, an SST methodology privileges a qualitative research design to understand and analyse the relation between the various elements/agents/structures in depth. It also provides a general approach to data collection and analysis.

SST provides researchers with the means to study the entrepreneuring process over time prioritizing the lived experience of entrepreneurs – social agents – through their actions (Orlikowski, 2010). The strong structuration cycle is ideally suited to case study research due to its flexibility and delimited time frame, its adaptability to a specific context and its focus on specific agents and structures within a localized issue or question (Brown, 2010). Single case studies allow for the capture of rich detail describing and accounting for how an issue might develop and change over time (Kouamé & Langley, 2018; Van de Ven, 1992; Mellahi & Sminia, 2009). Case studies also enable the exploration of remarkable episodes of entrepreneuring which warrant further in-depth study, for example, in terms of how particular outcomes emerged. SST also offers the 'meso-level of ontological abstraction' which allows for conceptualizing events across case studies, and the comparison of common themes of EaP practice from case comparison (Harris et al., 2016). Quantitative data might also be employed to ascertain entrepreneurial agents' perceptions of a variety of structural variables which reflect, for example, institutional contexts. Survey data might inform how entrepreneurial agents perceive both formal and informal institutions determining the constitution of exchange within their network (enabling or constraining) where such data can also be used to shed light on outcomes.

Studying the structuration cycle, and practices, may be guided by the following steps (adapted from Stones, 2005):

1. Sensing the entrepreneur's own understanding of the world around them, how they perceive their motivations, roles and self-imposed expectations and motives.
2. Understanding how these worldviews constrain or afford actions and the prioritization thereof.
3. Identifying relevant external structures within the immediate or far context of the entrepreneur.
4. Understanding how these structures constrain and offer possibilities of actions to the entrepreneur.

This strategy focuses on sequential relations between micro- and macro-level phenomena. The first two steps are guided by the research participants (data is provided by/collected from research participants and analysed by the researcher), while the third and fourth steps lean towards favouring the researcher's perspective on the case (collection of retrospective and documentary data by the researcher based on the first two steps, then analysis of these). Interviews and observations lend themselves to data generation covering the first two steps. It can also be useful to analyse background data through ethnographic observation to disentangle the agent's choices and actions. The researcher places the agent(s)-in-focus and their context at the centre of the data collection and analysis. The focus here is more micro in the sense that researchers zoom in (Nicolini, 2009) on the entrepreneurs and their practices. If we refer to some examples provided in Table 6.2 (a study in the wine industry), questions the researcher might pose include: How important is work–life balance? Does the entrepreneurial agent consider themselves a success in their career and how is this defined? What problems have been encountered over time and was the resolution considered successful? What are the agent's perceptions of their key competencies and how relevant are these to the current situation?

Data analysis is usually enabled by an agent's conduct analysis, a type of methodological bracketing. The emphasis is placed on the entrepreneur's reflexive monitoring of their own practices, their ordering of concerns, motives and desires and how they decide to interact with others in their network (Stones, 1996, 2005).

Identifying relevant external structures and their effects (steps 3 and 4) is likely to be achieved by collecting contextual longitudinal and retrospective documentary data. Data sources may be multiple and selected pragmatically to include combinations of documents, ethnographic field notes, semi-structured and other forms of interviews and surveys and multi-media such as video (Greenhalgh & Stones, 2010). Archival data may be particularly useful for tracing event chronologies, meanings and discourse over long periods of time (Langley et al., 2013). Retrospective data are important in understanding the historical forces that shape the studied actions of entrepreneurs (Stones, 2005). Additionally, quantitative data may be insightful and obtained from public sources. For example, the Longitudinal Small Business Survey (LSBS) UK panel reports provide key aspects of SMEs' paths to growth such as exporting and innovation performance, external finance acquisition, business support and employee training (see: https://www.gov.uk/government/collections/small-business-survey-reports). Such panel reports provide background from multiple units of analysis observed at different points in time. The four-year time span of observations from the 2,757 UK SMEs which comprise the LSBS panel offers insights into SME behaviour and strategic dynamics. Such information may be useful for comparative purposes.

Table 6.2 includes example questions for a study in the wine industry that the researcher may pose in steps 2 and 3, such as: What is expected from the owner-managers vis-à-vis other actors in their network? What are the technological advancements in wine-making that are affecting the industry? How are efforts of the wine professional bodies allowing or restraining practices enacted in wineries? Data analysis for these two steps is supplemented by another type of methodological bracketing: agent's context analysis. Here the focus of the analysis is on 'the terrain that faces an agent, the terrain that constitutes the range of possibilities and limits to the possible' (Stones, 2005, p. 122). Emphasis is placed on the constraints and opportunities imposed and offered by the structural elements within which the entrepreneur acts – a kind of zooming out (Nicolini, 2009) away from the practices that researcher is interested in.

It is, however, worth considering how to limit data collection scope at the macro level. Our experience suggests it is better to start from a particular topic/incident/action and trace back in time any related retrospective data at the macro level. For example, to understand why a small business manager made certain decisions, the researcher can explore questions to trace back (a) when this opportunity arose; (b) why; (c) how this opportunity presented itself; and (d) the manager's past experience of similar opportunities. For example, in our study within the wine industry, it was found that the owner-manager of our case company entered into cooperation with local vineyard owners. This, at first, seemed to be a practice which contrasted with the traditional adversarial nature of competition as found within the French wine industry. Actors typically try hard to protect their AOC appellations. On closer inspection, the decision of our case company was found to be based on the owner-manager's desire to internationalize his premium range of wine product. This meant using his best grapes from the 'terroir' which represented a smaller part of his vineyard hectarage. Collaboration, in this example, was perceived as a good way of leveraging resources. Sourcing grapes for his non-premium range from his neighbours allowed him to save his best grapes for his premium product range. From his networking with and learning from reputed geologists and oenologists, he knew that the 'terroir' of his smaller hectarage would produce premium grapes for producing a very high-quality wine which was expected to do well in the international market.

Consequently, in evidencing answers to questions, the researcher seeks to understand industry trends and national market conditions (a and b), internal organizational structure, strategizing processes, management systems and any changes to these in the past years (c) and questions the manager about their experience. Whilst the first two points relate to macro-level (external structures), the latter point (d) represents a type of internal structure (typification of things and drawing on previous experience). Point (c) combines both, as it represents what the organization set in place as priorities for growth (exporting, increased production, innovation, increased marketing) *and* the agents' knowledge of their own context (was it a deliberate decision to pursue internationalization based on the influence of formalized enablers or a decision linked to what other field actors were doing and thereby potentially meaning the business missing out on how the context can represent other opportunities for business growth?). Our wine industry example evidences a deliberate decision to internationalize based on a unique opportunity related to both the geography of the vineyard and the owner-manager's contextual knowledge and experience.

Unlike Giddens, Stones advocates for the use of the two types of methodological bracketing. By altering focus on both institutional and historical forces, and individual actions and practices, zooming in on and out of the agent-in-focus (Nicolini, 2009), researchers are better equipped to uncover any links between the two levels. It is important that the researcher carefully determines the boundaries of the action-horizons of the entrepreneurial agent in-situ so as to establish what they and/or the actors regard as the line between external and internal structures (Jack & Kholeif, 2007).

APPLYING SST IN EAP RESEARCH

A real value-adding application of SST concerns the meso-level ontology in-situ which allows the researcher to focus on the relative processual flow of entrepreneurial agents actively engaging in their structural context (Coad et al., 2016; Jack & Kholeif, 2007). This is made possible through the theoretical tools, concepts and vocabularies for exploring connections between levels; structures, agency, and practices and the outcomes of such practices. These levels are both informed by and inform the other. There are a variety of opportunities for researchers to conduct empirical work that can contribute to interpretative research in EaP either by adding to theory development or in applying that theory to new research studies.

EaP researchers can begin with a very specific research question concerned with one or more levels, and/or one or more elements of the structuration cycle. This then represents the starting point for exploring and expanding their investigation. Following the different points raised in the methodology section above, the researcher can then develop micro–meso–macro links, rather than limit their study to one aspect of the structuration cycle. Table 6.2 provides an example for observing EaP at one or more levels or structures from an example in the wine industry. It provides ideas for starting points, and what actions/structure/outcomes any exploration could involve. Other EaP examples might include a research focus on:

How and why do entrepreneurs transform and combine the various types of resources at their disposal?

The researcher's starting point could be the entrepreneur and their practices. Possible actions to examine could include meetings, decisions made during these communications, and justifications for resource allocation/use. The possible structures to observe to investigate the question might include formal and informal institutional trends, and using a variety of metrics. The outcomes to be examined could include continuity and transformation of business performance over time.

How do the institutional norms impact family succession practices?

A starting point might involve focusing on societal norms and the legal framework (including laws and taxes). Possible actions to examine could incorporate methods of ceding companies to family members, routines in passing on knowledge and experience. Potential structures to investigate might include the founding entrepreneur's experiences, regional and national family relationship norms, legal relief or taxation in changing ownership. Outcomes to examine might cover rate of succession at different stages of the SMEs' lifecycle, engagement in national and local networks, change of ownership structure.

What are the roles and mechanisms of entrepreneurship 'lobbying' agencies in supporting start-ups?

A starting point for this exploration might include a focus on the policies and procedures deployed by these agencies. Actions to examine might include talks and discussions during meetings, and informal communications between actors at this level. Structures to be investigated include cultural, political and economic change introduced into an industry or sector at the local level. The outcomes to examine could incorporate how change at local level influences national level changes or vice versa and/or how collective entrepreneurial agents' lobbying shapes national policies.

Returning to our wine industry example, institutional actors (for e.g. the wine-producing inter-professionals (CNIV), along with support from the Ministry of Agriculture and France AgriMer, have embarked on a National Plan against Vineyard Decline. The Plan translates the sector's willingness to act at all levels, in a concerted manner, with means to meet the challenges to combat the national decline of vineyards. A focus for an EaP research study might consider what this plan will mean for the practice of viticulture and the activities of winery managers, their power relations in-situ across and within the different producing regions of France.

SUMMARY AND CONCLUSIONS

This chapter presents SST (Stones, 2005) as an additional theoretical approach for exploring the EaP field and as a methodological guide for EaP research. The chapter introduces the quadripartite framework where SST is represented as a series of cycles. Each of these cycles involves four main elements: external structures, internal structure, active agency and outcomes. Structuration then becomes a framework for analysing empirical data and material. The value of SST for helping shape and guide practice research in entrepreneurship is presented through:

1. Emphasizing the different components of entrepreneurs' context. SST helps disentangle the different layers of the complex contextual background in which actions are implemented and how that implementation may be informed by wider contexts.
2. Advancing a structuration cycle model that makes explicit the processual unfolding of structuration over time. A structuration cycle may reproduce and maintain, or challenge and change existing structural conditions, external and/or internal. The effects may be intended or unintended.
3. Proposing methodological guidance to conduct empirical research through a focus on how entrepreneurial agents perceive and understand the constraints and possibilities that surround them (Stones & Turner, 2020; Coad et al., 2016).

Though not exclusively, SST methodology privileges a qualitative research design to understand and analyse the relations between the various elements/agents/structures in depth. It also provides a general approach to data collection and analysis.

The chapter explicates how empirical work might be carried out in EaP research using a reinforced version of Giddens' structuration theory. SST offers an 'ontology in-situ' which supports Giddens' 'ontology in general' since structure and action are not contemplated in abstract but studied in their concrete context. The chapter highlights SST as an alternative approach for observing EaP and as a promising means for the EaP researcher to study their field. For those who are interested in materiality, a development of SST in healthcare settings has incorporated material elements from Actor Network Theory (Greenhalgh & Stones, 2010). This theoretical development has also been empirically applied in the same settings (Greenhalgh et al., 2014a, 2014b, 2016).

REFERENCES

Adhikari, P., & Jayasinghe, K. (2017). 'Agents-in-focus' and 'agents-in-context': The strong structuration analysis of central government accounting practices and reforms in Nepal. *Accounting Forum*, *41*, 96–115.

Ahrens, T., & Chapman, C. S. (2007). Doing qualitative field research in management accounting: Positioning data to contribute to theory. In C. S. Chapman, A. G. Hopwood, & M. D. Shields (Eds.), *Handbook of Management Accounting Research* (vol. 1, pp. 299–318). Amsterdam: Elsevier.

Anderson, A. R., Dodd, S. D., & Jack, S. L. (2012a). Entrepreneurship as connecting: Some implications for theorizing and practice. *Management Decision*, *50*(5), 958–971.

Anderson, A. R., Jack, S. L., & Dodd, S. D. (2012b). The role of family members in entrepreneurial networks: Beyond the boundaries of the family firm. *Family Business Review*, *18*(2), 135–148.

Anderson A. R., & Starnawska, M. (2008). Research practices in entrepreneurship: Problems of defi-
nition, description and meaning. *International Journal of Entrepreneurship and Innovation*, *9*(4),
221–230.
Archer, M. S. (1995). *Realist Social Theory: The Morphogenetic Approach*. Cambridge: Cambridge
University Press.
Bhaskar, R. (1979). *The Possibility of Naturalism: A Philosophical Critique of the Contemporary Human
Sciences*. Atlantic Highlands, NJ: Humanities Press.
Brown, D. (2010). Strong structuration theory in educational research. Keynote presentation at La
Evaluación Formativa en el Contexto Internacional de la Convergencia Europea: V Congreso
Internacional de Evaluación Formativa en Docencia Universitaria, Universidad de Alcalá, Quadalajara,
Spain.
Champenois, C., Lefebvre, V., & Ronteau, S. (2020). Entrepreneurship as practice: Systematic literature
review of a nascent field. *Entrepreneurship & Regional Development*, *32*(3–4), 281–312.
Chatterjee, I., Kunwar, J., & den Hond, F. (2019). Anthony Giddens and structuration theory. In S. Clegg
& M. P. Cunha (Eds.), *Management, Organizations and Contemporary Social Theory* (pp. 60–79).
London: Routledge.
Chiasson, M., & Saunders, C. (2005). Reconciling diverse approaches to opportunity research using the
structuration theory. *Journal of Business Venturing*, *20*(6), 747–767.
Coad, A., Jack, L. J., & Kholeif, A. (2016). Strong structuration theory in accounting research.
Accounting, Auditing & Accountability Journal, *29*(7), 1138–1144.
Cohen, I. J. (1989). *Structuration Theory: Anthony Giddens and the Constitution of Social Life*.
Basingstoke: Macmillan.
Cowton, J., & Dopson, S. (2002). Foucault's prison? Management control in an automotive distributor.
Management Accounting Research, *13*(2), 191–213.
den Hond, F., Boersma, K., Heres, L., Kroes, E. H. J., & van Oirschot, E. (2012). Giddens à la carte?
Appraising empirical applications of structuration theory in management and organization studies.
Journal of Political Power, *5*(2), 239–264.
Dodd, S. D., & Anderson, A. R. (2007). Mumpsimus and the mything of the individualistic entrepreneur.
International Small Business Journal, *25*(4), 341–360.
Elbasha, T., & Avetisyan, E. (2018). A framework to study strategizing activities at the field level: The
example of CSR rating agencies. *European Management Journal*, *36*(1), 38–46.
Elbasha, T., & Wright, A. (2017). Reconciling structure and agency in strategy-as-practice research:
Towards a strong-structuration theory approach. *M@n@gement*, *20*(2), 107–128.
Feldman, M. S., & Orlikowski, W. J. (2011). Theorizing practice and practicing theory. *Organization
Science*, *22*(5), 1240–1253.
Feldman, M., & Worline, M. (2016). The practicality of practice theory. *Academy of Management
Learning and Education*, *15*(2), 304–324.
Franco, C. M., Feeney, O., Quinn, M., & Hiebl, M. R. W. (2017). Position practices of the present-day
CFO: A reflection on historic roles at Guinness, 1920–1945. *Accounting Magazine*, *20*(1), 55–62.
Gartner, W. B. (1988). Who is an entrepreneur? Is the wrong question. *American Journal of Small
Business*, *12*(4), 11–32.
Gedajlovic, E., Honig, B., Moore, C. B., Tyge Payne, M., & Wright, M. (2013). Social capital and entre-
preneurship: A schema and research agenda. *Entrepreneurship Theory and Practice*, *37*(3), 455–478.
Giddens, A. (1979). *Central Problems in Social Theory: Action, Structure and Contradictions in Social
Analysis*. Berkeley: University of California Press.
Giddens, A. (1984). *The Constitution of Society*. Berkeley: University of California Press.
Giddens, A. (1989). *Sociology*. Cambridge: Polity Press.
Greenhalgh, T., Shaw, S., Wherton, J., Hughes, G., Lynch, J., A'Court, C., Hinder, S., Fahy, N., Byrne,
E., Finlayson, A., Sorell, T., Procter, R., & Stones, R. (2016). SCALS: A fourth-generation study of
assisted living technologies in their organisational, social, political and policy context. *BMJ Open*,
6(2). doi:10.1136/bmjopen-2015-010208.
Greenhalgh, T., & Stones, R. (2010). Theorising big IT programmes in healthcare: Strong structuration
theory meets actor-network theory. *Social Science & Medicine*, *70*, 1285–1294.
Greenhalgh, T., Stones, R., & Swinglehurst, D. (2014a). Choose and book: A sociological analysis of
'resistance' to an expert system. *Social Science & Medicine*, *104*, 210–219.

Greenhalgh, T., Swinglehurst, D., & Stones, R. (2014b). Rethinking resistance to 'big IT': A sociological study of why and when healthcare staff do not use nationally mandated information and communication technologies. *Health Services and Delivery Research, 2*(39), 1–86.

Harris, E., Northcott, D., Elmassri, M. M., & Huikku, J. (2016). Theorising strategic investment decision-making using strong structuration theory. *Accounting, Auditing & Accountability Journal, 29*(7), 1177–1203.

Jack, L. (2017). Strong structuration theory and management accounting research. *Advances in Scientific and Applied Accounting, 10*(2), 211–223.

Jack, S. L., & Anderson, A. R. (2008). Role typologies for enterprising education: The professional artisan. *Journal of Small Business Development, 5*(2), 259–273.

Jack, S. L., Dodd, S. D., & Anderson, A. R. (2008). Change and the development of entrepreneurial networks over time: A processual perspective. *Entrepreneurship & Regional Development, 20*(2), 125–159.

Jack, S. L., & Kholeif, A. O. R. (2007). Introducing strong structuration theory for informing qualitative case studies in organization, management and accounting research. *Qualitative Research in Organizations and Management: An International Journal, 2*(3), 208–225.

Jarzabkowski, P., Kaplan, S., Seidl, D., & Whittington, R. (2016). On the risks of studying practices in isolation: Linking what, who and how in strategy research. *Strategic Organization, 14*(3), 248–259.

Johannisson, B. (2011). Towards a practice theory of entrepreneuring. *Small Business Economics, 36*(2), 135–150.

Johannisson, B. (2016). Limits to and prospects of entrepreneurship education in the academic context. *Entrepreneurship & Regional Development, 28*(5–6), 403–423.

Joseph, G. (2006). Understanding developments in the management information value chain from a structuration theory framework. *International Journal of Accounting Information Systems, 7*(4), 319–341.

Karataş-Özkan, M., Anderson, A. R., Fayolle, A., Howells, J., & Condor, R. (2014). Understanding entrepreneurship: Challenging dominant perspectives and theorizing entrepreneurship through new postpositivist epistemologies. *Journal of Small Business Management, 52*(4), 589–593.

Kholeif, A. O. R., & Jack, L. (2019). The paradox of embedded agency from a strong structuration perspective. *Qualitative Research in Accounting & Management, 16*(1), 60–92.

Kouamé, S., & Langley, A. (2018). Relating microprocesses to macro-outcomes in qualitative strategy process and practice research. *Strategic Management Journal, 39*, 559–581.

Langley, A., Smallman, C., Tsoukas, H., & Van de Ven, A. (2013). Process studies of change in organization and management: Unveiling temporality, activity and flow. *Academy of Management Journal, 56*(1), 1–13.

MacKay, B. R., & Chia, R. (2013). Choice, chance, and unintended consequences in strategic change: A process understanding of the rise and fall of NorthCo Automotive. *Academy of Management Journal, 56*(1), 208–230.

Makrygiannakis, G., & Jack, L. (2018). Designing a conceptual methodology for structuration research. *Meditari Accountancy Research, 26*(1), 70–87.

Manders, T. T., Wieczorek, A. A., & Verbong, G. G. (2020). Complexity, tensions, and ambiguity of intermediation in a transition context: The case of Connecting Mobility. *Environmental Innovation and Societal Transitions, 34*, 183–208.

McKeever, E., Jack, S., & Anderson, A. R. (2015). Embedded entrepreneurship in the creative reconstruction of place. *Journal of Business Venturing, 30*(1), 50–56.

Mellahi, K., & Sminia, H. (2009). The frontiers of strategic management. *International Journal of Management Reviews, 11*(1), 1–7.

Mouzelis, N. P. (1991). *Back to Sociological Theory: The Construction of Social Orders*. Basingstoke: Macmillan.

Nicolini, D. (2009). Zooming in and out: Studying practices by switching theoretical lenses and trailing connections. *Organization Studies, 30*(12), 1391–1418.

Nicolini, D. (2012). *Practice Theory, Work & Organization: An Introduction*. Oxford: Oxford University Press.

Nordqvist, M., & Melin, L. (2010). The promise of the strategy as practice perspective for family business strategy research. *Journal of Family Business Strategy, 1*, 15–25.

Orlikowski, W. J. (2010). The sociomateriality of organisational life: Considering technology in management research. *Cambridge Journal of Economics*, *34*(1), 125–141.

Parker, J. (2000). *Structuration*. Buckingham: Open University Press.

Price, C., Green, W., & Suhomlinova, O. (2019). Twenty-five years of national health IT: Exploring strategy, structure, and systems in the English NHS. *Journal of the American Medical Informatics Association*, *26*(3), 188–197.

Shepherd, D. (2015). Party on! A call for entrepreneurship research that is more interactive, activity based, cognitively hot, compassionate and prosocial. *Journal of Business Venturing*, *30*(4), 489–507.

Sminia, H. (2009). Process research in strategy formation: Theory, methodology and relevance. *International Journal of Management Reviews*, *21*, 267–291.

Steyaert, C. (2007). Entrepreneuring as a conceptual attractor? A review of process theories in 20 years of entrepreneurship studies. *Entrepreneurship & Regional Development*, *19*(6), 453–477.

Stones, R. (1996). *Sociological Reasoning: Towards a Past-Modern Sociology*. Basingstoke: Macmillan.

Stones, R. (2005). *Structuration Theory*. Basingstoke: Palgrave Macmillan.

Stones, R. (2012). Causality, contextual frames and international migration: Combining strong structuration theory, critical realism and textual analysis. IMI Working Papers. Oxford: International Migration Institute, University of Oxford.

Stones, R., Botterill, K., Lee, M., & O'Reilly, K. (2019). One world is not enough: The structured phenomenology of lifestyle migrants in East Asia. *British Journal of Sociology*, *70*, 44–69.

Stones, R., & Turner, B. S. (2020). Successful societies: Decision-making and the quality of attentiveness. *The British Journal of Sociology*, *71*(1), 183–199.

Suddaby, R., Bitektine, A., & Haack, P. (2017). Legitimacy. *Academy of Management Annals*, *11*, 451–478.

Thompson, N., Verduyn, K., Stam, E., & Gartner, W. B. (2016). Entrepreneurship as practice: Grounding contemporary practice theory into entrepreneurship studies. *Entrepreneurship & Regional Development*, *28*(9–10), 813–816.

Thrift, N. (1985). Bear and mouse or bear and tree? Anthony Giddens' reconstitution of social theory. *Sociology*, *19*(4), 609–623.

Tran, H. T., & Santarelli, E. (2014). Capital constraints and the performance of entrepreneurial firms in Vietnam. *Industrial and Corporate Change*, *23*(3), 827–864.

Van de Ven, A. H. (1992). Suggestions for studying strategy process: A research note. *Strategic Management Journal*, *13*, 169–188.

Watson, T. J. (2013). Entrepreneurship in action: Bringing together the individual, organizational and institutional dimensions of entrepreneurial action. *Entrepreneurship & Regional Development*, *25*(5–6), 404–422.

Whittington, R. (1996). Strategy as practice. *Long Range Planning*, *29*, 731–735.

Whittington, R. (2006). Completing the practice turn in strategy research. *Organization Studies*, *27*, 613–634.

7. Collective intentionality in entrepreneurship-as-practice

Steffen Farny and Ewald Kibler

INTRODUCTION

One great promise of the entrepreneurship-as-practice (EAP) perspective is that it helps advance understanding entrepreneurial activities and processes *within* an existing social reality. In most entrepreneurship research, social contexts are recognized mainly as sites or containers where entrepreneurial behavior takes place. To offer a conceptual alternative, EAP draws on practice theory to explain entrepreneurial processes as a nexus of actions that are linked through shared understandings and a teleoaffective structure (Schatzki, 2002; Thompson & Byrne, 2020). As such, entrepreneurial practices are "embodied, materially mediated arrays of human activity centrally organized around *shared* practical understanding" (Schatzki, 2001, p. 2, emphasis added). It follows that the determination of people's actions is attributed to something beyond the individual, and it "is not a set of properties of actors. It is, instead, the property of a practice" (Schatzki, 2002, p. 80). We therefore see the need to problematize conceptualizations of intentionality of the acting agent within the practice ontology of EAP.

Specifically, we argue in this chapter that the time is ripe for questioning *what entrepreneurship practices are*. Put differently, *what makes a practice a practice in EAP?* While versions of practice theory, e.g. Giddens' theory of structuration, Bourdieu's praxeology or Schatzki's theory of social practices, have been prominent for decades (Reckwitz, 2002), entrepreneurship scholars have only recently begun to systematically investigate entrepreneurship as a version of practice theory (cf. Johannisson, 2011; Thompson et al., 2020). So far, and to the best of our knowledge, this body of entrepreneurship research has mainly focused on what entrepreneurs do and what practices are good for – more evaluative and teleological questions – and failed to advance discussions of its practice ontology.

In addressing this challenge, we find the work by Raimo Tuomela (2007, 2013) particularly useful because it offers us a "we-perspective" in which people's practices are conceptually understood as representatives of a larger entity, a group. As Schatzki (2002, p. 84) emphasizes:

> who the participants in a practice are is only contingently related to people's opinions on the matter. Anyone who performs actions that are part of a nexus of activities organized by a collection of interlinked understandings, rules, and teleoaffective structure is by that fact alone a participant in that practice. This fact proscribes neither the contentiousness of judgments about who is a participant nor the use of explicit criteria (if any) to admit people into the practice.

As such, the intention of any performing individual to enact, or participate in, a practice, is related to something beyond the individual actor, a group. Group membership is here broadly defined as a person acting on behalf of a hierarchical group (e.g. large cooperation or state body), non-hierarchical groups (e.g. community, team, interest group), as well as people acting in collective dilemma situations (people with overlapping private interests).

Tuomela (2013) argues that a person's individual behavior can be described in intentional agency terms as a group agent (similar to how scholars usually describe the behavior of individual agents). In this case, acting always appears in *reference to a group*, whereby the form and strength of a person's beliefs and desires can occur in three broad forms of collective intentionality. In *shared intentions* an individual's reason to act together is primarily driven by private motives and happens to be similar or in line with another person's motives. With *joint intentions* people jointly act as part of the group by both being collectively committed to and mutually aware of acting jointly. It is thus necessary that individuals intend to do their own share and are, at the same time, certain the other does their part too. Last, *we-intentions* are a particular, strongly collective form of joint intentions, in which individuals intend to jointly perform if and only if one truly believes that group members collectively agree with the attitudinal state 'We will do X together as a group'. To varying degrees, collective intentionality unites the group members and 'cements' them together in all contexts where they function as group members, for example, in the contexts of cooperation (Tuomela, 2013, pp. ix–xi). This form of reasoning turns the individual acting agent into a "functional group agent". Conceptually, the acting agent is a representative acting for the group rather than a private point of view. "Simplistically put, the members act jointly with the purpose of achieving some shared goals according to some common beliefs, thereby functioning as a coherent, uniform unit" (Tuomela, 2013, p. 22).

Since EAP builds on the premise that entrepreneuring is a genuinely collective phenomenon (Johannisson, 2011), essentially composed of collaborative activities (Thompson et al., 2020), we argue it is worthwhile to develop our conceptual understanding of the functional group agent. Our chapter presents a middle-range approach (Merton, 1968 [1949]) by complementing Tuomela's theory with insights from our own research on collaborative forms of business venturing, such as entrepreneurial ecosystems (O'Shea et al., 2021), sustainability-oriented cooperatives (Farny et al., 2019b) or community-based enterprising (Farny et al., 2019a). By situating Tuomela's theory in the context of different cases and settings where we observed group agents employing joint entrepreneurial engagement, we particularly seek to develop a new theoretical understanding, resulting in three main propositions – *collectivity for, in and as joint practice* – which we hope informs further conceptual and empirical work on collective action in the field of entrepreneurship research.

Our chapter generates two contributions to the entrepreneurship literature. First, we suggest taking the (intuitive) idea that agents enact practices as functional group agents more seriously in the further development of the EAP perspective. This helps us move away from the dominant investigative focus of the individual entrepreneur to an analysis of entrepreneurship as an "interactively enacted shared reality" (Johannisson, 2011, p. 142). So far, the EAP literature has emphasized sharedness and togetherness but not yet sufficiently clarified the ontological and conceptual foundations of a reference group, or collective, inherent in practices. To this, we clarify three forms of collective intentionality in entrepreneurial practices, by distinguishing *shared intentionality (I-mode), joint intentionality (weak We-mode)* and *We-intentionality (strong We-mode)*. By adopting such a 'we-perspective', one ascertains that practices in EAP are conceptualized via people's shared understanding, in line with the practice ontology.

Second, our chapter unpacks and disambiguates various notions of intentionality at the joint and collaborative action level, i.e. collective enterprising (cf. Johannisson, 2011). Dominant entrepreneurial intention models suggest that to determine if a person will take entrepreneurial action to start a business is to inquire about their intention to do so (Van Gelderen et al., 2015), and the intention holds as a strong precondition for the realization of action, independent of the social, regional and institutional context (Kibler et al., 2014). However, when conceptualized at a collective level, the intention–action relationship is less clear, as collective intentionality sometimes refers to "an intention ascribed to a group or to a collective and sometimes to the group members collectively" (Tuomela, 2013, p. 63). Distinguishing three forms of collective intentionality allows us to explain (1) *how* and *why* shared intentionality can act as an important determinant *for* collective enterprising action, and (2) how and why joint and collective intentionality develop *in/through* and manifest *as* group ethos in collective entrepreneurial engagement. Put differently, our we-perspective framework suggests that, at the collective enterprising level, research requires a new theoretical and ontological understanding of intentionality in relation to collective action. The benefit of building on a collective level conceptualization is that a group agent has the capacity to act as a unit, making it easier to discuss interaction and interdependencies between various groups and social structures.

Taken together, we hope our work serves as an inspiration for the further development of entrepreneurship (practice) theory at the collective level (e.g. Cardon et al., 2017; Farny et al., 2019a; Kibler & Muñoz, 2020; Sarasvathy & Ramesh, 2019; Wigger & Shepherd, 2020).

UNDERSTANDING COLLECTIVE INTENTIONALITY THROUGH TUOMELA'S WE-PERSPECTIVE

In this section we seek to interrogate a 'we-perspective' for EAP, by deconstructing the nature of entrepreneurial intentions motivating and preceding enterprising practice. To this Tuomela suggests that in non-group settings, a person's intentionality is an *intrinsic* part of practices, because of the biological and bodily nature of human beings. However, since groups are not biological entities and real only in the sense of a social system capable of action, *intentionality of groups is a result of the intentionality of its members*. Hence, "the intentional properties of group agents, then, are not intrinsic but *extrinsic* in the sense that they are based on the members' (and possibly other people's) collective attribution of attitudes to the group" (Tuomela, 2013, p. 23). This speaks to the practice ontology of EAP, where "every practice implies a particular routinized mode of intentionality, i.e. of wanting or desiring certain things and avoiding others" (Reckwitz, 2002, p. 254). Building the connection, we understand Tuomela as suggesting that all practices imply, or are rooted in, a form of collective intentionality, which therefore can only be understood in reference to a functional group agent.

Following Tuomela, we distinguish three types of collective intentionality in this chapter: shared intentionality, joint intentionality and we-intentionality. We speak of *shared intentionality* when an individual's reason to act together is primarily driven by private motives and happens to be similar or in line with another person's motives. *Joint intentionality* refers to people jointly acting as part of a group by both being collectively committed to and mutually aware of acting jointly. Last, we talk about *we-intentionality* when individuals mutually agree with the attitudinal state 'We will do X together as a group'. In Tuomela's own words, these three forms of intentionality can be distinguished as "a group agent's intention, a joint intention ascribed to several individuals collectively, and a we-intention understood below as a kind of individual 'slice' of those individuals' joint intention and involving a participant's intention to take part in the jointly intended collective action" (Tuomela, 2013, p. 63). In all three types of collective intentionality, people's motives and reasons to act are conceptually understood in reference to a group, analytically a 'functional group agent'. This means that the intention notions interrelate and are dependent on the group, in contrast to purely private intentions not involving a group reference.

Tuomela argues that one can talk of people's shared, joint and we-intentionality, and not just their personal purposes, when three conditions apply: *group reason* (e.g. a unifying reason for entrepreneurs, collaborators and other practitioners to participate), a *collectivity condition* for all participants involved in joint activities (i.e. awareness of being or feeling in the 'same boat'), and *collective commitment* (i.e. the result of joint intentionality and participants' reason to be involved). For analytical purposes, it is thus important to describe the group reason, collectivity condition and collective commitment that constitute one's intentionality in a specific instance. In simple terms, the three conditions help understand how individual actors' intentions relate to (and overlap or conflict with) one another in their role as group members.

Together these three conditions make up the **intention state** to explain the strength of collective intentionality. In entrepreneurship research the emphasis is often placed on the intention content, such as the type of cooperation between actors. Yet, this intention content of cooperation can have different collective intention strengths, an important analytical nuance which would otherwise be lost. Hence, the explanation of the intention state, which presupposes the content, helps provide analytical depth by distinguishing strengths of collective intentionality (compare Table 7.1). As Tuomela (2013, p. 63) clarifies, "it is primarily on the 'jointness' level that the three criteria of collective commitment, group reasons, and the collectivity condition interact to bind together interdependent individual actions into normatively coherent and cohesive group action. From the group's point of view, the members must function together 'as parts of an organism'—*as a group*". To study and determine intentionality, Tuomela suggests looking at both the intention content and the attitude sense (the reference to a 'we'). Thus, differences in intention strength are conceptually linked to the intention state and can be analytically revealed via the group reason, collectivity condition and collective commitment (Table 7.1).

The weakest kind of collective intentionality is *shared intention*, in Tuomela's terms also called a pro-group I-mode intention, that depends fully on the intention content. For an individual, the reason to act together is primarily driven by private motives and happens to be similar or in line with another person's motives. For example, consider the case of a fallen tree blocking a road, which cannot be removed by a single person. When two or more drivers realize that they cannot continue their journeys without removing the tree from the street they intend to act together strictly because they have the same private objective, the continuation of their journey. Their intention does not contain a group reasoning that assigns attitudinal value to a collaborative act by their status of being a group member. We thus cannot argue for a collectivity condition nor a collective commitment in pro-group I-mode intentions. Strictly speaking, a collective intention state is therefore not satisfied, despite the shared intention content, hence the reference to 'I' in the concept (Tuomela, 2013). A person with a pro-group I-mode intention intends to act *because of* the right kind of group reason (reflecting the intention content). The formula for shared intentionality in joint action is:

(1) I have the intention to do X. (2) You have the same intention to do X. Therefore (3) we are both privately committed to our joint performance (as a group) of X.

Table 7.1   *Three kinds of intentionality in joint action*

		Shared Intentionality	Joint Intentionality	We-Intentionality
	Tuomela's technical terminology	Pro-group I-intentionality / Pro-group I-mode we-intentionality	We-mode joint-intentionality	We-mode we-intentionality
Intention content	Case Example	Two drivers from opposite directions need to jointly remove a fallen tree from the road	Professors teaching a joint seminar but independently grading assignments	Two people plan to paint a house together
	Reasoning for Group Formation	Contingent upon the shared intention content (I-mode reasoning)	Contingent upon belonging to the group (We-mode reasoning)	Contingent upon a match of private and groups' intentions (strong We-mode reasoning)
	Implicit reasoning of individuals	"What should I do as a private person acting in part for the group?"	"What should our group do?"	"What should I do as a group member as my part of our group's action?"
	Reasoning for Group Formation	Contingent upon the shared intention content (I-mode reasoning)	Contingent upon belonging to the group (We-mode reasoning)	Contingent upon a match of private and groups' intentions (strong We-mode reasoning)
Intention state	*Group Reason*	Because of the shared intention content, to continue their journeys, a group reason exists	The shared intention content of the group is to educate students	The shared intention content of the group is to see to it that the house gets painted
	Collectivity Condition	Non-existent	Pre-analytic collective acceptance of acting qua group member and not independently thereof	Pre-analytic collective acceptance of acting qua group member and believing that this intention is shared with (most) other members
	Collective Commitment	Non-existent	Each group member (directly or indirectly) participates in jointly educating students in reference to the university ethos	Each person intends to perform his/her share of the painting, knowing that the other one(s) will do the same in reference to their mutual belief in the group reason

Source: Inspired by Tuomela (2013).

A stronger kind of intentionality for joint action is jointly held intentions, in short, *joint intentions*. Joint intentions refer to a situation where it is necessary and sufficient for two or more people to intend to jointly act as part of the group by both being collectively committed to and *mutually aware* of acting jointly. Joint intention contains a circularity in that intention to act together must make reference to joint intentions, thereby establishing a collectivity condition for collective action that does not exist in pro-group I-intentionality. For example, a professor has the duty to teach a joint seminar and needs to grade the final assignments. She or he is motivated to do the grading work alone, but in another sense practices the grading as part of a larger activity jointly with other staff (Tuomela, 2013). Therefore, the professor functions as a group member for a particular group reason, here to promote the ethos of the university. Tuomela (2013, p. 76) clarifies that "we are functioning as group members for this group reason, we are necessarily 'in the same boat' concerning our joint performance of X. The joint intention is necessarily satisfied for you, for me, and for our dyad if and only if it is satisfied for you and for me. We are also collectively committed to satisfying our joint intention". Thus, in the case of joint intentions the important element is the having the same attitude sense. For an individual, joint intention requires both doing one's own part but also making sure, even pressure, the other one to do his/her part as well to be satisfied with the joint action. In analytical terms, we can say a person truly acting based on joint intention acts qua group member (Tuomela, 2013). It presupposes that each person accepts the We-mode group reasoning (and thus the intention content) as the condition for collective commitment to joint action. The formula for collectively accepted We-mode joint intentions in joint action is:

(1) We will do X jointly. (2) I am one of "us" (the present group). Therefore, (3) I will do my part of our joint performance of X.

The strongest kind of intentionality for joint action is *we-intentions* that generate reasons to function as a group member. We-intentions are "full-blown joint intentions [that] exist as *relational properties* between two or more individuals collectively viewed as forming a group, and individual agents are the only initiators of causal chains in this context" (Tuomela, 2013, p. 63). This important difference to joint intentions suggests that we-intentions are not subjective states of an individual but a 'slice' of group members' joint intentions. We-intensions are a particular, strongly collective form of joint intentions, in which individuals intend to jointly perform *if and only if* one truly believes that group members collectively agree with the attitudinal state 'We will do X together as a group'. Also, individuals have to believe that the group mutually believes in the effect of the joint action opportunity and, as a result, all will do a joint performance of X. For example:

> our collectively accepted intention to get the house painted provides me with a reason, indeed a group reason, which I would not have otherwise; and I intend to perform my share of the painting at least in part because of this group reason. [...] In addition to the presence of this group reason, there is also collective commitment to act for this reason; viz., we have voluntarily committed ourselves to seeing to it that the house gets painted as agreed. This collective commitment also entails for both parties the intention to see to it that mutual awareness of the satisfaction of the intention will eventually be achieved, or, if it turns out that it cannot be satisfied, to see to it that this fact will become mutually known. According to the collectivity condition, if the intention is satisfied, then it is necessarily satisfied for both of us. (Tuomela, 2013, p. 69)

We-intentions thus provide a world-to-mind fit, in which group members collectively accept 'We will do X together as a group', that satisfies all three intention state criteria, i.e. group reason, collectivity condition and collective commitment. In this intention state, the specific content of the intention is secondary. In short, the formula for we-intentionality is:

(1) I: We will perform X jointly. (2) You: We will perform X jointly. Therefore, (3) we both will do our parts of our joint performance of X.

In summary, Tuomela's work provides a generic understanding of intentionality both foundational to understanding practices in EAP as well as presupposing different types of collective action. Resembling only weakly collective I-mode intentionality, shared intentionality arises from sharing a particular *intention content* at a specific time and place. In turn, joint and we-intentionality contain a mutual awareness of the *intention state* and are thus experienced as more strongly collective forms of intentionality. Based on the above taxonomy, we argue that Tuomela's 'we-perspective' can be adapted to understand joint entrepreneurial practice. In the following we develop a practice theoretical account of joint action of human collectives.

COLLECTIVE INTENTIONALITY IN JOINT ENTREPRENEURIAL PRACTICE

In practice theories, collectivity and collective action is an implicit assumption inherent in the constitution of social practices. For example, Welch and Yates (2018, p. 298) argue that theories of practice have been generative for developing an understanding of dispersed collective activity to capture a "socially, spatially and temporally patterned character of practices and arrangements". In all its variations regarding the meaning and motivations of the various individual practices, such as getting to work, making a living, or feeding a family, there is a *shared element* that constitutes something as a practice (Welch & Yates, 2018). This constituting element relates to the people's shared, collective, practical understanding of activities and material arrangements that specific practices entail (Schatzki, 2001). In other terms, collectivity in its broader meaning – i.e. the joint experience of sociality, (omni)present in everyday life, its various forms of interactions and encounters – is a constitutive element of practices.

In this section, we build on the three kinds of intentionality to theorize an alternative practice foundation in dispersed, joint, and collective actions in entrepreneurship. We argue that all three types of intentionality possess an important role in developing a we-perspective in EAP, as we seek to illustrate in the following vignette. The vignette draws on insights from our recent study (together with Simon Down) that examines entrepreneurs' institutional creation practices as we witnessed them in the response and recovery to a major disaster in Haiti (Farny et al., 2019a).

Vignette 1. In the midst of disorder and despair, Gabi and Steve, two social entrepreneurs operating in the region, began improvising in the Limonade community immediately after a devastating earthquake had flattened most parts of the capital region. Facing similar private issues, a **shared intention** drew in additional community members to help in Gabi and Steve's rather dispersed improvising activities. The two entrepreneurs' practices were quickly recognized as being in line with motives of the local mayor and some locally operating international organizations, all aiming for the provision of disaster relief. Thus, due to their **joint intentions**, these stakeholders united in the entrepreneurs' needs assessment, advocating and leading work. Quickly, the joint enterprising actions led to a visible and coordinated disaster response, leading to a feeling of security and compassionate empathy in some community circles. As the two entrepreneurs further adjusted their enterprising practices during the recovery process, they were able to build and develop a strong level of collective trust and a collective vision for Limonade. Thus, when they started mobilizing engagement and synergizing operations between various local parties, **we-intentions** activated groups, such as the Rafaval cooperative, to coordinate their food processing efforts with the social entrepreneurs. It was clear for both parties that it was only if they collectively engaged in some enterprising activities that they could offer and further develop lasting solutions in Limonade.

In this vignette, we see interesting clues suggesting that advancing our conceptualizations of the *functional group agent* and understanding of the form of collective intentionality motivating and justifying practice enactment can be a fruitful way to explain whether people engage in *dispersed, joint,* or *collective* enterprising action. To improvise together is recognized as beneficial in some dispersed enterprising practice, in several circumstances, when individuals have overlapping private concerns (I-mode intentionality), such as organizing food for everyone after a disaster. In this case the group is neither formalized not yet known, but the improvising practices establish a reason to act as a part of this functional group agent. In contrast, joint and we-intentions formed around Gabi and Steve after they had established a level of trust and personal ties with many community members. Synergizing practices contain strongly collective we-intentions that serve as justification for people to substantively invest into a collective enterprising effort. This is recognized by all members acting on behalf of the group in the synergizing practice, thus creating a strong bond between group members (We-mode intentionality).

In the following we will draw on additional empirical insights to further elaborate our arguments and to develop more focused propositions on the relationship between the forms of collective intentions and differences in joint practices.

Shared intentions. In a previous study (O'Shea et al., 2021) of the purposive creation of an entrepreneurial ecosystem around nanocellulose in Finland, we identified various stakeholders' private motives to engage in co-intuiting, co-interpreting and co-integrating practices with the objective to develop a novel ecosystem serving each stakeholder and the region as a whole. In our study, we argued that shared sustainability intention operates as a fundamental enabler in progressing from mere opportunity beliefs to a greater level of opportunity confidence. Regarding the form of collective intentionality, the research team facilitated the co-creation of feasible products and services. In analytical terms, we thus emphasized the presence of a group reason in our practices which would bring people together in the first place, as exemplified in this vignette:

Vignette 2. At various stages of the ecosystem creation project, members of the project team facilitated dialogue and discussion through showrooms, exhibitions and public workshops. Exhibited were for example various sturdy colorful molds, a longer piece of gown with the famous Unikko design from Marimekko as well as lab samples showing the structures of the fiber. The team practiced co-intuiting, for example, in the interdisciplinary Cellulife workshop. Besides creating awareness of the stage of nanocellulose, the reason for the series of co-creation practices was to create a common vision for the future of Finland. Even though the diverse set of participants from private sector, civic society and university was changing, individuals engaged in these co-creation practices because of their overlapping private interests in contributing towards a more sustainable future for the country, as one participant stressed: "The big driver [to join the co-creation workshop] was to develop new added value uses for wood-based biomass in Finland because wood-based biomass is the biggest natural raw material source in Finland, or the only one, if you do not count the water". Practicing co-imagining in which products wood could replace plastic, such as bike frames, acoustic panels and medical castes, emerged around a group reason of developing feasible products around nanocellulose technologies. In few instances, the joint co-creation practices initiated the formation of joint intentionality of a few interdisciplinary teams who continued these developments in isolation. But, at a network or ecosystem level, the design practices of the research team were purely based on a unifying group reason, here shared sustainability intentions.

At the time, we did not specify that the sustainability intentions, at least originally, resembled "shared intention rather than joint intention in the I-mode case, because the collective commitment and the other unity-creating criterial elements of the we-mode are not present; the members are not 'glued' together in a strong sense of jointness" (Tuomela, 2013, p. 63). The ecosystem acts as the functional group agent in this case. As such, stakeholders opted to join ecosystem-forming events with the purpose to develop a new sustainability-oriented ecosystem that would help each member develop feasible products and services around nanocellulose technologies for themselves and survive in a competitive market. The stakeholders' shared intentions became evident for example in the reluctance of firms and research organizations to share patents and most recent research findings that could become the content for developing collective commitment and group membership. As the study shows, it took the coordinated effort and a series of interventions to create a stronger group reason and collective commitment that would resemble joint intentions so that people would assign value to belonging to this sustainable entrepreneurial ecosystem. In sum, mostly shared intentions served to attract stakeholders to exchange events and engage in co-intuiting, co-interpreting and co-integrating practices because of people's overlapping private motives (e.g. presenting their recent nanocellulose inventions and innovations in a joint exhibition).

Proposition 1 – I-mode intentionality for joint action: *Based on people's overlapping private interests in a particular intention content, shared intentions are likely to motivate people's joint entrepreneurial engagement.*

Joint intentions. In our study (Farny et al., 2019b) on entrepreneurial practices aiming to secure volunteer retention, we scrutinized prosocial entrepreneurs' and volunteers' joint intentions to engage in modern cooperative enterprises trying to lead the sustainability transition in the food and energy sectors. Our starting point was entrepreneurial groups who offered a compelling group reason to attract volunteers: only by working together, the cooperative is able to provide sustainable solutions to aspects of daily life that directly benefit the local population. We then analyzed the specific practices to manage organizational tensions apparent in sustainability-oriented ventures. We discovered that the entrepreneurs effectively narrated the cooperative endeavor as an overarching group reason that can only be achieved through group membership, illustrated in this vignette on 'La Ruche qui dit Oui!' (The Food Assembly) case.

Vignette 3. The founders Guilhem and Marc-David initiated their sustainable cooperative The Food Assembly to connect farmers and consumers directly to encourage local food distribution and consumers. Untypical for online platforms, the founders envisioned their enterprise to foster the emergence of several thousand micro-communities where people feel connected to one another, as they explained in one interview: "There were also always several volunteers who had some issues, often something psychological, for whom The Food Assembly was an oasis. I think it is also the intention to create a place where everybody feels comfortable". In organizing regular pop-up markets, their

Food Assemblies, they organized shopping experiences beyond typical transactions where a goal was to meet local producers and realize the pains and needs of local producers. Therefore they practiced energizing volunteers to organize these community-building encounters as they stressed: "You have to motivate core volunteer members of the community because they are going to help the community a lot, they are going to support it, they are going to participate in community activities, and once the community is there, there are more and more activities together, like visits to farms, special events, and special produce tastings. So, it's starting to be like a community place in a neighborhood but an easy one without too many constraints." The entrepreneurs effectively used the vehicle of volunteering, which here contains a place-based collective commitment, in organizing the Assemblies.

In all enterprise cases, the entrepreneurs implicitly accepted that all activities would occur via membership of the enterprise, satisfying the collectivity condition of joint intentions. For example, they had to coordinate new projects with volunteers as they had implemented a shared ownership structure. Taken together, opting to be part of and lead a community-based enterprise (collectivity condition) with the objective to provide more sustainable food and energy products and services (group reason), the entrepreneurs possessed a collective commitment to jointly act as a member of the cooperative. The cooperative enterprise thus acted as the functional group agent in these practices, as all enterprising practices were enacted on behalf of the group members belonging to the cooperative. As the study shows, the social entrepreneurs applied duality-focused and emotion-focused practices to maintain volunteer engagement despite experiencing conflicting organizational tensions.

Proposition 2 – Weak We-mode intentionality in joint action: *Based on people's collective commitment to the group's intention content, joint intentions are likely to be formed in and justify people's joint entrepreneurial engagement.*

We-intentions. In our study (Farny et al., 2019a) of community practices to recover from an earthquake (see also **Vignette 1**), we identified we-intentionality among a group of social entrepreneurs and several community members motivating the purposive creation of new community arrangements. Initially, we were surprised by people's willingness to contribute to joint efforts beyond their immediate daily tasks and work, in light of the turmoil present in post-disaster areas. Our analysis revealed that resourceful social entrepreneurs elicited collective emotional experiences that aligned people's concerns and objectives (Salmela, 2014). As such, their rather mundane disaster recovery practices, such as collaborating, reflecting and valorizing, provided a strong group reason: by joining this group effort we can together rebuild and even improve the daily life in our community. The social entrepreneurs did not get tired of reinforcing the necessity of people joining in order to progress with disaster recovery, thereby building a collectivity condition for people to join these practices and become part of this functional group agent, i.e. working collectively with the two social entrepreneurs. In the 2019a paper, we did not specify that the resulting 'joint intentions' are actually oftentimes we-intentions, a particular 'slice' of joint intentions in which individual and group intentions are fully aligned. Through the joint engagement in the creation of a new community arrangements (group reason) qua group membership in these particular practices (collectivity condition), they elicited and aligned community members' way of thinking and feeling about disaster response and recovery work (collective commitment). As Tuomela (2013, p. 77) argues, the "notion of collective commitment is the glue that binds the members of a we-mode

Table 7.2 *Three kinds of intentionality in entrepreneurship-as-joint-practice*

	Shared intentionality for joint practice	Joint intentionality in joint practice	We-intentionality as joint practice
Empirical example	Co-evolutionary practices shaping the formation of a sustainable entrepreneurial ecosystem (O'Shea et al., 2021)	Entrepreneurs duality-management practices securing volunteer retention in prosocial cooperatives (Farny et al., 2019b)	Community practices for institution building after a disaster (Farny et al., 2019a)
Boundaries of the group (unit of analysis)	Ecosystem as a latent network containing a group of self-selected actors	Venture as a bureaucratic organization containing a group of organizational members	Community as a social grouping sharing certain social practices
Group Reason	To develop feasible products and services around nanocellulose technologies and survive in a competitive market	To provide more sustainable products and services for themselves and others	To find local solutions to recover from the disaster that would serve the entire community
Collectivity Condition	Initially non-existent	These cooperatives offer a new organizational model to address sustainable transformation of the energy and food sector	Post-disaster practices are effectively organized via Sonje Ayiti Organization and its partners
Collective Commitment	Initially non-existent	By officially becoming a member of the cooperative, the members will jointly contribute to the organization's mission and objectives	By emotionally belonging to the coordinated group effort, people believe in the mutual commitment of most members to the group itself, and will act as a group member to find solutions for the community

group together in relation to the group's ethos". The study thus shows that collective emotions emerge from we-intentional practices and enable institution building.

Proposition 3 – Strong We-mode intentionality as joint action: *Based on people's mutual belief in their collective commitment being beneficial by default (person and group intention fully aligned), we-intentions are likely to be inherent to people's joint entrepreneurial engagement as embodied group ethos.*

It follows that the three kinds of intentionality are a conceptual clarification to further develop EAP as a distinct theoretical account to enterprising behavior. We argue that intentionality is a crucial element to understand practice variations. As a matter of fact, Tuomela (2013, p. 62) goes as far as to conclude that "we-mode reasoning and intending will in many cases lead to rationally and functionally better action equilibria than individualistic, I-mode reasoning and intending". Hence, in many situations, joint intentions and we-intentions are desirable intention states as they represent people's functionally aligned group reasons and collective commitment to enact a practice together. Viewing the kind of intention as a constituting element of practices, we therefore suggest distinguishing I-mode reasoning present in *shared intentional practice* from We-mode reasoning inherent in *joint intentional practice* and *we-intentional practice*. In Table 7.2, we develop an overview of intention features in entre-preneurship-as-*joint*-practice, based on the examples provided above.

CONCLUDING REMARKS

Practice theory suggests that entrepreneurship is best understood as social processes of embedded actors in spatial, temporal and socio-ecological contexts enacting practices of entrepreneuring (Johannisson, 2011; Thompson et al., 2020). Practice theoretical accounts assume that all practices take place in fields of shared understanding (Reckwitz, 2002; Schatzki, 2005). Therefore, it is essential to overcome ontological individualism in entrepreneurship research (entrepreneurial activities are predominantly conceptually equated with the entrepreneur), and forefront the notion of practices as fundamental to the ontology of *all* social phenomena (Thompson & Byrne, 2020; Thompson et al., 2020). This entails appreciating collectivity as a sensitizing device to view any social phenomenon in a different light (Alvesson & Kärreman, 2003).

In response, our chapter offers a nuanced understanding of collectivity informing researchers on how actors relate to each other in enterprising practices. Essentially, we suggest that different kinds of intentionality serve as a foundation to understand variations in strengths of collectivity underpinning joint action in entrepreneurship. In line with practice theory that avoids common dualities such as agency/structure or individual/collective (Thompson et al., 2020), we rather view collectivity as an important part of human sociality, an inherent feature of a practice ontology. Thus, weak and strong forms of collectivity are linked to actors' practical understandings, the internalized shared, embodied know-how on which practices rest (Johannisson, 2011; Reckwitz, 2002; Schatzki, 2005). "Hence, people ill-equipped with practical understanding as it relates to a particular practice often find it hard to decode meanings and participate with others (cf., being able to speak a language)" (Thompson et al., 2020, p. 249). In other words, two people could not carry out an enterprising practice if they could not build on the same practical understanding of what the practice entails, which provides a conceptual bridge between collectivity and intentionality. Each form of intentionality, that we introduced in this chapter, therefore assumes a similar shared, practical understanding of entrepreneurial practices which they are about to carry out and are carrying out.

Theorizing intentionality through Tuomela's (2013) social ontology is helpful in this regard as such a relational conception of the self is analytically linked to the intention content *and* intention state *for*, *in* and also *as* joint enterprising practices. We argue that in particular the intention state in joint action (based on group reason, collectivity condition and collective commitment) essentially views people's motivations through their relationship to and interaction with others. Based on this, we suggest to reverse the analytical logic in empirical studies in EAP. Instead of framing any practice in shared, group or collective terms, it is more reasonable to assume a collective framing of practices, based on people's shared understanding of what that practice actually is. As such, one would then argue about the strength of collective intentionality likely to drive people enacting that practice. In exceptional cases, empirical analysis would find entrepreneurs enacting enterprising practices in purely private, non-group contexts, and then have to clarify why a practice foundation is still warranted, instead of the other way around.

Moreover, we argue, many entrepreneurship studies tend to assume that actors share a similar understanding of e.g. commercial, social and/or ecological venturing objectives, as "something located in the individual mind, without attending to other components of social reality, such as body, things, discourse and structure" (Thompson et al., 2020, p. 249), and so additionally assign agency *a priori* to actors, instead of conceptualizing agency as a product of (ongoing, changing) social practices. Thus, we as scholars should not simply assume a shared practical understanding. In turn, we suggest that advancing understanding of the meaning and role of weak and strong collectivity in entrepreneurship as joint practice would offer an important epistemological shift from actor to action, conceptualizing agency as a product of social practices.

Going further down this road, we particularly emphasize the importance of distinguishing forms of collective intentionality for advancing our critical understanding of entrepreneurship in relation to sustainability topics. Building on our theorizations, we suggest that only joint intentions and we-intentions enable different sustainable enterprising practices. At the moment, we argue, the majority of activities (e.g. as codified in the Sustainable Development Goals) depart from people's shared intentionality, based on some implied conditionality criteria 'if you do X, then I also do X'. Instead the systemic and intergenerational magnitude aimed for in sustainability transitions requires more enterprising practices where individuals are convinced that at least 'a sufficient number of other will do X and therefore also intend to do X'. We thus stress that joint-intentionality and we-intentionality transpose we-feelings reaffirming people in their practices, motivating the further enactment of sustainability-oriented enterprising practices (Wigger & Shepherd, 2020). Unanimously, our work concurs with sustainable business studies (cf. Bansal, 2019) calling for entrepreneurial action to contribute to a sustainable transition of the dominant economic model (Salmivaara & Kibler, 2020), where a stronger focus on collective action is needed (cf. Farny et al., 2019a; Reinecke & Ansari, 2021). That is where we hope our conceptual work helps raise awareness of the need for developing our practical and theoretical understanding of collective intentions in entrepreneurship, which require agency transformations, where actors perceive a situation as a decision-making problem of the group and no longer as their own.

Within this context, we further conclude that developing an understanding of collectivity in EAP helps us better address that current theories in the social sciences struggle to provide guidance for such large-scale socio-technical adaptations, partly because they neglect the social dynamics of daily life in theorizing collective action (Welch & Yates, 2018). Instead, current research rather supports a model of individual and collective actors that is deliberative, rational and utilitarian (Welch & Yates, 2018), in which agency is assigned *a priori* to actors, rather than understanding agency as a product of their social practices (Reckwitz, 2002; Schatzki, 2005; Thompson et al., 2020). This is a major shortcoming as any sustainability transition requires an agency transformation leading to behavioral change of larger social entities. This calls for a 'collective action frame' that would help mobilize emotionally attached, widespread supportive action, as evidenced in social movement studies (Reinecke & Ansari, 2021). In conclusion, we concur with others who suggest that a collective approach to entrepreneurially address social and sustainability challenges is needed (Bansal, 2019; Kibler & Muñoz, 2020; Sarasvathy & Ramesh, 2019) and we hope our work will serve as inspiration for further research in this area.

REFERENCES

Alvesson, M., & Kärreman, D. (2003). Collectivity: A cultural and processual view. Institute of Economic Research Working Paper Series No. 8, Lund University.

Bansal, P. (2019). Sustainable development in an age of disruption. *Academy of Management Discoveries*, 5(1), 8–12.

Cardon, M. S., Post, C., & Forster, W. R. (2017). Team entrepreneurial passion: Its emergence and influence in new venture teams. *Academy of Management Review*, *42*(2), 283–305.

Farny, S., Kibler, E., & Down, S. (2019a). Collective emotions in institutional creation work. *Academy of Management Journal*, *62*(3), 765–799.

Farny, S., Kibler, E., Hai, S., & Landoni, P. (2019b). Volunteer retention in prosocial venturing: The role of emotional connectivity. *Entrepreneurship Theory and Practice*, *43*(6), 1094–1123.

Johannisson, B. (2011). Towards a practice theory of entrepreneuring. *Small Business Economics*, *36*(2), 135–150.

Kibler, E., Kautonen, T., & Fink, M. (2014). Regional social legitimacy of entrepreneurship: Implications for entrepreneurial intention and start-up behaviour. *Regional Studies*, *48*, 995–1015.

Kibler, E., & Muñoz, P. (2020). What do we talk about when we talk about community? *Academy of Management Discoveries*, *6*(4), 721–725.

Merton, R. K. (1968 [1949]). *Social Theory and Social Structure* (enlarged edition). New York: Free Press.

O'Shea, G., Farny, S., & Hakala, H. (2021). The buzz before business: A design science study of a sustainable entrepreneurial ecosystem. *Small Business Economics*, *56*, 1097–1120.

Reckwitz, A. (2002). Toward a theory of social practices: A development in culturalist theorizing. *European Journal of Social Theory*, *5*(2), 243–263.

Reinecke, J., & Ansari, S. (2021). Microfoundations of framing: The interactional production of collective action frames in the Occupy Movement. *Academy of Management Journal*, *64*(2), 378–408.

Salmela, M. (2014). The functions of collective emotions in social groups. In A. K. Ziv & H. B. Schmid (Eds.), *Institutions, Emotions, and Group Agents* (pp. 159–176). Dordrecht: Springer.

Salmivaara, V., & Kibler, E. (2020). "Rhetoric mix" of argumentations: How policy rhetoric conveys meaning of entrepreneurship for sustainable development. *Entrepreneurship Theory and Practice*, *44*(4), 700–732.

Sarasvathy, S. D., & Ramesh, A. (2019). An effectual model of collective action for addressing sustainability challenges. *Academy of Management Perspectives*, *33*(4), 405–424.

Schatzki, T. R. (2001). Practice theory: An introduction. In T. R. Schatzki, K. Knorr Cetina, & E. von Savigny (Eds.), *The Practice Turn in Contemporary Theory* (pp. 1–14). London: Routledge.

Schatzki, T. R. (2002). *The Site of the Social: A Philosophical Account of the Constitution of Social Life and Change*. University Park: Pennsylvania State University Press.

Schatzki, T. R. (2005). Peripheral vision: The sites of organizations. *Organization Studies*, *26*(3), 465–484.

Thompson, N. A., & Byrne, O. (2020). Advancing entrepreneurship as practice: Previous developments and future possibilities. In W. B. Gartner & B. T. Teague (Eds.), *Research Handbook on Entrepreneurial Behavior, Practice and Process* (pp. 30–55). Cheltenham, UK and Northampton, MA, USA: Edward Elgar Publishing.

Thompson, N. A., Verduijn, K., & Gartner, W. B. (2020). Entrepreneurship-as-practice: Grounding contemporary theories of practice into entrepreneurship studies. *Entrepreneurship & Regional Development*, *32*(3–4), 247–256.

Tuomela, R. (2007). *The Philosophy of Sociality: The Shared Point of View*. Oxford: Oxford University Press.

Tuomela, R. (2013). *Social Ontology: Collective Intentionality and Group Agents*. Oxford: Oxford University Press.

Van Gelderen, M., Kautonen, T., & Fink, M. (2015). From entrepreneurial intentions to actions: Self-control and action-related doubt, fear, and aversion. *Journal of Business Venturing*, *30*(5), 655–673.

Welch, D., & Yates, L. (2018). The practices of collective action: Practice theory, sustainability transitions and social change. *Journal for the Theory of Social Behaviour*, *48*(3), 288–305.

Wigger, K. A., & Shepherd, D. A. (2020). We're all in the same boat: A collective model of preserving and accessing nature-based opportunities. *Entrepreneurship Theory and Practice*, *44*(3), 587–617.

8. Improvisation, routines and the practice of entrepreneurship-as-practice

Richard T. Harrison and Suwen Chen

INTRODUCTION

Set in Regency England, Miss Elizabeth Bennet's relationship with Mr Fitzwilliam Darcy in Jane Austen's romantic comedy of manners *Pride and Prejudice* (1813) hinges on the difference between the superficial and the essential, whether this superficiality is seen in Mrs Bennet's obsession to follow social conventions and marry off her daughters, including Elizabeth, to 'suitable' husbands or in Elizabeth's own initial rejection of aristocratic land-owner Darcy on account of his excessive pride and arrogance, a rejection which is progressively overcome by Elizabeth's belief that the essential foundation of marriage was a matter of much reflection and serious thought (Brown, 1999). Given that Austen is a great believer in surface and depth, and favours depth over the superficial ('prejudice', after all, represents the failure to get beneath appearances), 'we are not, in fact, reading a morality tale in which Austen warns us of the perils of arrogance and blinkeredness ... Instead, we are undergoing a process in which we may if we are alert and willing give ourselves *practice in withholding judgement*' (Landy, 2020, p. 154, original emphasis). Reflecting a spirit of 'affective individualism', Austen, in the character of Elizabeth Bennet, held up a satiric mirror to the realities of her day, highlighting the foolishness of the superficial cultural notions these characters are bounded and blindly governed by, and pointing to the essential possibility that women can rise above the silly rules of a crippling social environment to think critically, question outcomes and have greater autonomy, evidenced in Elizabeth Bennet's demonstration that a woman is or can become just as capable as the most virtuous man in thinking intelligently and independently (Hansen, 2020). This distinction between the superficial and the essential is central to the novel:

> Because Darcy and Elizabeth attract to themselves people who share worthwhile values, their marriage is treated as an institution capable of preserving society as it best ought to be preserved. The novel shows then that marriage can be an institution more socially important than it is shown to be in novels that treat it as a romantic institution only; it suggests, in fact, that novels that treat marriage in such a limited way misunderstand the broader social and political nature of the institution [...] as precisely that which is most central to the preservation of the world as it ought to be, when the institution involves a husband and a wife who are willing to improve each other, [to] be improved [...] and to extend that mutual improvement to a larger community. (Shaffer, 1992, p. 66, cited in Hansen, 2020, p. 678)

In similar fashion, entrepreneurship research is only belatedly coming to appreciate the difference between the superficial (observed 'entrepreneurial phenomena') and the essential (the relational collaborative practices in which the phenomena are embedded). What *Pride and Prejudice* suggests is that marriage as an institution has the potential to improve not only the partners involved but the surrounding community as well, as the positive influences of the domestic can extend into the social and political realms (Shaffer, 1992, pp. 67–68). By analogy, the same argument can be made for entrepreneurship: the benefits are experienced not just by the immediate participants in the process but have wider implications for and impact on society. This shift from the superficial to the essential in entrepreneurship is particularly apposite in an intellectual climate which universalizes the notion of entrepreneurship and entrepreneurial phenomena: if, indeed, we 'are all entrepreneurs now' (Pozen, 2007) and focused on 'the entrepreneurship of the everyday' (Dodd et al., 2021), then we face the paradox that if everything is entrepreneurship then nothing is entrepreneurship (Harrison & Leitch, 2021). To paraphrase Williamson's (2003) discussion of the theory of absolute generality, excluding situations where there is a tacit reduction of 'everything' to a domain of contextually relevant objects (for example, the 'everything' you pack in your suitcase for a vacation), the claim that 'everything is X' is logically equivalent to the claim that 'everything is not-X'. If, however, we shift the focus from the phenomena to the underlying relational collaborative practices (as in Austen's 'marriage') this opens up the possibility of a new discourse based around process – the privileging of verbs over nouns, of becoming over being (Hjorth et al., 2015; Laine & Kibler, 2018; McMullen & Dimov, 2013; Steyaert, 2007) – and practice, the view that assigns ontological significance to practices, premised on the notion that social life 'is brought into being' through activities and practices (Feldman & Orlikowski, 2011, p. 1241).

Although there has been some engagement of entrepreneurship with this process and practice perspective (Champenois et al., 2020), the field has come late to the practice turn in social theory. As the lovechild of entrepreneurship's on–off dalliance with the society dandy, strategy (Landström, 2004, 2020), entrepreneurship-as-practice (E-A-P) is a relatively new but rapidly expanding interest (Figure 8.1). Apart from a very few scattered references since 2002 to 'entrepreneurship as practice' (without the connective '-') (Champenois et al., 2020), there is no E-A-P literature as such before 2011, by which time one in five of all 7,490 strategy-as-practice papers in a still expanding field had been published. Over 54 per cent of the 121 E-A-P citations on Google Scholar are from 2018 and 2019, compared with 16 per cent of S-A-P citations: relative to strategy-as-practice, entrepreneurship-as-practice is the new kid on the block. The attraction of S-A-P as a template is obvious, although rarely specifically acknowledged in E-A-P research (Champenois et al., 2020), given its micro orientation to the analysis of how interactions among individuals can influence competitive behaviour and decision-making (Suddaby et al., 2013) based on a rejection of economic rationality in recognition of the complex, often messy and convoluted, day-to-day decision-making processes of individuals and groups (Jarzabkowski et al., 2007).

But the relevance for entrepreneurship-as-practice of the practice turn in social theory in general, and in management and organization studies in particular, has deeper roots than S-A-P per se (Nicolini, 2012, 2017). Two waves of practice theory have been identified (Orlikowski, 2010; Postill, 2010): the so-called first generation practice theorists (Bourdieu, Foucault, Giddens, de Certeau, for example) have established the foundations of practice theory, upon which have been developed new extensions to the theory by second generation theorists (such as Ortner, Schatzki, Knorr Cetina and von Savigny). This includes the turn towards more processual understandings of management and organization (Weick, 1998; Hernes, 2014). The wider 'practice turn' in social science includes, for example: foundational studies such as Garfinkel's (1967) practical ethnomethodology of organizational life; Bourdieu's (2002 [1977]) theory of practice; Foucault's (1977) disciplinary archaeology; applications and developments such as Schatzki (2002) and Schatzki et al.'s (2001) practice theory; the feminist

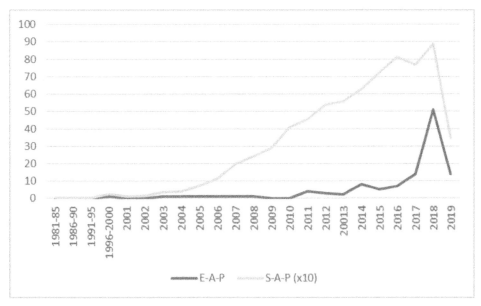

Note: For clarity the S-A-P data are shown at 1/10th scale.
Source: Google Scholar, 25 June 2019.

Figure 8.1   *Number of citations by year for 'entrepreneurship-as-practice' and*
              'strategy-as-practice' 1981–2009

emphasis on theorizing practice of Haraway (1997), Barad (2007), and Roy (2008); Clegg (1975) and Silverman and Jones' (1976) organizational sociology; and Mintzberg's (1973) analysis of the daily routines of managerial work (Carter et al., 2008). This is not to suggest that entrepreneurship scholarship is unmindful of these – on the contrary, many of them have been acknowledged as important influences in a number of recent studies (see, for example, Sklaveniti & Steyaert, 2020; Champenois et al., 2020). The point remains, however, that relative to other disciplines within and beyond management and organization studies, entrepreneurship has come very late to practice (Thompson et al., 2020). Entrepreneurship scholars have not necessarily neglected 'practice' – it is just that, like Molière's Monsieur Jourdain, in *Le Bourgeois Gentilhome* (1670), who was surprised to discover that he had been speaking prose all of his life, they have been studying practice without realizing it.

PRACTICE AND PRACTICES

One of the challenges in E-A-P research, to which we respond in this chapter, is defining exactly what a practice is. As the Introduction to this collection itself makes clear, 'there is no one definition of practice possible, they are fundamentally collaborative and relational activities, and not solely reducible to the agents who carry them out … [and] … bring together actors, activities and contexts, thus interrelating social structures and human agency' (see Tatli et al., 2014; Dodd et al., 2016; Hill, 2018). Entrepreneurial phenomena as practices are reproduced, transformed and have consequences across time, space and individuals as ways of doing and saying things (Gartner & Teague, 2019). There is congruence here with the strategy-as-practice literature, where '[t]he term "practice" implies repetitive performance in order to become practised; that is, to attain recurrent, habitual, or routinized accomplishments of particular actions' (Jarzabkowski, 2004, p. 531). Practices, in this sense, are 'routinized types of behavior' (Reckwitz, 2002, p. 249), ways of doing and saying things (Matthews et al., 2018), collaborative activities which can be reproduced and transformed across time, space and individuals, and which are fundamentally material and embodied (Schatzki, 2002, 2012).

Given this, practice, and the practical knowledge to which it gives rise, is knowing-in-action, embodied knowing which 'only manifests itself in, by, and during action in a particular situation' (Rix & Lièvre, 2008, p. 225). To illustrate, and introduce a major theme of this chapter, Oscar Peterson, the Montreal-born jazz pianist, in his autobiography, *A Jazz Odyssey* (2002), articulated this clearly in his account of the 'will to perfection' and the 'daredevil enterprise' of improvising individually and collectively in front of an audience: 'It draws on everything about you, not just your musical talent. It requires you to collect all your senses, emotions, physical strength and mental power, and focus them totally on the performance ... [Playing jazz] is so uniquely exciting that once it's bitten you, you never get rid of it. Nor do you want to, for you come to believe that if you get it all right, you will be capable of virtually anything' (cited in Hentoff, 2006, p. 6). Five postulates follow from this. First, *ethnomethodologically*, practice as 'situated action' (Suchman, 1987) is embedded in its context and it is impossible to understand a practice outside of its local setting (Garfinkel, 1967). To study practice is to experience the practice directly (Orlikowski, 2002), and to appreciate the social ontology of the nature, composition and basic structures of social phenomena (Schatzki, 2005). Second, *phenomenologically*, understanding a practice is not just a matter of observation but presupposes the understanding of what lies beneath, whether the private and unobservable subjective construal of the 'significant real-life sets' (Merleau-Ponty, 1965 [1942], p. 179) that shape embodied meaning, or the role of routines in capturing what is (at least temporarily) stable while recognizing the potential for change over time (Nelson & Winter, 1982). Third, *epistemologically*, the actor in the performance of a practice is a reflective practitioner (Schön, 1983) capable of recognizing their own activity from a new perspective and in so doing becoming aware of their own subjective experience. This, however, as we will demonstrate below, is 'not spontaneous, nor immediate, nor direct, nor easy' (Vermersch, 1999, p. 13, quoted in Rix & Lièvre, 2008, p. 227). Fourth, *psychologically*, practices invoke intentionality; they are cognitive, enacted by reflexive agentic persons, and are widely held to be rule-governed, the 'explicit formulations, principles, precepts, and instructions that enjoin, direct, or remonstrate people to perform specific actions' and that are not explicitizations, articulations of understandings or tacit or implicit formulas (Schatzki, 2002, p. 79). But there is a potential tension here with the view of routines as the basis for practices (which we elaborate below) which suggests a more habitual and deeply internalized perspective on practices. Fifth, *sociologically*, while a practice may be individualistic, it is more typically construed as interpersonal, intersubjective and relational, enacted with other actors in front of, in association and co-produced with and for the benefit of 'audiences'. As such, human coexistence 'transpires as and amid an elaborate, constantly evolving nexus of arranged things and organized activities' (Schatzki, 2002, p. xi); practices embody actions that are taken towards and in response to people, events and objects as they are encountered in specific settings, and these shape which particular intelligibility-determining factors configure what makes sense to actors to do, how they decide to act, their practices (Schatzki, 1988, p. 246, cited in Nama & Lowe, 2014).

Drawing on this wider practice perspective, S-A-P incorporates two additional elements in addition to practices themselves (Jarzabkowski et al., 2007; Whittington, 2006). *Praxis* is 'the concrete, unfolding activity as it takes place' (Suddaby et al., 2013, p. 332), which is unique, existing only in the present but informed and guided by pre-existing socially defined practices. *Practitioners* are the actors doing the work and uniquely engaging with it based on their background and experience (Balogun & Johnson, 2004). Although this underlying theoretical framework 'would be helpful ... in assessing the flow of activity in which entrepreneurial process and agency is accomplished' (Champenois et al., 2020, p. 301), the E-A-P literature has not for the most part drawn on this theoretical grounding in the parallel S-A-P literature.

This orientation to practices, praxis and practitioners is not without its difficulties, however. A key challenge in developing a practice orientation in this respect is problematizing the relationship between embodied practices (praxis) and theory. In some situations theory arises from practice (and vice versa) but theory and practice are often inseparable: 'the body, so unstable, fickle, and malleable, simultaneously stands as an individual with agency and as a member of multiple communities, located in diverse contexts, and intricate relationships. The personal, social, and cultural complexities of the situated body make embodied practices even more difficult to comprehend' (Hahn, 2016, p. 148). This suggests the existence of a liminal zone where theory and practice dwell within the body and where the 'very struggle of comprehending experience allows us to grow and creatively convey what we know in an embodied sense' (Hahn, 2016, p. 162). To ask the question 'what theories arise from practice?' implies a separation of theory from practice. Indeed, 'telling it like it is' and 'being closer to reality' rather than theorizing is a key feature of the S-A-P literature (Carter et al., 2008, p. 89). As with the renewed interest in phenomenon-driven (rather than theory-driven) research (Schwarz & Stensaker, 2014, 2016; Von Krogh et al., 2012), there is a very real, but not inevitable, danger, to which much of the S-A-P literature has fallen victim, of replacing theory with more or less complex naïve descriptions of phenomena and practices (Behfar & Okhuysen, 2018). However, this separation of theory and practice is culturally constructed and historically reinforced and magnifies the separation of mind and body: if theory and practice do indeed dwell within our entire body (as the materiality of, for example, Schatzki's (2002) approach suggests) then cognition itself is embodied (Briñol & DeMarree, 2012; Clark, 1997; Damasio, 1999; Gallagher, 2005); as we will argue in the final section of this chapter, this offers additional directions for E-A-P research (see also Thompson et al., 2020).

ROUTINES AND PRACTICES

If we follow this line that practices are, or give rise to, routines, then the performance of entrepreneuring (Steyaert, 2007) and its constituent practices can be construed as the routinization of activity undertaken under conditions of Knightian uncertainty (Alvarez & Barney, 2005). As such, entrepreneurial routines can be construed as sites of paradoxical relations (Holt & Zundel, 2017; Chen & Harrison, 2019), serving as both generators of stability (March & Simon, 1958) through organizational emergence, and as drivers of change (Feldman & Pentland, 2003). Stability, however, does not imply unchanging: routines are repetitive, recognizable patterns of interdependent actions, which could accomplish organizational work. However, these routines are not tight sets of rules but are flexible and persistent (Feldman & Pentland, 2003), accounting for the development of regular and predictable behaviour patterns in both established and newly emerging firms (Nelson & Winter, 1982), underpinning patterns for accomplishing work that achieves stability and change, and allowing for variation within and between practices as 'patterns created through the bringing together of a set of activities, materials, understandings and skills' (Hui, 2017, p. 52). This occurs by endogenous interaction between the performative (specific actions taken at specific times and places) and the ostensive (enacted patterns) (Rerup & Feldman, 2011). Furthermore, the performative aspect consists of two main characteristics: it is improvisatory, and an effortful accomplishment (Feldman, 2000; Orlikowski, 2000; Feldman & Pentland, 2003). Similarly, the ostensive can take two forms: explicitly embedded in the form of an artefact such as a standard operating procedure (SOP), and/or as a taken-for-granted norm such as tacit knowledge or individual understanding (Feldman & Pentland, 2003).

Routines as drivers of change are so in two respects. Reactively, they embody a truce between latent conflicts (Zbaracki & Bergen, 2010), represent the search for more efficient practices (Nelson & Winter, 1982) and represent the multiple entrepreneurial features that need to be coordinated (Gersick & Hackman, 1990). Proactively, routines are motors of organizational emergence and change (Adler et al., 1999), stimulating new routine configurations and innovation (Howard-Grenville & Parmigiani, 2011). As such, they both reflect and revise social enactments and are nested in and productive of social structures and social expectations. In terms of Nelson and Winter's (1982) evolutionary ecology of organizations, therefore, the value of routines is that they simultaneously capture that which is (at least temporarily) stable in organizations while recognizing the potential for change over time. The resulting tension between stability in the broad routine, variation in specific replications and the potential for either accumulated or punctuated change is a theme to which we return in examining improvisation as the basis for the practice of entrepreneurship as practice.

Building on this and drawing on Bateson's (1972) emphasis on system wisdom and an ecology of flexibility, it is clear that any account of routines/practices in the entrepreneurial domain will need to be cognizant of the fact that there is a hierarchical nesting of sub-routines within higher-order routines and schemas as ever-unfolding arrangements of mutually implicated nested systems. It follows that a routine or practice as such carries no information on the wider schemata at play, in terms of the extended macroscopic events that signify the wider patterns which constitute the wider system of relevance. There is, therefore, in both the analysis of routines per se and in the discussion of their transferability in particular, a danger in coding and formalizing routines, of privileging their stability aspect over their change dynamic: that is, to fossilize a few elements as if they were these wider schemata or classes, without questioning the nature of these classes (such as bureaucratic tradition, entrepreneurial culture, family values) themselves. If, as Bateson suggests, purely conscious control of the working process (of routine creation, embedding and innovation) is neither possible nor desirable, then we fall back on the suggestive construction of associations to represent the restless apparent order of organizations in emergence as open democracies rather than hierarchical structures (Ehrenzweig, 1967).

ROUTINES AND IMPROVISATION

In so doing, we return to a consideration of how this paradox of stability and change in entrepreneurship-as-practice is negotiated through improvisation, which we understand as 'the ubiquitous practice of everyday life, a primary method of meaning exchange in any interaction ... [it is] ... as close to universal as contemporary critical method could responsibly entertain ... [and is] ... a crucially important site for both humanistic and scientific study' (Lewis, 2008, p. 108). Consider by way of context one particular entrepreneurial practice, the entrepreneur's pitch for finance and other resources from angel investors and other potential stakeholders. As the entrepreneurial finance market has developed, angel investors – private individuals, usually but not always with an entrepreneurial background, acting alone or in concert with others to invest their own capital directly into unquoted ventures with which they have no family connection – have emerged as an important source of finance and business development support for start-up and growth aspiring ventures across a range of geographies (Edelman et al., 2017; Harrison, 2017a; Tenca et al., 2018; Wallmeroth et al., 2018; White & Dumay, 2017). With the emergence of investor networks, groups and syndicates (Mason et al., 2016; Mason & Harrison, 2019) and the expansion of research on angel investor decision-making (Maxwell et al., 2011; Harrison et al., 2015, 2016), the role and nature of the 'pitch' as an entrepreneurial practice has come under increasing scrutiny (Mason & Harrison, 2003; Jones, 2008; Teague et al., 2020; Pollock et al., 2020).

The pitch is an increasingly important part of the pre-investment stage of the angel investor decision-making process (Maxwell et al., 2011; Carpentier & Suret, 2015; Söderblom et al., 2016), providing entrepreneurs with the opportunity in a 10–20 minute presentation to communicate to prospective investors their credibility, trustworthiness and capabilities and the potential of their ventures (Clark, 2008; Harrison et al., 1997, 2015; Murnieks et al., 2016; Cardon et al., 2017; Eddleston et al., 2016; Cassar & Friedman, 2009). They are intentional and purposive, not (as is mistakenly assumed) because 'business angels take investment decisions during pitch presentations' (Lefebvre et al., 2020, p. 5), but because they are a means of continuing the dialogue with prospective investors into the due diligence and deal negotiation stages of the investment decision-making process (Harrison & Mason, 2017; Teague et al., 2020). As a practice, the pitch illustrates many of the characteristics of practice identified in Table 8.1: they are relational, as an impression management perspective has demonstrated (Mason & Harrison, 2003); they are processual not events (Teague et al., 2020) and they are routinized and rule-governed in ways that can constrain their effectiveness across different contexts (Pollock et al., 2020). Notwithstanding the formalization of the process, however, it is clear from observation that while these pitches, whether to angel investors (Teague et al., 2020) or industry analysts (Pollock et al., 2020), tend to retain enough sameness or commonality to be recognized as a common practice, there are variations that occur in each and every performance of the pitch, even when given by the same presenter about the same start-up, variations that reflect both the presenter's own self-understanding of the pitch and their response to audience interaction and real-time feedback.

It is in the possibility for variation within the practice (Hui, 2017) that the negotiation of the paradox of stability and change in entrepreneurship-as-practice through improvisation occurs. This is hardly a new insight: for example, the phenomenological sociologist Schutz (1964, p. 159) asserted that study of the social relationships associated with the musical process could lead to insights for understanding other forms of social intercourse. In anthropology this theme has been elaborated by Szwed (1980, p. 588) in terms of the combination of rewarding musical individualism within a framework of spontaneous egalitarian interaction, a tension which represents a disruptive 'diagonality in relation to the traditional parameters of vertical domination and horizontal equality ... [devising] collective forms of agency which articulate the

Table 8.1   Practice and the codification of practical knowledge: the entrepreneur's pitch

Dimension	Features of a practice	Application to the pitch
Ethnomethodological	Embedded in context as situated action based on distributed cognition.	The pitch is a situationally specific encounter between actors (entrepreneurs, investors, other stakeholders) curated by a third party (e.g. investment network manager). It is purposive, to communicate, engage and develop continuing relationships among the participants, ultimately leading to investment/endorsement.
Phenomenological	Go beyond observation of a practice to the shaping by significant underlying facets. This public and behaviourally observable practice is underscored by a private and non-observable one – a subsidiary awareness (Polanyi), embodied meaning (Merleau-Ponty), pre-reflected awareness (Vermersch) or an unformulated and largely inarticulate understanding (Tsoukas).	The practice is increasingly widely observed (at investor group meetings, via video recordings or in the edutainment form of *Dragon's Den*/*Shark Tank*). The pitch as (observable) practice is governed by a number of unobservables, including: The entrepreneur's investment readiness (their willingness and ability to accept an investor's ownership and involvement in their venture) (Mason & Harrison, 2001). The angel investors' better ability to articulate what they would *not* invest in than what they would (the 'I'll know it when I see it' approach to defining a 'good' investment), and their emphasis on finding reasons to reject an opportunity (the 'three strikes and you're out' rule) (Mason and Harrison, 1996).
Epistemological	The actor as a reflective practitioner, but qualified by the nature of subjective experience and tacit knowledge – the capacity to reflect on what they do and articulate those reflections, albeit problematic when the practice has not yet become the object of conscious awareness.	The 'gatekeeper' role (e.g. investment network manager) is one of preparation and rehearsal, working with the entrepreneur to improve and refine their pitch. For the investor, there is some evidence of investing as an informal and largely unconscious learning process (Botelho et al., 2018).
Psychological	Practices invoke intentionality; they are cognitive, enacted by reflexive agentic persons, and are widely held to be rule-governed; however, there is a more habitual and deeply internalized perspective on practices.	The pitch as practice is increasingly formalized and formulized – it is scripted, often follows a set template, and the entrepreneur is coached, prepared and rehearsed in its delivery (Teague et al., 2020).

Dimension	Features of a practice	Application to the pitch
Sociological	Intersubjective and relational – the construction of the actor as the product of narrative work through the practice. Explication rather than a discourse of rationalization and justification.	The pitch as impression management, overcoming the liability of newness by signalling quality, reliability and trust in an enacted dramaturgical performance (Turner, 1992; Gardner, 1992; Mason & Harrison, 2003).
Linguistic	The epistemological break between knowing-in-action (only manifest in, by and during action and hence implicit as not yet enacted) and discursive knowledge concerning the practice.	The irreducibility of a practice to a discourse – the reliance on discursive knowledge rather than the contextually specific knowledge-in-action underlies the failure of entrepreneurs to successfully transition from the first (finance-oriented) to the second (analyst-oriented) pitch (Pollock et al., 2020).

outstanding power of the participating singularities' (Citton, 2016, p. 171). More specifically, Orlikowski (1996), for example, has pointed to the capacity for improvisation whereby the routine is repeated but never the same and where the return of the performative to the ostensive is done through the validation of new routines as objects of specification and bearers of agency (Jouxtel, 2019). Weick (1998), in the most cited contribution to a special issue of *Organization Science* on improvisation and the theory and practices of management, has drawn attention to the aesthetics of imperfection and the role of trust, intuition and divergent thinking. Similarly, for Feldman (2000, p. 614), an improvisation and process approach helps unveil the hidden potential in routines as embodied will and intentions (Betta, 2019).

There is a traditional, or popular, conception of improvisation as something 'of the moment', undertaken at speed, and involving snap decisions, lightning reactions and quick-fire responses (Peters, 2017). This allows no time for thought, prolonged contemplation or agonizing over one's next move. This is not, however, a position taken in most contemporary analyses of improvisation, which see it as 'coherent collective thinking' based on fluidity and adaptability, commitment, creativity and change, community and team (or distributed – Bolden, 2011) leadership and mastery (Harrison, 2017b). As the example of the entrepreneur's pitch demonstrates, however carefully scripted and rehearsed the presentation there is always variation, adjustment and refinement (Teague et al., 2020). Improvisation is not 'performance without preparation' but relies on a lifetime of preparation, knowledge and playing behind every performance. It is the capability to have and give free rein to individual virtuosity without losing the coherence of and commitment to the integrity and unity of the group. This has wider implications for E-A-P to which we return below, but at this point signals an important implication. Knowledge, preparation, commitment, fluidity, mastery come together in-the-moment of performative practice of an unfolding improvisation, not as the experience of uncertainty, expectancy, risk-taking and surprise (which are as much part of the conventional understanding of entrepreneurship as of improvisation), but in 'the extraordinary *certainty* of the improviser, the *predictability* of the improvisation, and the *absence* of risk-taking' (Peters, 2017, p. 23). The discipline and disciplining that this entails allows an entrepreneur-improviser to 'begin and sustain a work with a degree of certitude that belies the uncertainty of its origin and gestation' (Peters, 2017, p. 24). Entrepreneurship has developed a number of 'origin stories' (based on resource availability, effectuation, self-actualization, bricolage among others) to account for the creation of new ventures under uncertainty. An improvisational perspective on this process sees it as the momentary and momentous fixing of arbitrary structures which 'emancipates contingency' and represents the transition from the unmarked to the marked space (Luhmann, 2000, pp. 309, 115–116), where this space is not pre-existent and to be occupied but is created performatively in the improvising moment.

The literature on improvisation is now wide-ranging and is not confined to music or the performing arts (Lewis & Piekut, 2016a, 2016b; Caines & Heble, 2015). As knowing and reflection in action, improvisation has been described as the on the spot surfacing, criticizing, restructuring and testing of our intuitive understandings of experienced phenomena (Schön, 1983), based on the substantive rather than temporal convergence of planning and execution (Miner et al., 2001). While rooted in the present, improvisation is also very much oriented to the creation of the future as action unfolds (Barrett & Lindquist, 2008). However, notwithstanding these scattered references, it remains largely the case that the routines literature and the improvisation literature (including bricolage as an important construct in entrepreneurship) in the study of organizations have remained discrete and non-integrated (Suarez & Montes, 2019), and relatively little of this literature has considered the entrepreneurial domain (Hmieleski & Corbett, 2006, 2008; Yu et al., 2020). This is consistent with the argument that improvisation is itself a paradoxical practice which belongs to the infra-ordinary – the everydayness that requires a kind of quixotic or excessive attention (Perec, 1997) – rather than the extraordinary (Cunha & Clegg, 2019). This paradoxical practice is increasingly being recognized as foundational in circumstances of addressing unplanned work or emerging issues in highly uncertain environments (Hamzeh et al., 2019), of organizational emergence (Gartner & Teague, 2019), of innovation and organizational change (Du et al., 2019), where established routines break down (Suarez & Montes, 2019) or are executed in ever-changing ways as conditions (including the 'mutable contexts' (Stańczyk & Stańczyk-Hugiet, 2019) of entrepreneuring) always differ (Wetzel & Tint, 2019). Improvisation in this sense is 'ineluctably embodied; its creative and political force is manifested through sounds and gestures that are the traces of experience at once relational and contextual' (Siddall & Waterman, 2016, p. 1). This embodiment, and the scope for agency within it, is 'the process whereby collective behaviors and beliefs, acquired through acculturation, are rendered individual and "lived" at the level of the body … [and where agency …] is the power to alter those acquired behaviors and beliefs for purposes that may be reactive (resistant) or collaborative (innovative) in kind' (Noland, 2009, p. 9). Specifically, this emphasis on embodied gestures rather than linguistic discourse supports an argument that gestural performativity, as a manifestation of Feldman's embodied routines, invokes improvisational techniques such as 'stylistic entrainment, code switching, adaptability, interoperability, close listening and responsiveness' (Siddall & Waterman, 2016, p. 6; Harrison, 2017b). This can be illustrated in the case of the entrepreneurial pitch as impression management (Mason & Harrison, 2003), where the creation of 'organizational facades' (Nystrom & Starbuck, 1984) that justify actions, gain discretion and leverage access to resources, is a dramaturgical process (Turner, 1992) 'wherein the key performance elements are the actor; the audience; the situation serving as the stage; the set of expectations serving as the script; the performance as constituted by the verbal, non-verbal and artifactual behaviors; and the reactions of the audience serving as the reviews' (Gardner, 1992, p. 33).

Building on this prior literature we set out a framework for the role of improvisation and routines in entrepreneurship as practice (Figure 8.2). We begin by arguing that there is a distinction to be made between convergent improvisation, conducted to maintain a status quo by improvisationally tackling threats to the perceived normalcy of organizational operations (Cunha & Clegg, 2019), and divergent improvisation, the 'messy engagement' (Moore,

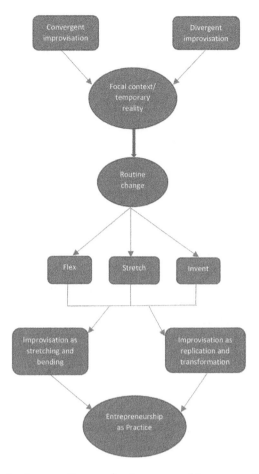

Figure 8.2   Improvisation, routines and entrepreneurship-as-practice

2019) with emergent situations, unpredictable content and complex products and assessments which require, as in the case of entrepreneuring, alternative forms of planning, support and implementation. In terms of the choreography of entrepreneurial organizations, improvisation represents the (at least) temporary suspension of deliberative thought and habitual and expected processes in favour of spontaneous, intuitive and non-routine activities that may lead to surprising results (Lavender, 2019; Albright & Gere, 2003; Belgrad, 1999; Lewis & Piekut, 2016a, 2016b; Caines & Heble, 2015). This represents, in effect, the establishment of a focal context, a constructed temporary reality that encompasses both the objective traits of the organization environment and the subjective perceptions organization members have of that environment (Suarez & Montes, 2019). Within this it then becomes possible to see both the routine enactment and routine transfer domains as the paradoxical practice of bricolage (Wolf & Beverungen, 2019) and improvisation of activities without deliberate pre-planning (Miner et al., 2008) on the one hand, and as the exercise of intentional choice on the other (Deken et al., 2016). In this, three modes of routine change can be identified (Chen & Harrison, 2019): flex (the adaptation of existing familiar actions), stretch (the application of actions that not all participants are familiar with), and invent (the creation of new activities and emerging patterns). The second pitch literature provides a very good example of this: in moving from the first pitch (to potential investors) to the second pitch (industry analysts) new technology-based ventures first flex, by relying on the same presentation but to a greater or lesser extent adapting the content/style/order of the presentation to tailor for the specific target audience; stretch, by moving beyond their comfort zone and adapting their presentation (often 'on the fly' in response to comments and challenges), for example, where the core of the pitch remains similar to the conventional pitch, the companies would add other elements or invite other people that are not required normally to join such as the product/IT manager to discuss with the analysts how to re-design/re-frame the product to better fit into the category and improve their market positioning; and finally invent, by developing a more contextually relevant and audience attuned presentation or, instead of delivering a conventional formal pitch, the companies would create new ways of engaging with the industry analysts such as attending professional conferences, having dinner together or joining the same sports club (Pollock et al., 2020).

Put another way, this resonates with stretching and bending as a style of improvisation (Peters, 2017, p. 101) and represents a process of replication and transformation within and across contexts (Blanche & Cohendet, 2019). This is based on recognizing the intent of the routine to be transferred, the existence of a dialogical dynamism that engages artefacts and memories of that intent, the existence of meta-routines that structures and enables the transfer of sub-routines across geographic and organizational distance, and a routine transfer and replication process through sharing a routine's ostensive aspect embedded in a professional culture. That this analysis has implications for our understanding of entrepreneurship-as-practice is obvious: in the remainder of this chapter we unpack this process of improvisation, of invention, transfer and replication.

IMPROVISATIONAL ANALYSIS AND ENTREPRENEURSHIP-AS-PRACTICE

We frame the discussion in the context of improvisation as the basis for approaching the analysis of entrepreneurship as practice and the practices of entrepreneurship under conditions of uncertainty. As the discussion above makes clear, the term 'improvisation' has many uses and interpretations. What runs through these definitions is a common emphasis on the idea of improvisation as 'spontaneous creativity within constraints' (Berkowitz, 2010, p. 2). It is, in other words, the creation of a musical work, or of the final form of a musical work, as it is being performed. As such, improvisation can refer to the immediate composition of the work by its performers, to the elaboration and adjustment of an existing framework, or to anything in-between: 'to some extent every performance involves elements of improvisation, although its degree varies according to period and place, and to some extent every improvisation rests on a series of conventions and implicit rules' (Nettl et al., n.d.). This emphasis on conventions and implicit rules is important: 'contrary to what one might expect from its spontaneous nature, musical improvisation depends very heavily on an implicit musical tradition, on tacit rules … It is only with reference to a thoroughly internalized body of works performed in a coherent style that improvisation can be performed by the musicians and understood by the audience' (Csikszentmihályi & Rich, 1997, p. 51). From a cognition perspective, these conventions, tradition and tacit rules are essential: in improvising, the performer must effect real-time sensory and perceptual coding, optimal attention allocation, event interpretation, decision-making, prediction (of the action of others), memory storage and recall, error correction and movement control, all the time integrating these into a seamless set of musical statements that reflect the performer's personal preferences and have the capacity to affect listeners (Pressing, 1984, 1998). Given the need to circumvent the limited human capacity for information processing and action, there is a need for tools and work-arounds to manage this process (Pressing, 1998). Two of these tools in particular have implications for how we practise E-A-P.

The first of these tools and work-arounds is that there are a number of processes that must be learned and rehearsed so as to develop formulae (or, to use the language of previous sections, routines) in improvised performances. For Pressing (1984) there are three such processes. Variation and recombination are reflected in Hui's (2017) analysis of the enactment of variations within and between practices in terms of the 'tolerable flexibility' that shapes the meaningful boundaries within which practices are conducted and understood. As the 'second pitch' literature suggests, entrepreneurs who exceed this tolerable flexibility, by assuming that the pitch that worked when addressing angel investors would also work for industry analysts, leads to miscommunication, negative impression management and relational dissonance (Pollock et al., 2020). Of particular interest in the present context is the third of Pressing's processes, transposition, which is fundamental to the tonal harmonic framework of jazz and Western classical music, and plays an important role in many other musical traditions (Berkowitz, 2010, pp. 40–41). Transposition 'indicates variations and shifts of scale in a discontinuous but harmonious pattern. It is thus created as an in-between space of zigzagging and of crossing' (Braidotti, 2006, p. 5). As a metaphor for the entrepreneurial process, it embodies five key characteristics. First, it is non-linear but not chaotic; discontinuity does not imply the absence of order and sensemaking. Second, it is nomadic, in the sense of a non-unitary subjectivity and a dispersed fragmented vision, but also committed and accountable in the development of a new form of ethical accountability in a technologically and globally mediated world. Third, it is a creative process, but not at the expense of cognitive validity, a tension that runs through the articulation of improvisation. Fourth, transposition is discursive but also materially embedded and embodied. Fifth, it is coherent but avoids falling into the trap of purely instrumental rationality. Taken together, transpositions are intertextual cross-boundary transfers, representing a leap from one code, field or axis into another, in a dance between the known and the unknown (Foster, 2003). Improvisation is an encounter with the unknown as we 'extend into, expand beyond, extricate ourselves from that which was known' (Foster, 2003, p. 4); but it is also a (re)encounter with the known as 'the performance of any action … contains an element of improvisation. The moment of wavering while contemplating how, exactly, to execute an action already deeply known, belies the presence of improvised action' (Foster, 2003, pp. 66–67). The improviser, in other words, shows the possibility of the mimetic transition from one thing to another, from the fixed to the unfixed, from the known to the unknown, 'in that moment of reflection, of hesitation, reservation and decision prior to each gesture' (Peters, 2009, p. 115).

For E-A-P as improvisation, the complex multiplicities of transpositions and the liminality of the in-between spaces of zigzagging and crossing require both an epistemological and a methodological shift: epistemologically, this places emphasis on non-linearity, nomadism, commitment and accountability, creativity and cognitive validity, discursiveness and coherence; methodologically, it suggests a deeper and wider engagement with improvisation theory and its multi-disciplinary applications. Transposition, as an integral part of this, is a theoretical perspective that 'stresses the experience of creative insight in engendering other, alternative ways of knowing ... [and] ... offers a contemplative and creative stance that respects the visible and hidden complexities of the very phenomena it attempts to study' (Braidotti, 2006, p. 6). As scholars, there are three implications of Braidotti's argument for our practice of E-A-P. First, transposition is a creative leap, the creation of an in-between space: what does that space look like? How do we navigate it? How do we communicate it? Second, transposition is centred on mobility and cross-referencing between disciplines and discursive levels: how do we connect philosophy with social realities? How do we relate theoretical speculation (for that does not disappear in E-A-P) with concrete plans? How do we connect concepts to imaginative figurations? Third, transposition implies a connection between the text and the social/historical context: how, fundamentally, do we develop modes of representation and forms of accountability that are adequate to the complexities of real-life worlds?

To answer that final question, we return to the second element of Pressing's (1984, 1998) discussion of improvisation tools and work-arounds. In terms of cognitive processes, Pressing (1998) unpacks the 'implicit rules' and 'tacit rules' referred to above. Specifically, he highlights the importance of referents, the formal structures that are used as the basis for improvisation, and of the knowledge base, the history of compositional choices and predilections defining the performer's personal style. Improvisation does not begin with the improvised performance but with the prior referents and knowledge base that shape and make it possible. E-A-P as improvisation, accordingly, is less a skill, technique, talent, idiom or style that is freely chosen, but a predicament of choice and decision: 'the performativity of choice ... is ontologically secondary to the *a-priority* of *decision*: improvisers *make* choices, but they are *made* by decisions' (Peters, 2017, p. ix). This concern with the event of improvisational E-A-P rather than with improvised situations per se turns the focus away from the in-the-moment free choices to the a priori decisive moments that ground the very possibility of these choices. If E-A-P is focused not on the thoughts, judgements and ideas hidden in the minds of individual entrepreneurs (although we have suggested above that the materiality of cognition is a legitimate focus for E-A-P research in which the neuropragmaticist emphasis on the embodiment of cognition and how it contributes to our comprehension of its practice in the way humans live (Shook & Solymosi, 2014) has much to offer), but on spontaneously expressed, visible, responsive and relational practices, then this predicament of choice and decision has to be addressed.

We do so initially by problematizing (bracketing, in Husserl's terms) the spontaneity of the expression of entrepreneuring practices. Following Peters (2017, pp. 7–9) our guide here is Heidegger (1999), who argued that the origin of a work of art was not in the past but now, as that which is always to come. This 'other beginning' represents an ontological shift such that a space of origination is highlighted now as another beginning within what has already been started. This introduces a disjuncture between 'starting' and 'beginning', often used synonymously, in which non-improvised work erases the difference between the start and the beginning and improvisation enacts it. Our understanding of entrepreneurial practices as improvisation, therefore, rests less on understanding the performance per se than on surfacing what happens between the start and the beginning, the enactment of the delay between the originary moment and the point where things simply got started. One of the key features of much of the current E-A-P research is its future orientation (Champenois et al., 2020): this may be teleoaffective, in terms of desired ends and affectivity (the acceptability of ends, means, beliefs and emotions) (Champenois et al., 2020, p. 283); it may be an emphasis on 'processes that unfold over time in an unfinalized open-ended trajectory of becoming' (Champenois et al., 2020, p. 284); or it may involve studying 'real situated practices unfolding over time' (Champenois et al., 2020, p. 293). We have already made reference to Luhmann's model of creativity as the marking of an unmarked space. Rereading this through the starting/beginning predicament, improvisation, both in E-A-P and in our practice of E-A-P, involves going forward while facing backward, using the path already trodden (the referents and knowledge base) to provide the improviser with the marks to shape the virgin space behind (relationally) which is in front (temporally).

For the entrepreneurial improviser this poses a challenge (Harrison, 2017b): 'as for the Future, your task is not to foresee, but to enable it' (de Saint-Exupéry, 1984, p. 50). This poses its own challenges, as the young king-to-be Arthur discovers from Merlyn the magician:

> 'Ah yes', said Merlyn. 'Now ordinary people are born forwards in Time, if you understand what I mean, and nearly everything in the world goes forward too. This makes it quite easy for the ordinary people to live. … But unfortunately I was born at the wrong end of time, and I have to live backwards from in front, while surrounded by a lot of people living forwards from behind.' (White, 1938, p. 40)

This perspective changes how the present is viewed. No longer just an accumulation of the past, the present is an enactment of the future, and the significance of present events and decisions is determined in the light of future states:

> The magician Merlyn had a strange laugh, and it was heard when nobody else was laughing. He laughed at the beggar who was bewailing his fate as he lay stretched on a dunghill; he laughed at the foppish young man who was making a great fuss about choosing a pair of shoes. He laughed because he knew that deep in a dunghill was a golden cup that would have made the beggar a rich man; he laughed because he knew that the pernickety young man would be stabbed in a quarrel before the soles of his new shoes were soiled. He laughed because he knew what was coming next. (Davies, 1990, pp. 652–653)

The improvisatory predicament of starting/beginning is reflected in the tension between living backward from in front and leveraging (or perhaps even transcending) the habits, marks, referents and knowledge base that is the path already trodden. These marks more generally are the product of repetition and habit:

> These thousands of habits of which we are composed – these contractions, contemplations, pretensions, presumptions, satisfactions, fatigues; these variable presents – thus form the basic domain of passive syntheses. The passive self is not defined simply by receptivity – that is, by means of the capacity to experience sensations – but by virtue of the contractile contemplation which constitutes the organism itself before it constitutes the sensations … there is a self wherever a furtive contemplation has been established, whenever a contracting machine capable of drawing a difference from repetition functions somewhere. (Deleuze, 2001, quoted in Peters, 2017, pp. 142–143)

In circling back to where we started, with the discussion of routines as practices, this raises the issue of the role played by these habits and marks in improvisation. As the S-A-P emphasis on praxis implies, and the place of mastery in improvisation requires, a practice needs to be practised.[1] This, of course, poses a conundrum: how does one reconcile the practise of a practice, especially a technical practice such as the entrepreneurial pitch, as a process by which habits are formed and ingrained with the more anticipatory future-oriented and possibility realizing practice of improvisation? One answer lies in the concept of 'woodshedding' in jazz circles

(Klemperer, 2014), signifying the bridge between technical practise and improvisation, the preparation for a performance to come (Peters, 2017, p. 146):

> Woodshedding is the nuts-and-bolts part of jazz, the place where you work out the techniques that form the foundation of your improvisational ability. The term woodshedding in jazz means more than just practicing. It is a recognition of the need to sequester oneself and dig into the hard mechanics of the music before you can come back and play with a group in public. There's something philosophical, almost religious, about the term. The musical treasures of jazz are not easily accessed. You have to dig deep into yourself, discipline yourself, become focused on the music and your instrument, before you can unlock the treasure chest. (Klemperer, 2014)[2]

This is both backward-looking, building on what is there and available, and oriented to a certain but indefinite future, making the best choices for and in advance of the 'in the moment' improvisation. For Peters (2017) this is preparation not rehearsal. Preparation is open to the future and its possibilities; it is anticipatory with 'its inherent futurity and focus on the *yet-to-happen*' (Peters, 2017, p. 147), an indefinite future where we know something will happen but we do not know exactly what or when. For E-A-P the futurity of preparation is reflected in practising. Where rehearsal is historical, circular and non-teleological, practising is inherently futural, progressive and teleological; it is intentional (in terms of seeking to progress within the parameters of given performance benchmarks), and it is a form of work in service to the mastery of a practice as a body of work (through which the verb becomes a noun, acts become things or skills, and experiments become routines). Rehearsal encompasses preparation in a way that is not reversible: 'to prepare is not necessarily to rehearse … but to rehearse is necessarily to prepare' (Peters, 2017, p. 147). At the most essential level, improvisation rests on the rehearsal of rehearsing itself – as a life-long task this represents a decisive commitment to develop the habit of rehearsing itself (which is more important than the choices made while actually rehearsing or performing) and through that to develop the contemplation necessary for the habitual to become transformative.

Drawing on Heidegger (1971) and Deleuze (2006), Peters (2017, pp. 153–158) adopts the Aristotelian distinction between *episteme* as a form of knowledge that is a universal truth, context-independent, rationally based, objective and expressed in propositional knowledge 'about' things, and *techne* as knowledge in the form of craftsmanship, precise codifiable techniques or practical instructions that are amenable to linguistic explication (Chia & Rasche, 2010; Flyvbjerg, 2008). In this analysis, practise is a form of preparation that allows the practitioner to rely on a body of existing knowledge (*episteme*) that can be put into practice, to transfer what is already known from one domain to another, and develop a practice stable enough and sufficiently recognizable to allow improvisation to take place. Rehearsal, by contrast, is seen as an enactment of *techne*, a form of knowing rather than a knowledge of the given that evokes the unfamiliar and the extraordinary. Given that improvisers may not have precise knowledge (*episteme*) of what is going to happen (they need to 'know how not to know' in the 'ignorance economy' (Peters, 2017, p. 154)), practice prepares them for the negotiation with the unknown in a way in which rehearsal does not: the improvisatory act (*techne*) is the creation of specific space-times, and the creative act is not what happens within the space-time of an improvised performance but the creation of the space-time within which the performance itself happens.

This has two consequences. First, it broadens the domain of improvisation itself as more than just the activity of an individual actor (such as an entrepreneur in the pitch to investors and other stakeholders) to include the space-time, the 'happening' that allows things to happen (Peters, 2017, p. 154). As such, this insight provides the basis for a broader understanding of what we mean by 'improvisation': 'The performance of any action, regardless of how predetermined it is in the minds of those who perform it and those who witness it, contains an element of improvisation. The moment of wavering while contemplating how, exactly to execute an action already deeply known, belies the presence of improvised action' (Foster, 2003, p. 4). What Peters (2017, p. 115) calls the 'contemplative wavering within predetermination' that characterizes improvisation is a moment of reflection, hesitation, reservation and decision prior to each gesture. The anteriority of history, and the creation of routines and habituated practices is important, but it is the concentration of that memory in the decisions of the here and now, the entering into the already known again and again that constitutes improvisation.

Second, this attention to *episteme* and *techne* points to the third of Aristotle's types of knowledge – *phronesis* – as a lens through which E-A-P as improvisation can be understood. *Phronesis* is practical wisdom or the ability to act appropriately in a given situation – in the form of tacit knowledge – that expresses the kind of person one is (Chia & Rasche, 2010) and represents the ability to think and act in relation to values and deliberate about things that are good or bad for humans (Flyvbjerg, 2008). Unlike *episteme* and *techne* which can be consciously learned, and hence forgotten, *phronesis* cannot as it is integral to a person's make-up. Similarly, *episteme* and *techne* distinguish between intention and behaviour, such that there is a separation between what one is and what one does. For *phronesis*, on the other hand, what one does is inextricable from who one is: it is the ability to know what is important, know how to bring it about and actually do so (Benson, 2020). This takes us back to praxis as the process by which *phronesis* as a construct becomes lived reality, where the focus of research is on practical activity and practical knowledge in everyday situations. In so doing, we come back to the position that a practice, and improvisation as both a practice and a metaphor for practice, is embedded, embodied and relational: 'the agent […] is constituted through the actions […] he becomes and discovers "who" he is through these actions. And the medium for this becoming through action is not one over which he is sovereign master; it is rather, a network of other people who are also agents and with whom he is bound in relationships of interdependence' (Dunne, 1993, pp. 262–263). This is consistent with Heidegger's (1962) argument that we first encounter the world in the very practical way of living in it and only then do we theorize about the world. For Benson (2020, p. 444), *phronesis* is improvisation, and improvisation is *phronesis*. First, it is the ability to take a given situation – the actors involved, the various circumstances and oneself – and decide on the right thing to do. Second, it requires an attentiveness, care and willingness to give ground and take direction from each other involved in the improvisation process (Becker, 2000) on the basis that our responsibility is first and foremost to other people not abstract rules (Levinas, 1979). Third, as music-making is a social activity (Cobussen & Nielsen, 2012) that requires being attuned to others (co-players, an audience), improvisation is not purely spontaneous: the improviser's freedom is checked by the existence of and responsibility to others and by the acceptance of the standards of excellence and rules that govern the practice (as MacIntyre (1984, p. 190) expressed it 'to enter into a practice is to accept the authority of those standards'). Fourth, improvisation is a form of communication or dialogue: in a reflection on the tension between routines and improvisation, stability and change, discussed earlier, effective communication rests on following conventions (such as grammar, syntax and context). Failure to follow grammatical rules or to understand context (as in the example of the pitch discussed above) will likely lead to miscommunication and misunderstanding (Sawyer, 2000). E-A-P as improvisation requires negotiating the tension between spontaneity and constraint, to develop a 'logical structure of openness' which brings forward something new in a 'state of indeterminacy' (Gadamer, 1989, pp. 362–363).

This has implications for us as practitioners, not least in our pedagogy as we work with other practitioners on our and their practice and praxis. Rehearsal is fundamentally and inescapably repetitive; woodshedding is about mastery through practise and preparation, developing improvisation through a mixture of predefined elements (the protocols, procedures and theoretical insights of our practice) and spontaneity (Harrison, 2017b). The jazz framework of 'improvisation based on underlying rhythmic and harmonic structure in an ensemble context … [is both] … a metaphor for organization and culture and a practical tool in … education' (van Ark & Wijnen-Meijer, 2019, p. 201). Our ability to fully exploit this framework is, however, limited by two weaknesses of the practice literature as it has developed in both the strategy and the entrepreneurship fields (Suddaby et al., 2013). First, there is a 'descriptive trap', the offering up of detailed micro-ethnographies so rich in contextualized description that they preclude wider sensemaking (Sklaveniti & Steyaert, 2020). Second, and relatedly, there is a 'coherence problem' that has made it difficult to build cumulative knowledge about specific areas and a recognition that in E-A-P most of the conceptual work remains to be done (Thompson et al., 2020).

CONCLUSION AND NEW DIRECTIONS

Throughout our discussion, we have taken the view that practice is not some mysterious agency but is simply what people do: in Veyne's (1997) terms objects, such as the state, the manager, the entrepreneur and so on, are only the correlative of a practice. Accordingly, the object is explained by its making, it is a reaction, a result of an assemblage of practices; only the process of objectifying and reifying these practices has led to what we think of as objects (Chia, 1996). This, of course takes us back to Miss Bennet and Mr Darcy and the development of the essential. To paraphrase Carter et al. (2008, p. 92), the object 'entrepreneurship' does not exist as a starting point – only the practices associated with the word make us believe 'entrepreneurship' is a thing that can be observed, crafted and managed whereas it is in fact only a projection of possible practices that might differ and change fundamentally from one setting to another. The problem is starting with the object 'entrepreneurship' and trying to explain how it got manufactured; rather we should forget for the moment the word entrepreneurship and see which practices produce enduring or recurring events that eventually turn into 'things' or 'events' that are then addressed as 'entrepreneurship'.

This leads us to a conclusion: entrepreneurship does not exist independently of a set of practices that form its base. E-A-P therefore should research those practices that constitute the object of entrepreneurship. Much of this hinges on the reconceptualization of actors and agency. Key questions to be addressed could include: which routines make an action or event entrepreneurial? What artefacts and symbols are involved in the creation and legitimization of entrepreneurship? Which performative language games are deployed in the creation of entrepreneurship? A corollary follows: this does not assume that given subjects, called 'entrepreneurs', are necessarily the authors of entrepreneurship, as in practice they have a limited degree of reflexivity about their relationship with the social structures they have created and a relative degree of capacity to change them (Suddaby et al., 2013, p. 338); it is the practices and rituals of entrepreneuring that might constitute a person as an 'entrepreneur'. This in turn suggests a reconsideration of the reification of entrepreneurial organizations, which can be recast as the 'contingent outcomes of ongoing interactions and inter-subjective interpretations of the individuals and social groups through which they are constituted' (Suddaby et al., 2013, p. 338). Mastering a certain language, tools and habitus (remembering that in Bourdieu's (2002 [1977], p. 78) terms, habitus forecloses the possibility of unpredictable novelty, in favour of 'a durably installed generative principle of regulated improvisations') might allow a person to position themselves as having the status of 'entrepreneur' ascribed to them. In other words a practice approach might finally help us understand what constitutes an entrepreneur as a subject, rather than assume them to be so a priori, and recognize that entrepreneurship only exists as an object constituted by a certain practice which itself is not a priori or beforehand entrepreneurial in any respect (Veyne, 1997).

In so doing, entrepreneurial relations display symbolic manifestations that generate a system of highly visible distinctions and discriminations that stratify the availability and appropriateness of the available discourses. Such a symbolic order is never fixed or stable but an effect of previous and current power relations and competitions in which actors seek to define and actualize their entrepreneuring. If this entrepreneuring is indeed world (or history) making as a cultural process (Spinosa et al., 1997), then we need to ask: Whose world? Whose history? Post-Foucault (1977), discourse analysis has dislodged belief in the 'natural' foundations of socially coded and enforced 'differences' and of the systems of scientific validity, ethical values and representation they support (Braidotti, 2002). As such, it rejects unitary identities indexed on a Eurocentric and normative humanist view of 'Man', and emphasizes diversity and difference in speaking of women, natives and other marginal subjects (Braidotti, 2013). The problem with humanism, in this sense, and the challenge for E-A-P, is that the dialectics of self and other and the binary logic of identity and otherness is predicated on the notion of 'difference' as pejoration and implied inferiority. As such, it acquires essentialist and lethal connotations for the others (the sexualized, the racialized and the naturalized): 'all humanisms have been imperial. They speak of the human in the accents and the interests of a class, a sex, a race, a genome. Their embrace suffocates those whom it does not ignore' (Davies, 1997, p. 141).

This humanist 'political economy of difference' (Braidotti, 2013, p. 28) remains an implicit or explicit orientation of current entrepreneurship thought and practice, notwithstanding the interest in entrepreneurship as emancipation (Rindova et al., 2009; Goss et al., 2011). It is reflected in the passing off of entire categories of human beings as devalued and disposable, the valorization of the dominant norm of the subject positioned at the pinnacle of a hierarchical scale that rewarded the ideal of zero-difference (Irigaray, 1993), the 'bellicose dismissiveness' (Said, 2004) of other cultures and civilizations in a process of epistemic and social de-humanization of non-Western others (Santos, 2014), and an enforced structural ignorance of and active production of half-truths about these others (Gilroy, 2010). For E-A-P specifically, as for the humanities and social sciences more generally, 'differences of location between centres and margins matter greatly' (Braidotti, 2013, p. 16): the dialectics of self and other of humanism can be replaced as an orientation by intersectionality, the methodological parallelism of gender, race, class and sexual factors, without flattening any differences between them but rather investing politically the question of their complex interaction (Crenshaw, 1995). One of the challenges for E-A-P is to articulate and implement movement between centres and margins and vice versa and to fully represent the complex interaction of the 'others'.

Entrepreneurship, as a transpositioning, zigzagging improvisational practice, is always a work in process, and the indetermination of entrepreneurships that follows from this is a piece of social construction that takes place in an already structured space of significations, privileges and practices. As the audience co-creates the performance with the improviser, so too it is not only officially formulated entrepreneurs who do entrepreneuring – entrepreneurship is a discourse in which some voices may not be heard or attended to for some time; E-A-P research therefore should explore not only what is done but what is not done, that which is not practised and that which is not said, in pursuit of what might be but is not. Understanding the unbearable lightness of being (Kundera, 2004) is important; more so is understanding the unpredictable process of becoming: an improvisational approach to E-A-P provides the basis for both, playing as it were both the notes and the spaces between the notes, for that is where the magic lies (Harrison, 1999, 2017b).

NOTES

1. We adopt the convention of using 'practice' as the noun and 'practise' as the verb.
2. Klemperer (2014) continues: 'At the same time, woodshedding is a process of demystifying the music … It is a humbling but necessary chore, like chopping wood before you can start the fire. Woodshedding is an outgrowth of the aural tradition in jazz, where a player works out by ear and intuition the music he or she heard played in public. While many jazz musicians have also been trained in written music, jazz improvisation developed aurally and orally, as older musicians passed on their innovations and discoveries to the younger, both through live performances and jam sessions and then, later, through recordings.'

REFERENCES

Adler, P. S., Goldoftas, B., & Levine, D. I. (1999). Flexibility versus efficiency? A case study of model changeovers in the Toyota production system. *Organization Science, 10*(1), 43–68.

Albright, A. C., & Gere, D. (Eds.) (2003). *Taken by Surprise: A Dance Improvisation Reader.* Middleton, CT: Wesleyan University Press.

Alvarez, S. A., & Barney, J. B. (2005). How do entrepreneurs organize firms under conditions of uncertainty? *Journal of Management, 31*(5), 776–793.

Balogun, J., & Johnson, G. (2004). Organizational restructuring and middle-manager sensemaking. *Academy of Management Journal, 47*, 523–549.

Barad, K. (2007). *Meeting the University Halfway: Quantum Physics and the Entanglement of Matter and Meaning.* Durham, NC: Duke University Press.

Barrett, L. F., & Lindquist, K. (2008). The embodiment of emotion. In G. Semin & E. Smith (Eds.), *Embodied Grounding: Social, Cognitive Affective, and Neuroscience Approaches* (pp. 237–262). New York: Cambridge University Press.

Bateson, G. (1972). *Steps to an Ecology of Mind.* Chicago: University of Chicago Press.

Becker, H. S. (2000). The etiquette of improvisation. *Mind, Culture, and Activity, 7*(3), 171–176.

Behfar, K., & Okhuysen, G. A. (2018). Discovery within validation logic: Deliberately surfacing, complementing, and substituting abductive reasoning in hypothetico-deductive inquiry. *Organization Science, 29*, 323–340.

Belgrad, D. (1999). *The Culture of Spontaneity: Improvisation and the Arts in Postwar America.* Chicago: University of Chicago Press.

Benson, B. E. (2020). Improvisation. In T. McAuley, N. Nielsen, & J. Levinson (Eds.), *The Oxford Handbook of Western Music and Philosophy* (pp. 437–450). Oxford: Oxford University Press.

Berkowitz, A. L. (2010). *The Improvising Mind: Cognition and Creativity in the Musical Moment.* Oxford: Oxford University Press.

Betta, M. (2019). Business, organization theory, and the current challenge of neocharisma. *Business and Society Review*, *124*(2), 261–281.

Blanche, C., & Cohendet, P. (2019). Remounting a ballet in a different context: A complementary understanding of routines transfer theories. In M. S. Feldman, L. D'Adderio, & K. Dittrich (Eds.), *Routine Dynamics in Action: Replication and Transformation* (pp. 11–30). Bingley: Emerald Publishing.

Bolden, R. (2011). Distributed leadership in organizations: A review of theory and research. *International Journal of Management Reviews*, *13*(3), 251–269.

Botelho, T., Harrison, R. T., & Mason, C. M. (2018). The business angel exit decision as a learning process: Does experience matter? *Frontiers of Entrepreneurship Research.* https://cdm16793 .contentdm.oclc.org/digital/collection/ferpapers/id/72/rec/6.

Bourdieu, P. (2002 [1977]). *Outline of a Theory of Practice.* Cambridge: Cambridge University Press.

Braidotti, R. (2002). *Metamorphoses: Towards a Materialist Theory of Becoming.* Cambridge: Polity Press.

Braidotti, R. (2006). *Transpositions: On Nomadic Ethics.* Cambridge: Polity Press.

Braidotti, R. (2013). *The Posthuman.* Cambridge: Polity Press.

Briñol, P., & DeMarree, K. (Eds.) (2012). *Social Metacognition.* New York: Psychology Press.

Brown, J. P. (1999). The narrator's voice. In C. Swisher (Ed.), *Readings on* Pride and Prejudice (pp. 103–110). San Diego: Greenhaven Press.

Caines, R., & Heble, A. (Eds.) (2015). *The Improvisation Studies Reader: Spontaneous Acts.* London: Routledge.

Cardon, M. S., Mitteness, C., & Sudek, R. (2017). Motivational cues and angel investing: Interactions among enthusiasm, preparedness, and commitment. *Entrepreneurship Theory and Practice*, *41*, 1057–1085.

Carpentier, C., & Suret, J.-M. (2015). Angel group members' decision process and rejection criteria: A longitudinal analysis. *Journal of Business Venturing*, *30*, 808–821.

Carter, C., Clegg, S. C., & Kornberger, M. (2008). Strategy as practice? *Strategic Organization*, *6*, 83–99.

Cassar, G., & Friedman, H. (2009). Does self-efficacy affect entrepreneurial investment? *Strategic Entrepreneurship Journal*, *3*, 241–260.

Champenois, C., Lefebvre, V., & Ronteau, S. (2020). Entrepreneurship as practice: Systematic literature review of a nascent field. *Entrepreneurship & Regional Development*, *32*(3–4), 281–312.

Chen, S., & Harrison, R. T. (2019). Disentangle the double dilemma of social enterprise: From intra-organisation routine adaptation to cross-organisation routine transfer to multi-organisation network creation. Paper presented to the 35th EGOS Colloquium, Edinburgh, Scotland, 4–6 July.

Chia, R. (1996). *Organizational Analysis as a Deconstructive Practice.* Berlin: De Gruyter.

Chia, R., & Rasche, A. (2010). Epistemological alternatives for researching strategy as practice: Building and dwelling worldviews. In D. Golsorkhi, L. Rouleau, D. Deidl, & E. Vaara (Eds.), *Cambridge Handbook of Strategy as Practice* (pp. 34–46). Cambridge: Cambridge University Press.

Citton, Y. (2016). Politics as hypergestural improvisation in the age of mediocracy. In G. E. Lewis & B. Piekut (Eds.), *The Oxford Handbook of Critical Improvisation Studies, Volume 1* (pp. 160–181). Oxford: Oxford University Press

Clark, A. (1997). *Being There: Putting Brain, Body, and World Together Again.* Cambridge, MA: MIT Press.

Clark, C. (2008). The impact of entrepreneurs' oral 'pitch' presentation skills on business angels' initial screening investment decisions. *Venture Capital*, *10*, 257–279.

Clegg, S. C. (1975). *Power, Rule and Domination.* London: Routledge & Kegan Paul.

Cobussen, M., & Nielsen, N. (2012). *Music and Ethics.* Farnham: Ashgate.

Crenshaw, K. (1997). Intersectionality and identity politics: Learning from violence against women of color. In M. L. Shanley, & U. Narayan (Eds.), *Reconstructing Political Theory: Feminist Perspectives* (pp. 178–193). Pennsylvania State University Press..

Csikszentmihályi, M., & Rich, G. J. (1997). Musical improvisation: A systems approach. In K. Sawyer (Ed.), *Creativity in Performance* (pp. 43–66). Greenwich: Ablex Publishing.

Cunha, M. P. E., & Clegg, S. (2019). Improvisation in the learning organization: A defense of the infra-ordinary. *The Learning Organization, 23*, 238–251.

Damasio, A. (1999). *The Feeling of What Happens: Body and Emotion in the Making of Consciousness.* New York: Houghton Mifflin Harcourt.

Davies, R. (1990). *The Deptford Trilogy: Fifth Business; The Manticore; World of Wonder.* New York: Viking Press.

Davies, T. (1997). *Humanism.* London: Routledge.

de Saint-Exupéry, A. (1984). *The Wisdom of the Sands.* Chicago: University of Chicago Press.

Deken, F., Carlile, P. R., Berends, H., & Lauche, K. (2016). Generating novelty through interdependent routines: A process model of routine work. *Organization Science, 27*(3), 659–677.

Deleuze, G. (2001). *Difference and Repetition.* Trans. B. Patton. London: Continuum.

Deleuze, G. (2006). What is a creative act? In *Two Regimes of Madness: Texts and Interviews 1975–1995.* Cambridge, MA: Semiotext(e).

Dodd, S., Anderson, A., & Jack, S. (2021). 'Let them not make me a stone': Repositioning entrepreneurship. *Journal of Small Business Management.* https://doi.org/10.1080/00472778.2020.1867734.

Dodd, S. D., Pret, T., & Shaw, E. (2016). Advancing understanding of entrepreneurial embeddedness: Forms of capital, social contexts and time. In F. Welter & W. B. Gartner (Eds.), *A Research Agenda for Entrepreneurship and Context* (pp. 120–133). Cheltenham, UK and Northampton, MA, USA: Edward Elgar Publishing.

Du, W. D., Wu, J., Liu, S., & Hackney, R. A. (2019). Effective organizational improvisation in information systems development: Insights from the Tencent messaging system development. *Information & Management, 56*(4), 614–624.

Dunne, J. (1993). *Back to the Rough Ground: Practical Judgement and the Lure of Technique.* Notre Dame, IN: University of Notre Dame Press.

Eddleston, K. A., Ladge, J. J., Mitteness, C., & Balachandra, L. (2016). Do you see what I see? Signaling effects of gender and firm characteristics on financing entrepreneurial ventures. *Entrepreneurship Theory and Practice, 40*, 489–514.

Edelman, L. F., Manolova, T. S., & Brush, C. G. (2017). Angel investing: A literature review. *Foundations and Trends® in Entrepreneurship, 13*, 265–439.

Ehrenzweig, A. (1967). *The Hidden Order of Art.* London: Trinity Press.

Feldman, M. (2000). Organizational routines as a source of continuous change. *Organization Science, 11*(6), 611–629.

Feldman, M., & Orlikowski, W. (2011). Theorizing practice and practicing theory. *Organization Science, 22*(5), 1240–1253.

Feldman, M., & Pentland, B. (2003). Reconceptualizing organizational routines as a source of flexibility and change. *Administrative Science Quarterly, 48*(1), 94–118.

Flyvbjerg, B. (2008). Phronetic organizational research. In R. Thorpe & R. Holt (Eds.), *The Sage Dictionary of Qualitative Management Research* (pp. 153–155). Los Angeles: Sage Publications.

Foster, S. L. (2003). Taken by surprise: Improvisation in dance and mind. In A. C. Albright & D. Gere (Eds.), *Taken by Surprise: A Dance Improvisation Reader* (pp. 3–10). Middletown, CT: Wesleyan University Press.

Foucault, M. (1977). *Discipline and Punish.* Harmondsworth: Penguin.

Gadamer, H.-G. (1989). *Truth and Method* (2nd edition). Trans. J. Weinsheimer & D. G. Marshall. New York: Continuum.

Gallagher, S. (2005). *How the Body Shapes the Mind.* Oxford: Oxford University Press.

Gardner, W. L. (1992). Lessons in organizational dramaturgy: The art of impression management. *Organizational Dynamics, 21*, 33–46.

Garfinkel, H. (1967). *Studies in Ethnomethodology.* Englewood Cliffs, NJ: Prentice Hall.

Gartner, W. B., & Teague, B. (Eds.) (2019). *Research Handbook on Entrepreneurial Behavior, Practice and Process.* Cheltenham, UK and Northampton, MA, USA: Edward Elgar Publishing.

Gersick, C. J., & Hackman, J. R. (1990). Habitual routines in task-performing groups. *Organizational Behavior and Human Decision Processes, 47*, 65–97.

Gilroy, P. (2010). *Darker than Blue.* Cambridge, MA: Harvard University Press.

Goss, D., Jones, R., Betta, M., & Latham, J. (2011). Power as practice: A micro-sociological analysis of the dynamics of emancipatory entrepreneurship. *Organization Studies, 32*(2), 211–229.

Hahn, T. (2016). Banding encounters: Embodied practices in improvisation. In G. Siddall & E. Waterman (Eds.), *Negotiated Moments: Improvisation, Sound, and Subjectivity* (pp. 147–167). Durham, NC: Duke University Press.

Hamzeh, F. R., Faek, F., & Al Hussein, H. (2019). Understanding improvisation in construction through antecedents, behaviours and consequences. *Construction Management and Economics, 37*(2), 61–71.

Hansen, K. (2020). Replacing romantic sentiments with just opinions: How Austen's novels function like Wollstonecraft's 'judicious person'. *Women's Studies, 49*(6), 652–685.

Haraway, D. (1997). *Modest_Witness@Second_Millennium: FemaleMan©_Meets_Oncomouse*. London and New York: Routledge.

Harrison, R. T. (1999). Playing the spaces between the notes: From competence to creativity in executive development. In R. E. Purser & A. Montuori (Eds.), *Social Creativity Volume II* (pp. 257–289). Creskill, NJ: Hampton Press.

Harrison, R. T. (2017a). The internationalisation of business angel investment activity: A review and research agenda. *Venture Capital: An International Journal of Entrepreneurial Finance, 19*, 119–127.

Harrison, R. T. (2017b). Leadership, leadership development and all that jazz. *Leadership, 13*, 81–99.

Harrison, R. T., Botelho, T., & Mason, C. M. (2016). Patient capital in entrepreneurial finance: A reassessment of the role of business angel investors. *Socio-Economic Review, 14*, 669–689.

Harrison, R. T., Dibben, M., & Mason, C. (1997). The role of trust in the informal investor's investment decision: An exploratory analysis. *Entrepreneurship Theory and Practice, 21*(4), 63–81.

Harrison, R. T., & Leitch, C. M. (2021). W(h)ither entrepreneurship: Accumulative fragmentalism on the road to nowhere? Working Paper, University of Edinburgh Business School.

Harrison, R. T., & Mason, C. M. (2017). Backing the horse or the jockey? Due diligence, agency costs, information and the evaluation of risk by business angel investors. *International Review of Entrepreneurship, 15*, 269–290.

Harrison, R. T., Mason, C. M., & Smith, D. (2015). Heuristics, learning and the business angel decision making process. *Entrepreneurship & Regional Development, 27*, 527–554.

Heidegger, M. (1962). *Being and Time*. Trans. J. Macquarrie & E. Robinson. New York: Harper & Row.

Heidegger, M. (1971). The origin of the work of art. In *Poetry, Language, Thought*. New York: Harper & Row.

Heidegger, M. (1999). *Contributions to Philosophy (from Enowing)*. Trans. P. Emad & K. Maly. Bloomington: Indiana University Press.

Hentoff, N. (2006). Introduction, in L. E. Tanner, *The Jazz Image: Masters of Jazz Photography* (pp. 6–7). New York: Abrams.

Hernes, T. (2014). *A Process Theory of Organization*. Oxford: Oxford University Press.

Hill, I. (2018). How did you get up and running? Taking a Bourdieuan perspective towards a framework for negotiating strategic fit. *Entrepreneurship and Regional Development, 30*, 662–696.

Hjorth, D., Holt, R., & Steyaert, C. (2015). Entrepreneurship and process studies. *International Small Business Journal, 33*(6), 599–611.

Hmieleski, K. M., & Corbett, A. C. (2006). Proclivity for improvisation as a predictor of entrepreneurial intentions. *Journal of Small Business Management, 44*(1), 45–63.

Hmieleski, K. M., & Corbett, A. C. (2008). The contrasting interaction effects of improvisational behavior with entrepreneurial self-efficacy on new venture performance and entrepreneur work satisfaction. *Journal of Business Venturing, 23*(4), 482–496.

Holt, R., & Zundel, M. (2017). What paradox? Developing a process syntax for organizational research. In W. K. Smith, M. W. Lewis, P. Jarzabkowski, & A. Langley (Eds.), *The Oxford Handbook of Organizational Paradox* (pp. 87–104). Oxford: Oxford University Press.

Howard-Grenville, J. A., & Parmigiani, A. (2011). Routines revisited: Exploring the capabilities and practice perspectives. *Academy of Management Annals, 5*, 413–453.

Hui, A. (2017). Variation and the intersection of practices. In A. Hui, T. Schatzki, & E. Shove (Eds.), *The Nexus of Practice: Connections, Constellations and Practitioners* (pp. 52–67). London: Routledge.

Irigaray, I. L. (1993). *An Ethics of Sexual Difference*. Ithaca, NY: Cornell University Press.

Jarzabkowski, P. (2004). Strategy as practice: Recursiveness, adaptation, and practices-in-use. *Organization Studies, 25*, 529–560.

Jarzabkowski, P., Balogun, J., & Seidel, D. (2007). Strategizing: The challenges of the practice perspective. *Human Relations, 60*, 5–27.

Jones, O. (2008). The entrepreneurial decision. *International Journal of Entrepreneurial Behavior & Research, 14*(2). https://doi.org/10.1108/ijebr.2008.16014baa.001.

Jouxtel, P. (2019). Rituals and routines: A joint approach to the rebellious life of teams in organizational stability and change. *Society and Business Review, 14*(1), 93–111.

Klemperer, P. (2014). Woodshedding and the jazz tradition. http://w.bigapplejazz.com/woodshedding.html.

Kundera, M. (2004). *The Unbearable Lightness of Being*. London: Faber and Faber.

Laine, L. J., & Kibler, E. (2018). Towards a mythic process philosophy of entrepreneurship. *Journal of Business Venturing Insights, 9*, 81–86.

Landström, H. (2004). Entrepreneurship research and its historical background. In T. Baker & F. Welter (Eds.), *The Routledge Companion to Entrepreneurship* (pp. 21–40). London: Routledge.

Landström, H. (2020). The evolution of entrepreneurship as a scholarly field. *Foundations and Trends® in Entrepreneurship, 16*(2), 65–243.

Landy, J. (2020). In praise of depth: Or, how I stopped worrying and learned to love the hidden. *New Literary History, 51*, 145–176.

Lavender, L. (2019). The emancipation of improvisation. In V. L. Midgelow (Ed.), *The Oxford Handbook of Improvisation in Dance* (pp. 275–294). Oxford: Oxford University Press.

Lefebvre, V., Certhoux, G., & Radu-Lefebvre, M. (2020). Sustaining trust to cross the Valley of Death: A retrospective study of business angels' investment and reinvestment decisions. *Technovation*. https://doi.org/10.1016/j.technovation.2020.102159.

Levinas, E. (1979). *Totality and Infinity: An Essay on Exteriority*. Trans. A. Lingus. The Hague: Martinus Nijhoff.

Lewis, G. E. (2008). *A Power Stronger than Itself: The AACM and American Experimental Music*. Chicago: University of Chicago Press.

Lewis, G. E., & Piekut, B. (Eds.) (2016a). *The Oxford Handbook of Critical Improvisation Studies, Volume 1*. Oxford: Oxford University Press.

Lewis, G. E., & Piekut, B. (Eds.) (2016b). *The Oxford Handbook of Critical Improvisation Studies, Volume 2*. Oxford: Oxford University Press.

Luhmann, N. (2000). *Die Politik der Gesellschaft*. Frankfurt am Main: Suhrkamp.

MacIntyre, A. (1984). *After Virtue* (2nd edition). South Bend, IN: University of Notre Dame Press.

March, J. G., & Simon, H. A. (1958). *Organizations*. New York: Wiley.

Mason, C. M., Botelho, T., and Harrison, R. T. (2016). The transformation of the business angel market: Empirical evidence and research implications. *Venture Capital: An International Journal of Entrepreneurial Finance, 18*, 321–344.

Mason, C. M., & Harrison, R. T. (1996). Why business angels say no: A case study of opportunities rejected by an informal investment syndicate. *International Small Business Journal, 14*(2), 35–51.

Mason, C. M., & Harrison, R. T. (2001). Investment readiness: A critique of government proposals to increase the demand for venture capital. *Regional Studies, 35*, 663–668.

Mason, C. M., & Harrison, R. T. (2003). Auditioning for money: What do technology investors look for at the initial screening stage? *Journal of Private Equity, 6*, 29–42.

Mason, C. M., & Harrison, R. T. (2019). The changing nature of angel investing: Some research implications. *Venture Capital: An International Journal of Entrepreneurial Finance, 21*, 177–194.

Matthews, R. S., Chalmers, D. M., & Fraser, S. S. (2018). The intersection of entrepreneurship and selling: An interdisciplinary review, framework and future research agenda. *Journal of Business Venturing, 33*(6), 691–719.

Maxwell, A., Jeffrey, S. A., & Lévesque, M. (2011). Business angel early stage decision making. *Journal of Business Venturing, 26*(2), 212–225.

McMullen, J. S., & Dimov, D. (2013). Time and the entrepreneurial journey: The problems and promise of studying entrepreneurship as a process. *Journal of Management Studies, 50*, 1481–1512.

Merleau-Ponty, M. (1965 [1942]). *The Structure of Behavior*. London: Methuen.

Miner, A. S., Bassof, P., & Moorman, C. (2001). Organizational improvisation and learning: A field study. *Administrative Science Quarterly, 46*(2), 304–337.

Miner, A. S., Ciuchta, M. P., & Gong, Y. (2008). Organizational routines and organizational learning. In M. C. Becker (Ed.), *Handbook of Organizational Routines* (pp. 152–186). Cheltenham, UK and Northampton, MA, USA: Edward Elgar Publishing.

Mintzberg, H. (1973). *The Nature of Managerial Work*. New York: Harper & Row.

Moore, D. C. (2019). Messy engagement. In *The International Encyclopedia of Media Literacy*. New York: John Wiley.

Murnieks, C. Y., Cardon, M. S., Sudek, R., White, T. D., & Brooks, W. T. (2016). Drawn to the fire: The role of passion, tenacity and inspirational leadership in angel investing. *Journal of Business Venturing*, *31*, 468–484.

Nama, Y., & Lowe, A. (2014). The 'situated functionality' of accounting in private equity practices: A social 'site' analysis. *Management Accounting Research*, *25*(4), 284–303.

Nelson, R. R., & Winter, S. G. (1982). *An Evolutionary Theory of Economic Change*. Cambridge: Cambridge University Press.

Nettl, B. et al. (n.d.). Improvisation. *Oxford Music Online*. http://www.oxfordmusiconline.com/subscriber/article/grove/music/13738.

Nicolini, D. (2012). *Practice Theory, Work, & Organization: An Introduction*. Oxford: Oxford University Press.

Nicolini, D. (2017). Practice theory as a package of theory, method and vocabulary: Affordances and limitations. In M. Jonas, B. Littig, & A. Wroblewski (Eds.), *Methodological Reflections on Practice Oriented Theories* (pp. 19–34). New York: Springer International.

Noland, C. (2009). *Agency and Embodiment: Performing Gestures/Producing Culture*. Cambridge, MA: Harvard University Press.

Nystrom, P. C., & Starbuck, W. H. (1984). Organizational facades. In J. A. Pearce & R. B. Robinson (Eds.), *Proceedings of the 44th Annual Meeting of the Academy of Management* (pp. 182–185). Boston: Academy of Management.

Orlikowski, W. J. (1996). Improvising organizational transformation over time: A situated change perspective. *Information Systems Research*, *7*(1), 63–92.

Orlikowski, W. J. (2000). Using technology and constituting structures: A practice lens for studying technology in organizations. *Organization Science*, *11*(4), 404–428.

Orlikowski, W. J. (2002). Knowing in practice: Enacting a collective capability in distributed organizing. *Organization Science*, *13*, 249–273.

Orlikowski, W. J. (2010). Practice in research: Phenomenon, perspective and philosophy. In D. Golsorkhi, L. Rouleau, D. Seidl, & E. Vaara (Eds.), *Cambridge Handbook of Strategy as Practice* (pp. 23–33). Cambridge: Cambridge University Press.

Perec, G. (1997). *Species of Places and Other Pieces*. Trans. J Sturrock. London: Penguin Books.

Peters, G. (2009). *The Philosophy of Improvisation*. Chicago: University of Chicago Press.

Peters, G. (2017). *Improvising Improvisation: From Out of Philosophy, Music, Dance and Literature*. Chicago: University of Chicago Press.

Peterson, O. (2002). *A Jazz Odyssey*. London: Continuum.

Pollock, N., Chapple, D., & Chen, S. (2020). The second most important pitch: How nascent digital ventures build credibility by briefing analysts. https://doi.org/10.5465/AMBPP.2020.10019abstract.

Postill, J. (2010). Introduction: Theorising media and practice. In B. Bräuchler & J. Postill (Eds.), *Theorising Media and Practice* (pp. 35–54). New York: Berghahn Books.

Pozen, D. E. (2007). We are all entrepreneurs now. *Wake Forest Law Review*, *43*, 283–340.

Pressing, J. (1984). Cognitive processes in improvisation. In R. W. Crozier & A. J. Chapman (Eds.), *Cognitive Processes in the Perception of Art* (pp. 345–364). Amsterdam: North-Holland.

Pressing, J. (1998). Psychological constraints on improvisational expertise and communication. In B. Nettl & M. Russell (Eds.), *In the Course of Performances: Studies in the World of Musical Improvisation* (pp. 345–366). Chicago: University of Chicago Press.

Reckwitz, A. (2002). Toward a theory of social practices: A development in culturalist theorizing. *European Journal of Social Theory*, *5*(2), 243–263.

Rerup, C., & Feldman, S. (2011). Routines as a source of change in organizational schemata: The role of trial-and-error learning. *Academy of Management Journal*, *54*, 577–610.

Rindova, V., Barry, D., & Ketchen Jr, D. J. (2009). Entrepreneuring as emancipation. *Academy of Management Review*, *34*(3), 477–491.

Rix, G., & Lièvre, P. (2008). Towards a codification of practical knowledge. *Knowledge Management Research & Practice*, *6*, 225–232.

Roy, D. (2008). Asking different questions: Feminist practices for the natural sciences. *Hypatia: A Journal of Feminist Philosophy, 23*, 134–157.

Said, E. (2004). *Humanism and Democratic Criticism*. New York: Columbia University Press.

Santos, B. de S. (2014). *Epistemologies of the South: Justice against Epistemicide*. Abingdon: Routledge.

Sawyer, R. K. (2000). Improvisation and the creative process: Dewey, Collingwood, and the aesthetics of spontaneity. *Journal of Aesthetics and Art Criticism, 58*, 149–161.

Schatzki, T. R. (1988). The nature of social reality. *Philosophy and Phenomenological Research, 49*, 239–260.

Schatzki, T. R. (2002). *The Site of the Social: A Philosophical Account of the Constitution of Social Life and Change*. University Park: Pennsylvania State University Press.

Schatzki, T. R. (2005). Peripheral vision: The sites of organizations. *Organization Studies, 26*(3), 465–484.

Schatzki, T. R. (2012). A primer on practices. In J. Higgs, R. Barnett, M. Hutchings, & F. Trede (Eds.), *Practice-Based Education: Perspectives and Strategies* (pp. 13–26). Rotterdam: Sense Publishers.

Schatzki, T. R., Knorr Cetina, K., & Savigny, E. von (Eds.) (2001). *The Practice Turn in Contemporary Theory*. London: Routledge.

Schön, D. (1983). *The Reflective Practitioner*. London: Temple Smith.

Schutz, A. (1964). Making music together: A study in social relationship. In A. Broderson (Ed.), *Alfred Schutz, Collected Papers 2: Studies in Social Theory* (pp. 159–178). The Hague: Martinus Nijhoff.

Schwarz, G., & Stensaker, I. (2014). Time to take off the theoretical straitjacket and (re-)introduce phenomenon-driven research. *The Journal of Applied Behavioral Science, 50*, 478–501.

Schwarz, G., & Stensaker, I. (2016). Showcasing phenomenon-driven research on organizational change. *Journal of Change Management, 16*, 245–264.

Shaffer, J. (1992). Not subordinate: Empowering women in the marriage plot–the novels of Francis Burney, Maria Edgeworth, and Jane Austen. *Criticism, 34*, 51–73.

Shook, J. R., & Solymosi, T. (2014). Neuropragmatism and the reconstruction of scientific and humanistic worldviews. In T. Solymosi & J. R. Shook (Eds.), *Neuroscience, Neurophilosophy and Pragmatism* (pp. 3–36). Basingstoke: Palgrave Macmillan.

Siddall, G., & Waterman, E. (2016). Introduction. In G. Siddall & E. Waterman (Eds.), *Negotiated Moments: Improvisation, Sound, and Subjectivity* (pp. 1–20). Durham, NC: Duke University Press.

Silverman, D., & Jones, J. (1976). *Organizational Work: The Language of Grading, the Grading of Language*. London: Collier Macmillan.

Sklaveniti, C., & Steyaert, C. (2020). Reflecting with Pierre Bourdieu: Towards a reflexive outlook for practice-based studies of entrepreneurship. *Entrepreneurship & Regional Development, 32*, 313–333.

Söderblom, A., Samuelsson, M., & Mårtensson, P. (2016). Opening the black box: Triggers for shifts in business angels' risk mitigation strategies within investments. *Venture Capital, 18*, 211–236.

Spinosa, C., Flores, F., & Dreyfus, H. (1997). *Disclosing New Worlds: Entrepreneurship, Democratic Action and the Cultivation of Solidarity*. Cambridge, MA: MIT Press.

Stańczyk, S., & Stańczyk-Hugiet, E. (2019). Organizational routines (ORs). In E. Stańczyk-Hugiet, K. Piórkowska, S. Stańczyk, & J. Strużyna (Eds.), *Evolutionary Selection Processes: Towards Intra-Organizational Facets* (pp. 35–68). Bingley: Emerald Publishing.

Steyaert, C. (2007). 'Entrepreneuring' as a conceptual attractor? A review of process theories in 20 years of entrepreneurship studies. *Entrepreneurship & Regional Development, 19*(6), 453–477.

Suarez, F. F., & Montes, J. S. (2019). An integrative perspective of organizational responses: Routines, heuristics, and improvisations in a Mount Everest expedition. *Organization Science, 30*, 573–599.

Suchman, L. (1987). *Plans and Situated Actions*. Cambridge: Cambridge University Press.

Suddaby, R., Seidel, D., & Lê, J. K. (2013). Strategy-as-practice meets neo-institutional theory. *Strategic Organization, 11*, 329–344.

Szwed, J. (1980). Josef Skvorecky and the tradition of jazz literature. *World Literature Today, 54*, 586–590.

Tatli, A., Vassilopoulou, J., Özbilgin, M., Forson, C., & Slutskaya, N. A. (2014). A Bourdieuan relational perspective for entrepreneurship research. *Journal of Small Business Management, 52*, 615–632.

Teague, B. T., Gorton, M. D., & Liu, Y. (2020). Different pitches for different stages of entrepreneurial development: The practice of pitching to business angels. *Entrepreneurship & Regional Development, 32*(3–4), 334–352.

Tenca, F., Croce, A., & Ughetto, E. (2018). Business angels research in entrepreneurial finance: A literature review and a research agenda. *Journal of Economic Surveys*, *32*, 1384–1413.

Thompson, N. A., Verduijn, K., & Gartner, W. B. (2020). Entrepreneurship-as-practice: Grounding contemporary theories of practice into entrepreneurship studies. *Entrepreneurship & Regional Development*, *32*, 247–256.

Turner, V. W. (1992). Dewey, Dilthey, and drama: An essay in the anthropology of experience. In V. W. Turner & E. M. Bruner (Eds.), *The Anthropology of Experience* (pp. 33–44). Urbana, IL: University of Illinois Press.

van Ark, A. E., & Wijnen-Meijer, M. (2019). 'Doctor Jazz': Lessons that medical professionals can learn from jazz musicians. *Medical Teacher*, *41*(2), 201–206.

Vermersch, P. (1999). Pour une psychologie phénoménologique. *Psychologie Française*, *44*, 7–18.

Veyne, P. (1997). Foucault revolutionizes history. In A. I. Davidson (Ed.), *Foucault and his Interlocutors* (pp. 146–182). Chicago: University of Chicago Press.

Von Krogh, G., Rossi-Lamastra, C., & Haefliger, S. (2012). Phenomenon-based research in management and organization science: When is it rigorous and does it matter? *Long Range Planning*, *45*, 277–298.

Wallmeroth, J., Wirtz, P., & Groh, A. P. (2018). Venture capital, angel financing, and crowdfunding of entrepreneurial ventures: A literature review. *Foundations and Trends® in Entrepreneurship*, *14*, 1–129.

Weick, K. E. (1998). Improvisation as a mindset for organizational analysis. *Organization Science*, *9*, 543–555.

Wetzel, R., & Tint, B. (2019). Using applied improvisation for organizational learning in the Red Cross Red Crescent Climate Centre. In E. P. Antonacopoulou & S. S. Taylor (Eds.), *Sensuous Learning for Practical Judgment in Professional Practice* (pp. 47–73). Cham: Palgrave Macmillan.

White, B. A., & Dumay, J. (2017). Business angels: A research review and new agenda. *Venture Capital: An International Journal of Entrepreneurial Finance*, *19*, 183–216.

White, T. H. (1938). *The Sword in the Stone*. London: William Collins.

Whittington, R. (2006). Completing the practice turn in strategy research. *Organization Studies*, *27*, 613–634.

Williamson, T. (2003). Everything. *Philosophical Perspectives*, *17*, 415–465.

Wolf, V., & Beverungen, D. (2019). Conceptualizing the impact of workarounds: An organizational routines perspective. In *Proceedings of the 27th European Conference on Information Systems (ECIS)*. Stockholm & Uppsala, Sweden, 8–14 June. https://aisel.aisnet.org/ecis2019_rip/72.

Yu, X., Li, Y., Su, Z., Tao, Y., Nguyen, B., & Xia, F. (2020). Entrepreneurial bricolage and its effects on new venture growth and adaptiveness in an emerging economy. *Asia Pacific Journal of Management*, *37*, 1141–1163.

Zbaracki, M. J., & Bergen, M. (2010). When truces collapse: A longitudinal study of price-adjustment routines. *Organization Science*, *21*(5), 955–972.

9. The artifacts of entrepreneurial practice

Henrik Berglund and Vern L. Glaser

INTRODUCTION

Historically, most explanations of venture development tend to focus on character traits or cognitive heuristics of individual entrepreneurs (Alvarez, Barney, & Anderson, 2012; Gartner, 1988; Sarasvathy, 2001), aspects of the environment that help shape the process (Ramoglou & Tsang, 2016; Venkataraman, 1997), or sequences of events and activities that mark venture development progress (Gartner, Shaver, Carter, & Reynolds, 2004). In recent years, practice-oriented scholars have instead sought to combine accounts of individuals, contexts, and activities by moving closer – both empirically and conceptually – to "the real-time doings and sayings of practitioners involved in entrepreneurship" (Champenois, Lefebvre, & Ronteau, 2020, p. 281). By doing so, the ambition is to develop more descriptively accurate and prescriptively useful entrepreneurship theories.

However, despite the practice tradition's commitment to sociomateriality and entrepreneurial practices as materially mediated (e.g., Thompson & Byrne, 2020), the central artifacts of entrepreneurial practice – such as pitches, business plans, business model diagrams, financial models, prototypes, minimum viable products, etc. – have received surprisingly little attention from not only mainstream entrepreneurship scholars, but also from scholars explicitly concerned with entrepreneurship-as-practice. This is surprising for several reasons. First, artifacts in the form of business model canvases (Osterwalder, 2013), minimum viable products (Blank, 2013; Ries, 2011), and prototypes (Savoia, 2019) are absolutely central in the thriving practitioner literature. In contrast, the neglect of entrepreneurial artifacts in the academic literature is striking. As a result, many entrepreneurship scholars grudgingly admit to teaching the Lean Startup methodology (Ries, 2011) or incorporating the Business Owner's Manual (Blank & Dorf, 2012) into their courses, because students are most interested in learning how to design products and businesses.

Second, entrepreneurship, when viewed as a management practice (as opposed to self-employment, an economic function, or the running of a small business), is essentially concerned with the design of new businesses in the face of uncertainty (Klein, 2008). From a design perspective (Berglund, Dimov, & Wennberg, 2018; Rindova & Martins, 2021; Wegener & Glaser, 2021), a focus on central entrepreneurial artifacts such as prototypes, business plans, and pitches is arguably quite natural and will likely improve our understanding of entrepreneurship. Analogous illustrations include how examinations of the constraints and affordances of Microsoft Excel helped explain the practice of financial evaluation (Spee, Jarzabkowski, & Smets, 2016), how investigating the use of whiteboards (Sapsed & Salter, 2004) and PowerPoint (Kaplan, 2011) helped develop theory about how collaborative work is enabled and constrained, and how studying algorithms and information systems has helped us understand the formation of organizational routines (Glaser, Valadao, & Hannigan, 2021).

Despite the obvious potential for practical utility as well as theoretical understanding, entrepreneurship research has so far been conducted without much attention paid to its central artifacts. Echoing Schumpeter (1942) and Baumol (1968), it is as if the Prince of Denmark had again been expunged from discussions of *Hamlet*. Only this time, it is not entrepreneurs who are missing from economic theories or textbooks, but artifacts that are missing from accounts of entrepreneurial practice. To rectify this situation, we first define entrepreneurial artifacts and describe them in terms of three broad categories: abstract, material, and narrative. Then, we discuss themes that we believe should be addressed to advance our conceptual understanding of entrepreneurial artifacts. We conclude the chapter by exploring the implications of our conceptual framework for the practice (and practice theory) of entrepreneurship.

ENTREPRENEURIAL ARTIFACTS

The value of considering artifacts in accounts of development and change has long been stressed by practice-oriented social theorists (e.g., Knorr Cetina, 2001; Latour, 1987; Schatzki, Knorr Cetina, & Savigny, 2001) as well as by organizational scholars from an increasingly broad set of perspectives (e.g., Carlile, 2002; D'Adderio, 2011; Glaser, 2017; Simon, 1996; Suchman, 2007; Whittington, 2003). In addition to making research more practically useful, there is much to be gained conceptually by making artifacts central to how we understand entrepreneurship as a practice, where such artifacts function as evolving boundary objects of sorts that relate individuals and environments as part of design-oriented practices (e.g., Bechky, 2003; Berglund, Bousfiha, & Mansoori, 2020; Knorr Cetina, 2001; Kostis & Ritala, 2020; Orlikowski & Lacono, 2001; Randhawa, West, Skellern, & Josserand, 2021; Rindova & Martins, 2021). In this spirit, we build on the work of Berglund et al. (2020, p. 828) and conceptualize the entrepreneurship concept of "opportunity" as the most abstract entrepreneurial artifact.[1] The abstract opportunity-as-artifact is then iteratively developed in an entrepreneurial design process that revolves around more concrete entrepreneurial artifacts – such as business models, prototypes, landing pages, pitches etc. – which serve connect and gradually stabilize the relationship between the organized individuals of the entrepreneurial venture and their external environment.

In our treatment, we define any artifact that serves to instantiate an abstract opportunity in a way that supports its further development as entrepreneurial (Berglund et al., 2020). While emphasizing the individual entrepreneur, Dimov's (2011, pp. 62–63) description resonates with ours:

> An opportunity epitomizes the symbolic aspect of the interaction between entrepreneurs and their environments. It can be regarded as an evolving blueprint for action, synthesizing the entrepreneur's sense of, expectations about, and aspirations for the future, and can help us understand what the entrepreneur does at every step of the way from within the worldview that the entrepreneur holds.

To further elucidate and make operable our understanding of entrepreneurial artifacts, we highlight three sub-categories: abstract artifacts, material artifacts, and narrative artifacts. While internally heterogeneous and partly overlapping, these broad types clarify our discussion and provide a stepping stone for entrepreneurship-as-practice scholars to better understand the entrepreneurial process. We illustrate each type of artifact using examples from academic and practitioner writings about entrepreneurship, and summarize this typology of entrepreneurial artifacts in Table 9.1.

Table 9.1   A typology of entrepreneurial artifacts

Entrepreneurial artifact	Definition	Examples
Abstract	Conceptual devices that help entrepreneurs develop theories of their ventures which in turn help them develop their organizations, create products and services, and communicate with external stakeholders	Business model Entrepreneurial identity
Material	"Things" whose corporeity and material substance are central to their function in the entrepreneurial process	Physical prototypes Digital prototypes
Narrative	Sensemaking devices that are not defined by their materiality, but rather by their ability to relate individuals, objects, and events in meaningful accounts	Business plans Rhetorical tropes: – Analogy, metaphor, synecdoche – Anomaly, paradox, and irony

Abstract Artifacts

Abstract entrepreneurial artifacts are conceptual devices that help entrepreneurs articulate theories of their ventures which in turn help them develop their organizations, create products and services, and communicate with external stakeholders. At the core of the entrepreneurial process is thus the development of "blueprints" (Dimov, 2011) or "theories" that "shape entrepreneurial action and strategy" (Felin & Zenger, 2009, p. 135). Specifically, to comprehend and describe entrepreneurial opportunities, entrepreneurs need to develop theories and models that make them concrete: "Entrepreneurs and managers originate theories and hypotheses about which activities they should engage in, which assets they might buy, and how they will create value" (Felin & Zenger, 2017, p. 258). Examples of abstract artifacts that instantiate an entrepreneurial theory are a *business model* and an *entrepreneurial identity*.

Academics and practitioners alike have used the concept of a *business model*, "the rationale of how an organization creates, delivers, and captures value" (Osterwalder & Pigneur, 2010, p. 14), to describe the theory of how a venture operates (for a more detailed history of the concept of business model, see DaSilva & Trkman, 2014). Academic understandings of business models suggest that they can be used to classify organizations, function as sources for analogical inspiration for strategic changes, or provide recipes for how to organize business processes and activities (Baden-Fuller & Morgan, 2010). Business models are used by entrepreneurs as market devices that facilitate the connections entrepreneurs make with other actors (Doganova & Eyquem-Renault, 2009), and recent research has begun to theorize the process of designing business models in nascent markets (McDonald & Eisenhardt, 2020). Academics thus have used business models to analyze and assess organizational performance.

Recently, business models have become increasingly central to the practices of entrepreneurship – specifically through the introduction of the business model canvas (Blank, 2013; Osterwalder & Pigneur, 2010). The business model canvas is an artifactual tool used to stimulate entrepreneurial articulation of the theory of the venture, asking questions about key partners, activities, and resources, value propositions, customer relationships, channels, customer segments, cost structures, and revenue streams that can be rapidly tested and evaluated (Blank, 2013). The business model canvas, when integrated with entrepreneurial practices intended to help would-be entrepreneurs recognize patterns, design novel business models, and re-interpret existing strategies through a business model lens, becomes a central means through which entrepreneurial practice is enacted (Osterwalder & Pigneur, 2010). The entrepreneurial artifact of the business model canvas (see Figure 9.1) thus has become a central part of entrepreneurship in practice, considering that the inventor of the canvas, Alex Osterwalder claimed that over 5,000,000 practitioners had downloaded it from the "strategyzer" website (Amarsy, 2015).

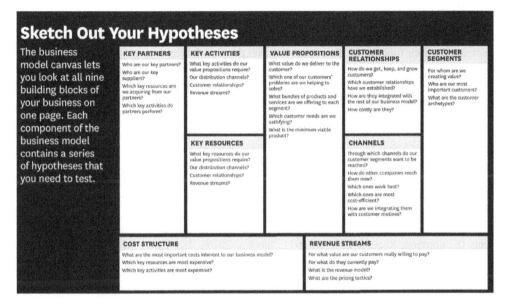

Source: Blank (2013).

Figure 9.1   The business model canvas

Another abstract artifact that can be associated with the theory of the entrepreneurial venture is *entrepreneurial identity* (Navis & Glynn, 2011). Entrepreneurs, when promoting novel innovations, need to concurrently promote the general legitimacy of their innovations while also maintaining their distinctiveness relative to other innovators (Navis & Glynn, 2010). Identity work is central to how entrepreneurs accomplish this, and existing research highlights its significance. Grimes (2018) showed that when engaging in the practice of entrepreneurship, founders often need to overcome the challenge of maintaining their distinctiveness while demonstrating their responsiveness to external feedback (see also McDonald & Gao, 2019; Snihur & Zott, 2020). Specifically, entrepreneurs use the abstract artifact of identity to enact practices of idea work (i.e., defending, repairing, and re-engineering) and identity work (i.e., transcending, decoupling, and professionalizing) in order to balance their needs to both differentiate and assimilate (Grimes, 2018, p. 1703). Collectively, the abstract entrepreneurial artifacts of business models and entrepreneurial identity provide an important framework from which to explore our understanding of entrepreneurship as practice.

Future research in this vein might explore how historical and contemporary analogs and antilogs (Mullins & Komisar, 2009) influence the design and use of abstract artifacts, including, but not limited to, popular business models (e.g., Chen, 2019) and founder identities (e.g., Carreyrou, 2020). Similarly, studies of cultural entrepreneurship exploring entrepreneurial possibilities (Lounsbury & Glynn, 2019) and optimal distinctiveness (Zhao, Fisher, Lounsbury, & Miller, 2017) might both enrich, and be enriched by, accounts of the influence and use of abstract artifacts.

Material Artifacts

Material entrepreneurial artifacts are those "things" whose corporeity and material substance are central to their function in the entrepreneurial process. In the strategy-as-practice literature (e.g., Vaara & Whittington, 2012; Whittington, 2003), scholars have long described how the materiality of PowerPoint presentations (Kaplan, 2011), spreadsheets (Spee et al., 2016), whiteboards (Hodgkinson & Wright, 2002), and other tools shape strategy work. Such artifacts can, of course, be relevant to entrepreneurial practice as well. However, to be properly considered as entrepreneurial artifacts in our framework, they must also be used to instantiate the opportunities being pursued. Key examples of material artifacts are *physical prototypes* and *digital prototypes*.

Physical prototypes are very common in the practitioner literature on entrepreneurship (e.g., Blank & Dorf, 2012; Kromer, 2019; Mansoori & Lackeus, 2020; Savoia, 2019) where they are usually designed to be distinct and unambiguous representations of the envisioned value proposition with a special emphasis on what are believed to be its most critical elements (Eisenmann, Ries, & Dillard, 2011; Savoia, 2019). Typically, the central focus is the envisioned product or user experience, and through their own or others' engagement with prototypes, entrepreneurs are able to evaluate assumptions, identify limitations, and surface opportunities for further development that otherwise would be easy to miss. An illustrative example is the wood and paper mockup of the Palm Pilot used by cofounder Jeff Hawkins during its early development (Jackson, 1998; Savoia, 2019) (see Figure 9.2).

Importantly, while material prototypes often represent the envisioned product in physical or digital form, their potential for generating insights during interactions with potential customers, users, partners, investors, and other external stakeholders goes beyond the product per se. In such situations, the entrepreneur can use the material artifact and descriptions of its intended functionality as a jumping-off point before segueing into more general discussions of the business as a whole. Enabling potential customers to vividly envision what it would be like to have a Palm Pilot and quite literally appreciate the difference it would make in their lives sets the stage for very concrete discussions of relevance to the entrepreneurial design process writ large, such as: typical use cases, preferred revenue models, complementary products and services, potential competitors, relevant marketing channels and key opinion leaders, product categorization and positioning, relevant trends in markets, technology, or regulations, etc. (Blank & Dorf, 2012; Moore, 2014).

Digital entrepreneurial artifacts have often been discussed in the context of experimentally testing explicit hypotheses, e.g., through landing pages or online ads for A/B testing, or more elaborate concierge or wizard of Oz MVPs (see Camuffo, Cordova, Gambardella, & Spina, 2020; Eisenmann et al., 2011; Kromer, 2019). However, due to their distributed nature and the relative ease by which software can be altered, digital artifacts can also be used to harness the transformational potential of collective creativity. Examples of such transformation-inducing digital artifacts include free and open-source software systems such as Linux and Wikipedia

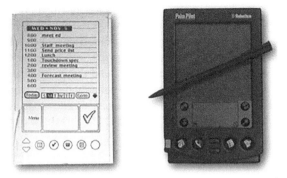

Source: Jackson (1998).

Figure 9.2   *Physical prototype of the Palm Pilot*

Source: TechCrunch Blog (2011).

Figure 9.3   *Digital prototype of the Dropbox video*

(Garud, Jain, & Tuertscher, 2008; Nambisan, 2017) as well as more delimited and focused artifacts such as software development kits (Franke & Piller, 2004; von Hippel & Katz, 2002) and digital probes (Jarvenpaa & Standaert, 2018) that entrepreneurs can use to explicitly invite others into the development process. An illustrative example of experimentation through digital artifacts is the video detailing the planned feature set and user experience of Dropbox (Figure 9.3), created by cofounder Drew Houston (Berglund et al., 2020; TechCrunch Blog, 2011). Being digital, the early Dropbox prototypes were shared and diffused to hundreds of thousands of potential users overnight, leading to validation of several critical business hypotheses. This example illustrates one of the advantages of digital over physical artifacts – namely, the speed and ease with which they can be distributed and transformed (Nambisan, 2017; Zittrain, 2006). With growing resources and userbases, startups often take full advantage of these affordances by running large numbers of simultaneous experiments (Thomke, 2001).

Future research in this vein might empirically explore how, for what purposes, and with what consequences physical and digital artifacts are used, thus probing deeper into the question of how the affordances and constraints of materiality artifacts makes them more or less suitable for various entrepreneurial design tasks. Based on such insights, scholars may also develop a typology with which to classify material artifacts and their affordances in the context of entrepreneurship (Berglund et al., 2020). Such efforts have been undertaken in many design-oriented fields. In information systems, the affordances of technologies that can enable informal network change across interdependent organizations have been categorized as individualized, collective, and shared (Leonardi, 2013), and the broad challenges of knowledge exchange, knowledge deliberation, and knowledge collaboration in large-scale collaborative efforts have similarly been matched with the affordances of knowledge collaging, purposeful deliberating, and knowledge interlacing (cf. Malhotra, Majchrzak, & Lyytinen, 2021).

Narrative Artifacts

By narrative entrepreneurial artifacts, we mean sensemaking devices that are not defined by their materiality, but rather by their ability to relate individuals, objects, and events in meaningful accounts. Depending on the purpose for which they are used, the function of narrative artifacts is to represent the opportunity with appropriate clarity, coherence, and stability (Ashforth & Humphrey, 1997). Due to their immaterial character, narratives can be recrafted very easily in principle, in the sense that the entrepreneur simply must tell a different story. In practice, however, the fact that narrative artifacts tend to be instantiated in physical documents or digital files – and are constrained by broader material and discursive circumstances that influence what can be meaningfully said – makes them more or less inert. Still, the material substrate is a contingent feature of any narrative artifact whose essence is captured in the account itself. In entrepreneurship, the archetypical narrative can be thought of as the business plan, and the narrative it uses employs a variety of literary devices to communicate a message or stimulate the generation of new insights (Garud, Gehman, & Giuliani, 2014).

The business plan tells a story that connects aspects of the past with present conditions in order to chart a plausible path toward the future. Echoing longstanding fault lines in the strategy field, business plans are often described as rational instruments that reflect the strategic intent of the firm and its founders, or as institutionally conditioned artifacts designed in response to external norms and pressures in order to appear legitimate to important stakeholders such as investors or partners (Honig & Karlsson, 2004). In discussions with such stakeholders, entrepreneurs are often advised to aim for optimal distinctiveness in the sense of constructing a narrative that balances the value of standing out as innovative and different with the value of being feasible and legitimate (Lounsbury & Glynn, 2001). Consequently, a business plan typically must cover a series of events and concepts that expand beyond and/or flesh out the entrepreneurial identity, as illustrated in "how-to" manuals prevalent in the practitioner literature (for an example, see Shelton, 2017), or in "the pitches" that entrepreneurs make to solicit investor fundings (e.g., Garud, Gehman, & Tharchen, 2018; Soublière & Gehman, 2020; van Werven, Bouwmeester, & Cornelissen, 2019).

Many consider a business plan to be a formal document containing five key elements (see Figure 9.4):

1. Business goals;
2. Reasons why these goals are attainable;
3. A plan for reaching these goals;
4. Data backing the uniqueness of the products and services to be sold; and
5. Supporting information about the organization and team attempting to reach these goals.

Key Lessons

Source: Shelton (2017, p. 27).

Figure 9.4   Example of a "how-to" business plan

To make novel or vague business ideas intelligible, entrepreneurs can develop narrative artifacts that make use of tropes such as analogies, metaphors, metonymies, or synecdoches that emphasize similarity with situations and concepts that are already understood (Gioia, 1986), thereby facilitating communication and development despite great uncertainty and ambiguity (Cornelissen & Clarke, 2010). To illustrate, analogies accomplish this through literal references to startups, such as an entrepreneur describing what they do as "X for Y," e.g., Uber for dogs or Airbnb for food (Chen, 2019) or by describing the applicability of concepts from one domain such as finance to another domain such as online advertising (Glaser, Fiss, & Kennedy, 2016). Metaphors instead rely on more figurative references by drawing parallels to less obviously related domains such as warfare, sports, or parenting when describing the products or services being developed, the organizations and overall ambitions of the entrepreneurs, and, not least, their "entrepreneurial journeys" (Bruni, Bonesso, & Gerli, 2019; Cardon, Zietsma, Saparito, Matherne, & Davis, 2005; Clarke & Holt, 2010; Santos & Eisenhardt, 2009).

In contrast, if the ambition is not to explicate or clarify a given idea, but to expand ideas and generate new insights, entrepreneurs may instead leave the "cognitive comfort zone" of similarity (Oswick, Keenoy, & Grant, 2002, p. 294) in favor of tropes such as anomaly, paradox, and irony. Executive taglines such as "impossible is nothing" (Nike) or "enjoy better" (Time Warner) are often used for marketing purposes by established companies, but can also be used by entrepreneurs to stimulate imagination and creative engagement (Berglund et al., 2020; Garud et al., 2008). Relatedly, instead of describing "what they do" using the idiom of the classical venture "pitch" – expecting some clarifying questions followed by either a yes or a no – entrepreneurs can use the idiom of "an ask" that explicitly invites the other person to "help shape the venture in return for their commitment to become involved in some way" (Dew, Ramesh, Read, & Sarasvathy, 2018, p. 400). To use the metaphor of dating, it is not hard to imagine the question "What would it take for you to go out with me?" opening doors to potential fruitful conversations that otherwise would remain firmly closed if one stuck to the traditional "Will you go out with me?"

Future research in this vein might explore how, for what purposes, and with what consequences narrative artifacts and linguistic strategies are developed and used in entrepreneurial processes. For instance, in a recent study of microlevel rhetoric in entrepreneurial pitches, van Werven et al. (2019) applied theories of argumentation (e.g., Brockriede & Ehninger, 1960; Perelman, 1982; Toulmin, 1958) to better understand of how types of arguments (e.g., analogy, classification, generalization, cause, sign, and authority) relate to the promotion of entrepreneurial ventures of differing degrees of novelty. Given the uncertainty and ambiguity of entrepreneurship (Berglund, 2015), it may be especially relevant to acknowledge how multiple narratives – e.g., as held and promoted by founders, employees, and investors – may coexist, compete, combine or otherwise relate to one and other. In addressing such questions, scholars may benefit from research on the role of narratives in organizational stability and change (Vaara, Sonenshein, & Boje, 2016) and on communication as constitutive of organizations (Cooren, Kuhn, Cornelissen, & Clark, 2011).

OPPORTUNITIES FOR ADVANCING OUR UNDERSTANDING OF ENTREPRENEURIAL ARTIFACTS

By conceptualizing entrepreneurship as artifact-centered design, we align ourselves with other profession-oriented fields such as engineering (Vincenti, 1990), medicine, architecture, human–computer interaction (Suchman, 2007), and information systems (March & Smith, 1995), which have long regarded as a central task: "to teach about artificial things: how to make artifacts that have desired properties and how to design" (Simon, 1996, p. 111). As for practitioners in these fields, the ultimate goal of practicing entrepreneurs is to design new artifacts, which typically involves employing a range of more or less concrete intermediate artifacts to guide the process. This pragmatic and instrumental attitude toward the object of inquiry highlights the conceptual difference between sciences of man-made design and of naturally existing things (Niiniluoto, 1993; Schön, 1984; Simon, 1996). To illustrate the difference, physicists *qua* natural scientists might be interested in describing and explaining the constituents and interactions of atomic nuclei, whereas physicists *qua* nuclear engineers combine such insights with human desires to develop principles and tools that guide the design of artifacts as different as nuclear power plants and hydrogen bombs.

Similarly, entrepreneurship research conducted as a "natural science" seeks to better understand how various things relate to one and other, so as to produce accurate descriptions and causal explanations of processes and outcomes. To illustrate, entrepreneurial opportunities are often treated as naturally existing, with the implication that researchers "need to know the magnitude of the force exerted by the opportunities themselves to accurately estimate the effect of the individual motivations on entrepreneurial decisions" (Shane, Locke, & Collins, 2003, p. 269; see also Berglund & Korsgaard, 2017; Ramoglou & Tsang, 2016; Shane & Venkataraman, 2000). In contrast, design-oriented entrepreneurship scholars gladly use insights from descriptive and explanatory research, but do so with an eye to developing pragmatically useful design theory. For example, the business model canvas is based on descriptive research that was used to develop, test, and refine a tool to enable effective communication, structure business assumptions, and guide entrepreneurial design work (Romme & Reymen, 2018). Similarly, Porter's (1979) five forces framework used explanatory research from industrial organization economics to develop a tool for assessing industry attractiveness and guide strategy development.

While a relatively recent perspective in the entrepreneurship field (see Berglund et al., 2020, 2018; Dimov, 2016; Rindova & Martins, 2021; Romme & Reymen, 2018), the focus on design-artifacts rather than natural things is quite common in other profession-oriented disciplines such as engineering, architecture, information systems, and medicine, where scholars are not primarily concerned with the world as it is, but as it ought to be – in terms of better cars, buildings, databases, or medical treatments (Niiniluoto, 1993; Simon, 1996). In what follows, we discuss how this perspective might be extended by studying the use of artifacts through experimentation and transformation, exploring the nature of artifacts as epistemic objects, and the embeddedness of entrepreneurial artifacts in assemblages.

The Design of Artifacts through Experimentation and Transformation

By describing in some detail how entrepreneurial artifacts can be conceptualized, we hope to provide entrepreneurship scholars who are interested in entrepreneurial action and practice with an alternative to the currently dominant concept of opportunity, which – stemming from its roots in economic theory (Dimov, 2011; Korsgaard, Berglund, Thrane, & Blenker, 2016) – has proven both conceptually and pragmatically problematic. Specifically, we hope that our elaboration of "entrepreneurial artifacts" proves to be both analytically and empirically productive for scholars who are interested in unpacking what might be called strategic entrepreneurship or venture development: entrepreneurial practices that revolve around artifacts that instantiate and develop the abstract "opportunity" pursued (Berglund et al., 2020).

Following design theorists and practice scholars, we see artifacts as interfaces that connect inner and outer systems in productive ways (Schön, 1984; Simon, 1996). In the specific context of entrepreneurship, this means that entrepreneurial artifacts relate the ideas and visions of the organized individuals comprising the emerging venture (inner system) to the customers, users, partners, regulators, institutions, technologies (outer system) comprising the context in which these artifacts are embedded and within which they must fit.

Clearly, entrepreneurial artifacts are intimately intertwined with entrepreneurial practice. Following Berglund et al. (2020), we find it useful to speak of such practices in terms of experimentation and transformation as broad categories or types of entrepreneurial design:

> Design principles in experimentation are analogous to those of scientists who gradually adapt and refine their tentative theories by articulating and iteratively testing the underlying assumptions on which they are based against empirical reality … On the contrary, transformation thrives on heterogeneity of both knowledge and perspectives … with the overarching aim of design principles being "to keep multiple evaluative principles in play and to exploit the resulting friction of their interplay" (Stark, 2009: 15). (Berglund et al., 2020, p. 833)

It often makes sense to design entrepreneurial artifacts that lend themselves especially well to either experimentation or transformation. Experimentation requires distinct and interpretively unambiguous artifacts that enable unbiased information gathering from, and adaptation of the artifact to, the external environment. In contrast, transformation relies on constructive negotiations centered around artifacts that are "underspecified, left incomplete, and retain tension" (Weick, 1979, p. 43).

However, actual practices of entrepreneurial design are not always as clear-cut as these ideal types suggest. Specifically, abstract, material, and narrative artifacts can be productively combined in different ways as part of experimental and transformational processes. To illustrate, the exact same entrepreneurial artifact (e.g., a physical product prototype) can be used to conduct a comprehension test or a usability test for purely evaluative purposes, or be used as a starting point for a creative conversation to the extent that it is narratively framed as part of a co-design and development process. Similarly, a business plan used to support a definitive vision and point of view in the context of pitching investors is very different from the same business plan framed as an initial stab where nothing is set in stone, and is used as a stimulus to engage investors in generative conversation.

The Nature of Artifacts as Epistemic Objects

As previously discussed, natural things are characterized by their essential qualities. Design-artifacts lack such essential qualities and are instead contingently defined and developed in relation to human purposes and situations. To help us further develop the notion of an entrepreneurial artifact, we need a vocabulary and an ontology that resonates with these purposive and contingent qualities. Here we believe that the notion of epistemic objects, as developed by Rheinberger (1997) and Knorr Cetina (2001) provides a good starting point.

Used to characterize the artifacts at the center of non-routine and novelty-generating activities – scientific research being the paradigmatic example – epistemic objects are characterized by an "unfolding ontology" in the sense that they are in the process of being defined, and as such, only exist in terms of various contingent instantiations that are, by definition, incomplete, thereby generating questions that drive further inquiry (Knorr Cetina, 2001; Rheinberger, 1997). In the words of Miettinen and Virkkunen (2005, p. 438):

> These objects are not things with fixed qualities but rather are open-ended projections oriented to something that does not yet exist, or to what we do not yet know for sure. For this reason, they are also generators of new conceptions and solutions and can be regarded as a central source of innovation and reorientation in societal practices.

To develop her argument, Knorr Cetina (2001) described the ontological status of epistemic objects as *unfolding*, *dispersed*, and *question-generating*. First and foremost, they are unfolding in the sense that they are essentially characterized by their lack of stability and incompleteness of being: they are not fixed, but in the process of being defined. One can think here of a "minimum viable product," a prototype, or some similar intermediate entrepreneurial artifact whose function is to elicit feedback and engagement that serves to gradually refine it (Berglund et al., 2020).

Second, entrepreneurial artifacts, as epistemic objects, are also dispersed in that they typically have multiple instantiations such as visions, business plans, pitches, simulations, prototypes, minimum viable products, etc. Such instantiations are always partial in the sense of not comprising the opportunity as a whole. However – and this is critical – these various instantiations are all there is. There is no more "real thing" that one may find by reaching beyond such manifestations. It is the epistemic object itself that unfolds through the various developments made possible by engaging with the more or less abstract representations comprising it.

Finally, epistemic objects are question-generating in that their very incompleteness, in more or less subtle ways, indicates what is lacking and suggests what ought to be done next. To illustrate, launching a minimum viable product to a set of users will quickly identify situations where it works to some extent, thereby revealing which activities ought to be undertaken, whether in terms of developing additional features, redefining the user segment, rethinking the revenue model, or something else (e.g., Comi & Whyte, 2018). These ontological commitments fit very well into our framework for entrepreneurial artifacts. They not only go beyond the popular (and simplistic) dualisms of discovery–creation and subjective–objective, but also are compatible with the view of entrepreneurship that is artifact-mediated and concrete, a practice that moves from something vague and simple to something gradually more concrete and intricate. Or, in the words of Knorr Cetina: "Objects of knowledge are characteristically open, question-generating, and complex. They are processes and projections rather than definitive things. Observation and inquiry reveals them by increasing rather than reducing their complexity" (Knorr Cetina, 2001, p. 181).

The Embeddedness of Artifacts in Assemblages

Another theoretical perspective that may be useful to extend the utility of our construct of entrepreneurial artifacts is assemblage theory (DeLanda, 2016; Deleuze & Guattari, 1987), which highlights that artifacts are always embedded in broader assemblages of actors, artifacts, theories, and practices (D'Adderio & Pollock, 2014; Glaser, 2017). For example, the aforementioned innovation of the Palm Pilot can be conceptualized as residing in a broader context that includes computers and phones, philosophies of planning (e.g., the Franklin planner), and different types of users. Whereas some research in entrepreneurship highlights the active power of the entrepreneur as an agent to influence outcomes and achieve goals through different types of thinking such as causation or effectuation (e.g., Sarasvathy, 2001), and other research highlights the affordances and material potential of the innovative product or service (e.g., Baker & Nelson, 2005), an assemblage perspective highlights that agency resides in the interaction of these components and is not reducible to the singular intention of particular actors or artifacts. To illustrate with our Palm Pilot analogy, an assemblage perspective would not overestimate either the rhetorical power of the "pitch" or the inherent affordances of the Palm Pilot: instead, it would focus on the embeddedness of the entrepreneurial artifacts within a broader sociomaterial context.

An example of the rich potential of taking an assemblage perspective on entrepreneurial innovation can be seen in Akrich, Callon, and Latour's (2002a, 2002b) analysis of the "key" to success in entrepreneurial innovation. They first showed how, in contrast with mainstream accounts that focus on the properties or characteristics of an innovation, a central component of success is the ability of entrepreneurs to enlist allies (Akrich et al., 2002a). Understanding the process of developing this broader network requires a theoretical conceptualization of entrepreneurial artifacts to understand how different types of abstract, material, and narrative artifacts are used in the process of developing a collaborative ecosystem. Additionally, they show how entrepreneurs must continually adapt their products to market demands (Akrich et al., 2002b). As highlighted earlier, these adaptation activities inherently require material prototypes, and consequently, entrepreneurial artifacts are central to understanding the phenomenon of entrepreneurial adaptation of an innovative assemblage. For instance, when deploying innovative products, Apple combines material prototypes (Garud et al., 2014) with media coverage of rumors (Hannigan, Seidel, & Yakis-Douglas, 2018; Seidel, Hannigan, & Phillips, 2018) and physical presentations (Wenzel & Koch, 2018).

Combining the concept of entrepreneurial artifacts with the assemblage concept offers promising potential to examine critical, transformative moments in entrepreneurship (D'Adderio, Glaser, & Pollock, 2019). For instance, Glaser, Pollock, and D'Adderio (2021) suggested that assemblages can be productively examined in terms of different "biographical moments" that highlight situations in which programs of action are layered into an assemblage; performative struggles are addressed and resolved; and assemblages "travel" to other locations. These moments are likely to be of particular import in the entrepreneurial process, and understanding the role of entrepreneurial artifacts could help scholars explain phenomena of interest.

CONCLUSION

As per our brief review, many entrepreneurship scholars appear to conceptualize entrepreneurship as an artifact-centered design practice, some more explicitly than others. However, what we largely lack is the vocabulary and conceptual tools to theorize the role of artifacts in entrepreneurial practice. In this chapter, we have defined entrepreneurial artifacts and developed a typology scholars can employ to address this gap. A natural next step is to build on this preliminary account of entrepreneurial artifacts through empirical and conceptual elaboration of their use in context. To this end, we suggested questions for future research related to abstract, material, and narrative artifacts. To better ground such efforts, we also discussed three opportunities for future conceptual development. Finally, we encourage the development and evaluation of pragmatic frameworks and process-models. Being explicitly prescriptive, these should relate artifacts and entrepreneurial practice in ways that support entrepreneurial design processes. Here, existing contributions (Berglund et al., 2020; Dimov, 2016; Romme & Reymen, 2018) can draw inspiration from practitioner models (Blank & Dorf, 2012; Ries, 2011) as well as examples from other design fields, such as Shneiderman's simple mantra for graphical user-interface design: "Overview first, zoom and filter, then details on demand" (Shneiderman, 2003, p. 365) or Eekels and Roozenburg's (1991) basic design cycle of analysis, synthesis, simulation, evaluation, and decision. In conclusion, we believe that understanding the nature and role of artifacts may be especially important to entrepreneurship compared to many other management activities, since entrepreneurial artifacts – i.e., those artifacts that serve to instantiate an abstract opportunity in a way that supports its further development – are integral to the constitution of the opportunity/venture/startup/business being designed. We hope this chapter can encourage and orient future research in this vein.

ACKNOWLEDGMENTS

We thank the editors Neil Thompson and Anna Jenkins for their insightful comments, which have contributed to this chapter. The authors would also like to acknowledge that this research has been supported in part by funding from the University of Alberta's Centre for Entrepreneurship and Family Enterprise.

NOTE

1. Using the opportunity concept to define entrepreneurial artifacts is a matter of convention; opportunity is the most common shorthand for describing the artifact being designed as abstractly as possible (Berglund et al., 2020; Stevenson & Jarillo, 1990). Alternatives might be "the venture" as preferred by many scholars, "the business" or "the startup" common among practitioners, or "the It," which is Alberto Savoia's charming term for the unknown thing entrepreneurs design (Savoia, 2011, 2019), as well as Karin Knorr Cetina's description of the detection equipment assemblage involved in high-energy physics experiments (Knorr Cetina, 2001, p. 182).

REFERENCES

Akrich, M., Callon, M., & Latour, B. (2002a). The key to success in innovation part I: The art of inter-essement (Trans. A. Monaghan). *International Journal of Innovation Management, 6*(2), 187–206.

Akrich, M., Callon, M., & Latour, B. (2002b). The key to success in innovation part II: The art of choosing good spokespersons (Trans. A. Monaghan). *International Journal of Innovation Management, 6*(2), 207–225.

Alvarez, S. A., Barney, J. B., & Anderson, P. (2012). Forming and exploiting opportunities: The implications of discovery and creation processes for entrepreneurial and organizational research. *Organization Science, 24*(1), 301–317.

Amarsy, N. (2015). Why and how organizations around the world apply the business model canvas. *Strategyzer.* https://www.strategyzer.com/blog/posts/2015/2/9/why-and-how-organizations-around-the-world-apply-the-business-model-canvas.

Ashforth, B. E., & Humphrey, R. H. (1997). The ubiquity and potency of labeling in organizations. *Organization Science, 8*(1), 43–58.

Baden-Fuller, C., & Morgan, M. S. (2010). Business models as models. *Long Range Planning, 43*(2), 156–171.

Baker, T., & Nelson, R. E. (2005). Creating something from nothing: Resource construction through entrepreneurial bricolage. *Administrative Science Quarterly, 50*(3), 329–366.

Baumol, W. J. (1968). Entrepreneurship in economic theory. *The American Economic Review, 58*(2), 64–71.

Bechky, B. A. (2003). Object lessons: Workplace artifacts as representations of occupational jurisdiction. *The American Journal of Sociology, 109*(3), 720–752.

Berglund, H. (2015). Between cognition and discourse: Phenomenology and the study of entrepreneurship. *International Journal of Entrepreneurial Behavior & Research, 21*(3), 472–488.

Berglund, H., Bousfiha, M., & Mansoori, Y. (2020). Opportunities as artifacts and entrepreneurship as design. *Academy of Management Review, 45*(4), 825–846.

Berglund, H., Dimov, D., & Wennberg, K. (2018). Beyond bridging rigor and relevance: The three-body problem in entrepreneurship. *Journal of Business Venturing Insights, 9*, 87–91.

Berglund, H., & Korsgaard, S. (2017). Opportunities, time, and mechanisms in entrepreneurship: On the practical irrelevance of propensities. *Academy of Management Review, 42*(4), 731–734.

Blank, S. (2013). Why the lean start-up changes everything. *Harvard Business Review*, May 1. https://hbr.org/2013/05/why-the-lean-start-up-changes-everything.

Blank, S., & Dorf, B. (2012). *The Startup Owner's Manual: The Step-by-Step Guide for Building a Great Company*. Hoboken, NJ: John Wiley & Sons.

Brockriede, W., & Ehninger, D. (1960). Toulmin on argument: An interpretation and application. *Quarterly Journal of Speech, 46*(1), 44–53.

Bruni, E., Bonesso, S., & Gerli, F. (2019). Coping with different types of innovation: What do metaphors reveal about how entrepreneurs describe the innovation process? *Creativity and Innovation Management, 28*(2), 175–190.

Camuffo, A., Cordova, A., Gambardella, A., & Spina, C. (2020). A scientific approach to entrepreneurial decision making: Evidence from a randomized control trial. *Management Science, 66*(2), 564–586.

Cardon, M. S., Zietsma, C., Saparito, P., Matherne, B. P., & Davis, C. (2005). A tale of passion: New insights into entrepreneurship from a parenthood metaphor. *Journal of Business Venturing*, *20*(1), 23–45.

Carlile, P. (2002). A pragmatic view of knowledge and boundaries: Boundary objects in new product development. *Organization Science*, *13*(4), 442–455.

Carreyrou, J. (2020). *Bad Blood: Secrets and Lies in a Silicon Valley Startup*. New York: Picador.

Champenois, C., Lefebvre, V., & Ronteau, S. (2020). Entrepreneurship as practice: Systematic literature review of a nascent field. *Entrepreneurship & Regional Development*, *32*(3–4), 281–312.

Chen, A. (2019). "Is your startup idea taken?" – And why we love X for Y startups. *Andrewchen*. https:// andrewchen.co/x-for-y-startup-ideas/.

Clarke, J., & Holt, R. (2010). The mature entrepreneur: A narrative approach to entrepreneurial goals. *Journal of Management Inquiry*, *19*(1), 69–83.

Comi, A., & Whyte, J. (2018). Future making and visual artefacts: An ethnographic study of a design project. *Organization Studies*, *39*(8), 1055–1083.

Cooren, F., Kuhn, T., Cornelissen, J. P., & Clark, T. (2011). Communication, organizing and organization: An overview and introduction to the special issue. *Organization Studies*, *32*(9), 1149–1170.

Cornelissen, J. P., & Clarke, J. S. (2010). Imagining and rationalizing opportunities: Inductive reasoning and the creation and justification of new ventures. *Academy of Management Review*, *35*(4), 539–557.

D'Adderio, L. (2011). Artifacts at the centre of routines: Performing the material turn in routines theory. *Journal of Institutional Economics*, *7* (Special Issue), 197–230.

D'Adderio, L., Glaser, V., & Pollock, N. (2019). Performing theories, transforming organizations: A reply to Marti and Gond. *Academy of Management Review*, *44*(3), 676–679.

D'Adderio, L., & Pollock, N. (2014). Performing modularity: Competing rules, performative struggles and the effect of organizational theories on the organization. *Organization Studies*, *35*(12), 1813–1843.

DaSilva, C. M., & Trkman, P. (2014). Business model: What it is and what it is not. *Long Range Planning*, *47*(6), 379–389.

DeLanda, M. (2016). *Assemblage Theory*. Edinburgh: Edinburgh University Press.

Deleuze, G., & Guattari, F. (1987). *A Thousand Plateaus: Capitalism and Schizophrenia* (Trans. B. Massumi) (2nd edition). Minneapolis: University of Minnesota Press.

Dew, N., Ramesh, A., Read, S., & Sarasvathy, S. D. (2018). Toward deliberate practice in the development of entrepreneurial expertise: The anatomy of the effectual ask. In K. A. Ericsson, R. Hoffman, A. Kozbelt, & A. M. Williams (Eds.), *The Cambridge Handbook of Expertise and Expert Performance* (2nd edition) (pp. 389–412). New York: Cambridge University Press.

Dimov, D. (2011). Grappling with the unbearable elusiveness of entrepreneurial opportunities. *Entrepreneurship Theory and Practice*, *35*(1), 57–81.

Dimov, D. (2016). Toward a design science of entrepreneurship. *Advances in Entrepreneurship, Firm Emergence and Growth*, *18*, 1–31.

Doganova, L., & Eyquem-Renault, M. (2009). What do business models do? Innovation devices in technology entrepreneurship. *Research Policy*, *38*(10), 1559–1570.

Eekels, J., & Roozenburg, N. F. (1991). A methodological comparison of the structures of scientific research and engineering design: Their similarities and differences. *Design Studies*, *12*(4), 197–203.

Eisenmann, T., Ries, E., & Dillard, S. (2011). *Hypothesis-Driven Entrepreneurship: The Lean Startup*. Boston, MA: Harvard Business School.

Felin, T., & Zenger, T. R. (2009). Entrepreneurs as theorists: On the origins of collective beliefs and novel strategies. *Strategic Entrepreneurship Journal*, *3*(2), 127–146.

Felin, T., & Zenger, T. (2017). The theory-based view: Economic actors as theorists. *Strategy Science*, *2*(4), 258–271.

Franke, N., & Piller, F. (2004). Value creation by toolkits for user innovation and design: The case of the watch market. *Journal of Product Innovation Management*, *21*(6), 401–415.

Gartner, W. B. (1988). Who is an entrepreneur? Is the wrong question. *American Journal of Small Business*, *12*(4), 11–32.

Gartner, W., Shaver, K., Carter, N., & Reynolds, P. (Eds.) (2004). *Handbook of Entrepreneurial Dynamics: The Process of Business Creation*. Thousand Oaks, CA: Sage Publications.

Garud, R., Gehman, J., & Giuliani, A. P. (2014). Contextualizing entrepreneurial innovation: A narrative perspective. *Research Policy*, *43*(7), 1177–1188.

Garud, R., Gehman, J., & Tharchen, T. (2018). Performativity as ongoing journeys: Implications for strategy, entrepreneurship, and innovation. *Long Range Planning*, *51*(3), 500–509.

Garud, R., Jain, S., & Tuertscher, P. (2008). Incomplete by design and designing for incompleteness. *Organization Studies*, *29*(3), 351–371.

Gioia, D. A. (1986). Symbols, scripts, and sensemaking: Creating meaning in the organizational experience. In H. Sims & D. Gioia (Eds.), *The Thinking Organization* (pp. 49–74). San Francisco, CA: Jossey-Bass.

Glaser, V. L. (2017). Design performances: How organizations inscribe artifacts to change routines. *Academy of Management Journal*, *60*(6), 2126–2154.

Glaser, V. L., Fiss, P. C., & Kennedy, M. T. (2016). Making snowflakes like stocks: Stretching, bending, and positioning to make financial market analogies work in online advertising. *Organization Science*, *27*(4), 1029–1048.

Glaser, V. L., Pollock, N., & D'Adderio, L. (2021). The biography of an algorithm: Performing algorithmic technologies in organizations. *Organization Theory*, *2*(2), 1–27.

Glaser, V. L., Valadao, R., & Hannigan, T. R. (2021). Algorithms and routine dynamics. In M. S. Feldman, B. T. Pentland, L. D'Adderio, K. Dittrich, C. Rerup, & D. Seidl (Eds.), *Cambridge Handbook of Routine Dynamics* (pp. 315–328). Cambridge: Cambridge University Press.

Grimes, M. G. (2018). The pivot: How founders respond to feedback through idea and identity work. *Academy of Management Journal*, *61*(5), 1692–1717.

Hannigan, T. R., Seidel, V. P., & Yakis-Douglas, B. (2018). Product innovation rumors as forms of open innovation. *Research Policy*, *47*(5), 953–964.

Hodgkinson, G. P., & Wright, G. (2002). Confronting strategic inertia in a top management team: Learning from failure. *Organization Studies*, *23*(6), 949–977.

Honig, B., & Karlsson, T. (2004). Institutional forces and the written business plan. *Journal of Management*, *30*(1), 29–48.

Jackson, D. S. (1998). Palm-to-palm combat. *TIME*, *151*(10), 42–44.

Jarvenpaa, S., & Standaert, W. (2018). Digital probes as opening possibilities of generativity. *Journal of the Association for Information Systems*, *19*(10). https://aisel.aisnet.org/jais/vol19/iss10/3.

Kaplan, S. (2011). Strategy and PowerPoint: An inquiry into the epistemic culture and machinery of strategy making. *Organization Science*, *22*(2), 320–346.

Klein, P. G. (2008). Opportunity discovery, entrepreneurial action, and economic organization. *Strategic Entrepreneurship Journal*, *2*(3), 175–190.

Knorr Cetina, K. (2001). Objectual practice. In T. R. Schatzki, K. Knorr Cetina, & E. von Savigny (Eds.), *The Practice Turn in Contemporary Theory* (pp. 175–188). London: Routledge.

Korsgaard, S., Berglund, H., Thrane, C., & Blenker, P. (2016). A tale of two Kirzners: Time, uncertainty, and the "nature" of opportunities. *Entrepreneurship Theory and Practice*, *40*(4), 867–889.

Kostis, A., & Ritala, P. (2020). Digital artifacts in industrial co-creation: How to use VR technology to bridge the provider–customer boundary. *California Management Review*, *62*(4), 125–147.

Kromer, T. (2019). The question index for real startups. *Journal of Business Venturing Insights*, *11*, e00116.

Latour, B. (1987). *Science in Action: How to Follow Scientists and Engineers through Society*. Cambridge, MA: Harvard University Press.

Leonardi, P. M. (2013). When does technology use enable network change in organizations? A comparative study of feature use and shared affordances. *MIS Quarterly*, *37*(3), 749–775.

Lounsbury, M., & Glynn, M. A. (2001). Cultural entrepreneurship: Stories, legitimacy, and the acquisition of resources. *Strategic Management Journal*, *22*(6–7), 545–564.

Lounsbury, M., & Glynn, M. A. (2019). *Cultural Entrepreneurship: A New Agenda for the Study of Entrepreneurial Processes and Possibilities*. Cambridge: Cambridge University Press.

Malhotra, A., Majchrzak, A., & Lyytinen, K. (2021). Socio-technical affordances for large-scale collaborations: Introduction to a virtual special issue. *Organization Science*, *32*(5), 1371–1390.

Mansoori, Y., & Lackeus, M. (2020). Comparing effectuation to discovery-driven planning, prescriptive entrepreneurship, business planning, lean startup, and design thinking. *Small Business Economics*, *54*, 791–818.

March, S. T., & Smith, G. F. (1995). Design and natural science research on information technology. *Decision Support Systems*, *15*(4), 251–266.

McDonald, R., & Eisenhardt, K. (2020). Parallel play: Startups, nascent markets, and the effective design of a business model. *Administrative Science Quarterly*, *65*(2), 483–523.

McDonald, R., & Gao, C. (2019). Pivoting isn't enough? Managing strategic reorientation in new ventures. *Organization Science*, *30*(6), 1289–1318.

Miettinen, R., & Virkkunen, J. (2005). Epistemic objects, artefacts and organizational change. *Organization*, *12*(3), 437–456.

Moore, G. A. (2014). *Crossing the Chasm*. New York: Harper Business.

Mullins, J., & Komisar, R. (2009). *Getting to Plan B: Breaking Through to a Better Business Model*. Boston, MA: Harvard Business Review Press.

Nambisan, S. (2017). Digital entrepreneurship: Toward a digital technology perspective of entrepreneurship. *Entrepreneurship Theory and Practice*, *41*(6), 1029–1055.

Navis, C., & Glynn, M. A. (2010). How new market categories emerge: Temporal dynamics of legitimacy, identity, and entrepreneurship in satellite radio, 1990–2005. *Administrative Science Quarterly*, *55*(3), 439–471.

Navis, C., & Glynn, M. A. (2011). Legitimate distinctiveness and the entrepreneurial identity: Influence on investor judgments of new venture plausibility. *Academy of Management Review*, *36*(3), 477–499.

Niiniluoto, I. (1993). The aim and structure of applied research. *Erkenntnis*, *38*(1), 1–21.

Orlikowski, W. J., & Iacono, C. S. (2001). Research commentary: Desperately seeking the "IT" in IT research – a call to theorizing the IT artifact. *Information Systems Research*, *12*(2), 121–134.

Osterwalder, A. (2013). A better way to think about your business model. *Harvard Business Review*, *91*(5).

Osterwalder, A., & Pigneur, Y. (2010). *Business Model Generation: A Handbook for Visionaries, Game Changers, and Challengers*. Hoboken, NJ: John Wiley & Sons.

Oswick, C., Keenoy, T., & Grant, D. (2002). Metaphor and analogical reasoning in organization theory: Beyond orthodoxy. *Academy of Management Review*, *27*(2), 294–303.

Perelman, C. (1982). *The Realm of Rhetoric*. Notre Dame, IN: University of Notre Dame Press.

Porter, M. E. (1979). How competitive forces shape strategy. *Harvard Business Review*, *57*(2), 137–145.

Ramoglou, S., & Tsang, E. W. (2016). A realist perspective of entrepreneurship: Opportunities as propensities. *Academy of Management Review*, *41*(3), 410–434.

Randhawa, K., West, J., Skellern, K., & Josserand, E. (2021). Evolving a value chain to an open innovation ecosystem: Cognitive engagement of stakeholders in customizing medical implants. *California Management Review*, *63*(2), 101–134.

Rheinberger, H.-J. (1997). *Toward a History of Epistemic Things: Synthesizing Proteins in the Test Tube*. Stanford, CA: Stanford University Press.

Ries, E. (2011). *The Lean Startup: How Today's Entrepreneurs Use Continuous Innovation to Create Radically Successful Businesses*. New York: Crown Business.

Rindova, V., & Martins, L. L. (2021). Shaping possibilities: A design science approach to developing novel strategies. *Academy of Management Review*, *46*(4). https://doi.org/10.5465/amr.2019.0289.

Romme, A. G. L., & Reymen, I. M. (2018). Entrepreneurship at the interface of design and science: Toward an inclusive framework. *Journal of Business Venturing Insights*, *10*, e00094.

Santos, F. M., & Eisenhardt, K. M. (2009). Constructing markets and shaping boundaries: Entrepreneurial power in nascent fields. *Academy of Management Journal*, *52*(4), 643–671.

Sapsed, J., & Salter, A. (2004). Postcards from the edge: Local communities, global programs and boundary objects. *Organization Studies*, *25*(9), 1515–1534.

Sarasvathy, S. D. (2001). Causation and effectuation: Toward a theoretical shift from economic inevitability to entrepreneurial contingency. *Academy of Management Review*, *26*(2), 243–263.

Savoia, A. (2011). *Pretotype it*. https://www.pretotyping.org/uploads/1/4/0/9/14099067/pretotype_it_2nd_pretotype_edition-2.pdf.

Savoia, A. (2019). *The Right It: Why So Many Ideas Fail and How to Make Sure Yours Succeed*. New York: HarperCollins.

Schatzki, T. R., Knorr Cetina, K., & von Savigny, E. (Eds.) (2001). *The Practice Turn in Contemporary Theory*. London: Routledge.

Schön, D. A. (1984). Design: A process of enquiry, experimentation and research. *Design Studies*, *5*(3), 130–131.

Schumpeter, J. A. (1942). *Socialism, Capitalism and Democracy*. New York: Harper & Row.

Seidel, V. P., Hannigan, T. R., & Phillips, N. (2018). Rumor communities, social media, and forthcoming innovations: The shaping of technological frames in product market evolution. *Academy of Management Review*, *45*(2), 304–324.

Shane, S., Locke, E. A., & Collins, C. J. (2003). Entrepreneurial motivation. *Human Resource Management Review*, *13*(2), 257–279.

Shane, S., & Venkataraman, S. (2000). The promise of entrepreneurship as a field of research. *Academy of Management Review*, *25*(1), 217–226.

Shelton, H. (2017). *The Secrets to Writing a Successful Business Plan: A Pro Shares a Step-by-Step Guide to Creating a Plan That Gets Results* (2nd edition). N.p.: Summit Valley Press.

Shneiderman, B. (2003). The eyes have it: A task by data type taxonomy for information visualizations. In B. Bederson & B. Shneiderman (Eds.), *The Craft of Information Visualization: Readings and Reflections.* https://learning.oreilly.com/library/view/the-craft-of/9781558609150/xhtml/B9781558609150500469.htm.

Simon, H. A. (1996). *The Sciences of the Artificial* (3rd edition). Cambridge, MA: MIT Press.

Snihur, Y., & Zott, C. (2020). The genesis and metamorphosis of novelty imprints: How business model innovation emerges in young ventures. *Academy of Management Journal*, *63*(2), 554–583.

Soublière, J.-F., & Gehman, J. (2020). The legitimacy threshold revisited: How prior successes and failures spill over to other endeavors on Kickstarter. *Academy of Management Journal*, *63*(2), 472–502.

Spee, P., Jarzabkowski, P., & Smets, M. (2016). The influence of routine interdependence and skillful accomplishment on the coordination of standardizing and customizing. *Organization Science*, *27*(3), 759–781.

Stark, D. (2009). *The Sense of Dissonance: Accounts of Worth in Economic Life*. Princeton, NJ: Princeton University Press.

Stevenson, H. H., & Jarillo, J. C. (1990). A paradigm of entrepreneurship: Entrepreneurial management. *Strategic Management Journal*, *11*, 17–27.

Suchman, L. (2007). *Human–Machine Reconfigurations: Plans and Situated Actions* (2nd edition). New York: Cambridge University Press.

TechCrunch Blog (2011). How DropBox started as a minimal viable product. *TechCrunch*. https://techcrunch.com/2011/10/19/dropbox-minimal-viable-product/.

Thomke, S. (2001). Enlightened experimentation: The new imperative for innovation. *Harvard Business Review*, February 1. https://hbr.org/2001/02/enlightened-experimentation-the-new-imperative-for-innovation.

Thompson, N. A., & Byrne, O. (2020). Advancing entrepreneurship as practice: Previous developments and future possibilities. In W. B. Gartner & B. T. Teague (Eds.), *Research Handbook on Entrepreneurial Behavior, Practice and Process* (pp. 30–55). Cheltenham, UK and Northampton, MA, USA: Edward Elgar Publishing.

Toulmin, S. E. (1958). *The Uses of Argument*. Cambridge: Cambridge University Press.

Vaara, E., Sonenshein, S., & Boje, D. (2016). Narratives as sources of stability and change in organizations: Approaches and directions for future research. *Academy of Management Annals*, *10*(1), 495–560.

Vaara, E., & Whittington, R. (2012). Strategy-as-practice: Taking social practices seriously. *Academy of Management Annals*, *6*(1), 285–336.

van Werven, R., Bouwmeester, O., & Cornelissen, J. P. (2019). Pitching a business idea to investors: How new venture founders use micro-level rhetoric to achieve narrative plausibility and resonance. *International Small Business Journal*, *37*(3), 193–214.

Venkataraman, S. (1997). The distinctive domain of entrepreneurship research. *Advances in Entrepreneurship, Firm Emergence and Growth*, *3*(1), 119–138.

Vincenti, W. G. (1990). *What Engineers Know and How They Know It: Analytical Studies from Aeronautical History* (Johns Hopkins Studies in the History of Technology). Baltimore, MD: Johns Hopkins University Press.

von Hippel, E., & Katz, R. (2002). Shifting innovation to users via toolkits. *Management Science*, *48*(7), 821–833.

Wegener, F., & Glaser, V. L. (2021). Design and routine dynamics. In M. S. Feldman, B. T. Pentland, L. D'Adderio, K. Dittrich, C. Rerup, & D. Seidl (Eds.), *Cambridge Handbook of Routine Dynamics* (pp. 301–314). Cambridge: Cambridge University Press.

Weick, K. E. (1979). *The Social Psychology of Organizing*. New York: McGraw-Hill.

Wenzel, M., & Koch, J. (2018). Strategy as staged performance: A critical discursive perspective on keynote speeches as a genre of strategic communication. *Strategic Management Journal*, *39*(3), 639–663.

Whittington, R. (2003). The work of strategizing and organizing: For a practice perspective. *Strategic Organization*, *1*(1), 117–125.

Zhao, E. Y., Fisher, G., Lounsbury, M., & Miller, D. (2017). Optimal distinctiveness: Broadening the interface between institutional theory and strategic management. *Strategic Management Journal*, *38*(1), 93–113.

Zittrain, J. (2006). The generative internet. *Harvard Law Review, 119*, 1974–2040.

PART III

NEW METHODOLOGICAL ADVANCES

10. Using conversation analysis to reveal talk in practice and talk as practice

Betsy Campbell

All professional work is conversational work (Donnellon, 1996). Entrepreneurial work is no exception, but only recently has language been recognized as an essential aspect of entrepreneurial practice (Thompson, Verduijn, & Gartner, 2020). Most analysts are probably more familiar with entrepreneurial interaction as it is demonstrated in pitch contests or media interviews than they are with the routine conversations that occur between team members in private. While public forms of expression are certainly part of an entrepreneurial skill set, they are not necessarily representative of the means by which founding teams enact the mundane and essential work of new venture creation. This chapter explains how to analyze the ordinary interactions of entrepreneurial teams in action and why such analyses matter to our understanding of entrepreneurship-as-practice.

Many everyday interactions of entrepreneurial teams occur in private contexts such as team meetings and working sessions. These include the basic and commonplace verbal exchanges that team members use to accomplish their shared goals and to talk their ventures into being (Heritage, 1984). They are "backstage" conversations (Goffman, 1956); unselfconscious and unrehearsed interactions that are essential to the actual work of a given organization and profession. Detailed studies of these ordinary conversations can reveal the practical means by which founders build new ventures. Such studies analyze entrepreneurial work as it is enacted and understood by the entrepreneurial team members in real time. As such they are as close as possible "to where things happen" (Johannisson, 2020; Steyaert & Landström, 2011). This enables analysts to observe the dynamic, complex, and idiosyncratic aspects of ordinary entrepreneurial work in action (Anderson & Starnawska, 2008) and to analyze these details as they emerge and are accomplished by real people in real contexts (Johannisson, 2011).

While some notable contributions exist in the literature (Campbell, 2019c, 2021; Chalmers & Shaw, 2017), few studies have considered the role of conversation as it relates to entrepreneurial practice. This may be, in part, because the practice turn in entrepreneurship is just beginning to gain significant traction (Champenois, Lefebvre, & Ronteau, 2020), or because people tend to think that talk is not worthy of analysis (Schegloff, 1996). However, it may be connected to uncertainty about the process of analyzing naturally occurring interaction in addition to the traditional difficulties of obtaining necessary forms of data for analysis.

This chapter provides an overview of the Ethnomethodological tradition of Conversation Analysis (EM/CA). It outlines the necessary elements and activities for a CA study and demonstrates how to do a CA treatment of entrepreneurial interaction. The chapter highlights several new developments in the EM/CA process including changes in technologies and techniques that may be especially relevant to studies of entrepreneurship-as-practice. It also offers an explanation of applied CA and its potential value. The chapter concludes with an invitation to embrace CA in studies of entrepreneurship-as-practice.

STUDYING CONVERSATION TO UNDERSTAND PRACTICE

The scholarly recognition of the importance of naturally occurring conversations to professional settings has its origins in the 1960s. At that time, sociologists began investigating the ways that real people did things in real settings; even just doing "being ordinary" (Sacks, 1984b). This turn toward the ethno-methods of ordinary people in everyday contexts anchored social actions in situated practices (Button, 1991). By studying the situated procedural aspects of common sense activities, Ethnomethodology (EM) made a revolutionary move; it moved all of the background details (long taken for granted in traditional forms of social science) into the focal point of scholarly investigations.

Drawing on this appreciation for context and everyday practices, a systematic science to study conversation began to emerge that linked ordinary verbal exchanges to people's ordinary methods of doing and being (Garfinkel, 1967). These studies spawned the awareness that ordinary people use language with "order at every point" to co-construct and make sense of real-world contexts (Sacks, 1984a, p. 22; Schegloff, 1991). Increasingly, social contexts and interactions were understood to be interdependent (Goffman, 1964, 1974). These insights about the context-creating and context-renewing capacity of interactions inspired investigations into the conversational structures that were relevant to participation in all social activities, including professional work.

Workplace interaction studies aim to reveal the structure of interactions in conjunction with organizational goals (Drew & Sorjonen, 1997). A significant body of literature has formed around the study of conversation in professional settings such as aviation, classrooms, medical offices, and legal settings (Atkinson & Drew, 1979; Macbeth, 2011; Nevile, 2004; Stivers, 2007). Workplace interaction studies have shown how professional accomplishments such as landing a plane, teaching a lesson, making a diagnosis, and conducting courtroom interrogations are conversationally produced and understood by members in action. They also have shown how the competent use of conversational moves signals professional identities (Psathas, 1990). What it is to be and be recognized as a pilot, teacher, doctor, or lawyer is, in part, the adherence to the conversational norms of these professions.

To contribute productively in the workplace conversations of one of these professions implies a kind of membership. An Ethnomethodological view of membership is forged out of the practices of participating and belonging. It is about the use of "a natural language" which is recognized by others as consistent with the ways that work is done in that context (Garfinkel & Sacks, 1970). Consequently, the term "member" in Ethnomethodological studies does not refer to a person as much as it refers to the mastery of a natural language that is necessary to accomplish a profession's tasks. This competence is recognized by people in context. It also is observable to analysts who have a member's sensitivity to the context; a kind of "unique adequacy" to understand the profession as a member does (Garfinkel & Wieder, 1992).

The body of work that investigates how workplace activities are rooted in socially observable interaction at work relies heavily on Conversation Analysis (CA) (Engeström & Middleton, 1998). Steeped in the traditional of Ethnomethodology, CA illuminates the structures and orders of interaction that members recognize as necessary to enact their shared work. EM/CA studies require analysts to suspend externally derived knowledge about the context being examined and study only the ways that members make the context relevant for themselves through their interactions. The concept is to examine a research object (e.g., prototyping, negotiating, or role or gender) as a situated interactional accomplishment of the members.

By attending to entrepreneurial work as it is understood by members for and by themselves in action, CA can reveal the endogenous construction of entrepreneurship.

THE ORIGINS OF CONVERSATION ANALYSIS

People do things with words (Austin, 1962). However, words can mean anything and only become meaningful – to members and analysts – when considered in the sequence of a particular interaction (Rawls, 2008). In order to understand an utterance as an answer, apology, compliment, criticism, or an infinite array of other things requires members and analysts to attend to what utterance has come before and what else is relevant in that setting at that time. In order to be intelligible, interactions have a design and structure that are reflexive, indexical, and accountable. Reflexivity is the process by which members interpret interactions in real time and respond accordingly. Because each utterance conveys a situated meaning and receives a situated response, interactions are the result of this reflexive process. Indexicality refers to the context-determined meaning of utterances. The pronouns I and we, for example, have meanings that continually change and can be understood only in an indexical way (Sacks, 1992). Accountability is the means by which members inform and display aspects of identity and activity as a means of achieving a local sense of order. In other words, members hold each other accountable for the joint achievement of their interaction in compliance with the "taken for granted" context they share (Garfinkel, 1967). These aspects of ordering interaction provide a practical means for creating, continuing, and evolving social identities and institutions and engender the contexts that beget cultures (Schegloff, 2006). How people in real time determine what another person is doing by saying this or that, in just those words, in just that way, at just this moment in this specific interaction is a core interest of Ethnomethodology and CA in particular (Schegloff, 2006).

CA shows how the sequence of talk matters to the conversation, the context, and a constellation of interconnected actions. Conversation is not merely a way to transfer information; it is a fundamental means of accomplishing shared goals and engendering social life (Wooffitt, 2005). To be clear, CA's focus is not on language as a tool that enables something else to occur, but on conversation as action which is itself the thing that is occurring. By studying the structures of interaction, analysts can reveal, "the way humans do things and the kinds of objects they use to construct order in their affairs" (Sacks, 1984a, p. 24). The analysis of the organization, sequence, and structure of interaction presents an account of the social practices that constitute related contexts such as an entrepreneurial venture and the entrepreneurial ecosystem.

Early studies of conversational organization, sequence, and structure mainly focused on turn-taking and adjacency pairs. Analysts explored the rules of interaction that enable ordinary people to navigate when a turn is completed and who talks next, for example (Sacks, Schegloff, & Jefferson, 1974). They also considered the recurring verbal characteristics that enable members to smoothly start or stop topical exchanges (Schegloff & Sacks, 1973). These studies into the fundamental machinery (Sacks, 1984a) of conversation demonstrate that conversational moves are both context creating and context renewing (Garfinkel, 1967). Utterances create contexts in that they cannot be understood except by their connections with the situated time and place in which they occur and in which members craft them. Similarly, utterances renew contexts in that they foster an enduring environment for future words and activities. Members in a conversation are akin to jazz musicians; their exact utterances and sequences are improvisationally contributed and experienced "for another first time" within an enduring architecture of rules (Garfinkel, 1967, p. 9).

Because conversation is systematically organized and the organizing properties are significant to members (Goodwin & Heritage, 1990; Sacks et al., 1974), there are no accidental details of interaction (Heritage, 1989). Moreover, because the organizing properties of conversations are recognizable to members utterance-by-utterance, they also are observable to analysts. This ability to orient to the perspectives and practices of members is at the heart of EM/CA.

To ensure the prioritization of members' perspectives and not analysts', CA studies utilize recordings. While audio recording became a standard way of collecting audible data, video recordings also have informed CA studies for decades (Goodwin, 1981; Sacks & Schegloff, 1975/2002). CA rejects any notion that language and the body in action are separate; gestures, gaze, and other embodied resources are used along with words by members as part of the co-construction intelligible interactions. Drawing on the Ethnomethodological stance that sees all human (inter)action as emergent and situated in a material environment, early video-based studies focused on co-speech gestures and gazes related to turn-taking and sequence organization. Over time, studies have considered body–material arrangements and have expanded the concept of interaction to include verbal utterances in conjunction with objects, motions, sensory experiences, and special configurations (Heath & Luff, 2000; Mondada, 2018a; Nevile, Haddington, Heinemann, & Rauniomaa, 2014).

Whether emerging from audio or audio/video data, CA studies embrace several guidelines (Psathas, 1995, pp. 2–3):

- Order is a produced orderliness
- This order is produced by members in context; it is situated and occasioned
- Members orient to the order themselves; analysts do not impose an order based on pre-formulated ideas about what roles or actions should exist
- The order is repeatable and recurring
- Discovering, describing, and analyzing the produced orderliness are the tasks of the analyst
- These tasks of discovering, describing, and analyzing the structures, the machinery, the organized practices, the formal procedures, and the ways in which order is produced take precedence over issues about how frequently or how often interactional phenomena occur
- The structures of social action, once identified in the members' interactions, can be articulated by the analysts in structural, organizational, logical, and topically countless, consistent, and abstract terms.

As these guidelines suggest, CA differs substantially from traditional forms of discourse analysis and other approaches that attend to matters of language. One vital difference that sets CA apart is that it is data driven and does not start with predetermined categories of interest to the analyst. CA does not guess about the thoughts, feelings or motivations of research subjects. Instead, it looks for evidence in the observable data that is available to members. A second core difference is that CA is concerned with the structure of interaction rather than the content. Conversation analysis focuses on sequential development of interaction; on seeing what happens and what happens next for and by the members as they construct and enact social practices (Drew & Heritage, 1992; ten Have, 2007). This is why CA is interested only in examining authentic interaction in context, and this requirement to stay close to the data informs how CA studies are done.

DOING CONVERSATION ANALYSIS

CA employs a rigorously empirical method. It relies on recordings of naturally occurring conversations in part because people are not good at inventing or remembering conversations (Sacks, 1984a). Audio or audio-and-visual recordings of members interacting in authentic settings make the analysis accountable to the details of actual occurrences. This means any data that has been produced for the benefit of the analyst – such as exchanges that are scripted or prompted – is not permissible as data. Similarly, data that comes from recollection without recordings is not usable. While a study might incorporate observations, interviews, or other ethnographic materials, a CA study must be based on the recorded data to reveal the ways that members develop and demonstrate their actions and understandings in real time as they (re) create the intelligibility and order of their shared experience. The recordings enable analysts to return to the interactions as they actually happened again and again. This is useful in the processes of transcription and analysis.

Transcription begins by giving the recordings attention that is "unmotivated" by existing theories or categories (Psathas, 1995). This initial step helps to familiarize the analyst with the data in a general way. It also allows the analyst to notice aspects of the interactions based on actual occurrence, not theory, and enables him/her to consider the situated nature of contexts and practices (Pomerantz & Fehr, 1997; ten Have, 2007). The analyst may recognize at this point that some parts of the recordings are not usable because of ambient noise or other problems that make the details of the conversation unclear. This unmotivated exploration also can point the analyst to sections of interaction that seem worthy of deeper investigation.

Because CA anchors analysis in the data, it is important to render the recorded interactions in great detail. Special symbol systems have been developed to capture the observable details of verbal conversation and embodied actions (Jefferson, 1984, 2004) (see Table 10.1). These details enable the members to interpret and understand each other in real time, and capturing them in the transcription makes it possible for the analyst to uncover the ways that members interactionally accomplish their work. In general, the more detail that the analyst can recognize in the recordings and render in the transcript, the better the analysis will be. However, each analyst needs to determine if a modified version of the notation systems would honor the conversation as it happened while making the transcript more accessible to their audience (e.g., readers of management literature who might resist the transcription conventions of CA). The process of transcription takes time and requires an iterative approach:

- Listen to and/or watch the recording and make a rough transcription that attributes specific utterances to individual members
- Revisit the data and prioritize the capture of the background elements such as audible breaths, clicks, laughs, and other sonic markers (mm, um, aa, etc.)
- Revisit the data and attend to overlaps and pauses. Note precisely where an utterance begins and how long a pause lasts. Pauses may happen between members' contributions or within a particular utterance

- Revisit the data and note the quality of voice used by each member over time. Features such as intonation, pitch, and speed all can play a role in the moment for the members in action
- Revisit the data and note any physical actions that play communicative roles
- Lastly, number the utterances and/or identify the speakers line by line.

As the transcription document becomes increasingly complete, the analyst continues to stay open to noticing important features in the utterances for the members. Once the analyst has noticed something to explore with greater intensity, s/he may begin to scan the transcript for other instances of the possible phenomenon. However, the aim is not to count the instances; it is to compare the structure and organization of the instances.

Table 10.1   *Jeffersonian notation (Jefferson, 1984, 2004) captures audible details of interactions*

Symbol	Descriptive name	Indication
[text]	Brackets	Start and end points of overlapping speech
=	Equal sign	Break and then continuation of a single utterance
(# of seconds)	Timed pause	Number within parentheses indicates seconds of pause in speech
(.)	Micropause	Brief pause, usually less than 0.2 seconds
. or ↓	Period or down arrow	Falling pitch or intonation
? or ↑	Question mark or up arrow	Rising pitch or intonation
,	Comma	Temporary rise or fall in intonation
-	Hyphen	Abrupt halt or interruption in utterance
text	Greater than / Less than	Speech within the marks was delivered more rapidly than usual for the speaker
text	Less than / Greater than	Speech within the marks was delivered more slowly than usual for the speaker
°	Degree symbol	Whisper, reduced volume, or quieter speech
ALL CAPS	Capitalized text	Shouted or increased volume of speech
underline	Underlined text	Emphasized or stressed speech
:::	Colon(s)	Prolongation of a sound
(hhh)	Hhh	Audible exhalation
˙ or (.hhh)	High Dot or period and hhh	Audible inhalation
(text)	Parentheses	Speech which is garbled, unclear, or in doubt
((*italic text*))	Double parentheses plus italics	Annotation of non-verbal activity

Understanding what is worth noticing can be summed up by the poignant question "why that now" (Schegloff & Sacks, 1973, p. 299). Members continually must work to recognize what action a particular utterance is being used to accomplish and why a particular utterance has been offered to accomplish it. By carefully attending to the matter of "why that now", analysts can begin to unpack the verbal means by which members accomplish shared goals.

Perhaps a short example would be helpful. The following three-line exchange between co-founders happens after a test of a prototype resulted in an unexpected outcome. The utterances are presented with a simplified version of Jeffersonian notation.

1. Ron: Do you have the stats on that?
2. Jan: (.hhh) It was wa::ay off (.) um (.)
3. Ron: We'll reschedule with the VCs. Let's review it with Ken↓

This exchange seems unremarkable at first glance. However, this brief interaction demonstrates how members orient to and accomplish much of the work of entrepreneurship. It reveals how entrepreneurial team members use their knowledge of entrepreneurial process as a resource to accomplish their shared goals that give rise to their venture. Simultaneously it shows how members constitute aspects of entrepreneurship as ordinary features of entrepreneurial work.

The utterances are uncomplicated. Ron opens the exchange with a question. After an audible inhalation that begins before Ron finishes his question, Jan offers an unmediated assessment and then pauses as she tries to gather the relevant specific information that would qualify as "stats". Rather than waiting for more detailed information, Ron closes the exchange with a declaration of next steps.

A deeper analysis of the exchange recognizes that these three turns of conversation reveal several rules and procedures related to this venture and to entrepreneurship more generally. In asking for detailed information on a just-completed test operation that did not go well, Ron is tapping into mundane knowledge about the process of building a flagship product, about demonstrating viability to influential organizations in the ecosystem, and about the necessity of raising venture capital to launch the venture. He doesn't explain to Jan what sort of information would be helpful or why he wants to know; he treats those things as part of the shared understanding of what it means to be working on this startup. Similarly, Jan does not ask Ron to be more specific or to offer reasons for wanting this information. The audible breath that precedes her initial summation signals that Jan knows the outcome of the test is not what they were hoping for (Heritage, 1989). Ron's next contribution starts before he gets the information he requested in his previous turn. Rather than respond to Jan's assessment, he proclaims the intention of rescheduling a fundraising meeting and a need to review what happened with an additional team member (Ken). Ron does this without needing to explain to her why a failed test is connected to the schedule for meeting with the VCs. Both team members actively understand the interdependencies between the tests and the team's ability to raise funds. Moment-by-moment Ron and Jan are referencing the ordinary requirements of organizing a venture in their interactions. They are oriented to these features of entrepreneurial practice and accomplishing them utterance-by-utterance.

What this tiny example highlights is that members of entrepreneurial teams (re)create, correct, and evolve their ventures through the structures of their interactions. Turn-by-turn, members display their situated knowledge of the ecosystem and use it as a resource in their entrepreneurial work, and they also constitute their venture – as a whole and as parts, in a given instance and in general – as a routine facet of entrepreneurship.

CA enables analysts to consider the members' perspective in entrepreneurship as it is practiced by real teams in real contexts. While concepts such as roles, functions, and processes are understood by analysts and entrepreneurs alike, CA enables analysts to see how these essential concepts are actively employed and accomplished by members for and by themselves. The exchange between Ron and Jan, for example, shows how these team members are oriented toward the role VCs play, the function of test results in the fundraising process, and the overall process of starting a venture by prototyping, relying on team mates' areas of expertise, and raising capital. This tiny example shows how CA provides a means to analyze language and social practices as "integrated elements of coherent courses of action" (Goodwin & Heritage, 1990, p. 301).

FROM INSTANCES TO INSIGHTS

When examining the exchange between Ron and Jan, an analyst might notice a variety of sequential puzzles while engaging in unmotivated looking (Psathas, 1995). For example, there are big leaps between each turn. Ron asks about "stats" of a failed test, and Jan gives her impression of the results. Jan offers this impression, and then Ron declares a postponement to a VC meeting. Noticing these structural gaps – what members are doing and saying through a situated sequence of utterances – is a necessary first step in the analysis process (Schegloff, 1996). The analyst needs to unpack the sequences to determine how the participants recognize what is being accomplished (e.g., affirming, arguing, etc.) (Sacks, 1984b). The meaning and impact of interactions are available to members (and to analysts) through the words themselves; specifically through the next-turn proof, whereby a member's understanding of a prior turn is displayed in the following turn (Sacks et al., 1974). Because the display of understanding is available to both members and analysts, the next-turn proof is also indicative of the validity of the findings (Peräkylä, 2011).

To move from an observation to the identification of a phenomenon for study, an analyst needs to return to the data. After recognizing a structural feature in the interactional data, the analyst seeks to understand how turns are constructed, sequences ordered, or identities categorized in other similar instances. For example, the next step to analyze the exchange between Ron and Jan would be to look for other instances in which undesirable feedback is addressed (or other instances in which the membership category of VC is handled). The goal is to uncover the systematic interactional ethno-methods that real people use to do things like manage undesirable feedback (or categorize VCs).

A final stage of analysis can connect the interactional data with wider social theory – providing that the analysis remains anchored in the observable data that is available to both members and analysts (Heritage, 2009; Clifton, 2006). Because people use language to signal their relative positions and emerging understandings, these verbal means of display "eventually get institutionalized into organizational rules" (Fairhurst & Uhl-Bien, 2012, p. 1045). The analysis of interaction then reveals how members continually orient to rules, roles, and systems but always "for another first time" (Garfinkel, 1967). Consequently, the analyst can point to the verbal means by which members talk their roles and organizations into being (Heritage, 1984). (For more on the mechanics of the Conversion Analysis process, see Psathas, 1995; Arminen, 2005; Schegloff, 2007; Heritage, 2010.)

NEW TWISTS IN THE PROCESS

In the early days of CA, analysts used tape recorders to gather data, facilitate transcription and analysis, and teach the process of doing CA (Sacks, 1984a, 1992). CA would have been hard to start even a decade earlier because the analytical process relies so heavily on recorded data, and only in the 1950s did tape recorders become somewhat portable and affordable. However, the tape recorder is not a sacred tool; it is used in CA because it makes available observable language as a basis for theorizing. As Sacks put it: "The tape-recorded materials constituted a 'good enough' record of what happened. Other things, to be sure, happened, but at least what was on the tape had happened" (Sacks, 1984a, p. 26).

While a reel-to-reel tape recorder still could capture the verbal interactions of members, technology and cultural norms have evolved. Today analysts can use digital audio recorders and video cameras, and they can leverage the popular use of self-recorded material (Burgess & Green, 2013). As more people engage in recording (with smart phones and wearable cameras) and even publicly sharing naturally occurring interactions, analysts have the chance to study more data and more intimate data than would be possible otherwise. Of course, in addition to the potential benefits of self-recorded data, embracing such files can introduce complexities into the processes of ensuring authenticity, gaining permission, and doing analysis (Chalfen, 2014). Not every file that is self-recorded and shared on a public platform will be unedited and completely natural. Analysts will need to find ways to verify the data before treating it as appropriate for CA. Of course, analysts can begin research relationships in traditional ways and empower research subjects to self-record for the study (Campbell, 2019b). In this case, the extraordinary intimacy of the collections of data may influence the way researchers think about and ensure the privacy and anonymity of research subjects. And as analysts begin to work with large collections of conversational data, new software and practices for analyzing the data may become a necessity.

The tools for transcription also have been evolving. Most analysts continue to listen to recordings in a slow playback mode and type transcriptions by hand in an iterative process. However, some analysts are experimenting with automated transcription services for some stages of the process. None of the current automated transcription services are accurate enough for the rigors of natural team conversation; nor are they attuned to the details of CA. But they can accelerate the speed at which a very rough rendering of main words can be completed. The analyst can put this inaccurate and incomplete transcript into the standard iterative process; correcting the utterances and adding the essential details (e.g., the pauses, false starts, and other audible features as well as markers of embodied communication). The final transcript needs to represent what really happened for and by the members in context as captured on the recording.

Another advance in transcription is the recent introduction of a marking system for multi-modal CA (see Table 10.2). The Mondada Multimodal Marking System (Mondada, 2018a) highlights the embodied silent actions that make interactions publicly intelligible. It offers a systematic interactional organization of silent, physical means of contributing to interactional accomplishment.

It is important to note that the quality of a recording matters regardless of the means by which it was captured and transcribed. The internal validity of a CA study is directly connected to the quality of the recorded data. Recordings that have muddled or otherwise inaudible portions cannot be repaired and are not usable. Similarly video recordings that have blurred images or action happening off-screen have limited use. Analysts therefore need to continue to manage the recording process with care.

In addition to adapting to a new generation of technologies, CA is incorporating new analytic strategies. Of particular relevance to scholars of entrepreneurship and business is the development of a Quantified Conversation Analysis (QCA). QCA studies begin with the traditional conversation analytic process and require a collection of instances (Schegloff, 1996). Only after all instances in the collection are analyzed in terms of sequence order and structure are features of the interactions coded and quantified. This phased approach differentiates QCA from text analysis or other methods that count occurrences of words or begin with predetermined categories of interest in the mind of the analyst.

Table 10.2   Mondada Multimodal Marking System (Mondada, 2018b) captures embodied actions essential for interactional intelligibility

Symbol	Name	Indication
* text *	Pair of asterisks or other symbols	Embodied movements described between a set of identical symbols that
+ text +		appear with corresponding speech (one symbol per participant)
text		
*---	Asterisk, dashes, and greater than	Beginning of an action that continues across utterances
---*	Dashes, greater than, and asterisk	End of an action that continues across utterances
	Double greater than	Action described begins before the utterance's beginning
---	Dashes and double greater than	Action described continues after the utterance's end
....	Periods	Preparation of a physical action
------	Dashes	Apex of a physical action is reached and maintained
,,,,,	Commas	Retraction of a physical action
ric	Letters ric	Participant doing embodied action who is not the speaker
fig #	Letters fig and number	Moment represented by screen shot (inserted after the textual representation)

CA scholars traditionally have tended to avoid quantification in order to prevent premature theorizing (Schegloff, 1993). However, QCA studies are becoming more common. Coding and quantifying CA data offers two primary advantages: it opens up opportunities to assess the connections between the structure of interactions and exogenous variables (individual attitudes, demographic groups, and organizational outcomes), and it enables a wider audience (of scholars and practitioners) to engage with CA findings (Stivers, 2015). Additionally, QCA findings provide for historical or cultural comparisons of organizational practices (Clayman, Elliott, Heritage, & Laurie, 2006; Heritage, 1999). This comparative basis of QCA studies aligns them with what some have called the interventionist edge of Applied CA (Antaki, 2011; ten Have, 2001).

APPLYING CA

Despite the tight focus of CA, findings from the study of interaction order speak to a constellation of professional practices and social problems (Maynard, 1988; Zimmerman, 2005). CA has been supporting productive changes in organizational settings for some time, especially in medicine (Heritage, Robinson, Elliott, Beckett, & Wilkes, 2007; Robinson & Heritage, 2014), counseling (Peräkylä, 1995), and aviation (Nevile, 2004). Examples include support for people with intellectual disabilities and their caregivers (Finlay, Walton, & Antaki, 2011), new mothers and support workers (Kitzinger & Kitzinger, 2007), doctors posing questions to young patients of different races (Stivers & Majid, 2007), and telephone helpline services (Hepburn, Wilkinson, & Butler, 2014). Any time CA findings are "applied to a practical problem as it plays out in interaction, with the intention of bringing about some sort of change" (Antaki, 2011, p. 1), the analyst is engaging in an intervention into practice.

To be clear: CA interventions tend to be informal interventions. They play out through workshops or continuing education courses and often include recommendations of specific conversational moves that members might adopt to achieve some preferred organizational outcomes. They do not tend to be interventions in the way that a hypothesis-driven research study might use the term. CA interventions often share five core features: (1) a practical problem exists in advance of the analyst's arrival, (2) the problem is recurring, (3) the basis of the problem lies in the sequential organization of talk, (4) a solution emerges through a process that includes members of the organization, and (5) both the analyst and the organizational members agree that the discovered solution(s) will address the problem (Antaki, 2011).

CA also can suggest new ways of teaching that lessen the gap between theory and practice. CA findings have informed educational experiences in medicine (Stivers, 2007), language instruction (Sert, 2013), aviation (Tuccio & Nevile, 2017), and even entrepreneurship at the college level (Campbell, 2019a). Many of these educational interventions build on a process first outlined by Stokoe (Stokoe, 2011) and have been adapted for specific professional contexts, including entrepreneurship (Campbell, 2019c). The basic flow of a CA-informed learning method begins with the recording of naturally occurring conversations and is followed by transcription of selected segments of interaction. At this point, learners are asked to share any general insights about the interaction that have emerged after seeing a transcript (e.g., overlapping speech, unequal turn-taking, and other common conversational features). In the next phase, the educator plays selected recordings while projecting the transcriptions for the class. This process is done slowly; revealing utterances in small segments. At each pause, learners are asked to formulate the function that the next turn of conversation will serve in context. After the educator plays the next turn of the recorded conversation, s/he pauses again to enable the learners to compare their expectations with the data. Class discussions then start to explore the conversational moves that the members use to enact particular practices and accomplish organizational goals. Because interactional patterns are relevant to organizational outcomes and practices (Heritage, 1999), these kinds of interventions provide the scaffolding that help learners develop competencies in the practices necessary for their profession (Tuccio & Nevile, 2017).

CA IN STUDIES OF PRACTICE

Studies of practice – including entrepreneurship as practice – prioritize relationships (e.g., between people, settings, and objects) and the dynamic interdependencies between activities and contexts (Cicourel & Knorr Cetina, 1981; Johannisson, 2011; Keating, Geiger, & McLoughlin, 2014; Watson, 2013). While studies might attend to matters of philosophy (the role of practices in the production of the social world) or theory (the impact of actions and outcomes that play out over time), they also can focus on empirical evidence (the things that people actually do) (Orlikowski, 2010). This final orientation – the empirical approach – emphasizes the centrality of members' actions and interactions in the (re)creation of organizations and outcomes. This attention to "what is actually done in the doing of work" anchors theories about practice in actual practice (Orr, 1998, p. 439). By providing an analytical, not simply descriptive, account of entrepreneurial practices, EM/CA identifies the social machinery that enables entrepreneurs to accomplish their immediate tasks and (re)create the larger contexts of their work (Mondada, 1998). EM/CA studies probe the complex and repeated patterns of saying and doing that are accepted and recognized as a way of enacting entrepreneurial work and being an entrepreneur.

While there is no single practice theory (Reckwitz, 2002), theories of practice share several principles. One is that ordinary actions are consequential in the (re)production of social order. Garfinkel's perspective is that social order emerges from members' constant attention to and competent display of ethno-methods in situated interactions (Garfinkel, 1967; Rawls, 2008).

Another principle is the rejection of dualisms (e.g., mind/body, thought/action, micro/macro). Ethnomethodology transcends the dualist framework: any empirically displayed (inter)action contains the social practices produced by and for those members and *all* matters of relevance for them in that context (Hilbert, 1990). In other words: "Both micro and macro sociological matters in whatever terms are always embedded in the immediate here and now settings of their productions" (Hilbert, 2009, p. 171). And an additional shared principle is that all practices are interconnected within a constellation of practices. In other words, the way of doing a particular activity, such as pitching, is connected to other practices that define what is recognized as a role, a venture, a culture, etc. According to Garfinkel, any habit, routine, or social activity only becomes socially intelligible within a universe of constitutive order (Rawls, 2008).

A core question of Ethnomethodologically informed studies is how mutually intelligible practices become recognizable for members in context and over time. CA often addresses this puzzle in entrepreneurship-as-practice studies as part of a methodological toolkit (Nicolini, 2012). CA is used to zoom in on the sequential details of verbal accomplishment of practices, and it is paired with other methodological approaches that zoom out to trace practices across time or space. These two lenses of zooming in and out enable analysts to examine the connections "between the here-and-now of the situated practicing and the elsewhere-and-then of other practices" (Nicolini, 2009, p. 1393). Together they provide multiple views on practice which, of course, is a multifaceted and multi-dimensional phenomenon.

One of the main reasons CA tends to be used as part of a toolkit is because its focus on phenomena such as social structures, institutions, and power as they are found only in the interactions of members is perceived as being too limited (Nicolini, 2009). While complementing CA with other methodologies can offer advantages to studies of entrepreneurship-as-practice, CA (QCA and multimodal CA) should not be ruled out as a stand-alone approach. Ethnomethodology with its analysis of the procedures members use to reflexively constitute social activities and settings is useful in understanding both local and general cultural contexts (Goodwin & Goodwin, 1992). Drawing on this tradition, CA provides a means to analyze (verbal, non-verbal, and embodied) language, culture, and social organization as "integrated elements of coherent courses of action" (Goodwin & Heritage, 1990, p. 301). It allows analysts to reveal organizations of practices through the sequence order of conversation and workplace interaction (Schegloff, Ochs, & Thompson, 1996).

In whatever ways CA is incorporated into studies of entrepreneurship-as-practice, it stands to add new details to existing constructs of entrepreneurship and entirely new ways of understanding entrepreneurship. CA can reveal the interactional means by which entrepreneurs recognize, create, and maintain an orderly yet dynamic world consisting of familiar identities (founder, customer), ordinary happenings (product validation, venture formation), and enduring contexts (entrepreneurial venture, accelerator contest) (Llewellyn, 2008). It can transform the impersonal and intra-personal constructs of entrepreneurship into interpersonal and relational accomplishments. Economic actions can be understood in terms of conversational structures (Huma, Stokoe, & Sikveland, 2019; Llewellyn, 2015). And, because there is nothing in people's "heads but brains" (Garfinkel, 1963, p. 190), cognitive stances can be reconsidered in terms of the situated and dynamic context of workplace interaction (Campbell, 2021; Lynch, 2006). Perhaps more importantly, CA can enable analysts to reveal new and unexpected facets to what is known about entrepreneurship-as-practice. These fresh findings can animate future scholarly debates, and they can inform entrepreneurship education, policy, and ideally the practices of founders in action.

Reflecting on the literature about workplaces, Heritage once noted a critical gap. The only things scholars of practice need to identify are "all the missing analyses of how the practitioners manage the tasks which, for them, are matters of serious and pressing significance" (Heritage, 1984, p. 299). CA provides a powerful way to investigate the empirical edges of practice and reveal the means by which entrepreneurs interactionally grapple with prototyping, negotiating, organizing, and the countless other interdependent practices that are essential to being an entrepreneur and doing entrepreneurial work within the ecosystem.

REFERENCES

Anderson, A., & Starnawska, M. (2008). Research practices in entrepreneurship: Problems of definition, description and meaning. *International Journal of Entrepreneurship and Innovation*, *9*, 221–230.

Antaki, C. (Ed.) (2011). *Applied Conversation Analysis: Intervention and Change in Institutional Talk*. New York: Palgrave Macmillan.

Arminen, I. (2005). *Institutional Interaction: Studies of Talk at Work* (Vol. 2). Farnham: Ashgate.

Atkinson, J., & Drew, P. (1979). *Order in Court: The Organisation of Verbal Interaction in Judicial Settings*. London: Macmillan.

Austin, J. (1962). *How to Do Things with Words*. Oxford: Oxford University Press.

Burgess, J., & Green, J. (2013). *YouTube: Online Video and Participatory Culture*. Cambridge: Polity Press.

Button, G. (Ed.) (1991). *Ethnomethodology and the Human Sciences*. Cambridge: Cambridge University Press.

Campbell, B. (2019a). EDUC 497: Accelerator Rap. Pennsylvania State University. Retrieved March 21, 2020, from https://lionpathsupport.psu.edu/.

Campbell, B. (2019b). *The Innovator's Discussion: The Conversational Skills of Entrepreneurial Teams*. London: Routledge.

Campbell, B. (2019c). *Practice Theory in Action*. New York: Routledge.

Campbell, B. (2021). Entrepreneurial uncertainty in context: An ethnomethodological perspective. *International Journal of Entrepreneurship Behavior and Research*, *27*(3), 648–667.

Chalfen, R. (2014). Your panopticon or mine? Incorporating wearable technology's Glass and GoPro into visual social science. *Visual Studies*, *29*(3), 299–231.

Chalmers, D., & Shaw, E. (2017). The endogenous construction of entrepreneurial contexts: A practice-based perspective. *International Small Business Journal*, *35*(1), 19–39.

Champenois, C., Lefebvre, V., & Ronteau, S. (2020). Entrepreneurship as practice: Systematic literature review of a nascent field. *Entrepreneurship & Regional Development*, *32*(3–4), 281–312.

Cicourel, A., & Knorr Cetina, K. (Eds.) (1981). *Advances in Social Theory and Methodology: Toward an Integration of Micro- and Macro-Sociologies*. London: Routledge & Kegan Paul.

Clayman, S., Elliott, M., Heritage, J., & Laurie, M. (2006). Historical trends in questioning presidents, 1953–2000. *Presidential Studies Quarterly*, *36*(3), 561–583.

Clifton, J. (2006). A conversation analytical approach to business communication: The case of leadership. *Journal of Business Communication*, *43*(3), 202–219.

Donnellon, A. (1996). *Team Talk: The Power of Language in Team Dynamics*. Boston: Harvard Business School Press.

Drew, P., & Heritage, J. (Eds.) (1992). *Talk at Work: Interaction in Institutional Settings*. Cambridge: Cambridge University Press.

Drew, P., & Sorjonen, M. L. (1997). Institutional dialogue. In T. A. Van Dijk (Ed.), *Discourse as Social Interaction: Discourse Studies: A Multidisciplinary Introduction* (pp. 191–216) (Vol. 2). London: Sage.

Engeström, Y., & Middleton, D. (1998). *Cognition and Communication at Work*. Cambridge: Cambridge University Press.

Fairhurst, G., & Uhl-Bien, M. (2012). Organizational discourse analysis: Examining leadership as a relational process. *The Leadership Quarterly*, *23*(6), 1043–1062.

Finlay, W., Walton, C., & Antaki, C. (2011). Giving feedback to care staff about offering choices to people with intellectual disabilities. In C. Antaki (Ed.), *Applied Conversation Analysis: Intervention and Change in Institutional Talk* (pp. 161–183). New York: Palgrave Macmillan.

Garfinkel, H. (1963). A conception of, and experiments with, "trust" as a condition of stable concerted actions. In O. Harvey (Ed.), *Motivation and Social Interaction* (pp. 187–238). New York: Ronald Press.

Garfinkel, H. (1967). *Studies in Ethnomethodology.* Englewood Cliffs, NJ: Prentice Hall.

Garfinkel, H., & Sacks, H. (1970). On formal structures of practical actions. In J. McKinney & E. Tiryakian (Eds.), *Theoretical Sociology: Perspectives and Developments.* New York: Appleton-Century-Crofts.

Garfinkel, H., & Wieder, D. (1992). Two incommensurable, asymmetrically alternate technologies of social analysis. In G. Watson & R. Seiler (Eds.), *Text in Context: Contributions to Ethnomethodology* (pp. 175–206). Newbury Park, CA: Sage.

Goffman, E. (1956). *The Presentation of Self in Everyday Life.* Edinburgh: Univeristy of Edinburgh SSRC.

Goffman, E. (1964). The neglected situation. *American Anthropologist, 66*(6), 133–136.

Goffman, E. (1974). *Frame Analysis: An Essay on the Organization of Experience.* Cambridge, MA: Harvard University Press.

Goodwin, C. (1981). *Conversational Organization: Interaction between Speaker and Hearers.* New York: Academic Press.

Goodwin, C., & Goodwin, M. (1992). Assessments and the construction of context. In A. Duranti & C. Goodwin (Eds.), *Rethinking Context: Language as an Interactive Phenomenon* (pp. 147–149). Cambridge: Cambridge University Press.

Goodwin, C., & Heritage, J. (1990). Conversation analysis. *Annual Review of Anthropology, 19,* 283–307.

Heath, C., & Luff, P. (2000). *Technology in Action.* Cambridge: Cambridge University Press.

Hepburn, A., Wilkinson, S., & Butler, C. (2014). Intervening with conversation analysis in telephone helpline services: Strategies to improve effectiveness. *Research on Language and Social Interaction, 47*(3), 239–254.

Heritage, J. (1984). *Garfinkel and Ethnomethodology.* Cambridge: Polity Press.

Heritage, J. (1989). Current developments in conversation analysis. In D. Roger & P. Bull (Eds.), *Conversation: An Interdisciplinary Perspective* (pp. 21–47). Philadelphia: Multilingual Matters.

Heritage, J. (1999). Conversation analysis at century's end: Practices of talk-in-interaction, their distributions, and their outcomes. *Research on Language & Social Interaction, 32*(1–2), 69–76.

Heritage, J. (2009). Conversation analysis as social theory. In B. S. Turner (Ed.), *The New Blackwell Companion to Social Theory* (pp. 300–320). Chichester: John Wiley & Sons.

Heritage, J. (2010). Conversation analysis: Practices and methods. In D. Silverman (Ed.), *Qualitative Research: Theory, Method and Practice* (pp. 207–226). London: Sage.

Heritage, J., Robinson, J., Elliott, M., Beckett, M., & Wilkes, M. (2007). Reducing patients' unmet concerns in primary care: The difference one word can make. *Journal of General Internal Medicine, 22*(10), 1429–1433.

Hilbert, R. (1990). Ethnomethodology and the micro–macro order. *American Sociological Review, 55,* 794–808.

Hilbert, R. (2009). Ethnomethodology and social theory. In B. S. Turner (Ed.), *The New Blackwell Companion to Social Theory* (pp. 159–178). Chichester: John Wiley & Sons.

Huma, B., Stokoe, E., & Sikveland, R. (2019). Persuasive conduct: Alignment and resistance in prospecting "cold" calls. *Journal of Language and Social Psychology, 38*(1), 33–60.

Jefferson, G. (1984). Transcript notation. In J. Heritage (Ed.), *Structures of Social Interaction* (pp. 191–222). New York: Cambridge University Press.

Jefferson, G. (2004). Glossary of transcript symbols with an introduction. In G. Lerner (Ed.), *Conversation Analysis: Studies from the First Generation* (pp. 13–31). Philadelphia: John Benjamins.

Johannisson, B. (2011). Towards a practice theory of entrepreneuring. *Small Business Economics, 36*(2), 135–150.

Johannisson, B. (2020). Searching for the roots of entrepreneuring as practice: Introducing the enactive approach. In W. B. Gartner & B. T. Teague (Eds.), *Research Handbook on Entrepreneurial Behavior,*

Practice and Process (pp. 138–167). Cheltenham, UK and Northampton, MA, USA: Edward Elgar Publishing.

Keating, A., Geiger, S., & McLoughlin, D. (2014). Riding the practice waves: Social resourcing practices during new venture development. *Entrepreneurship Theory and Practice, 38*(5), 1207–1235.

Kitzinger, C., & Kitzinger, S. (2007). Birth trauma: Talking with women and the value of conversation analysis. *British Journal of Midwifery, 15*(5), 256–264.

Llewellyn, N. (2008). Organization in actual episodes of work: Harvey Sacks and organization studies. *Organization Studies, 29*(5), 763–791.

Llewellyn, N. (2015). Microstructures of economic action: Talk, interaction and the bottom line. *The British Journal of Sociology, 66*(3), 486–511.

Lynch, M. (2006). Cognitive activities without cognition? Ethnomethodological investigations of selected "cognitive" topics. *Discourse Studies, 8*(1), 95–104.

Macbeth, D. (2011). Understanding understanding as an instructional matter. *Journal of Pragmatics, 43*(2), 438–451.

Maynard, D. (1988). Language, interaction, and social problems. *Social Problems, 35*(4), 311–334.

Mondada, L. (1998). Therapy interactions: Specific genre or "blown up" version of ordinary conversational practices? *Pragmatics, 8*(2), 155–166.

Mondada, L. (2018a). The multimodal interactional organization of tasting: Practices of tasting cheese in gourmet shops. *Discourse Studies, 20*(6), 743–769.

Mondada, L. (2018b). Multiple temporalities of language and body in interaction: Challenges for transcribing multimodality. *Research on Language and Social Interaction, 51*(1), 85–106.

Nevile, M. (2004). *Beyond the Black Box: Talk-in-Interaction in the Airline Cockpit.* Farnham: Ashgate.

Nevile, M., Haddington, P., Heinemann, T., & Rauniomaa, M. (Eds.) (2014). *Interacting with Objects: Language, Materiality, and Social Activity.* Philadelphia: John Benjamins.

Nicolini, D. (2009). Zooming in and out: Studying practices by switching theoretical lenses and trailing connections. *Organization Studies, 30*(12), 1391–1418.

Nicolini, D. (2012). *Practice Theory, Work, and Organization: An Introduction.* Oxford: Oxford University Press.

Orlikowski, W. J. (2010). Practice in research: Phenomenon, perspective and philosophy. In D. Golsorkhi, L. Rouleau, D. Seidl, & E. Vaara (Eds.), *Cambridge Handbook of Strategy as Practice* (pp. 23–33). Cambridge: Cambridge University Press.

Orr, J. (1998). Images of work. *Science, Technology, & Human Values, 23*(4), 439–455.

Peräkylä, A. (1995). *AIDS Counselling: Institutional Interaction and Clinical Practice.* Cambridge: Cambridge University Press.

Peräkylä, A. (2011). Validity in research based on naturally occurring social interaction. In D. Silverman (Ed.), *Qualitative Research: Theory, Method and Practice* (3rd edition) (pp. 365–382). London: Sage.

Pomerantz, A., & Fehr, B. (1997). Conversation analysis: An approach to the study of social action as sense making practices. In T. van Dijk (Ed.), *Discourse as Social Interaction: Discourse Studies 2 – A Multidisciplinary Introduction.* London: Sage.

Psathas, G. (Ed.) (1990). *Interaction Competence* (Vol. 1). Washington, DC: University Press of America.

Psathas, G. (1995). *Conversation Analysis: The Study of Talk in Interaction.* Thousand Oaks, CA: Sage.

Rawls, A. (2008). Harold Garfinkel, ethnomethodology and workplace studies. *Organization Studies, 29*(5), 701–732.

Reckwitz, A. (2002). Toward a theory of social practices: A development in culturalist theorizing. *European Journal of Social Theory, 5*(2), 243–263.

Robinson, J., & Heritage, J. (2014). Intervening with conversation analysis: The case of medicine. *Research on Language and Social Interaction, 47*(3), 201–218.

Sacks, H. (1984a). Notes on methodology. In J. M. Atkinson & J. Heritage (Eds.), *Structures of Social Action: Studies in Conversation Analysis* (pp. 21–27). Cambridge: Cambridge University Press.

Sacks, H. (1984b). On doing "being ordinary". In J. M. Atkinson & J. Heritage (Eds.), *Structures of Social Action: Studies in Conversation Analysis* (pp. 413–429). Cambridge: Cambridge University Press.

Sacks, H. (1992). *Lectures on Conversation* (Vol. 1. Fall 1964–Spring 1968). Oxford: Blackwell.

Sacks, H., & Schegloff, E. A. (1975/2002). Home position. *Gesture, 2*, 133–146.

Sacks, H., Schegloff, E., & Jefferson, G. (1974). A simplest systematics for the organization of turn-taking for conversation. *Language, 50*(4), 696–735.

Schegloff, E. (1991). Reflections on talk and social structure. In D. Boden & D. Zimmerman (Eds.), *Talk and Social Structure: Studies in Ethnomethodology and Conversation Analysis*. Cambridge: Polity Press.

Schegloff, E. (1993). Reflections on quantification in the study of conversation. *Research on Language and Social Interaction, 26*(1), 99–128.

Schegloff, E. (1996). Confirming allusions: Toward an empirical account of action. *American Journal of Sociology, 102*(1), 161–216.

Schegloff, E. (2006). Interaction: The infrastructure for social institutions, the natural ecological niche for language, and the arena in which culture is enacted. In N. Enfield & S. Levinson (Eds.), *Roots of Human Sociality: Culture, Cognition and Interaction* (pp. 70–96). Oxford: Berg.

Schegloff, E. (2007). *Sequence Organization in Interaction: A Primer in Conversation Analysis* (Vol. 1). Cambridge: Cambridge University Press.

Schegloff, E., Ochs, E., & Thompson, S. (1996). Introduction. In E. Ochs, E. A. Schegloff, & S. Tompson (Eds.), *Interaction and Grammar*. Cambridge: Cambridge University Press.

Schegloff, E., & Sacks, H. (1973). Opening up closings. *Semiotica, 8*(4), 289–327.

Sert, O. (2013). Integrating digital video analysis software into language teacher education: Insights from conversation analysis. *Procedia – Social and Behavioral Sciences, 70*, 231–238.

Steyaert, C., & Landström, H. (2011). Enacting entrepreneurship research in a pioneering, provocative and participative way: On the work of Bengt Johannisson. *Small Business Economics, 36*(2), 123–134.

Stivers, T. (2007). *Prescribing Under Pressure: Parent–Physician Conversations and Antibiotics*. New York: Oxford University Press.

Stivers, T. (2015). Coding social interaction: A heretical approach in conversation analysis? *Research on Language and Social Interaction, 48*(1), 1–19.

Stivers, T., & Majid, A. (2007). Questioning children: Interactional evidence of implicit bias in medical interviews. *Social Psychology Quarterly, 70*(4), 424–441.

Stokoe, E. (2011). Simulated interaction and communication skills training: The "conversation-analytic role-play method". In C. Antaki (Ed.), *Applied Conversation Analysis: Intervention and Change in Institutional Talk* (pp. 119–139). New York: Palgrave Macmillan.

ten Have, P. (2001). Applied conversation analysis. In A. McHoul & M. Rapley (Eds.), *How to Analyze Talk in Institutional Settings: A Casebook of Methods* (pp. 3–11). London: Continuum.

ten Have, P. (2007). *Doing Conversation Analysis: A Practical Guide*. London: Sage.

Thompson, N. A., Verduijn, K., & Gartner, W. B. (2020). Entrepreneurship-as-practice: Grounding contemporary theories of practice into entrepreneurship studies. *Entrepreneurship & Regional Development, 32*, 247–256.

Tuccio, W., & Nevile, M. (2017). Using conversation analysis in data-driven aviation training with large-scale qualitative datasets. *Journal of Aviation/Aerospace Education & Research, 26*(1), 1–47.

Watson, T. (2013). Entrepreneurship in action: Bringing together the individual, organizational and institutional dimensions of entrepreneurial action. *Entrepreneurship & Regional Development, 25*(5–6), 1–19.

Wooffitt, R. (2005). *Conversation Analysis and Discourse Analysis: A Comparative and Critical Introduction*. London: Sage.

Zimmerman, D. (2005). Introduction: Conversation analysis and social problems. *Social Problems, 52*(4), 445–448.

11. Using digital methods for the study of entrepreneurship-as-practice

Thomas Cyron

INTRODUCTION

A core argument of practice theory is that 'social life is tied to a context (site) of which it is inherently a part' (Schatzki, 2005, p. 466). Thus, practice-based studies of entrepreneurship face the challenge of transcending methodological individualism and achieving methodological situationism (Gartner, 1988; Steyaert, 2007). The goal is to emphasize the interplay of individuals and structures as they co-occur in practice-arrangement bundles (Schatzki, 1996, 2005). For this reason, practice-based research traditionally uses qualitative research methods such as ethnographies, conversation analysis, or interviews (Gherardi, 2012).

Such 'analogue' methods can run into some problems. First, they struggle to capture entrepreneurial practices that increasingly take place in digital sites. Digitalization has changed the ways in which people practise entrepreneurship (Nambisan, 2017): it opens up new ways of interacting with stakeholders (e.g., Drummond et al., 2018; Fischer & Reuber, 2011; Olanrewaju et al., 2020); enables new business models (e.g., Gustafsson & Khan, 2017; Kraus et al., 2019; Srinivasan & Venkatraman, 2018; von Briel et al., 2018); and facilitates crowdfunding (e.g., Mahmood et al., 2019; Mollick, 2014; Steigenberger & Wilhelm, 2018). The more tasks entrepreneurs perform digitally, the more difficult it becomes to observe digital sites with currently popular research methods unless the researcher always hovers behind an entrepreneur's shoulder and watches what happens on his or her computer screen.

A second problem of more traditional research methods concerns how far researchers can 'zoom out' of single real-time practice enactments and study the composition of wider nets of practice-arrangement bundles (Nicolini, 2009, 2012, 2017). Ideally, such research would retain observational detail while expanding on the (temporal) relations between practice-arrangement bundles (Kouamé & Langley, 2017). However, traditional methods are resource-intensive and often require the researcher to focus on one site, making it challenging to follow simultaneous unfoldings of practices across sites and cases (e.g., Keating et al., 2014). In addition, and more specific to entrepreneuring, entrepreneurs might work 'irregular' working hours or work from home where researchers cannot be physically with them at all times.

Digital research methods can partially mitigate these problems and offer two benefits. First, it becomes possible to capture what activities entrepreneurs perform digitally by accessing the digital platforms and tools that entrepreneurs use without the need for researchers to be physically present. This reduces the cost of data collection and focuses on the growing digitalization of entrepreneurial practices. Second, the reduced cost of digital methods can mitigate the problems associated with 'micro-isolationism' (cf. Seidl & Whittington, 2014) and idiosyncrasies in theorizing entrepreneurship as practice. Collecting digital traces of entrepreneurs provides cues about how practice-arrangement bundles connect across time and space, helping researchers 'get the bigger picture' (Thompson et al., 2020).

This chapter aims to introduce and encourage the use of digital methods in practice-based entrepreneurship research. It begins with an overview of qualitative digital research methods and outlines sources for collecting data via digital media. It then shows ways to use such data in connection with three research foci: (1) entrepreneuring in digital sites, (2) entanglements of digital and physical entrepreneurial practices, and (3) entrepreneuring across digital and physical sites. A concluding discussion outlines critical considerations for entrepreneurship-as-practice scholars who are considering embarking on the digital methods train.

QUALITATIVE DIGITAL RESEARCH METHODS: A BRIEF OVERVIEW

There are many ideas about what concerns digital methods that vary in breadth and depth. In some cases, authors describe comprehensive research approaches. For instance, netnography refers to a prescriptive and pragmatic step-by-step approach that provides guidelines for ethnographic research on digital media, including detailed templates for data collection, analysis, and interpretation (Kozinets, 2020). Other means of performing ethnographic work online are less prescriptive (Hine, 2000; Pink et al., 2016) but are still rooted in their respective methodological underpinnings. In contrast, others describe collections of digital tools without framing them within particular methodologies (Paulus et al., 2014; Rogers, 2019; Salmons, 2016). Finally, as digital methods continue to emerge from ongoing technological developments in society (Murthy, 2008), a growing number of articles and book chapters more narrowly describe specific methods of using digital media for data collection or analysis. Confusion about what concerns 'digital methods' thus stems from the various ways in which researchers have used computers and digital media in the past for various steps of the research process.

Concerning practice-based research projects, digital ethnography and its variants provide an appropriate methodological starting point because their ontological and epistemological underpinnings fit with practice-based research. Digital ethnographers seek 'to find a methodological common ground for scholars doing ethnographic research on, through and about digital media' (Abidin & de Seta, 2020, p. 8). Their key focus is theorizing the digital world and understanding how technology and digital media impact culture and society (Kozinets, 2020; Pink et al., 2016; Rogers, 2013).

In addition to digital ethnographies, there are other potential starting points because not all digital methods focus on theorizing digital phenomena exclusively. As Salmons (2016) points out, digital methods can also be used as a medium for collecting data without theorizing the digital world itself. Such a loose definition of what concerns 'digital methods' is useful when studying entrepreneurship as practice because researchers often have to monitor what is happening in physical sites as well. Therefore, it makes sense to consider any data collection technique via digital media as long as it helps researchers keep abreast of both physical and digital practices.

In line with such an open view of digital methods, the methods cited in this book chapter focus on collecting data via digital media, such as by putting a digital twist onto traditional methods (e.g., conducting interview studies through video chats, social media, or email (Deakin & Wakefield, 2014; Lynch & Mah, 2018) or conducting diary studies via email (Jones & Woolley, 2015), online blogs (Hookway, 2008), or dedicated smartphone apps (Do & Yamagata-Lynch, 2017; García et al., 2016)). The chapter also lists data collection methods more specific to studying digital phenomena, such as taking screenshots and web scraping (Kozinets, 2020) or issue crawling and URL fetching (Rogers, 2019).

Research can also involve multiple data sources using digital and 'analogue' methods, especially when the goal is to understand physical practices or their entanglements with digital sites. Researchers must then consider how to combine data effectively and how to analyse data from different sources. It might require researchers to reinterpret the affordances of data analysis software (e.g., Beneito-Montagut et al., 2017) by, for example, replacing physical archives with online databases and thus enabling new ways of understanding the data (Ernkvist, 2015).

COLLECTING DATA FROM DIGITAL SOURCES

Digital data collection can involve a wide range of data sources. A deliberate use of digital methods therefore involves (1) knowledge about different data sources, (2) the ability to deliberate about which and how many data sources to include in a research project, and (3) the acknowledgement of ethical standards and trust-building mechanisms concerning digital data sources. The following sections provide basic information concerning the three aspects.

An Overview of Digital Data Sources

Table 11.1 provides an overview of the data sources I discuss in this chapter. The goal is to offer an extensive though not exhaustive overview of typical digital data sources with a focus on how they can be used in qualitative research projects. For each data source, I outline (a) the nature of the data source, (b) the different types of data that can be gathered from each source, and (c) the degree of obtrusion depending on whether the data are naturally occurring or researcher generated.

Collecting information from (semi-)public profiles and blogs on social networking sites
Social networking sites (SNSs) are important sources of information, especially when studying phenomena in digital space. boyd and Ellison (2007, p. 211) define SNSs as 'web-based services that allow individuals to (1) construct a public or semi-public profile within a bounded system, (2) articulate a list of other users with whom they share a connection, and (3) view and traverse their list of connections and those made by others within the system'. SNSs include services such as Facebook, LinkedIn, Twitter, YouTube, Instagram and online blogs.

SNSs are key drivers of the growing entanglement between physical and digital entrepreneurial practices. For instance, platforms such as Facebook, Twitter, and LinkedIn change the ways entrepreneurs initiate and maintain social interactions with constituents and stakeholders (Fischer & Reuber, 2011). Furthermore, entrepreneurs have started to monetize their activities on SNSs and have created new business models (Gustafsson & Khan, 2017). SNSs have thus become entangled with physical entrepreneurial practices but also elicit new practices that largely take place in digital sites.

SNSs provide a variety of data, depending on the features and affordances of each platform (Evans et al., 2017). One type of data refers to user posts made on (semi-)public profiles. Such posts can include text, images, or videos that researchers otherwise would collect through diaries or observations. It is common for people to post updates on their whereabouts and activities on their social networking profiles. Such posts can provide cues that can help

Table 11.1   *Overview of digital data sources and characteristics*

Data source	Data types	Degree of obtrusion	Examples
(Semi-) public profiles and blogs on social networking sites	– User posts on profile pages or blogs (text, pictures and video) – Content shares – Comments and reactions	– Low, if used for covert observations – Medium to high, if the researcher interacts with users or if used for solicited diaries	– Facebook – LinkedIn – Instagram – Blogs – Online discussion forums
Back-channels	– Private one-to-one conversations – Private group conversations (e.g., team chats)	– Low to moderate, as it requires negotiating access but the researcher can subsequently be (mostly) invisible	– Facebook Messenger – WhatsApp – Slack – Microsoft Teams – Skype – Zoom
Productivity software	– To-do lists – Work structures – Responsibility assignments	– Low to moderate, as it requires negotiating access but the researcher can be (mostly) invisible	– Trello – Monday.com – Dapulse – Codingteam – Google Docs
Digital files from (online) data storage	– Letters – Business plans/business model canvasses – Instructions to team members/employees – Notes of ideas – Pitch presentations – Calculations	– Low to moderate, as it requires negotiating access but the researcher can be (mostly) invisible	– Physical hard drives – Cloud-based storage solutions
Digital tools and devices	– Interviews – Written accounts of experiences – Video recordings of practices	– High, due to the participants' direct involvement in the creation of data	– Emails – Messaging services – Video communication applications (Skype, Zoom, etc.) – Smartphone applications – Participant video recordings

researchers trace the activities of entrepreneurs across time and space. In addition to serving as spatial and temporal cues, the activities posted on SNSs can be seen as digital practices in themselves. For example, the curation of social networking profiles can be seen as a form of impression management because the (semi-)public nature of social networking profiles requires adaptations of social networking activities to the expectations of different audiences. The content from a personal account on Facebook or Instagram will likely differ from the impressions people maintain on LinkedIn, which focuses on a more professional audience. We can also expect differences in the ways in which entrepreneurs portray their personas and portray their ventures' images or brands.

In addition to posts, most SNSs also afford some form of interaction between people. Sharing content from other profiles and pages is one example. Researchers can study practices of sharing content to trace connections between groups of entrepreneurs and other stakeholders and to better understand, for instance, how they jointly raise awareness of a new product category. Another example relates to how SNSs allow us to trace the responses of people and thus capture interactions between entrepreneurs and their social media constituents. Platforms typically feature two types of responses. First, there are quick, low-cost responses, such as those made using the reaction buttons found on Facebook or using the heart buttons on Twitter and Instagram, whereby users can express their intuitive (emotional) reactions to a post. In addition, many platforms include a comment function that affords responses in the form of text, pictures, GIFs, strings of emoticons, or videos. Usually, comments signal a higher degree of user involvement relative to those providing more simplistic reactions.

Generally, the data available on SNSs allow for relatively unobtrusive research, especially when profiles are publicly accessible. Similar to the method of shadowing (Czarniawska, 2007), researchers can observe digital spaces from a distance without interfering or guiding the activities taking place, oftentimes without people even being aware of the presence of a researcher. In addition to studying user posts from a distance and 'as is', researchers can use SNSs for solicited modes of data collection. For example, Lackéus (2020) reports experiences of developing a scientific social media platform specifically for entrepreneurship research and education purposes. Additionally, Hookway (2008) recommends solicited studies of blogs-as-diaries where the researcher guides the diary writing process in line with the research aim.

Collecting information from backchannels
Backchannels describe digital communication that is less visible to the public because access is oftentimes restricted. Emails, video conferencing, private messages or closed discussion groups are some examples. Communication via digital backchannels has evolved over past decades with new software changing the ways that people communicate. The formatting of text provides a means to emphasize parts of what a person writes. In addition to text, people can use emoticons or animated GIFs to express themselves and respond to what another person has said before. People can add videos, pictures, voice messages and documents to the stream of communication. Some software, such as Slack, WhatsApp and Telegram, allows one to structure communication through multiple channels and limits access so that only specified group members can participate in related discussions. An administrator usually governs access and moderation rights.

Backchannels enable research on how digital spaces shape communicative and discursive practices, which are important aspects of entrepreneuring (Steyaert, 2007; Thompson et al., 2020). The relative importance of digital versus face-to-face communication hereby depends on the spatial distance between individuals. In some cases, digital communication occurs in addition and in parallel with face-to-face communication. Accessing digital backchannels then allows us to juxtapose the physical and digital and to understand how the affordances of different channels affect how individuals communicate and make sense of information. In other cases, such as in the case of remote working teams in which group members cannot meet in person, digital spaces provide the main channel for exchanging information and sensemaking, making digital methods a valuable tool for understanding how people create, develop, organize and implement new ventures.

Access to backchannels requires negotiating access with backchannel administrators and its users so that everyone is aware of the researcher 'listening in'. Nevertheless, collecting information from backchannels is a relatively unobtrusive mode of collecting data because here the silent lurking of a researcher is usually invisible to others. As long as researchers do not actively participate in the discussion, their existence is not noticeable except for their being listed as a group or chat member. This stands in contrast to traditional observation methods, where the presence of a researcher in physical space is more perceivable to a level at which this might influence how people behave and what they say.

Collecting information from productivity software

Closely related to backchannels is productivity software, such as task managers and project management tools. The boundary between backchannels and productivity software is blurry because many tools that are meant to organize the work of groups also feature means of communication. However, the focus of such productivity software is more on the organization of work tasks, responsibilities and timelines.

Researchers can use the information from productivity software in at least two ways. First, they can use it to monitor what people in an emerging organization are doing. For instance, many tools allow users to track when tasks emerge on an agenda, if tasks have a deadline and when people complete tasks. Sometimes, the ordering of tasks is specified because some might depend on the prior accomplishment of others. In this way, researchers can zoom out from individual doings and sayings and trace the connections and interdependencies between practices. Second, the researcher can also study how individuals and groups use tools. Although a particular software program might have distinct features, it does not mean that all people will use the technology in exactly the same way (Orlikowski, 2007). This raises questions as to what affordances the interactions of entrepreneurs with the productivity software elicit and how these differences interact with the development of new venture ideas and new venture creation. For example, studies can compare how different entrepreneurs and entrepreneurial teams make use of the same software as well as compare different software programs with different features to understand how the resulting affordances interplay with entrepreneurs.

Similar to backchannels, access to productivity software must be negotiated with the research participants. Once access is granted, the researcher's presence is usually unobtrusive.

Collecting digital files from (online) data storage

The more work is taking place in digital spaces, the more work is also being directed toward digital artefacts. Entrepreneurs create, share, revise, and delete these artefacts on an everyday basis, and each artefact shows how new ventures and ideas manifest in the world. As a result, the increasing digitalization of work leaves traces of archival data in the form of text documents, slideshow presentations, calculation sheets, databases, pictures, screenshots, lines of code, and much more. Document analysis can be a key means to understand such practices (Bowen, 2009). Access to the digital spaces in which such data are stored thus allows for the collection of more information.

Again, the analysis of such information can be threefold. First, such data allow for the tracking outcomes of entrepreneurial practices, i.e., the artefacts that entrepreneurs materialize along the way. Usually, the documents have timestamps, which also allow us to retrospectively track what entrepreneurs have done over time. In this way, digital artefacts can help trace entrepreneurial activities over time and space. Second, the ways in which entrepreneurs work with such artefacts can be used as another way to approach the data. Practices, such as pitching or business planning, can manifest in the similarities and differences between the artefacts that entrepreneurs and new venture teams create. Looking closer at the ways in which people compose and work with such artefacts might thus reveal patterns of how people practise entrepreneurship. Third, digital artefacts are a key link between digital and physical spaces. It often happens that these artefacts are presented in physical sites, such as at investor pitch presentations. When new venture teams meet in person, they might refer to digital arte-facts on their screens or projections on the wall, creating opportunities to study how the digital becomes entangled with the physical.

Collecting documents from online storage is an unobtrusive method, but it requires negotiating access to storage space. There are broadly two ways of obtaining access to such data. First, if the data are stored on a networked storage device, such as a company server or cloud-storage solution, the researcher can ask for remote access rights. This serves as a con-venient means to access information because it does not require the researcher to meet study participants in person. Second, if data are stored on a nonnetworked storage device, such as on the research participant's hard drive, researchers can ask the study participants to provide a copy of their data.

Collecting information via digital tools and devices
Nevertheless, there are some limitations of the aforementioned ways of collecting information from online sources. First, there are other digital sites that neither of the above techniques will capture. Searching for information on the web, for instance, is likely an important part of entrepreneurship. Researching this activity requires capturing the actions that entrepreneurs perform on their digital devices. Second, some practices are not performed in digital but physical sites. Some of the abovementioned techniques might offer cues about what happens in the physical world, but digital methods can also assist in capturing physical sites more directly. Third, relying on digital traces does not reveal why people perform activities or how they experience them. In relation to the study of entrepreneurship as practice, the previously mentioned ways of collecting information are limited with regard to understanding teleoaf-fective structures and the mental states of entrepreneurs while performing certain practices (Antonacopoulou & Fuller, 2020; Schatzki, 1996, 2012).

Researchers can overcome such limitations by using more digital media for solicited research. For example, developments in smartphone technologies and wearables provide new opportunities to collect data in line with experience sampling methods, which entrepre-neurship scholars have called for 10 years ago (Uy et al., 2010). Researchers can currently create their own smartphone applications and tailor the collection of data to research purposes (Do & Yamagata-Lynch, 2017; García et al., 2016). The applications can, for instance, ask participants to reflect on a given situation, share their emotional experiences, or take a photo or video of the physical spaces that they occupy. In this way, digital media creates a window into the physical world of entrepreneurship. Digital media can enable more frequent contact with research participants and strengthen relationships. For example, research participants in an email-based diary study reported that daily reminders and the possibility of tailoring diary content encouraged them to participate for prolonged periods of time (Jones & Woolley, 2015).

This suggests that researchers can refashion traditional data collection techniques through digital media. Conducting interviews via video chat or email, for instance, helps to more frequently contact research participants and reduce the time between when an event happens and when the researchers learn about it. Another method of data collection previously used in practice-based studies is video research, which allows for simultaneous observations of multi-ple sites and which has benefited from the decreasing costs of video technology (Jarzabkowski et al., 2015; LeBaron et al., 2018). The increasing abundance of video technology with many electronic devices invites further experimentation concerning how participants themselves can record their day-to-day activities.

Similarly, researchers performing conversation analyses have used screen capture software to understand turn-taking in digital communication (Garcia & Jacobs, 1999; Meredith, 2019). Such software essentially records everything that happens on the screen of a computer user. The method can help better reveal the processes by which messages are created and how people use their computers for their work, so as to understand how entrepreneurs use internet searches to find information pertaining to their new ventures.

Using digital media tools for such solicited research purposes is usually highly obtrusive. There is reason to believe that researchers should carefully build trust with their respondents over time before engaging in more interactive ways of using digital methods (Abidin, 2020). The challenge is to strike a balance between what is acceptable to the participants and at what point research activities start to interfere with their lives.

Deciding on the Use of Digital and Analogue Data Sources in a Research Project

From the above broad overview of digital data sources, I now shift my attention to decisions concerning which data sources to use and how many to include in a research project. This decision often depends on the openness of the research question with broad research questions requiring the use of vast amounts of data sources and narrower research questions focusing on single data sources.

Researchers can start from open research questions (e.g., 'How does digital media influence new venture team communication practices?'). In such a scenario, researchers might want to collect a vast amount of data from multiple sources and later in the analysis let 'the data speak for themselves'. On one hand, using such large amounts of data has the potential to overwhelm researchers (especially inexperienced ones) during analysis and thus make it difficult to discern important from unimportant information (Miles & Huberman, 1994). On the other hand, the broader span of such a research project is more suitable for zooming out of particular practices and tracing the connections between practices (cf. Nicolini, 2009, 2017).

The alternative is to start from a narrower research question (e.g., 'How does the use of GIFs enable emotional expression in new venture team communication?'). In such a scenario, researchers might select data sources more purposefully depending on the likelihood of data from any said data source providing appropriate answers to the research question (for example, only the backchannels of new venture teams; see explanation above). Such a narrower focus on fewer data sources restricts researchers' perceptions of connections to adjacent practices. However, it also decreases the risk of becoming overwhelmed because researchers focus on fewer data sources and analyse them from a more fixed starting point.

The data sources covered in a study do not have to be fixed in advance but can evolve throughout a research project. It is likely that as researchers focus on particular practices in digital sites, they will encounter adjacent practices that feed into or append the practice examined. In such cases, researchers can successively add new sources of data, both offline and online. For instance, it might be that a study focusing on the role of GIFs in new venture team communication finds traces of physical meetings that feed into and from conversations taking place online. In such cases, it could be valuable to observe physical meetings in addition to digital data.

Acknowledging Ethics and Trust in Naturally Occurring vs. Researcher-Generated Data

Similar to what must be exercised when using traditional qualitative research methods, researchers collecting data from digital sources must 'toe the line between being "insiders" with empathetic knowledge and intimate access to their community, and "outsiders" with more neutrality and a natural curiosity to critically examine cultural repertoire that is otherwise overlooked or presumed to be mundane' (Abidin, 2020, pp. 57–58). The distance between researchers and study participants will hereby differ depending on how researchers approach digital data sources. Broadly speaking, we can differentiate between two directions. First, there are *naturally occurring data*, which exist independent of the researcher and research purpose; second, there are *researcher-generated data*, which researchers actively and purposefully generate through interactions with research participants via digital tools (Paulus et al., 2014). As noted in the above overview, many digital data sources can be approached from either direction depending on the research focus.

In contrast to traditional methods for which researchers must first become 'invisible' by assimilating with the research context, the absence of a researcher's physical body within a digital site enables the collection of naturally occurring data without disrupting what is happening (Kozinets, 2020; Salmons, 2016). This approach offers unique opportunities for covert research. However, such use of digital methods requires special attention to research ethics. The General Data Protection Regulation (GDPR) is pushing researchers to focus on the amount of data collected depending on research purposes and to be more transparent about the intended use of data. Especially covert observations obtained from social media may cover a large number of users and thus make it unfeasible to collect informed consent from all. Although there is a general consensus that researchers may use publicly available online information without explicit consent, they must employ safeguards that ensure the privacy of participants and prevent wrongdoing, for example, by disguising user names and profile pictures (Ferguson, 2017; Kozinets, 2020).[1]

In contrast, digital media also enable close interactions. Researchers can communicate with people via digital media, interfere with what is happening, and encourage research participants to use digital media in solicited ways. In such cases, data collection often requires forging trusting relationships with research participants, and there are multiple ways to build such relationships via digital media, starting either from physical and face-to-face encounters or from meeting research participants online.

Many researchers can build on existing relationships with research participants that they know from offline settings and extend this trust to online sites. Usually, the stronger the relationship and level of trust between researchers and participants, the more likely research participants will be providing access to their digital data sources. Such participants can also act as evangelists of the research project if an online site is populated by other individuals with whom no previous relationship exists. However, it is crucial to inform all online participants of the research project and to obtain their informed consent, especially in settings that might involve sensitive information.

Another path toward developing trustworthy relationships with research participants begins in the digital realm. Especially when the goal is to become *immersed* in the research environment and obtain an intimate understanding of it (Kozinets, 2020), it is important to also interact with the people who populate a digital site. It can help to spend some time as a passive observant (a 'lurker') of such communities to identify core actors and their relations with other people online and to gain an understanding of the interpersonal dynamics governing the community. It can also help to better understand how the community credentials its members because the researcher will have to meet community members at eye level and know how to balance his or her identity as a researcher with a genuine interest in the community (Abidin, 2020). Sometimes, it might even help to participate in the research community before contacting potential research participants, as this can signal an authentic interest in the community. Researchers can then start immersing themselves more by contacting a few key individuals and successively moving from covert to overt research. Once the researcher has gained the trust of these core individuals, he or she can recommend and refer to other research participants. In this way, researchers can leverage the trust of those core individuals.

THREE WAYS OF STUDYING PRACTICES WITH DIGITAL METHODS

Entrepreneurship can be regarded as 'a nexus of activities performed by multiple people that are recognizable in particular social and material contexts' when adopting a practice lens (Thompson & Byrne, 2020, p. 37). Some of these performed activities remain bound to the offline world, which consists of bodily movements, face-to-face communication, and physical boundaries. However, many other activities have moved to the digital world, which consists of electrical currents, computer code, and onscreen projections. These relatively new sites of social life are not just mundane but, to borrow the language from Orlikowski and Scott (2015; see also, Scott & Orlikowski, 2014), have become *entangled* with and a driver of entrepreneurship.

Acknowledging that entrepreneurship spans digital and physical sites allows me to suggest three research foci with which researchers can employ digital methods: (1) entrepreneuring in digital sites; (2) entanglements of digital and physical entrepreneurial practices, and (3) entrepreneuring across digital and physical sites. The main idea here is one of zooming out successively from entrepreneurial practices in digital sites to their connections with practices in the physical world and finally to their embeddedness within even broader nets of practices.

Entrepreneuring in Digital Sites

The first perspective acknowledges that many entrepreneurial practices are becoming predominantly digital, sometimes leading to forms of pure digital entrepreneurship 'in which artifacts, digital platforms or both are the *new venture ideas* and market offers' (Nzembayie et al., 2019, p. 3, emphasis in original). We can study digital practices as what they are purely in digital sites or from what Nambisan (2017, p. 1032) identifies as digital infrastructures defined as 'digital technology tools and systems (e.g., cloud computing, data analytics, online communities, social media, 3D printing, digital maker spaces, etc.) that offer communication, collaboration, and/or computing capabilities to support innovation and entrepreneurship'. The importance of this perspective increases the more a venture depends on digital operations, for instance, due to the nature of its products or the geographical dispersion of team members.

The notion of affordances, originating from Gibson's (1979, 1986) ideas about ecological psychology, has proven useful to understand the effects of digital sites on communication (e.g., Evans et al., 2017; Meredith, 2017), organization (Boxenbaum et al., 2018; Leonardi & Vaast, 2017; Meyer et al., 2018), and strategy (Gulbrandsen et al., 2020; Jarzabkowski & Kaplan, 2015). Meredith (2019, p. 242) notes 'affordances suggests that any object affords particular possibilities for interaction, but what properties are relevant and how they are used only emerges through interaction between actors and those objects'. This underlines the relational nature of affordances, meaning they are not predetermined but emerge from idiosyncratic interactions between actors and objects. Surely enough, affordances emerge from features of (digital) objects and thus can also be regarded as somewhat stable; however, this does not preclude that in a different context governed by different teleological structures, different affordances between objects and actors might emerge (Evans et al., 2017). Affordances thus match the assumptions of practice theory.

Applying this notion to the study of entrepreneurship-as-practice in digital sites means better understanding what affordances digital sites offer for entrepreneuring. A topic that stands out due to its empirical relevance is the role that new media play in internal and external venture communication. For example, Matthews et al. (2018) argue that practice-based approaches can help better reveal the intersection between entrepreneurship and selling and specifically point out the need for research on how the context of social media affects the selling practices of entrepreneurs. Beyond the issue of selling, social media have impacted many other practices relevant to entrepreneuring. Social media also influence how new venture ideas emerge, shifting the focus from individual to distributed agency where an idea is no longer the product of an individual but of many minds (Autio et al., 2013). Social media have also enabled new business models (e.g., Gustafsson & Khan, 2017; Kraus et al., 2019; Srinivasan & Venkatraman, 2018). Overall, knowledge about the affordances of social media for entrepreneurship is limited (Olanrewaju et al., 2020), and past research has only partially exploited the potential of digital methods (Fischer & Reuber, 2011; Gustafsson & Khan, 2017).

From this perspective, there is an emphasis on digital data in analysis, although analogue data can complement an analysis (Kozinets, 2020; Pink et al., 2016). For instance, an in-depth understanding of affordance would require not only observing from the outside how people interact through digital media but also how the patterns we observe from interactions are the result of commonly shared understandings of how to use a particular technology. Such an approach would help reveal the role of 'lived' and situated cognition in entrepreneurship, where cognitive constructs (e.g., ideation, emotion, motivation, sensemaking, and learning) are understood in relation to the contexts in which they take place (Gartner et al., 2016; Thompson & Byrne, 2020; Welter et al., 2016). Interviews with users could help provide information about this process. Put differently, the researcher begins with data collection in the digital realm before moving to other methods, but in contrast to the second perspective, she or he maintains a focus on theorizing practices in digital sites.

Entanglements of Digital and Physical Entrepreneurial Practices

The second perspective focuses on the *entanglements* of physical and digital entrepreneurial practices. Practice theorists point out that nonhuman actors shape everyday practices, including media and communication technologies (Pink et al., 2016, p. 43). Barad's conception of *entanglements* is particularly relevant for practice theoretical approaches because she emphasizes the material-discursive practices that constitute boundaries and give rise to phenomena (Barad, 2003, 2007). Orlikowski and Scott (2015; Scott & Orlikowski, 2014) have been advancing Barad's critique of ontological boundaries between meaning/matter and humans/ nonhumans to explain the impact of technology on work practices. The critique emphasizes how boundaries dissolve in enactments of practices. Consequently, the focus problematizes a strict distinction between the 'physical' and 'digital' and instead views both as deeply entangled.

Uncovering and highlighting such entanglements is an important puzzle piece in the study of entrepreneurship-as-practice, especially given that many people increasingly use electronic devices as extensions of themselves, directing attention to the role of materiality and embodiment in entrepreneuring (Thompson & Byrne, 2020). As Nambisan (2017) points out, digital technologies have rendered entrepreneurship (1) less bounded and (2) less predefined, which reflects how entrepreneurs interact with digital technologies on an everyday basis. Many entrepreneurial practices are currently entangled in both physical and digital sites such that a full understanding of entrepreneurial practices requires access to both realms.

Approaching the entanglement of physical and digital sites can go one of two ways, either starting at the physical site of a phenomenon and moving toward the digital or starting at the digital and moving toward the physical. When collecting traditional observations of physical sites, the researcher could notice how physical practices are entangled with digital practices. For example, shadowing an entrepreneur's visit to trade fairs might show how the person uses SNSs, such as LinkedIn, to exchange contact information with other people. It could then be of interest to follow subsequent practices on digital sites and understand how an entrepreneur uses the platform to stay in touch with the new contact. For such purpose, the researcher would have to negotiate access to the relevant backchannels. From the other direction, researchers could also start with observations made in digital sites, such as by observing how entrepreneurs publicly interact on LinkedIn with other members of the SNS (e.g., by commenting, sharing the content of another member, or endorsing other members' skills). Researchers could then follow up on online observations to see if such interactions trigger in-person contacts and visits.

Similar to the first perspective, studying the entanglement of physical and digital practices likely requires triangulation between data from digital and physical sources. However, the data from digital media must not take a subordinate role but must be seen on par with the data collected via traditional research methods, which now show their limitations in capturing the details of digital practices. Common practice-based research methods are well suited to capture physical entrepreneurial practices. Traditionally, practice-based research projects rely much on observational methods (Gherardi, 2012; Nicolini, 2012). However, such analogue methods fail to capture other phenomena that include entanglements of the physical and digital as well as predominantly digital practices. For instance, observing how entrepreneurs use their computers or smartphones from a distance does not help reveal what they are doing with these devices. Digital methods are therefore necessary to fully understand the entanglements of physical and digital sites.

Entrepreneuring Across Digital and Physical Sites

Finally, researchers can zoom out further from digital sites and their entanglements with physical sites to view the physical and embodied enactment and entanglement of entrepreneurship across larger nets of practices. Entrepreneuring will involve an extensive combination of practices adopted on both the physical and digital sides from a bird's eye view. The challenge is to capture both 'zooming in' on individual instances of practices *and* 'zooming out' from their entanglements over time and across sites while avoiding retrospective interpretations (Thompson et al., 2020). A key element is to prolong the period of investigation beyond single enactments of practices to see how practices interconnect with one another from a longer-term perspective (Kouamé & Langley, 2017; Nicolini, 2009, 2017). Combining digital and analogue research methods can help overcome such challenges.

Such undertakings can be useful in identifying the practices involved in entrepreneurship while remaining open to practices that so far have not been considered important (Gartner, 2013; Gartner et al., 2016; Thompson et al., 2020; Welter et al., 2016). As indicated in the previous section, researchers can interpret data from digital media as cues about the sequencing of entrepreneurial practices. Such methods are also efficient in the sense that we can follow practices across multiple sites. For example, entrepreneurs who frequently update their profiles on SNSs also give away information about other activities in their lives. The pictures they post can provide information about where they are, what they do, and what preceded or followed an activity. Similarly, data collected from productivity software can offer information about the structure of planned activities and oftentimes also about their fulfilment. In such cases, the data work as an unsolicited diary that can help the research zoom out from particular activities.

It is advisable to triangulate such data with other solicited data because entrepreneurs might be more or less active on social media or might not update their productivity software in a timely manner. Interviews could serve as one alternative. For instance, prior entrepreneurship-as-practice research has used narrative interviews (Terjesen & Elam, 2009) and interviews in combination with archival data (Keating et al., 2014) to investigate the practices of entrepreneurs (see also Hill, 2018). Individual recalls, however, are subject to hindsight bias (Cassar & Craig, 2009), and 'insights into practices will not come about through asking for retrospective interpretations about previous experiences' (Thompson et al., 2020, p. 254). As an alternative, researchers can use smartphone applications (García et al., 2016; Lackéus, 2020) or email-based diaries (Jones & Woolley, 2015) to obtain more timely and relevant information on a more regular basis. Such solicited data collection methods using digital media can help one develop a stronger understanding of what types of practices are involved in entrepreneurship and how important they might be for different aspects of the process.

Such a perspective would also benefit from combination with more traditional research methods because digital data collection techniques often fail to 'zoom in' on physical practices. Digital data could, therefore, be used as a complement to in-person observations, which are better suited for zooming in on physical practices (Gherardi, 2012; Nicolini, 2012; Thompson et al., 2020). If the researcher cannot be physically present, however, it is possible to partly overcome physical boundaries by using digital media. For example, video conferencing technology can be installed at relevant sites.

Taken together, digital methods should take a supportive role in the study of entrepreneuring across wider nets of practices. Such research often zooms in on individual practices and is interested in embodied experiences and in their relations to material circumstances. Traditional methods still outperform their digital counterparts in these cases because the researchers themselves share the experiences of their research participants. However, data drawn from digital media can offer a valuable source for triangulation, which can be crucial for zooming out and understanding the relations between individual practices.

CONCLUSION: WHAT TO CONSIDER WHEN USING DIGITAL METHODS

This chapter has provided a brief introduction to digital methods and encourages their use in practice-based entrepreneurship research. I have taken a broad perspective of digital methods covering many types of data collection techniques adopting digital media and how to apply them for different research foci, including phenomena occurring in both physical and digital sites. Thinking about digital methods also sensitizes researchers to study the impact of digitalization on entrepreneurial practices. The mentioned research topics are by no means exhaustive and can hopefully inspire others to conduct practice-based entrepreneurship research through and about digital media.

As a concluding thought, I invite researchers to reflect on several aspects before using digital methods to study entrepreneurship as practice and thus to cope with the variety of approaches and interpretations about what concerns digital methods. Figure 11.1 shows the relationships between the three main considerations and summarizes the different options I have outlined throughout the chapter.

First, researchers need to consider how to employ digital methods for data collection to best satisfy the research purposes. There are different options in terms of where to collect online data or how to use digital tools for qualitative research purposes. Laying out these different options can help a researcher decide which tools to place in her or his methodological toolbox. Oftentimes, practice-based research projects benefit from multiple sources of information (Gherardi, 2012; Nicolini, 2012), which is why researchers must consider whether collecting data via digital media is sufficient or whether traditional methods must complement the data collection process.

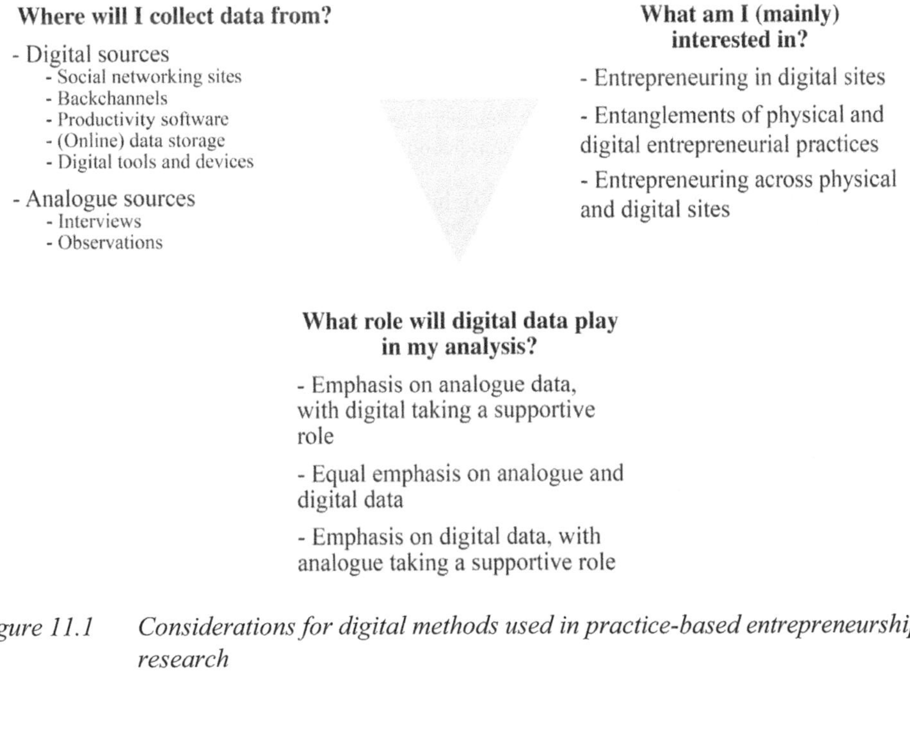

Where will I collect data from?

- Digital sources
  - Social networking sites
  - Backchannels
  - Productivity software
  - (Online) data storage
  - Digital tools and devices

- Analogue sources
  - Interviews
  - Observations

What am I (mainly) interested in?

- Entrepreneuring in digital sites

- Entanglements of physical and digital entrepreneurial practices

- Entrepreneuring across physical and digital sites

What role will digital data play in my analysis?

- Emphasis on analogue data, with digital taking a supportive role

- Equal emphasis on analogue and digital data

- Emphasis on digital data, with analogue taking a supportive role

Figure 11.1   *Considerations for digital methods used in practice-based entrepreneurship research*

Second, researchers should consider whether the main purpose of their study is to understand entrepreneuring in digital sites, whether they will use digital methods as a means to understand the entanglements of physical and digital entrepreneurial practices, or whether they are interested in entrepreneuring across physical and digital sites. The research focus is often in concert with the selection of data collection techniques. Sometimes, a researcher might stumble across interesting data and only later determine how such data might inform a research project. In other cases, researchers are interested in a particular phenomenon and then purposefully search for appropriate data. Regardless, a focus on either physical or digital phenomena influences the need to generate additional data via traditional methods and the relative importance of different data sources in the analysis and presentation of findings.

Finally, researchers must consider how digital tools can help with analysing and making sense of data and with presenting research findings. Given that most research projects will rely on multiple sources of information, it is important to consider what role data from each source will play in the analysis. In some cases, a study might emphasize analogue data and use digital methods to support the sensemaking process. In other cases, the emphasis might be on data collected from digital sites while using analogue methods as a supportive structure.

NOTE

1.   Chapter 6 in Kozinets (2020) provides more details about research ethics concerning data collection via digital methods and how to best implement ethical safeguards.

REFERENCES

Abidin, C. (2020). Somewhere between here and there: Negotiating researcher visibility in a digital ethnography of the influencer industry. *Journal of Digital Social Research*, *2*(1), 56–76.

Abidin, C., & de Seta, G. (2020). Private messages from the field: Confessions on digital ethnography and its discomforts. *Journal of Digital Social Research*, *2*(1), 1–19.

Antonacopoulou, E. P., & Fuller, T. (2020). Practising entrepreneuring as emplacement: The impact of sensation and anticipation in entrepreneurial action. *Entrepreneurship & Regional Development*, *32*(3–4), 257–280.

Autio, E., Dahlander, L., & Frederiksen, L. (2013). Information exposure, opportunity evaluation, and entrepreneurial action: An investigation of an online user community. *Academy of Management Journal*, *56*(5), 1348–1371.

Barad, K. (2003). Posthumanist performativity: Toward an understanding of how matter comes to matter. *Signs*, *28*(3), 801–831.

Barad, K. (2007). *Meeting the Universe Halfway: Quantum Physics and the Entanglement of Matter and Meaning*. Durham, NC: Duke University Press.

Beneito-Montagut, R., Begueria, A., & Cassián, N. (2017). Doing digital team ethnography: Being there together and digital social data. *Qualitative Research*, *17*(6), 664–682.

Bowen, G. A. (2009). Document analysis as a qualitative research method. *Qualitative Research Journal*, *9*(2), 27–40.

Boxenbaum, E., Jones, C., Meyer, R. E., & Svejenova, S. (2018). Towards an articulation of the material and visual turn in organization studies. *Organization Studies*, *39*(5–6), 597–616.

boyd, danah m, & Ellison, N. B. (2007). Social network sites: Definition, history, and scholarship. *Journal of Computer-Mediated Communication*, *13*(1), 210–230.

Cassar, G., & Craig, J. (2009). An investigation of hindsight bias in nascent venture activity. *Journal of Business Venturing*, *24*(2), 149–164.

Czarniawska, B. (2007). *Shadowing: And Other Techniques for Doing Fieldwork in Modern Societies.* Copenhagen: Copenhagen Business School Press.

Deakin, H., & Wakefield, K. (2014). Skype interviewing: Reflections of two PhD researchers. *Qualitative Research, 14*(5), 603–616.

Do, J., & Yamagata-Lynch, L. C. (2017). Designing and developing cell phone applications for qualitative research. *Qualitative Inquiry, 23*(10), 757–767.

Drummond, C., McGrath, H., & O'Toole, T. (2018). The impact of social media on resource mobilisation in entrepreneurial firms. *Industrial Marketing Management, 70*, 68–89.

Ernkvist, M. (2015). The double knot of technology and business-model innovation in the era of ferment of digital exchanges: The case of OM, a pioneer in electronic options exchanges. *Technological Forecasting and Social Change, 99*, 285–299.

Evans, S. K., Pearce, K. E., Vitak, J., & Treem, J. W. (2017). Explicating affordances: A conceptual framework for understanding affordances in communication research. *Journal of Computer-Mediated Communication, 22*(1), 35–52.

Ferguson, R.-H. (2017). Offline 'stranger' and online lurker: Methods for an ethnography of illicit transactions on the darknet. *Qualitative Research, 17*(6), 683–698.

Fischer, E., & Reuber, A. R. (2011). Social interaction via new social media: (How) can interactions on Twitter affect effectual thinking and behavior? *Journal of Business Venturing, 26*(1), 1–18.

Garcia, A. C., & Jacobs, J. B. (1999). The eyes of the beholder: Understanding the turn-taking system in quasi-synchronous computer-mediated communication. *Research on Language and Social Interaction, 32*(4), 337–367.

García, B., Welford, J., & Smith, B. (2016). Using a smartphone app in qualitative research: The good, the bad and the ugly. *Qualitative Research, 16*(5), 508–525.

Gartner, W. B. (1988). Who is an entrepreneur? Is the wrong question. *American Journal of Small Business, 12*(4), 11–32.

Gartner, W. B. (2013). Creating a community of difference in entrepreneurship scholarship. *Entrepreneurship & Regional Development, 25*(1–2), 5–15.

Gartner, W. B., Stam, E., Thompson, N., & Verduijn, K. (2016). Entrepreneurship as practice: Grounding contemporary practice theory into entrepreneurship studies. *Entrepreneurship & Regional Development, 28*(9–10), 813–816.

Gherardi, S. (2012). *How to Conduct a Practice-Based Study: Problems and Methods.* Cheltenham, UK and Northampton, MA, USA: Edward Elgar Publishing.

Gibson, J. J. (1979). The theory of affordances. In J. J. Gibson (Ed.), *The Ecological Approach to Visual Perception* (pp. 127–137). Boston: Houghton Mifflin.

Gibson, J. J. (1986). *The Ecological Approach to Visual Perception.* Mahwah, NJ: Lawrence Erlbaum Associates.

Gulbrandsen, I. T., Plesner, U., & Raviola, E. (2020). New media and strategy research: Towards a relational agency approach. *International Journal of Management Reviews, 22*(1), 33–52.

Gustafsson, V., & Khan, M. S. (2017). Monetising blogs: Enterprising behaviour, co-creation of opportunities and social media entrepreneurship. *Journal of Business Venturing Insights, 7*, 26–31.

Hill, I. (2018). How did you get up and running? Taking a Bourdieuan perspective towards a framework for negotiating strategic fit. *Entrepreneurship & Regional Development, 30*(5–6), 662–696.

Hine, C. (2000). *Virtual Ethnography.* London: Sage.

Hookway, N. (2008). 'Entering the blogosphere': Some strategies for using blogs in social research. *Qualitative Research, 8*(1), 91–113.

Jarzabkowski, P., Burke, G., & Spee, P. (2015). Constructing spaces for strategic work: A multimodal perspective. *British Journal of Management, 26*, 26–47.

Jarzabkowski, P., & Kaplan, S. (2015). Strategy tools-in-use: A framework for understanding 'technologies of rationality' in practice. *Strategic Management Journal, 36*(4), 537–558.

Jones, A., & Woolley, J. (2015). The email-diary: A promising research tool for the 21st century? *Qualitative Research, 15*(6), 705–721.

Keating, A., Geiger, S., & McLoughlin, D. (2014). Riding the practice waves: Social resourcing practices during new venture development. *Entrepreneurship Theory and Practice, 38*(5), 1207–1235.

Kouamé, S., & Langley, A. (2017). Relating microprocesses to macro-outcomes in qualitative strategy process and practice research. *Strategic Management Journal, 39*(3), 559–581.

Kozinets, R. V. (2020). *Netnography: The Essential Guide to Qualitative Social Media Research* (3rd edition). London: Sage.

Kraus, S., Palmer, C., Kailer, N., Kallinger, F. L., & Spitzer, J. (2019). Digital entrepreneurship: A research agenda on new business models for the twenty-first century. *International Journal of Entrepreneurial Behavior & Research*, *25*(2), 353–375.

Lackéus, M. (2020). Collecting digital research data through social media platforms: Can 'scientific social media' disrupt entrepreneurship research methods? In W. B. Gartner & B. T. Teague (Eds.), *Research Handbook on Entrepreneurial Behavior, Practice and Process* (pp. 199–241). Cheltenham, UK and Northampton, MA, USA: Edward Elgar Publishing.

LeBaron, C., Jarzabkowski, P., Pratt, M. G., & Fetzer, G. (2018). An introduction to video methods in organizational research. *Organizational Research Methods*, *21*(2), 239–260.

Leonardi, P. M., & Vaast, E. (2017). Social media and their affordances for organizing: A review and agenda for research. *Academy of Management Annals*, *11*(1), 150–188.

Lynch, M., & Mah, C. (2018). Using internet data sources to achieve qualitative interviewing purposes: A research note. *Qualitative Research*, *18*(6), 741–752.

Mahmood, A., Luffarelli, J., & Mukesh, M. (2019). What's in a logo? The impact of complex visual cues in equity crowdfunding. *Journal of Business Venturing*, *34*(1), 41–62.

Matthews, R. S., Chalmers, D. M., & Fraser, S. S. (2018). The intersection of entrepreneurship and selling: An interdisciplinary review, framework, and future research agenda. *Journal of Business Venturing*, *33*(6), 691–719.

Meredith, J. (2017). Analysing technological affordances of online interactions using conversation analysis. *Journal of Pragmatics*, *115*, 42–55.

Meredith, J. (2019). Conversation analysis and online interaction. *Research on Language and Social Interaction*, *52*(3), 241–256.

Meyer, R. E., Jancsary, D., Höllerer, M. A., & Boxenbaum, E. (2018). The role of verbal and visual text in the process of institutionalization. *Academy of Management Review*, *43*(3), 392–418.

Miles, M. B., & Huberman, A. M. (1994). *Qualitative Data Analysis* (2nd edition). London: Sage.

Mollick, E. (2014). The dynamics of crowdfunding: An exploratory study. *Journal of Business Venturing*, *29*(1), 1–16.

Murthy, D. (2008). Digital ethnography. *Sociology*, *42*(5), 837–855.

Nambisan, S. (2017). Digital entrepreneurship: Toward a digital technology perspective of entrepreneurship. *Entrepreneurship Theory and Practice*, *41*(6), 1029–1055.

Nicolini, D. (2009). Zooming in and out: Studying practices by switching theoretical lenses and trailing connections. *Organization Studies*, *30*(12), 1391–1418.

Nicolini, D. (2012). *Practice Theory, Work, and Organization: An Introduction*. Oxford: Oxford University Press.

Nicolini, D. (2017). Is small the only beautiful? Making sense of 'large phenomena' from a practice-based perspective. In A. Hui, T. R. Schatzki, & E. Shove (Eds.), *The Nexus of Practices: Connections, Constellations, Practitioners* (pp. 98–113). London: Routledge.

Nzembayie, K. F., Buckley, A. P., & Cooney, T. (2019). Researching pure digital entrepreneurship: A multimethod insider action research approach. *Journal of Business Venturing Insights*, *11*. https://doi.org/10.1016/j.jbvi.2018.e00103.

Olanrewaju, A.-S. T., Hossain, M. A., Whiteside, N., & Mercieca, P. (2020). Social media and entrepreneurship research: A literature review. *International Journal of Information Management*, *50*, 90–110.

Orlikowski, W. J. (2007). Sociomaterial practices: Exploring technology at work. *Organization Studies*, *28*(9), 1435–1448.

Orlikowski, W. J., & Scott, S. V. (2015). Exploring material-discursive practices. *Journal of Management Studies*, *52*(5), 697–705.

Paulus, T., Lester, J., & Dempster, P. (2014). *Digital Tools for Qualitative Research*. London: Sage.

Pink, S., Horst, H., Postill, J., Hjorth, L., Lewis, T., & Tacchi, J. (2016). *Digital Ethnography: Principles and Practice*. London: Sage.

Rogers, R. (2013). *Digital Methods*. Cambridge, MA: MIT Press.

Rogers, R. (2019). *Doing Digital Methods*. London: Sage.

Salmons, J. (2016). *Doing Qualitative Research Online*. London: Sage.

Schatzki, T. R. (1996). *Social Practices*. Cambridge: Cambridge University Press.

Schatzki, T. R. (2005). Peripheral vision: The sites of organizations. *Organization Studies*, *26*(3), 465–484.

Schatzki, T. R. (2012). A primer on practices. In J. Higgs, R. Barnett, S. Billett, M. Hutchings, & F. Trede (Eds.), *Practice-Based Education: Perspectives and Strategies* (pp. 13–26). Boston: Sense Publishers.

Scott, S. V., & Orlikowski, W. J. (2014). Entanglements in practice: Performing anonymity through social media. *MIS Quarterly*, *38*(3), 873–894.

Seidl, D., & Whittington, R. (2014). Enlarging the strategy-as-practice research agenda: Towards taller and flatter ontologies. *Organization Studies*, *35*(10), 1407–1421.

Srinivasan, A., & Venkatraman, N. (2018). Entrepreneurship in digital platforms: A network-centric view. *Strategic Entrepreneurship Journal*, *12*(1), 54–71.

Steigenberger, N., & Wilhelm, H. (2018). Extending signaling theory to rhetorical signals: Evidence from crowdfunding. *Organization Science*, *29*(3). https://doi.org/10.1287/orsc.2017.1195.

Steyaert, C. (2007). 'Entrepreneuring' as a conceptual attractor? A review of process theories in 20 years of entrepreneurship studies. *Entrepreneurship & Regional Development*, *19*(6), 453–477.

Terjesen, S., & Elam, A. (2009). Transnational entrepreneurs' venture internationalization strategies: A practice theory approach. *Entrepreneurship Theory and Practice*, *33*(5), 1093–1120.

Thompson, N. A., & Byrne, O. (2020). Advancing entrepreneurship as practice: Previous developments and future possibilities. In W. B. Gartner & B. T. Teague (Eds.), *Research Handbook on Entrepreneurial Behavior, Practice and Process* (pp. 30–55). Cheltenham, UK and Northampton, MA, USA: Edward Elgar Publishing.

Thompson, N. A., Verduijn, K., & Gartner, W. B. (2020). Entrepreneurship-as-practice: Grounding contemporary theories of practice into entrepreneurship studies. *Entrepreneurship & Regional Development*, *32*(3–4), 247–256.

Uy, M. A., Foo, M.-D., & Aguinis, H. (2010). Using experience sampling methodology to advance entrepreneurship theory and research. *Organizational Research Methods*, *13*(1), 31–54.

von Briel, F., Recker, J., & Davidsson, P. (2018). Not all digital venture ideas are created equal: Implications for venture creation processes. *Journal of Strategic Information Systems*, *27*(4), 278–295.

Welter, F., Baker, T., Audretsch, D. B., & Gartner, W. B. (2016). Everyday entrepreneurship: A call for entrepreneurship research to embrace entrepreneurial diversity. *Entrepreneurship Theory and Practice*, *41*(3), 311–321.

12. The challenges and methods of understanding, contextualizing and uncovering silent entrepreneurship practices

Nicole Gross

INTRODUCTION

> During the first few weeks of my 40-week immersion into a small high-tech firm, I often sat in compete silence. At first, I was highly uncomfortable with this silence, probably because I feared that it would impair my immersion processes or limit the data collection opportunities available to me. However, after a while I tried to understand the silence around me, explore its meaning and value for my data collection, and find ways to unsilence the practices around me. (Retrospective vignette of the author)

Studying what people do is difficult, especially when their work is done in complete silence. Finding, uncovering and capturing the technological as well as non-technological objects, artefacts and practices hidden in and behind silence is quite challenging (Lammi, 2018). However, there is more to silence than people working digitally or away from the researcher's view. The behavioural cues provided by silence are often highly ambiguous and researchers are prone to misattributing the motives that lie behind silence (Van Dyne et al., 2003). What is the role of silence? How does silence play out in the field? and How can researchers study 'things' and their use – to speak with Schatzki (2002, 2012) – if individual entrepreneurs or entrepreneurial teams sit fixed in position and quietly for hours on end?

In practice theory, researchers have tried to understand silence from a materialism and embodiment perspective. De Vaujany and Aroles (2019) for instance have discussed silence as a prominent feature of an ever-increasing range of work activities in open as well as collective spaces. Whilst silence is a part of modern workflows, it remains an understudied area (see Bigo, 2018; Kirrane et al., 2017). Applying his ideas to the context of institutional analysis, De Vaujany et al. (2019) suggest that the analysis of materiality has been elevated to a different level since the introduction and growth of digital technologies. Researchers are increasingly required to research practices, beliefs and dynamics to include the 'inert and invisible' (Friedland, 2012, p. 590). Researchers should start off by questioning what materiality actually is, including all its implications, and adopt a reflexive posture to researching it (Carlile et al., 2013). To penetrate into the deeper layers of materiality, entrepreneurship scholars need to understand ontological approaches to materiality, methods and epistemological stances. To that end, an open approach to researching materiality is appropriate as long as it supports the emergence of useful and insightful knowledge. De Vaujany et al. (2019) suggest looking at materiality by investigating (1) objects and artefacts, (2) digitality and information and (3) body and embodiment as they emerge over space and time. With regard to digitality, Yakhlef (2009) suggests that the invisible can be overcome by looking at the entanglement of the virtual and concrete, e.g. the situations, actions, ideas and artefacts that the virtual creates

(Jones, 2013). Despite having developed a preliminary understanding of the materiality associated with silence, field-researchers often overlook the importance of silence, fail to understand its role and meaning, and struggle with the unsilencing of practices.

This chapter reveals how the silence in entrepreneurial firms – whether it be created purposefully or as a result of modern, digital workflows – results in a new perspective on practice research. Moreover, the chapter puts forward strategies to uncover, in part at least, such silent practices. Based on the author's experience with practice research and auto-ethnographic data (Anderson, 2006), vignettes have been constructed to demonstrate important insights. Vignettes are particularly helpful to showcase specificity, context and minutiae, whether it be via the portrayal of characters, moods, objects, settings or descriptions of reality (Barter & Renold, 1999). Lastly, the chapter provides practical research suggestions poised to push the boundaries of the Entrepreneurship as Practice (EaP) field further.

THE ROLE AND VALUE OF SILENCE

The Oxford Dictionary defines silence as follows: 'a complete lack of noise or sound', 'a situation when nobody is speaking', 'a situation in which somebody refuses to talk about something or to answer questions' and 'a situation in which people do not communicate with each other by letter or phone' (Oxford Dictionary, n.d.). Silence is a key feature, not only in our conversations but also in our everyday life. In speech and communication theory, in psychotherapy but also in organizational research, researchers have explored silence as a purposeful tool rather than an obstacle. Silence, or leaving out the spoken word, can be quite powerful (Jaworski, 1993). For instance, it can used by people to shake up an existing order (Schlant, 1999), ostracize people (Williams, 2001), communicate hesitations (Mazzei, 2004), and even to purposefully conceal ideas or thoughts (Eagleton, 1983). Morrison and Milliken (2003, p. 1353) state that in organizations, 'people often have to make decisions about whether to speak up or remain silent – whether to share or withhold their ideas, opinions, and concerns. In many cases, they choose the safe response of silence, withholding input that could be valuable to others or thoughts that they wish they could express.'

From a political perspective, silence can even be used to influence mass communication (Noelle-Neumann, 1974). As it formulates dominant ideas as well as people's perception about those dominant ideas, it has the power to exclude particular groups or eradicate alternative ideas. With that, it can form a so-called 'spiral of silence' (Noelle-Neumann, 1974). In their research on silence in organizations, Bowen and Blackmon (2003) have shown that the decision of employees to openly and honestly speak up (or stay silent) is heavily influenced by the employee's perception of what their co-workers might think. If they fear ostracism or isolation, they will refrain from communicating their minority viewpoint. With that, silence becomes a collective as well as self-reinforcing mechanism (Morrison & Milliken, 2003).

From a pragmatic perspective though, according to Brooks (2007) at least, there is no such thing as empty time or empty space – there is always something to hear, observe or do. Brooks (2007) takes many of his examples from the study of music, poetry and prayer. He posits that silence is much more than an absence; it is a something, a presence that can be felt. Thus, it is a matter of note (Brooks, 2007). The first step that entrepreneurship researchers can do is to acknowledge the presence of silence and observe it. Is silence perhaps persistent or is it recurrent? Does silence emerge at different times of the day, or distinct stages of an organizational life and journey? Is it cyclical? Is it natural, e.g. due to separation of workers or type of work carried out; or is it constructed, e.g. due to individual choices not to speak? May silence be just a part of a company's organizational culture – the way things are done around here? What context, natural or artificial spaces does it invade? And how does silence impact the experience of the employees and the researcher? If silence invokes something, researchers have to listen.

Once researchers have acknowledged the presence of silence and reflected on its meaning as well as impact on the research, a next step can be to discover the materials, objects and practices which are hidden in and through the silence.

SOCIOMATERIALITY, TECHNOLOGY AND SILENCE

Practice research is inherently vague (Lammi, 2018). Alongside other discourses and streams (e.g. Gherardi, 2012; Nicolini, 2012; Schatzki et al., 2001; Shove et al., 2012), EaP has embraced the vagueness of work as it is 'done out there' in recent years (Thompson & Byrne, 2020). To that end, EaP seeks to (1) identify the everyday, contextually and socially situated nature of entrepreneurship; (2) recognize entrepreneurship practice, tools and methods that are used; and (3) relate and integrate these findings with the cognitions, behaviours, and/or skills of entrepreneurship practitioners (Gartner et al., 2016). Prominent EaP studies include, but are not limited to, the research of entrepreneurial bricolage enactment (Watson, 2013), new venture creation (De Clercq & Voronov, 2009), entrepreneurial marketing (Gross et al., 2014) and entrepreneurial networking (Keating et al., 2014). Other EaP studies have created new understandings of what makes an entrepreneurial firm entrepreneurial (Gross & Geiger, 2017) and lend perspectives on gendered entrepreneurship (Garcia & Welter, 2013). They also give insight into the entrepreneur's understanding of context (Chalmers & Shaw, 2017; Johannisson, 2011).

In examining practices, researchers tend to observe materials (e.g. tools, objects and things, bodies or infrastructures), capabilities (e.g. knowledge or understandings) and meanings (e.g. emotions, motivations or mental activities) in an ongoing, recursive and reflexive manner (Reckwitz, 2002; Shove et al., 2012). However, the nature of materiality in organizational research has been changing as organizations are now intertwined with 'multiple, emergent, shifting and interdependent technologies' (Orlikowski, 2007, p. 1435). Digital transformations, including the processes of 'datafication', have become part and parcel of many commercial (and entrepreneurial) processes and practices (Helles & Flyverbom, 2019; Flyverbom & Murray, 2018). Leonardi (2011) agrees, stating that only a few people are able to complete their work without the use of advanced information technologies.

There is a lot of materiality present in our immediate, observable environment, e.g. computers, laptops, speakers, mobile phones, chargers, scanners or printers. Less visible and observable are many other important flows that help researchers to develop an understanding of entrepreneurship practices as they exist 'out there', e.g. data, information or knowledge (Orlikowski, 2007; Orlikowski & Scott, 2008). These flows, processes and practices are, however, often cloaked in silence. Whether researchers adopt a techno-centric perspective (i.e. how technology influences human action) or human-centric perspective (i.e. how humans make sense of and interact with the technology) is perhaps less important in this respect. Important here is the constitutive and everyday material entanglement of humans with technology, and the silence that this entanglement brings along. Leonardi (2011) calls the interlock between humans and the technology 'imbrication'. Imbrication means 'to arrange distinct elements in overlapping patterns so that they function interdependently' (Leonardi, 2011, p. 150). Such intertwinements create new socio-technical arrangements, change the patterns of social interaction, establish new routines and activities, and redefine trajectories. With people and tools (including technologies) hanging so closely together (Orr, 2006), researchers ought to develop an understanding of sociomaterial practice-arrangement bundles and bundling (Lammi, 2018) as well as consider the contextual and institutional conditions that create and frame them (Leonardi, 2013).

Demonstrating the complexities of sociomaterial entanglements with the example of an 'information search online' further is Orlikowski (2007). To do this, people often go onto search engines such as Google and look for information. Whilst this may sound simple, it is in fact highly problematic for two reasons. First, whilst the 'searcher' has a locus of control and seems to delegate the search to Google, it is the search engine's set-up, algorithms, search engine optimization mechanisms and ranking features that ultimately controls what the searcher sees. In addition, due to personalization, every Google user may see different results (Orlikowski, 2007). Second, and perhaps an oversight by Orlikowski (2007), is that organizational researchers are often excluded from accessing these sociomaterial practice arrangements and bundles. Much of modern organizational work is done online and what is more, mobile communication technology has allowed workers to work virtually anywhere (Yakhlef, 2009). From a practical perspective, this leaves researchers potentially sitting in silence and/or with very limited access to data. Yet, digitalization is here to stay (Leonardi, 2011, 2013), therefore researchers will have to consider humans' entanglement with digital environment further (De Vaujany and Aroles, 2019), find novel ways to expand their analysis and deal with the presence of silent entrepreneurship practices.

The next section will present three vignettes which point towards the author's experience with silence in the field – its role and meaning but also how she was able to study 'things' and their use whilst entrepreneurs sat in complete silence.

Acknowledging, Understanding and Contextualizing Silence

As an academic researcher who was becoming immersed into the (work) life of a Geographical Intelligence Services (GIS) technology company, the author sought to develop an understanding of important sociomaterial practice arrangements (Lammi, 2018) but also the context, institutional settings and conditions which have created and framed them (Leonardi, 2013). The case company was an established, small Irish technology company which had recently adopted a software-as-service business model. Most of their clients were based in the UK and much of the communication was done online. Imbrication was evident (Leonardi, 2011) as digital technologies made up a significant, yet less observable part of the staff's everyday work, i.e. methods, tools and procedures, but also their 'entrepreneurship praxis' to speak with Whittington (2006). Praxis, in this respect, refers to the entrepreneurial strategy that was taken. Furthermore, the company had a particular and perhaps peculiar organizational culture where people preferred to communicate electronically than speak face-to-face. All of these elements had to be explored and understood by the author during her 40 weeks of immersion. With the concrete and virtual being very much entangled (Jones, 2013; Yakhlef, 2009) within the context and setting of this case firm, silence was a key feature during the first few weeks of the author's fieldwork. The following vignette demonstrates this point.

Vignette 1 – why is nobody helping me?

It is the first week into my fieldwork – I am assuming the work of a marketing executive. It is early April and I am stuck in an old, freezing Victorian building in Dublin. I have met the Chief Operations Officer so far who I quizzed about my position as a participant observer. I ask him what I should tell the other staff, e.g. the progammers, accountant and secretary, if they ask me who I am and what I do. He told me to tell them the truth. However, a few days in and no one has even asked me yet!

I get my desk in the management office. I am sitting with the Chief Executive Officer, the Commercial Director and the accountant. Our room is connected to the left with another room, some of the programmers sit there. All of the programmers, apart from two, are men. They seem very busy, typical IT-geeky, hacking away on their computers – people do not seem to talk much in the office. All you hear from in the office is 'click click click'. Computer screens are flashing brightly and the printer is whirring. To the right is a corridor that leads into another part of the building. According to the Chief Operations Officer 'all sorts of exciting things are happening in there, you won't be doing them'. He does not tell me any more but he introduces me to the Product Marketing Director. Later on at a meeting, the Product Marketing Director gives me an overview of the firm's four strategic business units and explains to me what the company does. He also gives me a brief overview of the company's history and some of the challenges he sees. Then he tells me he has a 'to do' list for me, which he later emails to me. I sit at my desk without really having a clue what is expected of me and how I am supposed to obtain the required information.

Over the coming days, I have to keep going back to the Product Marketing Director asking for more information, e.g. what to research, how to contact our printing suppliers, what has to be organized for a particular event, and how to raise a purchase order! I feel terrible having to ask him all the time. He is located a floor above me in the office, so I tend to walk up and ask. However, it is busy and at times, he seems annoyed with me. Also, due to his client-facing job, he is sometimes not there, so I end up emailing him. I feel lonely and this feeling of cluelessness is really uncomfortable for me.

It is difficult for any researcher, if not impossible, to discover practices without some kind of fieldwork or ethnographic immersion. However, and as can be seen through the first vignette, it takes time to understand people's behaviours and experiences (Arnould & Wallendorf, 1994), to move from 'they' (the researcher as outsider) to 'we' (the researcher as insider) (Schouten & McAlexander, 1995) and to see the world 'through the eyes' of the case firm (Fellman, 1999). Despite plentiful efforts of watching, listening and asking questions, many elements remained hidden to the author. Some practices stayed only hidden during in the first few weeks, whilst others remained out of her sight altogether. It took time to get to grips with the company's organizational culture, a culture where people worked hard, had high expertise and knew each other very well. The members worked proactively and creatively, researching and sensing the market, sharing information quickly and widely (though often electronically), and seeking to adapt their technology to explore emergent market opportunities. However, a persistent silence in the office was also a key feature which was observed. It took time for the researcher to understand convention (and resistances which existed) and 'listen' to the nuances inherent in those silence (Mazzei, 2004).

Beyond their high-tech set-up and particular organizational culture, the silence had other reasons too, as the author discovered later. As Morrison and Milliken (2000, 2003) previously put it, organizational forces can create climates of silence. In and around the time of the author's immersion, the firm had gone through a state of major organizational upheaval. Google maps had changed how their business model works. Their old proposition of printing maps had become more or less redundant. Not only did they have to rethink their value proposition altogether as well as finding new markets and customers, but they also had to redefine their revenue model in its entirety. In one of their new markets, the insurance market, they had only a handful of clients. Securing more clients was a lengthy and complicated process, especially since they were up against strong, international competitors who could afford to compete on price. In yet another newly defined market, transport, they had to collaborate with other market players in order to access government tenders. Furthermore, technology issues such as compatibility and integration were also causing upheaval. The top secret project was a radical new technology that was still being tested for functionality. No market had been defined for this technology yet.

The management did not always agree on strategic issues and at times, silence was a conscious choice. The Product Marketing Director, who was only six months in the company, had major concerns about the company's approach to opportunity seeking and value creation. However, and as he told the author in confidence, these concerns frequently got silenced by the other members of management, especially those who had been working much longer in the firm. Eventually, he stopped speaking up and after less than four weeks into the author's fieldwork, he decided to leave the company. Van Dyne et al. (2003) have called this silence 'disengaged behaviour based on resignation'. Without acknowledging, understanding and contextualizing the silence present in the firms – working through it and with it – the author would have missed important practices within the case firm.

Deconstructing Silence and Shaking Up the Status Quo

Firms are in effect 'small-scale societies'. It is therefore important for researchers 'to look beyond what people say to understand in the shared system of meanings' (Goulding, 2005, p. 298). Despite the author's journey of ethnographic immersion – learning the local vernacular, getting reflexively accustomed to the organizational culture and practices, and looking beyond appearances and reflections – becoming a real 'insider' was difficult as many important flows, especially the technology-mediated ones, were shielded from her and thus kept silent. The only way to locate the author more directly in the space of the phenomenon under research (Gille & O'Riain, 2002; Glaser & Strauss, 1967) was to address the issue of silence directly and ask for further participative insight. Vignette 2 demonstrates these issues.

Vignette 2 – vanishing in the 'reply to all'!

Six weeks into my fieldwork, I am still working on my own and mostly in silence. I sit at my desk and do not really know what other people actually do all day long. Most of the management meetings are held without me even knowing they were on. I am frustrated and disappointed. I speak to my academic supervisor about it and she tells me not to worry, immersion, deep and inclusion takes time. To address this issue, I make it a point to ask the management team every time I find out that a meeting had been on, what it was about and who had been there. Sometimes they tell me snippets, sometimes they tell me it was not relevant to my work and other times they are too busy to explain. On different occasions, I say it directly, e.g. to the accountant who was sitting at the desk beside me, that a management meeting had been on 'yet again' and I had not been invited. I also state that I was not getting enough insight. Around eight weeks into my fieldwork, I get included into my first insurance meeting though. The Chief Operations Officer came down and told me: 'We have an insurance meeting on later, it would be useful for you to come along'. After that, I am starting to get involved more and more, though undoubtedly still missing plenty of meetings and content.

Over the course of the fieldwork, I became included in two sales pipeline meetings, four board meetings and 27 formal team meetings. I also had six debriefing sessions with the management team. Around the eight week mark, I also became included into emails which were shared between the management team. For instance, the Commercial Director attached me to an email which discussed the two phases of the lead generation campaign in the insurance market. From then on, I often (though not always) got cc'd to the emails that flowed between the management team. As I became part of the 'reply to all' list, my presence as a researcher became somewhat forgotten. Over the course of time, I collected 767 emails altogether and 163 documents, most of which were sent electronically to me.

Deconstructing what is happening, acknowledging silence and drawing out the effects that silence has on a researcher's data collection is imperative. Researchers who are struggling to unearth practices and get included into the shared system of meanings have difficult choices to make. They can accept silence and find creative ways of working with and within silence. For instance, can the company's website or social media presence and content be analysed? Can publicly available documents be accessed, e.g. press releases, business plans, investor information or even profit and loss accounts (for some company types)? Can researchers look through the internet and engage in social listening – what do customers say in blogs or forums about the company as well as its value proposition?

Alternatively, the researcher can choose to break the silence and ask for increased (online and offline) access. Questioning and shaking up the status quo, as the author did, means drawing attention to the issue of silence, however. Whilst this can initiate change and therefore enable better access, this strategy is not without drawbacks. Drawing attention creates an impasse that the researcher is responsible for and which she must reflexively acknowledge. In his text *Reflexive Ethnography*, Davies (2002) highlights the precarious balance participant observers have to strike: living amongst the people studied and analysing their social structures and practices as they are (without disturbance) versus creating legitimacy as well as authority in order to become 'one of them'. Ethnographic practice in itself is vulnerable; therefore reflexivity is central to researchers' practice of research and subsequent analysis (Davies, 2002).

'Unsilencing' Practices

By nature, practices are embedded, fragmented and continuously evolving (Reckwitz, 2002; Schatzki et al., 2001). The immersed researcher therefore has to acknowledge that many practices can and will simply never be unsilenced. For instance, the strategy-making praxis of the entrepreneur or team might be cloaked in secrecy. Practitioners may work remotely and deploy methods, tools and procedures that are out of the researcher's view. Furthermore, some actions, e.g. online chats, networking or web research might be conducted real-time, thus are difficult to capture. Wherever and whenever it is possible, however, the 'unsilencing' of practices is a social process. This process unfolds within a specific context and over the course of time. The next vignette illustrates this.

Vignette 3 – discovering the 'stone soup'

Ten weeks into the fieldwork, the CEO sends me an email 'I think we tried (but didn't fully get there) to do a press release around the insurance launch in London. Has anyone got a copy of what was drafted here? Can you finish it and then add this to our web site? Please let me know.' I am delighted because I am becoming involved in the co-writing and publishing of press releases online. I also became involved in virtual brainstorming sessions, for instance, the CTO sent a document around called 'our stone soup'. In this document, he constructed a case study about the company's history, offerings and opportunities. He writes: 'Back in 2006 our main asset was the trust and intimacy it enjoyed with two major clients, who accounted for >80% of its revenue. A major challenge was to increase its number of clients beyond two and initiate revenue growth. Aside from two strong reference clients, we lacked any clear USP on which to develop business. New contacts struggled to see why they should engage with us over other local firms that appeared to provide equivalent skills and services. ... In early in 2007 MT recognized that it faced a strategic cross-road. ... Taking its lead from the "stone soup" proverb, we devised a proactive strategy. ... Our next move was to gather the villagers by building a fire in the town square.' As the team starts to email back and forth exchanging views and ideas, I can see what they believe, think and plan to do going forward. I think they are really starting to trust me.

Over time, I have various breakthroughs. For instance, I had been asked from the start to do some web research, e.g. to scout for emergent opportunities, map the competitive landscape or segment the market. I always email my findings around. Similarly, the management team and the programmers also email information and insights around that they think are worth sharing. Six months into the fieldwork, the CEO gives me his Google password and asks me to look through his collection of Google Alerts. Beyond that, I uncover further invisible elements of practice by gaining access to the company's website statistics. I become electronically connected with selected partners and suppliers, and even included into some email chains with insurance clients. Whilst silence was still a prominent feature in my daily work life, I gain more and more insight through electronic means. Other times, I have set-backs. There are days where I have nothing to do and no one is there to observe. The silence is getting to me. For instance, why would people sit right beside me and choose to send an email rather than talk to me? At times, they would also simply not respond to my emails. This frustrates me and makes me feel like they do not care.

In his work on silence and negotiation in relationships, Benjamin (2003) writes that silence can be part of a routine or a sign of an inner struggle. Unsilencing, in that respect, stands for the process of transformation: from a state of the unknown into a state of knowing, deciding and understanding. It is a social yet reflexive process in which emotions, beliefs and actions experience changes or shifts (Benjamin, 2003). As can be seen in vignette 3, unsilencing is complex and laden with ambivalence. Furthermore, it is likely that mere fragments are being unsilenced rather than complete actions or entire processes. Reflexivity in practice research (Carlile et al., 2013; Davies, 2002) is vital here once again, as the researcher's assumptions about practices need to be revealed as much as the elements of practice that are being uncovered. What is more, as Giddens (1984) points out: life is shaped by hierarchies and organizational hierarchies are no different. It takes time for researchers to gain or establish a position in the company's power hierarchy. At times the gaining of a social position is accompanied by achievements such as increased access. Other times the researcher may stay excluded, especially if the organization decides to keep the researcher (and perhaps others) in silence. Benjamin (2003) reinforces that power struggles and negotiation are imperative to the process of unsilencing, a point illustrated in vignette 2. The vignettes have also showcased some of the emotions which accompany the adjustment process (Kirrane et al., 2017). These include anger, disappointment and frustration but also the positive feelings that come with acceptance, validation, approval and capability.

DISCUSSION AND AVENUES FOR FUTURE RESEARCH

On the basis of the key ideas that emerged above, the chapter presents a model of unsilencing the silence associated with technology-induced sociomaterial assemblages. Figure 12.1 shows this model.

Technology-induced (but also non-technology-related) sociomaterial assemblages are present in most firms, including entrepreneurial ones. At the beginning of the research process,

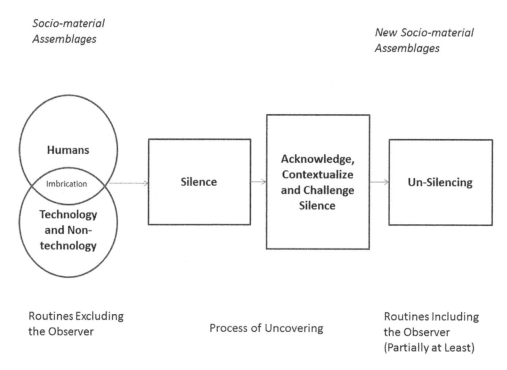

Figure 12.1   A model of unsilencing silence from sociomaterial assemblages

the researcher (as outsider), will find herself excluded from these assemblages. Through the imbrication process (Leonardi, 2011), organizational members are being routinely involved with their technology and other actions, activities and routines alone or with another, but not with the researcher, thus she might experience the presence of silence. This is illustrated on the left hand side as well as the middle section of the model. Future research could examine the concept of imbrication in entrepreneurship further as well as its impact on practices. What is more, does adopting a techno-centric perspective versus human-centric perspective, considered from an organizational view at least, change how silence unfolds in the field? What is clear though is the following: rather than considering silence as an obstacle, it should be seen as useful and fruitful data (Brooks, 2007). Silence stands for something and researchers ought to uncover what lies beyond the absence of spoken word.

The middle section of the model shows that researchers ought to acknowledge the presence of silence and understand the context in which silence takes place (Leonardi, 2011). The three vignettes have poignantly illustrated that silence reaches beyond modern workflows and the increased use of digital technologies. Thus, EaP researchers ought to explore the power and context of silence in the firm, whether it be to conceal ideas or thoughts (Eagleton, 1983), communicate hesitations (Mazzei, 2004), display corporate culture, ostracize people (Williams, 2001) or shake up an existing order (Schlant, 1999) – just to name a few. Reflection and contextualization matters in EaP research (Gartner et al., 2016) and only if silence is highlighted and challenged, can further access be considered and negotiated. The process of unsilencing can be achieved through the creation of the spoken word, e.g. talking rather than emailing, or meeting in person rather than online. However, limitations are evidence that this process may go 'against the grain' of the persons' choice or indeed their entire organizational culture.

Unsilencing can also be achieved by the researcher becoming part of silent practices through electronic means. For instance, the researcher may become cc'd to emails or gain access to statistics, platforms or shared drives. An interesting further research question here is how further personal as well as electronic access can be negotiated beyond the means which have been suggested earlier? Also, is there any difference between entrepreneurial and non-entrepreneurial firms when it comes better access to silent practices? And how does the firm's industry or approach to technology (e.g. high- versus low-tech) influence access to practices? In and through imbrication, the researcher is now, in part at least, included into technology- and non-technology-mediated silent routines. With that, new sociomaterial assemblages have been created (Orlikowski, 2007; De Vaujany et al., 2019). The right hand side of the model illustrates this point. Worth noting here is that vagueness (Lammi, 2018) will always be a key feature of practice research due to the variety and complexity of practices which exist out there. Vagueness is also present, however, as the unsilencing process is incomplete in itself. Whilst unsilencing can never be achieved entirely, an interesting research question could be how to uncover (more) coherent or adjoining bundles of practices.

Finally, this research has identified that ethnographic immersion is an important tool to discover and uncover practices. Whilst the value of ethnography for practice research has previously been discussed (e.g. Jarzabkowski et al., 2007; Rasche & Chia, 2009), a focus on silent practices is novel. The chapter has showcased that imbrication and exclusive sociomaterial assemblages require the researcher's transition from 'they' to 'we' (Schouten & McAlexander, 1995). However, beyond the need for extensive time commitments, researchers also need to be aware of the emotional investment that needs to be made to uncover silent practices (Kirrane et al., 2017). Future research could investigate the emotional side of dealing with those silent entrepreneurship practices further.

CONCLUSION

Mazzei (2004, p. 31) states so candidly: 'silence is all around us'. Beyond silence as an individual or organizational choice and strategy, modern workflows and the increasing digitalization of the workplace have created more silences around us than ever before. The absence of practices to hear or see cannot be equated with practices not being there, however. In the presence of silence, the process of observing, listening and researching has changed. This chapter has hopefully put forward theoretical as well as methodological tools and ideas to initiate such change.

REFERENCES

Anderson, L. (2006). Analytic autoethnography. *Journal of Contemporary Ethnography, 35*(4), 373–395.

Arnould, E. J., & Wallendorf, M. (1994). Market-oriented ethnography: Interpretation building and marketing strategy formulation. *Journal of Marketing Research, 31*, 484–504.

Barter, C., & Renold, E. (1999). The use of vignettes in qualitative research. *Sociology at Surrey: Social Research Update, 25*. http://sru.soc.surrey.ac.uk/SRU25.html.

Benjamin, O. (2003). The power of unsilencing: Between silence and negotiation in heterosexual relationships. *Journal for the Theory of Social Behaviour, 33*(1), 1–19.

Bigo, V. (2018). On silence, creativity and ethics in organization studies. *Organization Studies, 39*(1), 121–133.

Bowen, F., & Blackmon, K. (2003). Spirals of silence: The dynamic effects of diversity on organizational voice. *Journal of Management Studies, 40*(6), 1393–1417.

Brooks, W. (2007). Pragmatics of silence. In N. Losseff & J. Doctor (Eds.), *Silence, Music, Silent Music* (pp. 97–126). Aldershot: Ashgate.

Carlile, P. R., Nicolini, D., Langley, A., & Tsoukas, H. (Eds.) (2013). *How Matter Matters: Objects, Artifacts, and Materiality in Organization Studies.* Oxford: Oxford University Press.

Chalmers, D. M., & Shaw, E. (2017). The endogenous construction of entrepreneurial contexts: A practice-based perspective. *International Small Business Journal: Researching Entrepreneurship, 35*(1), 19–39.

Davies, C. A. (2002). *Reflexive Ethnography: A Guide to Researching Selves and Others.* London: Routledge.

De Clercq, D., & Voronov, M. (2009). Toward a practice perspective of entrepreneurship: Entrepreneurial legitimacy as habitus. *International Small Business Journal, 27*(4), 395–419.

De Vaujany, F.-X., Adrot, A., Boxenbaum, E., & Leca, B. (Eds.) (2019). *Materiality in Institutions: Spaces, Embodiment and Technology in Management and Organization.* Cham: Palgrave Macmillan.

De Vaujany, F.-X., & Aroles, J. (2019). Nothing happened, something happened: Silence in a makerspace. *Management Learning, 50*(2), 208–225.

Eagleton, T. (1983). *Literary Theory: An Introduction.* Minneapolis: University of Minnesota Press.

Fellman, M. W. (1999). Breaking tradition. *Marketing Research, 11*(3), 20–25.

Flyverbom, M., & Murray, J. (2018). Datastructuring: Organizing and curating digital traces into action. *Big Data & Society.* https://journals.sagepub.com/doi/full/10.1177/2053951718799114.

Friedland, R. (2012). The institutional logics perspective: A new approach to culture, structure, and process. *M@n@gement, 15*(5), 583–595.

Garcia, M. C. D., & Welter, F. (2013). Gender identities and practices: Interpreting women entrepreneurs' narratives. *International Small Business Journal, 31*(4), 384–404.

Gartner, W. B., Stam, E., Thompson, N., & Verduijn, K. (2016). Entrepreneurship as practice: Grounding contemporary practice theory into entrepreneurship studies. *Entrepreneurship & Regional Development, 28*(9–10), 813–816.

Gherardi, S. (2012). Docta ignorantia: Professional knowing at the core and at the margins of a practice. *Journal of Education and Work, 25*(1), 5–38.

Giddens, A. (1984). *The Constitution of Society: Outline of the Theory of Structuration.* Berkeley and Los Angeles: University of California Press.

Gille, Z., & O'Riain, S. (2002). Global ethnography. *Annual Review of Sociology, 28*, 271–295.

Glaser, B. G., & Strauss, A. L. (1967). *The Discovery of Grounded Theory: Strategies for Qualitative Research.* Chicago: Aldine.

Goulding, C. (2005). Grounded theory, ethnography and phenomenology. *European Journal of Marketing, 39*(3–4), 294–308.

Gross, N., Carson, D., & Jones, R. (2014). Beyond rhetoric: Re-thinking entrepreneurial marketing from a practice perspective. *Journal of Research in Marketing and Entrepreneurship, 16*(2), 105–127.

Gross, N., & Geiger, S. (2017). Liminality and the entrepreneurial firm: Practice renewal during periods of radical change. *International Journal of Entrepreneurial Behavior & Research, 23*(2), 185–209.

Helles, R., & Flyverbom, M. (2019). Meshes of surveillance, prediction, and infrastructure: On the cultural and commercial consequences of digital platforms. *Surveillance and Society, 17*(1–2), 34–39.

Jarzabkowski, P., Balogun, J., & Seidl, D. (2007). Strategizing: The challenges of a practice perspective. *Human Relations, 60*(1), 5–27.

Jaworski, A. (1993). *The Power of Silence: Social and Pragmatic Perspectives.* Newbury Park, CA: Sage Publications.

Johannisson, B. (2011). Towards a practice theory of entrepreneuring. *Small Business Economics, 36*(2), 135–150.

Jones, M. (2013). Untangling sociomateriality. In P. R. Carlile, D. Nicolini, A. Langley, & H. Tsoukas (Eds.), *How Matter Matters: Objects, Artifacts and Materiality in Organization Studies* (pp. 197–226). Oxford: Oxford University Press.

Keating, A., Geiger, S., & McLoughlin, D. (2014). Riding the practice waves: Social resourcing practices during new venture development. *Entrepreneurship Theory and Practice, 38*, 1–29.

Kirrane, M., O'Shea, D., Buckley, F., Grazi, A., & Prout, J. (2017). Investigating the role of discrete emotions in silence versus speaking up. *Journal of Occupational and Organizational Psychology, 90*(3), 354–378.

Lammi, I. J. (2018). A practice theory in practice: Analytical consequences in the study of organization and socio-technical change. Doctoral thesis, Företagsekonomiska Institutionen, Uppsala University. http://www.diva-portal.org/smash/record.jsf?pid=diva2%3A1192971&dswid=1585001572210.

Leonardi, P. M. (2011). When flexible routines meet flexible technologies: Affordance, constraint, and the imbrication of human and material agencies. *MIS Quarterly, 35*(1), 147–167.

Leonardi, P. M. (2013). The emergence of materiality within formal organizations. In P. R. Carlile, D. Nicolini, A. Langley, & H. Tsoukas (Eds.), *How Matter Matters: Objects, Artifacts and Materiality in Organization Studies* (pp. 142–170). Oxford: Oxford University Press.

Mazzei, L. A. (2004). Silent listenings: Deconstructive practices in discourse-based research. *Educational Researcher, 33*(2), 26–34.

Morrison, E. W., & Milliken, F. J. (2000). Organizational silence: A barrier to change and development in a pluralistic world. *Academy of Management Review, 25*(4), 706–731.

Morrison, E. W., & Milliken, F. J. (2003). Guest editors' introduction. Speaking up, remaining silent: The dynamics of voice and silence in organizations. *Journal of Management Studies, 40*(6), 1353–1358.

Nicolini, D. (2012). *Practice Theory, Work, and Organization: An Introduction*. Oxford: Oxford University Press.

Noelle-Neumann, E. (1974). The spiral of silence: A theory of public opinion. *Journal of Communication, 24*(2), 43–51.

Orlikowski, W. J. (2007). Sociomaterial practices: Exploring technology at work. *Organization Studies, 28*(9), 1435–1448.

Orlikowski, W. J., & Scott, S. V. (2008). Sociomateriality: Challenging the separation of technology, work and organization. *Academy of Management Annals, 2*(1), 433–474.

Orr, J. E. (2006). Ten years of talking about machines. *Organization Studies, 27*(12), 1805–1820.

Oxford Dictionary (n.d.). Silence. https://www.oxfordlearnersdictionaries.com/definition/english/silence_1?q=silence.

Rasche, A., & Chia, R. (2009). Researching strategy practices: A genealogical social theory perspective. *Organization Studies, 30*(7), 713–734.

Reckwitz, A. (2002). Toward a theory of social practices: A development in culturalist theorizing. *European Journal of Social Theory, 5*(2), 243–263.

Schatzki, T. R. (2002). *The Site of the Social: A Philosophical Account of the Constitution of Social Life and Change*. University Park: Pennsylvania State University Press.

Schatzki, T. R. (2012). A primer on practices. In J. Higgs, R. Barnett, S. Billett, M. Hutchings, & F. Trede (Eds.), *Practice-Based Education: Perspectives and Strategies* (pp. 13–26). Boston: Sense Publishers.

Schatzki, T. R., Knorr Cetina, K., & Savigny, E. von (Eds.) (2001). *The Practice Turn in Contemporary Theory*. London: Routledge.

Schlant, E. (1999). *The Language of Silence: West German Literature and the Holocaust*. London: Routledge.

Schouten, J. W., & McAlexander, J. H. (1995). Subcultures of consumption: An ethnography of new bikers. *Journal of Consumer Research, 22*, 43–61.

Shove, E., Pantzar, M., & Watson, M. (2012). *The Dynamics of Social Practice: Everyday Life and How it Changes*. London: Sage.

Thompson, N. A., & Byrne, O. (2020). Advancing entrepreneurship as practice: Previous developments and future possibilities. In W. B. Gartner & B. T. Teague (Eds.), *Research Handbook on Entrepreneurial Behavior, Practice and Process* (pp. 30–55). Cheltenham, UK and Northampton, MA, USA: Edward Elgar Publishing.

Van Dyne, L., Ang, S., & Botero, I. C. (2003). Conceptualizing employee silence and employee voice as multidimensional constructs. *Journal of Management Studies, 40*(6), 1359–1392.

Watson, T. J. (2013). Entrepreneurship in action: Bringing together the individual, organizational and institutional dimensions of entrepreneurial action. *Entrepreneurship & Regional Development*, *25*(5–6), 1–19.

Whittington, R. (2006). Completing the practice turn in strategy research. *Organization Studies*, *27*(5), 613–634.

Williams, K. D. (2001). *Ostracism: The Power of Silence*. London and New York: Guilford Press.

Yakhlef, A. (2009). We have always been virtual: Writing, institutions, and technology! *Space and Culture*, *12*(1), 76–94.

13. Entrepreneurship, practice theory and space: methodological principles and processes for spatial inquiry

Thomas Davis

INTRODUCTION

Approaches to studying entrepreneurial activity are traditionally classed in two difficult to reconcile methodological camps: one investigating characteristics of the entrepreneurial individual ('agent'); the other exploring environmental, social, network or economic conditions that contain the activity ('structure') (Tatli et al., 2014). In recent years, scholars have questioned the utility of these often-static structure-versus-agency divisions by focusing on social (entrepreneurial) practices as the unit of analysis – looking to combine both structural and agentic elements in research (Thompson et al., 2020).

Examples of entrepreneurship-as-practice research (see Champenois et al., 2020 for a review) include discursive-material approaches that treat activities such as pitching and storytelling as acts of sensemaking or language games and so emphasize how these play out as part of wider fabrics, for instance when garnering institutional support or legitimation in particular settings such as business clusters and networks (Chalmers & Shaw, 2017; Garud et al., 2014). There have also been inquiries into the underlying practices that support these infrastructures where entrepreneurial clusters or networks are understood as being constituted over time through much broader social and cultural practices (de Clercq & Voronov, 2009; Vincent & Pagan, 2018).

Practice approaches also highlight the role of time and space (Schatzki, 2005). Especially questions of time have started to receive more attention in the literature (e.g. by emphasizing the processual) but with few exceptions, the role of space in entrepreneurship is less well explored. For example, Steyaert (2007) conceptualizes entrepreneurship as a complex and non-linear process of 'becoming' – calling for contextualized and involved methodological techniques that witness unfolding entrepreneurial practices and activities as they occur in real time: 'all the meetings, the talking, the selling, the form-filling and the number-crunching by which opportunities actually get formulated and implemented' (Thompson et al., 2020, p. 247). There have been calls for entrepreneurship researchers to bring the role of space into greater focus including complex interactions concerning the relationship between entrepreneurship and especially the role played by the built environment, involving questions of how entrepreneurial practices emerge through an ongoing relating between people and such spatial settings (e.g. Korsgaard et al., 2020; Welter & Baker, 2021).

So, what is the relationship between space and entrepreneurial practising? How can we explore the influence of a space in relation to its current entrepreneurial activity? How might we understand the different aspects of space – this confluence between structural (space as objectively existing) and experiential (space as felt and understood) aspects? And methodologically, how can we begin to synthesize these different spatial aspects in a dynamic and unfolding entrepreneurial process? In this chapter, I elaborate one way that the interrelationship between space and entrepreneurship could be researched drawing upon Henri Lefebvre's (1991 [1974]) 'spatial triad'.

Lefebvre's (1991 [1974]) spatial triad is a conceptual and analytical frame for studying spatial phenomena over time that incorporates three interrelated 'spaces' in society: these are *perceived* space ('real' physical properties of space), *conceived* space ('imagined' mental representations of space) and *lived* space (the 'lived' experience of space in-between the real and imagined) (Lefebvre, 1991 [1974], pp. 38–39). Lefebvre's triad has been employed widely in organization studies to research how spaces such as buildings, architectures and other workspaces do not only contain organization but are also actively produced and changed by it, thus invoking a deeply reciprocal interrelationship between structural and agentic aspects of organizing as well as emphasizing a strong processual dimension (e.g. Liu & Grey, 2018; Petani & Mengis, 2016; Skoglund & Holt, 2021). This capacity to override traditional structure–agent dichotomies to study together phenomena that are so often treated as separate means that Lefebvre's triad has much potential for entrepreneurship-as-practice research.

In this chapter, I outline a set of methodological principles for mobilizing Lefebvre's triadic notion of space to investigate the temporal and spatial interrelations that give rise to and are simultaneously shaped by entrepreneurial practices; entrepreneurship as emerging in the space in-between, incorporating the mental and the physical yet irreducible to either, where space is both the outcome of time and the setting for the future (Lefebvre, 1991 [1974], pp. 91–92). These principles emphasize the need for researcher immersion and historicized methods as well as the importance of attending to wider geographical forces and the political implications of human action; following Lefebvre (1991 [1974], p. 66; 2003, p. 211), they are organized in a research process comprising three phases: beginning in a present space where entrepreneurial practices and activities are gathering, going back to investigate the historical development of this space before returning, armed with a historicized understanding, 'to rediscover the present, but elucidated, understood, explained' (Lefebvre, cited in Merrifield, 2006, p. 4).

I elaborate this method using empirical examples drawing on my own research investigating the entrepreneurial regeneration of the Cain's brewery building in Liverpool, UK. Cain's was once a highly entrepreneurial space and a substantial regional brewer throughout the nineteenth and twentieth century that entered administration in 2013 and subsequently fell into disuse. Today entrepreneurial practices and activities are gathering anew and Cain's is in the midst of a transformation from defunct brewery to important centre for leisure and employment orientated predominantly towards (but not exclusively on) the night-time economy: old cellars have become pubs and bars; horse stables are now co-working spaces and the cold storage facility is a food market. The entrepreneurial transformation of Cain's has acted as a catalyst for the regeneration of the surrounding area, which is currently one of the fastest growing districts in the city.

I investigate the interrelation between space and entrepreneurship at the Cain's brewery. More specifically, and by mobilizing the interplay of Lefebvre's triadic notion of space, I explore how we can understand the influence of a space, in this case a building, in terms of multiple and changing aspects including its design and layout, its location, its previous occupancy through time and how its current inhabitants relate to this space in the context of their present-day entrepreneurial practices and activities. My primary contribution is to attempt to show how entrepreneurship-as-practice scholars might utilize spatial inquiry to continue to unsettle structure–agent dichotomies, where space is treated as a dynamic and unfolding phenomenon actively shaping and in turn shaped by entrepreneurial practices and activities over time.

ENTREPRENEURSHIP AND PRACTICE THEORY

Entrepreneurship is considered a key economic contributor and entrepreneurs and their innovations have been recognized as important in technological and societal developments, even changing the course of history (Lippmann & Aldrich, 2016). The cultivation of entrepreneurship has become integral to policy and economic development and regeneration efforts as well as to business school curricula, and over the last fifty years entrepreneurship research has largely followed two distinct directions: one strand focused on psychological or behavioural theories to explain the agency of the individual entrepreneur (e.g. McClelland, 1961), describing intrinsic qualities or producing retrospective accounts of moments of decisive entrepreneurial decision and cognition in the subjective interpretivist tradition; a second strand examining the structural conditions (environmental, social, network, economic) containing the activity by drawing on functional principles such as classic theories of economic exchange (e.g. Kirzner, 1973), often sacrificing a richness in empirical insight. These two strands of research have produced a range of methodological approaches from psychological and trait-based perspectives (agentic approaches) on one end of the spectrum through to analysis of the economic and other environments (structural approaches) in which entrepreneurship takes place on the other (Tatli et al., 2014).

Some entrepreneurship researchers have voiced concerns that contemporary studies on either side of this structure–agency dualism produce insights that separate entrepreneurship from its context, thus compartmentalizing agentic and structural concerns, studying each separately in a static formulation that 'describes and explains a world that does not bear up under close scrutiny' (Thompson et al., 2020, p. 248). But researching entrepreneurship in a way that is able to apprehend the temporally and spatially specific, idiosyncratic, and often only post-hoc identifiable nature of the activities involved is notoriously difficult (e.g. Spinosa et al., 1997), and scholars have called for new approaches to apprehend the complexity and diversity of entrepreneurship as it unfolds in everyday life (Welter et al., 2016). In response a third strand of research, entrepreneurship-as-practice, has emerged that seeks to study entrepreneurial activities *in* context (Thompson et al., 2020).

Following practice-theoretical ideals, entrepreneurship researchers have explored discursive-material practices such as sensemaking (Cornelissen et al., 2012), pitching (Chalmers & Shaw, 2017) and storytelling (Garud et al., 2014). By conceiving of these entrepreneurial activities as discursive-material *practices* rather than a form of subjective interpretivism, these studies add to knowledge of how entrepreneurs use language in different ways to realize context-specific outcomes such as gaining institutional support for a fledgling venture (e.g. Cornelissen et al., 2012) or achieving legitimacy among peers (e.g. Garud et al., 2014).

In addition to tracing discursive-material connections, researchers have also investigated the underlying practices that support entrepreneurial contexts such as networks or clusters – entrepreneurship does not only emerge in specific contexts but also is constituted over time *through* wider social and cultural practices that give these contexts form and meaning (de Clercq & Voronov, 2009; Keating et al., 2014; Vincent & Pagan, 2018). This view emphasizes the processual dimension of practice where any notion of 'sensemaking', 'legitimacy' or 'institutional support' is in fact 'inconceivable without first considering the enactment and entanglement of various practices' (Thompson et al., 2020, p. 250).

Further studies have suggested that looking at process opens up an 'entrepreneuring' perspective (e.g. Steyaert, 2007; Johannisson, 2011; Verduijn, 2015). This approach conceives of entrepreneurship as 'a creative and social/collective organizing process that materializes in a venture' (Johannisson, 2011, p. 137). An entrepreneuring formulation further emphasizes the processual dimension of practice by treating entrepreneurship as a fundamentally unfinalized and open-ended act of 'becoming' that requires contextualized methodological techniques involving the researcher's active participation (Champenois et al., 2020, p. 299) – scholars should themselves be involved in the 'nitty-gritty work' of decision-making to witness entrepreneurship 'as it happens' (Thompson et al., 2020, p. 247).

ENTREPRENEURSHIP AND SPACE

The practice turn in entrepreneurship studies takes practices as the unit of analysis (Thompson et al., 2020, p. 249). In practice theory, 'practice' is understood as an organized, open-ended spatial-temporal manifold of human action that transpires in 'material arrangements': historical settings composed of built entities and physical orders (Schatzki, 2005, pp. 471–472). Practices 'acquire meaning only when understood as situated in context and in history, and as the collective accomplishments performed by multiple people' (Champenois et al., 2020, p. 283). So, while existing studies have elaborated the socialized human practices (e.g. rules, understandings, actions) involved in entrepreneurship very well, they often overlook the spatial and temporal dimensions of these practices. Research that is explicitly concerned with the relevance of wider social practices and their physical infrastructures for inquiring into locally situated entrepreneurship, taking in spaces such as cities, districts, local communities, buildings and other physical settings, is currently under-represented in entrepreneurship-as-practice studies (e.g. Champenois et al., 2020) as well as in entrepreneurship scholarship in general (e.g. Korsgaard et al., 2020; Welter & Baker, 2021).

A small number of studies have started to unpack the relationship between space and entrepreneurship. Johnstone and Lionais (2004) studied entrepreneurship enacted in various 'depleted communities' and observed how local socio-economic historical factors exerted a strong influence on the shape and form of entrepreneurship that emerged in each space: due to their institutional legacy depleted communities were found to be more conducive to community-based entrepreneurship orientated towards driving new forms of spatial development. Johnstone and Lionais (2004) therefore show that built spaces can cultivate locally specific idiosyncratic forms of entrepreneurship that are a product of their environment but also change it too.

Also in a study of a depleted community, this time 'Stanton' in New Zealand, Anderson, Warren and Bensemann (2019) observed how entrepreneurial activities were shaped and influenced by micro-level contextual factors in a study that was 'embedded in the history of Stanton' (Anderson et al., 2019, p. 1564). The authors found localized entrepreneurial practices where 'the role of place was central to the enactment' (Anderson et al., 2019, p. 1572). In Stanton, a material legacy comprising 'boarded up shops, dilapidated buildings, and peeling paintwork' (Anderson et al., 2019, p. 1564) discouraged entrepreneurship in the town centre, and new practices gathered on the outskirts of the town to capture the passing trade of motorists instead. Due to these material spatial realities, as well as other local factors, entrepreneurial activities worked inwards from the outskirts in a process that eventually produced new spatial changes in the town centre: 'economically and visually ... retailers of gifts, clothing and fancy goods have opened, the cafés are prospering, and local council have spruced up the town gardens, picnic areas and toilets' (Anderson et al., 2019, p. 1564).

These two studies demonstrate the beginnings of a movement from a mostly abstracted conception of space (e.g. the 'depleted communities' of Johnstone & Lionais, 2004) towards a more concrete treatment (e.g. 'Stanton' in Anderson et al., 2019), with this shift driven by investigating the actual concrete circumstances of entrepreneurial practices as they unfold in their natural settings (e.g. Watson, 2013, p. 17). In both instances a reciprocal relationship between act and setting is observed, establishing that there is an important relationship between entrepreneurship and space: entrepreneurship as shaped by space and shaping space in turn (see Welter & Baker, 2021, pp. 1165–1168). However, the structural side of this relationship tends to take precedent as a constraining or determining factor (see also Champenois et al., 2020, p. 299).

In his study of cultural entrepreneurs in Manchester, UK, Banks (2006) showed that structural characteristics, whilst important, are not the only way that we can understand space as shaping and influencing entrepreneurial practices. Banks's research investigated the role of spatial experience, finding that:

> Throughout, a sense of community, strong social and cultural ties and a regard for the 'can-do' and creative 'atmosphere' of Manchester were cited as incentives to action. Manchester's diverse configurations of social and spatial relations, underwritten by a rich history of images, myths and narratives, were often alluded to as a source of inspiration and value. (Banks, 2006, p. 464)

Banks (2006) described how the practices and activities of cultural entrepreneurs were infused with or 'underwritten' by their own spatial experiences of Manchester, including personal and collective perceptions of its rich musical heritage and long association with independent music that were tied to specific sites such as music venues and shops. Entrepreneurs had 'an abundance of collective memories and shared experiences cultivated through historical immersion in Manchester' which in the present became 'incentives to action' (Banks, 2006, p. 464):

> with many entrepreneurs expressing a strong, progressive sense of place it was not surprising that the desire to 'give something back' to the city was often expressed. To give some examples, entrepreneurs involved themselves in voluntary teaching and mentoring at local colleges, devoting services free to local arts and entertainment events, combining work with the provision of public art in the local community, driving a women's night-bus and, in the case of one local recording studio, working through colleges to offer local youth free use of their facilities. (Banks, 2006, p. 464)

This research suggests that the relationship between space and entrepreneurship is multiple and complex. The influence of a space, how it shapes and is in turn shaped by entrepreneurial practising unavoidably involves the everyday negotiation of its structural aspects (as in Johnstone & Lionais, 2004; also Anderson et al., 2019) but there are also important experiential considerations too, where an immersion in space over time leads to everyday entrepreneurial practices becoming infused with a sense of local culture, imagination and memory (Banks, 2006). This formulation requires a notion of space that accounts for but is at the same time not solely reducible to either of these two spatial aspects, but the continued study of this relationship between entrepreneurship and spatial-temporal aspects of practice, including important questions of how this multiplicity and complexity might be further conceptualized and analysed, has received little attention in the literature (e.g. Welter & Baker, 2021). I now turn to Henri Lefebvre.

HENRI LEFEBVRE'S TRIADIC NOTION OF SPACE

Henri Lefebvre is known among organizational scholars for his Marxist-inspired inquiries into the social practices that constitute daily life (*Critique of Everyday Life*), as well as his analysis of the political questions of emergent urban society throughout the 1960s (*The Right to the City*), but without doubt his most widely cited work in organization studies is *The Production of Space* (1991 [1974]). Against a backdrop of late 1960s/early 1970s industrial development in cities and towns, Lefebvre (1991 [1974]) employs and extends a Marxist notion of production to look for a way to investigate how urban space is produced in society that is able 'to get to the root of capitalist society, to get beyond the fetishisms of observable appearance, to trace out its inner dynamics and internal contradictions, holistically and historically' (Merrifield, 2006, p. 104).

To Lefebvre (1991 [1974], p. 27), spatial analysis has long suffered at the hands of an emphasis on either the physical (the 'realistic illusion') or the mental (the 'illusion of transparency'), and *The Production of Space* is his attempt to construct a unitary theory of space by harnessing what he calls a 'tridimensionality' (Lefebvre, 1991 [1974], p. 370). Lefebvre (1991 [1974], pp. 11–12) develops his threefold concept intended to supersede the separation of the physical and mental (which we can understand as broadly consistent with traditional notions of the structure–agent binary) by dialectically relating them through a third space: a disturbing force which works in-between, the space that 'the imagination seeks to change and appropriate' (Lefebvre, 1991 [1974], p. 39) that is 'occupied by sensory phenomena, including products of the imagination such as projects and projections, symbols and utopias' (Lefebvre, 1991 [1974], p. 12).

Lefebvre (1991 [1974]) introduces his 'spatial triad' as the conceptual and analytical frame to accommodate his unitary theory. The triad harnesses the simultaneous interplay of three 'spaces' in society, one of which is *conceived* space: the 'ideal' space of planning and conception that attempts to impose a form that may not naturally emanate from how a space is practised (Lefebvre, 1991 [1974], p. 33). This is space as conceived 'from above' by planners, urbanists and politicians, which means conceived space is 'the dominant space in any society' (Lefebvre, 1991 [1974], pp. 38–39). The triad also incorporates *perceived* space: the 'real' space of physical appearance and habitualized everyday routines that take place 'on the ground' (Lefebvre, 1991 [1974], p. 33). Perceived space is concerned with material empirical reality and becomes manifest through the realization of the conceived: comprising subjects moving through and negotiating physical space in the course of everyday routines (Lefebvre, 1991 [1974], p. 38). The triad dialectically relates these two spaces through a third, which is space as directly *lived*: this is space as it is experienced by users and inhabitants in-between the ideal and the real, the space in society that is pregnant with the potential for change and appropriation (Lefebvre, 1991 [1974], p. 39). For Lefebvre, lived space comes through the constant failure of idealized plans to be executed perfectly, and this disturbing quality drives the continuous development of any urban space in society in a process whereby the creative imagination of users and inhabitants 'overlays physical space, making symbolic use of its objects' (Lefebvre, 1991 [1974], p. 39). Due to its subversive potential lived space is often 'linked to the clandestine or underground side of social life' (Lefebvre, 1991 [1974], p. 33).

For Lefebvre, urban space is a process of 'endless production' (Lefebvre, 1991 [1974], p. 370) involving all three aspects of the triad in continuous interrelation. The analysis of any space in society must therefore account for but at the same time cannot be solely reducible to either of these three spaces as space is 'itself the outcome of past actions' (Lefebvre, 1991 [1974], p. 73) whilst also being 'at once a precondition and a result of social superstructures' (Lefebvre, 1991 [1974], p. 85). At the centre of this idea of space as a continuously unfolding phenomenon is the notion 'that a given plan must of necessity highlight either function, or form, or structure' (Lefebvre, 1991 [1974], p. 369), yet 'no plan could conceivably maintain a perfect balance between these diverse moments or "formants" of space' (Lefebvre, 1991 [1974], p. 369). This is precisely how we can understand lived space as the driver of change over time, as continuously unsettling, disturbing, working in-between the real and ideal, thus superseding their binary separation as '*use* corresponds to a unity and collaboration between the very factors that such dogmatisms insist on disassociating' (Lefebvre, 1991 [1974], p. 369, emphasis in original).

A number of organizational scholars have drawn on Lefebvre's work to investigate the temporal and spatial dimensions of organizing in spaces such as local authority planning departments (Petani & Mengis, 2016), university buildings (Liu & Grey, 2018) and workplace facilities such as toilets (Skoglund & Holt, 2021). Lefebvre's triad is able to apprehend how these spaces do not just contain organization but are actively produced and changed by it over time invoking a deeply reciprocal relationship between structural and agentic aspects of organizing; offering a dynamic conceptual and analytical frame for studying together phenomena that are so often treated as separate, shifting attention from the study of '*things in space* to the actual *production of space*' (Lefebvre, 1991 [1974]), p. 37, emphasis in original).

An illustrative example of the triad in action is Liu and Grey's (2018) study of the 'Founder's Building' – a Victorian-era UK university initially constructed to provide higher education to women. Liu and Grey suggest that the 'Lefebvrian "triad" enables organizational space to be studied as a condensation of all the social concepts and interrelationships through which it has emerged and evolved' (2018, p. 645), and they employ it to investigate the historical development of the Founder's Building revealing how 'the bricks and mortar have not changed, but their social and organizational meaning has' (2018, p. 662). The study describes how a space that was initially conceived of in terms of quite narrow gender proprietary is reconceived in terms of much broader notions of diversity and community over time at the hands of users and inhabitants, thereby demonstrating the inherent dynamism of Lefebvre's triadic formulation: the conceived, perceived and lived aspects constantly 'shift and change over time so that the organizational space is not just an "inheritance" but something whose meaning is amenable to re-working and re-interpretation' (Liu & Grey, 2018, p. 662).

More specifically for entrepreneurship studies, Beyes (2006) suggests that Lefebvre's spatial triad opens up new possibilities for research:

> it takes sites and spaces for entrepreneurship to happen, and at the same time sites and spaces are constituted and reorganized through entrepreneurial activities. Applying a spatial perspective therefore offers myriad opportunities for exploring the ways in which manifold forms, practices and concepts of entrepreneurship emerge. (Beyes, 2006, p. 269)

In particular, Beyes emphasizes the new possibilities (both conceptual and analytical) implied in Lefebvre's (1991 [1974]) notion of lived space with its capacity for creativity 'intertwining the real and the imagined without preferring the one over the other' (Beyes, 2006, p. 263). He suggests that researchers should 'look out' for lived spaces where new inventions or trans-formations of practices emerge 'connecting real and imagined spaces, contesting dominant discourses, producing subversion, provoking transformation, enabling social change' (Beyes, 2006, p. 264).

In one of few attempts to apply Lefebvre's triadic formulation to entrepreneurship, Beyes (2006) pays particular attention to the theoretical aspects of his work. There remain, however, substantial methodological questions pertaining to the mobilizing of Lefebvre's ideas for empirical research. In the section that follows, I attempt to build upon Beyes's work by first drawing out and then exemplifying some methodological principles and processes, with empirical examples, for entrepreneurship-as-practice researchers wishing to conduct an inquiry utilizing Lefebvre's spatial triad as a conceptual and analytical frame.

MOBILIZING LEFEBVRE'S 'SPATIAL TRIAD' FOR EMPIRICAL RESEARCH: METHODOLOGICAL PRINCIPLES AND PROCESSES

> For how *could* we come to understand a genesis, the genesis of the present, along with the precondi-tions and process involved, other than by starting from that present, working our way back to the past and then retracing our steps? (Lefebvre, 1991 [1974], p. 66, emphasis in original)

For Lefebvre (1991 [1974]), the core value of the triad lies in concretizing the seemingly abstract: the triad 'loses all force if it is treated as an abstract "model". If it cannot grasp the concrete ... then its import is severely limited' (Lefebvre, 1991 [1974], p. 40). Mobilizing the three interrelated aspects of the triad for empirical studies requires researchers to incorporate several spatial phenomena all at once and this is not an easy task; in organization studies 'many scholars whose studies are theoretically underwritten by Lefebvre seem hesitant to operation-alize a dialectic method' (Skoglund & Holt, 2021, p. 1015):

> to capture in thought the actual process of production of space ... it's a task that necessitates both empirical and theoretical research, and it's likely to be difficult. It will doubtless involve careful excavation and reconstruction; warrant induction and deduction; journey between the concrete and the abstract, between the local and the global, between self and society, between what's possible and what's impossible. (Merrifield, 2006, p. 108)

On the basis of my own research, which I will outline in detail below, I suggest four (certainly by no means exhaustive) guiding principles for operationalizing Lefebvre's triad. These prin-ciples emphasize researcher immersion and historicized methods, as well as the importance of attending to wider geographical forces and the political implications of human action. Following Lefebvre (1991 [1974], p. 66; 2003, p. 211), these principles are organized in a methodological process that describes a present space where entrepreneurial practices and activities are gathering, that then travels backwards to investigate the historical development of this space over time before returning armed with this historicized understanding to further elucidate present-day entrepreneurial enactments (see also Lefebvre, cited in Merrifield, 2006,

p. 4). Throughout this process, I mobilize the three interrelated aspects of the triad, unfolding the continuous interplay between the conceived, perceived, and lived.

I furnish this method with empirical evidence from my own research investigating the entrepreneurial regeneration of the Cain's brewery building in Liverpool, UK. Constructed in 1887, Cain's impressive red-brick structure is an unmistakable part of the local landscape and its fluctuating fortunes have entered local folklore as a metaphor for Liverpool's own rise, decline and re-emergence (e.g. *The Story of Liverpool in a Pint*: see Routledge, 2008). Cain's was once a highly successful brewery with its success peaking around the turn of the twentieth century, but the story of the ensuing years was of gradual decline before the demise of brewing operations in 2013. Today, new entrepreneurial practices and activities are gathering as the space is brought back into productive use at the hands of local entrepreneurship, with different parts of the brewery now occupied by an eclectic and growing mix of fledgling organizations trading out of old cellars, horse stables, cold storage facilities and brewing rooms. Cain's is in the midst of an entrepreneurial transformation from defunct brewery to important destination for culture and leisure with a particular emphasis on the night-time economy. The space has become a catalyst for the regeneration of the surrounding area which is now one of the fastest growing districts in the city.

I explore the relationship between space and entrepreneurship at the Cain's brewery. More specifically, I investigate how we can understand the influence of a space, in this case a building, in terms of multiple and changing spatial aspects including its design and layout, its location, its previous occupancy through time and how its current inhabitants relate to this space in the context of their present-day entrepreneurial practices and activities. The main thrust of this section is to further a research agenda for entrepreneurship-as-practice scholarship that can continue to unsettle structure–agent dichotomies (e.g. Thompson et al., 2020); mobilizing Lefebvre's triadic formulation of space to investigate the temporal and spatial interrelations that give rise to and are simultaneously shaped by entrepreneurial practices (e.g. Welter & Baker, 2021).

Starting in the Present

From the outset, Lefebvre (cited in Merrifield, 2006, p. 4) suggests approaching empirical material with a scrutiny guided by observation and a general theory; to engage closely with the phenomena under investigation, attentive to the small details, aware of possible connections, but at the same time retaining a certain openness and willingness to let the space speak on its own accord (see also Lefebvre, 2003, pp. 211–213). At the point of departure researchers could utilize methodological techniques such as observation, participation, shadowing and primary visual photography, activities that amount to a form of 'hanging around' (Johannisson, 2018, p. 393) that could even include the occasional pursuit of leisure, all the while producing detailed descriptions and visual records of observable entrepreneurial practices and activities as well as built surroundings.

On a typical day Cain's is a busy and bustling scene; initial impressions might summarize a variety of local and independent-focused shops, bars, nightclubs, shared creative workspaces and local artist space that collectively occupy a recently transformed and architecturally impressive Victorian-era industrial building. The main building is striking, many storeys high with a tower protruding from its centre – adorned with terracotta tiles arranged in ornamental style. On the walls is a stencilled piece of graffiti: 'Liverpool has its own story to tell.' On show are various traces of its industrious past as a substantial regional brewing outfit: large loading docks have become outdoor seating areas for recently established bars and restaurants located in vast brewing rooms; old stables and garage doors have been turned into main entrances; a cellar is now one of the larger pubs in the city. There are many cases of old architectural features and industrial functions being incorporated into the fabric of these newly established ventures. Other remnants from the Victorian industrial era comprising brewery equipment in various stages of decay are also on show: a deep well along with its rusted machinery is displayed under plexiglass in the cellar pub; commercial brewing artefacts (pulleys, motors, measuring instruments, brewing equipment – all of which date from the late nineteenth and early twentieth century) as well as old advertising hoardings have been strategically placed around the site. Yet alongside this rekindling and showcasing of the old, there are also some unreservedly modern developments and new construction in-progress to accommodate the ever-growing number of new arrivals.

We can begin to unpack these early observations by employing Lefebvre's (1991 [1974]) triadic formulation as a configuring frame. The first thing that strikes any visitor is the sheer size of this space; the brewery dominates the local landscape and its material stature invokes feelings that this is a building enacted as it was intended at the point of conception: to achieve market dominance, to impress, reminiscent of empire. However, up close, we can see that the building is indeed grand but there is still a patchwork roof, evidence of efflorescence and broken windows on upper levels. Despite the busy and bustling scene there are still large swathes of the building that remain unused and dilapidated and these sections of the brewery are cold, uninsulated, remote and inhospitable. This is a building that was once reminiscent of empire, alive to the confidence in British capitalism and industry that characterized the era of its construction, but today its physical stature speaks also to a faded grandeur. We can see the entrepreneurial as coming through this rupture: repairing, patching up, bringing back into productive use – a practice that 'overlays physical space, making symbolic use of its objects' (Lefebvre, 1991 [1974], p. 39).

So, how can we begin to understand the influence of this space in relation to its current entrepreneurial enactment? Cain's brewing history appears to be significant and this is certainly true in regard to aesthetic concerns, as evidenced through the proliferation of late nineteenth-century brewing paraphernalia. But there is also a sense of a symbolic significance to this entrepreneurial regeneration arising from the brewery's long association with the city of Liverpool. Indeed, 'Liverpool has its own story to tell' – and it is clear that much work had to be done to bring sections of this old and damaged building back into productive use, the majority carried out by new and fledgling local entrepreneurial ventures who characteristically possess limited financial resources. There is a notable absence of the national brands and chain stores that typically inhabit similar redevelopments in other cities in the UK – and perhaps this is why Cain's retains a certain DIY ethic, a rough-around-the-edges charm that is often absent in post-industrial retained-façade regeneration projects. Thus, we see entrepreneurial practices at Cain's at once attempting to rescue fragments of the past, to preserve and to showcase selected aspects, to exploit their commercial potential, but at the same time these practices imply an attempt to collectively articulate something new and different. To enact a new future for this space.

These insights gesture towards layers of meaning that are perhaps not so obvious at first but rather become more apparent over time, demonstrating the importance of immersive research practices that permit such spaces to begin to do their work. A single visit to Cain's might yield a surface understanding but it is by hanging around that researchers can begin to develop a sense for the possibility of multiplicity and complexity (e.g. Johannisson, 2018). This echoes prescriptions for entrepreneurship-as-practice research to endeavour to 'stay close to "what happens", that is, to real and concrete practices under study' (Champenois et al., 2020, p. 291). However, observed practices 'acquire meaning only when understood as situated in context *and in history*' (Champenois et al., 2020, p. 283, emphasis added). Thus, we can take these initial insights as further invitations to excavate the historical development of this space (Lefebvre, 2003, pp. 211–213): to journey into the past to situate observed practices in their specific historical conditions (e.g. Thompson et al., 2020, p. 247).

Excavating History

'If space is produced, if there is a productive process, then we are dealing with *history*' (Lefebvre, 1991 [1974], p. 46, emphasis in original). Writing in 1986, in the *Preface to the New Edition* of *The Production of Space*, Lefebvre affirms that his project seeks 'not only to describe the space we live in, and its origins, but to retrace the origins, through and by the space it produced' (2003, p. 211). For this task, research can draw upon primary archival as well as documentary and other secondary sources, which could comprise a wide variety of textual and visual materials such as newspapers, press releases, company reports, local authority papers, meeting minutes, historical photographs, local histories, oral histories as well as social media.

Company records show that the Cain's brewery building was designed in the late nineteenth century to accommodate vastly increased production and to establish the business as one of the largest in the region, with an elaborate Renaissance decoration that at the time would have been the height of fashion (Routledge, 2008). Cain's was constructed when Liverpool was a truly global city of significant power and influence and the physical attributes of this space embodied the confidence of this era:

> The brewery is a remarkable building, rightly considered one of Liverpool's finest. With its ornate terracotta tiles and brickwork, the elaborate crest, the tower and the pretty Brewery Tap pub nestling in one corner, it is a monument to the optimism of Victorian Liverpool. (Routledge, 2008, p. 1)

Mobilizing Lefebvre's (1991 [1974]) triadic formulation once more, we find that the conceived values of Cain's at the point of inauguration comprised a design for a visually attesting building; built high and wide, elaborate and decorative; requiring vast quantities of raw material but also fine craftmanship; invoking intended themes of dominance: over nature, over the immediate surroundings, over commercial rivals. These idealized conceptions of power, prestige and productivity can be envisaged as being more-or-less enacted at the perceived level: a large ornate building was constructed and its physicality asserted the brewery amongst the immediate surroundings; the interior housed state-of-the-art machinery for mass-production that enabled and enforced movements and work routines that greatly increased productive activity relative to competitors; market share grew as a result, and thereby profits (Routledge, 2008).

However, Cain's struggled through much of the twentieth century and eventually collapsed under the weight of its debts in 2013. The brewery building subsequently fell into disuse. It became the grand relic of a distant model of British industrial capitalism.

In 2014, new plans for Cain's were published to transform the space into a 'Brewery Village' in accordance with a more 'post-industrial' model of redevelopment driven by property investment. This reconception involved repurposing the brewery as a destination for high-end transient tourism and leisure; the roof of the building was to be cleaved off to make way for a cocktail bar; the inside gutted to house serviced luxury apartments and a supermarket installed underneath complete with a large glass frontage. Planning permission was granted by the local authority with £150m required from investors; promotional material was produced and there was significant fanfare online, particularly in local newspapers and on social media. But despite all this the brewery was eventually deemed ineligible for large-scale redevelopment, investors baulked at the state of disrepair and out-of-town location and the plans for the Cain's Brewery Village were quietly abandoned.

We can envisage this passage of time as bearing witness to the uncoupling of conceived and perceived space: no longer in harmonious agreement but now circling one another; sometimes even producing a direct opposition where the plans for a shiny, glossy retained-façade post-industrial redevelopment stand in stark contrast to an empirical reality of a cold, damp and decaying building located in the 'wrong' part of the city. Cain's size, its architecture and its decoration made it an attractive target for this proposed redevelopment – and we see much promotional material featuring the words 'iconic'. 'aspirational', 'ambitious' – but at the same time these features erected barriers to this plan: the space was deemed to be too large, too elaborate. The extent and scale of Cain's dilapidation meant that the prevailing view among investors was that there was too much work to be done, too many risks associated with proposed redevelopment; the project was a financially unappealing prospect for those seeking healthy returns on capital. Cain's soon found itself on the periphery; rather than attract investment as desired, its state of disrepair and abandonment lent itself much more readily to more subversive activities and documentary analysis revealed the proliferation of urban exploration and art installations, also uncovering flyers for warehouse parties advertising deejays from Detroit and Chicago – activities that define Lefebvre's notion of a lived space 'linked to the clandestine or underground side of social life, as also to art' (1991 [1974], p. 33).

At Cain's, we find that capitalist heritage and industry cast a long shadow, but we have also uncovered a contested historical process of a substantial regional brewery embodying a very British capitalism actually becoming intrinsically resistant to these forces; tracing entrepreneurial practices back to the spark first ignited by underground groups who found a creative use for a space that had been cast adrift by the conventional forces of urban redevelopment.

A Return to the Present

Having retraced our steps we can start to elaborate further on the entrepreneurial practices that are gathering at Cain's, situating present enactments in their historical conditions (e.g. Thompson et al., 2020) to 'rediscover the present, but elucidated, understood, explained' (Lefebvre, cited in Merrifield, 2006, p. 4). At this phase, research could conduct further phenomenological interviews with questioning guided by accumulated practical and historical knowledge of the entrepreneurial phenomenon under investigation gleaned over time from previous phases of inquiry.

The present experience of Cain's is constituted of multiple and complex interactions between geographical and political forces situated in history. Once a substantial regional brewing operation, a site for mass-production, the regulated movement of users – a most pure expression of capitalist power – Cain's is now in the process of an entrepreneurial transformation that is predicated on a different notion of what this space is and can become. The wreckage of Cain's industrial past and the inability of traditional forces of redevelopment to enact their plan for the future became a source of creativity and new possibility. With this historicized understanding we can now begin to appreciate the influence of the early reclamation practices of the underground groups that came before: they sought to make a rejected space their own and the entrepreneurial practices that followed channel this momentum; absorbing the spirit of resistance to traditional notions of redevelopment; articulating the new possibilities implied in this lived space onto much wider spheres. This process of regeneration manifested through entrepreneurial practices comprising many small spatial transformations: rebuilding among the ruin, altering existing material arrangements, appropriating the history of this space and its past industrial functions and re-representing them in a different way, creating new constellations. The accumulation of these many small transformations instituted a much broader project: an entrepreneurial enactment that collectively forms an expression of a new future for Cain's that is premised on a much more local notion of redevelopment – space as both the outcome of time and the setting for the future (Lefebvre, 1991 [1974], pp. 91–92).

Invoking Lefebvre, this process is an 'endless production' (1991 [1974], p. 370) that is still very much in motion, and the success of local entrepreneurship at Cain's means that the space is now showing signs of aggregating towards more traditional and mainstream ideals of redevelopment that its current inhabitants sought initially to oppose: where the clustering of entrepreneurial activity, generating increased footfall and favourable demographics, is encouraging the regrouping of conceived forces. The unrealized plans for a 'Cain's Brewery Village' are coming back to the table, already closer to realization than before, calling for new entrepreneurial formulations once more. This demonstrates the strong temporal dimension of Lefebvre's (1991 [1974]) dynamic triadic formulation, where the multiplicity and complexity of the present and into the future starts to become apparent through a historical treatment of constitutive spatial forces. These forces are always changing, interrelating in new ways. Thus, what we are left with in our return to the present is not 'the linear, time-based dialectic of thesis/anti-thesis/synthesis' (Beyes & Holt, 2020, p. 11), but rather 'a propulsive but undirected triadic awareness' (Beyes & Holt, 2020, p. 11).

Indeed, the efficacy of Lefebvre's triad (1991 [1974]) lies in its ability to visualize complexity, to offer a configuring frame for understanding the present as constituted of multiple forces that are all 'inscribed in the built landscape, literally piled on top of each other' (Merrifield, 2006, p. 105). Lefebvre invokes the image of a 'flaky *mille-feuille* pastry' (1991 [1974], p. 86, emphasis in original) to help us to envisage space as composed of these multiple layers where 'the local, the regional, the national and the world-wide interweave and overlap' (Lefebvre, 2003, p. 211) – and if we do not trace these wider connections there is a risk that research 'separates what is connected' (Lefebvre, 2003, p. 211) by treating local studies as isolated phenomena which can 'break up spatial networks, links and relations' (Lefebvre, 2003, p. 211). Thus, we can draw clear links between Lefebvre and an entrepreneurship-as-practice research agenda that seeks to apprehend entrepreneurial practising as not just an economic function, but a societal phenomenon situated among broader social, cultural, geographical as well as political forces (e.g. Champenois et al., 2020; Thompson et al., 2020).

With Lefebvre's (1991 [1974]) triad as the productive force for analysis, I have offered an attempt at not resting or settling, but continually shifting between three interrelated spatial aspects so that what this space 'is' and what its entrepreneurial practices 'amount to' remain curious, challenging, and unfinished (e.g. Johannisson, 2011). I have attempted to illustrate one way of exploring the spatial and temporal dimensions of entrepreneurial practising as emerging through a triadic set of tangles in a methodological process where there is a constant movement between the conceived, perceived and lived over time (e.g. Liu & Grey, 2018; Skoglund & Holt, 2021). Where going from an initial surface understanding to more immersive research practices mobilizes a historicized appreciation that moves towards becoming more questioning; taking in historical accounts of success and industry but also of decline and failure; shifting between local and global forces where one is not always dominant. Where among these continuously unfolding spatial forces, entrepreneurial practices emerge.

CONCLUSION

Previous research exploring the relationship between space and entrepreneurship has a tendency to emphasize built spaces as already objectively existing structural phenomena that entrepreneurial practices must negotiate or navigate, or conversely, to imply that the relationship is more premised on individual perceptions and experiences of space – where subjective representations prompt particular courses of individual entrepreneurial action (Welter & Baker, 2021). Conversant with practice-theoretical ideals, Lefebvre's (1991 [1974]) triad is not isolated or static but rather constituted of a cluster of relations which are always in dialectical interrelation, encouraging us to go looking for entrepreneurship as it emerges in-between binaries as a disruptive and transformational force (e.g. Thompson et al., 2020) – entrepreneurial practices as both a product of and also able to change space.

In this chapter, I have attempted to show one way of exploring the temporal and spatial interrelations that give rise to and are simultaneously shaped by entrepreneurial practices by mobilizing Lefebvre's (1991 [1974]) triadic notion of space, thereby elaborating a new opening for empirical investigations into the role of built spaces and their significance for present-day entrepreneurial enactments. Whilst this is not a full set of procedures or complete taxonomy, I have endeavoured to show what a methodological entry to the study of entrepreneurial practising through spatial inquiry could look like, and how this might unearth new forms of entrepreneurship-as-practice scholarship that continues to unsettle traditional dichotomies.

REFERENCES

Anderson, A., Warren, L., & Bensemann, J. (2019). Identity, enactment and entrepreneurship engagement in a declining place. *Journal of Small Business Management, 57*(4), 1559–1577.

Banks, M. (2006). Moral economy and cultural work. *Sociology, 40*, 455–472.

Beyes, T. (2006). City of enterprise, city as prey? On urban entrepreneurial spaces. In C. Steyaert & D. Hjorth (Eds.), *Entrepreneurship as Social Change. A Third Movements in Entrepreneurship Book* (pp. 251–270). Cheltenham, UK and Northampton, MA, USA: Edward Elgar Publishing.

Beyes, T., & Holt, R. (2020). The topographical imagination: Space and organization theory. *Organization Theory, 1*, 1–26.

Chalmers, D., & Shaw, E. (2017). The endogenous construction of entrepreneurial contexts: A practice-based perspective. *International Small Business Journal, 35*, 19–39.

Champenois, C., Lefebvre, V., & Ronteau, S. (2020). Entrepreneurship as practice: Systematic literature review of a nascent field. *Entrepreneurship & Regional Development, 32*(3–4), 281–312.

Cornelissen, J., Clarke, J., & Cienki, A. (2012). Sensegiving in entrepreneurial contexts: The use of metaphors in speech and gesture to gain and sustain support for novel business ventures. *International Small Business Journal, 30*, 213–241.

de Clercq, D., & Voronov, M. (2009). Toward a practice perspective of entrepreneurship: Entrepreneurial legitimacy as habitus. *International Small Business Journal, 27*, 395–419.

Garud, R., Schildt, H., & Lant, T. (2014). Entrepreneurial storytelling, future expectations, and the paradox of legitimacy. *Organization Science, 25*, 1479–1492.

Johannisson, B. (2011). Towards a practice theory of entrepreneuring. *Small Business Economics, 36*(2), 135–150.

Johannisson, B. (2018). Disclosing everyday practices constituting social entrepreneuring: A case of necessity effectuation. *Entrepreneurship & Regional Development, 30*, 390–406.

Johnstone, H., & Lionais, D. (2004). Depleted communities and community business entrepreneurship: Revaluing space through place. *Entrepreneurship & Regional Development, 16*, 213–233.

Keating, A., Geiger, S., & McLoughlin, D. (2014). Riding the practice waves: Social resourcing practices during new venture development. *Entrepreneurship Theory and Practice, 38*(5), 1207–1235.

Kirzner, I. (1973). *Competition and Entrepreneurship*. Chicago: University of Chicago Press.

Korsgaard, S., Hunt, R., Townsend, D., & Ingstrup, M. (2020). COVID-19 and the importance of space in entrepreneurship research and policy. *International Small Business Journal, 38*, 697–710.

Lefebvre, H. (1991 [1974]). *The Production of Space*. Oxford: Blackwell.

Lefebvre, H. (2003). Preface to the new edition: *The Production of Space*. In S. Elden, E. Lebas, & E. Kofman (Eds.), *Henri Lefebvre: Key Writings* (pp. 206–216). London: Continuum.

Lippmann, S., & Aldrich, H. E. (2016). A rolling stone gathers momentum: Generational units, collective memory, and entrepreneurship. *Academy of Management Review, 41*, 658–675.

Liu, Y., & Grey, C. (2018). History, gendered space and organizational identity: An archival study of a university building. *Human Relations, 71*, 640–677.

McClelland, D. (1961). *The Achieving Society*. New York: Van Nostrand.

Merrifield, A. (2006). *Henri Lefebvre: A Critical Introduction*. Abingdon: Routledge.

Petani, F., & Mengis, J. (2016). In search of lost space: The process of space planning through remembering and history. *Organization, 23*, 71–89.

Routledge, C. (2008). *Cain's: The Story of Liverpool in a Pint*. Liverpool: Liverpool University Press.

Schatzki, T. (2005). Peripheral vision: The sites of organizations. *Organization Studies, 26*, 465–484.

Skoglund, A., & Holt, R. (2021). Spatially organized future genders: An artistic intervention in the creation of a hir-toilet. *Human Relations, 74*(7), 1007–1032.

Spinosa, C., Flores, F., & Dreyfus, H. (1997). *Disclosing New Worlds: Entrepreneurship, Democratic Action and the Cultivation of Solidarity*. Cambridge, MA: MIT Press.

Steyaert, C. (2007). 'Entrepreneuring' as a conceptual attractor? A review of process theories in 20 years of entrepreneurship studies. *Entrepreneurship & Regional Development, 19*(6), 453–477.

Tatli, A., Vassilopoulou, J., Ozbilgin, M., Forson, C., & Slutskaya, N. (2014). A Bourdieuan relational perspective for entrepreneurship research. *Journal of Small Business Management, 52*, 615–632.

Thompson, N. A., Verduijn, K., & Gartner, W. B. (2020). Entrepreneurship-as-practice: Grounding contemporary theories of practice into entrepreneurship studies. *Entrepreneurship & Regional Development, 32*(3–4), 247–256.

Verduijn, K. (2015). Entrepreneuring and process: A Lefebvrian perspective. *International Small Business Journal, 33*, 638–648.

Vincent, S., & Pagan, V. (2018). Entrepreneurial agency and field relations: A realist Bourdieusian analysis. *Human Relations, 72*, 188–216.

Watson, T. (2013). Entrepreneurial action and the Euro-American social science tradition: Pragmatism, realism and looking beyond the 'entrepreneur'. *Entrepreneurship & Regional Development, 25*, 16–33.

Welter, F., & Baker, D. (2021). Moving contexts onto new roads: Clues from other disciplines. *Entrepreneurship Theory and Practice, 45*(5), 1154–1175.

Welter, F., Baker, T., Audretsch, D. B., & Gartner, W. B. (2016). Everyday entrepreneurship: A call for entrepreneurship research to embrace entrepreneurial diversity. *Entrepreneurship Theory and Practice, 41*(3), 311–321.

14. Interviewing as social practice

Irina Liubertė and Miriam Feuls

INTRODUCTION

Entrepreneurship as practice (EaP) researchers routinely refer to interviews as a method of gathering research materials through talking to research participants. Entrepreneurial practices are often difficult to observe in real time – normative rules and knowledge of how to accomplish work are mostly tacit; practices are scattered over space and time; and actions can begin before we even recognize their entrepreneurial nature. Interviews are a proven way to learn about entrepreneurial phenomena; however, it is risky for EaP researchers to unconditionally import the methodological principles of other ontological traditions. Therefore, in this chapter we suggest and elaborate the principles of how interviewing practices may be adapted in line with the onto-epistemological assumptions of practice theory in EaP research.

Interviewing is not a homogeneous concept, and it is primarily used in two ways: interviewing as a 'research instrument' for collecting opinions and other cognitively generated content; and interviewing as a 'social practice' for co-creating accounts of 'truths' and negotiated meanings (Talmy, 2010a). The guiding principles of interviewing as social practice are very distinct but frequently confused with the principles of interviewing as a research instrument due to the latter being used as a dominant approach that stems from an individualist research tradition. In line with the interviews-as-an-instrument approach, interviews may be seen as artificial conversation – 'contrived' or 'cheap' talk that is inferior to observed 'events' (Atkinson & Coffey, 2003; Holstein & Gubrium, 1997; Jerolmack & Khan, 2014). Such treatment of interviews implies a Cartesian separation of mind and body, resulting in the impossibility of reconciling cognitive and sensual experiences, and this downgrades researchers to mere spectators of or inquirers into social practices (Dewey, 1960). Consequently, this suggests that it must be possible to learn about the totality of practices from observing what people do, which goes against practice theory assumptions. It is therefore not surprising that the reputation of interviews is accompanied by doubt as to their potential as a source for creating knowledge about entrepreneurial practices (Johannisson, 2011; Teague, Gorton, & Liu, 2020; Thompson & Byrne, 2020; Thompson, Verduijn, & Gartner, 2020). Indeed, using interviews as a research instrument to study entrepreneurial practices is highly problematic and potentially harmful to EaP research because the methodological and paradigmatic foundations of the method are not aligned with the purpose of the inquiry (Johannisson, 2011). However, the suitability of any methodology for learning about practices lies not in the specific methods (interviews or observation) used in order to create materials for the analysis, but in how researchers engage with these methods. Therefore, EaP researchers must not abandon interviewing but must move beyond the interview-as-an-instrument approach and adapt their interviewing practices to their onto-epistemological assumptions.

During an interview encounter and when analysing texts of and discussions with other people, EaP researchers inevitably face the difficulty of 'stepping into another person's shoes'. Researchers find themselves at the interface of their own and another person's world, which is a complex space to enter, as we only have direct access to our own thoughts or senses and never to those of another human being. However, this does not prohibit researchers from disclosing their reflective voices and engaging with the method – in this case, interviewing – as a social practice. Like any other practice, interviewing is a 'site of the social' (Schatzki, 2002) in which we navigate in an intersubjective knowledge plenum (Davidson, 2001). If understood this way, interviews are not merely texts and materials that are independently observed but are a social and collaborative accomplishment of both the researchers and the research participants (Deppermann, 2013; Silverman, 2006; Talmy, 2010a). However, few studies clarify the specific interviewing and analytic techniques that make interview materials useful to their practice-based research studies; some examples of these rare exceptions are the studies by Gherardi (2015) and Jones and Clifton (2018).

The methodological principles of what interviewing entails in EaP research are scant and call for more analysis. Therefore, in this chapter, we formulate the principles of how interviews may productively be used to explore entrepreneurial practices and offer methodological guidance to EaP researchers. We highlight the social and collaborative nature of interviewing, using 'interviewing' as opposed to 'interview' when we need to highlight the active and interactive nature of the practice as well as when we want to refer to the research process as a whole – considering all the steps involved in planning the study, carrying it out and analysing the research materials.

To begin this chapter, we summarize the use of interviews in extant EaP research and the criticism that the method receives. We then offer arguments from general theories of practice that help us to conceptualize interviewing as social practice: first, interviews as sites of social and collaborative practice and second, as spaces for the intersubjective co-creation of knowledge. We conclude our chapter by describing six methodological principles with empirical examples and links to other useful methodological resources. By using the methodological principles outlined further in this chapter, researchers may encourage their research participants to engage in the co-creation of knowledge and work together to articulate the knowledge that is embedded in entrepreneurial practices.

INTERVIEWS IN EXTANT ENTREPRENEURSHIP AS PRACTICE RESEARCH

EaP scholars favour qualitative methods in their research and they creatively draw on a variety of qualitative research methodologies. However, in line with other practice-based research streams and in order to explore social practices in their immediate contexts, EaP scholars prioritize ethnographic studies and observational techniques over interviews (see Champenois, Lefebvre, & Ronteau, 2020; Thompson & Byrne, 2020; Thompson et al., 2020). Ethnographic methods are seen as an experience-oriented method of exploring practices, enabling researchers to 'directly' observe the enactment of 'real' practices as well as to immerse themselves in the practice and not simply reconstruct it with words (Champenois et al., 2020; Thompson & Byrne, 2020). On the contrary, interviews are mostly seen as complementary to observations and are considered a less helpful way of reflecting upon the significance that practices have for entrepreneurs rather than learning about the practices themselves.

Even though interviews are criticized as being less suitable than observations for exploring practices, they are widely used in empirical EaP studies,[1] especially as part of a wider methodological repertoire. The use of interviews is argued as being necessary in order to explore people's perceptions, sense-making, histories and lived experiences, as well as the meanings they assign to their actions. They can also serve as a source for triangulation with observational data. During analysis, even with a focus on observation in ethnographic or quasi-ethnographic studies (Champenois et al., 2020), interviews may still be used as a primary source to substantiate findings and, on some occasions, also as a primary source of theoretical insight.

As highlighted in the introduction, it is important to understand how interviewing is used in practice-based research. However, we have only identified two empirical studies and one conceptual paper that explicitly refer to the ways in which interviews may be used to explore entrepreneurial practices. Jones and Clifton (2018) draw on narrative inquiry by Bamberg (2011) in order to study gendered identity work. The authors make use of interview materials by analysing them in three ways: looking at the interaction in the interview, analysing identity work in interview narratives and exploring how wider narrative contexts are enacted by such identity work. Thus, interviewing is seen as a social practice in which the broader contexts brought to interview encounters help researchers enrich their analysis. Similarly, Gherardi (2015, p. 654) in her analysis of female entrepreneuring, accounts not only for the language of interviews but also for the 'relationships between interviewee, text, and researchers'. Whereas Hill (2018) conceptualizes how nascent entrepreneurs negotiate entrepreneurial processes and suggests conducting open interviews that leave space for deep reflections – a co-creational approach to generating knowledge between researcher and research participant. These studies demonstrate that it is possible to trace wider entrepreneurial contexts through the analysis of interview narratives, as well as that the researcher and research participant are equal partners in the co-creation that occurs during their interaction and that this interaction matters very much in the interpretation of the interview materials.

The use of interviews to explore social practices in EaP research has been critiqued for three main reasons. The first point of the critique is related to the understanding that studying practices requires 'empirical proximity to the practice' (Thompson & Byrne, 2020). Champenois et al. (2020) argue that a practice-based interview methodology supports the meaning-making of specific entrepreneurial practices but they only classify interviews as 'relatively close to the field' (Champenois et al., 2020). Understood in this way, interviews are distant from the actual context of action and they prohibit direct access to real-time practical accomplishments (Thompson et al., 2020) or, as Campbell puts it, 'interviews […] are not able to showcase how entrepreneurs […] accomplish their shared work in context' (2019, p. 9). Related to the above is the second point of the critique: that humans know what they do and why, but are not immediately capable of reflecting on what their practices entail – the doings behind their actions (Thompson & Byrne, 2020). Such a definition of interviews promotes them as a tool that supports researchers in understanding the consciously acknowledged sides of practice (Thompson et al., 2020) – the cognitive, sense-making or retrospective accounts of human experiences (Thompson & Byrne, 2020) but not the affective, embodied or material sides of entrepreneurial practice. The third point of the critique relates to the limitations of interviews in studying interactions and performativity (Johannisson, 2011; Thompson & Byrne, 2020). Interviews are seen as a reflection of the practitioners' vocabulary and their sense-making of the emerging processes of entrepreneuring, whereas a practice-based approach should centre on the process itself, its pattern-making or its materialization in the form of a certain outcome.

To summarize, EaP researchers speak of interviews and use interviews in different ways. However, the methodological challenges of using interviews to explore social practices and the critique of interviews as a method are largely connected to the issues that arise from the use of interviews as a fact-collecting tool – interviews as a 'research instrument' (Talmy, 2010a). The shortcomings of interviews are seen in the fact that they are carried out in staged contexts and therefore only allow access to the cognitive and retrospective interpretations of what people do, which does not help researchers grasp the actual doings from a practice perspective. However, the limitations of interviews may be addressed when using a practice theory-based methodological and epistemological research framework – as demonstrated by the few studies mentioned, which explicitly refer to the social nature of interviewing. Observational data provides researchers with the observable elements of practices – watching bodies, materials and communication in action – whereas interviewing allows researchers to access the more tacit elements of practices. Thus, further in this chapter, we address the aforementioned critiques of interviews by building on practice theory and applying it to interviewing.

PRACTICE THEORY APPROACH TO INTERVIEWING

What aligns the variety of practice-based studies is their unified focus on practices, which are both their unit of analysis and the focal phenomenon of study. Individuals and their surroundings connect through what they do and say – thus, both material and discursive practices matter. In the following section, we build on general theories of practice and discuss interviewing as being designed to narratively co-create what people think, feel, do and say, as well as something that constitutes a social site for intersubjective knowledge co-creation.

Interviewing as Site of the Social

Practices are 'materially mediated arrays of human activity centrally organized around shared practical understanding' and are social by nature (Schatzki, 2001, p. 11). Practices are interconnected and form 'bundles'. Activities, language, meaning, knowledge and other phenomena are parts of these bundles and represent the site of the social, in which social reality takes place (Schatzki, 2001, 2002). Additionally, practices are organized by several other social phenomena, which Schatzki defines as the following: first, practical understanding – comprehensibility of the practices; second, general understanding – assigning practices to a broader context, or the 'why' of doings and sayings; third, rules that refer to 'what' has to be done in certain circumstances in a non-judgemental but orienting way; lastly, teleo-affective structures that organize practices through affective and purposive engagement – the 'how' of practice, for example, purposes, projects, tasks, emotions and moods (Schatzki, 2002). As per Schatzki (2017), language, sayings and discourses belong to these organized nexuses of action and imply that they are guided by the same phenomena as material actions are.

So, when we speak of interviewing as a site of the social, there are several elements to consider. First and foremost, scholars are practitioners themselves – they are defined by their practices. Second, interviewing is part of a bundle of practices – what researchers and research participants do and say in their interaction is inextricably intertwined with their daily practices and each one is guided by their own practical understanding and purpose as well as by peer pressure and affective engagement. Third, both the researcher and the research participant go through a range of emotions – each experiencing their own hesitations, questioning what is taking place in the room and wondering how it is relevant to their own understanding of the interviewing practice. Fourth, interviewing is connected to and depends on both the researcher's and research participant's normative judgements of what the rules of the practice are – who needs to act, what they need to say, when and how they need to do it. The two parties in an interview do not necessarily have a similar understanding of these things and they negotiate their understandings during the interview: interviewing involves a process of establishing a shared understanding that begins with the introductory exchanges and carries on throughout the entire interaction. Lastly, interviewing comprises a material dimension expressed through bodily movements (e.g. gestures or facial expressions) and artefacts (e.g. interview guide, recording device). Thus, interviewing is not only a linguistic representation, but a 'language-in-use' (Schatzki, 2017) that is made up of the different contexts in which researcher and research participant act according to the elements of their own practice and in relation to the contexts.

In interviewing, knowledge is created through the negotiated meanings (Gherardi, 2008) of researcher and research participant – it is 'both sustained in practice and manifests itself through practice' (Nicolini, 2011, p. 602). Interviewing as a site of the social connects multiple sites of knowing (Nicolini, 2011) and offers an empirical ground on which to capture situational wisdom and its connectedness to the broader realms of practice (Gherardi, 2001, 2008). The challenge then remains of how to demonstrate and make believable that what we communicate as 'true' meaning through capturing the utterances and bodily engagement of research participants is not what we ourselves wish and believe to be true, but what is truthful for both parties as well as for our reader. We discuss this further as intersubjective knowledge co-creation.

Interviewing as Intersubjective Knowledge Co-Creation

In the Cartesian tradition, mind and body are separate entities and it is impossible to reconcile the asymmetry between the direct knowing of your own mind and the indirect knowing of other people's minds (Davidson, 2001). Drawing on the Cartesian perspective, the physical environment becomes external and 'foreign' to one's own understanding. Interviewing is therefore a meeting of two foreigners in which one party – the research participant – brings their knowledge, and the other – the researcher – attempts to acquire it and learn about the true body of the research participant's knowledge. The knowledge of the physical environment in which the researcher and participants actually perform their work is left behind: it cannot be transferred into the interview situation.

In contrast, in practice theory terms, practices connect knowledge, bodies and their material contexts, and researchers use different kinds of knowledge to inform themselves about different aspects of practice. Davidson (2001) distinguishes among three types of knowledge: subjective (first person), intersubjective (second person) and objective (third person). First-person knowledge is what people think, want, intend and feel, and it is accessible to them directly; second-person knowledge is the knowledge of another person's mind; lastly, third-person knowledge is our interaction with the environment through our senses. All three types of knowledge concern the same reality.

Drawing on Davidson's three types of knowledge, a discrepancy lies in the traditional approach to interviews as a research instrument in that research participants are seen as coping with their reality (first-person knowledge) while researchers reflect and interpret this new knowledge through their senses or, in other words, take a detached scientific approach to a research participant's reality (third-person knowledge). This way, researchers become 'objective' observers of the interviewees. The reality as it unfolds during the interaction between researchers and research participants (second-person or intersubjective knowledge) is put aside as an unfeasible source of learning about the practices of the research participants. Consequently, interviewing wrongly appears to be a way of reducing one type of knowledge (first person) to another type (third person) – even though, according to Davidson (2001), this is impossible.

There is no fundamental distinction between subjective and objective spaces because all knowledge 'could for the most part be expressed by concepts which have a place in a publicly shared scheme of things' (Davidson, 2001, p. xiii). All three types of knowledge concern the same object of research inquiry (e.g. practices) and allow us to learn about different aspects of practice. Thus, from a practice theory perspective, there is no reduction of one type of knowledge to the other type and interviewing does not have to be a method of accomplishing this reduction. Instead, interviewing is a complex practice in which researchers create an intersubjective practice space and collaborate with their research participants in the creation of new knowledge. Researchers can only demonstrate the 'truth' and communicate the meaning of their interview materials on their own normative ground.

We argue that interviewing as it is accepted in 'normalized sciences' is not appropriate for the exploration of social practices and it needs to be revised to suit the EaP research approach, which invites research participants to collaborate in the knowledge-creation process (Johannisson, 2011). Research participants need their voices to be heard but they are not a passive vessel of the knowledge they impart – they are active participants too. In the process of interviewing, researchers alternate between the use of first- and second-person knowledge, as do the research participants. The power and potential for the analysis of interview materials and the created artefacts is not in that this is 'true' knowledge of a (first-) person or that it may be objectively assessed by another (third-) person, but in that it is a co-creation of (intersubjective) reality in practice.

Based on what we discussed above, interviewing as social practice is an interactive, purposeful and affective engagement that allows for the co-creation of knowledge by researchers and research participants; it is situated at the crossroads of contexts that are brought into the interview encounter from both sides. Interviewing as social practice moves away from trying to resolve the divide between first- and third-person knowledge. The attempt to reduce one type of knowledge to another loses meaning if we appreciate the multiplicity of knowledge types related to the same reality – the kinds of knowledge we use to create and build our methodologies, guided by the general principles of practice theory.

METHODOLOGICAL PRINCIPLES OF INTERVIEWING AS SOCIAL PRACTICE

Conceptualizing interviewing as social practice means recognizing the interactive elements of interviewing and scrutinizing the performance or 'hows' of interviewing (Holstein & Gubrium, 1997). Guided by concerns about the feasibility of interviews to study practices (as analysed in the first section of this chapter) and the practice theory approach to interviewing (established in the second section), we determine six essential principles of interviewing as social practice that offer methodological reflections and guidance with regard to the interview encounter and subsequent analysis. We start with three principles that are focused on how researchers can help their research participants reveal their practices during the interview encounter (*by creating an open space for stories, prioritizing the language of research participants* and *using verbs*). We then present three principles that stem from an actual interview encounter but are more relevant to the analysis of interview materials (by *appreciating the holistic and multimodal nature of interviewing* and *reflexively interacting*).

The First Principle: Creating an Open Space for Stories

To reduce the inherent pressure of being questioned and create an open space in which research participants can freely share their stories, we can make use of different interviewing techniques. Some well-known examples of suitable interviewing techniques are conversational interviews, in which researchers rely on their interaction with research participants (Turner III, 2010), as well as 'life' or 'verbal' histories (for guidance, see e.g. McKenzie, 2007). The use of these techniques enables research participants to bring up their own stories (Gherardi, 2019) and it helps open up the space for the co-creation of narrative knowledge (Bruner, 1990). When dealing with complex phenomena like practices, stories are extremely helpful in understanding their roots (Czarniawska-Joerges, 1992) as well as the broader contexts in which they take place. Additionally, story-telling techniques, which largely rely on the natural flow of a story, facilitate the generation of rich contextual detail, which both complicates and enriches the research. On the one hand, research participants provide a variety of stories and create a wide range of knowledge in which it is not immediately clear what is most relevant to the research inquiry; on the other hand, with this method, research participants tend not to filter out the stories they see as 'irrelevant' based on their understanding of the research topic. Researchers must therefore apply their judgement as to what kind of knowledge is valuable to their research study.

Furthermore, knowing-in-practice researchers use a projective interviewing technique called 'interview to the double'. This is a technique in which researchers ask research participants to imagine that they have a double who has to replace them at work the next day and to whom they have to explain everything they do during their workday (for full methodological details, see Gherardi, 2019; Nicolini, 2009). According to Nicolini (2009) this technique supports the multifaceted presentation of practices, not only by providing a detailed description of activities, but also by taking into account the context in which practices unfold. Many other projective techniques may be used to engage research participants, such as 'think-aloud' or critical incident (for more information, see the Apprentice Genre interviews in Langley & Meziani, 2020) or using other language, drawing or acting exercises during interviews. These techniques are well known in personality psychology and are used in that field to tap into the underlying processes beneath the surface, but they are not yet widely used in researching entrepreneurial practices. One recent example of using metaphors and drawing, along with follow-up interviews, to study entrepreneurial identities is the study by Clarke and Holt (2017), as well as a subsequent study which expands on their methodological approach in the first study (Clarke & Holt, 2019). Although the authors focus more on the 'experiences' of entrepreneurs, the art-based techniques applied are valuable in exploring entrepreneurial practices as well, as they relieve the tension which stems from the necessity of responding to research inquiry during an interview, and allow people to creatively 'tell' stories about their daily practices through a medium – a drawing, a piece of writing or a role play. This engagement in the creation of material objects facilitates the creation of an open-ended space, helps mitigate the pressure of the interview situation and encourages spontaneous performances, which, we argue, are helpful to EaP researchers in studying entrepreneurial practices.

The Second Principle: Prioritizing the Language of Research Participants

When interviewing, 'a partly shielded situation' is created in which 'both parties agree to enter into a particular communicative form' (Cruickshank, 2012, p. 43) that suppresses other communicative forms. However, the meaning that can be drawn from interview materials lies not only within the interview situation and context but also outside of it (Chalmers & Shaw, 2017; Gee & Green, 1998); in other words, the performative aspects of entrepreneurial practices may be traced by attending to those broader contexts. The potential to gain an understanding of the hidden layers of entrepreneurial practices depends upon how we allow the broader entrepreneurial contexts to enter the interview situation – and this can be done through prioritizing the language of research participants. For example, practice-related knowledge is co-created when researchers allow themselves to maintain their curiosity about the ordinary and encourage research participants to talk about what may seem like boring, day-to-day, common-sense parts of their activities (Smagacz-Poziemska, Bukowski, & Martini, 2021). The less researchers are able to reveal about their own interpretations, the more space they leave for the research participant's voice.

One technique that helps in prioritizing the language of research participants includes a type of probing that relies on the research participant's linguistic repertoire. This probing technique is based on a psychological counselling technique and is not specific to practice-based qualitative interviewing; however, it is useful when probing for more details, as shown in the example provided below. The example is an extract from an interview in which the first author of this chapter is speaking with an entrepreneur and probing him about secrecy in his interaction with his partners in the biotechnology industry (Liubertė, 2018b):

> **Research participant**: '… they did not even tell us what [materials] they used. We create them a graph [that reflects the result of an experiment], provide them, and they say – oh, it is perfect.'
>
> **Researcher**: '*you say, they did not even tell [you] what they used?*'
>
> **Research participant**: 'Yes, they may tell us – we give you protein X. And that is it, and you can't do anything. With protein X you got 16, and with protein Y you got 18, and with protein Z you got 25. And they look then – ah, very good, it is as it should be. Or, the other way round – hah, why it is so, we will try now to think what is wrong in here. And that is it.' [Continues explaining the details of his interaction with the partner]

In this example, at first, the research participant offers a brief description of 'what' the practice is but does not reveal specific details about the interaction with his partners. By repeating the research participant's own phrase (italicized above) and not finishing the sentence, the researcher remains within the language of the research participant and invites him to provide a more detailed response. The research participant then offers an extended explanation of 'how' their partners enact the 'not telling' ('they did not even tell us', in the first response), which actually includes some 'telling' ('they may tell us', in response to the probing) and their own response to it in a codified form (naming products X, Y and Z). Such probing was useful to uncover the paradox laid in the practices that include both telling and not telling, and which may not have been realized if the researcher had tried to impose their linguistic repertoires when probing.

Furthermore, the example brings to our attention that it is important to consider not only the answers, but also the questions themselves, as well as the way in which these questions are asked during the interviews. If researchers articulate their questions using very different language than that of the research participants, the participants may then attempt to imitate the researcher's language or even become incapable of answering a query (read more on this in De Fina, 2009).

The Third Principle: Using Verbs

Interviewing is a dual practice: researchers create an open space in which research participants can use their own language but, at the same time, they still determine the rules of the practice and can deliberately use their influence to create language that is more favourable to creating practice-related knowledge. They can probe for specific examples of how people do things and, when doing so, it is beneficial to use verbs in interview questions. When using verbs, researchers encourage research participants to use more verbs too and, this way, divert their story-telling to what they do instead of who they are or what things should be like – so they are speaking in actions rather than 'entities'. There are also questions that are suitable for setting the tone of an interview, such as 'what do you do in a typical day' (referring to a person's actions) that are broad enough but still action oriented. Though this may not always be an easy journey – some people might switch to explaining who they are, begin describing their practice in a generic way, or even decide it is too personal to talk about what they do and pay no heed to the persistence of the interviewer.

Of course, not all languages are convenient for using verbs. Some, like English, have a gerund and present participle form of the verb (-ing) that are ideal to use in order to turn a conversation to discussing actions. Others, such as Lithuanian or German, express action in nouns and the nouns quickly turn a conversation to speaking about 'entities'; therefore, more mastery and 'workarounds' are required in order to identify probing words that would elicit answers about practices.

During analysis, researchers must build their strategy around the kinds of narrative, story-telling or coding techniques that have successfully captured actions, and consequently practices. One of the suitable coding techniques is process coding, which uses the gerund to connote action in interview materials, and which can be used both as sole technique and in combination with other analysis techniques. See more about 'active codes' in 'The logic of initial coding' chapter in Charmaz (2014) and the 'Process coding' chapter in Saldaña (2009).

The Fourth Principle: Appreciating the Holistic Nature of Interviewing

The strategies for the analysis of interviews often include some kind of coding – looking for themes and patterns in interview materials. Coding strategies are necessary in many cases and there is nothing wrong with them per se, but the use of coding may be dangerous in that it limits the researcher's attention to narrow segments of the interview materials. However, in interviews, responses to some research queries may not be immediate but delayed and may emerge over the course of conversation (Bakhtin, 1986). Therefore, the analysis of research materials must be accompanied by a more holistic approach to the research materials.

Integrating different parts of interviews may be accomplished through writing reflective research dairies, (re-)reading, (re-)analysing and appending them with new insights. When a respondent deviates from the planned flow of conversation, this may serve as a hint to the researcher as to where to explore to find out how different parts of the interviews are connected. For example, when discussing collaboration practices in one of the interviews in the first author's research (Liubertė, 2018b), a research participant was asked the same question several times but still deviated from the topic:

> I asked the research participant, '*can you please tell me more about the meetings that you mentioned earlier?*' but the answer quickly turned into sharing vivid examples about the conferences which I thought was an excursus to a different topic, and inquired again '*getting back to the meetings ...*'. The research participant continued '*oh, to the meetings ...*' but went on speaking about conferences two more times. At the end of the interview, he apologetically reminded himself that he was supposed to speak about their project meetings and not conferences. The meetings, though, he described without going into detail. *(Based on the interview transcript and the researcher's notes.)*

The example above illustrates how a research participant persistently replaced answering questions about project meetings, which are a dedicated space for collaboration, and substituted discussing the sharing of knowledge during these meetings with talking about his experiences during conferences. Curious about this segue, the author read over the whole interview multiple times and picked out how other parts of the conversation could have been relevant to the conferences, wrote multiple reflective notes on this topic and discussed it with other people. The analysis suggested that the conferences were a meaningful space for collaboration and that they largely replaced the function of the project group's meetings for this respondent, even if not explicitly acknowledged as such. Interviewing provided leads as to what the participant regarded as a significant space for collaborative practices, while observation would have yielded only a fraction of the practices that are observable during the project meetings. In connection to the overall flow of the interview, the analysis productively expanded the repertoire of collaboration spaces and, with it, extended the range of relevant practices to probe in subsequent interviews. Here, we illustrate just one way of tracing practices through going back to the interview as a whole; however, the methods of doing this are very individual and may depend on the interview context and the practices that are being explored.

The Fifth Principle: Appreciating the Multimodal Nature of Interviewing

A common practice is for interviews to be first recorded, then transcribed and then analysed using only the written transcripts. However, the transcription is already an interpretation and the choice of what to analyse and interpret is made by what is written down and how (Bucholtz, 2000; Ochs, 1979). Thus, not only the transcript, but also the original notes during and after an interview, as well as the audio or video recordings themselves are important sources of insight. The original recording of an interview is often the most neglected part of the research materials. In order to enhance the reflexivity and multiplicity of their interpretation, Revsbæk (2018) calls on researchers to listen to their interview recordings more than once as a standard practice.

Moreover, the observations of bodily and material engagement during interviewing is an additional source of insight. These are especially useful when the interview is conducted in the spaces in which the research participants' daily actions normally take place. For example, in one of the interviews (unpublished source by the first author), an entrepreneur was talking about his daily routine – filling out forms, writing to someone, revising documents, sending them out to someone else, and so on. The researcher also observed, and later reflected on in her notes, how the person spoke:

> While [the person] was talking, he sat by his working desk, his usual working place, and touched different papers, shelves – apparently related to the routine paperwork he was trying to describe in words. At a certain point, he turned his eyes from his table and his gaze was briefly distant, as if he were looking through the wall. The direction he looked in was the same as where his R&D laboratory room was. Then [the person] apologetically noted that he has no time for his invention at all. He turned his head to the researcher and provided a 'conclusion' of this elaborate story about his paperwork, which could briefly be summarized as 'you see, it is all about money'. *(Based on the researcher's notes.)*

The observation of this particular body language and other participants' bodily involvement during interviews, in combination with how the entrepreneurs expressed their activities in words, led to the realization that their daily practices, in fact, may mean being distant from the pursuit of opportunity (by creating their technology) but are nevertheless necessary in order to obtain support for their ideas. In the provided example, the entrepreneur did not reflect directly on the tensions in his daily practice; however, the complex of interaction, language and bodily involvement helped imply the non-immediate meanings of the entrepreneur's daily practices.

Convenient analysis strategies (e.g. coding) often lead us to prioritize transcripts, which exclude the actual interaction during the interview. It is also common to draw a clear line between the methods of text analysis (e.g. coding) and discourse analysis. Each holds different aims in itself – one reaches for the meaning to describe the essence of a research inquiry, and the other examines the language instruments research participants use to express the content. In interviewing as social practice, this hard distinction loses its value: the content has no value without the sensory information – how people recount things adds additional context and is an extra resource for analysis and interpretation.

The Sixth Principle: Reflexively Interacting

According to Nicolini, '[w]hen we study practice we thus always scrutinize two practices at the same time: our epistemic practice, and what we are concerned with' (Nicolini, 2009, pp. 196–197). In practice research, authors cannot choose to vanish from their analyses and texts (Golden-Biddle & Locke, 2007) due to the whole situated performance of interviewing as a result of interaction, which depends equally on researchers and research participants. We are not able to reconstruct entrepreneurial practices from a first-person view, whether it be our own or another person's entrepreneurial practices (Dimov & Pistrui, 2020). However, we can provide a more interactive account of entrepreneurial narratives from a second-person view (Davidson, 2001). Reflexivity about the interaction and our own participation as researchers in interviewing is essential in order to appreciate the complexity of an interview encounter.

Reflexivity in interviewing as social practice is not only about the interpretation of what a research participant says and does during an interview, it is also about the researcher's own input and, most importantly, about the encounter between the two of them. Scrutinizing 'what' happens and 'how' in interviewing is a contribution to research insights (Holstein & Gubrium, 1997). One of the interviews, which served as a basis for a case study by the first author (Liubertė, 2018a), is a vivid example of a reflexive interview encounter, which later provided input into the analysis of secrecy practices. The idea for this case study arose after one particularly difficult online interview with a biotechnology entrepreneur. The research participant did not feel comfortable with the conversation with the researcher, which also triggered tension and negative emotional reactions in the researcher: '*the minutes I spent just then felt worthless and I wished this interview had never happened to me*' (from the research diary which was later also used in the case analysis). The case uses conversational analysis techniques (see Campbell, Chapter 10 in this volume) to examine the researcher's responses to the participant's unfolding concerns and uncertainties, thereby exploring how the interview progressed. The analysis of this interaction led to the identification of two sources of the tension that has persisted throughout the interview: questions that are simultaneously 'too broad' and 'too specific', and the difficulty of separating social interaction (the focus of the interview) from technical information (potentially sensitive information) in his stories about his entrepreneuring. The insights that were related to the interview situation and interaction were also relevant to the investigation: the communication between entrepreneurs and their collaborative partners is also an interstitial space between speaking too broadly (not useful) and too specifically (dangerous to reveal confidential information). As can be seen from the example, reflexivity regarding the interaction during an interview may be helpful in figuring out the potential tensions that entrepreneurs experience in their daily lives.

CONCLUSIONS

It is critical for EaP scholars to consider the advances that practice theory offers (Thompson et al., 2020) not only in terms of formulating theoretical arguments but also in terms of accessing and analysing empirical phenomena. Attention is primarily directed towards the entrepreneurial practices of interest and the breadth of methodological approaches used to examine them; however, much greater consideration is required for the research practices themselves, such as interviewing, and the depth of their methodological approaches. Therefore, in this chapter we guided through the current use of interviewing in EaP research and the principles of practice theory in order to present a revised understanding of interviewing in practice theory terms.

As previously pointed out, the literature discusses interviewing from two different perspectives: (1) as a 'research instrument' and (2) as a 'social practice'. The first perspective sees interviewing as a research tool for collecting information from research participants: accounts of facts, attitudes and other cognitive representations. The analysis involved in this view then assumes a rather straightforward summary of the findings from the interview materials, which 'speak for themselves' (Talmy, 2010a). Conversely, the second perspective acknowledges interviews as social, collaborative and practical accomplishments, and is in line with the epistemological and ontological realm of practice theory. As such, interviewing is not a free-standing technique, but is a part of an analytically defined (practice theory) perspective (Silverman, 1998). Interviews are participatory encounters that include the interactional, multimodal, narrative and indirect elements and contexts that are brought into action (Gherardi, 2019; Holstein & Gubrium, 1997; Nicolini, 2009; Talmy, 2010b). Furthermore, researchers are not controlling bias and validating the 'truth' of research participants' accounts, rather they are grasping the elements of the knowledge that is actively and reflectively co-created. Thus, the purpose of interviewing is not to reproduce accounts of visible practices – these, as it was previously discussed, are more effectively observed and understood through participatory involvement and observation. On the contrary, interviewing allows researchers to grasp the hidden layers of practices, which are not easily accessible through observation (Deppermann, 2013) and which remain tacit for practitioners in their daily practice. Interviewing can be seen as an intervention that stimulates reflection about otherwise invisible elements of practices (Langley & Meziani, 2020). Nevertheless, interviewing should be approached with caution and should not be interpreted as a reflection of reality, as is done in the interview-as-research-instrument approach.

Drawing on practice theory, we argue that a depth of understanding can be achieved by exploiting the interactive and multimodal nature of interviewing; connecting discursive content with affective and bodily (material) aspects as they manifest during and outside of interview situations; and applying a second-person view that allows for the co-creation of knowledge. Consequently, the aforementioned critique actually becomes the strength of interviewing if looking through a practice theory lens.

To help EaP researchers efficiently identify and make use of the potential of interviewing as social practice, we present six essential principles of this method:

1. Creating an open space for stories, which refers to a favourable climate in which research participants can address what is important in their point of view rather than the researcher's.
2. Prioritizing the language of research participants, which refers to the deliberate support of the research participant's communicative forms as they manifest in interaction in order to facilitate the co-creation of knowledge about practices.
3. Using verbs, which refers to directing research participants to actively discuss what they do in order to avoid generalizations or speaking in 'entities'.
4. Appreciating the holistic nature of interviewing, which refers to looking at the bigger picture when analysing an interview situation in order to connect the pieces of the 'puzzle' that are scattered throughout the interview.
5. Appreciating the multimodal nature of interviewing, which refers to apprehending the bodily, material and affective elements of interviewing in order to 'read between the lines' of the immediate linguistic contents.
6. Reflexively interacting, which refers to accounting for both the researcher's and research participant's doings and sayings during the interaction in order to identify the connection between different contexts.

There is no one method fit for all. Interviewing as social practice gives us access to the layers of practices that are not observable: researchers and research participants engage and co-create knowledge during an interview. The method demands embeddedness and a reflective process of creating research materials – sound or video recordings for interpretation. Therefore, the principles of interviewing as social practice are more easily adapted for use in multi-method studies, in which we create research materials of multiple types. The complementarity of methods, though, does not infer the superiority of any of these methods of accessing, creating or analysing research materials and does not bestow superiority on any of the aspects of practices that we learn about from these different sources. Additionally, in this chapter, we assumed a dyadic interaction between a researcher and a research participant, as well as that the researcher would be the same person as the interviewer. There may certainly be other research study designs in which more than two people participate in the interaction; or in which a team of researchers combine their efforts and the interviewer and the analyst are not the same person. Such methodological approaches are not different in principle yet they do add complexity due to the multiplicity of the interactions.

Our contribution to EaP research is the development of a methodological approach to interviewing as social practice that is grounded in the principles of practice theory. This approach addresses the ways in which the method may be used to address the needs of EaP researchers. A knowledge of practices without learning about these practices from the people who enact them is incomplete. Therefore, by using the methodological principles of interviewing as social practice, a deeper theoretical understanding of entrepreneurial practices can be achieved.

NOTE

1. To analyse how interviews are used in extant empirical EaP research, we drew on 51 empirical EaP-related papers: 48 studies published between 2002 and 2018 and analysed in Champenois et al. (2020) and three studies published after 2018 – Teague et al. (2020), Sabella and El-Far (2019) and Ramírez-Pasillas, Lundberg and Nordqvist (2021). We sampled the additional three studies based on the list of journals used by the authors of the original review. Of these 51 articles, 39 draw on interview materials (27 use interviews along with observation or secondary data and 12 – as a single method), four articles used observational methods without interviews and eight draw exclusively on secondary materials. Two of these articles – Gherardi (2015) and Jones and Clifton (2018) – use interviews in the way that is relevant to interviewing as a social and interactive practice.

REFERENCES

Atkinson, P., & Coffey, A. (2003). Revisiting the relationship between participant observation and interviewing. In J. A. Holstein & J. F. Gubrium (Eds.), *Inside Interviewing: New Lenses, New Concerns* (pp. 415–428). Thousand Oaks, CA: Sage.

Bakhtin, M. (Ed.) (1986). *Speech Genres and Other Late Essays*. Austin: University of Texas Press.

Bamberg, M. (2011). Narrative practice and identity navigation. In J. A. Holstein & J. F. Gubrium (Eds.), *Varieties of Narrative Analysis* (pp. 99–124). Thousand Oaks, CA: Sage.

Bruner, J. S. (1990). *Acts of Meaning* (Vol. 3). Cambridge, MA: Harvard University Press.

Bucholtz, M. (2000). The politics of transcription. *Journal of Pragmatics, 32*(10), 1439–1465.

Campbell, B. (2019). *Practice Theory in Action: Empirical Studies of Interaction in Innovation and Entrepreneurship*. Abingdon: Routledge.

Chalmers, D., & Shaw, E. (2017). The endogenous construction of entrepreneurial contexts: A practice-based perspective. *International Small Business Journal, 35*, 19–39.

Champenois, C., Lefebvre, V., & Ronteau, S. (2020). Entrepreneurship as practice: Systematic literature review of a nascent field. *Entrepreneurship & Regional Development, 32*(3–4), 281–312.

Charmaz, K. (2014). *Constructing Grounded Theory*. London: Sage.

Clarke, J., & Holt, R. (2017). Imagery of ad-venture: Understanding entrepreneurial identity through metaphor and drawing. *Journal of Business Venturing, 32*(5), 476–497.

Clarke, J., & Holt, R. (2019). Images of entrepreneurship: Using drawing to explore entrepreneurial experience. *Journal of Business Venturing Insights, 11*, e00129. https://doi.org/10.1016/j.jbvi.2019.e00129.

Cruickshank, J. (2012). The role of qualitative interviews in discourse theory. *Critical Approaches to Discourse Analysis Across Disciplines, 6*(1), 38–52.

Czarniawska-Joerges, B. (1992). *Exploring Complex Organizations*. London: Sage.

Davidson, D. (2001). *Subjective, Intersubjective, Objective*. Oxford: Clarendon Press.

De Fina, A. (2009). Narratives in interview–the case of accounts: For an interactional approach to narrative genres. *Narrative Inquiry, 19*(2), 233–258.

Deppermann, A. (2013). Interviews als Text vs. Interviews als Social Interaction. *Forum qualitative Sozialforschung: FQS = Forum: Qualitative Social Research, 14*(3). https://doi.org/10.17169/fqs-14 .3.2064.

Dewey, J. (1960). *The Quest for Certainty*. New York: G. P. Putnam's Sons.

Dimov, D., & Pistrui, J. (2020). Recursive and discursive model of and for entrepreneurial action. *European Management Review, 17*(1), 267–277.

Gee, J. P., & Green, J. L. (1998). Chapter 4: Discourse analysis, learning, and social practice: A methodological study. *Review of Research in Education, 23*(1), 119–169.

Gherardi, S. (2001). From organizational learning to practice-based knowing. *Human Relations, 54*(1), 131–139.

Gherardi, S. (2008). Situated knowledge and situated action: What do practice-based studies promise? In D. Barry & H. Hansen (Eds.), *The SAGE Handbook of New Approaches in Management and Organization* (pp. 516–525). London: Sage.

Gherardi, S. (2015). Authoring the female entrepreneur while talking the discourse of work–family life balance. *International Small Business Journal, 33*(6), 649–666.

Gherardi, S. (2019). *How to Conduct a Practice-Based Study: Problems and Methods* (2nd edition). Cheltenham, UK and Northampton, MA, USA: Edward Elgar Publishing.

Golden-Biddle, K., & Locke, K. (2007). *Composing Qualitative Research* (2nd edition). Thousand Oaks, CA: Sage.

Hill, I. (2018). How did you get up and running? Taking a Bourdieuan perspective towards a framework for negotiating strategic fit. *Entrepreneurship & Regional Development, 30*(5–6), 662–696.

Holstein, J., & Gubrium, J. (1997). Active interviewing. In E. Silverman (Ed.), *Qualitative Research: Theory, Method and Practice* (pp. 113–129). London: Sage.

Jerolmack, C., & Khan, S. (2014). Talk is cheap: Ethnography and the attitudinal fallacy. *Sociological Methods & Research, 43*(2), 178–209.

Johannisson, B. (2011). Towards a practice theory of entrepreneuring. *Small Business Economics, 36*(2), 135–150.

Jones, K., & Clifton, J. (2018). Rendering sexism invisible in workplace narratives: A narrative analysis of female entrepreneurs' stories of not being talked to by men. *Gender, Work & Organization, 25*(5), 557–574.

Langley, A., & Meziani, N. (2020). Making interviews meaningful. *The Journal of Applied Behavioral Science, 56*(3), 370–391.

Liubertė, I. (2018a). Dealing with uncertainty in communication: A reflective account on talking about knowledge sharing and secrecy with an entrepreneur having secretive concerns. Paper presented at the ESU 2018 Conference and doctoral program on entrepreneurship: New Trends in European Research, Lodz, Poland.

Liubertė, I. (2018b). Organizing secrecy in inter-firm cooperation. Paper presented at the 78th Annual Meeting of the Academy of Management, Chicago, Illinois.

McKenzie, B. (2007). Techniques for collecting verbal histories. In H. Neergaard & J. P. Ulhoi (Eds.), *Handbook of Qualitative Research Methods in Entrepreneurship* (pp. 308–330). Cheltenham, UK and Northampton, MA, USA: Edward Elgar Publishing.

Nicolini, D. (2009). Articulating practice through the interview to the double. *Management Learning, 40*(2), 195–212.

Nicolini, D. (2011). Practice as the site of knowing: Insights from the field of telemedicine. *Organization Science, 22*(3), 602–620.

Ochs, E. (1979). Transcription as theory. In E. Ochs & B. Schieffelin (Eds.), *Developmental Pragmatics* (pp. 43–72). New York: Academic Press.

Ramírez-Pasillas, M., Lundberg, H., & Nordqvist, M. (2021). Next generation external venturing practices in family owned businesses. *Journal of Management Studies, 58*(1), 63–103.

Revsbæk, L. (2018). Resonant experience in emergent events of analysis. *Qualitative Studies, 5*(1), 24–36.

Sabella, A. R., & El-Far, M. T. (2019). Entrepreneuring as an everyday form of resistance. *International Journal of Entrepreneurial Behavior & Research, 25*(6), 1212–1235.

Saldaña, J. (2009). *The Coding Manual for Qualitative Researchers*. Los Angeles: Sage.

Schatzki, T. R. (2001). Practice theory: An introduction. In T. R. Schatzki, K. K. Cetina, & E. von Savigny (Eds.), *The Practice Turn in Contemporary Theory* (pp. 1–14). London: Routledge.

Schatzki, T. R. (2002). *The Site of the Social: A Philosophical Account of the Constitution of Social Life and Change.* University Park: Pennsylvania State University Press.

Schatzki, T. R. (2017). Sayings, texts and discursive formations. In A. Hui, C. R. Schwenk, & E. Shove (Eds.), *The Nexus of Practices: Connections, Constellations, Practitioners* (pp. 126–140). New York: Routledge.

Silverman, D. (1998). Qualitative research: Meanings or practices? *Information Systems Journal, 8*(1), 3–20.

Silverman, D. (2006). *Interpreting Qualitative Data: Methods for Analyzing Talk, Text and Interaction.* London: Sage.

Smagacz-Poziemska, M., Bukowski, A., & Martini, N. (2021). Social practice research in practice: Some methodological challenges in applying practice-based approach to the urban research. *International Journal of Social Research Methodology, 24*(1), 65–78.

Talmy, S. (2010a). The interview as collaborative achievement: Interaction, identity, and ideology in a speech event. *Applied Linguistics, 32*(1), 25–42.

Talmy, S. (2010b). Qualitative interviews in applied linguistics: From research instrument to social practice. *Annual Review of Applied Linguistics, 30*, 128–148.

Teague, B. T., Gorton, M. D., & Liu, Y. (2020). Different pitches for different stages of entrepreneurial development: The practice of pitching to business angels. *Entrepreneurship & Regional Development, 32*(3–4), 334–352.

Thompson, N. A., & Byrne, O. (2020). Advancing entrepreneurship as practice: Previous developments and future possibilities. In W. B. Gartner & B. T. Teague (Eds.), *Research Handbook on Entrepreneurial Behavior, Practice and Process* (pp. 30–55). Cheltenham, UK and Northampton, MA, USA: Edward Elgar Publishing.

Thompson, N. A., Verduijn, K., & Gartner, W. B. (2020). Entrepreneurship-as-practice: Grounding contemporary theories of practice into entrepreneurship studies. *Entrepreneurship & Regional Development, 32*(3–4), 247–256.

Turner III, D. W. (2010). Qualitative interview design: A practical guide for novice investigators. *The Qualitative Report, 15*(3), 754–760.

15. Capturing entrepreneurial practices' socio-materiality with ethnography-based research

Inge Hill

CONCEPTUALIZATIONS OF PRACTICES AND SOCIO-MATERIALITY

During my journey of becoming a socio-material researcher, I would have benefited from clarity as to the ontological choices the researcher needs to make before embarking on designing research questions and methodologies. For example, I made the following notes upon entering my research site:

> When I enter the research site through the black metal gates I always feel as if a time machine has transported me to a different time. Old, dark, grey single-storey buildings surround the main modern two-floor-building hosting the shop. The resident artisan entrepreneurs work in these small old buildings, built long before double glazing and insulation were invented, fighting with the seasons and temperature. Today it simply feels damp inside the artist's studio, as the electric heater has not been running for long. Since my last visit, three cigarette butts have been added to the six in the corner of studio 4.

Variance type research has dominated entrepreneurship research for decades, giving an impression of a static, disconnected interaction between institutions, individuals and processes, with variables influencing business performance. This perspective could be labelled a 'from without' viewpoint (Langley & Tsoukas, 2017); it would be helpful if these researchers were to make their ontological assumptions obvious, instead of hiding them under a cloud of 'objectivity'. Thus, differentiating the ontological perspectives and research assumptions at the start of the research is essential.

The term 'practice' is used in everyday language, denoting established ways of doing an activity. The meaning of 'practices' in academic research is, however, different. Practices are conceptualized as situated interconnected groups of activities enacted by group/field members (after Schatzki, 2002). Indeed, most conceptualization of practices share two common features (Schatkzi, 2018): they are indistinguishably entangled with the material context and with social relations. Practices constitute shared performances of activities by a group of people that are linked by these activities and form a field of power relations and positions. Thus, at research start, the researcher needs to actively construct the social business phenomena under investigation as practices, and home in on practices as units of analysis.

Most practice theory informed studies conceptualize agents as practitioners who have limited behavioural choices in contexts. This statement needs explaining further: those contexts are subsumed under 'field' in practice-based research (Bourdieu, 1990). 'Field' is a conceptualization of networks that homes in on the close entanglement of power relations as a special form of social relations and materiality. Fields allocate social positions to field practitioners or members. These social positions come with allocations of access to different types of resources. Bourdieu's theory of practice developed the notion of 'capitals' for resources held relationally and dynamically in fields (Bourdieu, 1990). In other words, leading field practitioners can hold positions of influence over which capitals can be accessed and by whom, determined to an extent by the field member's position.

An example from membership clubs with committees shows that chairs of a club often have the overview of activities and external influences; thus, they hold access to influential people and their resources and contacts (social capital). For example, chairs can allocate this access to some committee members, but not to members. This position gives them power over various capitals – such as the club economic resources, to provide a reduced membership fee (with committee agreement, economic capital). Similarly, they can allocate roles of prestige on the committee (symbolic capital), and influence elections. Being on the committee allows the development of behaviours suitable for gaining further influence and thus gaining embodied cultural capital, for example.

'Agency' homes in on the actions of practitioners, who are viewed as enacting the socio-material conditions and power relations of fields (Bourdieu, 1990). Agency is seen to link macrostructures and subjective lifeworlds (Hill, 2018); the concept incorporates personal structure and the perceived accessibility of capitals of practitioners. Agency enacts socio-materiality that it simultaneously recreates with its agency. Returning back to the initial statement at the start of the paragraph – practitioners (agents in fields) act from allocated positions with limited access to capitals, and need to engage in negotiations with other practitioners to change their position and increase their potential behaviour choices.

Socio-materiality is a concept widely used in sociology and management studies (Gherardi, 2012; Orlikowski, 2007; Orlikowski & Scott, 2016) to develop a sharper focus on dynamic microprocesses. 'The social' refers to social relations conceptualized as dynamic processes between people, material environment, and institutions; 'socio-material relations' denote these interactions with material artefacts. 'The material' denotes the tangible and visible aspects of the material environment, including technology and the internet (Gherardi, 2012). Whilst the 'social' and the 'material' are analytically separated, they are inseparably entangled in agency. Socio-materiality assumes an entanglement of the 'social' and the 'material' – in other words, social relations and materiality condition each other and do not exist separately (Barad, 2003; Orlikowski, 2007). Contexts thus encapsulate the inseparable nature of the social and material aspects of the environment.

To clarify the research focus, researchers ideally decide on assumptions regarding conceptualizations of the nature of practices (Nicolini & Monteiro, 2017): practices-as-entities or practices-as-accomplishments. This decision is most helpful for developing appropriate research questions and associated research methodologies. For practices-as-accomplishments, research often investigates mainly business activities at the micro-level, for example, pitching for investments or skiing (Nicolini & Monteiro, 2017). Practices as an 'object' studies the sum of accomplishments as one unit of analysis, such as competing in an industry (Smets et al., 2015, for reinsurance trading). These studies construct subsets of practices-as-accomplishments, for example, advertising as a subset to competing.

Moreover, the perspective taken towards the processes under investigation needs to be explicitly chosen, so that, indeed, valid insights can be gained. The 'from within' perspective focuses on how phenomena develop chronologically, and aims to establish what changed during a fixed period of time (Langley & Tsoukas, 2017). Studies with a 'from within' approach are interested in agents' experiences, either through their accounts or forms of active participation in a field. These studies aim for close proximity to present a view through the eyes of entrepreneurs. The level of engagement with the social processes under investigation is an important decision to make: the engagement can vary from this full engagement of enactive research to other forms of interactions. 'From outside' research (Langley & Tsoukas, 2017; see Table 15.1) avoids engagement and interruptions with the business processes by the research process.

To sum up, the researcher needs to answer the following questions before considering the choice of ethnography-based methods:

- Do I conceptualize social phenomena as practices-as-entities or practices-as-accomplishments?
- Am I interested in how practices come about ('in the flow') or how an outcome is achieved ('after the fact'; Langley and Tsoukas, 2017)?
- Do I study practices 'from within' or 'from without'? And what type of engagement with the actual business processes am I seeking?

Making the decisions on those outlined questions at the start of the research is significant for selecting ontological assumptions about the nature of social phenomena. The decisions need to guide the selection of appropriate research questions and designing aligned research designs. A sharpened lens and clearer findings are the result of making these decisions before starting fieldwork.

ENTREPRENEURSHIP-AS-PRACTICE RESEARCH

Process research in organization studies (Langley & Tsoukas, 2017; Weick, 1995), makes obvious the dynamic aspects of organizational phenomena in business through unpacking their emergent and fluid aspects (Steyaert, 2007). However, *how* business outputs are achieved, is less researched in entrepreneurship studies. Entrepreneurship-as-practice research (EAP) offers one solution, achieved through applying practice theory to the study of dynamic entrepreneurial activities. EAP is an applied field of research (Hill, 2018; Thompson et al., 2020), which breaks down the entanglement of sets of interconnected situated entrepreneurial activities, and how they are enacted (Champenois et al., 2020; Sklaveniti & Steyaert, 2020). It aims to demonstrate how the entanglement of agents (or practitioners), social relations and materiality lead to entrepreneurial outcomes and outputs. Yet, this detailed understanding of *how* entrepreneurs and small business owners enact business activities requires appropriate research questions, designs and methods. Thus, EAP research needs to explain *how* practices come about and are enacted, with reference to social relations and material artefacts in order to fully capture and explain the nature of entrepreneurial practices. Yet, few EAP studies explicitly direct attention to the significance of socio-material aspects of practices (but see Hill, 2021).

Conceptualizing practices as sets of situated interdependent and iterative activities and associated processes, contingent to contexts they are enacted within means that in EAP our units of analysis are entrepreneurial activities and processes carried out by entrepreneuring individuals in the context of running businesses (Thompson & Byrne, 2020; Thompson et al., 2020). Therefore, 'doing business' refers to a view of practices as an entity (Nicolini &

Monteiro, 2017). Research investigates how practices come about through a focus on how practitioners enact personal structure and temporary manifestations of contexts. Materiality in business can refer to the home office, the co-working space, technology, the internet and equipment to give some examples. 'Social relations' encompass work-related and personal relations. EAP research needs to capture the socio-material aspects of 'doing business', for all entrepreneurial activities.

Many EAP publications draw on Bourdieu's (Bourdieu, 1990) concepts of field, agency, and capitals (Champenois et al., 2020; Hill, 2018; Pret et al., 2016; Sklaveniti & Steyaert, 2020). Of particular importance for designing primary research is the concept of entrepreneurial capitals, which focuses attention on those aspects of general capitals that are brought into doing business (Hill, 2018). This latter relational focus on the practices and the resources located between people and not individually held by them is essential for the dynamic nature of practices EAP research highlights. These conceptualizations need to inform the methodology design.

Only few entrepreneurship research primary publications explicitly discuss *how* a researcher can capture the materiality of entrepreneuring, whereas methodology articles and chapters remain rather abstract on how to create tailored data gathering research instruments. Thus, for newcomers to EAP theory, getting started is particularly challenging. Researchers need to take account of the taken-for-granted material artefacts, such as pens, laptops, mobile phones and records. Only few entrepreneurship studies have addressed the journey and use of material artefacts. Surprisingly, I identified that even amongst those publications, very few offer insights on the practical implementation of capturing socio-materiality in the data gathering processes. The following pointers aim to address this oversight.

ETHNOGRAPHY AND ETHNOGRAPHIC RESEARCH

Ethnography has been painted as a form of qualitative research, traditionally emphasizing a deep and longitudinal level of engagement by researchers with the processes under investigation (Groenland & Dana, 2019; Pelly & Fayolle, 2020). Ethnography implies going into the field, watching, talking, thinking and experiencing the lifeworlds of entrepreneurs in close proximity to identify the ways in which people make sense of everyday life (Geertz, 1973). Rooted in naturalism, the social phenomena constructed as practices are studied in their 'natural setting' (Pelly and Fayolle, 2020). Mostly, ethnographers aim to create 'thick' interpretive description (Geertz, 1973) of identified patterns of behaviours, routines, rituals, which require deep understanding of the context. Thick descriptions are particularly relevant to studying and capturing entrepreneurial practices. Conceptualizing practices as collective and enacted by knowledgeable agents (Gherardi, 2012), researchers need to capture details of activities and their contexts. It is important to make the role of the ethnographic researchers more explicit – they are the 'research instrument' (Groenland & Dana, 2019). The question is how we make the findings from such ethnographic research valid and conclusions plausible, as the traditional view is that the researcher is 'there', integrated into the field, engaging with a subjective lens (van Maanen, 2011), and thus findings could be criticized for being not valid outside of this context.

More recently, researchers have developed different types of ethnography. Some types are differentiated by the time period covered, such as focused ethnography (done over short periods of time, e.g. two weeks of intense field engagement; Wall, 2015) to rapid (Ranabahu, 2017) or micro ethnography (LeBaron, 2011). The latter type focuses on microprocesses in small spatial units. Other differentiations address the theoretical roots, such as critical and feminist ethnography (Groenland & Dana, 2019). Most recently, team-based ethnographic research has emerged (Jarzabkowski et al., 2015b), and questions of the scale of ethnographic research are being discussed.

ETHNOGRAPHIC METHODS FOR EAP RESEARCH

This section discusses several methods for capturing entrepreneurial practices – both for ethnography and ethnographic studies (both are subsumed as ethnographic research) with a focus on data gathering methods applied face-to-face, whereas another chapter addresses digital methods (Cyron, Chapter 11 in this volume). Applying ethnographic research offers multiple benefits for investigating situated entrepreneurial practices. Their relevance follows from the aim of practice-based research – to provide research relevant for business (Thompson et al., 2020). A focus on conversations only, that is spoken words by research participants, is too limited in my view to be able to explain the situated nature of practices.

Tables 15.1 and 15.2 demonstrate the choices researchers have. Table 15.1 critically evaluates a selection of research strategies with their advantages and limitations and the research perspectives 'within' and 'without' outlined above. Table 15.2 then differentiates selected methods for ethnographic research by the levels of researcher intervention in the business processes and offers indicative examples of journal articles applying these methods. Researchers should start with a selection of a research strategy and a perspective from Table 15.1 and then select methods from Table 15.2 matching the chosen perspective.

Table 15.1 outlines the position of ethnographic research to other suitable research strategies for capturing entrepreneurial practices. For *enactive research*, the scholar adopts the social role and actions of an entrepreneur and launches, organizes and finalizes a venture (Johannisson, 2018), whilst this venture is simultaneously under investigation. Criticism of the approach suggests employing the term auto-ethnography to indicate its self-reflective nature (Poldner, 2020). *Interactive research strategies* indicate that researchers and practitioners share learning experiences and jointly create new knowledge whilst working on a project (Tillmar, 2020). *Case study strategy* can focus on a single case (from a business to a town or a country) or compare cases. Case study and ethnography-based research combined allow the researcher to identify relevant material artefacts and social relations (Hill, 2021).

Once researchers have identified the research strategy and the perspective, 'within' or 'without', they need to select data gathering methods that create a methodological fit. For this purpose, Table 15.2 differentiates five levels of intervention of a researcher with the investigated business processes, introducing labels for the role of the researcher. Levels 0, 1 and D are ways to examine business processes 'from without', whereas levels 2 and 3 allow the 'from within' perspective. These levels follow Davies' call (2008) for researchers to reflect on their possible influence on data collection.

Participant observation is regarded as a set of 'data collection techniques' (Davies, 2008) ranging from shorter to longer periods of living in a certain place. While it can be carried out covertly (without research participants knowing they are being observed), this chapter focuses

Table 15.1   *Research strategies and degrees of intervention in investigated business processes*

Research strategies	Relation of business to research processes and research perspective 'from within' (WI) or 'from without' (WO) Langley & Tsoukas (2017)	Advantages (A) and Limitations (L)
Enactive research (Fletcher, 2011; Johannisson, 2018)	Deep integration of business and research processes, (nearly) 100% intervention in business processes of an organization. The researcher(s) enact(s) a venture and research(es) the business processes with a variety of methods. Research and business activities are enacted simultaneously. WI	A – Dynamics of business processes can be studied in contexts and in-depth. L – The researcher positionality is too enmeshed with the field and processes enacted to offer insights relevant beyond the site. Research insights have rather limited transferability to different contexts.
Interactive research strategies (Tillmar, 2020)	Researchers and field agents / practitioners co-create the social phenomena under investigation. WI (WO)	A – Engaged interactions allow the research to empathize more with the entrepreneurs' experiences, assisting in creating more relevant research insights. L – A limited number of cases can be studied. Cases are contingent on practitioners and contexts; findings have limited transferability to different contexts.
Case study (Yin, 2012)	A wide range of possible perspectives: business processes can be just observed and researched, without any researcher intervention. Or, the researcher can employ an enactive approach. WI and WO	A – Context-related insights can be gained with a variety of research methods. L – A limited number of cases can be studied at micro- and macro-level.
Ethnography-based practice research (excluding auto-ethnography) (see the text for article examples)	A degree of interaction with the business processes is possible, through becoming part of the field community. WI and WO	A – A deep embeddedness is possible with the field; additional perspectives close to that of entrepreneurs can be developed. L – A limited number of cases can be studied at micro- and macro-level. The empirical findings have limited transferability to other contexts.

on overt applications only. Covert observations create a number of ethical challenges well documented (see, for example, Lloyd, 2012; Tillmar, 2020).

Shadowing, a particular form of observation, traditionally involves following entrepreneurs in their everyday occupations: the researcher moves with entrepreneurs through daily activities. Shadowing relies on the idea that research should be based on the recognition of differences in the understanding of a phenomenon by a researcher and a researched person (Czarniawska, 2007). When researchers 'go native' as in enactive research, they may lose their distance to the research field and therefore may lose a sense of surprise. Rather, they tend to accept incidents and conditions as 'normal' in line with the field members they investigate. Some researchers see shadowing as easier than participant observation, because shadowing focuses on observation only (Czarniawska, 2007). Increasingly, this approach is extended to shadow (quasi-)material objects and their journey within organizations (Bruni, 2005).

Interviews can be conducted with individual entrepreneurs and groups. The wide range of interview types is well documented (see Jarzabkowski et al., 2015a, 2015b; Tillmar, 2020).

Table 15.2   Research methods suitable for ethnography-based research for capturing entrepreneurial practices (selection)*

Research methods	Intervention in the business processes by researcher in five categories: 0 – None or negligible, non-participant observation from afar, Researcher as observer 1 – Minor – Researcher asks questions, Researcher as facilitator 2 – Medium – Researcher participates in business processes, researcher as influencer 3 – Major – Researcher changes business processes through intervention, such as training; Researcher as shaper D – Researcher as document collector	Indicative examples of journal articles with primary research using this data gathering method
Observation		
Observation (non-participant)	Category 0 – Covert Category 1 – Overt	Smets et al., 2015; Clarke, 2011; Hill, 2021; Katila et al., 2019; Reid, 2021
Shadowing, a type of observation	Category 0 No interaction with the business processes, passive researcher role.	Czarniawska, 2007; Smets et al., 2015
Participant observation, overt	Category 2 Interaction with business processes in a clearly defined role: acting as a full participant in the business and research processes, such as a workshop participant, is possible.	Hill, 2021; Karataş-Özkan, 2011; Teague et al., 2020
Photographs	Category 0	Katila et al., 2019
Self-observation of researcher sensations	Category 0	Katila et al., 2019; Valtonen et al., 2010
Interview forms		
Interview with individuals: (un- / semi-) structured	Category 1	Crawford et al., 2021; Hill, 2021; Reid, 2021; Vershinina and Rodgers, 2020
Interview with individuals: Life history Narrative Oral history	Category 1	Jesse, 2018; Ladstaetter et al., 2018; Lam, 2020; Webster, 2017
Focus group interviews (a group of research participants are interviewed)	Category 1	Jarzabkowski et al., 2015b
Self-observation and reflection by research participants		
Diary as tool of reflection (written, audio and video)	Category 1 Researcher sets questions for daily/weekly diary for entrepreneur.	De Rond et al., 2019
Self-interview by research participants	Category 1 Researcher sets questions for daily/weekly diary for entrepreneur.	Aubrey & Nowlan, 2011; Keightley et al., 2012
Mixed levels of engagement of researcher in business processes		

Research methods	Intervention in the business processes by researcher in five categories: 0 – None or negligible, non-participant observation from afar, Researcher as observer 1 – Minor – Researcher asks questions, Researcher as facilitator 2 – Medium – Researcher participates in business processes, researcher as influencer 3 – Major – Researcher changes business processes through intervention, such as training; Researcher as shaper D – Researcher as document collector	Indicative examples of journal articles with primary research using this data gathering method
Online research in all its forms, from observation, to fully engaging through creating online identities**	Categories 0 to 3	Kozinets, 2020
Video recording	Categories 0 to 3 possible: Using a video camera, and possible to combine with forms of observation and interaction, or being absent from business processes.	LeBaron et al., 2018; Thompson & Illes, 2021
Action research	Category 3	Blesia et al., 2021; Hill, 2021
Documentary data collection, Category D		
Social media and websites	Researcher is data collector and does not participate in the processes of data creation.	Lam, 2020; Olanrewaju et al., 2020
Unpublished *formal* company documents: policies, internal reports; process documentation etc. and *informal* company documents: meeting notes, emails, internal memos.	See above	Bowen, 2009; Smets et al., 2015

Note: * The selected references focus on entrepreneurship-related research where possible; ** Netnography is a subfield addressed by Cyron in Chapter 11 in this volume.

Self-interview by entrepreneurs accounts for professionals with little time for research participation and creates space/time for self-directed reflection and 'self-research', facilitated by researchers. More recently, the self-interview has been promoted as an effective tool to support everyday remembering for research participants (Keightley et al., 2012). This memory support is helpful for research participants to take account of what they actually do during a day.

Video ethnography is increasingly applied in entrepreneurship research (LeBaron et al., 2018; Thompson & Illes, 2021), as it foregrounds embedded behaviour and activity sequences. Videos offer the advantage of capturing all available movements in context, and the recording can be watched unlimited times. One limitation is that some research participants remain cautious and hold back in verbal and visible behaviour at all times. Thus, how to account for 'natural' versus performed behaviour in front of a camera is a matter of balance and experience.

The main feature of *documentary data* is the age and the timeline they can cover: documentary data mostly have been in the field before the start of the research process. More recently, the boundaries between online and printed communication have become significantly blurred, and all research benefits from considering social media communication as an extension of the verbal communication between entrepreneurs, gathered via interviews (Bowen, 2009; Smets et al., 2015).

The researcher selecting data gathering methods should be conscious of the data analysis methods these methods allow and ensure that the quality of the data and documents allows for this type of analysis.

CAPTURING RAW DATA FOR IDENTIFYING ENTREPRENEURIAL PRACTICES

This chapter limits the consideration of material artefacts to those that are essential for accomplishing entrepreneurial activities. Based on the above definition that practices are 'sets of situated interdependent iterative activities contingent to the contexts' enacted by a group of people within a field, research usually starts with an interest in a particular type of social phenomenon that is surprising, new or problematic looking for activities carried out regularly, stopped or material artefacts (Sandberg & Tsoukas, 2011). An example for an entrepreneurial activity would be marketing, and a related material artefact would be a website or a brochure. Related social relations may take shape in collaborative marketing between two companies, with complementary offers on one brochure. An intriguing study by Ladstaetter, Plank and Hemetsberger (2018), for example, began with examining an interrupted business practice. The breakdown reason was discovered to be increasing conflicts between social and economic objectives, which was addressed through linking all business activities back to the core business values.

An example of research starting with material artefacts: Cigarette butts, as indicated in the vignette at the chapter start, could be a starting point. The ethnographic data gathering process starts with the observation – there are cigarette butts – and then research may turn to discovering how these butts came to be on that ground. This investigation would use several methods: observations, standing or sitting in the site courtyard and watching the activities of customers and artists, interviews with artists and site manager to gain their insights on smoking on site, and lastly, studying any site policies or minutes of meetings (informal document gathering and analysis, see Table 15.2). Only after data has been gathered from at least two sources, and the analysis has been conducted, can a possible conclusion be drawn – that being that these cigarette butts do indeed matter for doing business on the site. The cigarette butts could be an interesting side product of a one-off event or two events, with no significance for important situated business activities. But until the analysis has finished, this conclusion is not possible. Consequently, the processes of data gathering need to be wide ranging in order to gather as much information and insight as possible. Ruling something out just because the researcher cannot see any links or significance for situated practices of 'doing business' would be unhelpful to the research. Cigarette butts in my research were indeed a significant indicator for site regulations and how some entrepreneurs complied with or undermined them.

Similarly, shadowing can be applied to material artefacts (Czarniawska, 2007). Researchers followed patient records from first digital entry to last in hospitals (Bruni, 2005), and invoices, (Frandsen, 2009). This (quasi-)object shadowing is a useful technique for identifying the significance of material artefacts in accomplishing entrepreneurial activities.

Clarke's study (2011) on the use of symbols in entrepreneurial performances analysed dress style, props (paintings, vehicles, prototype displays and framed company documents) and material settings within and outside of the office space. The findings reveal three overarching functions of these visual symbols: presenting an appropriate scene to stakeholders to appear professional and gain credibility through setting and props, creating professional identity and emphasizing control and regulating emotions. Presenting an appropriate scene involved practices functioning to explicitly expose some artefacts, such as patents framed on the wall, to gain credibility, and the attempts to conceal other aspects of settings they regarded as possibly damaging to the image the entrepreneurs tried to create, such as clutter (Clarke, 2011). These practices demonstrate a relational use of materiality, creating entrepreneurial symbolic capital (Hill, 2018) temporarily for particular social relations and settings.

These examples illustrate the integration of habitus and partial field understanding (Bourdieu, 1990; Hill, 2018) through the named beliefs regarding what is viewed as professional in a field, that is here the industry. These beliefs are integrated into enacting entrepreneurial activities, creating temporary symbolic (related to credibility) and social capitals in the interaction with different stakeholders (Hill, 2018).

HOW TO IDENTIFY MATERIAL ARTEFACTS AND SOCIAL RELATIONS THAT MATTER FOR ENTREPRENEURIAL PRACTICES

To start with, it is worth considering *how* to identify material artefacts and social relations that are relevant for entrepreneurial practices. How does a researcher identify what is important for enacting the particular entrepreneurial practice under investigation?

For example, craft entrepreneurs creating jewellery need materials and tools; these types of material artefacts are easy to identify. The need for a laptop and associated utensils (mouse, cable, etc.) might be less obvious. However, the fact that marketing and maintaining client contact via social media is an essential activity carried out at least bi-weekly, renders these material artefacts essential. The researcher is advised to collect insights on how often and where marketing is carried out, and if indeed the laptop is the most important material artefact (or possibly the smartphone?). Remaining with this example, the following information would be helpful to collect: the size and data capacity of the laptop, where and how often it is being used for what business purpose. While some of this information might be obvious (laptop size), other details need to be gathered through observation (when and how it is being used, for example) whereas others need to be collected through asking the artisan entrepreneur (laptop age, data capacity, etc. through an interview). To capture the meaning and thus significance of these artefacts can partially be learned through the existing literature on professions and industries (for example, on artisan entrepreneurs; Bell et al., 2018). Artefacts can simply be tools essential for carrying out the trade, or they can be totems with symbolic meaning going beyond the functional and business use (Robinson & Baum, 2020).

Social relations are an important element of entrepreneurial success, as represented in entrepreneurial social capital (Hill, 2018). How do researchers know which relations are significant for running the business? Following an open research approach, the researcher can ask about all the social relations the entrepreneur maintains, including the frequency of meetings (online/ via phone or in person). A direct question on which social relations are important is possible, however, due to social bias not all truly relevant individuals might be named. Indeed, once I had asked these questions, I learned through observations and frequent visits that people less involved in the business were not named. For example, a male entrepreneur did not mention his wife's role in business decisions when asked about significant social relations; his wife was neither an employee nor a director in the business. Yet, through asking more general questions about different business decisions, it turned out that she had a significant influence on selecting suppliers. My advice is to only focus on what is important to enacting entrepreneurial activities relevant to the research question under investigation.

To sum up, at the start of ethnography-based entrepreneurial practice theory studies, if limited insights exist into what are or are not relevant material artefacts and social relations, I suggest to widely capture insights on which elements might be relevant. Narrowing a wide range of artefacts and social relations down through observation combined with transcript analysis is easier than having to go back to an entrepreneur and ask more questions.

PRESENTING ETHNOGRAPHIC RESEARCH FINDINGS

Presenting ethnographic research findings is possibly one of the most important steps for getting published: we create new knowledge and extend existing concepts predominantly for academic researchers. Yet, as practice theory-based researchers we aim to also inform policy-makers and SME advocate networks to change societal ways of regulating 'doing business'. As a former entrepreneur, I consider both audience groups whenever possible. To capture socio-materiality, the document coding would need to include how material artefacts and social relations are integrated into entrepreneurial activities to become relevant for entrepreneurial practices.

Many findings sections focus on the detailed discussion of a small number of practices (2–5) and present their analysis in different ways. I present here three ways, which in many articles are combined. Researchers need to keep the research philosophy underpinning the practice theory when selecting analysis methods. Analysis methods vary between phenomenological analysis (Pret et al., 2016), content analysis, narrative analysis and thematic analysis. Here, I can only touch upon data analysis and findings presentation.

One way to give insights into how conclusions were reached involves writing vignettes (an experience-based text) and explaining these by applying the article's theoretical framework. Vignettes impress the reader with a vivid account of particular socio-material moments in the research. Some researchers focus the findings section on longer quotes by entrepreneurs, around which they organize the analysis (Essers et al., 2021). Other vignettes share the researchers' development journey of gaining insights while in the field, mixed with quotes from research participants (Harding et al., 2021; Jarzabkowski et al., 2015b). The use of vignettes allows researchers to show the richness of findings and consider the researcher's positionality for data generation as a co-production process.

An alternative method to give evidence of how conclusions were reached based on analysing qualitative raw data, is based on an article by Gioia et al. (2013). This way of findings presentation starts off with an explanation of codes and higher-level categories. The associated analytical account explains with reference to theory how these sets of activities have been identified as practices, what those practices consist of, and what the significance of these practices is for the entrepreneurs 'doing business'. What follows then is a presentation of how the categories have been used to select quotes accompanied by an analytical narrative explaining these quotes.

Giving an account of the temporality of insights with ethnographic methods is well illustrated when applying Stern's (2004) methodology of moments (see Harding et al., 2021). This account of the research explicitly considers the researchers' bodily presence and takes account of the performativity of human interaction through longer vignettes and shorter quotes.

CONCLUSIONS

This chapter discussed *ethnography-based practice research* for capturing situated entrepreneurial practices and how to capture these practices' socio-materiality – often not given sufficient attention in entrepreneurship research. This finding is surprising, as other studies portray the inextricable nature of practices and socio-materiality (Gherardi, 2012). Thus, a consideration of social relations and material artefacts must be an integrated part of researching entrepreneurial practices (Hill, 2021; Schatzki, 2018).

Discussions of research strategies, designs and methods revealed that differentiating researcher involvement in research is helpful. The role of the researcher as observer and integrated facilitator sheds light on how the researcher role defines which aspects of socio-materiality are important to the research. The term 'ethnography-based practice research' captures recent developments in ethnographic research, away from tradition (the individual researcher being fully integrated over at least one year in the field), to groups of researchers, new media for data capturing (video ethnography, digital ethnography) and different levels of involvement, from weeks to recurring visits (Jarzabkowski et al., 2015a; Wall, 2015).

This chapter could not cover all aspects of ethnography. Most importantly, I have indicated that presenting qualitative research findings on entrepreneurial practices is an art deserving further study (see Jarzabkowski et al., 2015b).

I hope those insights inspire more researchers to fully consider situated entrepreneurial practices and capture sufficient raw data on practices' deeply inextricable socio-materiality. These rich sources allow finer analysis of *how* entrepreneuring is accomplished.

REFERENCES

Aubrey, S., & Nowlan, A. G. P. (2011). An evaluation of audio diaries as a research method in language research. *Kotesol Proceedings*. https://www.researchgate.net/publication/332263263_An_Evaluation _of_Audio_Diaries_as_a_Research_Method_in_Language_Research.

Barad, K. (2003). Posthumanist performativity: Toward an understanding of how matter comes to matter. *Signs*, *28*(3), 801–831.

Bell, E., Gianluigi, M., Taylor, S., & Toraldo, M. L. (Eds.) (2018). *The Organization of Craft Work: Identities, Meanings and Materiality*. New York: Routledge.

Blesia, J. U., Iek, M., Ratang, W., & Hutajulu, H. (2021). Developing an entrepreneurship model to increase students' entrepreneurial skills: An action research project in a higher education institution in Indonesia. *Systemic Practice and Action Research*, *34*, 53–70.

Bourdieu, P. (1990). *The Logic of Practice*. Stanford, CA: Stanford University Press.

Bowen, G. A. (2009). Document analysis as a qualitative research method. *Qualitative Research Journal*, *9*(2), 27–40.

Bruni, A. (2005). Shadowing software and clinical records: On the ethnography of non-humans and heterogeneous contexts. *Organization*, *12*(3), 357–378.

Champenois, C., Lefebvre, V., & Ronteau, S. (2020). Entrepreneurship as practice: Systematic literature review of a nascent field. *Entrepreneurship & Regional Development*, *32*(3–4), 281–312.

Clarke, J. (2011). Revitalizing entrepreneurship: How visual symbols are used in entrepreneurial performances. *Journal of Management Studies*, *48*(6), 1365–1391.

Crawford, B., Chiles, T. H., & Elias, S. R. S. T. A. (2021). Long interviews in organizational research: Unleashing the power of 'show and tell'. *Journal of Management Inquiry*, *30*(3), 331–346.

Czarniawska, B. (2007). *Shadowing and Other Techniques for Doing Fieldwork in Modern Societies*. Copenhagen: Copenhagen Business School Press.

Davies, C. (2008). *Reflexive Ethnography: A Guide to Researching Selves and Others*. New York: Routledge.

De Rond, M., Holeman, I., & Howard-Grenville, J. (2019). Sensemaking from the body: An enactive ethnography of rowing the Amazon. *Academy of Management Journal*, *62*(6), 1961–1988.

Essers, C., Pio, E., Verduijn, K., & Bensliman, N. (2021). Navigating belonging as a Muslim Moroccan female entrepreneur. *Journal of Small Business Management*, *59*(6), 1250–1278.

Fletcher, D. E. (2011). A curiosity for contexts: Entrepreneurship, enactive research and autoethnography. *Entrepreneurship & Regional Development*, *23*(1–2), 65–76.

Frandsen, A.-C. (2009). From psoriasis to a number and back. *Information and Organization*, *19*(2), 103–128.

Geertz, C. (1973). Thick description: Toward an interpretive theory of culture. In C. Geertz, *The Interpretation of Cultures: Selected Essays* (pp. 3–30). New York: Basic Books.

Gherardi, S. (2012). *How to Conduct a Practice-Based Study: Problems and Methods*. Cheltenham, UK and Northampton, MA, USA: Edward Elgar Publishing.

Gioia, D. A., Corley, K. G., & Hamilton, A. L. (2013). Seeking qualitative rigor in inductive research: Notes on the Gioia methodology. *Organizational Research Methods*, *16*(1), 15–31.

Groenland, E., & Dana, L.-P. (2019). *Qualitative Methodologies and Data Collection Methods: Towards Increased Rigour in Management Research*. Singapore: World Scientific Publishing.

Harding, N., Gilmore, S., & Ford, J. (2021). Matter that embodies: Agentive flesh and working bodies/selves. *Organization Studies*. https://doi.org/10.1177/0170840621993235.

Hill, I. (2018). How did you get up and running? Taking a Bourdieuan perspective towards a framework for negotiating strategic fit. *Entrepreneurship & Regional Development*, *30*(5–6), 662–696.

Hill, I. (2021). Spotlight on UK artisan entrepreneurs' situated collaborations: Through the lens of conversion of entrepreneurial capitals. *International Journal of Entrepreneurial Behavior & Research*, *27*(1), 99–121.

Jarzabkowksi, P., Bednarek, R., & Cabantous, L. (2015a). Conducting global team-based ethnography: Methodological challenges and practical methods. *Human Relations*, *68*(1), 3–33.

Jarzabkowski, P., Burke, G., & Spee, P. (2015b). Constructing spaces for strategic work: A multimodal perspective. *British Journal of Management*, *26*(S1), S26–S47.

Jesse, E. (2018). The life history interview. In P. Liamputtong (Ed.), *Handbook of Research Methods in Health Social Sciences* (pp. 1–17). Singapore: Springer.

Johannisson, B. (2018). *Disclosing Entrepreneurship as Practice: The Enactive Approach*. Cheltenham, UK and Northampton, MA, USA: Edward Elgar Publishing.

Karataş-Özkan, M. (2011). Understanding relational qualities of entrepreneurial learning: Towards a multi-layered approach. *Entrepreneurship & Regional Development*, *23*(9–10), 877–906.

Katila, S., Laine, P.-M., & Parkkari, P. (2019). Sociomateriality and affect in institutional work: Constructing the identity of start-up entrepreneurs. *Journal of Management Inquiry*, *28*(3), 381–394.

Keightley, E., Pickering, M., & Allett, N. (2012). The self-interview: A new method in social science research. *International Journal of Social Research Methodology*, *15*(6), 507–521.

Kozinets, R. V. (2020). *Netnography: The Essential Guide to Qualitative Social Media Research* (3rd edition). London: Sage.

Ladstaetter, F., Plank, A., & Hemetsberger, A. (2018). The merits and limits of making do: Bricolage and breakdowns in social enterprise. *Entrepreneurship & Regional Development*, *30*(3–4), 283–309.

Lam, A. (2020). Hybrids, identity and knowledge boundaries: Creative artists between academic and practitioner communities. *Human Relations*, *73*(6), 837–863.

Langley, A., & Tsoukas, H. (2017). Introduction: Process thinking, process theorising and process researching. In A. Langley & H. Tsoukas (Eds.), *The SAGE Handbook of Process Organisation Studies* (pp. 2–20). London: Sage.

LeBaron, C. (2011). Microethnography. In V. Jupp (Ed.), *The SAGE Dictionary of Social Research Methods* (pp. 178–179). London: Sage.

LeBaron, C., Jarzabkowski, P., Pratt, M. G., & Fetzer, G. (2018). An introduction to video methods in organizational research. *Organizational Research Methods*, *21*(2), 239–260.

Lloyd, A. (2012). Working to live, not living to work: Work, leisure and youth identity among call centre workers in North East England. *Current Sociology*, *60*(5), 619–635.

Nicolini, D., & Monteiro, P. (2017). The practice approach: For a praxiology of organisational and management studies. In A. Langley & H. Tsoukas (Eds.), *The SAGE Handbook of Process Organisation Studies* (pp. 110–126). London: Sage.

Olanrewaju, A.-S. T., Hossain, M. A., Whiteside, N., & Mercieca, P. (2020). Social media and entrepreneurship research: A literature review. *International Journal of Information Management*, *50*, 90–110.

Orlikowski, W. J. (2007). Sociomaterial practices: Exploring technology at work. *Organization Studies*, *28*(9), 1435–1448.

Orlikowski, W. J., & Scott, S. V. (2016). Digital work: A research agenda. In B. Czarniawska (Ed.), *A Research Agenda for Management and Organization Studies* (pp. 88–95). Cheltenham, UK and Northampton, MA, USA: Edward Elgar Publishing.

Pelly, D. R. M., & Fayolle, A. (2020). Ethnography's answer to the plus zone challenge of entrepreneurship. In W. B. Gartner & B. T. Teague (Eds.), *Research Handbook on Entrepreneurial Behavior, Practice and Process* (pp. 82–101). Cheltenham, UK and Northampton, MA, USA: Edward Elgar Publishing.

Poldner, K. (2020). Performing affirmation: Autoethnography as an activist approach to entrepreneurship. In W. B. Gartner & B. T. Teague (Eds.), *Research Handbook on Entrepreneurial Behavior, Practice and Process* (pp. 102–137). Cheltenham, UK and Northampton, MA, USA: Edward Elgar Publishing.

Pret, T., Shaw, E., & Dodd, S. D. (2016). Painting the full picture: The conversion of economic, cultural, social and symbolic capital. *International Small Business Journal*, *34*(8), 1004–1027.

Ranabahu, N. (2017). 'Rapid' but not 'raid': A reflection on the use of rapid ethnography in entrepreneurship research. *Qualitative Research Journal*, *17*(4), 254–264.

Reid, S. (2021). The generative principles of lifestyle enterprising: Dialectic entanglements of capital-habitus-field. *International Journal of Entrepreneurial Behaviour & Research*, *27*(3), 629–647.

Robinson, R. N. S., & Baum, T. (2020). Work(ing) artefacts: Tools of the trade, totems or trophies? *Human Relations*, *73*(2), 165–189.

Sandberg, J., & Tsoukas, H. (2011). Grasping the logic of practice: Theorizing through practical rationality. *Academy of Management Review*, *36*(2), 338–360.

Schatzki, T. R. (2002). *The Site of the Social: A Philosophical Account of the Constitution of Social Life and Change*. University Park: Pennsylvania State University Press.

Schatzki, T. (2018). On practice theory, or what's practices got to do (got to do) with it? In C. Edwards-Groves, P. Grootenboer, & J. Wilkinson (Eds.), *Education in an Era of Schooling: Critical Perspectives of Educational Practice and Action Research. A Festschrift for Stephen Kemmis* (pp. 151–165). Cham: Springer.

Sklaveniti, C., & Steyaert, C. (2020). Reflecting with Pierre Bourdieu: Towards a reflexive outlook for practice-based studies of entrepreneurship. *Entrepreneurship & Regional Development*, *32*(3–4), 313–333.

Smets, M., Jarzabkowski, P., Burke, G. T., & Spee, P. (2015). Reinsurance trading in Lloyd's of London: Balancing conflicting-yet-complementary logics in practice. *Academy of Management Journal*, *58*(3), 932–970.

Stern, D. N. (2004). *The Present Moment in Psychotherapy and Everyday Life*. New York: W. W. Norton.

Steyaert, C. (2007). 'Entrepreneuring' as a conceptual attractor? A review of process theories in 20 years of entrepreneurship studies. *Entrepreneurship & Regional Development*, *19*(6), 453–477.

Teague, B. T., Gorton, M. D., & Liu, Y. (2020). Different pitches for different stages of entrepreneurial development: The practice of pitching to business angels. *Entrepreneurship & Regional Development*, *32*(3–4), 334–352.

Thompson, N. A., & Byrne, O. (2020). Advancing entrepreneurship as practice: Previous developments and future possibilities. In W. B. Gartner & B. T. Teague (Eds.), *Research Handbook on Entrepreneurial Behavior, Practice and Process* (pp. 30–55). Cheltenham, UK and Northampton, MA, USA: Edward Elgar Publishing.

Thompson, N. A., & Illes, E. (2021). Entrepreneurial learning as practice: A video ethnographic analysis. *International Journal of Entrepreneurial Behavior & Research*, *27*(3), 577–599.

Thompson, N. A., Verduijn, K., & Gartner, W. B. (2020). Entrepreneurship-as-practice: Grounding contemporary theories of practice into entrepreneurship studies. *Entrepreneurship & Regional Development*, *32*(3–4), 247–256.

Tillmar, M. (2020). Practicing participant observations: Capturing entrepreneurial practices. In W. B. Gartner & B. T. Teague (Eds.), *Research Handbook on Entrepreneurial Behavior, Practice and Process* (pp. 168–181). Cheltenham, UK and Northampton, MA, USA: Edward Elgar Publishing.

Valtonen, A., Markuksela, V., & Moisander, J. (2010). Doing sensory ethnography in consumer research. *International Journal of Consumer Studies*, *34*, 375–380.

van Maanen, J. (2011). Ethnography as work: Some rules of engagement. *Journal of Management Studies*, *48*(1), 218–234.

Vershinina, N., & Rodgers, P. (2020). Symbolic capital within the lived experiences of Eastern European migrants: A gendered perspective. *Entrepreneurship & Regional Development*, *32*(7–8), 590–605.

Wall, S. (2015). Focused ethnography: A methodological adaptation for social research in emerging contexts. *Forum Qualitative Social Research*, *16*(1), Art. 1. http://nbn-resolving.de/urn:nbn:de:0114 -fqs150111.

Webster, N. A. (2017). Rural-to-rural translocal practices: Thai women entrepreneurs in the Swedish countryside. *Journal of Rural Studies*, *56*, 219–228.

Weick, K. E. (1995). *Sensemaking in Organizations*. Thousand Oaks, CA: Sage.

Yin, R. K. (2012). Case study methods. In J. L. Green, G. Camilli, & P. B. Elmore (Eds.), *Handbook of Complementary Methods in Education Research* (pp. 111–122). Mahwah, NJ: Lawrence Erlbaum Associates.

PART IV

NEW EMPIRICAL ADVANCES

16. Unpacking collective judging practices in entrepreneurial pitching competitions: a social practice perspective

Lars Hamacher, Jarrod Ormiston and Deniz Iren

INTRODUCTION

This chapter applies a practice perspective to investigate how judges make decisions in entrepreneurial pitching competitions. Previous research on entrepreneurial pitching has tended to explain pitching outcomes based on judges' perceptions of both entrepreneurs and their business plans (Brooks et al., 2014; Chen et al., 2009; Clarke, 2011; Mitteness et al., 2012). This focus on judges' perceptions of entrepreneurs fails to appreciate the individual preferences and social dynamics that play out between judges as they attempt to reach a consensus in their decisions (Pollack et al., 2012; Huang & Pearce, 2015). To overcome this gap in understanding, this research focuses on unpacking the social practices involved as groups of judges at entrepreneurial pitching competitions actually make their decisions. The study is guided by the following research question: *What are the practices involved in making collective judging decisions in entrepreneurial pitching competitions?*

We extend a stream of research that emphasizes the importance of judges' perceptions in determining the outcomes of entrepreneurial pitching competitions. This research has shown how displays of passion and preparedness can influence judges' perceptions of entrepreneurs (Chen et al., 2009; Mitteness et al., 2012; Sudek, 2006). Beyond their reactions to the entrepreneurs, this research suggests that the personal preferences and interests of the judges may shape the outcomes of pitching competitions (Pollack et al., 2012; Huang & Pearce, 2015; Brooks et al., 2014). However, these studies tend to focus on either the preferences and interests of individual judges and/or how they perceive entrepreneurs. We know, however, that most entrepreneurship competitions involve panels of judges. This study therefore seeks to explore the collective practices enacted by groups of judges as they attempt to reach collective decisions.

In order to understand the *collective* judging practices in entrepreneurial pitching competitions we adopt a practice perspective. At the heart of a practice perspective is an attention to the everyday doings and sayings of people and things (Sandberg & Dall'Alba, 2009). Practice theory emphasizes that practice is social, and that the interconnectedness of social practice is central to theorizing human activity (Jarzabkowski & Seidl, 2008; Nicolini, 2012; Schatzki, 2001; Whittington, 2011). A practice perspective thereby encourages us to move beyond understanding at the level of the individual judge or entrepreneur and turn our attention to the shared social practices that are enacted in the world of entrepreneurship. In applying a practice perspective to the study of entrepreneurial pitching we engage with the emerging stream of research on entrepreneurship as practice (Gartner et al., 2016; Thompson & Byrne, 2020).

The study draws on audio recordings of judging discussions at a three-day hackathon event involving 250 contestants across 30 entrepreneurial teams. Utilizing a conversation analysis approach (Sacks et al., 1978), we zoom in on the relational and temporal practices that play out in judging discussions to understand the practices involved in moving from individual perceptions of pitches towards consensus decisions between judges. Our findings map out the key phases that play out on judging discussions, before identifying three practices (*Alliance Building*, *Politicking*, and *Undermining*) that shape collective judging decisions. The findings contribute to research on entrepreneurial pitching by highlighting the collective practices involved in judging. Further, we open up novel avenues for entrepreneurship-as-practice research by moving beyond the methodological individualism that pervades entrepreneurship research and highlighting the relevance of studying non-entrepreneurial actors that influence entrepreneurial outcomes.

The chapter is organized as follows. First, we provide a short review of the literature on entrepreneurial pitching and practice theory. Second, we outline the research site and our research methods. Third, we unpack the core practices involved in collective judging. Finally, we discuss the implications of this study for our understanding of entrepreneurial pitching and entrepreneurship-as-practice.

LITERATURE REVIEW AND THEORETICAL FRAMING

Entrepreneurial Pitching

Entrepreneurs are consistently searching for people to back their ideas, be it with money (investor) or knowledge (partner). Pitching is thereby a critical activity for early-stage entrepreneurs in order to acquire resources and convince investors about the value of their idea (Balachandra et al., 2019; Clarke et al., 2018; Pollack et al., 2012). Pitching is the practice of telling the story of an entrepreneurial idea in just a few minutes, and allows the pitcher to provide the 'receiver' (often an investor or judge) with an overview of the whole idea in just a few bullet points so that they will remember the most important information (Clark, 2008; Eckhardt et al., 2006; Williams, 2013). Pitches vary in their length and purposes, from short one-minute elevator pitches and longer five-minute competitive pitches, to even longer 20+ minute investment pitches (Clark, 2008). In this study we zoom in on early-stage competitive pitching that takes place during entrepreneurial hackathons.

Research on pitching has highlighted various factors that determine pitching outcomes. Most of these studies focus on what the entrepreneurs say and do during their pitch (Ormiston & Thompson, 2021). These studies emphasize the role of language used by entrepreneurs, showing how rhetoric and narratives shape pitching success (Katila et al., 2019; Pollack et al., 2012; van Werven et al., 2019). This stream of research also shows how entrepreneurs utilize non-verbal elements such as gestures and facial expressions to persuade investors (Clarke et al., 2018: Stroe et al., 2020).

Moving beyond an analysis of the entrepreneurs themselves, judges are viewed as playing an important role in pitching competitions (Mitteness et al., 2012). Persuading judges about the quality of an idea is thereby a key element of pitching success (Williams, 2013). Previous research on entrepreneurial pitching shows how the results of pitching competitions are influenced by judges' perceptions of entrepreneurs (Brooks et al., 2014; Cardon et al., 2009; Chen et al., 2009; Clarke, 2011). For example, Brooks et al. (2014) showed how judges preferred attractive male pitchers, over other pitchers. Furthermore, Cardon et al. (2009) and Chen et al. (2009) have explored how displayed (entrepreneurial) passion and preparedness influences judges' decisions. Finally, Clarke (2011) has shown how entrepreneurs applied visual symbols to enrich their story and influence judges' decisions. These studies illustrate how judges' decisions are influenced by different non-content-related criteria.

This short review reveals that previous research on entrepreneurial pitching has tended to explain pitching outcomes based on judges' perceptions of both entrepreneurs and their business plans. This focus on judges' perceptions of entrepreneurs fails to appreciate the social dynamics that play out between judges as they attempt to reach a consensus in their decisions. We argue that we need a practice perspective to better understand the social practices involved as groups of judges actually make their decisions.

A Social Practice Perspective on Judging Decisions in Entrepreneurial Pitching

A practice perspective focuses on the everyday, often mundane, talk, actions and interactions of social actors (Sandberg & Dall'Alba, 2009). Practice perspectives gained initial momentum in entrepreneurship through the work of Johannisson (2011) and Steyaert (2007) who put forward the concept of entrepreneuring as a way of understanding entrepreneurial endeavor as a process or practice, rather than focusing on outcomes or individuals. Practice-based research is characterized by three core foci: (i) a focus on everyday sayings, doings, and interactions of social actors; (ii) an appreciation of the embodied and material nature of these actions; and (iii) an understanding that everyday action is inherently social (Miettinen et al., 2009; Nicolini, 2012; Whittington, 2011). Neatly capturing these three themes, Schatzki describes practice as "embodied, materially mediated arrays of human activity centrally organized around shared practical understandings" (2001, p. 11). A practice perspective thereby rejects the methodological individualism that dominates entrepreneurship scholarship and turns our focus onto the relational and social nature of entrepreneurial endeavor (Steyaert, 2007).

In particular we adopt Schatzki et al.'s (2001) perspective on practice as social, which prioritizes the role of social interactions in understanding practice. Schatzki's work builds on Heidegger's notion of *being-with* (Heidegger, 1962 [1927]), which moves us beyond an overly individual perspective of the world, and allows us to understand entrepreneurship as inherently social. Schatzki (2007) translates *being-with* as 'coexistence', stating that "human existence is essentially social: an essential feature of an individual life is that other lives bear on it" (p. 234). Schatzki (2007) describes four main ways that others bear on our existence: (i) one encounter others; (ii) one acts towards others; (iii) one shares the world with others; and, (iv) 'worldhood', or sense of the world, is largely the same for all involved. If we appreciate these four ways of *being-with*, or coexistence, we realize the need to move our attention away from the individual entrepreneur, to understand how entrepreneurs are always-already entangled and concerned with others (Watts, 2011). Through this Schatzkian perspective, we as entrepreneurship scholars need to appreciate the shared world of entrepreneurs, appreciating the myriad others they encounter and act towards, and alongside, and who shape their entrepreneurial journey.

Through a social practice perspective, our study of entrepreneurial pitching moves away from examining the entrepreneurs themselves, and instead shifts the focus to other social actors, the judges, and the interactions between both the entrepreneurs and the judges, and the interactions between the judges themselves. In looking at the social interactions involving judges, we aim to uncover the 'black box' of judging decisions in entrepreneurial pitching by focusing on the, usually private, judging discussions. To date, studies of entrepreneurial pitching have focused on verbatim transcripts of what the entrepreneurs said in their pitch (Kanze et al., 2018; van Werven et al., 2019) or observations of what the entrepreneurs did while pitching (Clarke et al., 2018). Some studies have explored the interactions between entrepreneurs and judges by looking at the question and answer sections that play out following a pitch (Cardon et al., 2017; Chalmers & Shaw, 2017; Kanze et al., 2018). Whilst we have some understanding of the interactions between entrepreneurs and judges, research to date has failed to explore the interactions that play out *between judges* as they attempt to reach consensus decisions. The next section reveals how we accessed judging discussions to unpack the collective judging practices in entrepreneurial pitching competitions through conversation analysis.

METHODS

In order to understand judges' collective decision-making practices, we collected video and audio recordings of entrepreneurial pitches and judging discussions at a three-day hackathon event involving 250 contestants across 30 entrepreneurial teams.

Research Site

We collected video and audio recordings from a hackathon held in the Netherlands in 2018. Over 250 contestants participated in the three-day event. The participants were presented with four real-life business and societal challenges from different social and public institutions. They were also provided with real data sets on the nature of the four challenges. The participants then worked in 30 entrepreneurial teams over the weekend to generate innovative solutions for the problems. The entrepreneurial teams used the weekend to come up with an idea and prototype, with the support of expert coaches. The weekend culminated with each team pitching to a panel of judges within each of the four social challenge categories.

A different panel of judges was responsible for determining the winners of each of the four challenges. Each of the judging panels consisted of five people with different backgrounds relating to the particular challenge. They had no previous knowledge about what the teams were working on, only the general challenge provided upfront. After each pitch the judges were able to ask questions of the participants. Following the questions, the judges had a brief moment together (approximately two minutes) to share their initial comments on the pitch they just saw. After the judges had watched all pitches, they had the chance to debate for about fifteen minutes to decide on the top three pitches for the challenge. The top three pitches from each challenge were then able to enter the pitching finals, where they were given the chance to pitch in front of the whole audience. The winner for each challenge was then selected by two representatives relating to the topic.

Data Collection

Throughout the hackathon event we made video recordings of the pitches and questions and answer segments. We also made audio recordings of the judging discussions after each indi vidual pitch, as well as the final judging discussion. In total we recorded 30 pitches and over six hours of audio and video recordings (as indicated in Table 16.1). In this chapter we analyze the audio recordings of the 'Final Judging Discussions' that took place after all of the pitches were completed as they revealed the social practices of collective judging decisions. In these final judging discussions the judges were able to voice their opinions on the relative merit of the pitches and make collective decisions. In total we recorded four of these final judging discussions which ran for a combined total of 71 minutes.

Table 16.1   *Overview of recorded pitches and judges' discussions*

	Challenge 1	Challenge 2	Challenge 3	Challenge 4	Total
Number of pitches	6	8	8	8	**30**
Average length of pitches (including Q&A) (minutes)	12:56	8:04	7:33	9:16	**292:30**
Average length of small judging discussion (minutes)	1:34*	2:00**	1:33	N.B.***	**27:58**
General judging discussion length (minutes)	14:50	30:01	15:36	10:52	**71:19**

Note: * Only one small discussion; ** Only seven small discussions; *** No small discussions included.

In order to understand the practices of judges' decision-making we relied on these audio recordings rather than relying on surveys, interviews, or observer's notes. Using the audio recordings allowed us to listen to the interactions between judges multiple times to gain an understanding of the practices. This enabled us to understand the doings and sayings of entrepreneurial judging as it happened (Gartner et al., 2016; Thompson & Byrne, 2020).

Data Analysis: Conversation Analysis

Building on the work of Chalmers and Shaw (2017) we utilize conversation analysis as a method to reveal "actual instances of practice in entrepreneurship scholarship" (Chalmers & Shaw, 2017, p. 19). Conversation analysis provides a means for unpacking everyday, often mundane, social action through examining recordings of naturally occurring conversations and interactions (Chalmers & Shaw, 2017). Conversation analysis builds on Goffman's (1983) work on interaction orders and Garfinkel's (1967) study of practical reasoning (Sidnell, 2010). Through conversation analysis we can reveal social practices by zooming in on turn-taking or talk-in-interaction within social interactions (Goodwin & Heritage, 1990; Sacks et al., 1978). Our use of audio recorded judging discussion aligns with the two key features of conversations analysis: (i) the data were naturally occurring which allows for a focus on the actual practices; (ii) the data are recorded, which allows the researcher to study the precise details of the social interaction (Toerien, 2014).

The data analysis involved multiple, overlapping stages. The first stage of data analysis involved the transcription of the audio recordings. The lead author did the transcription by himself, paying attention to who said what and when. He also made interpretive memos as interesting moments emerged, for example long silences, irritation, sarcasm, and alliance building.

The second stage of analysis involved the creation of an 'event history database' (Garud & Rappa, 1994). Mapping the events playing out in the transcripts allowed us to understand what was going on in the judging discussions as a whole. We mapped the events that played out in the large judging discussion. Through this open coding we generated the first-order categories in Figure 16.1.

In the third stage axial coding was applied, and links were sought between these broad categories, which grouped them into themes (Strauss & Corbin, 1990). This axial coding helped define the second-order themes, which correspond to the key phases in the judges discussion (e.g. Framing, Redirecting, Wrapping Up). Figure 16.1 provides an overview of the phases.

In the final stage, we utilized the conversation analysis approach to unpack the underlying practices enacted throughout the pitch. This revealed the underlying practices of *Alliance Building*, *Politicking*, and *Undermining* which judges enact to shape the final collective decisions. Within each of the four judging discussions we sought to analyze when and why these practices emerged, and how they influenced the final outcomes of the judging discussions. In the second part of our results section, we outline each of these three practices using illustrative turn-by-turn excerpts from the judging discussions to show how these practices shaped the accomplishment of collective judging decisions.

RESULTS

Part 1: Key Phases in Reaching Collective Judging Decisions

Figure 16.1 provides an overview of the key phases that emerged during the judges' discussions. The figure presents the general flow of conversation as it arose throughout the general judging discussions as the judges moved back and forth through the key phases of: (i) Framing, (ii) Redirecting, (iii) Wrapping Up.

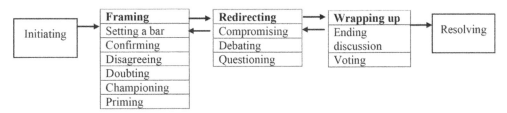

Figure 16.1   *Key phases in collective judging decisions*

We noticed common conversational phases across all four judging panels. Table 16.2 provides exemplar quotes for each of the key phases throughout the collective judging conversation.

Table 16.2   Quotes related to key phases

Theme			Example
	Framing		
1.	Setting a bar	A.	[Pitch B5], [Pitch B8], [Pitch B3], [Pith B4] [Providing the pitches this judge prefers].
		B.	What I like about [Pitch C4], although it is solely about studying texts and who is going to do it, the children of highly educated parents, so, it only increases the gap. However, it is an awesome idea. [Pitch 3.3] was a mess, the idea was not all too bad, some kind of TripAdvisor for education if you can manage it well a feasible idea. I see the potential on the idea, however, the pitch was such a mess. They linked upcoming students to current students, so, they could chat and ask questions.
2.	Confirming	A.	Me neither since it is not an applicable tool for us.
		B.	Yes, we already do that.
3.	Disagreeing	A.	No, I do not agree, I do not like the idea at all. However, the majority of the votes has it.
		B.	No, in my opinion, they did a good job, that is also what I gave back to them.
4.	Priming	A.	What do we do with [Pitch B2]?
		B.	[Pitch B3]? I voted them the highest, together with [Pitch B5], but I do not know how you ranked them?
5.	Doubting	A.	I think we could use small parts of it, just for the profit it would generate. Nevertheless, within a year we would be shut down and arrested as a result of the law on competition.
		B.	The only downside is the fact that they have no business plan.
6.	Championing	A.	[Pitch A4] is implementable as an add-on on our website.
		B.	I liked them, it was practical, and I believe it is a feasible idea.
	Redirecting		
1.	Compromising	A.	You know what the problem is when I look at the bottom line, and I am checking with my fellow judges, [Pitch B5] should be in.
		B.	Well look we could of course make them second.
2.	Debating	A.	I do not fully believe in their idea, however, I have got to give them credits for diving into this domain, which is quite hard.
		B.	Well, I have to say education is a cultural problem, it has nothing to do with technical features. However, we force people to come up with technical solutions. So, we have to convert technical ideas into cultural solutions. In my opinion, the guys from [Pitch C7] were able to show us this.
3.	Questioning	A.	Would it not be an idea to first check out the other criteria?
		B.	Implementability is indeed harder, however, I believe that this pitch does not need the monetary reward. We could implement it ourselves within three weeks.
	Wrapping Up		
1.	Ending Discussion	A.	So, this will be our third name then?
		B.	For now, we got [Pitch B5] in the first place, we still have to determine the number two and three.
2.	Voting	A.	Shall we just vote?
		B.	Can we go on with voting, otherwise we will not be done in the next hour or so.

Framing

The first step in every discussion is initiating/starting it. This step is similar in all reviewed judges' discussions. One of the judges interrupts the conversation which is going on – mostly small talk – by mentioning the reason to be here today.

'Well, let us [judges] start discussing on what we came here for today.'

Once the initiating is done, the *framing* phase begins. In this phase, one judge starts by talking about one pitch or their personal top-three. This plays the function of *setting a bar* for others, a reference point by which other opinions get compared.

> 'What I liked about [Pitch C4], although it is only reading texts and who is willing to do that, the kids of the higher educated parents, therefore it only increases the gap between poor and rich. … [talks about other pitches] I liked their idea, however, the presentation was a mess.'

By bringing attention to particular pitches, this step can be interpreted as *priming*, as judges mention their preference for certain pitches in an attempt to influence others.

> '[Pitch B3]? I ranked them the highest together with [Pitch B5], however, I do not know how you feel about that?'

Other judges can display their opinion on the comments of the first judge in several ways. They can *confirm* or *disagree* on the thoughts, this does not add to the flow of the discussion.

> 'I do not like it either, it is not an applicable tool.'

> 'No, I do not fully agree, however, the most votes count. I do not like it'.

Alternatively, other judges might add to the discussion through *doubting* (negative) or *championing* (positive), through which they attempt to strengthen or weaken the previous arguments:

> 'We could apply some parts of it since they are lucrative. Nevertheless, we will be shut down within a year as a result of the law on competition.'

> 'I liked [Pitch A4], the idea was very applicable and in my opinion feasible.'

Redirecting

After the *framing* phase is over, the bar is set and most pitches have been discussed. The discussion then moves to the next phase, the *redirecting* phase. In this phase, the discussion moves from one topic to another to cover all questions and concerns and discuss all different viewpoints. During this process, certain judges direct and redirect the discussion based on their individual and collective interests. This redirecting can be done through politicking, debating, and questioning. In this phase the subjectivity of entrepreneurial pitches becomes clear. Our findings reveal how the same pitch could be judged completely differently by different judges as a result of their personal criteria.

There are several themes which belong to the redirecting phase. First, *questioning* guides the discussion in a different direction by asking something that does not relate to the topic of discussion. In this sense, judges play a role in questioning the judging process.

> 'Would it not be a good idea to first have a look at the other criteria before going into this much detail?'

Next, *debating* is enacted by countering the current topic with another topic and thereby redirecting the discussion. A judge counters the argument made with a different argument, on which other judges can build and thus redirect the discussion.

'I do not believe in the applied method, however, we can give them [pitching team] the credits for diving into this hard domain.'

During this redirecting phase we also saw compromises emerge as judges sought to find a middle ground when there was no clear consensus. The following example is a *compromise* proposed by one of the judges. This judge compromises by voting a pitch into the top-three in exchange for letting his personal preference win the competition:

'You know what the problem is when I look at the bottom line, and I am checking with my fellow judges, [Pitch B5] should be in. The other two to present would then be [Pitch B3] and [Pitch B4]. However, I suggest that we let [Pitch B5] win then.'

Wrapping up
In the last phase, the *wrapping up* phase, one of the judges mentions the discussion has come to an end by indicating the time is up or everything has been said.

'Shall we just vote, otherwise we will be still discussing in an hour.'

The quote shows an attempt to *end the discussion*, which can often be neglected by the other judges who start discussing again. Then the initiator might try one or several times again to make the discussion end to begin the *wrapping up* phase. Once this happens, a *voting round* is initiated. Often, a judge might attempt to drag the discussion back into a previous phase by *priming* or *debating*, however, after a short time the discussion is *wrapped up*, a top-three is determined, and the discussion ends.

The following standardized judging discussion vignette provides an insight into how the discussion builds and transfers from one phase to another.

Discussion

P1: Well, let us [judges] start talking about what we came here for today.

P2: What I liked about the first pitch, although it did not completely fit the framework as proposed by the organization, is the core of their idea.

P3: Yes, I agree with that.

P1: To a certain extent I agree, however, at some points they did not score that well.

P4: We could apply some parts of the idea, however, implementing the whole plan would not be feasible.

P5: Well, I liked the idea and also think it is very applicable!

P3: Maybe it is a good idea to move on to the other pitches?

P4: I liked the second pitch best, their idea was the most feasible in my opinion.

P2: I do not know, I do not feel that this idea suits the criteria we should be judged on.
....

P1: Shall we just vote? Otherwise, we will be still discussing in an hour or two. We need to come up with a top-three now.
...

P3: So, we all agree on this top-three? Then, I guess this was it!

Phases

Initiating – In this step, the discussion is initiated by one of the judges, by interrupting the ongoing conversation.

Framing – In the framing phase, a frame of reference is shaped. This is done by setting a bar, by discussing a certain pitch. One judge starts about this pitch and others display their personal opinions about it.

Redirecting – After the bar is set other pitches/criteria are discussed. Also, the remaining questions are answered. This phase helps to shape an overall picture of all pitches and rank them.

Wrapping up – After the discussing is done or the time has run out, the discussion is wrapped up. Mostly by interrupting the ongoing discussion and mentioning that the judges should start voting.

Ending Discussion – Once the voting is done and the top-three is determined and agreed upon, the discussion is ended.

Part 2: Underlying Practices of Collective Judging Decisions

We now turn to the underlying practices that appear to shape the accomplishments of collective decisions by the judges: *Alliance Building, Politicking, Undermining*.

Alliance building

Alliance building was a practice that many judges engaged in when there remained debate about the best pitches after multiple conversation turns. Through this practice of alliance building, judges with similar 'top' choices joined forces to ensure the least negative outcomes based on their perceptions. Alliance building tended to be utilized as a practice when there was a disagreement over the merits of a particular pitch. Often a back-and-forth disagreement would play out between two judges, then another judge might join forces with one of the disputing judges to form an alliance that helps to cement a positive view of a particular pitch.

The conversation extract below shows how two judges (P2 and P1) are having a disagreement about the merits of a particular pitch (Pitch 1). To overcome the disagreement, we see another judge (P4) enter the conversation and work together with one of the other judges (P2) to build an alliance that eventually guarantees a higher ranking for the pitch (Pitch 1).

Discussion	Phases and practices
P2: By the way, I thought at that [Pitch 1] that we could achieve a lot of results …	**Priming** – this judge (P2) moves the conversation onto another pitch (Pitch 1) of which they have a favorable opinion.
P1: This actually comes a bit from [another idea they were discussing earlier] that you have a fluent transition between the hospital … I think this is very American, I see little application in [the Netherlands], I am also curious who those parties are that are joining.	**Doubting** – a particular judge starts to dismantle the merits of the pitch.
P2: That would be [an accepted approach]	**Disagreeing** – referencing a standard practice in the Netherlands that this idea aligns with.
P1: No, but how you organize that all the elements in that program	**Doubting** – the disagreeing judge continues to raise doubts about the pitch.
P4: I was recently in [small town] at that department where those people have been lying for so long, they also have track and trace there they asked for permission. This is a very big problem.	**Disagreeing** – another judge (P4) joins the discussion, disagreeing with the doubting judge (P1) and lending support to the argument of the judge (P2) supporting the pitch.
P2: This is really a big problem.	**Confirming** – **Alliance Building** – Judges P2 and P4 begin to work together to cement the high ranking of the pitch.
P4: For money, for life days, when we come to make it [tries to intimidate by slamming his fist on the table ?]. In financial terms I think [Pitch 1] is the top.	**Championing** – **Alliance Building** – making strong argument for the pitch in terms of both social and economic benefits.
P2: Yes agreed.	**Confirming** – **Alliance Building**
P4: That transition from hospital to home that is killing. That lasts weeks!	**Confirming** – **Alliance Building**

Throughout the different judging discussions, the shift towards the *wrapping up* phase often relied on *alliance building*, which served to move a certain pitch high in the rankings, thereby narrowing down the possible winners.

Politicking

Politicking was another common practice enacted within the discussions, where a judge might guide the conversation into a different direction by drawing on powerful actors outside the room. The use of politicking as a practice was observed when a certain judge aimed to either strongly support or strongly denounce a certain pitch. Through drawing on outside actors, judges engaging in politicking as a practice would attempt to lend weight to either their positive or negative view of a pitch. In this sense, politicking can be viewed as similar to alliance building. However, rather than aligning with another judge in the room, an alliance of sorts is made with political actors not directly present in the conversation. In doing so, the judges utilize politicking as a means of appealing to the higher status of other actors (e.g. the Ministry).

The following conversation highlights an instance of politicking as a practice that served to elevate a particular pitch (Pitch 1) higher in the ranking in order to appease the local governmental officials. This example shows how certain judges can draw on politicking as a practice to protect their own interests in ways not necessarily consistent with their opinions about a particular pitch.

Discussion	Phases and practices
P2: What do we think about [Pitch 1]?	**Priming** – this judge (P2) moves the conversation onto another pitch (Pitch 1). With limited indication of their opinion.
P3: I don't fully believe in the method, but you could give them credit for diving into this difficult domain.	**Doubting** – the judge (P3) raises questions about the value of the idea, but respects the direction of the pitch.
P4: I have the same thing, what they claim doesn't work (yes) but they have started to think specifically about this challenge. They did stick their necks out.	**Confirming** – another judge (P4) agrees with the perspective of the previous speaker (P3).
P5: I am not allowed to reason politically, but these guys who visit [us] and say [the chamber] has not even mentioned us. Politically it is just nice if we put them on 3, that's just neat.	**Politicking** – yet another judge enters the conversation, joking about not making a politically based decision, but then clearly and openly suggesting that this pitch should be given a positive ranking.
P3: To be able to come up with this, you have to understand something.	**Championing** – this judge (P3) is persuaded by the political argument.
P5: … and the Ministry could blame us for not giving them [pitching team which is linked to the ministry] more credit.	**Politicking** – By adding to their previous remark.
P6: So this will be our third name? (yes)	**Wrapping up** – and accepting the political argument.
P4: I think it's a very good one.	**Confirming – Politicking** – a change of tone from this judge (P4) compared to initial doubts raised above.

Whereas the previous example illustrates how politicking was used to elevate the ranking of a particular pitch, politicking was also used to paint certain pitches in a negative light. Framing a pitch in a negative light occurred when a judge perceived that certain political actors might not agree with their selection, or judges felt that they might suffer negative consequences from certain pitches being celebrated or commended. The following excerpt reveals a case where politicking was used to caution against voting for an entrepreneurial team that was critical of the Ministry:

P1: Yes, but it's about who do we put on stage now, who gets the press and the attention.

P5: Good that you say that, press and attention, the [Pitch 4] story has a chance of reputation damage for the [Ministry]. Because the first time we heard them talk very condescendingly about the Ministry], if they do that to the press, then you as a [Ministry] will not benefit from it.

Throughout the judging discussions we saw instances of how politicking can shift the tone of the overall discussion, highlighting how other actors outside of the room are also shaping decision-making.

Undermining

A final practice that emerged multiple times in the judging discussions was *undermining*. Undermining involves belittling the opinion of someone else to downgrade their argument and strengthen one's own argument (Duffy et al., 2006). Our findings revealed that during the judging discussions there is a lot of disagreement as a result of different opinions among the judges, which is to be expected. However, some judges make inappropriate remarks at some point, which might be sarcastic or can even be interpreted as painful. In doing so they aim to *undermine* the argument made by the other judge, to strengthen their argument. Judges engaging in undermining practices sought to eliminate pitches they felt strong negative opinions towards.

The following excerpt shows an example of undermining that resulted in a particular pitch being removed from consideration. A judge with strong negative perceptions of a particular pitch shuts down another judge's positive perception of that pitch using strong language and illustrating a lack of respect for the other judge.

Discussion	Phases and practices
P3: I thought the thought was perhaps the strongest about [Pitch 1].	**Championing** – this judge (P3) sings the praises of a particular pitch (Pitch 1) as the conversation draws towards a close.
P1: Maybe I thought that was the worst, [they] just said some general shit. How do you want to do it at all? No idea, people have been working on that for years	**Undermining** – Very strong use of undermining by disrupting the previous arguments in a somewhat disrespectful way.
P2: I thought that was weak indeed. Confirming; which is strange because previously this judge primed the group.	**Confirming** – Another judge (P2) is heavily swayed by the undermining practices and ends up agreeing with the undermining judge (P1) despite originally being a supporter of this pitch earlier in the judging discussion.

Undermining was not always directly displayed in the judging discussions; it was also displayed indirectly via an emotional comment, a sarcastic remark, or laughing, as illustrated in the following interaction which led to the elimination of a pitch that was perceived positively by other judges.

P2: does anyone see [Pitch 1] still winning?

P3: [Pitch 1] is a way of … measuring the emotions of the children based on AI so that they can ask questions more intelligently and know better how children react to things … that doesn't work (laughter).

Undermining evokes a feeling of superiority, as judges try to show that their opinion is better than someone else's. By engaging in this practice, judges hope that others are inclined to support their arguments over the argument of another judge whose opinion is being undermined. For example, one judge was being very enthusiastic about an idea of one of the pitchers, nevertheless, their presenting skills were not overly strong. Therefore another judge commented on the positive remark:

'However, the presentation was a big letdown. It just made me sad.'

By making this remark the positive view of the idea/pitch is erased and even replaced by negative feelings of the pitching skills, leading other judges to focus on the negative aspect of the pitch, instead of the good idea the pitching team proposed.

Overall, undermining practices emerged when judges were passionately against particular pitches receiving a high ranking. In this sense, the practice was more than just the regular disagreement, but an intentional practice that shaped the final collective decisions.

DISCUSSION AND CONCLUDING COMMENTS

This study aimed to unpack the social practices involved as groups of judges at entrepreneurial pitching competitions actually make their decisions. Our findings reveal the core conversational phases of the collective judging process and highlight three dominant practices that shape collective decisions: *Alliance Building*, *Politicking*, and *Undermining*.

Our findings suggest that whilst the persuasiveness of an entrepreneur's pitch can shape the initial *framing* phase of judging discussions (Brooks et al., 2014; Cardon et al., 2009; Chen et al., 2009; Clarke, 2011), it is actually the group dynamics that play out between judges that has the strongest influence on final collective decisions. The practices of *Alliance Building*, *Politicking*, and *Undermining* that are enacted through the process of judging steer collective decision-making in directions that might depart from the quality of the pitches or the ideas. We thereby highlight how the social practices that play out behind closed doors in judging discussions shape the accomplishment of collective judging decisions.

Our study contributes to research on entrepreneurial pitching by showing the importance of examining the role of non-entrepreneur actors, such as judges, in determining entrepreneurial outcomes. By focusing on these non-entrepreneur actors, our study extends research on how social interactions influence pitching outcomes (Pollack et al., 2012; Huang & Pearce, 2015). We add to this research by examining a previously unexplored interaction, the interaction *between judges* behind closed doors. Our findings highlight the importance of focusing on judges' perceptions and preferences when examining entrepreneurial pitching. These findings align with the work of Clark (2008), who found that to be successful, an entrepreneur is dependent on the judging team. Our findings support the work of Huang and Pearce (2015) which suggested that every judge emphasizes different factors, which makes it hard for a pitching team to prepare the right approach. Further, our findings extend prior practice-based research on entrepreneurial pitching (e.g. Teague et al., 2020) by highlighting how it is not only interactions between entrepreneurs and the judges that shape pitching outcomes, but also interactions between the judges themselves.

Our study contributes to research on entrepreneurship-as-practice by focusing on the everyday sayings and doings that play out in entrepreneurial pitching competitions. The study emphasizes the importance of shifting the analysis away from the entrepreneurs and onto the judges involved in entrepreneurial pitching competitions. In doing so we highlight the inherently social nature of entrepreneurial pitching. We unpack how entrepreneurial pitching is a shared social practice that takes place at the intersection of various actors including entrepreneurs and their audience. Future research should expand on this finding to explore interactions with other actors involved in entrepreneurship pitching including teammates, other teams, mentors, coaches, sponsors, organizers and audiences.

Finally, we make a methodological contribution to the study of entrepreneurial practice by accessing the generally 'behind closed doors' practices of collective judging discussions. We showcase how audio recordings allow us to capture entrepreneurial practices as they unfold in real time and the ways in which the discussions shape entrepreneurial outcomes. In doing so, we add to a growing stream of entrepreneurship research that utilizes audio and video recordings to capture entrepreneurship as it happens (Chalmers & Shaw, 2017; Clarke, 2011; Clarke et al., 2018; Ormiston & Thompson, 2021). By focusing on the interactions between entrepreneurs and judges, and between judges themselves, we offer a practical example of how entrepreneurship scholars can move away from the methodological individualism that dominates entrepreneurship research, and focus instead on the relational, social interactional elements of entrepreneurial endeavor (Steyaert, 2007).

This research is limited by its focus on one hackathon event, in one country, and only four panels of judges. Future research could benefit from researching a range of entrepreneurial pitching competitions and diverse groups of judges. Further, our study relied on audio recordings of judging discussions. This restriction was imposed by the event organizers to decrease the interference with the judging process. Future research should incorporate non-invasive video recordings of collective judging discussions to examine how non-verbal elements such as body language, facial expression, gestures, and material objects influence the judging process.

REFERENCES

Balachandra, L., Briggs, T., Eddleston, K., & Brush, C. (2019). Don't pitch like a girl! How gender stereotypes influence investor decisions. *Entrepreneurship Theory and Practice, 43*(1), 116–137.

Brooks, A. W., Huang, L., Kearney, S. W., & Murray, F. E. (2014). Investors prefer entrepreneurial ventures pitched by attractive men. *Proceedings of the National Academy of Sciences, 111*, 4427–4431.

Cardon, M. S., Mitteness, C., & Sudek, R. (2017). Motivational cues and angel investing: Interactions among enthusiasm, preparedness, and commitment. *Entrepreneurship Theory and Practice, 41*(6), 1057–1085.

Cardon, M. S., Sudek, R., & Mitteness, C. (2009). The impact of perceived entrepreneurial passion on angel investing. *Frontiers of Entrepreneurship Research, 29*(2), art. 1.

Chalmers, D., & Shaw, E. (2017). The endogenous construction of entrepreneurial contexts: A practice-based perspective. *International Small Business Journal, 35*, 19–39.

Chen, X. P., Yao, X., & Kotha, S. (2009). Entrepreneur passion and preparedness in business plan presentations: A persuasion analysis of venture capitalists' funding decisions. *Academy of Management Journal, 52*(1), 199–214.

Clark, C. (2008). The impact of entrepreneurs' oral 'pitch' presentation skills on business angels' initial screening investment decisions. *Venture Capital, 10*(3), 257–279.

Clarke, J. (2011). Revitalizing entrepreneurship: How visual symbols are used in entrepreneurial performances. *Journal of Management Studies*, *48*(6), 1365–1391.

Clarke, J. S., Cornelissen, J. P., & Healey, M. P. (2018). Actions speak louder than words: How figurative language and gesturing in entrepreneurial pitches influences investment judgments. *Academy of Management Journal*, *62*(2), 335–360.

Duffy, M. K., Ganster, D. C., Shaw, J. D., Johnson, J. L., & Pagon, M. (2006). The social context of undermining behavior at work. *Organizational Behavior and Human Decision Processes*, *101*(1), 105–126.

Eckhardt, J. T., Shane, S., & Delmar, F. (2006). Multistage selection and the financing of new ventures. *Management Science*, *52*(2), 220–232.

Garfinkel, H. (1967). *Studies in Ethnomethodology*. Englewood Cliffs, NJ: Prentice Hall.

Gartner, W. B., Stam, E., Thompson, N. A., & Verduijn, K. (2016). Entrepreneurship as practice: Grounding contemporary practice theory into entrepreneurship studies. *Entrepreneurship & Regional Development*, *28*(9–10), 813–816.

Garud, R., & Rappa, M. A. (1994). A socio-cognitive model of technological evolution: The case of cochlear implants. *Organization Science*, *5*, 344–362.

Goffman, E. (1983). The interaction order: American Sociological Association, 1982 presidential address. *American Sociological Review*, *48*(1), 1–17.

Goodwin, C., & Heritage, J. (1990). Conversation analysis. *Annual Review of Anthropology*, *19*, 283–307.

Heidegger, M. (1962 [1927]). *Being and Time* (J. Macquarrie & E. Robinson, Trans.). Oxford: Blackwell.

Huang, L., & Pearce, J. (2015). Managing the unknowable: The effectiveness of early-stage investor gut feel in entrepreneurial investment decisions. *Administrative Science Quarterly*, *4*, 634–670.

Jarzabkowski, P., & Seidl, D. (2008). The role of meetings in the social practice of strategy. *Organization Studies*, *29*(11), 1391–1426.

Johannisson, B. (2011). Towards a practice theory of entrepreneuring. *Small Business Economics*, *36*(2), 135–150.

Kanze, D., Huang, L., Conley, M. A., & Higgins, E. T. (2018). We ask men to win and women not to lose: Closing the gender gap in startup funding. *Academy of Management Journal*, *61*(2), 586–614.

Katila, S., Laine, P.-M., & Parkkari, P. (2019). Sociomateriality and affect in institutional work: Constructing the identity of start-up entrepreneurs. *Journal of Management Inquiry*, *28*(3), 381–394.

Miettinen, R., Samra-Fredericks, D., & Yanow, D. (2009). Re-turn to practice: An introductory essay. *Organization Studies*, *30*(12), 1309–1327.

Mitteness, C., Sudek, R., & Cardon, S. M. S. (2012). Angel investor characteristics that determine whether perceived passion leads to higher evaluations of funding potential. *Journal of Business Venturing*, *27*, 592–606.

Nicolini, D. (2012). *Practice Theory, Work, and Organization: An Introduction*. Oxford: Oxford University Press.

Ormiston, J., & Thompson, N. A. (2021). Viewing entrepreneurship 'in motion': Exploring current uses and future possibilities of video-based entrepreneurship research. *Journal of Small Business Management*, *59*(5), 976–1011.

Pollack, J. M., Rutherford, M. W., & Nagy, B. G. (2012). Preparedness and cognitive legitimacy as antecedents of new venture funding in televised business pitches. *Entrepreneurship Theory and Practice*, *36*, 915–939.

Sacks, H., Schegloff, E. A., & Jefferson, G. (1978). A simplest systematics for the organization of turn taking for conversation. In J. Schenkein (Ed.), *Studies in the Organization of Conversational Interaction* (pp. 7–55). New York: Academic Press.

Sandberg, J., & Dall'Alba, G. (2009). Returning to practice anew: A life-world perspective. *Organization Studies*, *30*(12), 1349–1368.

Schatzki, T. R. (2001). Practice theory: An introduction. In T. R. Schatzki, K. K. Cetina, & E. von Savigny (Eds.), *The Practice Turn in Contemporary Theory* (pp. 1–14). London: Routledge.

Schatzki, T. R. (2007). Early Heidegger on sociality. In H. L. Dreyfus & M. A. Wrathall (Eds.), *A Companion to Heidegger* (pp. 233–247). Malden, MA: Blackwell Publishing.

Schatzki, T. R., Knorr Cetina, K., & Savigny, E. von (Eds.) (2001). *The Practice Turn in Contemporary Theory*. London: Routledge.

Sidnell, J. (2010). Conversation analysis. In N. H. Hornberger & S. L. McKay (Eds.), *Sociolinguistics and Language Education* (pp. 492–527). Bristol: Multilingual Matters.

Steyaert, C. (2007). 'Entrepreneuring' as a conceptual attractor? A review of process theories in 20 years of entrepreneurship studies. *Entrepreneurship & Regional Development, 19*(6), 453–477.

Strauss, A., & J. Corbin (1990). *Basics of Qualitative Research: Grounded Theory Procedures and Techniques.* Thousand Oaks, CA: Sage.

Stroe, S., Sirén, C., Shepherd, D., & Wincent, J. (2020). The dualistic regulatory effect of passion on the relationship between fear of failure and negative affect: Insights from facial expression analysis. *Journal of Business Venturing, 35*(4), 105948.

Sudek, R. (2006). Angel investment criteria. *Journal of Small Business Strategy, 17*, 89–103.

Teague, B. T., Gorton, M. D., & Liu, Y. (2020). Different pitches for different stages of entrepreneurial development: The practice of pitching to business angels. *Entrepreneurship & Regional Development, 32*(3–4), 334–352.

Thompson, N. A., & Byrne, O. (2020). Advancing entrepreneurship as practice: Previous developments and future possibilities. In W. B. Gartner & B. T. Teague (Eds.), *Research Handbook on Entrepreneurial Behavior, Practice and Process* (pp. 30–55). Cheltenham, UK and Northampton, MA, USA: Edward Elgar Publishing.

Toerien, M. (2014). Conversations and conversation analysis. In U. Flick (Ed.), *The SAGE Handbook of Qualitative Data Analysis* (pp. 327–340). London: Sage.

van Werven, R., Bouwmeester, O., & Cornelissen, J. P. (2019). Pitching a business idea to investors: How new venture founders use micro-level rhetoric to achieve narrative plausibility and resonance. *International Small Business Journal, 37*(3), 193–214.

Watts, M. (2011). *The Philosophy of Heidegger.* Durham: Acumen.

Whittington, R. (2011). The practice turn in organization research: Towards a disciplined transdisciplinarity. *Accounting, Organizations and Society, 36*(3), 183–186.

Williams, A. (2013). A study on the art and science of pitching new businesses. *MIT Sloan School of Management, 10*(3), 3–55.

17. Entrepreneuring practices: interconnected bundles for digital servitization

Katja Maria Hydle, Magnus Hellström, Tor Helge Aas and Karl Joachim Breunig

INTRODUCTION

Corporate entrepreneurship (CE) refers to firm-level entrepreneurial activities and encompasses both new business within an existing firm and the transformation of the existing firm (Covin & Wales, 2018; Ramachandran et al., 2006). CE describes entrepreneurial behaviour inside established large and mid-sized organizations (Morris et al., 2011). When CE activities are conceptualized, they often include innovation, corporate venturing and strategic renewal activities (Covin & Wales, 2018). Sharma and Chrisman (1999, p. 18) found that CE 'is the process whereby an individual or a group of individuals, in association with an existing organization, create a new organization or instigate renewal or innovation within that organization'. The definition focuses on the individual and the association between individuals and the existing organization.

Further, Bouchard and Fayolle (2018, pp. 27–28) explain that CE involves two different approaches: one is an intrafirm process resulting in innovation and business creation; the other is a characteristic of the firm's strategy, referring to the orientation towards innovation, risk-taking and responsiveness. The authors problematize how traditional CE research consists of many conceptual articles defining CE and developing models that expose the relationship between internal organizational processes and external variables (Bouchard & Fayolle, 2018, p. 30). In addition, they expose how a large part of the CE literature is based on quantitative studies aiming to find correlations between CE and other variables, while another part of the literature is based on single or multiple case studies describing the processes that create new activities within existing organizations. The authors then call for more qualitative approaches to capture the complex and elusive processes of CE, which need to be better understood.

These CE approaches communicate the understanding that CE rests on social ontological individualism, claiming that social life is an aggregate of individuals' actions. Hence, CE research includes the underlying assumption that entrepreneurship as a social phenomenon can be explained by properties of individual people, their mindset, their behaviours and their relations (Schatzki, 2005; Thompson et al., 2020). This chapter uses another ontology: a social practice ontology giving primacy to practices. A social practice ontology is an alternative to individualism in which not all social phenomena are constructed of individuals and their relations, but rather holding that there is something beyond individuals that one needs in order to understand the organizational phenomenon under scrutiny (Schatzki, 2005). Schatzki (2005) calls this site ontology. Since there are multiple people involved in performing one specific practice, practices as phenomena are social. Schatzki (2005) explains that practices are non-individualist phenomena. 'It is people, to be sure, that perform the actions that compose a practice. But the organization of a practice is not a collection of properties of individual people. It is a feature of the practice, expressed in the open-ended set of actions that composes the practice' (Schatzki, 2005, p. 480). To follow a practice ontology, it is necessary to focus on different people's ways of performing particular activities, as well as the events and processes that form part of the practices. Thus, this chapter uses a practice approach to view corporate entrepreneuring and is part of the entrepreneurship-as-practice research domain (Gartner et al., 2016; Thompson & Byrne, 2020).

Using practice theory has the advantage of going deeper into CE to uncover the interrelated activities of practitioners and thus further enhance our knowledge of CE activities as social phenomena (Corradi et al., 2010; Fortwengel et al., 2017; Schatzki, 2012, 2017). Using practice theory to grasp the enacted CE practices is a powerful frame that may expose entrepreneurial activities involved in creating new business within existing corporate structures (Johannisson, 2011, 2012, 2014; Keating et al., 2014; Steyaert & Landström, 2011).

To view the practices of CE, we focus on the transition that manufacturing firms go through when developing new revenue streams from services. This transition from product- to service-oriented business is called servitization (Lightfoot et al., 2013). Servitization describes the transition when manufacturing firms shift focus from tangible products to intangible services (Partanen et al., 2017). A widely studied phenomenon, servitization entails a strategic shift for manufacturing companies (Rabetino et al., 2017), as well as the development of new business within an existing corporate structure. Servitization is well suited for studying new dimensions of CE in a specific setting. So far, such attempts have remained scarce. The related literature has focused more on organizational transformation processes (Baines et al., 2017, 2020) and less on the agency and the practices therein. To our knowledge CE activities that form interdependent practices leading towards new services have not been examined. The research question is: How are corporate entrepreneuring practices enacted when manufacturing firms develop new service-oriented business ventures?

This chapter leans on Schatzki's practice theory (2010, 2012, 2016, 2017, 2019), which emphasizes how practices and arrangements bundle, and how these bundles emerge and interrelate. This chapter reports findings from five different firms in transition, including their emergent practices when they develop and establish new service-oriented business ventures.

The chapter proceeds with a description of certain parts of practice theory relevant to this study on entrepreneuring practices and explains what perspectives the study may provide on the phenomenon of servitization. Then, we explain our method and describe the empirical material we have collected. Next, we explore the four entrepreneuring bundles of practices we found in the empirical material, after which we further analyse their interrelations. We discuss our contribution to practice theory and CE theorizing before concluding with the limitations of this study and outlining future research avenues.

PRACTICE THEORY

From a practice theoretical perspective on servitization, it is important to grasp the practices involved when manufacturing firms are changing focus from products to services. Uncovering particular practices in servitization entails focusing on the activities that hang together while developing intangible services in manufacturing firms.

A practice is composed of multiple activities that hang together in a teleological order that is normative in relation to the activities performed (Schatzki, 2012; Schatzki et al., 2001).

Customer relationship management can be considered a practice composed of multiple activities, such as customer contact, project follow-up, and so on, that are normative to the practice. Practices are thus sets of organized activities (Schatzki, 2012; Schatzki et al., 2001). A practice consists of multiple activities, and an activity is the performing, the doing, while an action is what is done. Basic bodily actions of doings and saying (such as holding a phone, talking on the phone and typing on a keyboard) form activities, while multiple activities following an accepted and prescribed teleological order are understood as part of a practice (e.g. customer relationship management). Focusing on servitization implies identifying the emergence of new practices related to services (Schatzki, 2013). Practice emergence will expose the locus of change and hence the servitization transition, which in turn highlights how firms expand into new business and CE phenomena.

Practices use, react to, and are inseparable from material arrangements, while material arrangements prefigure practices. Material arrangements are things, artefacts and even human bodies. Practices and material arrangements bundle, meaning they are bound together. Following Schatzki (2010, p. 77), 'a practice-arrangement bundle is linked sets of organized doings and sayings that are performed amid interconnected … material arrangements'. Organizations and firms are understood as bundles of practices and material arrangements. People's lives hang together through bundles and interconnected practices and arrangements (Schatzki, 2016, p. 5). Bundles overlap when actions are part of the practices of different bundles (Schatzki, 2010) (e.g. talking to a customer may be a part of customer relationship management practices, of accounting practices and of project management practices). Interactions, learning and experiences take place in bundles while people perform actions. Further, bundles of practices and arrangements are defined by their relatedness and how dense these relations are, although the patterns of relations are relatively durable (Schatzki, 2016, p. 6).

Practice-arrangement bundles do not just emerge. Often there are periods in transitions, such as the introduction of new technology, before bundles emerge. 'Periods of ferment or transition give way to new bundles as people's activities, often without their knowledge, come to be governed by common rules, teleological structures and general understandings' (Schatzki, 2013, p. 39). Since practices are performed by multiple people, and since people's reactions to events and happenings are different and their activities form sequences, it takes time for commonalities to emerge. This is why experimentation and unpredictability often precede stability and organization. New practical understanding by the participants also needs to evolve, such as knowing how to use new technology.

We will use these insights to understand servitization as entrepreneuring practices – the material arrangements and the bundles that the practices and arrangement form – leading to the establishment of new service-oriented business ventures. We focus on different participants' activities, how these activities form practices, how different practices are connected and bundled with material arrangements, and how these bundles evolve.

METHODS

The empirical setting was an industrial cluster of oil and gas suppliers within the Norwegian energy and maritime sectors. The strength of uncovering bundles of practices and arrangements across firms was being able to identify the same types of activities, practices, material

Table 17.1   *An overview of the companies and empirical material*

Name	Offering	Discussion meetings	Workshops	Semi-structured interviewees
Alpha	Engineering, procurement, fabrication, transportation, construction, installation supervision, project management (on an engineer-to-order basis).	3	3	15
Beta	Tailor-made drilling equipment and systems, and related life-cycle services such as training and remote diagnostics and online support.	3	3	17
Gamma	Lifting equipment and related life-cycle services such as training, remote diagnostics and online support.	3	2	11
Delta	Custom-made operator chairs in small series.	2	1	7
Epsilon	Lay flat hoses. Sensored hoses as future prospects.	3	1	16
All	*Experience exchange workshop*		2	
Total		14	12	66

arrangements and bundles during their efforts to change from product centricity to a service focus through new service-oriented business ventures. More specifically, we were able to uncover entrepreneuring practices in five firms, retrospectively (see Table 17.1). The firms were at different stages of servitization, which is why we chose to interview and capture oral histories where the researchers participated over an extended period of time, asking questions, uncovering what happened and collecting accounts that shed light on issues of concern (Rasche & Chia, 2009; Schatzki, 2012). The different bundles of practices and material arrangements were found in retrospect (Tsoukas, 2010), while we discussed these uncovered practices and the bundles with the practitioners during discussion meetings, workshops and later rounds of interviews. The understanding of the practices used, related material arrangements and labels of the bundles hence emerged during the years we worked with the firms. We did not follow or shadow the different servitization activities within the five firms; instead, we chose to have different rounds of interviews in the firms, workshops, and discussion meetings with the practitioners involved in servitization to capture the practices in retrospect; we used practice theory to understand the different findings and to uncover the bundles of practices and material arrangements.

We collected data through two separate rounds of semi-structured in-depth interviews with employees involved in servitization and corporate entrepreneuring. The first round was in fall 2018, the second in spring 2020. The aim of these two rounds was to capture the transition from products to services and identify the commonalities between the firms without needing to perform observations in five firms over a two-year period. The interviewees were mainly people involved in servitization along with some others representing the current product focus, ranging from service engineers, IT engineers, product engineers, and middle management to top management. In addition to interviews, we had several discussion meetings involving 8–14 people in the firms, participation at internal workshops regarding specific digital service innovation activities, interaction arenas between the firms discussing common challenges, several guided tours of the firms and presentations of the different services and document studies.

The empirical material was analysed abductively (Alvesson & Kärreman, 2011; Peirce, 1978) in different iterative rounds, comparing findings with different theoretical insights. The empirical material was examined in relation to our research question, balancing the empirically grounded findings with theoretically driven research practices. We used literature on servitization (Baines et al., 2017, 2020; Lightfoot et al., 2013; Vandermerwe & Rada, 1988) for the context of our companies, literature on CE (Covin & Wales, 2018; Kuratko & Audretsch, 2013; Kuratko et al., 2014; Kuratko & Morris, 2018; Morris et al., 2011) to frame the study, and practice theory to grasp the practices, the related material arrangements and the bundles these formed, and emergent phenomena. We analysed different types of activities and practices involved in servitization within each firm.

Our analysis also helped identify regularities across the firms. Although there were large variations between the firms regarding how far they achieved the transition to servitization, we were surprised by the similarities of the activities and practices across the firms leading towards new business within the existing corporations. The bundles were uncovered at different times of the research and the order of their uncovering is described successively. We began by uncovering the first bundle of practices and arrangements, prospecting the ecosystem while visiting the firms, inquiring about different internal and external research and innovation projects, talking with senior employees and interviewing several employees. Prospecting the ecosystem yielded observations of bundles of different practices that led to understanding the markets in new ways, retrospectively. Next we slowly identified the fourth bundle, establishing the new service-oriented business venture, through visits, interviews and discussions. These findings, which were mainly based on the first round of interviews, one experience exchange workshop and a few discussion meetings with the firms, were later extended with the second bundle of practices: development activities. Several different internal company workshops in 2019 enabled us to shed light on their activities developing their new service-oriented business ventures. This is in line with Schatzki's emphasis that it takes time for commonalities to emerge (2013). Towards the end of our research, we uncovered the third bundle, transforming the existing organization, since we identified the effects of these practices – hence, uncovering them in retrospect – in the final discussion meetings and workshops with the firms.

These findings, the bundles of practice-arrangements, were inquired about through open-ended questions and also discussed with different top managers, middle managers and employees involved in servitization to validate the data's veracity and enhance the trustworthiness of the analysis (Lincoln & Guba, 1985). These inquiries and discussions gave valuable insights about interconnection and interrelations between the different bundles. The four bundles of practice-arrangements are described and discussed in the next sections.

FINDINGS

Across the firms, we uncovered four different interrelated entrepreneurial practice-arrangement bundles that were often performed in parallel, related to servitization. These bundles are: (1) prospecting the industry and innovation ecosystem for servitization, (2) developing the new service-oriented business venture based on deep needs understanding, (3) transforming the organization for servitization, and (4) establishing the new service-oriented business venture.

Prospecting the Industry and Innovation Ecosystem for Servitization

The first entrepreneurial bundle of practice-arrangement of servitization was related to foreseeing new markets for services based on understanding the entire industry, the related ecosystem across the traditional value chain and the possibilities for new directions for the firm. The practices of the bundle involve understanding the market, collaborators and competitors, customers, and end-users' needs, all of which is necessary for firms to be able to provide services. This is in sharp contrast to the earlier situation, where the company's model was to deliver products to the customer without having to consider the surrounding environment or the customer's needs and situation. The practices of the bundle were undertaken by expert engineers, those who had spent major parts of their professional lives in the firm or within the industry without a formal expert title, but with a lot of weight internally in the firms.

The practices consist of participating in both internal and external research and development projects. Within these projects, the experts are, for example, creating simulations to develop solutions for different future scenarios. They use simulation tools to plan future operations and verify these by using sensors to measure whether they effectively simulate different operations, analyses and tools to support decision making. One example is from crane operations on boats in Gamma. These operations entail heavy lifts from the sea floor, vulnerable to weather and mistakes. The most complicated lifting operations may take up to two years to prepare. The focus was much more on conformance (to requirements) than on overall performance. As explained by one expert:

> After all, the critical phases of a lift are when lifting from the deck and underwater. Then you have to know that the sea condition is good and that the equipment can cope with current conditions. Surely you can use simulation technology and make the right decisions: 'Now it looks a bit rough, but is it okay to do that?' That kind of question we sit and work on and we have specific projects. We have also done simulations of marine operations and we have done similar measurements with sensors. We can estimate this here. Then we have another project with many partners. There we have measurements on the vessel and can look at the waves coming towards the vessel; we also detect the size of the waves and how they will develop towards the vessel. Then we have other partners who see how the vessel will move. Then we have others who make simulation models to simulate the effect of the waves coming on the vessel. So, there are long chains then. Anyway, it gives you a window that lets you say that: 'Within five minutes, we can do that operation.' It usually takes five minutes to get it done. Then you reckon you might save 30 per cent because you are often waiting for the weather. Especially in the winter. Then one can use such systems. Such operations benefit the industry. I think we manage to combine that type of service ... and we put ourselves in a much better competitive situation than others who have only one requirement. We have more of a total package.

Innovating new digitally enhanced services essentially requires new externally oriented practices. Some of the expert engineers were entrepreneurial and initiated practices internally in the firms to delve into challenges in new ways. One of these experts in Beta portrayed himself as follows: 'He [the CEO] has told me several times that he can only afford one of me.' He points at the need for questioning current external relationships by using the car industry as an example:

> My claim in the latest technology strategy, which I presented to our board, came with a rather strong claim. The claim is that the specifications we receive from our customers are wrong. Sure, when you buy a car, do you really think you are better in specifying that car than those who do research on cars and come up with improvements all the time? You're not better than BMW's R&D department. But

we have a tendency in this industry to just take the specifications and deliver according to it. We do not even ask questions.

The expert further explains how they work with customers' situations:

Getting to a customer who has a business model where he does not profit from being more efficient is a difficult sale. It is only when the [oil] downturn began, that they started to focus on it and then they started to buy these services. So, we work through and made some processes on how and in what order we should do things. Then we started to develop some tools to make the process more efficient. Then we have used the simulator technology to implement improvements, show the customer the improvements and enable them to do the calculations on efficiency internally.

Another such expert from Gamma described the importance of prospecting customer needs:

It's about getting closer to the customer and about offering several types of services related to this. We see that there are some challenges that our customers have today. They have high debt, they have products and solutions that are outdated, and it is difficult to use new technology because they are locked-in because they made earlier investments. One method, which I have thought about, is to switch to more service-based, to sell it as a service. Then this could be a platform and introduce new technologies, so that we who have these services and the knowledge of the technology, could make use of this to get a more efficient service which in turn had been beneficial to our customers. It could also improve our competitive position in relation to doing so.

These expert engineers initiate practices internally in the firms to delve into challenges in a new externally oriented and systemic way. Their practices involve knowing, viewing and prospecting the entire ecosystem and determining how their firm can take a new role towards customers and within the ecosystem. Furthermore, the practices are inseparable from the material arrangements used, such as the sensors, simulation tools and simulator technology (virtual reality). This bundle of practices-arrangements is closely related to the strategy of the firms and to top management decision making, since these practices lay the ground for future services. The practice-arrangement bundle can even be understood as the strategizing practices of conducting internal and external research projects for future prospects.

Developing New Service-Oriented Business Ventures Based on Deep Needs Understanding

The second entrepreneurial bundle of practices involves fostering and developing digital services by understanding the challenges and customer needs in depth. The practices involved in this bundle were exploring the problem, finding options to solve the challenge, testing different solutions, presenting a solution and further developing the service. As an example from Beta regarding oil platforms and drilling, one practice was about exploring the customer challenges:

Before, we focused on the top of the [oil platform] deck. Now, we focus on what is going on down in the [drill] well and what we can support. There are 20–30 men on land with the same focus. And it's all about the logistics, the crane being moved, and it's so complex. All of them have to collaborate; everyone has their systems, something on paper, something oral, things change, they have to get in all the information, some are really tired, they meet onshore every day, and a lot happens on many levels, for the driller and the supervisor.

Two people from Beta, here called development engineers, visited different rigs and followed the different drilling practices on the rigs to be able to assist the drillers better. A drilling crew consists of a core of 20–30 people. In addition, there are some others on the rig who have support tasks and others as well in the office onshore. The development engineers from Beta noticed that they used whiteboards to plan and go through daily operations, that they had a lot on paper, Post-it notes, and that they used the phone to communicate between each other as well as several different screens. As one Beta engineer explained about the driller: 'When he drives, there is so much, and adding an extra screen has no function. They have an incredible need for visualization and detailed drawings.'

The practices of the development engineer at the customer site were following and observing different drilling crews using a design methodology in five phases: define concept, get insights, translate findings, test ideas and choose concept. These two developers first stayed at the rig over several weeks, following and observing the different workers within various drilling crews and how they worked, met, talked and cooperated. The development engineers from Beta were taking a lot of notes and photos to visualize the working practices at the oil platforms and in the onshore offices. They tested ideas with the drillers, had workshops with the assistant drillers and collaborated closely with the crews both offshore and onshore.

The development engineers developed 'StayAlert', the new digital service business venture as a result of and after following the customers' drilling practices. The practices and related material arrangements of fostering digital services were about knowing the customer needs, designing and developing the software and finding out how to price the software in the market.

> StayAlert: It is a result of having started working with services and seeing that in the working life of the driller or those doing the operation, there is a sea of different services information input. Some are digitized, some are analogue, others have yellow Post-it patches on the wall. So, it is a wonderful collection of sources of error. These are recreated at different levels and different versions, often in multiple environments on the same rig: Down at the drill leader, drills, you have [an] assistant who sits in your own office and has theirs. So, there is simply a significant danger potential for making mistakes. There, this product has taken aim at gathering these on a platform that allows all 'stakeholders' to get the information and collect information on the platform, to retrieve and collect exactly what they need. Then it is also adapted to the drill which is completely dependent on the present to read the information to be used. There, the system will provide necessary information that is customized wherever they are, at any time. Then you have these others who are more observers, who can pick up and deliver and choose a little more what they want to see and at what time. So, it's a pretty exciting product that is definitely a result of that.

The development engineers undertook practices to develop new solutions for these highly complex operations, which inevitably comes with a need to cope with uncertainty. A developer from Gamma explained the practices and the uncertainty involved in developing new solutions:

> I am basically a creator skull … [T]here is something better that needs to be found out as we approach the goal somehow, then it crystallizes … I do not need to know that the product should be like this when it is finished, as long as the gut feeling that we must go in that direction … And so, I've experienced so many times that no matter how much time we spend in mapping and analysis, using process charts in the start-up, with financial analysis and so on and so forth. Never hit. You may end up at 60, 70, 80 per cent, but there is always a factor of uncertainty that you do not notice until you start.

The practices of developing new service-oriented business ventures involved an interesting connection between top management and the expert engineers developing the new ventures. As is evident from the above quote by the developer at Gamma, despite rigorous studies of user needs, there is always lots of uncertainty attached to the development of these types of solutions. Hence, a fair share of trust and support is needed from the top management to let the trial and error aspects of development activities go on. This entails that the practice-arrangement bundle of developing new service-oriented business ventures, such as StayAlert, be closely related to the practices performed by top management signifying trust and support of such development. We identified various expert developers in all companies undertaking development practices, and we also found promoters among senior management who enabled the sometimes rather long development lead times to get the new venture going. Hence, the practice-arrangement bundle of developing new service-oriented business ventures is closely related to the bundle of practices of transforming the organization for servitization.

Transforming the Existing Organization for Servitization

The third practice-arrangement bundle we uncovered involved facilitating the organizational transformation and following up internal changes in the organization to enable development of new service-oriented business ventures. Coping with challenges proved to be an essential part of this practice-bundle. A middle manager in Gamma describes the challenges for the required organizational transformation that had just started due to an increased service orientation:

> And then we have what we call internal barriers which would be solved by having a solid, large, global, all-inclusive service organization, and then we build the organization on it. And then some of us say that we rather think we need to think about segmentation. Look at the segments. A rig operator in the North Sea is not the same as a container ship operator in Greece, right. There are two different markets. There are two different customers. There are two different needs. There are different business models to achieve. There may be different services we should sell. So, then we have to think more about the segments, like matrices. We need to think more vertical rather than horizontal. I believe in matrices. Then it is not certain that it is right. Maybe an intermediary. But it is one ongoing process. And there is a lot of maturation that is needed to get there, I think.

The practices we found are related to the organizational transformation necessary to enable the new digital services that are under development. One middle manager in Alpha explained:

> Digitization is first and foremost to have order internally. The fact that we are digitalizing is to connect the various departments together, so that everyone works immediately or follows the same red thread.

Another middle manager from Alpha described the reason behind a project management practice and the use of material arrangements such as the project implementation model and digital tools:

> When I started last year trying to find out what someone wanted, find out what we should do, it took the direction of working with and improving the project implementation model because it is the big ugly wolf. We are simply too bad. We are not good enough to manage and implement our projects. In order to be good at it, we have to take advantage of the opportunities that lie in the digital tools today. So, it has in a way more and more crystallized. In the beginning, I think many people had expectations

that the answer was robots, or the answer was in some way that kind of thing, but what is the thing is that robots can help us if we are basically good at managing projects.

The practices of connecting departments internally and changing the way of working on projects were found in every firm. A manager for Beta described the challenges for internal improvements between departments regarding services and the need for new types of competence:

> For me personally, it is most important to make use of synergies. When it comes to 'Operation', those who develop our products in after-sales service, I can say that there is potential for improvement. One of the reasons for this is that we have got some new projects, so they develop into the 'ongoing' project and we must fight to get our part of the cake to deliver services on operations. Then there is this resource problem … and capacity. It is not an unwillingness … When it comes to critical competence, I find that we are not good at defining what competence we need. It's not that simple to just say that we suddenly need a software designer … but we need to know more about what kind of profiles we are looking for.

Another manager from Beta highlighted the same challenge when integrating new technology: 'We cannot staff ourselves because we are part of a total package. It is linked to some organizational designs on how far we can go.' A middle manager in Epsilon highlights how they are challenged by organizational transformation and tries to address some of the missing competences by training.

> There is a lot of work for certain individuals, since there are ever more requirements, then there are many new employees who do not see the big picture and the connections. Thus, we are doing a lot of training where we try to work on what we are going to do. After all, the solution is not just to employ more people. It is so specialized, what we are doing. So, there are a few individuals who really [know] what matter. I just see that we in the management team are 6–7 people.

This practice of transforming the organization towards providing new services and using digitalization is only performed by middle managers.

Establishing the New Service-Oriented Business Venture

The fourth entrepreneurial bundle of practice-arrangement was fusing the various services and adopting, integrating and using digital technology for service provision. These practices relate to the actual services and expose how digital technology needs to be more integrated in service performance and used to provide the services. One informant from Beta explains the integration and use of digital technology for providing different services:

> We have to hurry up. After all, all this is about working smart. You know this particular customer deal. We are responsible for maintenance and the customer is not specific about what we do. From our part, we have to work smart … We want to gather technology and expertise around what we call a 'Smart Operation Centre' which will improve our strengths and expertise and digitization. The services we have that affect our efficiency are 'Work Boost', which is strengthened by the 'Work Investigator', but also 'Dedicated Support' which has also been strengthened by the 'Work Investigator'.

The informant describes an existing large customer and how they now deal with maintenance service through the different branded services of Work Boost, Work Investigator and

Dedicated Support and continues to explain how this can be performed in the future through virtual services and special tools being material arrangements, such as smart online glasses with picture and sound (artificial reality):

> So, we see that we want to make something special on 'Virtual Special Services' which means that we can help the customer in a better way than today. Today, we take the phone and help the customer by using the tool called 'Symptomatic' to monitor the logic of their control system [offshore]. What is a problem for our customers is when they have a real problem which we cannot solve that way [over the phone] and we must tell them that they have to wait to until we manage to get a man out there [by plane, boat or helicopter]. Then time and money fly. Then we see that with the help of glasses, we can help this person by seeing what he sees, hearing what he hears, use our expertise [onshore] with him and hopefully ...

The Virtual Special Services that are described here will thus enable Beta to monitor, help and assist customers during their operations offshore, while the experts are located onshore. Gamma has similar services under development, although for an entirely different market. Instead of offshore platforms, they service ships and they have just completed a project regarding autonomous ships with other large actors. A manager described the service situation as follows:

> If we get the products digitized in a good way and we can offer services and to a great extent sit and monitor the equipment for the customer, then we get the aftermarket as well. It's important. Then we see how it develops here in the world with autonomous ships ...   As soon as there is no more crew on board, it is unlikely to send ... service engineers on board either. Then we, as a company, must have another 'Interface' towards that ship.

Other types of maintenance and controlling services using sensors are under development both in Beta and Gamma. Epsilon has innovation projects integrating sensors in the products to secure and monitor leakages, for instance: 'And then it is of course exciting with sensors, but there we just have to go out and find something that exists and embed these into the hoses.' The quotes indicate services that are under development and how these services are being or will be developed by integrating existing technology in a new way, thus establishing the new service venture. The technology enables an entire set of new services and new ways of working, both for the service firm and for their customer. The practices internally are highly entrepreneurial since such integration of technology is new in these specific markets and the services that are under development have not been rendered before. The informants involved in these different practices are employees working directly with the services.

ANALYSIS

Analysing these four practice-arrangement bundles, using a practice theoretical lens, gives an understanding of the emergence of new service-oriented business ventures. Practice theory establishes that practice-arrangement bundles often emerge after periods of transition, such as the introduction of new technology (Schatzki, 2013). The industry and the companies we studied are going through major transitions from product-oriented to more service-oriented deliveries, and more recently 'digital servitization' (Kohtamäki et al., 2019). Technologies such as sensors, IoT, virtual reality, simulations, artificial reality and automation and robotics all enable the development of new services, as illustrated above. However, the companies experience different realities; some drive the transition internally in the organization without a demanding industrial customer asking for new servitized solutions, while others have a customer expecting such new business services. A top manager in Beta explained:

> So, there is a sea of difference between saying, 'We believe in this, so we spend money on it', where everyone should understand what solution to believe in and everyone should 'buy in' and all that, and saying, 'We have agreed with our Customer [anonymized] to make this', so you have to join! Then, you do not need to get everyone's 'buy in' in all decisions ... say, 'This, we need answers to. We need answers to this now.' [With a customer onboard:] Just thunder on, make that thing there and then, find out if the solution had any value and then we can answer the question afterwards. But this is much more difficult if we decide to make a big effort without having a customer. Then we had to have someone running around and make it happen. Someone who was loyal to the idea and had a lot of ownership to make it happen.

Using practice theory, we identified four important bundles of practice-arrangements for new service business venture development. These different bundles are composed of several different practices and material arrangements. The first bundle of practice-arrangements is related to the multi-layered innovation ecosystem. Prospecting the market, the industry, the customers and end-user needs obtained by expert engineers with long experience within the industry constituted the necessary impetus to be able to provide the services. These practices concern the reasons why certain services are needed. The main practices involved are research project management, simulating scenarios, verifying the results and convincing other stakeholders about the viability of the findings, while the main material arrangements used, apart from bodies, PCs, furniture and papers, are simulation tools and sensors.

The second entrepreneuring bundle of practice-arrangements is related to developing a prototype or solution, using technology and understanding the different aspects of the challenges. It was described by those involved in development. Further, top management and middle managers also referred to these activities and the people involved, due to their reliance on the solutions as well as the related costs. The main practices found were exploring the problem, finding options to solve the challenges, finding different solutions, presenting a solution and further developing the services. These bundled practices of developing solutions are closely related to the practices performed by middle managers in transforming the organization. Following Schatzki (2016, p. 6), bundles of practices and arrangements are defined by their relatedness since relations between the bundles are relatively durable. Regarding the interrelations between the bundles of developing solutions and of transforming the organization, one manager explained: 'Those who knew (the solutions) the best, communicated the worst with people ... These are people with relatively large capacity in general and then something needs to be simplified or communicated ... [I]t is clear that they are missing some link from their box to the world around them.' The 'world around them' refers to involving the entire organization in the developments. Hence, for the development bundle to succeed, the transforming the organization bundle must involve the organization.

The third bundle is related to the organizational transformation to enable services and was performed by the middle managers. In order to transform the organization, enable new collaborations and facilitate coordination between divisions to develop and provide new services, their focus was on how to further enhance learning, experience exchange and develop new competences related to new technology and developing solutions. A member of a top management team openly talked about how enabling the transition is related to development activities:

> Those in development [do] not have competence on change … They have no management experience. But they are put into the group because they have the nerdy development skills. While now I think we are starting to take some lessons from the processes that we have gone through and then maybe we can do it in a better way.

The fourth bundle is related to the service orientation and how digital technology will be more integrated into the products and also used to provide the services. This practice-arrangement bundle was performed by those supplying the services. These employees were deeply involved in service provision to the customers and worked on which services should be offered. A top manager in Beta commented, exposing the relation between the second and the fourth practice-bundles: 'We have people who understand the technology in depth. Then we have someone who understands the customer value in depth, so we have to put them together.'

Bundles of practices and arrangements are defined by their relatedness, how dense these relations are, although the patterns of relations are relatively durable (Schatzki, 2016, p. 6). Each of the bundles we uncovered are interrelated and interconnected with the others. Without the transforming organization, the developing activities would not see light. Without the developing activities and the transforming organization, the integration of services would not happen. Without the understanding of the ecosystem, the other bundles would not be successful. When asked about how they managed to come up with a servitized solution, one manager talked about the persons involved in his firm, indirectly exposing the activities and the interrelations between the practices and bundles:

> The developer job, we have two specifically that are sitting here working on that service. On the Dedicated Support service, if it … had not been for that group there, this would not have worked. Had it not been for the four people with Tom in the lead and Ole and Rolf … They are the ones making this here. It is Ole who understands the customer and their challenges. Not least, also how to improve internal processes. Ole and Rolf are developing what he envisions. And Tom, who is facilitating … But it's just a small group who manages to perform this. [Names anonymized.]

The bundled practices and how these interrelate are summed up after inquiring about the findings with a top management team member in Alpha:

> After all, we depend on benevolence on every level to achieve it. You can have a good idea, have faith in it and the customer signals that they want it, but if we do not get access to the resources that can help to do the job … You need to have the experts who hand out the solution and the concept. Then you have to have the execution link that is actually testing it out in a pilot and preferably offshore or in a simulator. Then you have to have access and the will to put those resources in place. Then you have to have a willingness in the company to take that cost. Everything has a cost.

The quote exposes how all the bundles are interrelated with dense relations. The experts need to have an understanding of the solution and the concept, the developers need to develop the solution, the different technologies need to be integrated in relation to the customer expectations, and the managers have to assure that the right people are involved and the necessary resources are used to achieve the servitized solution.

DISCUSSION AND CONCLUSIONS

We set out to answer the question: How are corporate entrepreneuring practices enacted when manufacturing firms develop new service-oriented business ventures? We explored five different firms over a two-year period while they were striving to develop new service business ventures. Although the firms were at different stages in the servitization process, we found four common bundles of practice-arrangements related to servitization within the firms.

These bundles were composed of several practices, and their related material arrangements and the bundles were interrelated. We used practice theory to expose entrepreneuring servitization practices as interconnected bundles. Schatzki (2012, 2013, 2017) explains well how bundles develop and emerge, what the bundles consist of and how the bundles interrelate. Practice theory enabled us to uncover the four bundles and their emergence, exposing the development of new service business ventures. Our contribution to CE theory is thus using practice theory to uncover different emergent bundled practices and related material arrangements in servitizing organizations, interconnections among the different bundles, and ways organizations develop through such bundles. This extends CE theorizing (Bouchard & Fayolle, 2018; Covin & Wales, 2018; Kuratko & Audretsch, 2013; Kuratko et al., 2014; Kuratko & Morris, 2018; Morris et al., 2011) by using practice theory to shed light on entrepreneuring activities building future business.

These four bundles for new service business venture development were prospecting the industry, developing the service-oriented business venture, transforming the organization and establishing the business venture. These bundles were found due to a social practice ontology, focusing on how different people perform activities, how these activities form part of practices, and how these practices form larger bundles together with the related material arrangements. The focus is quite different from viewing the mindset or behaviour of entrepreneurial leaders or the various strategic roles of managers which related to a social ontological individualism in CE.

The four practice-arrangement bundles identified in this chapter also expose that there are different types of practitioners involved in the four corporate entrepreneuring practices: the first involved the senior engineers focusing on the markets; the second, engineers with development responsibility; the third, middle managers working with the organizational transformation; and the fourth, the employees performing the services. Through our findings, with a focus on the practices performed, we uncovered different sets of employees with strategic roles in corporate entrepreneuring. However, the roles of the practitioners are not in focus, but their activities, which constitute the practices forming larger practice-bundles, are. The second contribution of this chapter is identifying that different employees have different strategic roles when focusing on the practices and not on the practitioners' roles. This empirical extension may seem commonsensical; however, practices and enacted activities often reflect common sense once uncovered, which highlights how and why practice theory is such a powerful lens; the theoretical descriptions may seem abstract, while the empirical expositions are close to the observed phenomena.

For CE and entrepreneurship-as-practice theorizing, our findings expose four different corporate entrepreneuring bundles of practices and related arrangements, the ways these practices and arrangements emerge and bundle, and the actors involved. The implications for CE theorizing are to use practice theory as a tool to further grasp and uncover entrepreneuring activities within corporations. The implications for practitioners are to understand the four different corporate entrepreneuring bundles that need to be enhanced for transition – in this case, servitization.

A limitation of this study is that we have not conducted ethnographic studies of practices within the firms. An ethnographic study of entrepreneuring practices would bring much to the field since traditional research methods are not able to uncover interrelated activities and the practices at stake. Each of the researchers could have been present in each firm over a longer period of time to uncover the different bundled practice-arrangements, although it would be time-consuming and allow fewer possibilities for identifying the emergent while regular practices across the firms. Future research could therefore use both practice-based studies and practice theory to study corporate entrepreneuring bundles, practices and related material arrangements at length and in depth. Another fruitful avenue is to focus on other types of transitions, to identify other types of bundles of practices and material arrangements, enabling firms to diversify into new areas. Corporate entrepreneuring practices are interesting phenomena on the edge of change.

REFERENCES

Alvesson, M., & Kärreman, D. (2011). *Qualitative Research and Theory Development: Mystery as Method.* London: Sage.

Baines, T., Ziaee Bigdeli, A., Bustinza, O. F., Shi, V. G., Baldwin, J., & Ridgway, K. (2017). Servitization: Revisiting the state-of-the-art and research priorities. *International Journal of Operations & Production Management, 37*(2), 256–278.

Baines, T., Ziaee Bigdeli, A., Sousa, R., & Schroeder, A. (2020). Framing the servitization transformation process: A model to understand and facilitate the servitization journey. *International Journal of Production Economics, 221*, 107463.

Bouchard, V., & Fayolle, A. (2018). *Corporate Entrepreneurship.* London: Routledge.

Corradi, G., Gherardi, S., & Verzelloni, L. (2010). Through the practice lens: Where is the bandwagon of practice-based studies heading? *Management Learning, 41*(3), 265–283.

Covin, J. G., & Wales, W. J. (2018). Crafting high-impact entrepreneurial orientation research: Some suggested guidelines. *Entrepreneurship Theory and Practice, 43*(1), 3–18.

Fortwengel, J., Schüßler, E., & Sydow, J. (2017). Studying organizational creativity as process: Fluidity or duality? *Creativity and Innovation Management, 26*(1), 5–16.

Gartner, W. B., Stam, E., Thompson, N. A., & Verduijn, K. (2016). Entrepreneurship as practice: Grounding contemporary practice theory into entrepreneurship studies. *Entrepreneurship & Regional Development, 28*(9–10), 813–816.

Johannisson, B. (2011). Towards a practice theory of entrepreneuring. *Small Business Economics, 36*(2), 135–150.

Johannisson, B. (2012). Tracking the everyday practices of societal entrepreneuring. In K. Berglund, B. Johannisson, & B. Schwartz (Eds.), *Societal Entrepreneurship: Positioning, Penetrating, Promoting* (pp. 60–88). Cheltenham, UK and Northampton, MA, USA: Edward Elgar Publishing.

Johannisson, B. (2014). The practice approach and interactive research in entrepreneurship and small-scale venturing. In A. Carsrud & M. Brännback (Eds.), *Handbook of Research Methods and Applications in Entrepreneurship and Small Business* (pp. 228–258). Cheltenham, UK and Northampton, MA, USA: Edward Elgar Publishing.

Keating, A., Geiger, S., & McLoughlin, D. (2014). Riding the practice waves: Social resourcing practices during new venture development. *Entrepreneurship Theory and Practice, 38*(5), 1207–1235.

Kohtamäki, M., Parida, V., Oghazi, P., Gebauer, H., & Baines, T. (2019). Digital servitization business models in ecosystems: A theory of the firm. *Journal of Business Research, 104*, 380–392.

Kuratko, D. F., & Audretsch, D. B. (2013). Clarifying the domains of corporate entrepreneurship. *International Entrepreneurship and Management Journal, 9*(3), 323–335.

Kuratko, D. F., Hornsby, J. S., & Covin, J. G. (2014). Diagnosing a firm's internal environment for corporate entrepreneurship. *Business Horizons*, *57*(1), 37–47.

Kuratko, D. F., & Morris, M. H. (2018). Corporate entrepreneurship: A critical challenge for educators and researchers. *Entrepreneurship Education and Pedagogy*, *1*(1), 42–60.

Lightfoot, H. W., Baines, T., & Smart, P. (2013). The servitization of manufacturing: A systematic literature review of interdependent trends. *International Journal of Operations & Production Management*, *33*(11–12), 1408–1434.

Lincoln, Y. S., & Guba, E. G. (1985). *Naturalistic Inquiry*. Beverly Hills, CA: Sage.

Morris, M. H., Kuratko, D. F., & Covin, J. G. (2011). *Corporate Entrepreneurship and Innovation: Entrepreneurial Development within Organizations*. Mason, OH: South-Western Cengage Learning.

Partanen, J., Kohtamäki, M., Parida, V., & Wincent, J. (2017). Developing and validating a multi-dimensional scale for operationalizing industrial service offering. *Journal of Business & Industrial Marketing*, *32*(2), 295–309.

Peirce, C. S. (1978). *Collected Papers* (Vol. V, pp. 180–212). Cambridge, MA: Harvard University Press.

Rabetino, R., Kohtamäki, M., & Gebauer, H. (2017). Strategy map of servitization. *International Journal of Production Economics*, *192*, 144–156.

Ramachandran, K., Devarajan, T. P., & Ray, S. (2006). Corporate entrepreneurship: How? *Vikalpa*, *31*(1), 85–97.

Rasche, A., & Chia, R. (2009). Researching strategy practices: A genealogical social theory perspective. *Organization Studies*, *30*(7), 713–734.

Schatzki, T. (2005). Peripheral vision: The sites of organizations. *Organization Studies*, *26*(3), 465–484.

Schatzki, T. (2010). *The Timespace of Human Activity: On Performance, Society, and History as Indeterminate Teleological Events*. Lanham, MD: Lexington Books.

Schatzki, T. (2012). A primer on practices: Theory and research. In J. Higgs, R. Barnett, S. Billett, M. Hutchings, & F. Trede (Eds.), *Practice-Based Education: Perspectives and Strategies* (pp. 13–26). Rotterdam: Sense Publishers.

Schatzki, T. (2013). The edge of change: On the emergence, persistence, and dissolution of practices. In E. Shove & N. Spurling (Eds.), *Sustainable Practice: Social Theory and Climate Change* (pp. 31–46). New York: Routledge.

Schatzki, T. (2016). Keeping track of large social phenomena. *Geographische Zeitschrift*, *104*(1), 4–24.

Schatzki, T. (2017). Practices and people. *Teoria e Prática em Administração*, *7*(1), 26–53.

Schatzki, T. (2019). *Social Change in a Material World*. London: Routledge.

Schatzki, T. R., Knorr Cetina, K., & Savigny, E. von (Eds.) (2001). *The Practice Turn in Contemporary Theory*. London: Routledge.

Sharma, P., & Chrisman, J. J. (1999). Toward a reconciliation of the definitional issues in the field of corporate entrepreneurship. *Entrepreneurship Theory and Practice*, *23*(3), 11–28.

Steyaert, C., & Landström, H. (2011). Enacting entrepreneurship research in a pioneering, provocative and participative way: On the work of Bengt Johannisson. *Small Business Economics*, *36*(2), 123–134.

Thompson, N. A., & Byrne, O. (2020). Advancing entrepreneurship as practice: Previous developments and future possibilities. In W. B. Gartner & B. T. Teague (Eds.), *Research Handbook on Entrepreneurial Behavior, Practice and Process* (pp. 30–55). Cheltenham, UK and Northampton, MA, USA: Edward Elgar Publishing.

Thompson, N. A., Verduijn, K., & Gartner, W. B. (2020). Entrepreneurship-as-practice: Grounding contemporary theories of practice into entrepreneurship studies. *Entrepreneurship & Regional Development*, *32*(3–4), 247–256.

Tsoukas, H. (2010). Practice, strategy making and intentionality: A Heideggerian onto-epistemology for strategy-as-practice. In D. Golsorkhi, L. Rouleau, D. Seidl, & E. Vaara (Eds.), *The Cambridge Handbook of Strategy as Practice* (pp. 47–62). Cambridge: Cambridge University Press.

Vandermerwe, S., & Rada, J. (1988). Servitization of business: Adding value by adding services. *European Management Journal*, *6*(4), 314–324.

18. 'You are angels': understanding the entanglement of family and enterprise in an early-stage family-run coworking space

Boukje Cnossen and Julian Dominik Winter

INTRODUCTION

Academic research on family enterprises reflects the idea that running a successful enterprise, and adhering to family roles, are at odds with one another. The literature warns, for example, that family-owned enterprises must be careful not to be absorbed by family dynamics (Miller & Le Breton-Miller, 2003) or have the business-ownership scattered over too many family members (Lubatkin, Schulze, & Dino, 2003). The literature also states that family enterprises have a strong tendency towards altruistic behaviour, which can also result in actions that damage the enterprise, specifically when such altruistic behaviour focuses on the benefit of other family members instead of the long-term success of the enterprise (Siebels & Knyphausen-Aufseß, 2012).

Although there are conflicting ideas (Miller & Le Breton-Miller, 2003) about the advantages and disadvantages of family-owned enterprises (which make up between 65 and 90 per cent of all businesses in the world; Salvato, Chirico, Melin, & Seidl, 2019), the common denominator is that there is a separation or boundary between the realm of the family and the realm of the enterprise. Family and enterprise are understood as separate entities or domains, each with their own aims and rules. While this might seem reasonable at first sight, especially when the enterprise or the family is demarcated in space (people enter the firm, or enter their home), these boundaries are not so clear in cases of early-stage enterprises, where family members put unpaid labour into the business, or in enterprises where the service or product sold is about providing a home-like place with a familial atmosphere. Both these things are the case in the setting we studied.

Therefore, we turned to practice-theoretical approaches that see enterprises not as separate, pre-existing entities, but rather ask how enterprises emerge and are maintained through practices (Champenois, Lefebvre, & Ronteau, 2020). We build on this approach in order to investigate an early-stage family-run coworking space in Hamburg, Germany.

Our research is based on a month of fieldwork in a family-run coworking space in Winterhude, a residential area of Hamburg, Germany's second-largest city. The fieldwork was conducted by the second author, who became a member at this coworking space. He engaged in participant observation to capture the day-to-day practices and processes going on (Tillmar, 2020). He took an analytical autoethnographical approach (Anderson, 2006), meaning that his own experiences, thoughts, and emotions as a new member were seen as pathways into an understanding of the culture of the coworking space, whilst also using his position as a newcomer to engage in conversations with the managers. In the fieldwork, we focused on the family dynamics of the managers – mother and daughter – which were a central part of the day-to-day character of the space, and of the ways in which they interacted with their customers and shaped the coworking space.

We will draw attention to the entanglement of the enterprise and the family by building on the call of practice scholars (Gherardi, Murgia, Bellè, Miele, & Carreri, 2019; Reckwitz, 2016, 2017a) to bring a focus on affects into the empirical study of social practices. In our case, an attention to affect helps understand practices of caretaking and managing as both contributing to the family, as well as to the enterprise. In what follows, we will first offer a concise overview of the main tenets of the entrepreneurship-as-practice literature, and how it relates to a practice-theoretical understanding of other social phenomena. Second, we will introduce Reckwitz's practice theory, with a particular focus on the affective nature of practices. Third, we will describe our research design and offer relevant details of our empirical setting. This is also where we explain how our focus on practices came into the picture, and how we presented and analysed the empirical material collected. Fourth, we will present our findings in the form of three accounts, which we subsequently analyse by drawing on the work of the German practice theorist Andreas Reckwitz. Finally, we will discuss the implications of our analysis for the field of entrepreneurship-as-practice and will indicate possible opportunities for research.

HOW DO ENTREPRENEURSHIP PRACTICES RELATE TO OTHER SOCIAL PRACTICES?

The recent practice turn in entrepreneurship research (Champenois et al., 2020; Johannisson, 2011; Verduyn, 2015) has been challenging the ontological individualism in the entrepreneurship literature (Thompson, Verduijn, & Gartner, 2020). Moving away from a focus on the individual level of analysis, the unit of analysis of the entrepreneurship-as-practice literature, are practices themselves. This allows entrepreneurship scholars to move away from questions of motivation or personality – in which the individual entrepreneur is taken as the main explanandum of entrepreneurial outcomes – as well as away from economic approaches – in which market forces are meant to explain everything – towards the understanding of entrepreneurial agency as 'relational, embodied, and improvisational' (Thompson et al., 2020, p. 251). Drawing on a variety of practice theories with roots in European sociology (Nicolini, 2012), researchers in this vein see entrepreneurship as a set of ongoing social practices of recognizing and reaping opportunities (Johannisson, 2011; De Clercq & Voronov, 2009). A focus on the 'doing' of entrepreneurship conceptualizes entrepreneurship as a continuous accomplishment.

Given this focus on doing, it has been acknowledged that the doing of entrepreneurship can also intersect with other social accomplishments, such as doing gender (Bruni, Gherardi, & Poggio, 2004), doing place-making (Barinaga, 2017), or doing ethics (Clarke & Holt, 2010). However, how this works is still a puzzle. Bruni et al. (2004) show that in a conservative industry, female entrepreneurs engage in the performing of their gender while conducting business. They reveal that '"doing gender" and "doing business" are […] tied together through tacit knowledge' (Bruni et al., 2004, p. 265), for example in the case of two female business owners in the construction industry who choose to pose as secretaries and let their engineers handle negotiations. Bruni et al. speak of the 'intertwining' of practices into five overarching processes, with each singular practice still being conceived of as belonging to either the symbolic construction of gender, or that of entrepreneurship (Bruni et al., 2004, p. 210).

Based on their analysis of the narratives of entrepreneurs in different industries in the United Kingdom, Clarke and Holt (2010) argue that entrepreneurial and ethical concerns are not at odds, but rather interwoven. Relying on the work of Immanuel Kant, they conceptualize ethics itself as a practice and speak furthermore of entrepreneurial practice (p. 319) and business practice (p. 327) to develop their understanding of ethical entrepreneurial practice. However, different from what practice-theoretical research approaches advise (Nicolini, 2012), they do not engage in an empirical investigation of the different social practices that would then 'scale up' (Cooren, Kuhn, Cornelissen, & Clark, 2011, p. 1159) to larger entrepreneurial and organizational phenomena, such as ethical practice.

In other words, how the practices of entrepreneurship relate to the other social practices that make up the social world, such as ethics or gender, remains unclear. This is understandable given the focus of entrepreneurship-as-practice scholars on entrepreneurial phenomena, yet surprising at the same time, because entrepreneurship-as-practice research sees 'ventures, firms or startups [as] not ontologically separate phenomena from the performance of everyday, materially accomplished and ordered practices' (Thompson et al., 2020, p. 247). So the question is, if the doing of entrepreneurship relates to other forms of doing social life, how can we identify this? We turn to the work of Andreas Reckwitz and in particular his recent insistence on the role of affects (2016, 2017a), to answer this question.

RECKWITZ'S THEORY OF SOCIAL PRACTICES AND PRACTICE THEORY'S 'BLIND SPOT' FOR AFFECT

Andreas Reckwitz's research is mostly published in German (e.g. Reckwitz, 2012b, 2019), although recent translations (Reckwitz, 2017a, 2017b, 2020) and English-language contributions (Wenzel, Krämer, Koch, & Reckwitz, 2020; Reckwitz, 2002) have made his ideas available for wider academic audiences. Within management and entrepreneurship research (as well as in other parts of the social sciences, see e.g. Lamers, van der Duim, & Spaargaren, 2017; Hitchings, 2012; Warde, 2005), it is mostly Reckwitz's article published in 2002 that is cited (Feldman & Orlikowski, 2011), and its uptake is centred mostly in the strategy-as-practice literature (Jarzabkowski, Balogun, & Seidl, 2007; Vaara & Whittington, 2012; Whittington, 2006).

In his 2002 article, Reckwitz argues that although they stem from diverse theoretical backgrounds, practice theories all share a concern with the mundane (p. 244). This 'culturalist view', he states, is opposed to two other theories of action, which he refers to as purpose-oriented and norm-oriented, interpreting individual motivations to act as either defined by a specific purpose or goal, or by values and norms, respectively. In contrast, the culturalist concept Reckwitz argues for emphasizes the cultural contexts of actions (2002, p. 245). Actions have a certain cultural meaning that they convey by being carried out, regardless of the agent's intention. Thus, practices shed light on the tacit structures of meaning that they stem from (pp. 249–250).

Reckwitz initially (2002) developed his practice-theoretical framework along seven 'theoretical ideal-types' (p. 250) or focal points along which to analyse practices, being the body, the mind, things, knowledge, discourse, structure vs. process, and the agent. More recently, however, Reckwitz (2012a, 2016) has started to argue for practice theorists to pay attention to affects, not as an aspect or part of practices, but as an integral quality of them:

My basic claim is that it is not enough just to take affects 'into account' in social theory; the crucial insight is rather that every social order as a set of practices is a specific order of affects. If we want to understand how practices work, we have to understand their specific affects, the affects which are built into the practices. (Reckwitz, 2016, p. 166)

An English translation of Reckwitz's 2016 chapter became part of an edited volume of recent contributions in practice theory (Hui, Schatzki, & Shove, 2017) and here, his insistence on affect is categorized by the editors as one of several suffusing phenomena or phenomena which are intangible yet permeate different sets of practices, providing 'pervasive links' between them (Hui et al., 2017, p. 4). The intangible nature of the 'affectivity' (a translation of the original *affektualität* (Reckwitz, 2016, p. 166) which does not feature in the English) is likely a part of the reason why the social sciences, in general, have a blind spot for affect (Reckwitz, 2016). At the same time, Reckwitz sets his argument apart from the vast and different approaches to affect theory that have existed over the decades and stresses that a practice-theoretical approach to affects, or affectivity, always entails asking the question who is being affected, and by whom or what. Counter to other scholars, affects are thus inherently social, and part and parcel of the maintenance as well as the potential disruption of existing social orders (Reckwitz, 2017a).

Reckwitz is not alone in his quest for integrating affects and affectivity into the study of social practices (Gherardi et al., 2019; Thompson & Willmott, 2016). However, in his call for an analytical attention to affects, Reckwitz sees a special role for spatial atmospheres in the generation of affects:

In the case of spatial atmospheres, the individual things are less important as isolated entities, but their location in three-dimensional space, their interrelations, the way they constitute an environment. This space is then not so much 'used', but rather entered into by people and experienced. Naturally, spaces like apartments and offices are made for specific purposes, but their holistic, three-dimensional character endows them with a special capacity to produce [...] 'atmospheres'. (Reckwitz, 2016, p. 175)

Reckwitz's discussion of spatial atmospheres takes a more historical perspective, as he links the role of spaces in their capacity to generate affects to the development of modernity (see also Reckwitz, 2012a), but his explicit focus on spaces as affect generators is one among few to offer guidance as to how explicitly practice-based studies can account for affect (for an exception see Katila, Kuismin, & Valtonen, 2019). In what follows, we draw attention to the explicitly affective nature of a family-run and early-stage coworking space, to show how the practices of the managers relate to both the doing of family and the doing of entrepreneurship.

METHODOLOGY AND EMPIRICAL SETTING

Methodological Approach

In his guide for organizational researchers interested in practice theory, Nicolini (2012) advises using different theoretical lenses to look at empirical material. His method of 'zooming in and out' (2009) is to be understood not as advice to move between levels of analysis, but rather as a recommendation to use the different focal points of different practice theorists productively. In line with this advice, our engagement with Reckwitz's work should not be taken as a 'testing' of his theory, as a positivist epistemology would entail. Rather, after engaging with several practice-theoretical concepts, Reckwitz's recommendations, and in particular his advice to pay attention to affectivity (Reckwitz, 2017a), was taken as a theoretical lens to analyse and present our observations.

Access to the field and data collection

We conducted fieldwork at the CoWork Bude14 in Hamburg. 'CoWork Bude' is German for coworking booth and will be abbreviated as CWB from here on. The CWB is a relatively new coworking space that opened in January 2019; six months before the start of our fieldwork. It is 275 square metres large and located on the third floor of a large complex building in a residential area of a rather wealthy district of central Hamburg, called Winterhude. The area has about 55,000 inhabitants and lies close to the Alster river (Hopert, 2019). It is filled with boutiques and cafés and is close to a recreational area and park, making it a calm and comfortable part of the city. The CWB offers two fixed office spaces, a conference room, a meeting room and open space divided with fixed and variable desks. The two offices were rented out, while the open space was usually occupied by only two to three customers at a time. In the centre of the room is a large reception counter and a lounge area.

The second author encountered the CWB when searching online for coworking spaces in Hamburg. Two out of seven coworking spaces responded positively to his request for fieldwork access. He visited both spaces to speak to the managers and selected the CWB because it granted us the best access. The second author was able to join as a member for a reduced rate and could go there every weekday. Furthermore, as the coworking community was still in the early stages of its development, we expected that establishing contact with other customers would be relatively easy.

Ethnographic research at the CWB was conducted in July 2019. During this month, the second author spent an average of three full days per week at the coworking space. He worked in the open space and attended several events organized by the space or its partners/customers. He relied on participant observation (Laurier, 2010; Tillmar, 2020) and documented his observations and initial thoughts in the form of ethnographic field notes, aiming to capture specific moments and scenes happening in the space, as well as his own emotions, thoughts, and experiences. For this approach, he relied on analytic autoethnography (Anderson, 2006), meaning that the researcher's personal experiences as a new member gave him the perspective of an insider of the coworking space while remaining an outsider to the management team. His feelings as a newcomer were an additional source of information next to interview data and observations of the day-to-day happenings of the coworking space in general (Anderson, 2006, p. 389).

As per Anderson's suggestions (2006, pp. 385–386), the second author engaged in many conversations to validate and contrast his observations. He also conducted three semi-structured interviews, one with each of the two managers and one with a customer of the CWB. The semi-structured interviews could 'unfold in a conversational manner offering participants the chance to explore issues they feel are important' (Longhurst, 2010, p. 103). Each interview lasted about thirty minutes and was recorded and transcribed. All field notes and interviews were written and conducted in German and some excerpts were translated into English during the analysis process. Finally, pictures of the space were taken to be able to document and analyse the physical details of the space later. Content presented on the venue's website and social media channels was also collected and inspected.

Data analysis

After discussing preliminary observations and reflections, we decided to focus on the mother and daughter running the CWB. This was driven by pragmatic reasons at first, as both managers were a stable presence at the space, but also resulted from our emerging interest in the patterns of interaction between them and how their relationship affected their caretaking and managing practices. These were all geared towards maintaining and growing the coworking space and varied from day-to-day caretaking practices to strategic decision-making, to advertising practices. We analysed our data again, this time with an attention to practices, and asking ourselves how the managers accomplished their enterprise through practice. In particular, we were puzzled (Alvesson & Kärreman, 2011) by how the practices the managers engaged in scaled up to their family dynamics, as well as the early-stage enterprise that was the coworking space. Following this mystery invited us to challenge the assumption (Sandberg & Alvesson, 2011) that the family and the enterprise are separate realms to begin with.

From this list, and inspired by the work of Bruni et al. (2004) on how the doing of entrepreneurship intersects with the doing of gender, we selected those practices that best exemplified the co-occurrence of doing family and doing entrepreneurship. In line with ethnographic research in organizational and entrepreneurial settings (e.g. Bourgoin, Bencherki & Faraj, 2019; Cnossen & Bencherki, 2019), we chose to present these in the form of three vignettes, or scenes. These are short and condensed narratives based on several observations and conversations in the field. Each account is composed of observed sayings and doings and written so as to show how doing family and doing entrepreneurship intersect. Since the second author conducted the fieldwork, the narratives are written in the first person.

Keeping in mind prior research on the intertwining of different domains of social practice (Bruni et al., 2004; Clarke & Holt, 2010), we composed the scenes of those observed practices that related to doing family, as well as doing entrepreneurship.

THREE SCENES AT THE CWB

First Scene: Installing a Cupboard

It is 9.30 a.m. on a hot summer day and I arrive at the CWB. I have been here for quite some time now and have built up a relationship with the managers so that I don't feel uncomfortable or nervous anymore when I enter the space. As I find my favourite seat in the open space, I greet the manager Birte, a tall woman with long hair in her sixties, who is the mother of Anneke, the official founder and main manager. Her daughter is currently busy pacing through the space, carefully watering the plants and tearing off old leaves to make sure everything looks perfect. She also walks up to the customer in the open space and asks him whether she can open the window and move around some of the new air conditioners to optimize the temperature and air quality and make sure the customers are most comfortable. I wave my hand to her and then also say hi to Merit, a young and energetic woman who is renting out one of the fixed office spaces. The women are all dressed very casually, wearing colourful summer dresses and flip-flops.

Both women are moving through the space quickly, then disappear into Merit's office. I follow them to see what is going on and as I peek inside the small, untidy room, I see a man I have heard a lot about but never met personally. It is Rainer, Birte's husband. He is a carpenter who had his workshop in this space for a long time before their family turned it into a coworking space about a year ago. While he is busy tightening screws to build a large storage rack for the shoes Merit sells, she and Birte are unpacking large boxes filled with tiny children's sandals and sneakers, and Merit makes extensive expressions of gratitude to her two helpers. 'You are angels,' she says gratefully and happily. Rainer silently proceeds with his work as his wife contentedly replies that she is happy to finally be able to set up the office just as Merit wanted it to be.

When they start to tidy up the room, Merit puts some of the shoes into a cardboard box and then walks to the front desk where Anneke is now seated working on the computer. 'Annie' – this is what she always calls her as though they have known each other forever, even when Merit has only been here for 4 months – 'Can I borrow your duct tape?', she asks in a friendly manner. Anneke does not hesitate to get up and hand her the tape with a smile.

After the shelf is finally set up, Rainer stays a little bit longer and chats with his wife while sipping on a coke at the counter. I now walk up to the counter to ask Anneke a random question to initiate a conversation and we engage in a little small talk about the space. She explains how all of her family contributed to building the space last year: Anneke's sister came up with the idea to create a coworking space, her husband and her father did most of the DIY, she took care of all the formalities, and her mother contributed to the design. 'We all complemented each other in this combination. That's why we were able to do almost everything ourselves,' she says proudly.

Anneke also describes how the space's design incorporates a lot of allusions to the history of the space. She explains that her father's carpenter workshop was located here before, so they tried to keep some details and furniture from the workshop. She adds that when her father moved his business, they didn't want to give up the premises and started thinking about possible ways to keep and use the facilities. 'We had the space and didn't know what to do with it,' she says. The fact that they chose to turn it into a coworking space is fitting since her father also already rented out space to other small enterprises, she says. In a way, coworking already was a familiar concept to her family.

At this point, Birte, who seems to have been listening to our conversation, suddenly stands up and declares that the ideal of sharing makes a lot of sense given the high rents and lack of space in the city. She makes no effort to hide her excitement saying, 'I immediately found the idea to share this space great and worth supporting because of my personal values and the way that I've lived before. It only makes sense and I don't see a reason why we should not have done it!' Her eyes light up when she nostalgically describes how they shared their apartments, too, when she was younger. In that sense, she sees the CWB as a continuation of the family history as it promotes family values and convictions.

Second Scene: The Breakfast Event

Today, I am attending a breakfast event for start-up founders hosted by the CWB. As I arrive, Anneke and Birte have already set up a carefully arranged buffet. Besides the three of us, five founders show up to the event and engage in small talk. After a couple of minutes, Anneke tries to structure the conversation by asking what events a founder should attend in Hamburg in order to build a network. In so doing, Anneke seems to switch between the role of fellow founder, who has ideas to offer to the others, and the role of host. The conversation seems very rigid at times as Anneke often has to refer to new topics or ask direct questions to keep the exchange going. The visitors struggle to find a rhythm for the conversation and develop a dynamic where they proactively shape the chat and do not rely on the host's guidance. They talk about Hamburg's start-up scene, good workshops to attend, and mutual acquaintances they have in this community. Anneke invites the visitors to serve themselves at the buffet multiple times, but no one reacts, which noticeably irritates her, although she does not eat either. After half an hour, Anneke finally gets up to get some food, and then the others follow.

To my confusion, Birte quietly stands behind the front desk and observes the event from a distance without introducing herself and only rarely reacting to the conversations taking place. It takes about an hour until Birte slowly starts engaging in the discussion. As the talk opens up to more general topics, she even begins to participate strongly, while Anneke gradually gives up her leading role in the conversation and participates much less. Finally, when one visitor explains she is a freelancer who is bored with working from home, Birte enthusiastically talks about the coworking values and concepts. She talks about the sharing ideology and her love for the community idea behind coworking. About two hours later, when the first attendees have left the event, Anneke notices she hasn't asked for donations to fund the breakfast and reluctantly asks the remaining people to give some money.

After all the visitors have left, the space is filled with quietness as the managers and the customers dedicate themselves to their work again. However, after some time the stillness is broken by a young couple entering the space with their baby. It is Anneke's sister Gesa, with her husband and child. Birte and Anneke happily greet their family and Birte even introduces me to her other daughter saying, 'This is faithful Julian!' They then withdraw to the meeting room to not distract the customers with their laughter and the baby's cries. After a while, the women walk over to the kitchen with the child to change her diapers. Then, Anneke carries her niece around the space affectionately cuddling and kissing her and presenting her to me from afar with the proud smile of an aunt. The family ends up staying for several hours.

In the evening, as I prepare to leave, I stop by the counter and we have our usual small talk before I go home. We end up talking about the breakfast event from the morning and I ask why Birte did not sit with the others but remained standing behind the counter instead. A little surprised, she answers: 'I have to watch out for Coco [the cat] because not everyone likes it when the pets run across the space up to the visitors.' She thanks me for the question because it enables her to reflect on her own actions and says that originally they were forced to bring the pets to work because they couldn't stay home alone all day, but then it simply became a habit that they did not question. However, they learned that the pets often make for good conversation starters and help in building a friendly atmosphere. I nod in response and continue asking about how their family situation impacts their business. Birte explains that they are both depending on their husbands. 'I'm living off of his generosity,' she says laughing. 'Otherwise it wouldn't work! It's the same for Anneke, her husband earns the money and she has to work another job in addition to this one. I do minor tasks for my husband's business, too.'

Third Scene: Curing a Cold

It is one of my final days in the space and the heat in the space is intense and everyone seems very exhausted. Anneke makes every effort to make the temperature more bearable but is not very successful. As though surrendering to the weather the managers walk into the kitchen and shortly after come out with ice cream which they offer to me and the other customer. We both get up to stand by the counter with the managers and enjoy the cold treat and have a break and some small talk. Birte expresses her gratitude that I am there even under such uncomfortable circumstances while also highlighting their own commitment to be there. Anneke asks me what I plan to do after my fieldwork. I believe both are sad that I am leaving, although Birte expresses that more openly and passionately than Anneke. Birte laments, 'We already miss you,' after I said I would not be able to continue to come after I completed my study because I wouldn't be able to afford the membership fee.

All of a sudden, the other customer standing by the counter drops his cup and spills his coffee. Birte immediately turns her attention to him saying, 'Oh no! Did you get something on your shirt?' Remarkably, she first makes sure the man is fine before she takes care of the space and the furniture which could have been damaged.

After this incident, we return to our conversation and talk about Anneke and Birte's ideas and plans for the space and the challenges that they face. I try to encourage them to hang in there and tell them how much I have loved coming here in the past month. 'Aw, that's cute,' Birte replies visibly moved by my empathy. Later in the conversation, Anneke explains that she has been thinking about ways to enable me to keep coming despite my not being able to pay for the tickets. She offers me a discount under the condition that I encourage my friends to come, too, trying to reconcile their financial need with their desire to have me there in the future.

Finally, after I mentioned that I was not feeling too well and that I had a cold, Birte sympathetically offers me to make me a tea but then suggests I go home already to recover from my cold. 'Yes, mummy!,' says Anneke then, mocking Birte for handing out motherly advice. She then looks at me and says jokingly with an ironic smile on her face, 'Have some tea, Julian! Put on your scarf!' We laugh and I end up following their advice, pack up and say goodbye feeling sad that my time here is ending.

Analysis

While the vignettes presented above are already the result of an analytic process (Vásquez, Schoeneborn, & Sergi, 2016), we also coded the vignettes above (see Cnossen & Bencherki, 2019, for a similar approach) and grouped them into clusters. Building on Reckwitz (2002), we assert that actions carry certain cultural meanings and that these meanings are conveyed as the actions are carried out, regardless of the agent's intention. After several rounds of coding between the two authors, in which we engaged in a discussion and verified possible interpretations, we identified four clusters of practices, of which the two largest by far were labelled 'caretaking practices' and 'management practices'. Two much smaller clusters which, for the sake of conciseness and focus were not included in the tables in this chapter, related to the personal style of the managers, and the blurring of private and professional space. Table 18.1 and Table 18.2 offer a schematic representation of the observed practices described in our vignettes, along with an analysis of the consequences of these practices. In line with Bruni et al.'s (2004) investigation of the entanglements of doing gender and doing entrepreneurship, we ask ourselves how 'doing entrepreneurship' and 'doing family' were accomplished. In line with Reckwitz (2017a), we asked for every observed practice who is being affected, and how. The columns on the right-hand side of both Table 18.1 and Table 18.2 show the answers to these questions.

Table 18.1   Caretaking practices

Observed practices	Who is affected and how?	Relation to 'doing' entrepreneurship	Relation to 'doing' family
Birte's husband builds a cupboard for one of their customers.	The customer is aware that the managers help her out without needing to and that a family member is brought in to do so. She very clearly shows her gratitude.	The managers do their best to make the space their customers work in as nice as possible and respond to their requests for modification.	Birte's husband was asked to do this and he agreed to help out.
Birte and Anneke let a customer borrow duct tape.	Lending out tools without giving it a second thought gives people a sense of being at home and attaches them to the space.	The managers help their customers to make the space as comfortable for them as possible.	The managers seem glad to be able to help and support their customers to make themselves at home.
The managers adjust the lighting and air-conditioning, water the plants, and clean the space.	Highlighting the physical condition of the space helps the managers create a nice space for the customers. The physical condition and atmosphere of the space are an integral part of the service that they sell, but in taking care of it they also show and reinforce their attachment to the place.	Anneke creates a comfortable and pleasant space for the customers.	Maintaining the space and selling access to it is a way of holding on to a place the family already owned. 'We didn't want to leave this place,' the managers say.
The managers invite family over to the space. They drink coffee, have conversations, kiss one another, and play with the children.	The coworking space is characterized by an informal atmosphere.	The managers actively shape the atmosphere of the space by having family members over for coffee.	The managers use the space for private gatherings.
When I have a cold, Birte offers to make tea and gives me advice on how to recover from it. As a result, Anneke mocks Birte's 'mommy'-like behaviour.	The managers' close relationships create an informal atmosphere for someone who just joined.	Offering to make tea shows empathy.	The managers draw on their family roles even while at work, as exemplified by Anneke's comment about her mother's behaviour.

Table 18.2   Management practices

Observed practices	Who is affected and how?	Relation to 'doing' entrepreneurship	Relation to 'doing' family
The managers say they are aware of their own bias as family members and therefore challenge themselves and extensively discuss and test the arguments for their decision-making.	Anneke can feel that her mother cares about the enterprise and her development as a manager.	Engaging in discussions regarding the running of the space may help them to come up with efficient strategies to reach their business's goals.	Birte says she intentionally questions Anneke's opinion at times to help her daughter make good decisions and prevent themselves from making decisions based on instinct. She adds that the latter might happen since they usually share an opinion as they both come from the same 'stable'.
Birte and Anneke say they both rely on their husbands to 'feed' them, because their own income does not suffice 'Otherwise it wouldn't work', Birte says. Birte also mentions she does not receive a salary at all.	Birte's expressions about her free labour and about the fact that both her and Anneke are financially dependent on their husbands could make her daughter feel grateful.	The managers make sacrifices for the sake of the success of the coworking space. It seems they prioritize the long-term success of the enterprise over immediate financial benefits.	Birte says that it was self-evident that a mother helps her daughter.
Anneke tries to get the conversation going among the participants at the breakfast event. While Anneke is leading a meeting, Birte takes care of the pets.	By taking care of the space and the pets, Anneke is placed in the centre of attention and feels slightly put on the spot, as exemplified by the rigid nature of the conversation.	Anneke tries to build the community by shaping a certain type of atmosphere and taking the initiative to steer the conversations. She does not leave the talks to chance but actively tries to attract and satisfy new customers.	Birte wants to give her daughter the chance to lead the event. Her staying in the background causes some confusion as if she is not engaged enough, but she later explains she wants to mind the animals so as to enable her daughter to pursue the business's professional vision and not be distracted.
Anneke shows the manuals she has made to guide potential employees in the future.	Birte's freedom in changing her daughter's routines might leave Anneke feeling undermined.	As Anneke is still learning about the requirements and tasks associated with her role, the tools can help maintain this knowledge as well as efficiently guide any future employees she hopes to have someday.	Concerning the manuals, Birte says that Anneke is a 'perfectionist'. She takes the freedom to adapt the routines her daughter creates, even though her daughter is in charge.
Anneke tries to get me to convince friends to become customers as well.	As a new member, you can feel inclined to bring in your personal network as new clients.	The managers offer me a special deal if I were to bring friends to the CWB who would become paying customers as well.	Anneke and Birte bring their friends and family to the space. Encouraging customers to do the same can be seen as an extension of this already common practice.

DISCUSSION

Whilst entrepreneurship-as-practice has started to reveal the 'how' of entrepreneurial endeavours (Champenois et al., 2020), we wondered how the emergence and maintenance of entrepreneurship through practices relates to the emergence and maintenance of other social phenomena. Given our empirical setting, we specifically looked at the relation between, following the phrasing of Bruni et al. (2004), doing entrepreneurship and doing gender. Looking at the affective effects of observed practices, we show how practices can contribute both to the doing of entrepreneurship, and to the doing of family. Hence, rather than seeing an intertwining of practices of one kind and practices of another (Bruni et al., 2004), we see that practices cannot be divided in that way. As a result, our observations lead us to challenge our view of the family and the enterprise as two separate domains.

Recent practice-theoretical thinking (Hui et al., 2017) describes affect as a suffusing phenomenon, meaning it permeates different sets of practices and provides pervasive links between them. We think the notion of suffusing is a useful first step in thinking about the interconnectedness of these social domains. However, our analysis shows that this interconnectedness in fact exists on the level of the individual observed practice, meaning that, in our case, the suffusing does not happen between sets of practices, but seems to be located within or at the practice itself. To make sense of this, we have started to think about Karen Barad's notion of entanglement (2007) as a way to conceptually think together the doing of family and the doing of entrepreneurship. We admit these reflections result from our setting and can thus be highly contextual, while Barad's notion of entanglement results from an ontological argumentation; we believe new vocabulary is needed to think together those previously separately conceived realms or spheres, in our case the family and the enterprise.

Too often, entrepreneurship research, like many other parts of the social sciences, conveniently separates, at least on a conceptual level, those domains that are outside of the focus from the phenomenon of interest. In the case of entrepreneurship, and especially in early-stage enterprises or enterprises relying on family history, as in our case, everyday life cannot be separated from entrepreneurial endeavour.

Practice theory, and specifically the more recent calls for an understanding of practices as inherently affective (Gherardi et al., 2019; Reckwitz, 2016, 2017a), helps entrepreneurship researchers move beyond a conceptualization of a cross-over or an intersection of pre-existing domains (i.e. the family domain 'combined with' the entrepreneurship domain), and towards an understanding of their entanglement. Our case shows this entanglement as specific to its setting, but further theorizing in line with Barad's work (2007) might be able to develop an understanding of practice-based views of entrepreneurship as ontologically inseparable from other areas of (social) life.

CONCLUSION

In this chapter, we have investigated a mother and daughter running a coworking space together. By adopting Reckwitz's definition of practices as inherently affective, we have been able to look at actions as carrying cultural meaning beyond and apart from agents' intentions. By doing so, we have brought in a focus on the affective nature of social practices, in order to show the entanglement of the 'doing' of entrepreneurship, and the 'doing' of family.

Ours is only a small-scale study, and future practice-based research in the family entrepreneurship field could build on our insistence that entrepreneurship is not an unstable endeavour alongside the fixed system of family relations, but that both are entangled and ongoing accomplishments that continuously emerge through practice.

REFERENCES

Alvesson, M., & Kärreman, D. (2011). *Qualitative Research and Theory Development: Mystery as Method.* London: Sage.

Anderson, L. (2006). Analytic autoethnography. *Journal of Contemporary Ethnography, 35*(4), 373–395.

Barad, K. (2007). *Meeting the Universe Halfway: Quantum Physics and the Entanglement of Matter and Meaning.* Durham, NC: Duke University Press.

Barinaga, E. (2017). Tinkering with space: The organizational practices of a nascent social venture. *Organization Studies, 38*(7), 937–958.

Bourgoin, A., Bencherki, N., & Faraj, S. (2019). 'And who are you?' A performative perspective on authority in organizations. *Academy of Management Journal, 63*(4), 1134–1165.

Bruni, A., Gherardi, S., & Poggio, B. (2004). Entrepreneur-mentality, gender and the study of women entrepreneurs. *Journal of Organizational Change Management, 17*(3), 256–268.

Champenois, C., Lefebvre, V., & Ronteau, S. (2020). Entrepreneurship as practice: Systematic literature review of a nascent field. *Entrepreneurship & Regional Development, 32*(3–4), 281–312.

Clarke, J., & Holt, R. (2010). Reflective judgement: Understanding entrepreneurship as ethical practice. *Journal of Business Ethics, 94*(3), 317–331.

Cnossen, B., & Bencherki, N. (2019). The role of space in the emergence and endurance of organizing: How independent workers and material assemblages constitute organizations. *Human Relations, 72*(6), 1057–1080.

Cooren, F., Kuhn, T., Cornelissen, J. P., & Clark, T. (2011). Communication, organizing and organization: An overview and introduction to the special issue. *Organization Studies, 32*(9), 1149–1170.

De Clercq, D., & Voronov, M. (2009). Toward a practice perspective of entrepreneurship: Entrepreneurial legitimacy as habitus. *International Small Business Journal, 27*(4), 395–419.

Feldman, M. S., & Orlikowski, W. J. (2011). Theorizing practice and practicing theory. *Organization Science, 22*(5), 1240–1253.

Gherardi, S., Murgia, A., Bellè, E., Miele, F., & Carreri, A. (2019). Tracking the sociomaterial traces of affect at the crossroads of affect and practice theories. *Qualitative Research in Organizations and Management, 14*(3), 295–316.

Hitchings, R. (2012). People can talk about their practices. *Area, 44*(1), 61–67.

Hopert, T. (2019). *Villen und Backstein rund ums grüne Zentrum.* https://www.hamburg.de/sehenswertes -winterhude/.

Hui, A., Schatzki, T., & Shove, E. (Eds.) (2017). *The Nexus of Practices: Connections, Constellations, Practitioners.* Abingdon: Routledge.

Jarzabkowski, P., Balogun, J., & Seidl, D. (2007). Strategizing: The challenges of a practice perspective. *Human Relations, 60*(1), 5–27.

Johannisson, B. (2011). Towards a practice theory of entrepreneuring. *Small Business Economics, 36*(2), 135–150.

Katila, S., Kuismin, A., & Valtonen, A. (2019). Becoming upbeat: Learning the affecto-rhythmic order of organizational practices. *Human Relations, 73*(9), 1308–1330.

Lamers, M., van der Duim, R., & Spaargaren, G. (2017). The relevance of practice theories for tourism research. *Annals of Tourism Research, 62*, 54–63.

Laurier, E. (2010). Participant observation. In N. Clifford, S. French, & G. Valentine (Eds.), *Key Methods in Geography* (2nd edition) (pp. 116–130). London: Sage.

Longhurst, R. (2010). Semi-structured interviews and focus groups. In N. Clifford, S. French, & G. Valentine (Eds.), *Key Methods in Geography* (2nd edition) (pp. 103–115). London: Sage.

Lubatkin, M., Schulze, W. S., & Dino, R. N. (2003). Exploring the agency consequences of ownership dispersion among the directors of private family firms. *Academy of Management Journal, 46*(2), 179–194.

Miller, D., & Le Breton-Miller, I. (2003). Challenge versus advantage in family business. *Strategic Organization, 1*(1), 127–134.

Nicolini, D. (2009). Zooming in and out: Studying practices by switching theoretical lenses and trailing connections. *Organization Studies, 30*(12), 1391–1418.

Nicolini, D. (2012). *Practice Theory, Work & Organization: An Introduction*. Oxford: Oxford University Press.

Reckwitz, A. (2002). Toward a theory of social practices: A development in culturalist theorizing. *European Journal of Social Theory, 5*(2), 243–263.

Reckwitz, A. (2012a). Affective spaces: A praxeological outlook. *Rethinking History, 16*(2), 241–258.

Reckwitz, A. (2012b). *Die Erfindung der Kreativität*. Frankfurt: Suhrkamp.

Reckwitz, A. (2016). Praktiken und ihre Affekte. In H. Schäfer (Ed.), *Praxistheorie. Ein soziologisches Forschungsprogramm* (pp. 163–180). Bielefeld: Transcript.

Reckwitz, A. (2017a). Practices and their affects. In A. Hui, T. Schatzki, & E. Shove (Eds.), *The Nexus of Practices: Connections, Constellations, Practitioners* (pp. 114–125). London: Routledge.

Reckwitz, A. (2017b). *The Invention of Creativity*. Cambridge: Polity Press.

Reckwitz, A. (2019). *Die Gesellschaft der Singularitäten*. Frankfurt: Suhrkamp.

Reckwitz, A. (2020). *The Society of Singularities*. Cambridge: Polity Press.

Salvato, C., Chirico, F., Melin, L., & Seidl, D. (2019). Coupling family business research with organization studies: Interpretations, issues and insights. *Organization Studies, 40*(6), 775–791.

Sandberg, J., & Alvesson, M. (2011). Ways of constructing research questions: Gap-spotting or problematization? *Organization, 18*(1), 23–44.

Siebels, J.-F., & Knyphausen-Aufseß, D. (2012). A review of theory in family business research: The implications for corporate governance. *International Journal of Management Reviews, 14*(3), 280–304.

Thompson, M., & Willmott, H. (2016). The social potency of affect: Identification and power in the immanent structuring of practice. *Human Relations, 69*(2), 483–506.

Thompson, N. A., Verduijn, K., & Gartner, W. B. (2020). Entrepreneurship-as-practice: Grounding contemporary theories of practice into entrepreneurship studies. *Entrepreneurship & Regional Development, 32*(3–4), 247–256.

Tillmar, M. (2020). Practicing participant observations: Capturing entrepreneurial practices. In W. B. Gartner & B. T. Teague (Eds.), *Research Handbook on Entrepreneurial Behavior, Practice and Process* (pp. 168–181). Cheltenham, UK and Northampton, MA, USA: Edward Elgar Publishing.

Vaara, E., & Whittington, R. (2012). Strategy-as-practice: Taking social practices seriously. *Academy of Management Annals, 6*(1), 285–336.

Vásquez, C., Schoeneborn, D., & Sergi, V. (2016). Summoning the spirits: Organizational texts and the (dis)ordering properties of communication. *Human Relations, 69*(3), 629–659.

Verduyn, K. (2015). Entrepreneuring and process: A Lefebvrian perspective. *International Small Business Journal, 33*(6), 638–648.

Warde, A. (2005). Consumption and theories of practice. *Journal of Consumer Culture, 5*(2), 131–153.

Wenzel, M., Krämer, H., Koch, J., & Reckwitz, A. (2020). Future and Organization Studies: On the rediscovery of a problematic temporal category in organizations. *Organization Studies, 41*(10), 1441–1455.

Whittington, R. (2006). Completing the practice turn in strategy research. *Organization Studies, 27*(5), 613–634.

19. Sustainable entrepreneuring: alternative world making through shifting associations of practice

Dominik Mösching and Chris Steyaert

INTRODUCTION

In a world of rising inequalities (Piketty, 2014), geopolitical uncertainties (Rodrik, 2011), ecological challenges (Harris, 2007) and a general fragility of interrelated ecological, economic and social systems (Rogers, Jalal, & Boyd, 2008), novel practices of creating and organizing societal transformations and responding to ecological changes are in high demand. In entrepreneurship studies, the conviction that other worlds are needed and, in fact, possible, strongly resonates with readings of the entrepreneurial endeavor as a force of "world making" (Cálas, Smircich, & Bourne, 2009; Sarasvathy, 2015; Spinosa, Fernando Flores, & Dreyfus, 1997). At the same time, the assessment how, and under which conditions, entrepreneurship can constitute a "disruptive" (Hjorth & Steyaert, 2009a, 2009b) force that brings about "transformative" change – or rather reproduces "old" worlds – is highly contested (Cálas & Smircich, 2003; Cálas et al., 2009). As entrepreneurial practice is not performed in a tabula rasa situation, this chapter aims to understand how entrepreneurial world making can be enacted as it deals with and aims to overcome existing and often dominant organizational practices.

In particular, these struggles between existing and potential worlds become apparent in those entrepreneurial projects that subscribe to some of the functional logics of markets, but at the same time try to overcome them partially. Scholars have therefore increasingly been interested in such contexts as "social" (Dey & Steyaert, 2018; Osburg, 2014), "values-led" (Tennant, 2015), "activist" (Dey & Mason, 2018) or "sustainable" entrepreneurship (Nicholls, 2008) to understand how transformations are instilled towards "better" worlds. However, understanding how other worlds become possible remains both conceptually and empirically a complex challenge (Dey & Mason, 2018). Specifically, we aim to understand how entrepreneuring creates new organized worlds through asking the question whether this is a matter of developing new organizational practices and/or whether existing organizational practices can be significant as well. In this chapter, we analyze entrepreneuring, understood as organizing new ways of world making, by focusing on how this process unfolds in everyday entrepreneurial activities and their associations. By applying the conceptual framework of social practice theory (Hui, Shove, & Schatzki, 2017; Reckwitz, 2002), we are able to respond to the increasing call of entrepreneurship scholars to develop a processual view of entrepreneurship (Hjorth, Holt, & Steyaert, 2015), and, in particular, to study the process of entrepreneurial world making "as it happens" (Steyaert, 2004). The advantage of a social practice approach is that it offers a "theory-method package" (Nicolini, 2012) to conceive the entrepreneurial endeavor as a (bundle of) practice(s) where components such as discourse, matter, values, people, ideas or tools are jointly enacted in sociomaterial practice "associations" (Nicolini,

2017a) which always take shape in situated performances (Alkemeyer & Buschmann, 2017). Seen as a sociomaterial practice, entrepreneurial world making thus plays out in the ways that practices (and their components) are associated across time and space, whereby new (modes of) associations enable different worlds to become.

To study entrepreneurial world making as sociomaterial practice, we enter the empirical context of an entrepreneurial project aiming to change the dominant form of coffee production, distribution and consumption by turning to alternative, more sustainable and socially equal forms of organizing. Empirically, we ask the question "How, and to what effect, do entrepreneurial practices associate established and alternative organized worlds?" in a site like the one of coffee where the interest in a sustainable and fair approach to all aspects of the coffee-cycle is rising considerably. By means of a multi-sited ethnography, we trace this process of entrepreneurial world making along a migrant-led direct trade coffee business (Thurston, Morris, & Steiman, 2013) in Colombia and Switzerland, and analyze its modes of association through a configurationally oriented social practice lens (Nicolini, 2017b, p. 29). This "case" enables us to make visible an experimental, yet also marginal entrepreneurial endeavor as it tries to imagine and invent a new form of organizing coffee handling through direct trade, strongly in contrast to the dominant ways of handling coffee, as it is known from commodity trade. Based on the empirical analysis, the chapter develops two interrelated contributions. First, we theorize how alternative world making can be understood through shifting the mode of associations rather than through adopting new singular practices. Second, underlining the political aspect of social practice (theory), we propose that entrepreneurship as social practice comes with different effects that redistribute power, understood as agential potential in world making, and that thus enable alternative organized worlds or rather reproduce dominant ones. Taken together, our analysis suggests that novel agential potentials in world making can develop even when singular practices themselves are not changing.

In the following, we will first review the literature on entrepreneurship as a "frictional" process of world making and then move to the specific conceptualization of practice-based theory we take on in this study. After the description of our methodology, the results section presents two modes of organizing worlds which we operationalize through our conceptual framework as two modes of association, namely concentrated and dispersed, and contrasts their roles in the different configurations of "old" commodity coffee world versus the "new" direct trade coffee world. In the discussion, we address the theoretical contributions of this chapter and, in the conclusion, their implications for future research.

ENTREPRENEURING AS A FRICTIONAL PROCESS OF WORLD MAKING

The impact of entrepreneurship is no longer seen in purely economic terms but its effects come to be associated with social change (Steyaert, 2007; Steyaert & Hjorth, 2006) and societal transformation (Steyaert & Katz, 2004). This interest in the role entrepreneurial projects play in instilling social transformation and change towards a different or even "better" world has also incisively altered the outlook of entrepreneurship studies. Therefore, the focus of entrepreneurship studies has expanded and led to a range of quickly growing (sub)fields, such as social, civic, community-based, public and ecological entrepreneurship, making entrepreneurship into a matter of public concern (Dey & Mason, 2018).

However, this expansion of entrepreneurship in all aspects of societal life is also opening up space for important conceptual questions and debates. For instance, new theoretical questions and conceptual openings are required to address the increasing assessment and contestation of how, and under which conditions, entrepreneurship can constitute a "disruptive" (Hjorth & Steyaert, 2009a) or "transformative" (Tobias, Mair, & Barbosa-Leiker, 2013) force towards newly organized worlds. Recently, the conceptual understanding of entrepreneurship-as-world-making has therefore been framed as a "method" of disclosing new worlds (Spinosa et al., 1997) or as an ensemble of "practices" that seeks "gaps and breaches, and watches out for openings" (Weiskopf & Steyaert, 2009, p. 210) where presences and absences intersect and co-produce novelty.

Especially, critical scholars, asking what type of social change is actually enabled through entrepreneurial world making (Cálas & Smircich, 2003; Cálas et al., 2009), suggest new vocabularies that emphasize the processual and emancipatory nature of entrepreneuring as it aims to subvert or transform dominant organizational arrangements. They underline that mainstream takes on entrepreneurship as "the discovery, creation and exploitation of opportunities to create future goods and services" (Shepherd & Patzelt, 2017, p. 156), as a device to create new markets through "environmental" (Hockerts & Wüstenhagen, 2010) or "social" (Osburg, 2014) innovation, or as a "source for creative destruction" (Hart & Milstein, 1999) fail to acknowledge the conflictive negotiations between multiple views, voices and interests necessarily implied in entrepreneurship-as-world-making.

In such areas as political economy and decolonial theory, critiques that take an even more radical stance put forward that entrepreneurial practices *per se* produce at best a form of novelty that can be sold, but that they thereby often perpetuate powerful capitalist commodification processes (Escobar, 2018; Zanoni, Contu, Healy, & Mir, 2017). The underlying assumption is that entrepreneurial world making colonizes an "outside" environment, imagined as open, unchartered territory, and translates it into a zone of influence to exploit by means of business (Maldonaldo-Torres, 2010). By thus subjecting the not-quite or not-yet commodified "other" under the entrepreneurial trajectory of progress, entrepreneurship enters in a consequential friction with "other" – environmental, social, cultural, political – logics (Rindova, Barry, & Ketchen, 2009).

Therefore, entrepreneurial world making cannot be understood without considering its political effects and requires looking at those entrepreneurial projects that subscribe to some of the existing organizational processes, but at the same time try to overcome them, as they allow us to trace the ongoing and everyday struggles between existing and potential worlds. Any form of entrepreneurship with an implicit or explicit outlook at social change consists of frictional processes that transpire in everyday entrepreneurial practices of mobilizing resources and enrolling actors (Gherardi & Nicolini, 2005) at and beyond the margins of capitalist production (Tsing, 2015). In studying and understanding these frictions, the ontological force of entrepreneurial world making comes to define whom or what is empowered to take ownership of the world and the newness that enters it.

PRACTICE-BASED THEORY: UNDERSTANDING SOCIOMATERIAL PERFORMANCES

In order to study these frictional forms of world making, we argue that a coherent theory-method package is needed to develop theoretical explanations that are grounded in what is empirically observable but also enable us to understand the theoretical logic of practice (Janssens & Steyaert, 2019). Drawing upon the expansive range of practice-based approaches, we argue that a focus on frictions and conflicts should not be done in a dualistic way by opposing the old and the new, but by acknowledging that entrepreneurial world making can be realized by inscribing existing practices in new modes of association.

Social practice theory is rather an umbrella term to refer to a group of loosely connected theoretical approaches which have been established around the idea of a "practice turn" (Schatzki, Knorr Cetina, & von Savigny, 2001), claiming that the site of the social is located in social practices and their performance (Hui et al., 2017; Nicolini, 2012; Shove, Pantzar, & Watson, 2012). Such a performative view assumes that the creation of newly organized worlds "always takes shape in situated performances of practices" (Alkemeyer & Buschmann, 2017, p. 21). Building upon the Heideggerian and Wittgensteinian tradition, it is assumed that practices are oriented towards forming and performing a common sense, but that such sense "always manifests itself as part of an ongoing practical endeavor" (Nicolini, 2012, p. 162). Therefore, Nicolini further specifies "that practices, and neither sense nor the individuals that enact the sense-making, are the starting points for the investigation and understanding of human and social affairs. It is thus to the accomplishment of real-time practices that we need to turn if we want to understand human conduct and social order" (Nicolini, 2012, pp. 163–164).

Instead, in the vein of a post-dualistic (Janssens & Steyaert, 2019) and "flat ontology" (Nicolini, 2017a, p. 99), discourse, matter, values, people, ideas or tools all equally join the inclusive "club" of "practice components" (Schatzki, 2017, p. 137) to be enacted in emerging practices. Their processual status depends on how they perform and are performed, not on a howsoever-imagined pre-practical substance. This also implies that the material side of things plays a key role in the agency that is (per)formed in practice. For Gherardi (2017), proponents of a sociomaterial practice view the debate less about whether materiality matters for agency and power: it does. Instead, the question is whether materiality mediates human agency (as in human-centered social practice theory) or is constitutive of agency (as in posthuman social practice theory). Gherardi emphasizes that "a posthumanist approach instead interrogates how all the elements within a practice hold together and acquire agency in being entangled" (2017, p. 50). This does not mean that the specificity of humans as creative and sometimes improvising actors is irrelevant for a posthuman approach: "If practices are to persist, they need to recruit people willing and able to keep them alive" (Shove et al., 2012, p. 62).

Such a sociomaterial understanding implies a processual and performative view on practice, as the analytical interest lies in "performances connected in space and time, not mysterious entities called practices" (Nicolini, 2017b, p. 25). For Morley (2017), a more rhizomatic, assemblage-infused understanding of practice revolves much less around the concrete list of components that make up a practice, but rather asks how components interlink in practice, and how practices associate to wider collectives of practices. For Nicolini, the affordance of such a relational view is to go beyond the "agonizing" (2017b, p. 25) boundary work of defining what a practice *is* or not by preferring to look at what is *done* in practice. In that vein, the unit of analysis shifts from "a practice" to a vast array of performances inscribed in interconnected bodies, minds, objects and texts, which become resources for another in a "nested relational" way (Jarzabkowski, Bednarek, & Spee, 2015). These practice collectives are commonly conceived as "bundles and constellations" (Schatzki, 2017), "connective tissue" (Blue & Spurling, 2017), "nexuses" (Hui et al., 2017) or as "associations" (Nicolini, 2012), which we will use to emphasize the performative nature of how practices are associated. It implies what could be called "association work", enacted through negotiations and a certain temporality in the sense that associations have to be maintained to live on, and that they can be dissociated as well.

World making from a practice perspective is therefore not a grand gesture of heroic entrepreneurial individuals or larger-than-life structures. Rather it forms an ongoing accomplishment where the bodily situatedness of participants interact with the surrounding material arrangements and particular, situated "normative demands that open up and close off certain possibilities" (Alkemeyer & Buschmann, 2017, p. 20). This implies that world making is often not enacted as an explicit discourse, but collectively performed in nonverbal, minimal and subtle movements, in affective reverberances and "attunements" (Brice, 2014) of the involved actors in the situation. Therefore, social practice theory helps to understand how other, possible worlds are enacted through "[e]mpowerment, scope for agency and voice [which] are effects of practice and how they are associated" (Nicolini, 2017b, p. 31). Therefore, we propose that entrepreneuring as a process of world making plays out in the ways that practices (and their components) are associated across time and space and that different (modes of) associations enable different worlds to become – with different implications for enabled agency. As a consequence, our research questions can be formulated in an intertwined way, as we ask, first, what different modes of associations are empirically identifiable and, second, what effects these different forms of associating produce in a case of entrepreneurial world making, and the site of coffee in particular, to which we now turn.

EMPIRICAL FIELD AND METHODOLOGY

Empirical Field: Making New Coffee Worlds in Direct Trade Entrepreneuring

We contend that the field of direct trade (DT) coffee is a suitable empirical field to trace modes of associating in entrepreneurial world making. World coffee markets have been among the first empirical contexts where entrepreneurial practice has been effectively conceived as a force of world making (Daviron & Ponte, 2005; Thurston et al., 2013). Sooner than in the case of other commodities, environmental and social conditions gained consumers' attention as early as in the 1980s and started to trigger entrepreneurial innovations (Lernoud et al., 2017). From niche to mainstream in thirty years, a big number of initiatives enabling "ethical", "fair" or "sustainable" consumption have been developed, promoted and monitored by non-profit enterprises as well as, increasingly, by multinational companies through their own programs (Raynolds, 2002; Samper & Quiñones-Ruiz, 2017). Although dominant agri-businesses have been pushed to lift the "commodity veil" obscuring unfair pricing and unequal value distributions (Van der Ploeg, 2009) or exploitative and unsafe work practices (Burnett & Murphy, 2014), consumers are increasingly overwhelmed with the diversity of labels and what they stand for. At the same time, it is argued that the impact of certification efforts on livelihoods as well as work and labor practices has been limited (Fridell, 2007; Jaffee, 2014). For some, this is because set standards and their implementation protocols are not sensitive enough to the context-specific needs and conditions along the value chain (Samper, 2003).

A more fundamental critique perceives schemes such as "fair trade" as a continuation of Northern/Western domination over Southern producer countries by means of masking hard economic power with a more subtle epistemological approach (Maldonaldo-Torres, 2010; Mignolo, 2000, 2002). The core claim is that certification efforts may depart from a well-meant impetus to transform coffee markets, but effectively actualize established power relations and distributive logics as they perform North Western dominance in updated forms (Jaffee, 2014).

In part, as an answer to these challenges of "old" ways of handling coffee, and enabled by the emergence of new communication technologies that lowered transaction costs, the model of DT has gained momentum in the coffee sector. DT is part of a movement known as "Third Wave Coffee", trying to replace coffee-as-commodity (first wave) and coffee-as-certified-commodity (second wave) with coffee-as-traceable-high-quality-product (Artusi, 2014). The movement is essentially oriented towards affluent customers who are interested in distinctive status consumption. In so doing, it generates additional value mainly for the craft roasters and "hipster" baristas in their Northern neighborhoods and some surplus in the producer countries (Watts, 2013).

DT aspires to create and organize new worlds of coffee making by establishing direct producer–buyer relations by guaranteeing a "single origin", meaning that the journey of the coffee is transparent and the traveling product is not blended with coffee beans from other origins along the way (Watts, 2013). Whereas in first and second wave commodity coffees the (Northern) buyers are usually interested in coffee as a raw material to be refined in roasting, differentiated in quality classes rather than origins and therefore to be sourced around the world rather than from specific places, in DT the location of production is central in commodifying its value. Its location and taste profile are the unique selling proposition towards the customers (Peterson, 2013). By focusing on a direct relation between quality-oriented producers and quality-sensitive consumers, DT coffee emerges as "specialty coffee" (Poltronieri & Rossi, 2016) originating from somewhere vis-à-vis "commodity coffee" originating potentially from anywhere (Steiman, 2013).

Methodology: Empirical Case, Data Collection and Analysis

This study addresses these questions by means of a multi-sited ethnography (Falzon, 2009) of a migrant-led DT coffee business (Thurston et al., 2013) in Colombia and Switzerland. The single case follows entrepreneurial practices along the entrepreneurial endeavor initiated by Joaquín (pseudonym), a Colombian migrant living in Switzerland. Set in the context of established corporate networks active in both countries, it started as an import venture, was later complemented by a coffee shop in Switzerland and, finally, by re-starting a coffee farm in Colombia, *Finca Manantial*, to produce its own *Café Don Miguel* to change the way coffee is "handled" both in the producer region and in the global market.

As a DT coffee business, the focal case is part of the third wave of coffee. At the same time, it is not a typical third wave project as it is initiated and coordinated by a migrant from the South instead of the common DT entrepreneur without migratory experience from the North, making it marginal also within the niche market of DT coffee. In that sense, the chosen case might be atypical for the DT market, but serves as a typical example of marginal entrepreneurship as it unfolds in the often-silenced contexts of precarious and/or migrant lives (Durepos,

Prasad, & Villanueva, 2016). Engaging in a multi-sited ethnography is suitable to empirically trace practices and their associations, as it shares with the theory-method package (Nicolini, 2012) of social practice theory a rhizomatic sensitivity for the "living connection of performances and what keeps them together" (Nicolini, 2017a, p. 102). Furthermore, it allows for a combination of thick descriptions of lived realities with techniques to do fieldwork on the move in order to trace the connections in the multiple sites where the practices are performed (Falzon, 2009), and the orientation towards crafting a rich theoretical repertoire "by adding together ever shifting cases and learning from their specificities" (Heuts & Mol, 2013, p. 127).

The ethnographic fieldwork was realized by the first author in a "spiraling" (Falzon, 2009) series of participant observation visits at the coffee shop over sixteen months, 25 focused conversations with the owner, a five-week instance of ethnographic fieldwork in Colombia including dozens of "interviews with the double" (Nicolini, 2009) to retrace network activities, as well as on- and offline documentary research. The generated data include around 150 pages of field notes and field sketches from observing, and participating in, coffee practices, a total of 44 semi-structured and unstructured interviews, jottings from several dozen focused conversations with coffee farmers, workers, businessmen, villagers, researchers and a Colombian senator, and audio-visual materials, videos and soundbites from the field. The ethical stance guiding field access and positionality was informed by decolonial methodologies (Escobar, 2010) and more-than-representational research (Vannini, 2015). The responsibility of the researcher included "listening" to marginal subjects rather than "giving voice" (Yehia, 2006, p. 101) in full acknowledgment that "[i]t is not us who give the other a voice. It is they who give us ours" (Rose, 2016, p. 144).

The data analysis was conducted in iterations of multi-data triangulation, analytical vignette and memo writing, open inductive coding and evocative storytelling (Emerson, Fretz, & Shaw, 2011). Repeated instances of vignette writing/reading in varying intensities and analytical depth have put the empirical data in dialogue with practice-based concepts by "zooming in and out" (Nicolini, 2012) and "allowed a certain trajectory of thought to transpire" (Rose, 2016, p. 138). Applying a configurational practice analysis (Nicolini, 2017b), the analysis focuses on tracing practices plus their relationships in order to flesh out how practices are linked and how they act together in different types of association (Hui, 2017). This conceptual framework integrates both the spatially and temporally immediate reality of the social world (Watson, 2017) and the amplification and extension of action by practice components on the move.

THE EFFECTS OF SHIFTING MODES OF ASSOCIATION

By tracing coffee handling activities along the marginal direct trade (DT) business in the context of established commodity trade (CT) frameworks, the analysis shows how the entrepreneurial making of alternative worlds can be understood through shifting the mode of practice associations, rather than through introducing and enforcing new singular practices. Based on the ethnographic analysis of the empirical material, the interpretation shows how "old" CT practices and their components, rather than being replaced, become part of the "new" DT world. In particular, we suggest two modes of association: concentrated and dispersed association. The first part of the results section describes how, as they associate the same practices in different ways, these two modes "make" different worlds, and therefore bring different coffee qualities into being – commodity and direct trade coffee. Two examples of key practices along the coffee value chain, which remain mainly unchanged, but are associated differently, underline this point: quality testing and controlling the harvest. The second part describes the effects of different modes of association in terms of the worlds they enable to become, particularly concerning transparency, marginality and neocolonial stereotyping.

Concentrated and Dispersed Modes of Association

The empirical analysis of the researched DT case suggests that enhanced transparency and a more explicit orientation towards coffee quality have not transformed long-standing commodity-oriented practices along the value chain. While general orientations along the commercial networks have (partially) changed towards DT coffee understandings, and new associations as situated performances are being woven together differently, most coffee handling performances have remained without drastic changes. Two of the most important practices along coffee value chains exemplify the contrast between CT and DT association work: the practice of quality testing and the practice of controlling the coffee harvest.

First, the practice of quality testing, traced in several places along DT networks, enacts the same components – materials, skills, protocols and norms – as in CT coffee. However, our analysis suggests that in DT, the particular quality testing performances are associated differently along the value chain. In DT, the practice of quality testing is dispersed over instances, which are oriented towards each other relationally, and performed by intermediaries who know each other. In CT, quality testing happens in concentrated, but disconnected instances, which serve as bottlenecks between different, rather isolated production practices. A representative example for concentrated CT quality testing unfolds at the coffee cooperative in the village where commodity farmers typically sell the weekly harvest as dried, but not yet hulled "parchment coffee". As soon as the sale is completed, the connection between the specific bean and the specific origin is lost on both sides. Neither knows the buyer down the road from which farm the coffee originated, nor knows the farmer where her coffee goes after the cooperative. When zooming in onto the CT sales procedure, quality testing emerges as the key practice of associating concrete places with abstract standards in CT coffee, transforming a weekly harvest, produced by particular socioecological entanglements, into a class of goods that can be unequivocally localized on a one-dimensional, universal classification system. As a cooperative staffer groups a sample of the delivery into "good" and "bad" beans in a quick and routinized desk procedure, each delivery is assigned a given quality class with a related price tag, determined daily by world market prices and the exchange rate between Colombian Peso and US Dollar. As cooperative staff, traders and farmers equally confirm, farmers usually do not turn down the deal, even the more affluent ones who are not directly dependent on the sale, as they need sufficient liquid to pay the harvesters and sustain the family in the week to come. Because turning down would mean to take all the bags back to store them somewhere and, in the meantime, to look for some private dealers "on the street" – who are usually very well informed about the price dynamics at the cooperatives. Much traveling, transporting and hassle for the uncertain prospect of getting a better deal.

In the case of DT, the coffee is not sold at the village cooperative as raw material of green coffee, but it is directly exported to Switzerland as refined, roasted coffee. As the ethnographic tracing of entrepreneurial activities indicates, instead of a clear-cut selling instance where the responsibility (and visibility) of the farmer ends such as in CT, the DT activities are related by more components than just the physical product of the bean in its various stages. Actually, all instances of quality testing – at the farm, in the hulling factory, at the roaster – lie in the entrepreneur's responsibility. In addition, they are coordinated by a small number of people who know each other well. Therefore, beans, knowledge and information produced in one practice are "allowed" to travel beyond single sites of performance with fewer restrictions: bottlenecks such as the highly powerful quality/price determination in village cooperatives are bypassed.

What is crucial here is that key components of "old" practices, such as CT export regulations and quality norms, are also enrolled to ensure DT traceability and serve as a common orientation point for the relational coordination of the interdependent DT activities across time and space. David, owner of the hulling plant where *Café Don Miguel* is processed, explains: "When I am going to export, or when the farmer hands [the coffee] over to the client at the port, all the documents have to coincide with [...] a [FNC] transit guide from the origin of the coffee to the port where it will be shipped". In this sense, "old" commodity components serve as an associative glue for the "new" DT activities, performed at dispersed moments and places along the coffee value chain. Interestingly, the combination of bypassing commodity markets to get rid of intermediaries – and redistribute the value across the chain – with the elevated traceability and quality standards does apparently not lead to less, but to differently associated intermediating practices along the way:

> There have been a lot of ups and downs in the life of coffee. [...] Before, one arrived and bought the coffee and simply said: OK, let's do it. [He claps his hands.] Today, no. The cup tests have arrived, the laboratories have stuck around, and the norms are different now. Before, the norms were more flexible around exporting. No, now, the norms are stricter, more demanding. That's why so many have come to stick around in the chain. Before, the taster [catador] did not exist, the barista did not exist. No one did exist for the internal production control in a plant. All these requirements have created these types of work. (José David, coffee trader)

Second, as one of the most important instances on the way to bringing high-quality coffee into being (Peterson, 2013), the practice of controlling the harvest is a particular focus of alternative DT world making. As in the example of quality testing, the empirical material shows that coffee picking and the respective controls at *Finca Manantial* have remained to be performed overwhelmingly according to "old" CT coffee ways. Yet, as a difference to picking on CT farms, controlling the quality of the harvested coffee cherries is performed in instances that are much more dispersed in time and space. In Colombian CT coffee, other than in most producer countries, the traditional ways of harvesting have always been oriented towards "quality" – interpreted as a manual bean-by-bean picking of all-ripe, red cherries – for a number of reasons (amongst which the rugged topography and widespread family ownership of small farms are the most important (Ocampo Villegas, 2015)). On Colombian farms, thus, the all-red mature cherry becomes the crystallization point towards which the practice of harvesting is oriented. It translates the abstract and ambiguous general understanding of "quality" to the specific setting of the plantation (Peterson, 2013).

Up to a certain point, to enroll the "traditional" national pride of Colombia as a high-quality coffee country, materializing in everyday talk, in marketing and political campaigns and official reports, has proven functional for the DT business studied. However, as the DT model strives to guarantee minimal quality and profile variation from harvest to harvest, DT businesses tend to have resource-intensive trainings of the farm workers in place which internalize control by orienting "minds and skills" (Joaquín) towards high-quality procedures. In our case, owner Joaquín calls farm administrator Francisco sometimes up to two hours a day for mentoring and training calls and regularly interacts via WhatsApp with the farm workers. Yet, the "new" DT framework to be enacted at *Finca Manantial* has not changed the way they work compared to the traditional ways of handling commodity coffee. Whether it is DT or CT coffee they help to bring into being is mostly irrelevant to their understanding of what they are doing at the plantation. As they are mostly paid per kilo, they have a vital interest in maximizing their harvest per day. What is more, a number of conversations have shown that often, they do not know where the coffee goes beyond the farm, not even that it does not go to the cooperative.

What this analysis shows is that these regular remote contacts between the farm owner in Switzerland and the "Colombian side" (Joaquín) are relevant for the establishment of the DT business, but not because of their content, but much rather because they are an associative glue for the "new" DT practices. As such calls regularly reach Francisco during the harvesting time, he loses direct grip in supervising the pickers, a practice that is performed like on "old" CT farms: embodied, authoritative and personalized. At the same time, the remote presence of an invisible, yet very powerful owner enhances Francisco's power because for every order he gives it becomes clear that he is Joaquín's agent and that everybody is ultimately responding to the latter. In the way that the call and the harvest supervision compete for the practitioner's attention, they intersect. Precisely in this intersection, control transcends the visibility of the supervisor, it becomes disembodied and present all the time and collectively performed in affective reverberances and "attunements" (Brice, 2014). This "nested relationality" (Jarzabkowski et al., 2015) of dispersed control instances is a marked contrast to CT where focused instances of embodied control associate in a sequential manner ("first here, then there") pickers, coffee bushes, reaped cherries and the future income prospects on coffee markets.

The Effects of Different Forms of Entrepreneurial Associating

As the ethnographic tracing of two key practices along the coffee value chain – quality testing and harvesting – has illustrated, alternative ways of coffee handling do not need to include a shift in single practices by replacing one way of handling with another, but by differently associating them. Dispersed and concentrated modes of association come also with particular effects. While different associations of the same practices often imply continuities in terms of agency and power in the worlds that become, shifting modes of association are not only performing "old wine in new tubes" but also redistribute agential potential in world making. Concerning the worlds that are enabled to become, we identify three interrelated implications of dispersed and relational associations as identified in the case of DT coffee: first, a shift to an enhanced bidirectionality of transparency, second, a shift from global to local marginality, and third, only a modest shift in agency of producers as neocolonial stereotypes continue to be reproduced (see Table 19.1).

First, concerning the bidirectionality of transparency, the typical CT handling is to sell the harvest at the cooperative and to transform the particular product of a week's work at the farm into representations of standardized quality classes. For the farmers, further travels are hidden behind a "commodity veil", and the world of "raw" production is subsequently made invisible along the CT value chains. More dispersed and relational DT associations, on the other hand, lift the "commodity veil" for them:

Joaquín's project is special. You know where the coffee goes to. [...] Usually the federation organizes the exportation through the cooperatives. One never knows the end, and where the coffee goes to ... if one doesn't know, one doesn't really pay attention to the product. If one would know more about the consumer, one would value quality more [...] That's special about working for Joaquín. He explains us many things and tells us how things should be for the consumer. Coffee is an "aliment". It has to be good. (Francisco, DT farm administrator)

Compared to his CT colleagues at other farms, DT farmer Francisco has a much clearer idea of the final consumer of his coffee (rather than only the consumer having an idea of the producer such as in Fair Trade schemes). Joaquín's entrepreneurial activities open up a connection to the consumers, and this results in an acknowledgment of a commonality that triggers an enhanced quality orientation: both consumers and producers are aware of each other. Thus, coffee transforms from being an unspecific mass of cherries harvested to generate some income into "an aliment" that "has to be good". In addition, the DT model differs from the commodity model in the transparency of the pricing. Although the price is still fixed elsewhere like in commodity coffee, it is set by a particular other, at Joaquín's desk in Switzerland. Therefore, Francisco does not have to rely on anonymous economic forces at the commodity and currency markets or the bureaucratic or political norm making in hidden offices.

Second, concerning the localization of marginality, more transparency has associated temporally and spatially distant practices closer together by relationally orienting them towards each other, which has, in turn, lowered the marginalization in the global coffee markets for the producers. At the same time, the empirical material shows that, locally, frictions with interests and social connections have risen, which has marginalized actors involved in altered practice associations at the local places of enactment. One evening, Francisco's wife Luisa explains that the relation of Francisco to the village has changed after he stopped going to the cooperative to sell coffee every Saturday. She underlines that his quality had always been very good, but that the rumors in the village first were that he or the new farm could not deliver anymore. In enrolling Francisco, Joaquín pulled their whole family in a situation of marginality in the village, and they have started to see their farm as a proof of concept to show the village that change from within is possible ("they will not stop to smile" when they see the results,

Table 19.1   Effects of different modes of association: shifting from CT to DT redistributes agential potential in world making

	Concentrated association (CT)	Dispersed association (DT)
Shifting transparency from none/unidirectional to (potentially) bidirectional	None. Coffee comes from and goes to "anywhere" Buyers have unique bargaining power, producers don't have ownership of process and quality	Yes, but typified. Coffee comes from and goes to "somewhere" Producers have higher bargaining power (single origin needed), take ownership of process and quality
Shifting marginality from global to local	Binary here/there frictions Producers are marginalized in world markets and global value chains	Multiple us/them frictions Producers become marginalized in local communities, but gain connections beyond them
Shifting agency for producers: Continued neocolonial stereotyping, but blurring boundaries	Fixed boundaries South is always producer of raw materials, North is always refiner and consumer	Blurred boundaries South is partner in production both raw and refined, but "incompetent and unreliable". North is boss + consumer

Francisco). In that sense, the DT practitioners in the village started to perceive a gap between them and the "others" in terms of "punch and persistence" (Luisa). Taken together with similar experiences along the DT network, marginalities of people, ideas or products in their local contexts serve as a glue that effectively associates them together trans-locally. In that sense, it has been an explicit entrepreneurial practice to associate female farmers, village outsiders, value-driven factory owners (huller, roaster) and alternative consumers and restaurants in Switzerland into "webs of solidarity" (Joaquín, on the DT business).

Third, concerning the reproduction of neocolonial stereotypes, the performance of long-standing colonial understandings has appeared to be crucial components for key entrepreneurial practices in the DT case while reproducing established power formations in CT coffee. As indicated by the "commodity veil" phenomenon, CT coffee performs an othering of production places and countries that builds on centuries of colonial exploitation of the Global South as mere raw material producers, with the North being the exclusive place for refining producers and enlightened consumers. The world of CT coffee thereby builds on long-standing general understandings, which assign different world making agency along the "Orientalist" (Said, 1978) line between the West as historical subject and the Rest as historical object. In the empirical case, there are clear indications that for the DT business to succeed, business owner Joaquín continues to perform colonial othering, painting the Global South as "underdeveloped" children who are too self-interested and too immature to grow up. In most interactions with the "Colombian side", he positions himself as the clever idealist from outside, whose emancipative ideas are not comprehended by the ignorant population back in his region. In addition, they are "unreliable" and "can't be trusted", which is why his distance from the actual everyday enactments throughout the network may cause problems in compliance, in understanding and add transaction costs, or may even be used strategically by "dishonest" actors. Yet, the marginal position as the outsider who – in neocolonial frames – had the chance to be enlightened through his migration to the North is made functional: playing the card as "Swiss" enhances his reputation and helps him to put the vision of entrepreneur-driven social change in Colombia into practice. In that context, the partial invisibilities in organizing a value chain from abroad are enrolled for the sake of the project, because the entrepreneur's own marginal position as a migrant in Switzerland is essential to remain a strong and credible voice in Colombia:

> They don't see me. They think that I do everything like a director in a big office building [...] look at me, I am a civil engineer and I am here, cleaning mugs and the floor, putting on the apron. In Sneakers. Well, they don't see me ... I can't change things by telephone, but they do respect me there. I don't have much money, but ... (Joaquín, reflecting on his position in-between Colombia and Switzerland)

Neocolonial stereotypes continue to be reproduced on the Colombian side of the business in a self-directed fashion as well. One of the most telling indications of such "self othering" as performed in the daily accomplishments at the farm and in the village are the so-called *pasilla* or low-quality beans. They are separated early in the process, but not thrown away as they can still be sold to local buyers as "third quality" at much lower prices. Pasilla loosely translates to "coffee that doesn't pass", referring to something that is othered by the dominant system but is still of some value. "The bad coffee stays here", Francisco once said, and then sighed between fatalism and guilt: "Pasilla es nuestro café. Nos toca esto." ("Pasilla is our coffee. This is our destiny.")

DISCUSSION

To summarize the analysis, we have empirically identified two modes of associations that distinguish the worlds of CT and DT coffee, respectively: concentrated and dispersed associating. We have framed the dynamic interplay between both worlds by applying the theory-method package of social practice theory to expand the understanding of entrepreneurship-as-world-making, reading it as a sociomaterial performance in which diverse practice components are associated and dissociated to jointly bring worlds into being. Our analysis of the ethnographic material suggests that alternative DT worlds are not established in clear-cut dissociations from CT practices, but in novel modes of associating extant practices and their components. In particular, it has been shown how "old" CT practices and their components, rather than being replaced, become part of the "new" DT world – but in associations that shift from concentrated (as in CT) to dispersed (as in DT) modes. Our conceptual contribution is then to emphasize how alternative world making can be understood through shifting the mode of associations rather than through adopting new singular practices.

In terms of our first research question – what different modes of associations are empirically identifiable – we zoomed in on two exemplary practices along the coffee value chain. In the cases of quality testing and controlling the coffee harvest, we illustrated how in CT, association work is a question of weaving together the world of the farm and the "global" coffee markets in concentrated association work. Association is practiced in one particular weekly instance, namely the quality testing at the cooperative on Saturdays during the sales procedure, which can be thought of as an "eye of a needle" between worlds. As an outcome, coffee is first a particular agricultural product produced somewhere and then becomes ontologically translated into a representation of a universal quality class, together with thousands of tons of coffee produced anywhere. Whereas CT others coffee into a commodified raw product and the farmer into a voiceless producer of raw materials, DT maintains the voice of product and producer audible. In DT, association work has been analyzed as enacted in dispersed ways across time and space. This "nested relationality" (Jarzabkowski et al., 2015) of DT associations establishes a temporal and spatial discontinuity which leads to a routinized flow of association activities throughout the harvest season, and even throughout the year, compared to the uniquely powerful quality/price setting at the cooperative or embodied harvest supervising in CT coffee.

Both the practices of probing and harvesting show that the contrast between "old" CT associations and "new" DT associations does not lie in the replacement of one set of singular practices through another. The marked contrast lies in the modes of entrepreneurial associating of practices always already in place. The ethnographic data retraced in the studied case suggests that, while CT coffee associations are performed in more focused singular instances, the DT project shows much more dispersed association work. Such activities are performed in relational instances by intermediaries which are relationally aware and dependent of each other, which is a counter-intuitive finding considering the aspiration of DT coffee businesses to bypass intermediaries along the value chain altogether. It seems that the more different – and potentially competing – generalized and abstract norms are co-present, the bigger the demand for embodied (and skilled) quality control work to translate these abstract universals into practice. As an outcome, DT association work performs coexisting worlds: before a harvest is even quality tested and has physically become high-quality specialty *Café Don Miguel*, it is already performed as *Don Miguel* in that all the performances are oriented to it as if it was already what it aspires to become. It is, but not yet; it is virtually, but not yet actually. Until the moment that the roasted coffee is brewed, the "concept of specialty coffee is locked up as a possibility" (Poltronieri & Rossi, 2016, p. 14). Commodity coffee, as a result of CT association work, is first this and then that. DT coffee, as a result of DT world making is this and that at the same time. It is multiple.

But has DT effectively led to changes in coffee handling practices, actualizing or resisting dominant political economies in the coffee system? If so, how can these new forms be pathways towards more sustainable, equitable and just worlds? As for our second research question – what effects do these different forms of entrepreneurial associating produce in a case of entrepreneurial world making (and the site of coffee in particular) – our interpretation asserts that the implications of such a multiplicity for the worlds allowed to become are not trivial. Shifting modes of association do not solely perform "old wine in new tubes". They have shown possibilities to develop novel agential potentials in world making, even when the single practices performed are not changing. What we have called "association work" can be seen as the activities that bring together or pull apart components and practices. In that vein, how power is performed is an outcome of "the range of elements [components] in circulation, the ways in which practices relate to each other and the careers and trajectories of practices and those who carry them" (Shove et al., 2012, p. 19). In particular, practice associations hang together in that practices "produce" components that are performed by other practices "downstream" (Watson, 2017). As our take on social practice theory has shown, the club of possible components to be performed in practice is not restrictive. Practices not only perform matter in practice, but also components, which are typically described as discursive or cultural: skills, meanings and so on. In putting all of these components in motion, practices bring into being the conditions of possibility for other practices, or more particularly, the conditions of possibility to perform a practice in this way or another. They perform power.

In particular, we have identified three interrelated implications of more dispersed and relational associations as in the studied DT coffee case. First, the "commodity veil" in DT is lifted bidirectionally at least on the level of the typified consumer or producer. This shift enhances transparency, but also makes everyday enactments more ambiguous and fractured than the corresponding CT performances because a whole range of practice components travels with the bean. In turn, this means that the involved actors are made responsible for a wider array of activities – and, crucially, the connections between them. Second, the analysis has indicated a notable shift in marginal positions of Southern producers in DT, which is related to the enhanced transparency. Whereas CT producers are silenced and marginalized in global coffee markets – with the respective lack of bargaining potential in negotiating higher shares of the produced value along the chain – DT producers are marginalized locally, as they engage in altered practice associations that challenge habitual orientations, interests and social connections at the local places of enactment.

And, third, the performance of neocolonial stereotypes, either directed at "others" or at oneself (self othering), reproduces dominant power structures and disempowers marginalized actors even in the researched case of an emancipative DT project. While the disclosure of associated practices fosters a (potentially decolonizing) understanding of qualified producers along the chain, the work ethics and agential potential of the "Colombian side" is constantly questioned. What is more, the subject position of the consumer remains distinctively Northern, as the high-quality consumption that all production practices are oriented to, is Northern, while the consumer of the beans that fail along the way is Southern: Othered beans for othered customers. From a critical view on power relations along the value chain we contend here, the market segmentation in high- and low-quality coffee alone is not the problem; the problem is that these quality classes binarily lock in with the performance of neocolonial stereotypes. Without the belief in self-efficacy, it is hard if not impossible to take over responsibility over the world one co-enacts through the practices one performs – or to internalize orientations one enacts, as empowering as they may be. In that sense, a closer look at the way both associations are practiced shows differences, but also similarities with respect to agential potentials in world making.

CONCLUSION

How, and under which conditions, does entrepreneurship constitute a "disruptive" (Hjorth and Steyaert, 2009a) force that brings "transformative" (Tobias et al., 2013) newness into the world (Dey and Mason, 2018)? By suggesting that alternative DT worlds are not established in clear-cut dissociations from CT practices, but in novel modes of associating extant practices and their components, this chapter contributes to the debate by studying how other worlds are enacted as an effect of how everyday entrepreneurial practices are differently associated. Entrepreneurial attempts at making other worlds have to consider the (multiple) performances of visible and less visible social fabrics: The "old" power relations are always already in place, and associating practices towards making other worlds is a matter of creatively working with them. Tactics of radical connection can be radically subversive, as they themselves might contain the seed to counter the binary bifurcation between established and possible worlds. Multiplication instead of division: making worlds in which many worlds fit necessarily is a multiple performance. In order to "make the multiple possible and enable the potential of the multiple" (Steyaert, 2012, p. 159), we would therefore argue that the dualism of disruption and gradual transformation might be more a conceptual difference than an ontological one. Put in more explicit terms, we suggest that the making of new worlds is possible through fresh associations of existing practices rather than by designing, developing and adopting new singular practices. In addition, our analysis suggests that different associations have different effects: novel agential potentials in world making can develop even when the single practices and components performed are not changing. "Old" and "new" worlds influence each other, steal from each other and live from each other. They don't seem to replace each other in a Schumpeterian way through creative destruction, but form and perform a "pluriverse" (Escobar, 2018) of interacting and intersecting worlds.

In order to show how practice associations are formed, and performed, by such a joint enactment of "old" and "new" components, our research has been driven by the assumption that understanding the (political) effects of entrepreneurship requires tracing the ongoing struggles between existing and potential worlds – particularly in entrepreneurial projects at the margins of capitalist production. They subscribe to some of the functional logics of markets, but at the same time try to overcome them (Rindova et al., 2009; Tsing, 2015). We agree with critical scholarship that, more than has been acknowledged by mainstream entrepreneurial studies, fields such as sustainable, social, civic, community-based, public and ecological entrepreneurship are prime environments where struggles between different modes of world making play out, and that there is a vast potential for further research in this regard (Cálas et al., 2009; Dey & Steyaert, 2018).

Finally, we have argued that social practice theory, especially in its relational-configurational form (Nicolini, 2017b) is a coherent and suitable theory-method package to study the world making force of entrepreneurship without refraining to dualisms like "material and ideal", "object and subject", "structure and agency" or "body and mind" (Durepos et al., 2016). We put forward that the potential of social practice theory is far from being exploited in entrepreneurial studies (Luethy & Steyaert, 2019), as it enables us to develop grounded theoretical explanations of how the ontological force of entrepreneurial world making comes to define who or what acts and has effect, who or what is responsible for retention or change and accountable for outcomes, and who or what is empowered to engage in entrepreneurship-as-world-making practice.

REFERENCES

Alkemeyer, T., & Buschmann, N. (2017). Learning in and across practices: Enablement as subjectivation. In A. Hui, T. Schatzki, & E. Shove (Eds.), *The Nexus of Practices: Connections, Constellations, Practitioners* (pp. 8–23). London: Routledge.

Artusi, N. (2014). *Café. De Etiopía a Juan Valdez: La Historia Secreta de la Bebida más Amada y más Odiada del Mundo*. Bogotá: Editorial Planeta.

Blue, S., & Spurling, N. (2017). Qualities of connective tissue in hospital life: How complexes of practices change. In A. Hui, T. Schatzki, & E. Shove (Eds.), *The Nexus of Practices: Connections, Constellations, Practitioners* (pp. 24–37). London: Routledge.

Brice, J. (2014). Attending to grape vines: Perceptual practices, planty agencies and multiple temporalities in Australian viticulture. *Social and Cultural Geography*, *15*(8), 942–965.

Burnett, K., & Murphy, S. (2014). What place for international trade in food sovereignty? *The Journal of Peasant Studies*, *41*(6), 1065–1084.

Cálas, M. B., & Smircich, L. (2003). To be done with progress and other heretical thoughts for organization and management studies. In E. A. Locke (Ed.). *Postmodernism and Management: Pros, Cons and the Alternative* (pp. 29–59). Oxford: Elsevier.

Cálas, M. B., Smircich, L., & Bourne, K. A. (2009). Extending the boundaries: Reframing "Entrepreneurship as social change" through feminist perspectives. *Academy of Management Review*, *34*(3), 552–569.

Daviron, B., & Ponte, S. (2005). *The Coffee Paradox: Global Markets, Commodity Trade, and the Elusive Promise of Development*. London: Zed Books.

Dey, P., & Mason, C. (2018). Overcoming constraints of collective imagination: An inquiry into activist entrepreneuring, disruptive truth-telling and the creation of "possible worlds". *Journal of Business Venturing*, *33*(1), 84–99.

Dey, P., & Steyaert, C. (Eds.) (2018). *Social Entrepreneurship: An Affirmative Critique*. Cheltenham, UK and Northampton, MA, USA: Edward Elgar Publishing.

Durepos, G., Prasad, A., & Villanueva, C. E. (2016). How might we study international business to account for marginalized subjects? Turning to practice and situated knowledges. *Critical Perspectives on International Business*, *12*(3), 306–314.

Emerson, R. M., Fretz, R. I., & Shaw, L. L. (2011). *Writing Ethnographic Fieldnotes*. Chicago, IL: University of Chicago Press.

Escobar, A. (2010). Worlds and knowledges otherwise: The Latin American Modernity / Coloniality Research Program. In W. Mignolo & A. Escobar (Eds.), *Globalization and the Decolonial Option* (pp. 33–64). New York: Routledge.

Escobar, A. (2018). *Designs for the Pluriverse: Radical Interdependence, Autonomy, and the Making of Worlds*. Durham, NC: Duke University Press.

Falzon, M. A. (2009). *Multi-Sited Ethnography: Theory, Praxis and Locality in Contemporary Research*. Aldershot: Ashgate.

Fridell, G. (2007). *Fair Trade Coffee: The Prospects and Pitfalls of Market-Driven Social Justice*. Toronto: University of Toronto Press.

Gherardi, S. (2017). Sociomateriality in posthuman practice theory. In S. Hui, E. Shove, & T. R. Schatzki (Eds.), *The Nexus of Practices: Connections, Constellations, Practitioners* (pp. 38–51). London: Routledge.

Gherardi, S., & Nicolini, D. (2005). Actor-networks: Ecology and entrepreneur. In B. Czarniawska & T. Hernes (Eds.), *Actor-Network Theory and Organising* (pp. 285–306). Copenhagen: Liber.

Harris, G. (2007). *Seeking Sustainability in an Age of Complexity*. Cambridge: Cambridge University Press.

Hart, S. L., & Milstein, M. B. (1999). Global sustainability and the creative destruction of industries. *Sloan Management Review*, *41*(1), 23–33.

Heuts, F., & Mol, A. M. (2013). What is a good tomato? A case of valuing in practice. *Valuation Studies*, *1*(2), 125–146.

Hjorth, D., Holt, R., & Steyaert, C. (2015). Entrepreneurship and process studies. *International Small Business Journal*, *33*(6), 599–611.

Hjorth, D., & Steyaert, C. (2009a). Entrepreneurship as disruptive event. In D. Hjorth & C. Steyaert (Eds.), *The Politics and Aesthetics of Entrepreneurship* (pp. 1–12). Cheltenham, UK and Northampton, MA, USA: Edward Elgar Publishing.

Hjorth, D., & Steyaert, C. (Eds.) (2009b). *The Politics and Aesthetics of Entrepreneurship*. Cheltenham, UK and Northampton, MA, USA: Edward Elgar Publishing.

Hockerts, K., & Wüstenhagen, R. (2010). Greening Goliaths versus emerging Davids: Theorizing about the role of incumbents and new entrants in sustainable entrepreneurship. *Journal of Business Venturing*, *25*, 481–492.

Hui, A. (2017). Variation and the intersection of practices. In A. Hui, T. Schatzki, & E. Shove (Eds.), *The Nexus of Practices: Connections, Constellations, Practitioners* (pp. 52–67). London: Routledge.

Hui, A., Shove, E., & Schatzki, T. (Eds.) (2017). *The Nexus of Practices: Connections, Constellations, Practitioners*. London: Routledge.

Jaffee, D. (2014). *Brewing Justice: Fair Trade Coffee, Sustainability, and Survival*. Berkeley, CA: University of California Press.

Janssens, M., & Steyaert, C. (2019). A practice-based theory of diversity: Respecifying (in)equality in organizations. *Academy of Management Review*, *44*(3), 518–537.

Jarzabkowski, P., Bednarek, R., & Spee, P. (2015). *Making a Market for Acts of God: The Practice of Risk Trading in the Global Reinsurance Industry*. Oxford: Oxford University Press.

Lernoud, J., Potts, J., Sampson, G., Garibay, S., Lynch, M., Voora, V., Willer, H., & Wozniak, J. (2017). *The State of Sustainable Markets: Statistics and Emerging Trends 2017*. Geneva: International Trade Centre.

Luethy, C., & Steyaert, C. (2019). The onto-politics of entrepreneurial experimentation: Re-reading Hans-Jörg Rheinberger's understanding of "experimental systems". *Entrepreneurship & Regional Development*, *31*(7–8), 652–668.

Maldonaldo-Torres, N. (2010). On the coloniality of being: Contributions to the development of a concept. In W. D. Mignolo & A. Escobar (Eds.), *Globalization and the Decolonial Option* (pp. 94–124). New York: Routledge.

Mignolo, W. D. (2000). *Local Histories/Global Designs: Coloniality, Subaltern Knowledges, and Border Thinking*. Princeton: Princeton University Press.

Mignolo, W. D. (2002). The geopolitics of knowledge and the colonial difference. *South Atlantic Quarterly*, *101*(1), 57–96.

Morley, J. (2017). Technologies within and beyond practices. In A. Hui, T. Schatzki, & E. Shove (Eds.), *The Nexus of Practices: Connections, Constellations, Practitioners* (pp. 81–97). London: Routledge.

Nicholls, A. (2008). *Social Entrepreneurship: New Models of Sustainable Social Change*. Oxford: Oxford University Press.

Nicolini, D. (2009). Articulating practice through the interview to the double. *Management Learning*, *40*(2), 195–212.

Nicolini, D. (2012). *Practice Theory, Work, & Organization: An Introduction*. Oxford: Oxford University Press.

Nicolini, D. (2017a). Is small the only beautiful? Making sense of "large phenomena" from a practice-based perspective. In A. Hui, T. Schatzki, & E. Shove (Eds.), *The Nexus of Practices: Connections, Constellations, Practitioners* (pp. 98–113). London: Routledge.

Nicolini, D. (2017b). Practice theory as a package of theory, method and vocabulary: Affordances and limitations. In M. Jonas, B. Littig, & A. Wroblewski (Eds.), *Methodological Reflections on Practice Oriented Theories* (pp. 19–34). Cham: Springer International Publishing.

Ocampo Villegas, M. C. (2015). *La Promesa del Café. Estrategia Comunicativa detrás de la Cultura Cafetera*. Chía, Colombia: Universidad de la Sabana.

Osburg, T. (2014). Sustainable entrepreneurship: A driver for social innovation. In C. Weidinger, H. Fischler, & R. Schmidpeter (Eds.), *Sustainable Entrepreneurship: Business Success through Sustainability* (pp. 103–115). Berlin: Springer.

Peterson, P. (2013). Strategies for improving coffee quality. In R. W. Thurston, J. Morris, & S. Steiman (Eds.), *Coffee: A Comprehensive Guide to the Bean, the Beverage, and the Industry* (pp. 13–19). Lanham, MD: Rowman & Littlefield.

Piketty, T. (2014). *Capital in the Twenty-First Century*. Cambridge, MA: The Belknap Press of Harvard University Press.

Poltronieri, P., & Rossi, F. (2016). Challenges in specialty coffee processing and quality assurance. *Challenges*, *19*(7), 1–22.

Raynolds, L. T. (2002). Consumer/producer links in Fair Trade coffee networks. *Sociologia Ruralis*, *42*(4), 404–424.

Reckwitz, A. (2002). Toward a theory of social practices: A development in culturalist theorizing. *European Journal of Social Theory*, *5*(2), 243–263.

Rindova, V., Barry, D., & Ketchen, D. J. (2009). Entrepreneurship as emancipation. *Academy of Management Review*, *34*(3), 477–491.

Rodrik, D. (2011). *The Globalization Paradox: Democracy and the Future of the World Economy*. New York: W. W. Norton.

Rogers, P., Jalal, K. F., & Boyd, J. (2008). *An Introduction to Sustainable Development*. London: Earthscan.

Rose, M. (2016). A place for other stories: Authorship and evidence in experimental times. *GeoHumanities*, *2*(1), 132–148.

Said, E. (1978). *Orientalism: Western Conceptions of the Orient*. Harmondsworth: Penguin.

Samper, L. F., & Quiñones-Ruiz, X. F. (2017). Towards a balanced sustainability vision for the coffee industry. *Resources*, *6*(17), 1–28.

Samper, M. K. (2003). The historical construction of quality and competitiveness: A preliminary discussion of coffee commodity chains. In W. G. Clarence-Smith & S. Topik (Eds.), *The Global Coffee Economy in Africa, Asia, and Latin America, 1500–1989* (pp. 120–156). Cambridge: Cambridge University Press.

Sarasvathy, S. D. (2015). Worldmaking. *Entrepreneurial Action*, *14*, 1–24.

Schatzki, T. (2017). Sayings, texts and discursive formations. In A. Hui, T. Schatzki, & E. Shove (Eds.), *The Nexus of Practices: Connections, Constellations, Practitioners* (pp. 126–140). London: Routledge.

Schatzki, T. R., Knorr Cetina, K., & Savigny, E. von (Eds.) (2001). *The Practice Turn in Contemporary Theory*. London: Routledge.

Shepherd, D. A., & Patzelt, H. (2017). Researching entrepreneurship's role in sustainable development. In D. A. Shepherd & H. Patzelt (Eds.), *Trailblazing in Entrepreneurship: Creating New Paths for Understanding the Field* (pp. 149–179). Basingstoke: Palgrave Macmillan.

Shove, E., Pantzar, M., & Wilson, M. (2012). *The Dynamics of Social Practice: Everyday Life and How It Changes*. London: Sage.

Spinosa, C., Fernando Flores, F., & Dreyfus, H. (1997). *Disclosing New Worlds: Entrepreneurship, Democratic Action and the Cultivation of Solidarity*. Cambridge, MA: MIT Press.

Steiman, S. (2013). What is specialty coffee? In R. W. Thurston, J. Morris, & S. Steiman (Eds.), *Coffee: A Comprehensive Guide to the Bean, the Beverage, and the Industry* (pp. 102–105). Lanham, MD: Rowman & Littlefield.

Steyaert, C. (2004). The prosaics of entrepreneurship. In D. Hjorth & C. Steyaert (Eds.), *Narrative and Discursive Approaches in Entrepreneurship* (pp. 8–21). Cheltenham, UK and Northampton, MA, USA: Edward Elgar Publishing.

Steyaert, C. (2007). "Entrepreneuring" as a conceptual attractor? A review of process theories in 20 years of entrepreneurship studies. *Entrepreneurship & Regional Development*, *19*(6), 453–477.

Steyaert, C. (2012). Making the multiple: Theorising processes of entrepreneurship and organisation. In D. Hjorth (Ed.), *Handbook on Organisational Entrepreneurship* (pp. 151–168). Cheltenham, UK and Northampton, MA, USA: Edward Elgar Publishing.

Steyaert, C., & Hjorth, D. (Eds.) (2006). *Entrepreneurship as Social Change: A Third Movements in Entrepreneurship Book.* Cheltenham, UK and Northampton, MA, USA: Edward Elgar Publishing.

Steyaert, C., & Katz, J. (2004). Reclaiming the space of entrepreneurship in society: Geographical, discursive and social dimensions. *Entrepreneurship & Regional Development, 16*(3), 179–196.

Tennant, M. G. (2015). Values-led entrepreneurship: Developing business models through the exercise of reflexivity. *Local Economy, 30*(5), 520–533.

Thurston, R. W., Morris, J., & Steiman, S. (Eds.) (2013). *Coffee: A Comprehensive Guide to the Bean, the Beverage, and the Industry.* Lanham, MD: Rowman & Littlefield.

Tobias, J. M., Mair, J., & Barbosa-Leiker, C. (2013). Toward a theory of transformative entrepreneuring: Poverty reduction and conflict resolution in Rwanda's entrepreneurial coffee sector. *Journal of Business Venturing, 28*(6), 728–742.

Tsing, A. (2015). *The Mushroom at the End of the World: On the Possibility of Life in Capitalist Ruins.* Princeton: Princeton University Press.

Van der Ploeg, J. D. (2009). *The New Peasantries: Struggles for Autonomy and Sustainability in an Era of Empire and Globalization.* London: Earthscan.

Vannini, P. (Ed.) (2015). *Non-Representational Methodologies: Re-envisioning Research.* New York: Routledge.

Watson, M. (2017). Placing power in practice theory. In A. Hui, T. Schatzki, & E. Shove (Eds.), *The Nexus of Practices: Connections, Constellations, Practitioners* (pp. 169–182). London: Routledge.

Watts, G. (2013). Direct trade in coffee. In R. W. Thurston, J. Morris, & S. Steiman (Eds.), *Coffee: A Comprehensive Guide to the Bean, the Beverage, and the Industry* (pp. 121–127). Lanham, MD: Rowman & Littlefield.

Weiskopf, R., & Steyaert, C. (2009). Metamorphoses in entrepreneurship studies: Towards an affirmative politics of entrepreneuring. In D. Hjorth & C. Steyaert (Eds.), *The Politics and Aesthetics of Entrepreneurship* (pp. 202–220). Cheltenham, UK and Northampton, MA, USA: Edward Elgar Publishing.

Yehia, E. (2006). De-colonizing knowledge and practice: A dialogic encounter between the Latin American Modernity/Coloniality/Decoloniality Research Program and actor network theory. *Journal of the World Anthropology Network, 1*(2), 91–108.

Zanoni, P., Contu, A., Healy, S., & Mir, R. (2017). Post-capitalistic politics in the making: The imaginary and praxis of alternative economies. *Organization, 24*(5), 575–588.

Index

Aas, T. H. 15
abstract artifacts 170–72
accountability 69, 79, 87–8, 153–4, 190, 192, 343
Achtenhagen, L. 71
active agency 112, 117–18, 123
activity chains *see* chains of activity
Actor Network Theory 123
affect 100–101, 103–4, 315–18, 325, 332, 337
affirmative critique 97–101, 103
agencement 8, 22, 29–31, 33
Akrich, M. 179
Alberoni, F. 28
altruism 314
Alvesson, M. 22–3, 63, 73
Anamorphosis project 65–70, 73
Andersen, C. E. 9–10
Anderson, A. 59, 238–9
Anderson, L. 318
angel investors 147–8, 153
applied CA 188, 197
argumentation 22, 176, 325
Aristotle 61, 82, 87–8, 156–7
Aroles, J. 222
artifacts 11–12, 25, 30, 86, 117, 146, 150, 152,
 158, 168–80, 209–10, 213, 222, 244,
 254–5, 267–70, 274–7, 300
artificial reality 308
assemblages 12, 29–30, 43–4, 60, 99, 103, 158,
 177, 179–80, 229–31
association work 332, 335, 340–41
Austen, J. 141–2, 158
autoethnography 9, 62–3, 223, 270–71, 314, 318
automation 308
axiological issues 67–71

Baker, T. 58
Bamberg, M. 252
Banks, M. 239
Barad, K. 32, 215, 325
Baron, R. 55
Bateson, G. 146
Baumol, W. J. 169
Becattini, G. 59
Benjamin, O. 229
Bensemann, J. 238–9
Benson, B. E. 157
Berger, P. 23
Berglund, H. 11, 63, 66, 169, 177
Beyes, T. 241–2

biases 55, 63, 68, 177, 216, 261, 276, 324, 330,
 342
Blackmon, K. 223
blogs 13, 205–8, 228
Blue, S. 43, 51
Bouchard, V. 298
Bouchicki, H. 59
Bourdieu, P. 8, 11, 21–4, 32, 44–5, 61, 127, 142,
 159, 267, 269
Bowen, F. 223
Boye, K. 54
Braidotti, R. 94, 96, 98–9, 103, 154
brainstorming 48, 228
Breunig, K. J. 15
bricolage 61, 149–51, 224
Brooks, A. W. 284
Brooks, W. 223
Brown, J. 62
Bruni, A. 315, 319, 322, 325
Bueger, C. 44
bundles 4, 8–9, 15–16, 21, 42–52, 56, 82, 114,
 204, 225, 231, 253, 298–312, 328, 332
Burgelman, R. 54
business model canvas 11, 168, 170–71, 177, 207
business models 6, 11, 168–72, 177, 204, 206–7,
 214, 225–6, 304, 306
Business Owner's Manual 168
business plans 11, 14, 168, 170, 174–5, 178, 207,
 209, 228, 282, 284, 288

Calás, M. B. 104
Callon, M. 179
Campbell, B. 12, 252
capitalism 68, 87, 99, 240, 244–7, 330, 342
Cardon, M. S. 284
Carlsson, S. 72
Carter, C. 158
causality 23, 46–7
chains of activity 8, 45, 47–8, 50, 52, 87
Chalmers, D. 286
Champenois, C. 252
Charmaz, K. 258
Chen, S. 10
Chen, X. P. 284
Chia, R. 54, 62
Chrisman, J. J. 298
Clark, C. 294
Clarke, J. 256, 275, 284, 316
Clifton, J. 251–2

Printed and bound by CPI Group (UK) Ltd, Croydon, CR0 4YY

16/04/2025

14658393-0003